Quantitative techniques for management decisions

Quantitative techniques for management decisions

Frank S. McLaughlin

Robert C. Pickhardt

University of North Florida

HOUGHTON MIFFLIN COMPANY   BOSTON

Dallas   Geneva, Illinois   Hopewell, New Jersey   Palo Alto   London

Cover photograph by Michael Malyszko

Printed in the U.S.A.

Library of Congress Catalog Card Number: 78-69586

ISBN 0-395-26669-6

Table of contents

Preface

Quantitative Techniques for Management Decisions was written to serve as a textbook for a course or a sequence of courses introducing the student to management science. Different schools, programs, or instructors will use this textbook in different ways. We anticipate, however, that its major use will be in coursework that is a required part of a broad major, such as business administration, public administration, engineering, technology, or accounting.

Quantitative analysis is playing an increasingly important role in the curriculums of programs that prepare students for service in business firms and public organizations. At least one course in the area of quantitative analysis is now a required part of most of these curriculums. There are two reasons for this increasing emphasis. First, quantitative analysis provides the student with knowledge of a body of material that has direct applications in business and government. Second, a study of the process of quantitative methods helps the student become more proficient in analyzing decision situations and solving problems. This textbook was designed to help the student master both of these learning objectives.

Every effort has been made to make this a readable book. The text assumes that the reader's only mathematical background is a good course in college algebra. As with any textbook on this subject, additional mathematical training, for example, an introductory statistics course, will enhance the learning process. However, a prior course in statistics is certainly not a necessity. Except for the algebra, any needed mathematical or statistical tools are developed in the textbook. Thus, readers with no mathematical training beyond college algebra should have little difficulty with the level of mathematics in this text.

This book contains several interesting features that result from our belief that the easiest way to learn and retain material is through plentiful examples and applications. Each chapter or major section of a chapter begins with an example (minicase) that illustrates the use of a quantitative tool of analysis. The concepts underlying the management science technique are developed as the decision situation is being analyzed. Thus, the reader first is introduced to a situation that requires a management solution. Then the reader acquires a knowledge of quantitative techniques that can be helpful in analyzing this and similar situations.

A number of sample problems, along with their solutions, are placed at appropriate locations throughout the text. These problems serve as additional learning examples. They also allow readers to test their knowledge in one section before proceeding to another section of the text.

The book contains 448 end-of-chapter exercises. Considerable time and effort have been given to developing problems that are logical and consistent with the material covered in the text. Of the major chapters, only the one on simulation has less than 24 end-of-chapter problems. Most chapters have approximately 35 exercises. These problems have been selected to illustrate a wide variety of management science applications.

This textbook includes all of the material that is normally covered in introductory courses. Chapter 1 introduces the student to management science.

Chapters 2 and 3 are concerned with probability analysis and decision theory. Inventory models are the subject of Chapter 4. Chapters 5, 6, and 7 form a unit on linear programming and the transportation method. Goal programming, integer programming, and dynamic programming are all discussed in Chapter 8. Chapters 9 through 13 deal, respectively, with network analysis, queuing theory, simulation, Markov analysis, and game theory. Chapter 14 differs from other chapters. It is intended to serve primarily as a self-study unit for readers who feel they need help with statistical tables or statistical distributions. Chapter 15 is concerned with the problems of model selection and implementation. The problems at the end of this chapter are unique and are designed to assist the reader in developing skills in model selection. In order to analyze these problems the reader may have to use a technique or combination of techniques discussed in one or more of the preceding chapters.

There are many ways in which this textbook may be used. For a one-term course, the instructor will probably use the material on decision theory and linear programming and then select appropriate topics from the remainder of the book. Chapter 2 is a prerequisite for Chapter 3. Chapter 5 is a prerequisite for Chapters 6, 7, and 8. Otherwise, the chapters may be covered in any desired sequence. The book is arranged so that it is possible to use part of a chapter without using the entire chapter. For example, the instructor of an introductory course may choose to use most of Chapter 6, but omit the section on sensitivity analysis or the section on special types of linear programming formulations. Sections of Chapter 14, with associated end-of-chapter problems, may be assigned as the instructor desires.

A second logical way of using this material is to start at the beginning and work straight through the book. Used in this manner, the text contains sufficient material for a two-term course, provided good use is made of the problems and exercises at the end of each chapter.

A comprehensive Instructor's Manual is available for the instructor. This manual includes a set of figures that are presented in a form suitable for preparing overhead transparencies. The majority of these are drawn from selected end-of-chapter exercises, while other figures contain fully documented new problems. These visuals should be helpful in illustrating concepts discussed in the textbook.

We are grateful for the help we received from many people. We would especially like to thank the reviewers: Myron Cox of Wright State University; Donald Miller of Emporia State University; Andrew Thacker of the University of Houston; and Ronald Zigli of Appalachian State University. Their suggestions led to a greatly improved manuscript. Myron Cox deserves a special thank you for his assistance at several stages of the project. Finally, we would like to thank our families. Without their patience and understanding, this book would never have been completed.

F. S. M.
R. C. P.

Chapter 1

Introduction to quantitative managerial analysis

This is a book about decision making. It focuses on using quantitative methods in managerial decisions. *Decision making* occurs when management makes a judgment about what action to follow in a given situation. It is a process that results in the selection of a specific course of action from a set of possible alternatives. We assume that decisions are made by rational individuals. The purpose of decision making is to achieve personal or corporate objectives. Although our emphasis is on managerial decisions, the principles discussed also apply to situations in everyday life. The basic structures of all decision situations are similar, whether the setting is business, government, or the home.

Almost all business decisions involve both quantitative factors and qualitative factors. Some decisions, such as the selection of personnel, the design of an organizational structure, or the choice of a color for the company logo, are almost exclusively qualitative. Other decisions, such as production scheduling and capital budgeting, tend to be much more quantitative. The decision maker should never disregard either the qualitative or the quantitative aspects of a decision. An improvement in either area should improve the overall decision-making process.

Quantitative techniques do not make decisions; they assist in the decision-making process. The manager should never blindly adopt the results of a quantitative model. The final decision belongs to the manager. While overreliance on quantitative methods may be harmful, failure to make good use of them is also harmful. Some individuals have a tendency to ignore or disregard the results of a quantitative model. This reluctance may be more detrimental to decision making than "overquantifying." In short, while quantitative methods cannot substitute for the judgment of the decision maker, they can be a valuable asset.

Scope and history of management science

The use of quantitative methods in business is often referred to as management science or operations research. For our purposes, the two terms can be used interchangeably. They have been defined in various ways, and many of these definitions are broad enough to include all efforts to apply the scientific method to decision making. In this textbook, we favor a narrower definition. *Management science*, or *operations research*, is the application of quantitative methods to managerial problems.

There is no general agreement about when people first used management science to assist them in problem solving. Many scholars insist that management science is as old as society. Others argue that it was first used during the early years of World War II. Various writers trace the origin of operations research to Adam Smith in 1776, to Charles Babbage in 1832, or to Frederick Taylor in the early part of the twentieth century. We are not concerned with an exact history of management science. Nevertheless, knowing a few significant accomplishments in the area will add to our understanding and appreciation of the subject.

Frederick Taylor is often referred to as the father of scientific management. He was primarily interested in operating management, or how the worker should perform his or her task. He believed that there is one best way to do a job. Many of his studies were directed at finding this single most efficient means of performing a task. Taylor is noted for applying the scientific method to managerial problems, and one of his best known studies concerned yard shovelers at the Bethlehem Steel Company. Before Taylor, no one had tried to determine the best type of shovel for yard shovelers. Taylor concluded that a full shovel should weigh 21 pounds and that the shape of the shovel should vary, depending on the material to be moved. Implementation of these findings resulted in significantly increased productivity.

Henry Gantt was a contemporary of Frederick Taylor. He is best known for his "Gantt charts," which were developed for use in managerial planning. Gantt's outlook was broader in scope than Taylor's. While Taylor was looking at a particular task, Gantt was interested in finding an optimal relationship among tasks. His charts were most often used for job scheduling. They followed a particular job from station to station and gave the planner a means of minimizing delays. Gantt charts were forerunners of many of the production planning and control charts used today. Certain quantitative techniques such as network analysis are also derivatives of Gantt's work.

Some students of management science maintain that operations research began with the British in the early part of World War II. At that time, technological advances made possible the introduction of new devices into battle. This new equipment included radar, sonar, and rockets. The use of these devices in warfare was not fully understood. The British formed interdisciplinary study groups containing military strategists, natural scientists, and social scientists charged with the task of performing research on military operations and learning how to better utilize the resources available to the military.

The most famous of these groups was called Blackett's circus. Headed by the distinguished physicist P. M. S. Blackett, the group included physicists, army officers, mathematicians, and a surveyor. The recommendations of this group were highly valued, and Blackett's circus was credited with giving British forces a decisive advantage in several key World War II battles. The success of this group contributed greatly to the popularity of operations research during World War II. This popularity continued into the postwar years and led to many advances in management science that are used in industry today.

In the years after the war, substantial progress was made on many techniques used in quantitative business analysis. George Dantzig's development in 1947 of the simplex method of solving linear programming problems best exemplifies this progress. The development of the simplex method gave management a powerful and proven means of analyzing many large-scale problems. In addition, the simplex method could be used efficiently on electronic computers, which were being developed during this period. Linear programming can be used on many types of managerial problems, and its versatility contributed greatly to its popularity.

A significant development in management science occurred shortly after 1950, when the United States Navy successfully used the program evaluation and review technique (PERT) in the Polaris missile project. At that time, the navy was faced with the task of designing, building, and making operational a fleet of Polaris missile submarines. The project involved coordinating the work of thousands of private contractors and navy units. Prior to this time, the experience of the military with complex research and development projects had been unsatisfactory. Project completion times and project costs consistently exceeded original estimates by substantial margins and created major allocation and planning problems.

PERT was designed to assist in the planning and control of large, complex projects. It was developed by the special projects office of the U.S. Navy in cooperation with the consulting firm of Booz, Allen & Hamilton. PERT has been given the major credit for allowing the navy to finish this project approximately two years ahead of schedule. The success of this program gave impetus to the use of PERT or related techniques on large government and private projects.

These advances in the theory of management science are only some of the reasons for its widespread use in government and industry today. What is generally referred to as the computer revolution is another reason. Quantitative analysis often requires a large amount of mathematical computation. These complex calculations simply cannot be performed by hand. Today we have computers that can perform calculations millions of times faster than people can. Computers allow today's analysts to perform functions that were impossible or unprofitable before.

Comments about the future can only be speculative. No one can say with certainty what role management science will play in the lives of individuals and organizations. It seems apparent, however, that the world will continue to become more complex. Change seems destined to occur at an accelerating pace, and the world's storehouse of knowledge will grow at an ever-increasing rate. The organization of the future will exist in a climate of increased government regulation and social responsibility. In order to meet these challenges, managers will need better information and better techniques to assist them in the decision-making process.

It seems clear that there will be an increased need for management science to assist managers and decision makers in the future. Operations research must continue to grow and develop. We can expect further improvements and refinements in techniques presently in use, allowing management scientists to analyze larger and more complex problems. The discipline must go further, however, and develop new procedures. Some of these procedures will improve mathematical efficiency, while others will be concerned with problem analysis and implementation.

Future developments in management science must be linked to advances in computer hardware and software. During the past three decades, the capabilities and efficiencies of computer systems have increased dramatically. Even today, however, the computational requirements of some management science projects are so large as to make the projects impractical. Advances in the theory of operations research and in computer technology will make more and more problems amenable to analysis by management science procedures.

Models in management science

A *model* is an abstraction or a simplified representation of reality. Models are used extensively in management science. An analyst can study a model and then make inferences or draw conclusions about the portion of the real world that the model represents. For example, an industrial chemical manufacturer might construct a small-scale or pilot plant model of a proposed manufacturing process. Such a model allows the design engineer to observe the process without incurring the cost of building and operating an expensive chemical operation. Likewise, a carpet salesperson can use the floor plan of a house to estimate the amount of carpet needed for wall-to-wall installation.

Classification of models

Various methods have been used to classify models into types or categories. The simplest procedure is to classify a model as a member of one of three groups. A *physical* or *iconic model* looks like the part of reality that it represents. A scale model of a building is a physical representation of a real building. Likewise, model airplanes and trains are physical replicas of real objects and a pilot plant operation is often used to represent an actual manufacturing operation.

Analog models differ from iconic models in that their physical appearance is different from that of the object they represent. An oral fever thermometer is an analog model. Distances on the thermometer are used to represent degrees of temperature. Likewise, a slide rule is an analog model, because it substitutes distances for numerical quantities. Many graphical representations are analog models in that they represent numerical data pictorially.

Symbolic models represent a real situation by symbols such as words or mathematical relationships. The use of symbolic models is the essence of the quantitative approach to decision making, and much of this textbook is devoted to them.

Mathematical models are the most commonly used models in management science. There are two major reasons for their popularity. First, there is in the discipline of mathematics an inherent rigor that forces the decision maker to specify the important elements of the problem and the relationships that exist among these elements. Second, mathematics is a powerful technique for manipulating data and deriving conclusions from given premises. With high-speed computers, it is possible to handle models of great complexity. Thus, many large industrial situations can be analyzed with the use of a mathematical model.

It is interesting to note that the historical trend is away from iconic models toward symbolic (especially mathematical) models. It is often pointed out that the Wright brothers accumulated much of their data by actually flying their airplane. Years later, researchers obtained the same kinds of data by using scale models of airplanes in wind tunnels. Today, analysts can derive much of the same information by manipulating mathematical models on high-speed computers.

Characteristics of management science models

A good management science model must blend the sometimes opposing characteristics of *accuracy* and *simplicity*. The model should be as simple as possible and still represent reality well enough to be useful to the decision maker.

The characteristics of a good model are illustrated by the familiar road or highway map. Suppose we are driving from Denver to Buffalo. What do we want from the model that will guide us along the way? First, the model must be an abstraction. An exact duplication of reality would do us no good since we cannot fold reality up and put it into the glove compartment of our car.

Second, the model should contain enough detail to allow the decision maker to accomplish her or his objectives. Our road map should obviously include all possible major routes and intersecting roads, and for some purposes this may be enough. In other cases, we may need more details, such as mileage figures and the location of motels and gasoline service stations. If we are tourists, we may be interested in historic sites along the prospective route.

The third characteristic of a good model is that it should be simple. Enough useful details should be included, but there is no reason for a highway map to contain every little curve, every advertising billboard, or every stop sign. This information provides little or no assistance to the decision maker and would only make the model more cumbersome.

Choosing between simplicity and detail

Simplicity may be obtained by eliminating certain factors from the model. Elimination of these factors, however, will reduce the extent to which the decision maker's objectives can be achieved. Assume that a limited travel budget and the price of gasoline lead us to adopt the objective of selecting the shortest route. The map we selected does not show all existing roads, and one or more of the omitted roads might be short cuts between points included in our travel plan. Our carefully selected route may be the best alternative shown on the map, but it is not necessarily the minimum-distance route available.

We could avoid this difficulty by selecting detailed topographical maps showing all existing roads. Unfortunately, we will need a large number of these maps, and the process of selecting the shortest route becomes complex and time-consuming. It may even be impossible. We must ask ourselves if we are willing to spend a week locating a route that reduces travel distance by 20 or 30 miles. Like all decision makers, we must strike a balance between model accuracy and simplicity. As the model is simplified, the solution process is simplified, which is often necessary if a model is to be solved at all. In order to achieve the desired balance, the decision maker should try to include only critical factors in the model and to simplify it by eliminating secondary factors, the omission of which creates only minor inaccuracies.

Using submodels is one way to achieve a proper blend of simplicity and detail. A large model may sometimes be broken down into smaller segments, or submodels. In traveling from Denver to Baltimore, for example, it would not usually be necessary to include the residential areas of all the towns along the way. Suppose, however, that we wanted to stop and visit a friend in Kansas City. A street map of Kansas City might be quite helpful. This street map is a submodel. *Submodels* are used to represent one section of reality in a way that is different from the way we have chosen to represent the major portion of the item being modeled.

Utilizing a mathematical model

In the following sections, we will illustrate one of the simplest mathematical models. It is often called the break-even model. It mathematically represents the relationship between sales volume, cost, and profit. We chose this model primarily for pedagogical reasons. It is simple and easy to understand, and it is relevant to certain types of business problems.

For purposes of illustration, we will abstract a business operation to its most elementary state. In this form, the business manufactures a product at a given cost per unit. This cost is a *per-unit variable cost. Total variable costs* are so named because they vary as volume of output changes. For example, assume production costs are $2 per unit. It would cost $200 to produce 100 units and $600 to produce 300 units. The firm also incurs a *fixed cost* for such items as property tax and the president's salary. These costs are "fixed" in the sense that they do not change with varying production or sales quantities. For example, rent on the production facilities may be $150. This fee is fixed and does not vary with the number of units produced. The firm sells all that it produces and generates revenue from these sales. *Profit* for a given period may be thought of as total revenue less total cost.

In mathematical models, it is convenient and helpful to symbolically represent certain of the items being modeled. In this example, we will use the following symbols:

P = Profit

R = Total revenue

C = Total cost

F = Fixed cost

X = Number of units produced or sold in a given production period

S = Selling price of a unit of production

V = Cost of a unit of production

Perhaps the easiest way to construct a simple mathematical model is first to verbalize the relationship and then to transform this verbal statement into a mathematical statement. For example:

"Profit is obtained by subtracting total cost from total revenue."

Profit = Total revenue − Total cost

$$P = R - C$$

"Total revenue is obtained by multiplying the number of units produced by the selling price."

Total revenue = Selling price × Units produced

$$R = SX$$

"Total cost is the sum of fixed cost and variable cost. Variable cost is obtained by multiplying the number of units produced by the cost per unit."

Total cost = Fixed cost + (Cost per unit × Units produced)

$$C = F + VX$$

The relationships for profit, total revenue, and total cost may be combined as follows:

$$P = R - C$$
$$P = SX - (F + VX)$$

This equation is a simple mathematical model. It expresses the relationship among profit, sales volume, fixed cost, cost per unit, and price per unit. Its use is illustrated in the following example. A firm has a monthly fixed cost of $20,000. Units are produced at a cost of $6 per unit and sold for $10 per unit. We will use our mathematical model to answer several questions.

What will be the value of profit if 8000 units are produced and sold?

$$P = SX - (F + VX)$$
$$P = 10(8000) - [20,000 + 6(8000)]$$
$$P = 80,000 - (20,000 + 48,000) = \$12,000$$

How many units must the firm produce and sell in order to break even? The break-even position implies that profit is zero. Thus, we set P equal to zero and solve for X, the number of units produced.

$$P = SX - (F + VX)$$
$$0 = 10X - (20,000 + 6X)$$
$$0 = 4X - 20,000$$
$$X = 5,000$$

Finally, suppose fixed cost increases to $28,000. How large would the selling price have to be for the firm to break even at a sales volume of 4000 units? In this example, $P = 0$ and $X = 4000$. We must solve for S.

$$P = SX - (F + VX).$$
$$0 = S(4000) - [28,000 + 6(4000)]$$

$$0 = 4000S - 52,000$$
$$S = \$13$$

In this example, we used algebra and common sense to analyze a simple managerial problem. As we proceed through the text, the examples will become more complex and we will use a variety of techniques and models. We hope, however, that the reasoning will remain straightforward and clear. This textbook will concentrate on those models that have minimal mathematical requirements.

The management science process

This textbook is primarily concerned with the construction and use of specific models in management science. The process of management science is broad, however, and includes the general management functions of problem analysis, model building, model solving, and model implementation. We shall briefly discuss each of these areas.

Problem analysis

The first step in problem analysis is to obtain a good definition of the problem. This includes recognizing that a problem exists, assessing its magnitude, determining what factors are relevant to its solution, and deciding which of these factors can be controlled by the decision maker. At this initial step, it is important to understand the objectives of the study, that is, to understand what the analyst can accomplish by applying management science to the problem.

Proper problem definition can lead to unexpected results. In some cases an actual problem may not exist, or the problem may be so simple that a solution is obvious. Quite often, problem analysis will reveal that the real problem is different from what it was originally thought to be.

Once the problem is properly defined, the analyst must determine whether it is amenable to solution by management science techniques and whether the expected benefits are worth the cost of performing the analysis. The management scientist should realize that the costs of obtaining a solution may exceed the savings resulting from that solution. In such cases, the appropriate decision may be to abandon or scale down the project. If the project is determined to be feasible, however, the modeling process can begin.

Model building

Model building, or *model formulation,* involves constructing a model that represents the problem being considered. As we have stated, the emphasis in model building should be on practicality. The model should be a proper blend of simplicity and detail so that the objectives of the decision maker can best be achieved. Earlier in the chapter, we discussed and illustrated the formulation of a simple mathematical model. Normally, this phase of the management science process does not end with construction of the model. The model must be tested and revised until the researcher is convinced that it is a practical and useful representation of the real system it represents. Testing and refining can be one of the most difficult and time-consuming aspects of the model-building process.

Model solving

Once the model is formulated, it must be solved. Solving a model involves prescribing a course of action that the decision maker should follow in order to achieve the objectives of the project. Models that can be solved are referred to as *normative* or *analytical models*. They must contain a decision criterion for selecting the one best, or optimal, alternative. They should also contain a method of proving that this alternative is optimal. Many analytical models utilize an algorithm to determine the optimal solution. An *algorithm* is a structured, step-by-step procedure used to reach an optimal solution.

Some management science models are descriptive rather than normative. *Descriptive models* are not solved in the traditional sense. Their function is to describe the characteristics of a system. Most descriptive models have the capacity to describe the characteristics of a system under varying operating conditions. They are used primarily to explore the consequences of management alternatives. Descriptive models help managers to understand a system better and to test for a good or satisfactory solution. They differ from analytical models, however, in that they do not solve for the one best, or optimal, solution.

An important aspect of the model-solving process is determining how the solution reacts to variations in input data or operating conditions. This is referred to as sensitivity analysis. *Sensitivity analysis* determines how much the solution will change for a given change in input data, that is, how sensitive the solution is to change. In developing a production schedule, for example, a decision maker may assume a demand of 100,000 units per month for a particular product. It would be helpful to know how the solution would change if actual demand turned out to be 90,000 or 120,000 units. Sensitivity analysis is useful in determining the stability of a solution, the degree of accuracy required of input data, and the value of additional resources.

Model implementation

The final step in the management science process is putting the model to work. The work performed in all of the foregoing stages is of little value unless the model is implemented. Implementation should be the most rewarding aspect of the process. It can also be the most difficult. The management scientist must ensure that the solution is expressed in a form that operating personnel can understand and implement. These individuals must understand many aspects of the model, including its strengths and weaknesses, the assumptions on which it is based, and the conditions under which it can operate. The last chapter of this book contains a more thorough discussion of implementation and offers several suggestions for improving this facet of the management science process.

Management science in today's world

In virtually all types of organizations, quantitative analysis has been applied to problems that vary considerably in importance and complexity. The resulting returns range from minor improvements in efficiency to major reductions in operating cost. It is often difficult to evaluate accurately the total benefit of quantitative analysis to the organization, because many of the returns — such as improved service or control, reduced customer waiting time, and faster response time — are intangible and difficult to quantify.

The following examples are intended to illustrate the diversity and importance of management science techniques. We realize that terms such as *linear programming, queuing theory,* and *simulation* may not mean much to the uninitiated reader. They are types of management science models that will reappear later in the text. Our primary concern here is not the type of model used, but rather its application to a real problem.

National Airlines has developed and applied a linear programming model used to select fueling points, vendors, and fuel quantities for each of its flights. The model also provided a means of immediately evaluating price and supply changes, and National realized multimillion dollar savings over a two-year period.[1]

A variety of quantitative models were used to improve the deployment of New York City fire companies. The program improved fire protection, eased the workload on fire companies, and reduced annual operating cost more than $5 million. Principal changes involved the relocation of 7 fire companies and the elimination of 6 of the 375 companies. Another development was the implementation of an

[1] D. W. Darnell and C. Loflin, "National Airlines Fuel Management and Allocation Model," *Interfaces,* 7 (February 1977), 1–16.

adaptive response policy used to determine the number of fire companies to dispatch to a fire.[2]

A simulation model was a key feature in a study of the collection and disposal of solid waste in Cleveland, Ohio. Implementation of the results of the study is estimated to have saved $14.6 million between 1971 and 1974. The waste collection work force was reduced from 1640 to 850 employees.[3]

A Swedish steel mill, Fagersta AB, used a mixed-integer programming model to determine the best mix of available raw materials to use in meeting product specifications. Implementation of the model reduced annual raw-material costs by $200,000. In addition, the overall planning process was substantially simplified.[4]

Cleveland Trust Company used a system model incorporating several management science techniques to improve check processing for its branch banks. Over a five-year period, savings of approximately $1 million were realized in messenger and transportation costs alone. Improved control also resulted in a number of indirect savings. The average daily float was reduced by roughly $30 million. Cost reductions in check processing were also achieved.[5]

A shift scheduling system was applied to telephone operators at 43 locations of the General Telephone Company of California. This resulted in annual cost savings in excess of $170,000. It also allowed for a 6% increase in work force productivity. Most of the efficiency was obtained by reducing clerical and supervisory costs.[6]

A simulation model applied by Air Canada to aircraft maintenance planning yielded a 5% reduction in labor and material costs in a multimillion dollar operation. The time needed to prepare a five-year plan was reduced from three weeks to a few hours, and more frequent replanning is possible in response to changing conditions.[7]

A linear programming model was developed for Swift Chemical Company's phosphate mining and sales operation. It is used to plan short- and long-range sales strategies and to optimize the mining and blending of phosphate rock. This mathematical model generated an

[2]E. Ignall, et al., "Improving the Deployment of New York City Fire Companies," Interfaces, 5 (February 1975), 48–61.
[3]R. M. Clark and J. I. Gillean, "Analysis of Solid Waste Management Operations in Cleveland, Ohio: A Case Study," Interfaces, 6 (November 1975), 32–42.
[4]C. Westerberg, B. Bjorklund, and E. Hultman, "An Application of Mixed Integer Programming in a Swedish Steel Mill," Interfaces, 7 (February 1977), 39–43.
[5]J. A. Svestka, "A System Model for Controlling the Operations of Check Processing in a Branch Bank Network," Interfaces, 7 (insert of November 1976), 69–79.
[6]E. S. Buffa, M. J. Cosgrove, and B. L. Luce, "An Integrated Work Shift Scheduling System," Decision Sciences, 7 (October 1976), 620–630.
[7]N. J. Boere, "Air Canada Saves with Aircraft Maintenance Scheduling," Interfaces, 7 (May 1977), 1–13.

annual profit increase of several million dollars over what would have resulted from using the former manual planning approach.[8]

The preceding examples are only a sampling of the applications of quantitative analysis. Subsequent chapters of this book will develop useful and widely applied techniques that are available to the decision maker. This material should also suggest further applications. The potential uses of these techniques are limited mainly by the decision maker's own ingenuity.

Summary

This chapter has provided an introduction to management science. We discussed the history of management science and briefly speculated about the future. We also discussed the management science process and noted the importance of its four stages: problem analysis, model building, model selection, and model implementation.

A large portion of this chapter dealt with management science models, with emphasis on the mathematical model. This is proper because the use of mathematical models is a distinguishing characteristic of management science. We chose a simple model, the break-even model, to illustrate the basics of quantitative managerial analysis. We hope that its inclusion in this introduction may encourage the hesitant reader to conclude, "I understand this. Maybe quantitative managerial analysis isn't so bad after all!"

Finally, we briefly discussed several situations wherein organizations achieved substantial cost savings and/or improvements in service by using quantitative techniques in the decision-making process. These examples should illustrate the prevalence and importance of management science in today's world.

Problems and exercises

1. Explain the following terms:

management science	scientific management
operations research	descriptive model
model	analog model
abstraction	mathematical model
iconic model	physical model
variable cost	implementation
fixed cost	normative model

[8]J. M. Reddy, "A Model to Schedule Sales Optimally Blended from Scarce Resources," *Interfaces*, 6 (November 1975), 97–107.

2. From reference sources in the library, determine the contributions to management science made by each of the following individuals:

Charles Babbage	A. K. Erlang
F. W. Lanchester	Chester Barnard
Thomas Edison	Henri Fayol
Peter Drucker	Lyndall Urwick
Mary Parker Follett	Elton Mayo
Lillian Gilbreth	R. A. Fisher
Alfred Sloan	

3. From your other studies, are you familiar with individuals who have contributed to management science? If so, list these individuals and their contributions.

4. Name or describe a number of models used in everyday life.

5. Discuss the difference between analytical and descriptive models.

6. Give some examples of quantitative approaches that you have used to make decisions in your personal life.

7. Why should quantitative techniques alone not be allowed to dictate the decisions that managers make?

8. Consider the simple break-even model discussed in this chapter. Suppose a firm has a variable cost of $2 per unit, a selling price of $6 per unit, and a fixed cost of $900. Determine the following:
   a. Profit when sales are 300 units.
   b. Profit when sales are 100 units.
   c. The break-even point in units of sales.
   d. The amount the selling price would have to increase to break even at 200 units. All costs remain constant.

9. Consider a firm that buys units for $12 and sells them for $18. There are no other variable costs. Fixed costs are $3000. Use the simple break-even formula discussed in this chapter to determine the following:
   a. Sales volume when profit is $9000.
   b. Profit when sales are 400 units.
   c. The break-even point.
   d. The amount by which variable cost per unit has to be decreased in order for the firm to break even at 300 units. Selling price and fixed cost remain constant.

10. A business firm produces and sells a particular product. Variable cost is $20 per unit. Selling price is $30 per unit. Fixed cost is $60,000. Use the simple break-even model discussed in this chapter to determine the following:
    a. Profit when sales are 9000 units.
    b. The break-even point.
    c. Sales when profits are $9000.
    d. The amount by which fixed cost would have to be reduced to allow the firm to break even at a sales volume of 5000 units. Variable cost per unit and selling price remain constant.

11. Consider the simple break-even model discussed in this chapter. Suppose a firm sells a particular product for $.60 per unit. Variable cost is $.40 per unit. Total fixed cost is $1200. Determine the following:
    a. The break-even point in units of sales.
    b. Profit when sales are 10,000 units.
    c. Profit when sales are 5000 units.
    d. The amount by which selling price would have to increase for the firm to break even at 4000 units. Assume all costs remain the same.
    e. The amount by which fixed cost would have to decrease in order for the firm to break even at a sales volume of 4000 units. Assume selling price remains $.60 per unit and variable cost remains $.40 per unit.

Supplementary readings

Ackoff, R. L., and P. Rivett. *A Manager's Guide to Operations Research*. New York: Wiley, 1967.

Cook, T. M., and R. A. Russell. *Introduction to Management Science*. Englewood Cliffs, N.J.: Prentice-Hall, 1977.

Gupta, S. K., and J. M. Cozzolino. *Fundamentals of Operations Research for Management*. San Francisco: Holden-Day, 1974.

Hartley, R. V. *Operations Research: A Managerial Emphasis*. Pacific Palisades, Calif.: Goodyear Publishing Company, 1976.

Hillier, F. S., and G. J. Lieberman. *Introduction to Operations Research*. San Francisco: Holden-Day, 1974.

Johnson, R. H., and P. R. Winn. *Quantitative Methods for Management*. Boston: Houghton Mifflin, 1976.

Levin, R. I., and C. A. Kirkpatrick. *Quantitative Approaches to Management*, 3d. ed. New York: McGraw-Hill, 1975.

Turban, E., and J. R. Meredith. *Fundamentals of Management Science*. Dallas, Texas: Business Publications, 1977.

Wagner, H. M. *Principles of Management Science*. Englewood Cliffs, N.J.: Prentice-Hall, 1975.

Chapter 2
Decision theory

Illustrative example: ROBBINS DEVELOPMENT CORPORATION

The Robbins Development Corporation (RDC) is a well-established research and development (R&D) contractor located approximately 100 miles from Washington, D.C. It specializes in developing new products for large manufacturing organizations. Independent R&D contracting is a high-risk, high-yield business. Receiving a bid and subsequently developing a product can result in significantly large profits for the firm. On many occasions, however, the company incurs the cost of preparing a bid but does not receive the contract. An even costlier but less frequently occurring situation arises when the firm receives the contract but cannot develop the technology to produce the product. Quite often, there is a penalty clause associated with accepting a bid and then failing to produce the desired product.

Dr. J. K. Ekey is vice president of operations for RDC. He is faced with deciding whether or not to bid on the development of a new "summer product" for a large manufacturing firm. Based on his experience, Dr. Ekey feels that if a proposal is submitted, there is a 40% chance that RDC will receive the contract. He also estimates that it will cost RDC $40,000 to prepare the proposal. Unfortunately, none of this cost can be recovered if the contract is awarded to another contractor.

One risk inherent in R&D contracting is that the contractor is almost never 100% sure that the product can actually be developed. In this case, two known methods of development exist, but there is only enough time to try one method, since the product must be ready for the summer season.

The "standard" method of development was perfected several years ago by RDC's chief chemist, Nina Kennedy. Based on experience with this method, Dr. Ekey estimates that there is an 80% chance that the product can be successfully developed using this standard method. Obviously, there is also a 20% chance that this method will not be successful. Dr. Ekey estimates that using the standard method of development will cost the firm $260,000. Recently Harry Jung, a young engineer with RDC, proposed a "revised" method of development. This method is less expensive but also less likely to yield positive results. Dr. Ekey estimates the cost of this method to be $160,000. Unfortunately, he can only assign a 50% probability to its success.

Dr. Ekey knows that successful development of this product will result in payment of $600,000 to the firm. If the firm should receive the contract but fail to produce the product, it must pay a penalty of $100,000. The immediate question facing Dr. Ekey is whether or not to prepare a bid. Before making this decision, he decides to think the whole process through with the aid of a managerial tool of analysis known as a decision tree.

In Chapter 1, we indicated that decision making is a very important aspect of a manager's job. Students of managerial decision making have described four environments within which all decision making takes place. These environments are conditions of certainty, uncertainty, risk, and conflict. A decision maker is operating in a condition of *certainty* when all of the facts surrounding a decision situation can be exactly specified, that is, when each alternative is associated with only one possible outcome. In such cases, the decision process is a matter of simply selecting a single act from among all available alternatives. Although no decisions are made in an absolute state of certainty, many managerial decision situations approach this state. At the other end of the spectrum is the condition of *uncertainty*. In this state, each strategy leads to several possible outcomes, and the likelihood of any one of these outcomes occurring is unknown or cannot be specified.

Most management decisions are made in an environment known as the state of *risk*. In this state, strategy choices have several possible outcomes, but evidence exists that allows the decision maker to assign probabilities to the various possible outcomes. The body of knowledge known as *decision theory* is primarily a study of decision making in this environment or state of risk.

Decision under *conflict* constitutes a special class of decision problems. In this state, two or more decision makers are involved. Each of these individuals is, at least to some degree, competing with the others. The outcome of a decision under conflict depends not only on the choice made by a particular individual, but also on the choice made by his or her competitor.

Decisions under conflict and decisions under uncertainty are discussed in Chapter 13. Linear programming, discussed in Chapters 5 and 6, is the best known of the many models that assume a condition of certainty. This chapter and the next are primarily concerned with decisions made in the state of risk.

Decision tree analysis

A *decision tree* is a graphical representation of a decision situation. It structures the decision process for the decision maker, provides a view of the total process, and thereby helps the decision maker examine all possible outcomes. Most important, it allows the decision maker to impose an orderly, rational process on the decision situation.

Drawing the decision tree

The immediate problem Dr. Ekey of RDC faces is whether or not to prepare a proposal and make a bid. This simple situation is diagrammed in Figure 2.1. Graphically, *a rectangle represents a decision point,* or a place where a choice must be made. The two arrows leading out of the rectangle represent the only two possible alternatives: Dr. Ekey can choose to prepare the proposal or he can decide not to submit a bid. The letters A, B, and C in the decision tree are illustrative aids only. We will refer to them in our discussion, but they would not normally be included in a diagram that is actually being used for decision analysis.

Dr. Ekey should not make his decision until he considers the possible consequences and ramifications of the two alternatives. Figure 2.2 extends the graphical representation of the decision situation. If Dr. Ekey had chosen not to prepare the bid, he would have moved from position A to position C in Figure 2.2. At that position, the decision situation would have ended.

Suppose, however, that Dr. Ekey had chosen to prepare the bid. He would then have moved from position A to position B in Figure 2.2. At that point, a chance event would occur. Either RDC would win the contract or the contract would be awarded to a competitor. This type of situation is referred to as a *chance event* because the outcome is beyond the control of the decision maker. Graphically, *chance events are represented by circles.*

In this situation, the chance event has only two outcomes: RDC will either be awarded the contract or not. These outcomes are represented by the two arrows leading out of the circle at position B in Figure 2.2.

Figure 2.3 is a further extension of the graphical representation of the decision situation. If RDC does not receive the bid, Dr. Ekey will move from position B to position E in Figure 2.3. Here the decision situation would again stop, because if the bid is not received, there is no place to go. If the bid is received, however, the decision maker will move from

Figure 2.1 *Schematic of the initial decision point in the RDC problem*

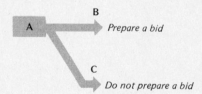

Figure 2.2 *First extension of the RDC decision tree*

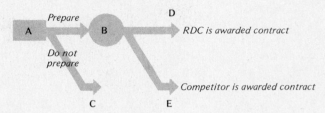

position B to position D, where Dr. Ekey is faced with another decision point. He must decide whether to use the standard method or the revised method to develop the new product. These two alternatives are represented by the arrows leading out of the rectangle at position D.

In Figure 2.4, the graphical representation includes the total decision situation. If Dr. Ekey chooses the standard method of development, he will move from position D to position F in Figure 2.4. At position F, there is another chance event. Either the method will succeed and the product will be produced, or the method will fail and RDC will be unable to produce the product. Likewise, if Dr. Ekey chooses the revised method of development, he will move from position D to position G, where another chance event will occur. Either the product will be developed or it will not be developed.

The graphical representation of the decision situation given in Figure 2.4 can be quite helpful to the managerial analyst. It structures the decision process and allows the analyst to view the whole problem before making the initial decision. At this point, the tree is not sufficient to allow the analyst to apply a logical decision process to the decision situation. Before doing this, we must add two items to our decision tree. First, we must consider the likelihood, or probability, of a chance event having a particular outcome. Second, we must consider

Figure 2.3 *Second extension of the RDC decision tree*

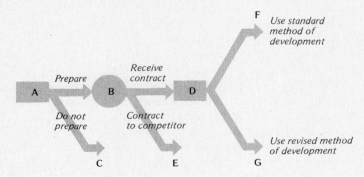

Figure 2.4 *Complete decision tree of the RDC problem*

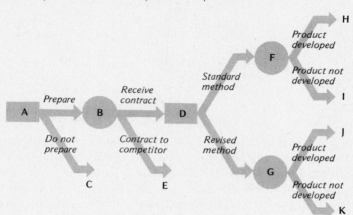

the costs and revenues associated with the various outcomes and alternatives.

Assigning probabilities in decision analysis

There are two basic types of probability: objective and subjective. *Objective probabilities* are those probabilities for which there are definite historical precedents and experience. The assignment of objective probabilities is based on historical precedent. If we flip a fair coin, we assume the probability of it landing heads is 1/2. If we roll a fair die, we assume the probability of rolling an ace (one) is 1/6. Likewise, if we choose a single card at random from a standard deck of 52 cards, we assume the probability of drawing a diamond is 13/52. These are objective probabilities. Experience based on historical evidence has taught us that if these events are repeated enough times, the coin will land heads half of the time, an ace on the die will come up one-sixth of the time, and a diamond will be drawn one-quarter of the time.

In many situations, there is no direct historical evidence on which to base a probability assumption. In these situations, a decision maker must rely on his or her own best estimate of the likelihood that various possible outcomes of a chance event will occur. This type of probability assessment is known as a *subjective* or *judgmental probability*.

We use subjective probabilities daily. At lunch time, we estimate the probability of a particular restaurant being crowded. We wonder if the chance of making a sale is high enough to justify driving a long distance to make a sales call. We wonder if a particular malady is serious enough to warrant a physician's attention. In all of these situations, we assign a subjective probability to each possible outcome of the chance event and

Figure 2.5 *RDC decision tree with probabilities and financial data (values in thousands of dollars; losses shown in brackets)*

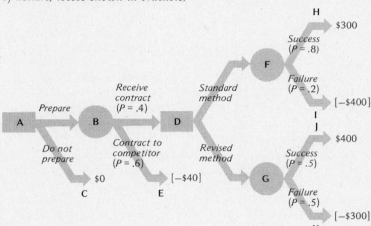

make decisions based on the probabilities we have assigned. Subjective probabilities are educated guesses based on an individual's knowledge and experience. Using subjective probabilities in decision analysis is risky, but it is much better than using nothing.

In the RDC problem, Dr. Ekey has stated that the probability of a bid proposal being accepted is 40% and that the probability of it being rejected is 60%. Likewise, we know that the standard method of development has an 80% chance of succeeding and a 20% chance of failing to produce the product. The revised method has a 50-50 chance of producing the product. These *probability estimates* have been entered in the decision tree diagram shown in Figure 2.5.

Adding financial data to the decision tree

Note that there are six positions where the RDC problem can end in Figure 2.5. For example, position H represents the end of the chain of events, "the bid was prepared, it was accepted, the standard method of development was used, and a successful product was produced." The costs[1] and revenues associated with this chain of events are a cost of $40,000 for preparing the bid, a cost of $260,000 for developing the product by the standard method, and a revenue of $600,000 for success-

---

[1] In this example, we have ignored the "time value" of money. One hundred dollars received on January 1 is more valuable than an identical sum received on July 1 of the same year. The first $100 could be invested, and the interest it earned in six months would make it worth more than $100 on July 1. In complex analysis, all financial data should be "discounted" to a fixed point in time.

ful development of the product. The net financial result is a gain of $300,000. This value, which has been entered in Figure 2.5, is known as a *conditional value* or *conditional profit*.

As another example, let us consider position K in Figure 2.5. The chain of events and resulting financial data are, "the bid was prepared at a cost of $40,000, it was accepted, the revised method of development was used at a cost of $160,000, and it did not succeed, resulting in a penalty cost of $100,000." The net result is a conditional loss of $300,000, which has also been entered in Figure 2.5. By a similar analysis, we find that the appropriate conditional values at positions I and J are a loss of $400,000 and a gain of $400,000 respectively.

Position E represents the end of the chain of events, "a bid was prepared, but it was not accepted." This would result in a $40,000 loss. Position C represents a position where no bid was prepared, so there was no resultant gain or loss. The addition of financial data adds clarity and substance to our decision process. We must now combine these data with the probability estimates we have made.

Combining probabilities and monetary values

The most common method of combining probabilities and conditional monetary values is to calculate the expected monetary value of chance events. The *expected monetary value* of a chance event is the weighted average of the conditional values of all possible outcomes. Each conditional value is weighted by the probability that it will occur. Mathematically, expected value (EV) can be determined by the following relationship:

$$EV = \sum_{i=1}^{n} P_i V_i$$

In this relationship, V_i is the conditional value of event i and P_i is the probability of occurrence of that particular event.

A few simple examples will help to clarify the concept. Suppose a fair coin is flipped, and we are to receive $4 if it lands heads and $6 if it lands tails. The expected monetary value is obtained by multiplying the payoff for a particular outcome by the probability of that particular outcome and summing for all possible outcomes. The expected monetary value of this simple coin-tossing event is $5. The calculations we use to arrive at this value are illustrated in Table 2.1.

$$EV = (.5 \times \$4) + (.5 \times \$6) = \$2 + \$3 = \$5$$

Expected monetary value has special significance in decision theory because it is used to establish indifference relationships. In an *indiffer-*

Table 2.1 *Calculations of expected value for the coin-tossing example*

Event	Probability (P_i)	Payoff (V_i)	P_iV_i
Obtain heads	.5	$4	$2
Obtain tails	.5	6	3
			EV = $5

ence relationship, two events are equally attractive to an individual and he or she should not prefer one to the other. In our example, the assumption is that a decision maker would have no preference between a sure sum of $5 and a chance situation offering a 50% chance of receiving $4 and a 50% chance of receiving $6. Later in the chapter we will question this assumption, but the establishment of indifference relationships makes this type of decision analysis possible.

As a second example, let us consider one of the chance events in the RDC decision tree. Assume that RDC received the bid and chose the standard method of development (position F in Figure 2.5). There is now an 80% chance of success with a resultant conditional profit of $300,000. There is also a 20% chance of failure with a resultant conditional loss of $400,000. The expected value of this chance event is $160,000. (The calculations appear in Table 2.2.) The indifference relationship implies that Dr. Ekey would be indifferent in choosing between a sure sum of $160,000 and a chance event offering an 80% chance of a profit of $300,000 and a 20% chance of a loss of $400,000. The EV of this chance is determined algebraically as follows:

$$EV = \sum_{i=1}^{2} P_iV_i = P_1V_1 + P_2V_2$$

$$= .8(\$300,000) + .2(-\$400,000)$$

$$= \$240,000 - \$80,000 = \$160,000$$

Table 2.2 *Calculations of expected value for the standard development method in the RDC problem*

Event	Probability (P_i)	Payoff (V_i)	P_iV_i
Product successfully developed	.8	$300,000	$240,000
Firm unable to develop product	.2	-400,000	-80,000
			EV = $160,000

Figure 2.6 *First reduction in the RDC problem (values in thousands of dollars)*

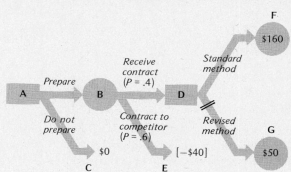

The backward reduction method of decision analysis[2]

Once we have completed the decision tree, we can begin the decision analysis process. This is best accomplished by the *rollback* or *backward reduction method. The purpose of the backward reduction method of decision analysis is to reduce a complex decision situation to an elementary decision situation.* It is based on two simple assumptions. The first assumption concerns indifference relationships. The assumption is that for every chance situation, an indifference relationship can be established such that a decision maker would be indifferent between a certain sum of money and the chance event. Thus, we can replace each chance event by a fixed sum of money. The second assumption is that a decision maker will prefer a larger sum of money to a smaller sum. We will return to the RDC problem to illustrate how these two assumptions reduce Dr. Ekey's decision to a very simple problem.

In our discussion of expected value in the preceding section, we showed how the chance situation at position F in Figure 2.5 could be equated to a fixed sum of $160,000. Using the expected value concepts, we can also equate the chance situation at position G in Figure 2.5 to a fixed sum. Position G is the chance event of the success or failure of the revised method of product development. There is a 50% chance of success with a resultant payoff of $400,000 and a 50% chance of failure with a resultant loss of $300,000. The expected value of this chance situation is therefore $50,000.

At this point, we are ready for our first "reduction." The first reduction is made by replacing two chance events by their expected values. These expected values are shown in the circles at positions F and G in Figure 2.6. Note that we have reduced the decision tree by "snipping off" the arrows that represent the outcomes of the chance events.

---

[2]The term *reduction* is used to emphasize the procedure followed in this analysis. The term *backward induction* is often used for similar analysis.

Figure 2.7 *Removal of the chance event with the lower expected value (values in thousands of dollars)*

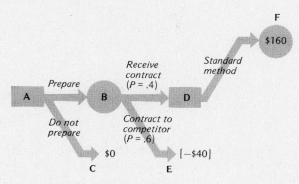

The second reduction is even simpler to effect. Position D represents a decision point. Dr. Ekey will choose the standard method of development because of its higher EV. The lower branch may therefore be discarded. The two slash marks in the lower branch in Figure 2.6 mean that we are removing this part of the decision tree. The tree with this branch removed is shown in Figure 2.7. A decision has been made at this point, and there is no need to keep the arrow running from position D to position F. Before snipping off the branch, however, we must remember that it leads to a sum of $160,000. We therefore insert the $160,000 value into the rectangle at position D. This is illustrated in Figure 2.8.

We perform the third reduction in the RDC problem by using an indifference relationship. Position B in Figure 2.8 is a chance event. The EV of this chance situation is $40,000, which is obtained as follows:

$$EV = (.4 \times \$160,000) + [.6 \times (-\$40,000)] = \$40,000$$

We can now place this value in the circle at position B and make the third reduction as shown in Figure 2.9.

We have succeeded in reducing the rather complex decision situation shown in Figure 2.5 to the elementary situation shown in Figure 2.9. In

Figure 2.8 *Second reduction in the RDC problem (values in thousands of dollars)*

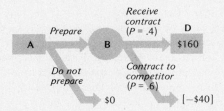

Figure 2.9 *Third (final) reduction in the RDC problem (values in thousands of dollars)*

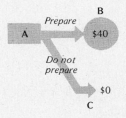

Figure 2.9, Dr. Ekey is faced with a choice between a "sum equivalent" of $40,000 for preparing the proposal and one of $0 for not preparing the proposal. Thus, he will prepare the proposal, since this alternative has the higher expected value. Dr. Ekey is aware of the risks involved. The outcome of the chance events may not be in his favor. He has, however, rationally considered the odds, and he knows that consistent use of rational procedures is the best long-range bidding philosophy.

In our discussion of this decision situation, we drew a number of figures to illustrate the reduction of the decision situation by snipping off branches. Of course, it is not necessary to redraw a figure each time a reduction is made. The standard procedure is to "prune" the tree by drawing two short lines through the branch to be discarded. This is the procedure we will follow in the remainder of this chapter.

Sample problem 2.1   THE McMILLAN COMPANY

The McMillan Company is approached by an individual who wishes to sell a patent for a new holiday product for $100,000. If the patent is purchased, the product must be developed. Development can be undertaken internally at a cost of $200,000, and the company is 50% certain that it can develop the product. The McMillan Company also has the option of contracting the product development to an independent R&D contractor. This contractor is also 50% certain that it can develop the product and will charge the McMillan Company $300,000. No charge will be made, however, if the R&D contractor fails to develop the product. The monetary return to the McMillan Company depends on the amount of snowfall during the holiday season. It is estimated that with a light snowfall, the net return will be $500,000, including all costs except for purchase of the patent and product development. With a heavy snowfall, estimated revenue is $900,000, which again includes all costs except for purchase of the patent and product development. The probability of a heavy snowfall is .4, and the probability of a light snowfall is .6. Draw a decision tree of the decision situation. Add probabilities and financial data to the decision tree. Use the backward reduction method to analyze the decision situation.

SOLUTION

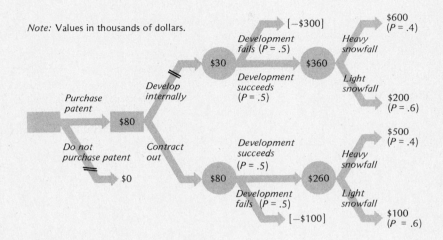

Note: Values in thousands of dollars.

[−$300]
Development fails (P = .5)

$600
(P = .4)
Heavy snowfall

$30

$360

Develop internally

Development succeeds (P = .5)

Light snowfall

$200
(P = .6)

Purchase patent

$80

$500
(P = .4)

Do not purchase patent

Contract out

Development succeeds (P = .5)

Heavy snowfall

$0

$80

$260

Development fails (P = .5)

Light snowfall

[−$100]

$100
(P = .6)

The value of information

In the preceding sections, we illustrated how Dr. Ekey could use decision theory to analyze the problem at RDC. At RDC, Dr. Ekey operates in an environment of risk; that is, probabilities are involved in the analysis. Better decisions can be made if the degree of risk can be reduced or eliminated. For this reason, it is generally wise to search for additional information that could be used to refine the probability estimates. To illustrate, we will modify the RDC problem slightly.

Let us assume there is a clause in the contract stating that no penalty payments will apply if the successful bidder gives notice within six weeks after receiving the contract that it cannot develop the product. Furthermore, Dr. Ekey knows of another R&D company (The Warren Company) that has performed extensive research on both the standard and the revised methods of development. For a fee, the Warren Company will tell Dr. Ekey whether the standard method or the revised method, or both, can be successfully used for product development. This information is *perfect* in the sense that it can be accepted as absolutely correct. At the moment, we do not know what price the Warren Company will charge, so we will proceed as though the information is free. Although we know this will not be the case, the assumption will allow us to determine how much Dr. Ekey should be willing to pay for this information.

Diagramming the decision to buy information

The decision tree shown in Figure 2.10 incorporates this modification; that is, it includes the option for Dr. Ekey to buy information from the Warren Company. There is a new decision point at position P. Here Dr. Ekey must decide whether to buy the information or to go ahead and choose a method of development without the benefit of the information that the Warren Company has to sell.

Position Q in Figure 2.10 represents a chance event. If Dr. Ekey chooses to buy the information, he may receive any one of four different answers: None of the methods will be successful, only the standard method will be successful, only the revised method will be successful, or both methods will be successful.

The arrow leading to point R represents the outcome that the product cannot be developed by any method. This outcome would result in a

Figure 2.10 *Decision tree of RDC problem, showing the option to buy perfect information (values in thousands of dollars)*

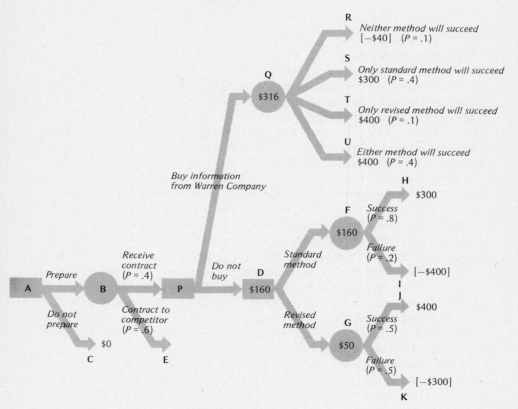

loss of $40,000 to the firm. Since Mr. Warren's information is perfect, RDC would not undertake to develop the product and no development cost would be incurred. Furthermore, RDC would not have to pay the $100,000 penalty, because it could obtain the Warren Company's information before the six-week deadline.

The arrow leading to position S in Figure 2.10 represents the outcome that only the standard method will be successful. This would result in a profit of $300,000 to the firm (a $600,000 payment to RDC less the bid preparation cost of $40,000 and the development cost of $260,000). The arrow leading to position T represents the outcome that only the revised method will be successful. The payoff here is $400,000.

Finally, the arrow leading to position U represents the outcome that both methods will result in successful development of the product. In this case, either method of development will assure success. RDC will therefore choose the revised method; it is cheaper and will yield a profit of $400,000, compared to $300,000 for the standard method. The $400,-000 value is therefore entered at position U in Figure 2.10.

Determining informational probabilities

In order to perform decision analysis, the analyst must assign probabilities of occurrence to all possible outcomes of the chance event at position Q. These probabilities are known as *informational probabilities,* and there is a definite relationship between them and the event probabilities discussed earlier. Dr. Ekey must use his subjective beliefs about the outcome of the two development processes to predict the likelihood of receiving each report from the Warren Company. He can then use these probabilities to estimate the value of the information.

Dr. Ekey has already stated that he believes there is an 80% chance that the standard method of development will be successful. He has also stated that he believes there is a 50% chance of success with the revised method of development. The probability of both methods being successful is therefore .40 (that is, .8 × .5). To be consistent, Dr. Ekey must believe that there is a 40% chance that the Warren Company report will indicate that both methods will result in successful product development. The .4 probability is entered by the arrow extending from position Q to position U in Figure 2.10.

By the same logic, the probability of receiving a report that neither method will be successful is equal to the probability that the standard method will fail (.2) multiplied by the probability that the revised method will fail (.5), which equals .10. The probability of receiving a report that only the standard method of development will succeed is .40. Likewise, the probability of the Warren Company reporting that only the revised method will be successful is .10.

Analyzing the decision to buy information

We are now ready to begin our backward reduction method of decision analysis. The lower half of the original version of the tree may be collapsed exactly as before so that position D in Figure 2.10 has an expected value of $160,000. We can easily obtain EV of the chance event at position Q by multiplying the conditional profit or loss values by their probabilities and summing the results of all possible outcomes. The EV of this chance event is $316,000.

As illustrated in Figure 2.10, Dr. Ekey, at position P, is faced with deciding whether to buy the information from the Warren Company or to proceed without the information. We have assumed the information could be obtained at no cost. Under this assumption, the alternative of buying the information has an expected value of $316,000. The alternative of proceeding without the information has an expected value of $160,000. Obviously, under these conditions, Dr. Ekey should obtain the information before proceeding.

Finding the expected value of perfect information

It is much more likely that Mr. Warren would charge Dr. Ekey a fee for the information, and we want to determine the maximum amount that Dr. Ekey should be willing to pay for it. For the purpose of this analysis, we have assumed that *the Warren Company's information is perfect —* that it is infallible. The company can predict the relevant events with 100% certainty. For this reason, the maximum amount that Dr. Ekey would be willing to pay for this information is known as the *expected value of perfect information (EVPI)*. The EVPI is obtained by subtracting the EV of proceeding without the information from the EV of obtaining the perfect information before proceeding. In the RDC problem, the EV of Mr. Warren's perfect information is $156,000, which is $316,000 − $160,000. In other words, Dr. Ekey should purchase the information for any amount up to $156,000.

Since no information is perfect, *we would never pay the full EVPI value for any information.* The concept is quite useful in decision analysis, however. It puts a "cap" or ceiling on the amount we would pay for information. It also allows analysts to incorporate the decision to buy information into the total decision process in a logical and rational way.

Sample problem 2.2   THE McMILLAN COMPANY (Continued)

Consider the McMillan Company problem given in Sample Problem 2.1. Assume that after it purchases the patent but before it makes a decision on product development, the McMillan Company has an opportunity to purchase a perfect holiday weather forecast and learn whether there will be a heavy snow or a light snow. Draw a decision tree and determine the EV of this perfect information.

SOLUTION

The decision tree is given here. The EV of proceeding with no information is exactly the same as that of proceeding with perfect information. The EV of perfect information is zero. Note that the same decision (contract out) would be made with or without the benefit of the weather information and regardless of its content (heavy or light snow).

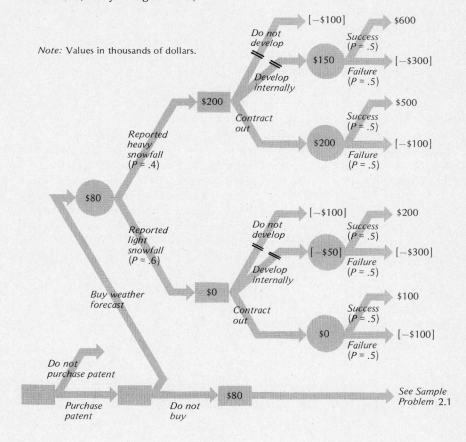

Note: Values in thousands of dollars.

Analysis using conditional and expected monetary tables

Subjective probabilities were an integral part of the RDC problem. We shall now introduce a problem that is very similar to the decision that concerned Dr. Ekey at Robbins Development Corporation. There is one major difference; in this situation, there is definite historical evidence on which to base probabilities. Thus, the probabilities are objective rather than subjective. The very simple structure of the problem also allows for special tables that simplify the calculations.

Illustrative example: JOHN'S LITTLE PEACH MARKET

Several years ago, John Edwards retired from his position as professor of accounting at a major university. He began operating a peach stand at a popular intersection in a major metropolitan area of California.

Mr. Edwards refers to his business as "John's Little Peach Market." Every morning, he goes to the wholesale produce market and purchases 10 bushels of peaches for $6 a bushel. He opens his market promptly at 8:00 A.M. and sells peaches for $10 a bushel until closing time at 4:00 P.M.

On several occasions, Mr. Edwards has sold his tenth and last bushel just before 4:00 P.M. On such days, he remains open until 4:00 P.M., but he has never had requests for more than 10 bushels of peaches in any one day. On a number of occasions, however, he has not been able to sell all the peaches that he purchased in the morning. Unfortunately, the peaches are a "one day" variety. Any peaches remaining unsold at the end of the day must be discarded.

Recently, economic conditions have made Mr. Edwards more concerned about maximizing profit contribution. He wonders if it might not be wise to make a daily purchase of fewer than 10 bushels. He knows that during the past 100 working days, 7 bushels were demanded on 20 days, 8 bushels were demanded on 40 days, 9 bushels were demanded on 30 days, and 10 bushels were demanded on 10 days. Mr. Edwards believes that he may be able to utilize decision theory to determine how many bushels of peaches to purchase daily.

The problem given in "John's Little Peach Market" could be analyzed with the aid of a very simple decision tree. In this tree, there would be only one decision point, located where Mr. Edwards must decide whether to purchase 7 bushels, 8 bushels, 9 bushels, or 10 bushels. In addition, there is only one chance event; that is, demand will be either 7, 8, 9, or 10 bushels.

Decision tree analysis is usually reserved for complicated situations involving sequential decisions. In simple cases such as "John's Little Peach Market," it is generally more convenient to use conditional profit and expected monetary tables than to draw the entire decision tree. We should recognize, however, that these tables are nothing more than compact methods of presenting and analyzing the information that would be found in a decision tree.

The conditional profit table

The conditional profit table for John's Little Peach Market is given in Table 2.3. This is a two-way table with a row for each possible demand condition and a column for each possible stock action. It is easy to obtain the conditional profit values of the various outcomes of the chance events. For example, suppose Mr. Edwards chose to purchase 8 bushels and demand was for 7 bushels. *Conditional profit* would be $22: 7 bushels sold at $10 (a revenue of $70) less 8 bushels purchased at $6 (a cost of $48). If he purchased 8 bushels and demand was for 8 bushels, total revenue would be $80 and total cost $48, resulting in a conditional profit of $32.

The situation wherein demand is greater than quantity available requires special attention. If Mr. Edwards only purchased 8 bushels, he cannot sell more than eight bushels even if demand is for 9 or 10 bushels. Thus, when 8 bushels are purchased, conditional profit is $32 regardless of whether demand is for 8, 9, or 10 bushels.

The expected monetary table

The expected monetary table provides a convenient method of determining the EV of the chance events in a decision situation. Table 2.4 gives the expected monetary table for Mr. Edwards' decision situation. Each column in the table is nothing more than a convenient place to record the values necessary for calculating the EV of a particular action. We obtain the values in an expected monetary table by multiplying the probabilities of occurrence of a particular demand by the corresponding values in the conditional profit table. For example, the conditional profit of stocking 8 bushels in a situation where 7 bushels are demanded is given in Table 2.3 as $22. The probability that 7 bushels will be demanded is .20. Thus, $4.40 is entered in Table 2.4 at the intersection of the "Demand values" row 7 and the "Stock 8" column. As a second example, let us consider determination of the value at the intersection of the "Demand values" row 8 and the "Stock 8" column. From Table 2.3, we know that the conditional profit of stocking 8

Table 2.3 *Conditional profit table for John's Little Peach Market*

Demand values	Probability	Possible stock actions			
		Stock 7	Stock 8	Stock 9	Stock 10
7	.20	$28	$22	$16	$10
8	.40	28	32	26	20
9	.30	28	32	36	30
10	.10	28	32	36	40

Table 2.4 *Expected monetary table for John's Little Peach Market*

Demand values	Probability	Possible stock actions			
		Stock 7	Stock 8	Stock 9	Stock 10
7	.20	$ 5.60	$ 4.40	$ 3.20	$ 2.00
8	.40	11.20	12.80	10.40	8.00
9	.30	8.40	9.60	10.80	9.00
10	.10	2.80	3.20	3.60	4.00
Expected value		$28.00	$30.00	$28.00	$23.00

bushels in a demand situation of 8 is $32. The probability of 8 bushels being demanded is .40. Thus, the proper value is $12.80; that is, $32 × .4 = $12.80.

The last row in Table 2.4 represents the EV of the four possible stock actions available to Mr. Edwards. Each value is the sum of all the other values in the same column. We assume that Mr. Edwards will choose the alternative with the highest EV; that is, he will choose to maximize his long-run profits by purchasing 8 bushels of peaches daily.

Formula determination of expected value We could have determined the EV of each of the four stock actions by using the mathematical expression for EV,

$$EV = \sum_{i=1}^{n} P_i V_i$$

As an example, the EV for a stock action of 9 bushels is

$$EV = \sum_{i=1}^{4} P_i V_i = P_1 V_1 + P_2 V_2 + P_3 V_3 + P_4 V_4$$

$$= .2(\$16) + .4(\$26) + .3(\$36) + .1(\$36)$$

$$= \$3.20 \ + \$10.40 \ + \$10.80 \ + \$3.60 = \$28$$

Selected use of conditional and expected monetary tables

In the following sections, we will illustrate some of the many uses of decision analysis. In these discussions, we will use both conditional profit tables and expected monetary tables extensively. We should remember, however, that each of these decision situations could be analyzed with the assistance of a decision tree.

Analyzing a problem with salvage value In "John's Little Peach Market," we noted that Mr. Edwards had to discard his unsold peaches at the end of each day. Let us now assume that *Mr. Edwards has been able to locate a salvage market* for these peaches. At the end of each day, a local agricultural distributor will buy unsold peaches for $4 a bushel. The distributor uses the peaches for certain types of animal feed.

If a product has salvage value, we must take this salvage value into consideration when we calculate the conditional profit. For example, let us assume that Mr. Edwards decides to purchase 9 bushels daily. His total daily cost is therefore $54. If demand is for 7 bushels, Mr. Edwards will have a total revenue of $78. Of this amount, $70 will result from the sale of 7 bushels at $10 each in his regular trade. The other $8 will result from the sale of 2 bushels at $4 each in the salvage market. In this situation, conditional profit is $78 revenue less the $54 cost, which equals $24. After we consider salvage revenue, we set up the conditional profit and expected monetary tables exactly as we did in the preceding section.

The algebraic determinations of the EVs of the four possible stock actions are as follows:

$$EV = \sum_{i=1}^{4} P_i V_i = P_1 V_1 + P_2 V_2 + P_3 V_3 + P_4 V_4$$

Stock 7: EV = .2($28) + .4($28) + .3($28) + .1($28) = $28.00

Stock 8: EV = .2($26) + .4($32) + .3($32) + .1($32) = $30.80

Stock 9: EV = .2($24) + .4($30) + .3($36) + .1($36) = $31.20

Stock 10: EV = .2($22) + .4($28) + .3($34) + .1($40) = $29.80

The existence of a salvage market will always increase average daily earnings. The *value of a salvage market* is the difference between the EV of the optimal stock action with salvage value and the EV of the optimal stock action with no salvage value. In Mr. Edwards' problem, the optimal action with a $4 salvage value is to stock 9 bushels, and the EV of this action is $31.20. Thus, the value of a salvage market would be $1.20, the difference between $31.20 and $30.00. In many cases, the value of a salvage market is less than we might expect. It is wise to estimate this value before spending a great deal of time and effort searching for a salvage market.

Sample problem 2.3   THE WILLIAMS COMPANY

Ms. Williams operates a small novelty shop. Each morning she purchases a small quantity of "daily computerized horoscopes" at a cost of $15 per item. She resells them later in the day for $25 per horoscope. For the past 200 days, Ms. Williams' demand has been for 6 items on 60 days, 7 items on 60 days, 8 items on 40 days, 9 items on 20 days, and 10 items on 20 days. The horoscopes come in packages of 2, which forces Ms. Williams to purchase an even number, and the horoscopes are salable for one day only. At the end of each working day, however, Ms. Williams can sell any remaining horoscopes to a "night-owl peddler" for $10 per item. Construct a conditional profit table and an expected monetary table. What is the optimal stock action?

SOLUTION

Conditional profit table

Demand values	Probability	Possible stock actions		
		Stock 6	Stock 8	Stock 10
6	.30	$60	$50	$ 40
7	.30	60	65	55
8	.20	60	80	70
9	.10	60	80	85
10	.10	60	80	100

Expected monetary table

Demand values	Probability	Possible stock actions		
		Stock 6	Stock 8	Stock 10
6	.30	$18.00	$15.00	$12.00
7	.30	18.00	19.50	16.50
8	.20	12.00	16.00	14.00
9	.10	6.00	8.00	8.50
10	.10	6.00	8.00	10.00
	Expected value	$60.00	$66.50	$61.00

A stock action of 8 is optimal.

Determining the expected value of perfect information The expected value of perfect information (EVPI) is the difference between the EV of making a decision with perfect knowledge of the outcome of a future chance event and the EV of making the decision knowing only the probability distribution in advance. In the case of John's Little Peach Market, if Mr. Edwards had perfect information about demand before he made his morning purchase, he would always purchase exactly the right amount. Thus, if demand for the day were going to be 8 bushels, Mr. Edwards would make a morning purchase of 8 bushels. Likewise, if demand were going to be 9 bushels, he would purchase 9 bushels. Demand would still vary randomly from 7 to 10 bushels a day. Demand would be for 7 bushels 20% of the time, 8 bushels 40% of the time, 9 bushels 30% of the time, and 10 bushels 10% of the time. The major difference is that Mr. Edwards would know how much would be demanded and would purchase exactly as many peaches as he needs.

Table 2.5 contains the calculations for the expected value with perfect information (EVWPI). If demand is known to be 8 bushels, Mr. Edwards will choose a stock action of 8 bushels. Since he will buy 8 and sell 8, the conditional profit will be $32. Likewise, if demand is known to be 9, the proper stock action is to purchase 9 bushels and the conditional profit is $36. We obtain the EV as before, by multiplying each conditional profit by its probability of occurrence and summing for all possible outcomes. For this example, the EVWPI is $33.20.

The algebraic expression for determining the EVWPI follows. In this relationship, V_i' is the conditional profit associated with the optimal stock action for each possible demand. P_i is the probability of occurrence of that particular level of demand.

$$\text{EVWPI} = \sum_{i=1}^{4} P_i V_i'$$

$$= .2(\$28.00) + .4(\$32.00) + .3(\$36.00) + .1(\$40.00)$$

$$= \$5.60 \quad + \$12.80 \quad + \$10.80 \quad + \$4.00 = \$33.20$$

When Mr. Edwards did not have the benefit of perfect information, his optimal stock action was to purchase 8 bushels daily. This alternative had an expected value of $30. The optimal purchasing procedure with perfect information has an expected value of $33.20. Thus, the daily EVPI is $3.20. We must repeat that *no information is perfect.* Calculating EVPI is very useful, however, because it sets a ceiling on the amount we would pay for any information. It is also a good starting point from which to estimate the value of "imperfect" information.

Table 2.5 *Perfect information table*

Known demand	Probability	Stock action	Conditional profit	Expected value
7	.2	7	$28	$ 5.60
8	.4	8	32	12.80
9	.3	9	36	10.80
10	.1	10	40	4.00
				EV = $33.20

Sample problem 2.4   THE WILLIAMS COMPANY (Continued)

Consider the Williams Company problem given in Sample Problem 2.3. Assume that Ms. Williams had perfect information about daily demand before making her morning purchase. What is the expected value of acting with perfect information (EVWPI)? What is the expected value of perfect information (EVPI)?

SOLUTION

Perfect information table

Known demand	Probability	Stock action	Conditional profit	Expected value
6	.3	6	$ 60	$18.00
7	.3	8	65	19.50
8	.2	8	80	16.00
9	.1	10	85	8.50
10	.1	10	100	10.00
				EVWPI = $72.00

EVPI = $72.00 − $66.50 = $5.50

Analyzing by minimizing the value of regret If Mr. Edwards purchases 9 bushels in the morning and demand is actually for 8 bushels, then he will "regret" purchasing the ninth bushel. The *amount of regret* is the monetary difference between the purchasing action that was taken and the correct or "perfect" purchasing decision. If demand is for 8 bushels and 9 bushels are purchased, there will be a profit of $26. If Mr. Edwards had acted "perfectly," he would have purchased 8 bushels and the resulting profit would have been $32. Thus, the amount of regret is $6.

The concept of regret provides an alternative method of solving for the optimal stock action. Rather than maximizing expected profit, we can minimize the value of regret. Two types of losses may be involved in any decision. *Opportunity losses* result from the opportunity forgone when Mr. Edwards does not have a bushel of peaches to sell to a customer who is willing to buy. For example, assume that Mr. Edwards purchased 8 bushels and 9 bushels are demanded. He cannot sell the ninth bushel because he does not have it in stock. If it had been in stock, it would have added $4 to profit ($10 revenue less $6 cost). Thus, Mr. Edwards regrets by an amount of $4 that he did not stock the ninth bushel.

Real losses, sometimes called obsolescence losses, result from stock-

Table 2.6 *Conditional loss (regret) table*

Demand values	Probability	Possible stock actions			
		Stock 7	Stock 8	Stock 9	Stock 10
7	.20	$ 0.00	$ 6.00	$12.00	$18.00
8	.40	4.00	0.00	6.00	12.00
9	.30	8.00	4.00	0.00	6.00
10	.10	12.00	8.00	4.00	0.00

ing a bushel of peaches that cannot be sold. For example, if 10 bushels are purchased and demand is for 8 bushels, then 2 bushels cannot be sold. The loss is $6 per bushel for each bushel bought but not sold. Thus, the action of buying 10 bushels and selling only 8 results in a real loss of $12.

Table 2.6 is a conditional loss table for John's Little Peach Market. The regret value is always zero when the stock action is identical to quantity demanded. Thus, this conditional loss table has a "zero diagonal." Values above the diagonal represent real losses that result from purchasing more peaches than could be sold. Values below the zero diagonal represent opportunity losses that result from stocking fewer peaches than could be sold. The conditional loss table may be converted to an expected regret table by the same methods we used previously. The expected regret table for Mr. Edwards' problem appears in Table 2.7.

Mr. Edwards wants to minimize his regret, so he will choose the stock action with the smallest expected regret value. The action of stocking 8 bushels daily has the smallest regret value and is the optimal stock action. Note that this is the same stock action that we determined to be optimal when we used a conditional profit table and an expected monetary table.

The *expected regret value* of any stock action is the difference between the expected profit value for that stock action and the EV of acting with perfect information. Thus, if we take the expected monetary values from Table 2.4 and add to them the expected regret values, we should in

Table 2.7 *Expected monetary (regret) table*

Demand values	Probability	Possible stock actions			
		Stock 7	Stock 8	Stock 9	Stock 10
7	.20	$ 0.00	$ 1.20	$ 2.40	$ 3.60
8	.40	1.60	0.00	2.40	4.80
9	.30	2.40	1.20	0.00	1.80
10	.10	1.20	.80	.40	0.00
	Expected value	$ 5.20	$ 3.20	$ 5.20	$10.20

Table 2.8 *Illustration of the relationship among conditional profit values, regret values, and EVWPI*

	Possible stock actions			
	Stock 7	*Stock 8*	*Stock 9*	*Stock 10*
Expected conditional profit	$28.00	$30.00	$28.00	$23.00
Expected regret	5.20	3.20	5.20	10.20
EVWPI	$33.20	$33.20	$33.20	$33.20

all cases obtain the EV of acting with perfect information. This is illustrated in Table 2.8. *The minimum regret value will always equal the value of perfect information.* This must be true, because perfect information eliminates any possibility that the decision maker will suffer regret.

Sample problem 2.5 **THE WILLIAMS COMPANY (Continued)**

Use the method of minimizing regret to solve the Williams Company problem given in Sample Problem 2.3.

SOLUTION

Conditional loss (regret) table

Demand values	Probability	Possible stock actions		
		Stock 6	*Stock 8*	*Stock 10*
6	.3	$ 0.00	$10.00	$20.00
7	.3	5.00	0.00	10.00
8	.2	20.00	0.00	10.00
9	.1	25.00	5.00	0.00
10	.1	40.00	20.00	0.00

Expected monetary (regret) table

Demand values	Probability	Possible stock actions		
		Stock 6	*Stock 8*	*Stock 10*
6	.3	$ 0.00	$ 3.00	$ 6.00
7	.3	1.50	0.00	3.00
8	.2	4.00	0.00	2.00
9	.1	2.50	0.50	0.00
10	.1	4.00	2.00	0.00
		$12.00	$ 5.50	$11.00

The use of marginal values in decision analysis

A basic principle of economics is that an entrepreneur can maximize profits by scheduling operations so that marginal cost equals marginal revenue. *Marginal cost* is the additional or incremental cost of increasing output by one unit. *Marginal revenue* is the additional or incremental revenue obtained by producing and selling one additional unit. If an entrepreneur is operating at a production level where marginal revenue is greater than marginal cost, production should be increased until marginal revenue equals marginal cost. Likewise, if present operations result in a marginal cost greater than marginal revenue, production should be decreased until the two are equal. By following these two decision rules, the entrepreneur will always reach an optimal level of production where marginal cost is equal to marginal revenue.

Expected marginal profit (EMP) and expected marginal loss (EML)

The marginal approach is also quite useful in decision analysis. Instead of marginal cost and marginal revenues, however, we must use the concepts of expected marginal profit and expected marginal loss. The term *marginal profit* (MP) denotes the profit received from stocking and selling an additional unit of merchandise. In the case of John's Little Peach Market, the profit realized from stocking and selling an additional unit is $4. The *expected marginal profit* (EMP) is the marginal profit for stocking and selling an additional unit multiplied by the probability that the unit will be sold. For example, if the marginal profit of a unit is $4 and there is a 50% chance that the unit can be sold, then the expected marginal profit is $2.

In the example of John's Little Peach Market, there was a 20% chance of selling exactly 7 bushels, a 40% chance of demand for exactly 8 bushels, a 30% chance of demand for exactly 9 bushels, and a 10% chance of demand for exactly 10 bushels. The probability of demand for 7 bushels or more is therefore equal to 1.00 (the probability of 7, 8, 9, or 10 bushels being demanded). This type of probability is a *cumulative probability*, because it represents the sum of the probabilities of several events. The cumulative probability of a particular demand is important, because it is the probability that a specific unit of inventory will be sold. Therefore, the probability that Mr. Edwards will sell the seventh bushel is 1.00. The cumulative probability of selling 8 or more bushels is .80. Thus, the probability of selling the eighth bushel is .80. Likewise, the probability of selling the ninth bushel is .40, and the probability of selling the tenth bushel, if stocked, is .10. These values have been entered in Table 2.9. We obtain the *expected marginal profit* (EMP) for each unit of peaches by multiplying the marginal profit value of $4 by each respective probability value. These values are shown in Table 2.10.

Table 2.9 *Probabilities of demand for John's Little Peach Market*

Bushels demanded	Probability of this specific demand	Cumulative probabilities
7	.20	1.00
8	.40	.80
9	.30	.40
10	.10	.10

The *marginal loss* (ML) associated with a particular unit of merchandise is the loss resulting from stocking an additional unit and then not being able to sell it. In our example, Mr. Edwards buys a bushel of peaches for $6. If he is unable to sell it, he takes a loss of $6 per bushel. Thus, the marginal loss is $6 per bushel. The *expected marginal loss* (EML) is obtained by multiplying the ML by the probability of not being able to sell the unit. If we let P represent the marginal probability of being able to sell a particular unit, then $(1 - P)$ will represent the probability of not being able to sell that unit. The EML can be obtained by multiplying the ML by $(1 - P)$.

The use of EMP and EML in decision analysis

The EMP and EML values for John's Little Peach Market are given in Table 2.10. A general decision rule for the "buy or no buy" decision could be stated as follows: Mr. Edwards should continue to purchase additional bushels as long as the EMP from stocking the additional unit is greater than the EML. Mr. Edwards should purchase the seventh and eighth bushels, because, in each of these cases, the EMP is greater than the EML. He should not purchase the ninth and tenth bushels, however, because the EMP is less than the EML.

Table 2.10 *Calculations of marginal profit and marginal loss for John's Little Peach Market*

Bushels demanded	Marginal probability of sale (P)	Marginal probability of no sale (1 − P)	Marginal profit	Marginal loss	Expected marginal profit	Expected marginal loss
7	1.00	.00	$4	$6	$4.00	$0.00
8	.80	.20	4	6	3.20	1.20
9	.40	.60	4	6	1.60	3.60
10	.10	.90	4	6	.40	5.40

For analytical purposes, it would be helpful to solve for the value of P that would equate EMP and EML. We will refer to this particular value of P as P'. Once we have determined this value, we can express the "buy or no buy" decision rule in an alternative way. We can say that purchases should be increased as long as P is greater than P'. If P' is greater than P, then purchases should be reduced until the two are equal. We will use John's Little Peach Market to illustrate this concept.

The first step is to find P', the value where EMP is equal to EML.

$$\text{EMP} = \text{EML}$$
$$P'(\text{MP}) = (1 - P')\text{ML}$$
$$P'(\text{MP}) = \text{ML} - P'(\text{ML})$$
$$P'(\text{MP}) + P'(\text{ML}) = \text{ML}$$
$$P'(\text{MP} + \text{ML}) = \text{ML}$$
$$P' = \text{ML}/(\text{MP} + \text{ML})$$

In our example,

$$\text{MP} = \$4 \qquad \text{and} \qquad \text{ML} = \$6$$
$$P' = \frac{6.00}{(4.00 + 6.00)} = \frac{6}{10} = .60$$

We should continue to purchase additional bushels as long as P, the probability of a sale, is greater than P'. Thus, the optimal stock action is the largest stock action with a P value greater than P'. From Table 2.10, we know that a stock action of 8 has a P value of .8. This is the largest stock action with a probability of sale greater than .6, the value of P'. It is the optimal stock action, and it is the same stock action that we determined to be optimal when we used conditional profit tables and expected monetary tables.

The "marginal way of thinking" is quite useful in decision analysis. In most managerial situations, we are concerned with the future rather than the past. We are concerned with the next increment, the next unit, or the next step. In most cases, if the next step is profitable, we should take it. Marginal analysis allows us to determine how far to proceed in a given direction and at what point further progress down a given path will be unprofitable. If we are walking down a path of 1000 stepping stones, it may be much easier to determine where to stop than to choose the optimal one of 1000 stones. In the case of John's Little Peach Market, we had only four possible stock actions and four possible sales levels. In many situations, the number of these values may well increase to 100 or more. Rather than evaluate each of the possible alternatives, we might turn to the marginal approach, wherein each additional item stocked can only result in an increase or decrease in profit.

Decision analysis with continuous variables

In the example of John's Little Peach Market, demand is a repeating event; that is, it recurs day after day. It is therefore known as a random variable. A *random variable* is a repeating chance event with a numerically defined outcome. In many business problems, the random variables have a very large number of possible outcomes. For example, the number of orders received per day at a catalog distribution center can vary by as much as 10,000 units. Because of this, it may be practically impossible to analyze the problem using conditional profit tables and expected monetary tables. An alternative method of analysis is to approximate the discrete distribution of the random variable with a continuous distribution and then perform decision analysis on the continuous distribution.

Comparison of discrete and continuous distributions

A random variable has a *discrete distribution* if it can assume only certain values within a given range. It is sometimes easier to give a backwards definition. A distribution is discrete if there are certain values within a given range that the random variable cannot assume. The distribution of the number of students in various classes is discrete, because there cannot be 27.34 or any other fractional number of students in a given class. The distribution of the number of rainy days per month is also discrete.

A random variable has a *continuous distribution* if it can take on any value within a given range. The amount of daily rainfall is a continuous random variable because it can take on any value from zero to the maximum daily amount of rainfall. Likewise, the distribution of the amount of fuel oil in each of 1000 80-gallon tanks is a continuous distribution, because the random variable can take on any value between 0 and 80.

The normal distribution

The best known continuous distribution is the normal distribution represented by the bell-shaped curve. The normal curve is widely used because it is often a good approximation of reality. Many real distributions can be approximated by the normal distribution. Both the heights and the weights of individuals tend to be normally distributed. Student grade-point averages, daily sales values, and golf scores in a professional tournament also tend to be normally distributed. Since the normal curve closely approximates many business phenomena, we can often use it in decision analysis.

Many readers of this text are probably familiar with the normal distribution. Those who are not should refer to Chapter 14 of this book.

The first section of Chapter 14 describes the normal distribution and its role in managerial analysis. It also explains the use of Table A in the Appendix, which gives areas under the normal curve. This material will also be helpful to those who wish to review the subject.

The use of the normal distribution in decision analysis

Let us assume that Ms. Dalton owns a large peach stand. She buys peaches for $14 a bushel and sells them for $20 a bushel. There is no salvage value. In the past, Ms. Dalton's demand has averaged 140 bushels per day with a standard deviation of 20 bushels. This demand distribution is represented by the normal curve shown in Figure 2.11. Ms. Dalton wonders what her optimal daily stock action should be in order to maximize daily profit contribution.

We know that Ms. Dalton should continue to stock additional bushels until she reaches a level where the probability of selling an additional bushel is equal to ML/(MP + ML). The ML resulting from purchasing a bushel that cannot be sold is $14. The MP resulting from purchasing and selling an additional unit is $6. Therefore,

$$P' = \frac{ML}{(MP + ML)} = \frac{14}{(6 + 14)} = .70$$

This P' value represents the probability of selling the next unit. Thus, in Figure 2.11, we are trying to determine the value that divides the distribution so that 70% of the curve lies to the right of the value and 30% lies to the left of the value. In Figure 2.11, we have labeled the 30-70 "split value" as position X. Since 30% of the area is less than X, it must be true that 20% of the area is between the mean (140) and X. From Table A in the Appendix, we learn that .52 standard deviation units encompass approximately 20% of the measurements (19.85%, to be more precise). Thus, the number of standard deviation units between the mean and X is .52. Since the standard deviation of demand is 20,

Figure 2.11 *Illustration of optimal stock action with no salvage value*

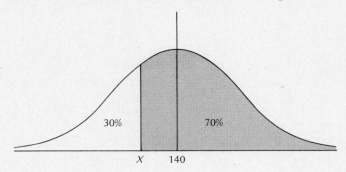

30%   70%

X 140

the numerical value of X is 129.60; that is, $140 - (.52)(20) = 129.60$. At this point, the probability of selling an additional unit is .70. Ms. Dalton's optimal stock action is to stock approximately 129 bushels of peaches.

As another example, suppose that Ms. Dalton is able to locate a salvage market where peaches unsold at the end of the day may be disposed of for a salvage price of $10 a bushel. Ms. Dalton still has a marginal profit of $6 if she buys an additional unit and is able to sell it in the regular market. The marginal loss of stocking a unit that cannot be sold in the regular market is now $4, because it can be disposed of for $10 in the salvage market. We can calculate our new P' value as follows:

$$P' = \frac{ML}{(MP + ML)} = \frac{4}{(6 + 4)} = .4$$

Figure 2.12 illustrates the situation Ms. Dalton faces when there is a salvage value for her peaches. She will want to continue to purchase additional units until the probability of selling an additional unit has decreased to .40. Position Y represents the value that divides the distribution so that 40% of the distribution lies to the right and 60% lies to the left of the given value. Since 40% of the distribution lies to the right of Y, it must be true that 10% of the measurements lie between the mean (140) and Y. From Table A in the Appendix, we know that .25 standard deviation units contain 10% (9.87%, to be precise) of all measurements. Thus, the distance from the mean (140) to Y is .25 standard deviation units. The numerical value of Y is 145.00. Ms. Dalton's optimal stock action is to purchase 145 bushels daily. Under present demand conditions, she can do no better.

In these examples, we used the normal distribution, which serves as a good approximation of many business phenomena. Some business

Figure 2.12 *Illustration of optimal stock action with salvage value*

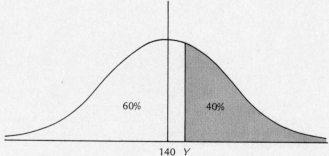

situations are better approximated by other distributions, such as the *Poisson distribution* and the *beta distribution*. If an analyst is in doubt, there are tests to determine if a particular distribution is appropriate to the problem under consideration. Having selected the distribution, the analyst can use tables that are available.

Sample problem 2.6 THE B & F COMPANY

The B & F Company is a large wholesaler of fresh seafood. The company purchases a certain type of seafood for $125 a case and resells it for $200 a case. All resales must be made the same day the seafood is received. Past daily demand has been normally distributed with an arithmetic mean of 650 cases a day and a standard deviation of 120 cases a day. Determine the optimal daily purchase action if:

1. There is no salvage value.
2. There is a daily salvage value of $120 per case.

SOLUTION

1. $MP = 75$ $ML = 125$ $P' = 125/(75 + 125) = .625$
   Area to the left of the mean is $.625 - .500 = .125$
   From tables: .32 standard deviation units
   Optimal stock action is $650 - (.32)(120) = 611$ cases
2. $MP = 75$ $ML = 5$ $P' = 5/(75 + 5) = .0625$
   Area to the right of the mean is $.5000 - .0625 = .4375$
   From tables: 1.53 standard deviation units
   Optimal stock action is $650 + (1.53)(120) = 833$

The use of expected value in decision analysis

Throughout this chapter, we have assumed that the concept of EV can be used to determine indifference relationships. For example, we have assumed that an individual would be indifferent between a sure sum of $10 and a chance situation wherein there is a 50% chance of receiving $20 and a 50% chance of receiving nothing. We have also assumed that given two or more alternatives, an individual will select that alternative with the highest expected value. The following examples may make us question these assumptions.

Assume that Sam Rideshort is approached by Harry Horsetrader, who makes the following proposition. A fair coin will be tossed. If the coin lands heads, Sam will collect $100. If the coin lands tails, Sam will lose $6. This simple decision situation is diagrammed in Figure 2.13.

Figure 2.13 *Sam Rideshort's problem*

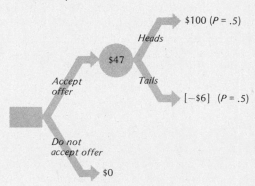

Sam has two alternatives. He may accept the offer, which has an EV of $47, or he may choose not to accept the offer, in which case the payoff is a sure sum of $0. Our EV decision analysis tells us that Sam should accept the proposition.

Now imagine that Sam and Harry live in the days of the Old West. Sam Rideshort is a horse thief who has been caught and is to be hanged at sunrise. Fortunately for Sam, the owner of the horse is a benevolent individual who asked for and obtained Sam's temporary release. Sam was told that if he could earn $6 to pay for the horse before sunrise tomorrow, he would not be hanged. Sam has worked diligently to earn the $6. He is ready to pay the money to the owner when he meets Harry Horsetrader. Harry has a proposition for him. A fair coin will be flipped. If it lands heads, Sam Rideshort will collect $100. If it lands tails, Sam will lose $6. Monetarily, this situation is identical to the situation diagrammed in Figure 2.13. Nevertheless, we doubt that Sam would elect to accept the proposal with the highest EV.

In this example, Sam simply could not risk the gamble. We can easily imagine business examples of the same type. From an EV perspective, fire insurance may not be a good buy, but the possibility of fire destroying a business may make it not only a good buy but a necessity.

Individuals and organizations have various attitudes toward risk. Some people are born gamblers and like to take risks. Others tend to be more conservative and prefer to avoid risk. The EV concept is sometimes criticized for not taking into consideration the decision maker's attitude toward risk. When necessary, we can consider attitude toward risk by incorporating utility theory with the EV concept.

In *utility theory*, a *preference curve* is developed for the decision maker. This curve is a summary of his or her attitudes toward risk. This curve can be used to determine *certainty equivalents* for chance events in the decision problem. Then we can apply the methods of decision analysis discussed in this chapter to the decision situation.

Knowledge of utility theory and preference curves is necessary for the person specializing in decision analysis. Many excellent discussions of utility theory are available in professional journals and more advanced textbooks. For most of us, however, knowledge of the decision process is the most important consideration. In many cases, the EV concept serves as a very effective means of determining indifference relationships. When necessary, we can incorporate utility theory or obtain the assistance of a specialist in the field.

Problems and exercises

1. Explain the following terms:

   certainty
   uncertainty
   risk
   decision tree
   decision point
   chance event
   objective probability
   subjective probability
   perfect information
   EVPI
   informational probabilities
   expected value

   indifference relationship
   random variable
   continuous distribution
   discrete distribution
   normal distribution
   conditional profit
   regret value
   opportunity losses
   marginal analysis
   expected marginal profit
   expected marginal loss
   EVWPI

INSTRUCTIONS FOR PROBLEMS 2–13

Draw a decision tree for each of the following decision situations. Show each decision point and each chance event. Insert all probability values and financial data. Use the backward reduction method to analyze each decision situation.

2. The Randolph Concession Company is considering bidding on the concessions at the homecoming game. There is no cost to bid preparation. The company can bid for either the beverage concession or the hot dog concession, but not both. There is a 40% probability of either bid being accepted. The company's estimates of net profits depend on whether it is a rainy day or a clear day. For the beverage concession, the company estimates a profit of $2000 on a clear day and a loss of $2000 on a rainy day. For the hot dog concession, the company estimates a profit of $1000 regardless of weather conditions. Past experience indicates that during this time of year, 70% of the days are clear and 30% of the days are rainy. Should the company prepare a bid, and if so, should it be for beverages or hot dogs?

3. In problem 2, suppose the company knows that if it bids for beverages, and if its bid is accepted, it can choose either cold beverages or coffee (but not both). If it chooses cold beverages, then net profits will be $2000 for a clear day and losses will be $2000 for a rainy day. If coffee is chosen, net profit will be $2000 for a rainy day and $1000 (profit) for a clear day. All other factors remain the same. Should the company bid for beverages, bid for hot dogs, or prepare no bid at all?

4. The Pickering Company is considering the purchase of mineral rights on a piece of property for $100,000. The price includes a seismic test to indicate whether the property has a type A geological formation or a type B geological formation. The company will be unable to tell the type of geological formation until after the purchase is made. It is known, however, that 40% of the land in this area has a type A geological formation and 60% of the land has a type B geological formation. If the company decides to drill on the land, it will cost $200,000. If the company does drill, it may hit an oil well, a gas well, or a dry hole. Drilling experience indicates that the probability of bringing in an oil well is .4 on an A formation and only .1 on a B formation. The probability of hitting gas is .2 on an A formation and .3 on a B formation. The estimated return (discounted cash value) from an oil well is $800,000 and from a gas well is $500,000. This includes everything except the cost of the mineral rights and the cost of drilling. Should the company purchase mineral rights?

5. The Marshall Company is planning to build a new plant to manufacture a new product. At the moment, it has two options. It can build a large plant or it can build a small plant. Its expected return depends on the ability of the competition to develop a similar product. If it builds a large plant and no competition develops, management feels that the net return (discounted cash value) will be $800,000. If competition develops, net return will be $300,000. If the company builds a small plant, it has two additional options. It can maintain the small plant for the life of the product, or it can expand its plant after three years. With competition, the expected return is $100,000 with plant expansion and $300,000 with no plant expansion. With no competition, the expected return is $600,000 with plant expansion and $350,000 with no expansion. There is a 50% chance of the competition developing the product within the first three years. It is known that competitors will not develop the product unless they do it in the first three years. What course of action should the Marshall Company follow?

6. The Smith Company is an independent R&D contractor, which has been asked to submit a proposal for developing a new product. It will cost the company $10,000 to prepare this proposal. It is estimated that if the Smith Company submits the proposal, the chances are 50-50 that it will receive the contract. It is not certain that the product can actually be developed, but there are three known methods of development that can be followed.

Method A will cost $140,000 and the company is 80% certain that it will be successful. Method B will cost $70,000 and the probability of success is .60. Method C will cost $30,000 and the probability of success is .40. Because of time limitations, the Smith Company can try only one of these three methods. If the company receives the contract and supplies the product, it will receive $300,000. No penalty is charged for failing to produce the product. Should the Smith Company prepare a proposal?

7. The Clay Manufacturing Company has been approached by an individual who has an idea for a new "summer product." He wants to sell this idea for $20,000. If the idea is purchased, the product must be developed. The company can develop the product at a cost of $50,000, and company engineers are 50% certain that they can develop it in time for the summer market. An independent R&D firm has offered to develop the product. This will also cost $50,000, but they are only 30% certain that they can get the product ready for the summer market. No charge will be levied unless they are successful. If the product is developed, it must be advertised. The advertising manager has proposed two advertising plans for the new product. Plan A will cost $50,000. With this plan, the marketing manager feels the probability of the product being a success is .70. Plan B costs $30,000 and the probability of success is .50. Management believes that if the product is a success, the net return will be $300,000 (including all costs except purchase, development, and advertising). Even if the product is not a success, management believes that enough sales will be made so that the only loss will be the costs of purchasing, developing, and advertising. Should Clay Manufacturing purchase this idea?

8. Assume that the company in problem 2 has the option of buying a perfect weather forecast before deciding which bid to prepare. Should it buy this information? What is the EVPI? What other actions should the company take?

9. Assume that *if* the company in problem 3 makes and receives a beverage bid, it will then have the option of buying a perfect weather forecast before deciding on coffee or cold beverages. What is the EVPI? Should the company pay $300 for this information?

10. Suppose that the company in problem 4 could obtain the results of the seismic test that would correctly determine which formation exists before purchasing the mineral rights. What is the expected value of this information?

11. Suppose that the Pickering Company in problem 4 could obtain perfect information about whether it would hit a dry hole, a gas well, or an oil well, and that it could obtain this information before deciding whether to purchase mineral rights. What is the EV of this perfect information?

12. Assume that the Smith Company in problem 6 can buy perfect information about whether method A, method B, or method C can be used successfully

for product development. The company is considering purchasing this information before deciding on whether to prepare a proposal. What is the EVPI?

13. Assume that the cost of the information in problem 12 is $10,000. Should the Smith Company purchase the information before preparing the proposal or after the proposal has been prepared and a decision on acceptance or rejection has been received? Suppose the cost of the information were reduced to $300. When should the information now be purchased?

INSTRUCTIONS FOR PROBLEMS 14–18

In each of the following problems, determine the EV of the event described.

14. A coin is flipped, and $2 is paid for a head and $4 for a tail.

15. Two coins are flipped simultaneously, and $2 is paid for each head and $4 for each tail.

16. A single card is drawn from a standard deck of 52; $52 is paid for an ace and $26 for any other face card (king, queen, or jack). A loss of $13 is charged for any other card (2 through 10).

17. The Livingston Company is planning to drill an oil well at a certain location. From past experience, analysts know that there is a 10% chance of hitting a combination well, a 20% chance of hitting an oil well, a 30% chance of hitting a gas well, and a 40% chance of the well not producing. It is estimated that the return to the company would be $800,000 for a combination well, $600,000 for an oil well, $400,000 for a gas well, and nothing for a nonproductive well.

18. The McLane Company spends $40,000 to prepare a bid on a construction project. If the contract is awarded, estimated profit will be $200,000. If the contract is not awarded, the company will lose the $40,000. There is a 40% chance that the company will receive the contract.

INSTRUCTIONS FOR PROBLEMS 19–31

Analyze each of the following problems by constructing an appropriate table(s), such as an expected monetary table, a conditional profit table, a perfect information table, and/or a regret table.

19. The Forsyth Company operates an apple stand at the corner of Main and Fifth Streets. The company buys apples for $6 a bushel and sells them for $12 a bushel. At the end of each day, all unsold apples must be discarded. There is no salvage value. Past demand has been for 5 bushels on 40 days, 6 bushels on 60 days, 7 bushels on 60 days, and 8 bushels on 40 days. Using the EV concept, find the optimal daily stock action.

20. Suppose that the manager of the Forsyth Company in problem 19 could obtain a perfect daily demand forecast before deciding how many bushels of apples to purchase. What is the value of this perfect information?

21. Construct a regret table for problem 19 and solve for the optimal stock action by minimizing the expected regret value.

22. Assume that in problem 19 there is a salvage market wherein apples unsold at the end of the day may be disposed of at a salvage value of $2 a bushel. What is the optimal daily stock action? What is the EV of the salvage market?

23. The Webster Company operates a newsstand at the corner of Central and Sixth Streets. Every week it purchases a given quantity of *Corrick's Weekly* for 30 cents a copy and sells the newspapers during the week for 50 cents a copy. The company may order either 12 copies or 15 copies each week. Copies left over at the end of the week must be discarded with no value. Experience has indicated that the probability of demand for 11 through 16 copies is as follows:

Copies	11	12	13	14	15	16
Probability	.1	.2	.2	.2	.2	.1

What is the EV of the optimal weekly stock action?

24. In problem 23, suppose copies that remain unsold at the end of the week may be sold as scrap paper for 5 cents a copy. What is the optimal daily stock action?

25. In problem 24, assume that a perfect weekly forecast for *Corrick's Weekly* could be obtained and used in determining the amount (12 or 15 copies) of newspapers purchased each week. What is the EVWPI? What is the EVPI?

26. Construct a regret table for problem 24, and solve for the optimal stock action by minimizing the expected regret value.

27. The Upshur Company owns a watermelon stand at the corner of Richmond Avenue and Lakeshore Boulevard. The company buys watermelons for $10 a bushel and sells them for $18 a bushel. Watermelons not sold at the end of the day must be discarded at no salvage value. Demand for the past 150 days has been as follows: 9 bushels for 30 days, 10 bushels for 45 days, 11 bushels for 45 days, and 12 bushels for 30 days. Using the concept of EV, what is the optimal daily stock action?

28. In problem 27, assume that a perfect sales forecast is available before Upshur Company must decide how many watermelons to purchase. What is the maximum amount that the company should pay for this information?

29. Construct a regret table for problem 27, and solve for the optimal daily stock action by minimizing the EV of regret.

30. The Ajax Company is trying to determine which of three overall marketing strategies to adopt for next year. The profit expected from each of these strategies will be significantly affected by economic conditions that develop during the year. Ajax's economists have estimated that the odds are 20%, 50%, and 30% for poor, average and good economic conditions respectively. The following decision matrix represents Ajax's view of the problem. Payoffs are corporate profits in millions of dollars.

		Economic conditions		
		Poor (.2)	Average (.5)	Good (.3)
Strategy	S_1	10	15	20
	S_2	5	20	30
	S_3	−10	10	50

a. What is the EV of the best decision?

b. What is the expected regret of the best decision?

c. What is the expected profit if a perfect forecasting device is available?

d. How much would Ajax be willing to pay for a perfect forecast?

31. In problem 27, what is the EV of the optimal stock action if a salvage market can be found where unsold watermelons can be disposed of at $2 a bushel? What is the expected daily value of this salvage market?

INSTRUCTIONS FOR PROBLEMS 32–42

Each problem deals with a concept discussed in this chapter. Answer the question asked.

32. In problem 19, determine the EMP and EML of each bushel of apples. Use this information to determine the optimal stock action. Repeat the procedure for problem 22 (where there is salvage value).

33. In problem 27, determine the EMP and EML of each additional watermelon stocked. Use this information to determine the optimal stock action.

34. Characterize each of the following as having either discrete or continuous distributions.

    a. Number of runs scored in major league baseball games

    b. Baseball players' batting averages

    c. Distance traveled by home run balls

    d. Amount of popcorn sold at baseball games

    e. Amount of weight gained by spectators from eating popcorn at a baseball game

35. Past daily demand (for the last 1000 days) has averaged 3600 with a standard deviation of 800. Assume that demand can be approximated by the normal curve. What percent of daily demand values have been:

    a. Greater than 3600?   c. Between 3200 and 6000?

    b. Greater than 4600?   d. Greater than 2200?

36. Past daily demand has an arithmetic mean of 550 with a standard deviation of 50 and can be approximated by the normal distribution. What percent of daily demand values have been:

    a. Less than 475?   c. Greater than 475?

    b. Between 475 and 575?   d. Between 475 and 550?

37. Assume that the data in problem 35 represent the daily demand situation for the Calhoun Company, an importer of highly perishable flowers. The

company's cost is $3 per flower, and its selling price is $8 per flower. The flowers cannot be saved from day to day, and there is no salvage value. What is the optimal level of stock for the firm to carry?

38. In problem 37, assume that a salvage market has been located where flowers left at the end of the day can be sold for $2 per flower. With this salvage market, what is the optimal level of stock for the firm to carry?

39. Assume that the data in problem 36 represent the daily demand situation for John's Big Peach Market. Peaches are bought for $5 a bushel and sold for $9 a bushel. Peaches remaining unsold at the end of the day must be destroyed, and there is no salvage value. What is the optimal daily stock action?

40. In problem 39, assume that a new city ordinance requires that all peaches remaining at the end of the day be destroyed by incineration. The charge for incineration is $2 per bushel. What is the optimal daily stock action?

41. The Clayton Company sells the new magazine *George's Weekly* at its news-stand. Past weekly demand has averaged 70 copies with a standard deviation of 12 copies. The Clayton Company purchases the magazine for 20 cents and sells it for 50 cents. Magazines remaining at the end of the week are discarded with no salvage value. What is the optimal weekly stock action?

42. In problem 41, assume that magazines not sold during the week can be sold for scrap for 5 cents a copy. What is the optimal weekly stock action?

Supplementary readings

Anderson, D. R., D. J. Sweeney, and T. A. Williams. *An Introduction to Management Science*. St. Paul, Minn.: West, 1976.

Brown, R. V., A. S. Kahr, and C. Peterson. *Decision Analysis for the Manager*. New York: Holt, 1974.

Brown, R. V. "Do Managers Find Decision Theory Useful?" *Harvard Business Review*, 48 (May–June 1970), 78–89.

Chernoff, H., and L. E. Moses. *Elementary Decision Theory*. New York: Wiley, 1957.

Hammond, John S. "Better Decisions with Preference Theory." *Harvard Business Review*, 45 (November–December 1967), 123–141.

Lapin, L. L. *Quantitative Methods for Business Decisions*. New York: Harcourt Brace Jovanovich, 1976.

Levin, R. I., and C. A. Kirkpatrick. *Quantitative Approaches to Management*, 3d. ed. New York: McGraw-Hill, 1975.

Luce, R. D., and H. Raiffa. *Games and Decisions*. New York: Harcourt Brace Jovanovich, 1973.

Magee, John F. "Decision Trees for Decision Making." *Harvard Business Review*, 42 (July–August 1964), 126–138.

Mendenhall, W. and J. E. Reinmuth. *Statistics for Management and Economics*. Belmont, Calif.: Wadsworth, 1971.

Raiffa, H. *Decision Analysis: Introductory Lectures on Choices Under Uncertainty*. Reading, Mass.: Addison-Wesley, 1968.

Schlaifer, R. *Analysis of Decisions Under Uncertainty*. New York: McGraw-Hill, 1961.

Swalm, R. O. "Utility Theory — Insights into Risk Taking." *Harvard Business Review*, 44 (November–December 1966), 123–136.

Chapter 3

Probabilities and decision analysis

Illustrative example: JOSE'S MAGIC URN

According to legend, the Spanish pirate Jose owned two apparently identical mosaic urns. One of the urns had mystical powers, however. When taken on a voyage, the magic urn ensured that the seas on which Jose sailed would always be calm, even in the middle of a raging storm. Needless to say, the magic urn became one of Jose's most treasured possessions.

The second urn, which Jose called the common urn, possessed no magic or mystical powers. Jose had often thought of discarding the common urn. He decided, however, that discarding the common urn might arouse suspicion and therefore kept both urns in the cabin of his ship. In order to distinguish between the two urns, Jose placed seven gold and two silver nuggets in the magic urn. In the common urn he placed four nuggets, three of which were silver and one of which was gold.

Jose's ship was sunk in deep water years ago. Until recently, all attempts at salvage failed. Seven years ago, however, one of the mosaic urns was recovered. This urn is being offered for sale in an antique shop in a Midwestern city.

Ms. Janice Kelly is the curator of a nautical museum located in the northern portion of the Cumberland Mountains. She has petitioned her board of directors for the money to purchase Jose's urn. Unfortunately, Ms. Kelly cannot guarantee that the urn for sale is the magic urn. She must admit that there is a 50% chance that the urn for sale is the common urn. The directors of the museum are unwilling to purchase the urn unless there is a "reasonable belief" that the urn for sale is the magic urn rather than the common urn. They have informed Ms. Kelly that she can purchase the urn only if she is 75% certain that it is the magic urn.

Ms. Kelly has one hope. She knows that every leap year, on Halloween night, a nugget is drawn at random from the urn and given to the governor of the state. The first nugget was drawn three years ago, but the governor refused to say whether it was silver or gold. This year, however, he has promised to reveal whether the nugget is gold or silver. Ms. Kelly hopes she can use this information to revise her estimate of the probability that the urn for sale is the magic urn.

In Chapter 2, we discussed the importance of subjective probabilities in decision making. We noted that before deciding to visit a restaurant for lunch, we make a mental judgment about the probability of the restaurant being crowded. Likewise, we may wonder if the likelihood of a physical malady being serious is great enough to warrant a trip to the family physician. In the first case, we might telephone the restaurant and then revise our probability estimate on the basis of the information we receive. In the second case, we might also delay a decision until we have more information. If our temperature goes down, for example, it might decrease our probability estimate of something serious being wrong. If our temperature goes up, it would increase our belief (probability) that the malady is serious, and we might decide to seek the advice of a physician.

Probability revision in decision analysis

There are many business and management situations wherein additional information about a chance event may become available. For example, many companies revise sales estimates as new economic data become available. Good management practice requires that we use new information to revise our probability estimates about the outcomes of chance events. Good decision making depends on good subjective probability estimates, and good probability estimates depend on proper use of available information.

Probability trees

We will use a probability tree to analyze the problem faced by Ms. Kelly in the case of "Jose's Magic Urn," but first we should distinguish between a probability tree and a decision tree. A *decision tree* contains both chance events and decision points. A *probability tree* represents a situation with only chance events. Figure 3.1 represents the initial and second stages of the problem situation Ms. Kelly is investigating. One of Jose's two urns has been found and offered for sale. Without further knowledge, we have to assume a 50% chance that it is the magic urn and a 50% chance that it is the common urn. Thus, the probability of moving from position A to position B in Figure 3.1 is .50, and the probability of moving from position A to position C is also .50.

Figure 3.2 extends our representation of the magic urn problem to the third stage by including the possible outcomes of the governor's first draw. In the second stage, we do not know if the magic urn was found (position B) or if the common urn was found (position C). If it was the magic urn, however, we know that one of two events could have occurred. The governor could have drawn either a gold nugget or a

Figure 3.1 *Schematic representation of the first stages of the probability tree for "Jose's Magic Urn"*

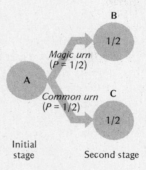

Initial
stage

Second stage

silver nugget from the urn. Since a total of 9 nuggets were in the magic urn, the probability of drawing a gold nugget from the magic urn is 7/9, and the probability of drawing a silver nugget from the magic urn is 2/9. We obtain the probability of the chain of events, "find the magic urn and draw a gold nugget," by multiplying the probability of finding the magic urn (1/2) by the probability of drawing a gold nugget from the magic urn (7/9). The probability of this chain of events is therefore 7/18.

As a second example, consider the chain of events, "find the common

Figure 3.2 *Expansion of the probability tree for "Jose's Magic Urn"*

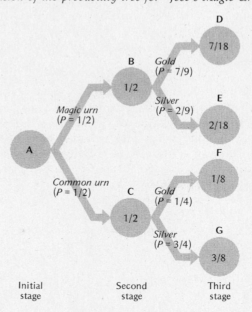

Initial
stage

Second
stage

Third
stage

urn and select a silver nugget," which leads to position G in Figure 3.2. The probability of finding the common urn is 1/2. The probability of selecting a silver nugget from the common urn is 3/4. Thus, the probability of both finding the common urn and selecting a silver nugget is 3/8. By the same method, the probability of "finding the magic urn and selecting a silver nugget" is 2/18, and the probability of "finding the common urn and selecting a gold nugget" is 1/8. These values have been entered at positions E and F respectively in Figure 3.2.

Figure 3.3 is a complete representation of the probability situation in the case of "Jose's Magic Urn." It includes all possible outcomes of the second (forthcoming) drawing by the governor. Position D represents the chain of events, "find the magic urn and select a gold nugget on the first draw." At this point, there are 8 nuggets left in the urn and 6 of them are gold. The probability of selecting another gold nugget is therefore 6/8, and the probability of selecting a silver nugget is 2/8. Thus, the probability of the chain of events, "find the magic urn, select a gold nugget on the first draw, and select a gold nugget on the second draw," is $[(1/2) \times (7/9) \times (6/8)]$, which is 42/144. Likewise, the probability of the chain of events, "find the magic urn, select a gold nugget on the first draw, and select a silver nugget on the second draw," is 14/144. These probabilities are entered in Figure 3.3 at positions J and K.

The situation at position F in Figure 3.3 may require special attention. At this position, the common urn has been found and a gold nugget has been drawn. There are now three nuggets left in the urn and all of them are silver. Thus, the probability of selecting another silver nugget is 1.0, or 3/3, and the probability of selecting a gold nugget is 0.0, or 0/3. The probability of the chain of events, "find the common urn, select a gold nugget on the first draw, and select a silver nugget on the second draw" is 3/24.

The remaining probabilities at positions L, M, R, and S in Figure 3.3 were determined by the same procedure. In order to simplify further analysis, all probabilities have been converted to a common denominator of 144. The column to the right of the fourth stage is a summary of the chain of events that led to a particular terminal position. For example, the M, G, and S at position K indicate that "the magic urn was found, a gold nugget was selected on the first draw, and a silver nugget was selected on the second draw."

Sample problem 3.1   THE MM & BL COMPANY

The MM & BL Company makes equal use of three available processes to grow zroids, which are microorganisms used in medical research. A culture grown by

Figure 3.3 *Complete probability tree for "Jose's Magic Urn"*

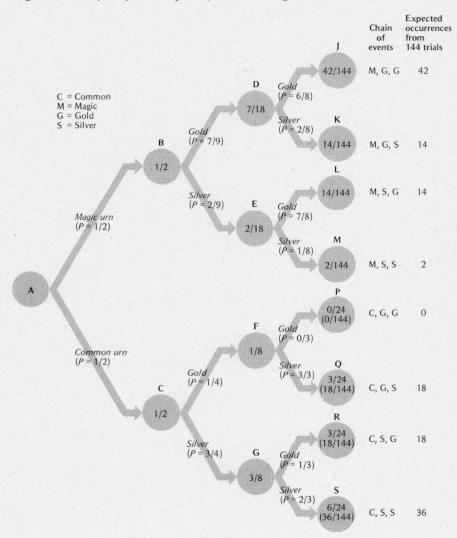

	Chain of events	Expected occurrences from 144 trials
J 42/144	M, G, G	42
K 14/144	M, G, S	14
L 14/144	M, S, G	14
M 2/144	M, S, S	2
P 0/24 (0/144)	C, G, G	0
Q 3/24 (18/144)	C, G, S	18
R 3/24 (18/144)	C, S, G	18
S 6/24 (36/144)	C, S, S	36

C = Common
M = Magic
G = Gold
S = Silver

Gold (P = 6/8)
Silver (P = 2/8)
D 7/18
Gold (P = 7/9)
B 1/2
Silver (P = 2/9)
E 2/18
Gold (P = 7/8)
Silver (P = 1/8)
Magic urn (P = 1/2)
A
Common urn (P = 1/2)
Gold (P = 0/3)
Silver (P = 3/3)
F 1/8
Gold (P = 1/4)
C 1/2
Silver (P = 3/4)
G 3/8
Gold (P = 1/3)
Silver (P = 2/3)

process 1 contains 62.5% red zroids, 25% yellow zroids, and 12.5% green zroids. Cultures from process 2 contain 50% red zroids and 50% yellow zroids. Cultures from process 3 contain 75% yellow zroids and 25% green zroids. A culture is randomly chosen from a large lot. One zroid is then selected from the culture and tested for color. Draw a probability tree for this problem situation.

SOLUTION

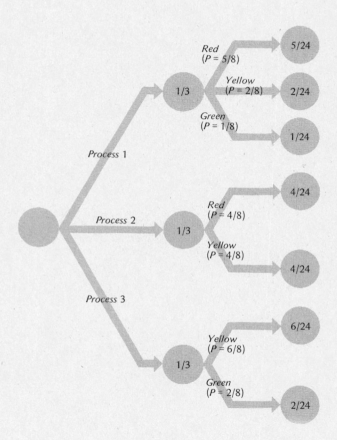

Utilizing trees in probability analysis

Assume that a situation identical to the situation described in "Jose's Magic Urn" was repeated 144 times. We would expect to arrive at position J in Figure 3.3 on 42 of those 144 occasions. We obtain this figure by multiplying the number of times a particular event is repeated (144 in this example) by the probability of occurrence of a particular outcome (42/144 for this particular chain of events). By a similar analysis, the numbers of times we would expect to arrive at positions K, L, M, P, Q, R, and S are 14, 14, 2, 0, 18, 18, and 36 respectively. This information is entered in the far right-hand column of Figure 3.3.

If a chance event is repeated a large number of times, then *the probability of a particular happening* (such as a gold nugget) *can be determined by the formula*

$$P = s/N$$

The denominator, N, is the number of times the chance event was repeated. The numerator, s, is the number of times a particular outcome occurred. Thus, the probability of a gold nugget being selected on the second draw is 74/144. We obtain the 74 by summing the number of occurrences of the chains of events that include a gold nugget on the second draw. These chains are represented by positions J, L, P, and R in Figure 3.3. Their respective numbers of occurrences are 42, 14, 0, and 18, which total 74. Likewise, the probability of a silver nugget being drawn on the second draw is 70/144.

Probability trees and probability revision

In the case of "Jose's Magic Urn," we know that Ms. Kelly should assign a value of .50 to the probability that the magic urn was found. We also know that a nugget was drawn from this urn three years ago, but Ms. Kelly does not know whether it was gold or silver. A second nugget will be drawn later this year, and whether it is gold or silver *will* be revealed. If possible, Ms. Kelly wants to use this information to revise her estimate of the probability that the magic urn was found.

Suppose the governor draws the second nugget and it is gold. Ms. Kelly then knows (with certainty) that we are *not* at position K, M, Q, or S in Figure 3.3, because all these positions represent the ends of chains of events that include a silver nugget selected on the second draw. *These outcomes may be eliminated from further consideration.* The only possible outcomes are now represented by positions J, L, P, and R. Instead of having 144 possible outcomes, we now only have 74 (the total for these four positions). Of these 74 possible outcomes, 56 of them (42 at position J and 14 at position L) represent a chain of events that includes finding the magic urn. Thus, if we know that a gold nugget was selected on the second draw, then the *revised probability* that the magic urn was found is 56/74, or .7568.

In this example, Ms. Kelly used new information to revise her probability estimate that the magic urn was recovered and is now for sale. Her board of directors had indicated that if she was at least 75% certain that the magic urn was for sale, she could purchase the urn. Based on new information, she now believes, with about 76% certainty, that it is the magic urn. The board of directors will authorize purchase. Note that if a silver nugget had been drawn, the probability that the magic urn had been found would have been only 16/70, which is approximately .23. In this case, the board would not have approved purchase of the urn.

Before going on, we should explore a few other examples of using new information to revise probability estimates. Each of the following questions refers to the case of "Jose's Magic Urn."

If it was known that the first nugget drawn and the second nugget drawn were both silver, what is the probability that they were drawn from the magic urn?

In Figure 3.3, positions M and S represent the ends of the only two chains of events that include the drawing of two silver nuggets. Thus N, the denominator of the equation $P = s/N$, is 38 (2 at M plus 36 at S). Of these two chains of events, only the one leading to position M includes finding the magic urn. Thus, the numerator s is 2 and the probability is 2/38, or .053.

If it is known that the second nugget is silver, what is the probability that the first nugget was also silver?

In Figure 3.3, positions K, M, Q, and S represent the ends of the only chains of events that include drawing a silver nugget on the second draw. Therefore N, the denominator, is 70. Since only positions M and S represent chains of events wherein both nuggets were silver, the numerator s is 38. Thus, the probability is 38/70 that the first nugget was silver if the second nugget is silver.

If the first nugget drawn was gold, what is the probability that the second nugget is also gold?

Positions J, K, P, and Q represent chains of events wherein the first nugget drawn was gold. Of these, J and P represent gold nuggets being drawn on both occasions. Thus, the probability is 42/74 that gold will be drawn on the second draw if the first nugget was gold.

We have been using a probability tree to help us use new information to revise our probability estimates. In the following sections, we will discuss other methods of using information to revise probability estimates. Which method to use is up to the individual. The important thing is to use the available information properly.

Sample problem 3.2   *THE MM & BL COMPANY (Continued)*

Consider the case of the MM & BL Company given in Sample Problem 3.1. Use the probability tree in the example to answer the following questions.

1. What is the probability that the zroid will be red?

2. If it is known that process 3 was *not* used, what is the probability that the zroid will be yellow?
3. If the zroid was red, what is the probability that process 1 was used?
4. If the zroid selected was green, what is the probability that the culture was developed using process 1? process 2? process 3?

SOLUTION

1. $(5 + 4)/24 = 9/24$

2. $(2 + 4)/(5 + 2 + 1 + 4 + 4) = 6/16 = 3/8$

3. $5/(5 + 4) = 5/9$

4. Process 1: $1/(1 + 2) = 1/3$

   Process 2: $0/(1 + 2) = 0/3$

   Process 3: $2/(1 + 2) = 2/3$

Review of probability terms and concepts

If authors, instructors, readers, and practitioners are to communicate effectively, a statement must mean exactly the same thing to the person who reads it as it does to the person who wrote it. For this reason, we should familiarize ourselves with certain terms, definitions, symbols, and concepts used in probability analysis. (The symbols used in this chapter are listed at the end of the chapter.)

Prior and posterior probabilities

Prior probabilities are probabilities assigned to the possible outcomes of chance events before additional information is obtained. *Posterior probabilities* are probabilities that have been revised in light of additional information. In the case of "Jose's Magic Urn," Ms. Kelly assigned a prior probability of 1/2 to the event that the magic urn had been found. After receiving the information that a gold nugget was drawn on the second draw, she revised her probability estimate to .7568. This revised probability estimate is known as a posterior probability.

As a second example, we might assign a high value (such as .95) to the probability that a production line is operating correctly. If we sampled items coming off the production line and found that all of the items we selected were bad, we would revise our probability estimate based on this new information. The probability estimate we made before sampling the product is a prior probability. The probability estimate we made after we obtained sampling information is a posterior probability. Since posterior probabilities are made with the benefit of additional information, we expect them to be better estimates than prior probabilities.

Marginal, unconditional, and conditional probabilities

The term *marginal probability* is often used to describe a simple, ordinary, or *unconditional probability*. The marginal probability is simply the probability that an event will happen. It is not "conditioned" on any prior knowledge or on the prior occurrence of any particular event. In the case of "Jose's Magic Urn," the marginal probability that the magic urn was found is 1/2. Likewise, the marginal probability of rolling an ace (one) on a single roll of a fair die is 1/6.

We let $P(A)$ stand for the marginal probability that event A will occur. The symbol $P(\bar{A})$ is often used for the probability that the event A will not occur. Similarly, we might use the following symbols for the events described.

$P(M) =$ Marginal probability that the magic urn was found

$P(H) =$ Marginal probability of obtaining a "heads" on a toss of a coin

$P(\bar{2}) =$ Marginal probability of not obtaining a two on a single roll of a die

A *conditional probability* implies that certain additional information must be considered before the assignment of a numerical probability. Thus, in the case of "Jose's Magic Urn," we cannot state the probability of a gold nugget being drawn from an urn until we know from which urn the nugget is being drawn. Likewise, we cannot determine the probability of drawing a gold nugget on the second draw (from either particular urn) until we know what type of nugget was obtained on the first draw. In drawing from the magic urn, the probability of the second nugget being gold is 7/8 if the first nugget was silver and 6/8 if the first nugget was gold. There is a difference because the probability is "conditioned" on the outcome of the first draw.

A conditional probability is written $P(A|B)$ and is read, "the probability that event A will occur, given the information that event B has occurred." We might symbolically describe other conditional probabilities as follows:

$P(G_1|M) =$ Conditional probability that a gold nugget will be drawn on the first draw, given the information that the magic urn was found

$P(G_2|S_1) =$ Conditional probability that a gold nugget will be drawn on the second draw, given the information that a silver nugget was drawn on the first draw

$P(H_2|D_1) =$ Conditional probability that a heart will be drawn on the second draw, given the information that the first card drawn was a diamond

Independent, dependent, and mutually exclusive events

If two events are *statistically independent*, then the outcome of the first event has no effect on the outcome of the second event. If two events are *dependent,* then the outcome of one event does affect the probability that the other event will occur. For example, flipping two coins represents two independent events, because the outcome of the first coin (heads or tails) in no way affects the probability of the second coin landing heads (or tails). Likewise, two successive rolls of a die are independent, because the outcome of the first roll should not affect the probability distribution of the second roll of the die.

If two events (A and B) are independent, then

$$P(A|B) = P(A) \qquad \text{and} \qquad P(B|A) = P(B)$$

As an example, suppose we flip a nickel and a dime. Let

A = Obtain heads on the nickel

B = Obtain heads on the dime

The marginal probability of B (obtaining heads on the dime) is 1/2. Thus, $P(B) = 1/2$. Even if we have information that the nickel landed heads, $P(B|A)$ is still 1/2, because A has no effect on B. Thus, the information that A has occurred does not affect the probability estimate that B will occur. *For independent events, therefore, the conditional probability that B will happen, given that A has happened, is equal to the marginal or unconditional probability that B will happen.* We have already represented this relationship symbolically in saying that when events A and B are independent, $P(B|A) = P(B)$.

It should be pointed out that if two events are independent, then we cannot use the results of one event to revise our probability estimates about the other event. If we flip a fair coin, the probability of it landing heads on any particular toss is .5. This is true regardless of the outcome of any and all previous tosses. Thus, the results of previous flips in no way affect our probability estimate of the outcome of the next toss. Since the information received from one independent event cannot be used to revise the probability of a particular outcome of another independent event, we pay little attention to independent events in our discussion of probabilities and decision making.

Drawing two cards from a standard deck of 52 cards (without replacement) represents two *dependent events,* because the probability of a particular occurrence (such as the outcome "draw a heart") on the second card depends on the outcome of the first draw. If the first card was a heart, then $P(H_2|H_1)$ — the probability of obtaining a heart on the second draw given the information that a heart was obtained on the first draw — is 12/51. If the first card was a spade, then $P(H_2|S_1)$ is 13/51. The two card drawings are dependent events, because the probability of obtaining any particular outcome on one draw is dependent on the outcome of the other draw.

Two events (such as A and B) are *mutually exclusive* if the occurrence of one event excludes the possibility that the other event will occur. In other words, if A happens, B cannot happen; and if B happens, A cannot happen. Obtaining heads *and* obtaining tails on a flip of a single coin are mutually exclusive events, because both cannot be obtained at once. Likewise, the events "win" and "lose" for a single team in a single game are mutually exclusive. They cannot both happen.

Joint probability

Joint probability is the probability that two (or more) events will both happen. Such an occurrence is referred to as the *intersection of A and B*. Symbolically, we will let $P(AB)$ represent the probability of the joint event that both A and B will happen. Other symbols, such as $P(A$ and $B)$ and $P(A \cap B)$, are often used to represent the probability of the same joint event. Obviously, if A and B are mutually exclusive events, they cannot both happen, and the probability of the joint event AB is zero. In the case of "Jose's Magic Urn," if M represents the event, "the magic urn was found," and G represents the event, "a gold nugget was drawn on the first draw," then the joint event MG is the event, "the magic urn was found and a gold nugget was drawn on the first draw." The joint event MG_1S_2 is the event, "the magic urn was found, a gold nugget was drawn on the first draw, and a silver nugget was drawn on the second draw." As another example, the joint event H_1H_2 is the event, "two coins are flipped and both of them land heads."

Use of formulas in probability revision

We have been using probability trees to assist us in making and revising probability estimates. Probability trees are quite helpful in learning the concepts of probability analysis. They can also be very useful in analyzing probability situations. Many times, however, it may be more useful or convenient to use a formula or a combination of formulas in probability analysis. (The formulas discussed in this chapter are summarized at the end of the chapter.)

Multiplicative law of probability

The joint event AB is the event that both A and B will happen. The probability of the joint event AB is obtained by multiplying the marginal probability that A will happen by the conditional probability that B will happen given that A has happened. This relationship is often called the *multiplicative law of probability* and can be stated as follows:

$$P(AB) = P(A) \cdot P(B|A)$$

In the case of "Jose's Magic Urn," the probability of having the magic urn and obtaining a gold nugget on the first draw is given by the formula

$$P(MG_1) = P(M) \cdot P(G_1|M)$$
$$= \left(\frac{1}{2}\right) \cdot \left(\frac{7}{9}\right) = \frac{7}{18}$$

As another example, the probability of drawing two successive diamonds without replacement from a standard deck of 52 cards can be obtained by the formula

$$P(D_1D_2) = P(D_1) \cdot P(D_2|D_1)$$
$$= \left(\frac{1}{4}\right) \cdot \left(\frac{12}{51}\right) = \frac{12}{204}$$

In the special case where A and B are independent events, we know that $P(B|A) = P(B)$. Thus, *for independent events only, the multiplicative law of probability may be stated as follows:*

$$P(AB) = P(A) \cdot P(B)$$

Since flipping coins represents independent events, the probability of flipping two successive heads can be obtained as follows:

$$P(H_1H_2) = P(H_1) \cdot P(H_2)$$
$$= .5 \cdot .5 = .25$$

Likewise, if we draw a card from a deck of 52, replace the card, and reshuffle before drawing a second card, then these two events are independent. The probability of drawing a spade and a diamond (with replacement) in that order can be obtained as follows:

$$P(S_1D_2) = P(S_1) \cdot P(D_2)$$
$$= .25 \cdot .25 = .0625$$

Additive law of probability

The additive law of probability refers to the event, "either A will happen or B will happen or they both will happen." This "and/or" event is properly referred to as the *union of A and B.* We represent it symbolically as $(A \text{ or } B)$. [Many textbooks use $P(A + B)$ or $P(A \cup B)$.] The *additive law of probability* can be stated as follows:

$$P(A \text{ or } B) = P(A) + P(B) - P(AB)$$

Suppose we roll a die and let

A = The event of obtaining an odd number

B = The event of obtaining a 3 or less

We know that

$$P(A) = \frac{3}{6} = \frac{1}{2}$$

$$P(B) = \frac{3}{6} = \frac{1}{2}$$

$$P(B|A) = \frac{2}{3}$$

$$P(AB) = P(A) \cdot P(B|A) = \frac{1}{2} \cdot \frac{2}{3} = \frac{1}{3}$$

We can, therefore, use the additive law of probability to determine the probability that either A will occur, or B will occur, or they will both occur.

$$P(A \text{ or } B) = P(A) + P(B) - P(AB)$$
$$= \frac{3}{6} + \frac{3}{6} - \frac{2}{6} = \frac{4}{6}$$

Intuitively, we know this is correct. Of the six possible outcomes, four of them (1, 2, 3, and 5) satisfy either A (1, 3, and 5 are odd numbers) or B (1, 2, and 3 are $\leq$ 3). For this simple problem, the additive law of probability confirms what we would expect, that $P(A$ or $B)$ is 4/6.

If the events A and B are mutually exclusive, then the joint probability of both A and B happening is zero; that is, $P(AB) = 0$. Thus, *for mutually exclusive events only, the additive law may be stated as follows:*

$$P(A \text{ or } B) = P(A) + P(B)$$

Suppose we roll a die and let

A = The event of rolling a 6

B = The event of rolling an odd number

Since A and B are mutually exclusive,

$$P(A \text{ or } B) = P(A) + P(B)$$
$$= \frac{1}{6} + \frac{3}{6} = \frac{4}{6}$$

Bayes' theorem

The multiplicative law of probability was previously stated as follows:

$$P(AB) = P(A) \cdot P(B|A) \text{ or } P(AB) = P(B) \cdot P(A|B)$$

To obtain a formula for conditional probability, we rearrange the multiplicative law to read

$$P(A|B) = \frac{P(AB)}{P(B)}$$

This formula for conditional probability is generally referred to as *Bayes' theorem.* The theorem was named for the Reverend Thomas Bayes, an English mathematician and Presbyterian minister. Bayes' essays on conditional probability did not appear until after his death in 1761.

In the case of "Jose's Magic Urn" (see Figure 3.2), we can obtain the posterior probability that the magic urn was found, after being given the information that a silver nugget was drawn on the first draw, by using the formula

$$P(M|S_1) = P(MS_1)/P(S_1)$$

The event S_1 may occur in two different ways. The silver nugget may be drawn from the magic urn (MS_1) or it may be drawn from the common urn (CS_1). Using the additive law of probability,

$$P(S_1) = P(MS_1) + P(CS_1)$$

$$= \frac{8}{72} + \frac{27}{72} = \frac{35}{72}$$

Thus,
$$P(M|S_1) = \frac{(8/72)}{(35/72)} = \frac{8}{35}.$$

Bayes' theorem can be expanded to include multiple possible outcomes. First, let us consider two sequential dependent events A and B, where A represents event A happening, $\bar{A}$ represents event A not happening, B represents event B happening, and $\bar{B}$ represents event B not happening. Bayes' theorem can be written as follows:

$$P(A|B) = \frac{P(A) \cdot P(B|A)}{[P(A) \cdot P(B|A)] + [P(\bar{A}) \cdot P(B|\bar{A})]}$$

Let us use this statement of Bayes' theorem to rework the foregoing example drawn from the case of "Jose's Magic Urn." The question is: "What is the posterior probability that the magic urn was found, after being given the information that a silver nugget was drawn on the first draw?" Let

A = The event that the magic urn was found

$\bar{A}$ = The event that the magic urn was not found (that is, that the common urn was found)

B = The event of drawing a silver ball on the first draw

Thus,

$$P(A|B) = \frac{(1/2)(2/9)}{(1/2)(2/9) + (1/2)(3/4)} = \frac{8/72}{35/72} = \frac{8}{35}$$

This statement of Bayes' theorem assumes that the first event has only two possible outcomes; either event A happens or it does not happen. In some cases, the first event (or chain of events) may have multiple outcomes. *For multiple outcomes, Bayes' theorem may be restated as follows:*

$$P(A_i|B) = \frac{P(A_i) \cdot P(B|A_i)}{\sum_{i=1}^{n} [P(A_i) \cdot P(B|A_i)]}$$

As an example, assume that 3 identical urns are placed on a table. All 3 urns contain 2 red balls. However, urn 1 contains 1 green ball, urn 2 contains 4 green balls, and urn 3 contains 10 green balls. An urn is selected at random and then a ball is drawn from the selected urn. The ball is red. What is the probability that it came from urn 1?

In this case, the first event (A) is the selection of an urn, and it has three possible outcomes. A_1, A_2, and A_3 represent the outcomes of the first, second, and third urns being selected. We can use Bayes' theorem (for multiple outcomes) to determine the probability that urn 1 was selected, given that the ball drawn was red.

$$P(A_1|R) = \frac{P(A_1) \cdot P(R|A_1)}{[P(A_1) \cdot P(R|A_1)] + [P(A_2) \cdot P(R|A_2)] + [P(A_3) \cdot P(R|A_3)]}$$

$$P(A_1|R) = \frac{(1/3)(2/3)}{[(1/3)(2/3)] + [(1/3)(2/6)] + [(1/3)(2/12)]}$$

$$P(A_1|R) = \frac{8/36}{14/36} = \frac{8}{14}$$

Sample problem 3.3   THE MM & BL COMPANY (Continued)

Consider the MM & BL Company problem given in Sample Problems 3.1 and 3.2. Use the appropriate probability formulas to answer the questions asked in Sample Problem 3.2. Compare these answers with the results you obtained using the decision tree.

SOLUTION

1.
$$P(R) = P(1R) + P(2R) + P(3R)$$

$$\frac{5}{24} + \frac{4}{24} + \frac{0}{24} = \frac{9}{24}$$

2.
$$P(Y|\bar{3}) = P(Y\bar{3})/P(\bar{3})$$
$$P(Y\bar{3}) = P(1Y) + P(2Y)$$
$$\frac{2}{24} + \frac{4}{24} = \frac{6}{24}$$
$$P(\bar{3}) = P(1) + P(2)$$
$$\frac{1}{3} + \frac{1}{3} = \frac{2}{3}$$
$$P(Y|\bar{3}) = \frac{(6/24)}{(2/3)} = \frac{3}{8}$$

3.
$$P(1|R) = \frac{P(1R)}{P(R)}$$
$$= \frac{(5/24)}{(9/24)} = \frac{5}{9}$$

4. Process 1: $P(1|G) = P(1G)/P(G)$
$$\frac{(1/24)}{(3/24)} = \frac{1}{3}$$

Process 2: $P(2|G) = \dfrac{P(2G)}{P(G)}$
$$\frac{(0/24)}{(3/24)} = \frac{0}{3}$$

Process 3: $P(3|G) = \dfrac{P(3G)}{P(G)}$
$$\frac{(2/24)}{(3/24)} = \frac{2}{3}$$

Sample problem 3.4   COMMUNITY RESCUE SERVICE

1. Two rescue squads are normally available for emergencies in a certain community. Due to demands on their time, the probability of the first squad being able to respond to a particular emergency is .9. The probability of the second squad being able to respond is .8. Assume that the probability of one squad being able to respond is independent of the probability of the other squad being able to respond. Also let A be the event that the first squad can respond and B be the event that the second squad can respond. In the event of an emergency, determine
    a. The probability that both rescue squads can respond
    b. The probability that neither will be available
    c. The probability that at least one rescue squad will be available
2. In Problem 1 assume that the availabilities of the rescue squads are not independent. The probability of the first squad being available is .8. The probability of the second squad being available is .6 if the first squad is

available and .5 if the first squad is not available. If it is known that the second squad is available, what is the probability that the first squad is also available?

SOLUTION FOR PROBLEM 1

a. $P(AB) = P(A) \times P(B)$ (independent events)

$$= .9 \times .8 = .72$$

b. $P(\overline{AB}) = P(\bar{A}) \times P(\bar{B})$

$$= .1 \times .2 = .02$$

c. $P(A \text{ or } B) = P(A) + P(B) - P(AB)$

$$.9 + .8 - .72 = .98$$

SOLUTION FOR PROBLEM 2

$$P(AB) = P(A) \times P(B|A) = .8 \times .6 = .48$$
$$P(\bar{A}B) = P(\bar{A}) \times P(B|\bar{A}) = .2 \times .5 = .10$$
$$P(B) = P(AB) + P(\bar{A}B) = .48 + .10 = .58$$
$$P(A|B) = \frac{P(AB)}{P(B)} = \frac{.48}{.58} = .83$$

Illustrative example: WALES MACHINE PARTS, INC.

Wales Machine Parts, Inc. is a manufacturer of precision parts used in large industrial furnaces. These parts are basically starters used to ignite the furnaces. Mr. J. E. Boyte is chief operating engineer for the Wales plant. One of his major concerns is the correct operation of a particular machine that must be set up at the beginning of each production shift. "Setting up" is a delicate and costly adjustment and calibration process.

From past experience, Mr. Boyte knows that the machine is correctly set up 70% of the time. On the other occasions, an incorrect setup is made. If the setup is made correctly, the machine is known to produce 90% acceptable parts and 10% defective parts (parts that do not meet quality specifications). If the machine is set up incorrectly, it produces 40% acceptable parts and 60% defective parts.

The company would like to ensure that the machine is set up correctly, because it must make refunds on all defective parts. Unfortunately, the starters can only be used once. Since testing destroys these devices, it is impossible to test each part. Mr. Boyte knows, however, that he can sample and test a few parts and then revise his probability estimate of correct machine setup based on the results of this sample. Since the parts are expensive to produce, Mr. Boyte decides to begin this procedure by testing two parts after each setup.

Machine setups: typical applications of probability revision

By this time, the reader should be aware of the importance of probability revision in decision analysis. Throughout the rest of this chapter, we will describe and analyze several situations that represent many real problem areas wherein probability revision is helpful. One area of application is in a broad category known as machine setup problems. In these problems, we will typically use information obtained from a sample to estimate the probability that a particular machine or production line is operating properly (or has been set up correctly). This analysis should make us more aware of the many other situations wherein we can use information to revise estimates about the probability of the occurrence of a particular event.

In the case of Wales Machine Parts, Inc., a machine is set up at the beginning of each shift. Two parts are then sampled and tested in an effort to determine if the machine has been set up correctly. In this case, assume that *both parts are found to be defective.* If Mr. Boyte uses this information, what will he find to be the revised probability that the machine is set up correctly?

Before taking the sample, Mr. Boyte must assume that the probability of a correct setup is .70. This is a prior probability. What he wants to calculate is the posterior probability that was revised on the basis of the two-element sample. We are assuming that the outcome of each element sampled is dependent on the type of machine setup (either correct or incorrect) but is independent of the other element sampled. Thus, if a correct setup has been made, the probability of the second element being defective is .1 regardless of whether the first element sampled was good or defective.

A probability tree for the machine setup problem

One method of revising prior probabilities is to use a probability tree. Figure 3.4 is a probability tree of the situation faced by Mr. Boyte at Wales Parts. From Figure 3.4, we note that only two chains of events include the drawing of two defective parts. These are the chains of events leading to positions L and Q. Since two defective parts were sampled, we must be at either position L or position Q in Figure 3.4. Therefore, the denominator in the formula $P = s/N$ is .115 (.007 + .108). Of the two relevant chains of events, only one (position L) includes a correct machine setup. The numerator must be .007 and the revised probability of a correct setup is now $P = .007/.115 = .06$.

In this example, Mr. Boyte has used information from a sample to revise his probability estimate about an improper machine setup. Before obtaining the sample information, he assigned a value of .70 to the probability of having a correct machine setup. After obtaining two

Figure 3.4 *Complete probability tree for the machine setup in Wales Machine Parts, Inc.*

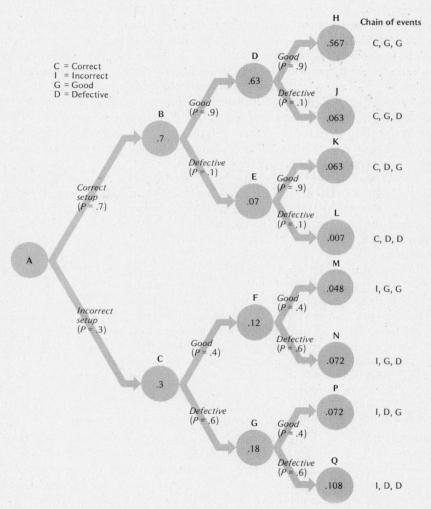

defective parts, he revised that probability estimate downward to .06. He now has three options. First, he can assume that the machine is set up properly and allow it to continue to run. It is doubtful that he would do this because of the very low revised probability of a correct machine setup. Second, he can continue to sample and obtain more information with which to revise his probability estimate. Third, he can shut the machine down and perform a new setup. The choice among these three alternatives depends on the economics involved. It is likely that some type of decision rule will be developed. For example, if the revised estimate of a correct setup is above a certain level (such as .95), Mr. Boyte will assume that a correct setup has been made and let the machine run. If it is below a certain level (such as .40), he will ask for a new setup. If the probability estimate is somewhere between these limits, he may wish to obtain more information by additional sampling.

Posterior probability tables

It should be evident that using an entire probability tree is a cumbersome way to analyze the machine setup problem. In Figure 3.4, a number of calculations were made that were never used. For example, the probability of the chain of events leading to position H was determined to be .567, but this value was never used in revising the probability estimate concerning a correct machine setup. In fact, the only relevant chains of events were those leading to positions L and Q. Mr. Boyte's probability revision could have been obtained by using the reduced probability tree shown in Figure 3.5. This reduced tree abstracts all of the relevant information from Figure 3.4. Given the information that both parts sampled were bad, we can obtain the probability of a correct setup from either Figure 3.4 or Figure 3.5 as

$$P = \frac{.007}{(.007 + .108)} = \frac{.007}{.115} = .06$$

We can carry this simplified procedure of using the reduced probability tree one step further by constructing a *posterior probability table.* Table 3.1 is a posterior probability table for Mr. Boyte's machine setup

Figure 3.5 *Reduced probability tree for Wales Machine Parts, Inc.*

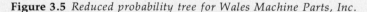
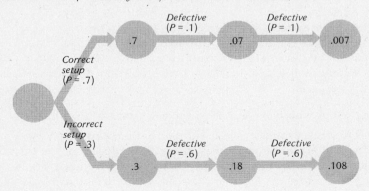

Table 3.1 *Posterior probability table for the machine setup example*

Event	P(E)	P(G|E)	P(D|E)	P(DD|E)	P(E,DD)
Correct	.7	.9	.1	.01	.007
Incorrect	.3	.4	.6	.36	.108
					.115

$$P(C|DD) = \frac{P(C,DD)}{P(DD)} = \frac{(.007)}{(.007 + .108)} = .06$$

E = The event; either a correct or an incorrect setup
G = A good part is sampled
D = A defective part is sampled
P(E,DD) = Probability of the event and two defective parts

problem. This table extracts and summarizes all of the relevant information from Figure 3.4. Calculating the revised probability as shown in Table 3.1 is a direct application of Bayes' theorem, discussed earlier in this chapter. We stated Bayes' theorem as follows:

$$P(A|B) = \frac{P(A) \cdot P(B|A)}{[P(A) \cdot P(B|A)] + [P(\bar{A}) \cdot P(B|\bar{A})]}$$

Suppose we let

A = A correct setup
$\bar{A}$ = An incorrect setup
B = The joint event (DD) of obtaining two defective parts

Then

$$P(A|B) = \frac{(.7) \cdot (.01)}{[(.7) \cdot (.01)] + [(.3) \cdot (.36)]} = \frac{.007}{(.007) + (.108)} = .06$$

Posterior probability tables provide us with a simple and convenient way to calculate revised or posterior probabilities. In short, *a posterior probability table extracts from a probability tree only those branches that are needed* to analyze the particular problem of concern. Thus, we simplify our analysis by eliminating material we do not need. Because of their simplicity, we will continue to use these tables in the discussions that follow.

Machine setups with more than two elements sampled

In the foregoing example, we assumed that only two parts were sampled after the machine setup was made. The procedure we have been using can be easily extended to situations wherein more than two elements are sampled. Assume that Mr. Boyte decided to sample four

Table 3.2 *Posterior probability table for a situation wherein more than two elements are sampled*

Event	$P(E)$	$P(G|E)$	$P(D|E)$	$P(GGGD|E)$	$P(E,GGGD)$
Correct	.7	.9	.1	.0729	.05103
Incorrect	.3	.4	.6	.0384	.01152
					.06255

$$P(C|GGGD) = \frac{P(C,GGGD)}{P(GGGD)} = \frac{.05103}{.06255} = .82$$

Table 3.3 *Posterior probability table wherein order of sampling is not specified*

Event	$P(E)$	$P(G|E)$	$P(D|E)$	$P(3G,1D|E)^*$	$P(E,3G,1D)^*$
Correct	.7	.9	.1	.2916	.20412
Incorrect	.3	.4	.6	.1536	.04608
					.25020

$$P(C|3G,D)^* = \frac{.20412}{.25020} = .82$$

*The notation 3G,D means 3 good and 1 defective without regard to order.

parts and found the first three of the elements good and the last element defective. Table 3.2 is a posterior probability table for this particular example. The two joint probabilities in the far right-hand column represent the probabilities of the only two relevant chains of events. Determination of the revised probability of a correct setup, $P(C|GGGD)$, is again a direct application of Bayes' theorem.

This example assumes a *specific sampling order* of three acceptable parts followed by a defective part. Suppose the *sampling order is unknown.* All that is known is that three of the parts sampled were acceptable and the other one defective. The probability of sampling one defective and three good elements without regard to order is equal to $P(GGGD) + P(GGDG) + P(GDGG) + P(DGGG)$. These probabilities have been used in Table 3.3. The net result is to multiply both the numerator and the denominator of Bayes' theorem by four. The probability of a correct setup remains .82.

Sample Problem 3.5   THE CLEMMENTS COMPANY

The Clemments Company purchases and ships industrial parts that have been classified as defective (they usually have only minor blemishes) or as manufacturer's surplus. Seventy percent of the trucks are shipped from the south warehouse, and 30% of the shipments come from the west warehouse. Shipments from the south warehouse contain 80% surplus parts and 20% defective parts. Shipments from the west warehouse contain 40% surplus parts and 60% defective parts. Mr. Fabian is interested in bidding on a particular truckload. He would like to have a better estimate of which warehouse this truckload was shipped from. Three parts were selected at random. Find the revised probability that the shipment came from the south warehouse if

1. The sampled parts were found to be surplus, defective, and defective, in that order.
2. Two parts were defective and one was surplus, but the order of sampling is unknown.

SOLUTION

Event	$P(E)$	$P(S\|E)$	$P(D\|E)$	$P(SDD\|E)$	$P(E,SDD)$	$P(2D,1S\|E)^*$	$P(E,2D,1S)^*$
South warehouse	.7	.8	.2	.032	.0224	.096	.0672
West warehouse	.3	.4	.6	.144	.0432	.432	.1296
					.0656		.1968

1.
$$P(\text{South, SDD}) = \frac{P(\text{South}|SDD)}{P(SDD)}$$
$$= \frac{.0224}{.0656} = .34$$

2.
$$P(\text{South}|2D,1S)^* = \frac{P(\text{South},2D,1S)^*}{P(2D,1S)}$$
$$= \frac{.0672}{.1968} = .34$$

*The notation 2D, 1S means 2 defective and 1 surplus without regard to order.

An application of the Bernoulli process

In Table 3.2, the probability of the joint event $(E,GGGD)$, was obtained by the multiplicative law of probability as follows:

$$P(E,GGGD) = P(E) \cdot P(GGGD|E)$$

The conditional probabilities $P(GGGD|E)$ were easily obtained, because the sample was composed of only four elements. If the sample size increased to 10, 20, or 50, it would obviously become more difficult to calculate this conditional probability. Fortunately, once the machine setup has been made (either correctly or incorrectly), the sampling behavior is an example of a type of process known as the Bernoulli process. We may, therefore, use a special formula to simplify the calculation of this joint probability. This formula is known as the *binomial theorem*.

A review of the binomial theorem and the binomial probability distribution appears in Chapter 14. The material in that chapter is provided for readers who would like more information on these sub-jects. Chapter 14 also explains how to use Table B in the Appendix. This is a table of values of the cumulative binomial distribution.

Before applying the binomial theorem, we must ensure that the process we are investigating has all the characteristics of a Bernoulli process. *All Bernoulli processes possess the following properties:*

1. Each trial (in this case, sampling a part) has only two possible outcomes. We will refer to one outcome as a success and to the other as a failure.
2. The probability of a particular outcome, such as a success or a failure, on any trial remains fixed from trial to trial. We shall refer to the probability of a success as p and to the probability of a failure as q, which is $(1 - p)$.
3. The trials are independent.

Once the machine setup has been made in the Wales problem, the sampling process has the characteristics we have just described. With a correct machine setup, we have a specified number of samples (such as 4); each sample must be either good or defective; the probability of a good part (.9) remains constant from trial to trial; and the trials are assumed to be independent of each other.

For a Bernoulli process, we may calculate probability by the following formula:

$$P(r) = \frac{n!}{r!(n - r)!} \, p^r q^{n-r}$$

where

    $P(r) = $ Probability of r successes in n trials

      $p = $ Probability of success on any trial

      $q = $ Probability of failure on any trial

      $n = $ Total number of trials

      $r = $ Number of successes in n trials

This formula is known as the *binomial probability formula*. With it, we can calculate the probability of r successes in n trials *without regard to order.* Later in this chapter, we will show how we can simplify our calculations by using a table for the cumulative binomial distribution. At that time, it will be necessary to *choose our definitions of success and failure such that p will always be less than or equal to .5 and q will always be greater than or equal to .5.* We should adopt that practice at this time.

As an example, suppose that Mr. Boyte sampled 4 parts and wanted to obtain *the probability of obtaining exactly 3 good parts and 1 defective part without regard to order.* If we assume a correct machine setup, then

$p = .1 =$ Probability of a defective part (success)

$q = .9 =$ Probability of a good part (failure)

$n = 4 =$ Number of trials

$r = 1 =$ Number of successes (defective parts) in n trials

$$P(1) = \frac{4!}{1! \, (4 - 1)!} \, (.1)^1 (.9)^3$$

$$P(1) = \frac{(4 \times 3 \times 2 \times 1)}{(1)(3 \times 2 \times 1)} \, (.1)^1 (.9)^3 = .2916$$

The value of .2916 is the probability of obtaining 3 good parts and 1 defective part in any order. Previously, we determined the probability of 3 good parts and 1 defective part in a specific order to be .0729. The first probability (.2916) is 4 times greater than the second (.0729). This is logical because there are 4 specific ways of obtaining 3 good parts and 1 defective part: GGGD, GGDG, GDGG, and DGGG.

For a second example of the binomial theorem, suppose we *assume an incorrect machine setup.* Mr. Boyte samples 5 parts, and he wants to know the probability of obtaining 3 good parts (successes) and 2 defective parts (failures) in any order. In this case,

$p = .4 =$ Probability of a success (good part)

$q = .6 =$ Probability of a failure (defective part)

$n = 5 =$ Number of trials

$r = 3 =$ Number of successes (good parts) in 5 trials

$$P(3) = \frac{5!}{3! \, (5 - 3)!} \, (.4)^3 (.6)^2 = .2304$$

Utilizing the cumulative binomial table

As a final illustration of the Bernoulli process, let us consider a production line that operates correctly 80% of the time and incorrectly 20% of the time. When operating correctly, the production line produces 95% good parts and 5% defective parts. When operating incorrectly, the

Table 3.4 *Posterior probability table for a Bernoulli process*

Event	$P(E)$	$P(G|E)$	$P(D|E)$	$P(3D,7G|E)^*$	$P(E,3D,7G)^*$
Correct	.8	.95	.05	.0105	.00840
Incorrect	.2	.40	.60	.0425	.00850
					.01690

$$P(C|3D,7G)^* = \frac{P(C,3D,7G)^*}{P(3D,7G)^*} = \frac{.00840}{(.00840 + .00850)}$$

$$= \frac{.00840}{.01690} = .497$$

*The notation 3D,7G means 3 defective and 7 good parts sampled without regard to order.

production line produces 40% good parts and 60% defective parts. On one occasion, 10 parts are sampled and 3 are found to be defective. What is the revised probability that the production line is operating correctly?

Table 3.4 is a posterior probability table for the foregoing example. The conditional probabilities $P(7G,3D|E)$ were determined by using the binomial distribution. Instead of using the binomial probability formula, however, we may find it more convenient to use a table for the cumulative binomial distribution (Table B in the Appendix). The use of this table is explained in Chapter 14.

In Table 3.4, the conditional probabilities $P(3D,7G|E)$ were obtained by using the cumulative binomial tables. Once these values were obtained, the table was completed by means of the same procedures we have described. The joint probabilities $P(E,3D,7G)$ were obtained by multiplying the event probabilities $P(E)$ by the conditional probabilities $P(3D,7G|E)$. Determination of the probability of a correct setup, given 3 defective and 7 acceptable parts, is again a direct application of Bayes' theorem.

A setup problem with more than two basic settings

Let us return to the machine setup problem in the case of Wales Machine Parts, Inc. In the previous example, we assumed that as a result of the machine setup, only one of two events could occur; either the machine setup was made correctly or it was made incorrectly. Now let us assume that any one of four grades of adjustment could be made on the machine setup. A grade A adjustment is only accomplished 10% of the time, but it produces 100% acceptable parts. A grade B adjustment is accomplished 50% of the time and produces 80% acceptable parts and 20% defective parts. A grade C adjustment happens 30% of the time and produces 50% acceptable parts and 50% defective parts. A grade D adjustment is performed only 10% of the time, but when this adjustment is made, the machine produces 10% acceptable parts and 90% defective parts. Suppose 3 parts are sampled and the first 2 are acceptable and the third defective. What is Mr. Boyte's revised probability estimate about the grade of the machine setup that was made?

Table 3.5 is a posterior probability table for this example. The joint probabilities $P(E,GGD)$ are obtained by using the multiplicative law of probability. The conditional probabilities $P(E|GGD)$ are obtained by using Bayes' theorem. Before the sample is taken, Mr. Boyte assigns values of .10, .50, .30, and .10 to the respective probabilities of a grade A, grade B, grade C, and grade D machine setups. After receiving the sample information, he revises these estimates to .0, .625, .366, and .009. The effect of this revision is that with the sample information, he is almost certain that the setup is either grade B or grade C. And the odds are almost two to one that it is a grade B setup.

Generality of the machine setup problem

The examples we have discussed are all concerned with a particular type of problem, the machine setup problem. The machine setup problem is a typical example of how we can use information to revise a probability estimate. The same principles apply to many other real problems the manager will face. The active manager continually revises probability estimates on the basis of information received from many sources: market research surveys, consumer complaints, frequency of machine breakdown, and so on. The sample problems in this chapter and the exercises at the end of the chapter will provide further examples of probability revision.

Table 3.5 *Posterior probability table for an event with more than two basic outcomes*

Event	$P(E)$	$P(G|E)$	$P(D|E)$	$P(GGD|E)$	$P(E,GGD)$
Grade A	.1	1.0	0	.000	.0000
Grade B	.5	.8	.2	.128	.0640
Grade C	.3	.5	.5	.125	.0375
Grade D	.1	.1	.9	.009	.0009
					.1024

$$P(A|GGD) = \frac{.0000}{.1024} = .000 \qquad P(C|GGD) = \frac{.0375}{.1024} = .366$$

$$P(B|GGD) = \frac{.0640}{.1024} = .625 \qquad P(D|GGD) = \frac{.0009}{.1024} = .009$$

Indirect probability assessment

Our discussion of probability analysis has dealt primarily with probability revision and statistical decision theory. Before concluding these two chapters, we should discuss two other management applications of probability analysis. The first concerns the use of probability theory in improving subjective probability estimates. In our past discussions, we have used probability trees to aid us with probability revision and decision analysis. It may seem (and rightfully so) that we have overlooked a very obvious application of probability trees, helping us assess, or estimate, the likelihood of occurrence of complex events. This procedure is often referred to as *indirect probability assessment.* It is based on the principle that a complicated problem can be broken into component parts in such a way that it is more effective to estimate the probability of the component parts than to try to estimate the probability of the original problem.

When asked to directly estimate a subjective probability, an individual often answers that the proper estimate is dependent on certain other events. A probability tree is quite helpful in indirect probability assessment, because it allows the decision maker to consider this dependence by first estimating the probability of the component parts and then combining these estimates to obtain a probability estimate of the original, more complex problem.

To illustrate, let us consider a simple example. Suppose that Mr. Doyle, an industrial purchaser of vegetables, approaches Mr. Hodges, a farmer who grows a particular type of vegetable, to discuss the possibility of buying 1000 bushels of this vegetable from Mr. Hodges' next crop. Early in the discussion, Mr. Hodges is asked to assess the probability that he will have a crop of 1000 bushels or more. His answer is, "That depends." Mr. Hodges considers a yield of 1000 or more bushels to be a large crop. He believes that with a rainy growing season, there is an 80% chance of producing 1000 bushels or more. With a dry growing season, he feels that there is only a 30% chance of producing the 1000 bushels. Further questioning reveals that in the past, approximately 60% of the growing seasons have been what Mr. Hodges considers rainy and approximately 40% have been what he considers dry.

This problem is an example of indirect probability assessment. Mr. Hodges is unwilling to make a direct estimate of the probability of his crop being 1000 bushels or more. He is, however, willing to estimate the likelihood of occurrence of the component parts of the larger problem. Figure 3.6 is a probability tree for this example. Note that there are two positions (D and F) in Figure 3.6 that represent the harvesting of a large crop. The probability of a large crop, therefore, is simply the sum

Figure 3.6 *Probability tree for Mr. Hodges' problem*

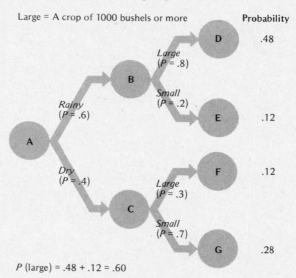

Large = A crop of 1000 bushels or more

Probability

Large *(P = .8)* — D — .48

Small *(P = .2)* — E — .12

Rainy *(P = .6)*

B

A

Dry *(P = .4)*

C

Large *(P = .3)* — F — .12

Small *(P = .7)* — G — .28

P (large) = .48 + .12 = .60

of the probability of reaching position D and the probability of reaching position F in Figure 3.6. By indirect assessment, we can say that Mr. Hodges believes there is a 60% (.48 + .12) chance of producing the 1000 bushels.

In this example, we have used our knowledge of probability trees and probability concepts to make a probability assessment of a complex event by first estimating the probability of the component parts of the complex event. Experience has shown that this type of probability estimate is often more accurate than trying to directly estimate the probability of occurrence of the complex event. Our example was concerned with subjective probability estimates. The same type of analysis is also useful when the probabilities are objective rather than subjective. We can calculate the overall reliability (probability of successful operation) of a rocket, for example, by determining the reliability of component parts and then combining these probability values to determine a reliability factor for the total system.

Sample problem 3.6 THE MOONBEAM COMPANY

The Moonbeam Company has designed a lantern that the astronauts plan to carry to Mars. It has a primary and a secondary battery and a main and a reserve light bulb. The probability that the primary battery will function properly is .8.

If the primary battery works properly, the probability that the main bulb will operate is .9. If the main bulb fails, the reserve bulb will be used, and the probability it will work from the primary battery is .5. If the primary battery fails to operate, the secondary battery will be used. The probability of it working properly is .7. The main light bulb will not operate from the secondary battery, so the reserve light bulb must be used. It has a .9 probability of working from the secondary battery. What is the probability that the lantern will function, allowing the astronauts to read?

SOLUTION

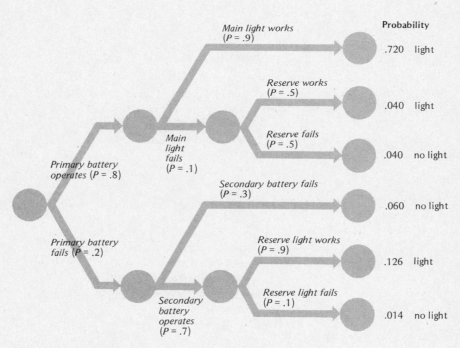

P (light) = .720 + .040 + .126 = .886

Replacement analysis

Another useful application of probability analysis is in devising replacement schedules for items that fail over time. Obvious examples are light bulbs above football stadiums and the light bulbs above the playing surfaces of large indoor basketball arenas. An industrial example is the replacement of process thermometers in a chemical manufacturing plant. The latter example may differ from the first two in one important aspect. In the case of the light bulbs, it may be feasible to operate with a few burned-out bulbs. The thermometers, on the other hand, might have to be replaced as they fail, since proper temperature control is essential to the chemical production process.

In each of these examples, the replacement process may involve a large setup cost; that is, a fixed cost will be involved regardless of the number of bulbs replaced. If all the bulbs or thermometers were replaced at one time, the labor cost per bulb would be much smaller than if the bulbs were replaced as they burned out. This potential reduction in setup costs suggests that we should investigate the economic feasibility of periodic mass replacement. Probability theory will help us with this analysis.

Consider the problem faced by the production manager at the Kent Chemical Company. Kent Chemical's manufacturing plant utilizes 1000 industrial process thermometers that must be replaced as they burn out. Cost records indicate that replacement cost is $1.50 per thermometer if replacement is done on a mass basis such that all 1000 elements are replaced at once. If the thermometers are replaced on an individual basis, however, replacement cost rises to $5 per unit. Kent Chemical Company also has records that indicate how rapidly the thermometers tend to fail. These data are presented in Table 3.6.

Replacement as they burn out

Our *method of analysis* will be to calculate first the total cost of a managerial policy of replacing the thermometers as they burn out. We can then compare this cost with the cost of other alternatives, such as mass replacement every month, mass replacement every quarter (three months), and so on. Initially, the Kent Company installed 1000 new units. These will be replaced as they fail, however, and eventually the company will be replacing approximately the same number of elements each month. In order to determine this number, we first need to

Table 3.6 *Life expectancy of thermometers at the Kent Company*

Month after replacement	Percent of thermometers that fail in that month
1	5
2	10
3	15
4	20
5	25
6	25

calculate the average life of the thermometers. Using the information in Table 3.6, we calculate the average life of the thermometers as follows:

$$.05 \times 1 \text{ month} \quad = \quad .05 \text{ month}$$
$$.10 \times 2 \text{ months} = \quad .20 \text{ months}$$
$$.15 \times 3 \text{ months} = \quad .45 \text{ months}$$
$$.20 \times 4 \text{ months} = \quad .80 \text{ months}$$
$$.25 \times 5 \text{ months} = 1.25 \text{ months}$$
$$.25 \times 6 \text{ months} = \underline{1.50 \text{ months}}$$
$$4.25 \text{ months}$$

Over time, the company will be replacing 1000/4.25 = 235 units per month (in this section, we will round our answers to the nearest integer). Replacing bulbs as they burn out, then, would result in an average monthly replacement cost of $1175. The company should now compare this average monthly cost with the cost of such alternative policies as mass replacement every month, mass replacement every two months, and so on.

Periodic mass replacement

Assume that the Kent Company decides to investigate a policy of periodic (for instance, semiannual) mass replacement. Two types of replacement costs would be involved. At the beginning of each period, the company would incur a *mass replacement cost*. The mass replacement cost would be the cost of replacing 1000 thermometers at $1.50 each, for a total cost of $1500. The company would also incur a *maintenance replacement cost*. This cost arises because the company must replace the elements that fail during the interval between mass replacements. In order to determine this cost, we must first calculate the number of units that would have to be replaced each month.

Table 3.7 gives the calculations by which we determine the number of thermometers that must be replaced each month. One thousand new thermometers are installed at the beginning of the replacement period. For illustrative purposes, assume this was done on January 1. During the first month, 5% (or 50 units) will fail and have to be replaced. During the second month of the replacement period (February), 10% of the original 1000 elements (.10 × 1000 = 100) will fail and have to be replaced. In addition, 5% of those installed the previous month will also have to be replaced. In our example, 50 new replacement thermometers were installed in January. Of these, 5% (.05 × 50 = 2.5, which we will round to 3) will fail in February. Thus, the total number to be replaced in the second month is 103 (100 + 3).

During the third month (March), the Kent Company must replace

Table 3.7 *Determination of the number of thermometers to be replaced monthly at the Kent Company*

Month	Calculations	Replacements
0	(Initial mass replacement)	1000
1	(1000)(.05)	
	50	50
2	(1000)(.10) + 50(.05)	
	100 + 3	103
3	(1000)(.15) + 50(.10) + 103(.05)	
	150 + 5 + 5	160
4	(1000)(.20) + (50)(.15) + (103)(.10) + (160)(.05)	
	200 + 8 + 10 + 8	226
5	1000(.25) + 50(.20) + (103)(.15) + 160(.10) + 226(.05)	
	250 + 10 + 15 + 16 + 11	302
6	(1000)(.25) + (50)(.25) + (103)(.20) + (160)(.15) + (226)(.10) + (302)(.05)	
	250 + 12 · + 21 + 24 + 23 + 15	= 345

15% of the original items, 10% of those installed in the first month and 5% of those installed in the second month. Thus, the number of replacement thermometers installed in the third month is 160 (150 + 5 + 5). The number of replacement units installed in succeeding months may be determined by the same procedure. All of these calculations are given in Table 3.7.

Table 3.8 compares the costs of various replacement policies available to the management of the Kent Company. To illustrate the calculations, consider the data for the policy of mass replacement every 2 months. At the beginning of each 2-month period, the Kent Company would replace all 1000 units at a cost of $1.50 each. This results in a replacement cost of $1500. From Table 3.7, we note that during the 2-month period, 153 thermometers (50 in the first month and 103 in the second month) would have to be replaced as they wear out, at a cost of $5.00 per item. Thus, the 2-month maintenance replacement cost is $765. Total cost for the 2-month period is the sum of the mass replacement cost and the maintenance replacement cost, or $2265. Since a 2-month period is involved, the average monthly cost is $1132.

Table 3.8 *Cost of alternative replacement policies at the Kent Company*

Replacement policy	Mass replacement cost	Maintenance replacement cost			Total cost	Average monthly cost
		Thermometers	$/unit	Cost		
Every month	$1500	50	$5	$ 250	$1750	$1750
Every 2 months	1500	153	5	765	2265	1132
Every 3 months	1500	313	5	1565	3065	1021
Every 4 months	1500	539	5	2695	4195	1049
Every 5 months	1500	841	5	4205	5705	1141
Every 6 months	1500	1186	5	5930	7430	1238

As another example, consider the cost calculations for the policy of mass replacement every 5 months. Again, the mass replacement cost is $1500. The number of thermometers replaced as they wear out is 841, the sum of the number that wear out during each of the five months. Maintenance replacement cost is $4205 and total cost is $5705. Average monthly cost is $1141, obtained by dividing total cost by 5.

Optimal replacement policy

The optimal replacement policy is the policy that results in the lowest average monthly cost. Management of the Kent Company has determined that a policy of replacing a thermometer only when it fails results in an average monthly cost of $1175. From Table 3.8, we learn that a policy of mass replacement every 3 months results in the minimum average monthly cost, $1021. We would expect the management of the Kent Company to strongly consider adopting a policy of replacing all thermometers at the beginning of each 3-month period.

In this example, we considered only six alternative policies. If potential cost savings were great, the analyst might wish to break the problem down to a weekly or even a daily basis. If the analysis were made on a weekly basis, it would not be necessary to investigate all possible alternatives. We would only need to investigate those alternatives (such as 11 and 13 weeks) that are close to the apparent minimum-cost policy of mass replacement every 3 months.

Symbols and formulas used in probability analysis

We have used a number of different symbols and formulas in this material on probability analysis. For convenient reference, here is a list of those symbols and formulas.

$P(A)$ = Marginal, simple, or ordinary probability that event A will happen

$P(\bar{A})$ = Probability that event A will not happen

$P(A|B)$ = Conditional probability that event A will occur, given the information that event B has occurred

$P(AB)$ = Joint probability that both A and B will happen; the intersection of A and B

$P(A$ or $B)$ = Probability that A will happen, or B will happen, or they will both happen; the union of A and B

The multiplicative law of probability:

$$P(AB) = P(A) \cdot P(B|A)$$

If A and B are independent, then

$$P(AB) = P(A) \cdot P(B)$$

The additive law of probability:

$$P(A \text{ or } B) = P(A) + P(B) - P(AB)$$

If A and B are mutually exclusive, then

$$P(A \text{ or } B) = P(A) + P(B)$$

Bayes' theorem for conditional probability:

$$P(A|B) = \frac{P(AB)}{P(B)}$$

If event A has multiple outcomes, then

$$P(A_1|B) = \frac{P(A_1) \cdot P(B|A_1)}{\displaystyle\sum_{i=1}^{n} [P(A_i) \cdot P(B|A_i)]}$$

Problems and exercises

1. Explain the following terms:

   probability tree   intersection of A and B

   prior probability   union of A and B

   posterior probability   additive law of probability

   marginal probability   multiplicative law of probability

   conditional probability   Bayes' theorem

   unconditional probability   Bernoulli process

   independent events   binomial theorem

   dependent events   mass replacement cost

   mutually exclusive events   maintenance replacement cost

   posterior probability tables   optimal replacement policy

2. Three identical urns are placed on a table. Urn 1 contains 2 red balls and 1 green ball. Urn 2 contains 1 red ball and 1 green ball. Urn 3 contains 5 red balls and 1 green ball. An urn is selected at random and a single ball is drawn from the selected urn.

   a. Draw a probability tree for this problem.
   b. What is the probability that the ball was red?
   c. Given the information that urn 1 was selected, what is the probability that the ball was red?
   d. Given the information that the ball drawn was red, what is the probability that urn 1 was selected?

    e. Given the information that either urn 1 or urn 2 was selected (it is known that urn 3 was not selected), what is the probability that the ball was red?

3. Two identical boxes are placed on a table. The first box contains 2 red, 2 green, and 2 white marbles (total = 6). The second box contains 2 red marbles and 1 green marble (total = 3). A box is selected at random and a marble is drawn from the selected box.

    a. Draw a probability tree of the problem, showing the probabilities of all events.

    b. What is the probability that a red marble was selected?

    c. If a red marble was selected, what is the probability that box 1 was selected?

    d. If a red marble was drawn and then, without replacement, another marble was drawn from the same box, what is the probability that it was also red?

4. Two identical urns are sitting in a bookcase. The first urn contains 1 green, 1 black, and 4 red balls. The second urn contains 2 red and 4 black balls. One urn is selected at random and 2 balls are drawn in succession from the selected urn.

    a. Draw a probability tree of this problem, showing the probabilities of all events.

    b. What is the probability that the second ball drawn will be black?

    c. If the second ball was actually black, what is the probability that urn 1 was selected?

    d. If the second ball was actually black, what is the probability that the first ball was also black?

    e. What is the probability of selecting two balls of the same color (two red, or two black, or two green)?

    f. If it is known that both balls are the same color, what is the probability that urn 1 was selected?

    g. If it is known that both balls were the same color, what is the probability that the color was red?

5. Three identical cigar boxes are placed on a counter. One box is selected at random, and then a cigar wrapper is chosen from the selected box. The first box contains 5 red wrappers and 1 silver wrapper. The second box contains 4 red wrappers, 1 green wrapper, and 1 silver wrapper. The third box contains 2 red wrappers and 4 green wrappers. Draw a probability tree of this problem and then answer the following questions.

    a. What is the probability that the wrapper drawn was red?

    b. If the wrapper drawn was red, what is the probability that box 1 was selected?

    c. If the wrapper drawn was red, what is the probability that the selected box also contains a silver wrapper?

    d. Suppose a silver wrapper was drawn and then, without replacement, another wrapper was drawn from the selected box. What is the probability that the second wrapper was green?

6. Two identical hats are placed in a closet. The first hat contains 6 quarters and 2 dimes. The second hat contains 4 dimes and 2 quarters. A hat is selected at random and then 2 coins are drawn from the selected hat. Draw a probability tree for this problem and then answer the following questions.

    a. What is the probability that the two coins had a total value of 20 cents?

    b. If the total value of the 2 coins is 35 cents, what is the probability that the first hat was selected?

    c. If one of the coins was a quarter, what is the probability that the other coin was a dime?

    d. If two quarters were selected, what is the probability that they came from the second hat?

7. An 8-member congressional committee consists of 3 male senators, 2 female senators, 2 male representatives, and 1 female representative. Assume that the names of the committee members are put in a hat, and answer the following questions.

    a. What is the probability that a name selected at random will be that of a man?

    b. Given that the name drawn is that of a man, what is the probability that that man is a senator?

    c. When two names are drawn, what is the probability that they are both names of senators?

    d. The clerk draws a name and then leaves the room before announcing the name (he takes the name with him). A second name must be drawn. What is the probability the second name drawn will be that of a man?

8. A "minideck" of 8 cards contains the king, queen, jack, three, and two of hearts and the jack, eight, and six of spades. Remember that kings, queens, and jacks are considered face cards.

    a. One card is drawn from this minideck. What is the probability that it is a heart?

    b. One card is drawn from the minideck, and it is known to be a face card. What is the probability that it is also a heart?

    c. One card is drawn from the minideck, and it is known to be a heart. What is the probability that it is also a face card?

    d. One card is drawn from the minideck and discarded without anyone looking at it. A second card is then drawn. What is the probability that this second card is a heart?

    e. Two cards are simultaneously drawn from the minideck. What is the probability that they are both face cards?

    f. Two cards are drawn in succession, without replacement, from the minideck, and it is known that both are face cards. What is the probability that one of the cards is a spade?

9. A minideck of cards contains 5 red cards (hearts), 2 black cards (clubs) and 1 green card (joker). Two cards are selected in succession without replacement. (That is, one card is drawn and looked at, and a second card is drawn without the first being replaced.)

a. If the second card drawn was a green card, what is the probability that the first card was a red card?

b. What is the probability of drawing a red card and a green card *in any order?*

c. What is the probability that either the first card or the second was a red card (or that both were red cards)?

10. Roll a single die and define events A and B as follows:

A = Obtain an even number

B = Obtain a number of 4 or less

Determine each of the following probabilities: $P(B)$, $P(A$ or $B)$, $P(AB)$, $P(B|A)$, and $P(A|B)$.

11. Simultaneously flip a coin and randomly draw 1 card from a standard deck of 52. Define events A, B, and C as follows:

A = Obtain heads on the coin

B = Obtain a club on the card draw

C = Obtain a face card on the card draw

Determine each of the following probabilities: $P(A)$, $P(B)$, $P(C)$, $P(A$ or $B)$, $P(B$ or $C)$, $P(AC)$, $P(BC)$, $P(A|B)$, $P(B|A)$, $P(B|C)$, and $P(C|B)$.

12. In the Webster Company, the jacket and pants to a man's suit are made on different machines by different people. The probability of the pants to a particular suit being made without a defect is .9. The probability that the jacket will have no defect is .8. What is the probability of the following events?

a. Neither the pants nor jacket are defective.

b. Both are defective.

c. One or the other (or both) is defective.

13. Assume that both pants and jacket in problem 12 are made on the same machine so that the events are dependent. The probability of the pants being made without defect is .9. If the pants have no defect, the probability of the jacket having no defect is .9. If the pants are defective, the probability of the jacket being defective is .6. Determine the following probabilities:

a. The probability that neither pants nor the jacket has a defect

b. The probability that one or the other (or both) has a defect

c. Given the information that the jacket is free of defects, the probability that the pants are also free of defects

14. The Marcy Company has asked two contractors to bid on a construction project. From past experience, it is anticipated that the probability of company A submitting a bid is 60% and the probability of company B submitting a bid is 70%. If these probabilities are independent, determine the respective probabilities of exactly 0, 1, and 2 bids being submitted.

15. In problem 14, assume that the probabilities of company A and company B submitting bids are not independent. The probability that company A will submit a bid is .8, and the probability that company B will submit a bid is .9. The probability that they will both submit a bid is .6. Suppose it is known that company A submitted a bid. What is then the probability that company B also submitted a bid? Suppose it is known that company B submitted a bid. What is then the probability that company A also submitted a bid?

16. The Cass Company has a production line that operates effectively 80% of the time and ineffectively 20% of the time. When it is operating effectively, it produces 90% acceptable parts and 10% defective parts. When it is operating ineffectively, it produces 40% acceptable parts and 60% defective parts. Two parts are selected at random and both found to be defective. What is the revised probability that the production line is operating effectively? What would this revised estimate be if both parts had been acceptable?

17. In problem 16, suppose 4 parts were sampled and 2 were found acceptable and 2 unacceptable. What is the revised probability that the production line is operating effectively?

18. The Seward Company has a precision machine that stamps paper clips from sheet metal. The machine is set up correctly 70% of the time and incorrectly 30% of the time. When a correct setup is made, the machine produces 80% good parts and 20% rejects. When an incorrect machine setup is made, the machine produces 50% good parts and 50% rejects. Three parts are sampled and all found to be good. What is the revised probability that a correct setup has been made?

19. Suppose the paper clips in problem 18 had been good, reject, and good, in that order. What is the revised probability of a good machine setup?

20. In problem 19, suppose a fourth paper clip is sampled after it is known that the first 3 were good, reject, good. What is the probability that the fourth paper clip will have to be rejected?

21. The local probability club has a wheel game that is played with either one of two apparently identical spinning wheels. The star wheel lands red 50% of the time and green 50% of the time. The moon wheel lands red 70% of the time and green 30% of the time. From past history, it is known that the club uses the star wheel 60% of the time and the moon wheel 40% of the time. Suppose that on 2 spins, the wheel lands red both times. What is the revised probability that the star wheel is being used? How would this probability change if 4 consecutive spins were red?

22. In problem 21, what is the revised probability that the star wheel is being used if a sample of 2 spins results in 1 red and 1 green (in any order). How would this probability change if a sample of 4 resulted in 2 reds and 2 greens?

23. Suppose that the first 2 spins in problem 21 were red. What is the probability that the third spin will be red?

24. The Washburne Company has 3 machines (A, B, and C) that produce the same part. Machine A produces 60% of the total volume and produces 80% acceptable parts and 20% rejects. Machines B and C each produce 20% of the total volume. Machine B produces 60% acceptable parts and 40% rejects. Machine C produces 50% acceptable parts and 50% rejects. Three elements were sampled from a particular production lot and all were tested and found to be acceptable. What is the revised probability that the lot was produced by machine A? by machine B? by machine C?

25. In problem 24, assume that the 3 parts sampled consisted of 2 acceptable parts and 1 reject. What is the revised probability that the lot came from machine A? machine B? machine C?

26. The local probability club has a game wherein a single cube, which resembles a die, is tossed. On any given occasion, the club may use any 1 of 4 cubes (dice). The Mars cube is a standard six-sided die. The probability of obtaining an odd number on this cube is therefore 1/2. The probabilities of obtaining an odd number on a single roll of the Venus, Jupiter, and Pluto cubes are 4/6, 2/6, and 1/6 respectively. It is known that the club uses the Mars cube 50% ($\frac{4}{8}$) of the time, the Venus cube 25% ($\frac{2}{8}$) of the time, the Jupiter cube 12.5% ($\frac{1}{8}$) of the time, and the Pluto cube 12.5% ($\frac{1}{8}$) of the time. Suppose that a particular cube lands even on 2 successive rolls. What is the probability that the cube in use is the Mars cube? the Venus cube? the Jupiter cube? the Pluto cube?

27. Solve problem 26 assuming that the cube was rolled 3 times and landed even, odd, and even, in that order.

28. Mr. True, a sales representative for the Fish Company, is known to sell a refrigerator on 40% of his sales calls. If he makes 12 sales calls, what is the probability that he will make 6 or more sales? What is the probability that he will make exactly 6 sales? (*Note:* Use the cumulative binomial tables.)

29. Ms. Martin, a sales representative for the Evarts Company is known to sell a dishwasher on 55% of her sales calls. If she makes 20 sales calls, what is the probability that she will make at least 12 sales? What is the probability that she will make exactly 12 sales? (*Note:* Use the cumulative binomial tables.)

30. Consider the Seward Company in problem 18. Assume that 25 paper clips are sampled and that 16 are found to be acceptable and 9 defective. What is the revised probability that the machine is set up correctly?

31. Suppose the wheel in problem 21 is spun 20 times and lands red on 13 occasions and green on 7 occasions. What is the revised probability that the wheel in use is the star wheel?

32. Consider the Washburne Company in problem 24. Assume that 20 parts are sampled and that 15 are acceptable and 5 are rejects. What is the revised probability that the lot was produced by machine A? by machine B? by machine C?

33. The Blaine Company sells items on a door-to-door basis. Before sending their sales representatives out to make sales calls, the company mounts a newspaper and television advertising campaign. From past experience, the company estimates that the probability of an individual buying an item is 20% if he or she has seen neither of the advertising campaigns, 30% if he or she has seen either the newspaper campaign or the television campaign (but not both), and 50% if he or she has seen both the television and the newspaper advertising. The Blaine Company estimates that 40% of the population will see the newspaper advertising and that 50% will see the television advertising. What is the probability that an individual will buy an item when called on by a sales representative from the Blaine Company?

34. In problem 33, suppose it is known that a customer saw some advertising, but it is not known whether it was in the newspaper, on television, or both. What is the revised probability that the customer will buy an item?

35. The product manager of the Bayard Company is asked to assess the probability of the success of a new summer product. His answer is, "That depends on the advertising support we get." He feels that with a good television and newspaper advertising campaign in May, there is an 80% probability of success. With television only or with newspaper only, there is a 50% chance of success. With no advertising, he believes there is no chance of success. The advertising manager is asked to assess the probability of Bayard Company being able to mount the advertising campaigns in May. Her answer is, "That depends on the personnel manager." She believes that with additional help by the end of the month, there is an 80% chance of getting the newspaper advertising and a 50% chance of getting the television advertising. With no additional help, she believes that the probability of getting newspaper advertising is only 40% and that there is no chance of getting the television advertising in May. The personnel manager assesses the probability of obtaining additional advertising help to be 80%. Combine these estimates to assess the probability of success of the new summer product.

36. A farmer sprays his crop 3 times a year. Each spraying is 50% effective (that is, 50% of the time it kills all of the pests and 50% of the time it kills none). If 2 of the 3 (or all 3) of the sprays are effective, the farmer is 100% sure that his crops will survive. If only 1 of the sprays is effective, there is still a 64% chance that the crops will survive. If no spray is effective, the farmer is certain that his crops will not survive. What is the probability that his crops will survive?

37. A student must pass a final exam to graduate. The probability of passing is 90% if the exam consists of multiple-choice questions, 60% if it consists of essay questions, and 75% if it is a mixture of multiple-choice and essay

questions. Past experience indicates that 50% of the professor's exams are essay, 25% are multiple-choice, and 25% are a combination of the two. What is the student's estimate of the probability that she will graduate?

38. Ms. Green, a construction project director with the Foster Company, wants to assess the probability of completing a project by November 1. The land preparation supervisor estimates that there is a 60% chance of finishing his work by June 1 and a 100% chance of finishing by July 1. The building erectors will begin work after land preparation is complete. It will take either 1, 2, or 3 months to erect the building, and the respective probabilities are 20%, 30%, and 50%. After the building is completed, it must be painted, which will take either 2 or 3 months. The probability that the painting will take 2 months is 70% and the probability that it will take 3 months is 30%. What is Ms. Green's estimate of the probability of completing the project by November 1?

39. The Gresham Company is considering drilling a well at a certain location. It is known that in this area, 30% of wells drilled result in an oil well, 10% result in a gas well, and 60% result in a dry well. It is also known that 80% of seismic tests performed on oil wells result in "positive soundings" while 20% result in "negative soundings." When seismic tests are performed on gas wells, 50% are positive and 50% are negative. Likewise, 10% of dry wells produce positive soundings for a seismic test, while 90% produce negative soundings. If a seismic test is taken, what is the probability that the result will be a positive sounding? If the result is a positive sounding, what is the revised probability of a gas well?

40. The Sherman Company uses 2000 sensitive pressure gauges in its production process. These pressure gauges tend to fail in time and must be replaced. The company has estimated that the replacement cost is $3 per gauge if all gauges are replaced on a mass replacement basis during one of the company's scheduled downtimes. Any gauges that must be replaced during production require additional cost, and the total replacement cost is $20 per gauge. Past history indicates that 10% of the gauges fail during the first month of operation. Likewise, 20%, 30%, 30%, and 10% fail respectively during the second, third, fourth, and fifth months of operation. Recommend a replacement policy for the Sherman Company.

41. The Day Company must replace the bearings on a particular type of machine used in its manufacturing operation. The company has 5000 of these machines. Experience indicates that 40% of the bearings fail during the first month of operation, 30% fail during the second month, and 30% fail during the third month. Mass replacement cost of the bearings is $2 per machine. If bearings are replaced as they wear out, however, replacement cost is $10 per machine. Recommend a replacement policy for the Day Company.

42. The Hay Company has 1000 overhead lights in its customer showroom. For goodwill purposes, these lights must be replaced as they wear out. The company is investigating the advisability of a policy of periodic mass

replacement. Cost data indicate that if all bulbs are replaced on a mass basis, replacement can be done for $1 per bulb. If each bulb must be replaced as it burns out, however, replacement cost rises to $6 per bulb. Consider the data given in the following table, and then recommend a replacement policy for the Hay Company.

	Month after replacement					
	1	2	3	4	5	6
Percent of original bulbs that fail in that month	10	10	10	30	30	10

43. The Bacon Company uses 3000 thermometers in its chemical production process. These thermometers are delicate, high-temperature thermometers that have a short life. Data indicate that 10% must be replaced during the first week of operation, 20% during the second week, 30% during the third week, and 40% during the fourth week. Mass replacement cost is $8 per thermometer, and the cost of replacing thermometers as they wear out is $65 per thermometer. Recommend a replacement policy for the Bacon Company.

Supplementary readings

Anderson, D. R., D. J. Sweeney, and T. A. Williams. *An Introduction to Management Science*. St. Paul, Minn.: West, 1976.

Bell, C. E. *Quantitative Methods for Administration*. Homewood, Ill.: Irwin, 1977.

Bierman, H., C. P. Bonini, and W. H. Hausman. *Quantitative Analysis for Business Decisions*. Homewood, Ill.: Irwin, 1977.

Braverman, J. D. *Probability, Logic, and Management Decisions*. New York: McGraw-Hill, 1975.

Brown, R. V., A. S. Kahr, and C. Peterson. *Decision Analysis for the Manager*. New York: Holt, 1974.

Lapin, L. L. *Quantitative Methods for Business Decisions*. New York: Harcourt Brace Jovanovich, 1976.

Mendenhall, W., and J. E. Reinmuth. *Statistics for Management and Economics*. Belmont, Calif.: Wadsworth, 1971.

Schlaifer, R. *Introduction to Statistics for Business Decisions*. New York: McGraw-Hill, 1961.

Winkler, R. L. *Introduction to Bayesian Inference and Decisions*. New York: Holt, 1972.

Chapter 4

Inventory models

Illustrative example: EAST ORANGE NURSERY

The East Orange Nursery specializes in selling small potted palms to tourists in central Florida. These palms are grown from seed for indoor use. When they are approximately 18 inches high, they are transplanted from the firm's planting bed to a porcelain decorative planting vase. When fully grown, they are approximately 4 feet high. The porcelain vase that East Orange uses is very attractive, and most purchasers continue to use the vase when displaying the palms in their homes.

East Orange Nursery is open 360 days a year and sells, on the average, 400 potted palms a day. The nursery purchases the porcelain vases from a nearby manufacturer for $.70 per vase. The manufacturer charges $112 per lot to deliver the vases to the East Orange Nursery. This is a flat charge; it is $112 regardless of the number of vases delivered. The company's present policy is to purchase a six-month supply of vases each time they place an order. The reason the company orders so many at a time is to take advantage of its existing warehouse space and to reduce the yearly delivery cost.

Phyllis Baughman, the owner of the nursery, has recently become concerned about the company's ordering policy. She knows that her cost of capital is 18% per year, and she believes that the money tied up in inventory may be put to better use. She has asked a consultant from a local bank to investigate the company's ordering and inventory policy. She hopes that the consultant will suggest the best inventory policy for East Orange Nursery, including the proper number of vases to order at a time.

The maintenance of inventory is a necessary function of virtually all business operations. Financing and maintaining inventories often represent a major cost of doing business. For large companies, the cost associated with inventories can run into the millions of dollars. Even for smaller companies, proper management of inventories often makes the difference between a successful and an unsuccessful operation. Because of the potential savings involved, most organizations are quite concerned with proper inventory management. Most issues in inventory management fall into one of two categories:

1. What is the proper quantity of inventory to order at any given time?
2. When is the proper time to order this quantity?

A wide range of inventory models are available to assist managers in making these decisions. In many cases, it is possible to make quite accurate decisions with relatively simple models. The following sections introduce several of the more commonly used elementary models. As noted in Chapter 1, developing a simple model generally requires that we make assumptions about the characteristics of the operating situation. The manager must ascertain whether the model's assumptions are reasonable in a particular situation. If they are not, the manager will have to adopt a more complex model.

Our procedure will be first to discuss the costs associated with inventories and then to discuss each of the major inventory questions. The problem of how much to order will lead us to a discussion of the proper "economic order quantity." Discussion of when to place the order will include the important topic of maintaining "safety stocks" as insurance against running out of stock.

Costs associated with inventories

Good inventory management controls and minimizes costs directly associated with the organization's inventory. These costs are generally classified as either carrying costs or ordering costs. Proper inventory management also takes into account an indirect inventory cost, the cost of lost sales that result from running out of inventory. We will defer consideration of this cost, which is called *stockout cost,* until later in the chapter.

Carrying cost

A firm incurs *carrying cost* simply because it is holding inventory. For this reason, carrying cost is often referred to as *holding cost.* All types of carrying costs have one common characteristic. *Carrying costs increase as the size of the inventory increases.* In other words, as the inventory grows larger, so does the carrying cost. A major contributor to carrying cost is the *interest* on money invested in the inventory. In some cases, the firm borrows money to finance the inventory. In this case, interest cost can be computed directly. In most cases, the firm simply uses money that it could invest in other ways. The proper charge is then the amount of return that the money would bring in if it were otherwise invested. Ms. Baughman, at East Orange Nursery, believes that the money invested in her firm is earning 18% per year. This is the proper charge to inventory.

A second major source of carrying cost is *storage cost,* which may include rent (or, alternatively, the value of the space if it were used for other than inventory purposes). It may also include the cost of heat, lights, refrigeration, and personnel needed to maintain, protect, and keep records of the inventory. Other sources of carrying cost include the *taxes* and *insurance* that have to be paid on the inventory. In some cases, *obsolescence* or *deterioration* of inventory may contribute to carrying cost.

Carrying cost is usually expressed, on an annual basis, as a percentage of average inventory. If the rate of inventory usage was steady, and if the new order was received exactly as the old lot was depleted, average inventory would be half of the amount ordered. This concept is illustrated in Figure 4.1.

For basic analysis, it is sufficiently accurate and convenient to assume that *average inventory is equal to half of maximum inventory.* As we shall show, this generalization has useful analytical applications even though it may not be exactly true in a given case. Figure 4.2 illustrates two patterns of inventory usage wherein the rate of demand is not constant. In practice, there are many acceptable methods of determining average inventory for these conditions. One of the most common is to measure the level of inventory at the beginning of each month and then obtain an average of these 12 measurements. (Figure 4.2 also illustrates the use of a safety stock to guard against variations in demand.)

Figure 4.1 *Maximum and average inventory levels with constant usage*

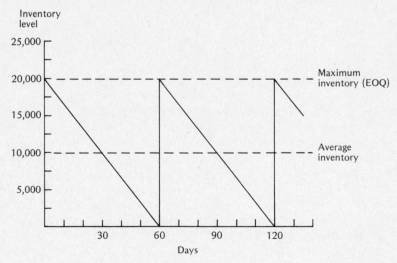

Figure 4.2 *Inventory with varying use rate and safety stock*

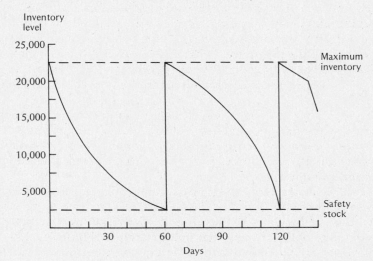

Ordering cost

Ordering costs are those costs associated with getting an item into the firm's inventory. Total *ordering cost* is composed of many cost items, such as issuing a purchase order, shipping, receiving, setting up equipment, and getting payment to the supplier. For all of these items, *cost increases as the number of orders per year increases.* In other words, the more orders placed in a given year, the greater the cost incurred. Ordering cost may apply to material supplied by an outside vendor or by another section of the same firm. Ordering cost is normally expressed as a dollar cost per order.

The economic order quantity

The objective of determining the proper order quantity is to minimize the sum of ordering cost and carrying cost. As we know, ordering cost decreases as we decrease the number of orders placed per year. On the other hand, decreasing the number of orders per year increases the average inventory value and therefore the annual carrying cost. To find the proper order quantity, it is necessary to trade off, or balance, these two types of costs. The order size that minimizes the sum of ordering cost and carrying cost is known as the *economic order quantity*, or simply EOQ. We will use the East Orange Nursery to explain how to determine this quantity.

Before proceeding, we should set up symbolic notation for factors that appear often in inventory situations. We will use these symbols in the discussion that follows.

A = Annual sum of ordering and carrying costs

B = Total yearly ordering cost

C = Total yearly carrying cost

H = Annual inventory requirements in units of inventory

K = Cost of carrying inventory expressed as a percent of average inventory value

P = Value (price) of a unit of inventory expressed as dollars per item

Q = Order quantity

S = Per-lot ordering cost expressed as dollars per order

We will introduce new symbols as we proceed with our analysis of inventory problems in this chapter. (All these symbols are listed at the end of the chapter.)

Determining the ordering cost

Yearly ordering cost is determined by multiplying the number of orders per year by the per-lot cost of ordering and receiving the inventory. We can determine the number of orders required per year by taking the total yearly requirements in units and dividing by the lot size, or number of items ordered at one time. Yearly ordering cost is expressed mathematically as follows:

$$\text{Ordering cost} = \underset{\text{year}}{\text{Orders per}} \times \underset{\text{order}}{\text{Cost per}}$$

$$B = \frac{H}{Q} \qquad \times S \qquad = \frac{HS}{Q}$$

Let us consider the East Orange Nursery problem. The firm requires 144,000 vases annually. Present policy is to order a six-month supply, or 72,000 vases, at a time. Total ordering cost for this policy is:

$$B = \frac{HS}{Q}$$

$$B = \frac{(144{,}000)(\$112)}{72{,}000} = \$224$$

Table 4.1 indicates what would happen to total ordering cost if the lot size were reduced. As expected, yearly ordering cost increases as the lot size decreases.

Table 4.1 *Ordering cost for various lot sizes at East Orange Nursery*

Order quantity (Q)	Orders per year (H/Q)	Days' supply per order*	Cost per order (S)	Annual ordering costs (B = HS/Q)
72,000	2	180	$112	$ 224
36,000	4	90	112	448
24,000	6	60	112	672
16,000	9	40	112	1008
12,000	12	30	112	1344
8,000	18	20	112	2016

*Based on 360 days per year

Determining annual carrying cost

Annual carrying cost is determined by multiplying the average inventory value by the percentage carrying cost per year. We obtain the value of the inventory at its maximum level by multiplying the lot size in units by the per-unit value of the inventory item. If we assume that average inventory is equal to half of maximum inventory, then carrying cost is mathematically expressed as follows:

$$\text{Carrying cost} = \begin{array}{c} \text{Average} \\ \text{inventory} \\ \text{value} \end{array} \times \begin{array}{c} \text{Percentage} \\ \text{carrying} \\ \text{cost} \end{array}$$

$$C = \frac{PQ}{2} \times K = \frac{KPQ}{2}$$

We may again use the East Orange Nursery for an illustration. Present policy is to order twice a year, which yields lot sizes of 72,000 units. The percentage carrying cost is .18. Thus, carrying cost for this policy is

$$C = \frac{KPQ}{2} = \frac{(.18)(.70)(72,000)}{2} = \$4536$$

Annual carrying cost for different lot sizes for the East Orange Nursery are given in Table 4.2. As expected, the annual carrying cost decreases as the lot size decreases.

Determining total annual inventory cost

Total annual inventory cost is simply the sum of carrying cost and ordering cost. For the East Orange problem, annual inventory cost is expressed mathematically as follows:

$$\text{Annual cost} = \text{Ordering} + \text{Carrying}$$
$$\text{cost} \qquad \text{cost}$$
$$A = B \qquad + C$$
$$A = \frac{HS}{Q} \qquad + \frac{KPQ}{2}$$

For a lot size of 72,000, we obtain annual inventory cost as follows:

$$A = B + C = \$224 + \$4536 = \$4760$$

Table 4.2 shows annual inventory cost for various lot sizes at the East Orange Nursery. Of the alternatives shown, a lot size of 16,000 vases has the minimum total inventory cost. We can conclude that the bank consultant should recommend that each order be for 16,000 vases. This would result in the company ordering 9 times a year, or once every 40 days. Annual ordering cost and annual carrying cost would each be $1008, and total cost would be $2016.

This procedure is known as a tabular solution. Unfortunately, solving an inventory problem this way may require numerous lengthy calculations to determine the optimal solution, or even a good solution. For this reason, we usually solve inventory problems by deriving an optimal economic order quantity, or EOQ. We will first illustrate the concept of EOQ by graphical methods and then determine EOQ by mathematical methods.

Graphical representation of inventory costs

Figure 4.3 is a graph of ordering, carrying, and total annual inventory costs for the East Orange Nursery. This visual representation of inventory costs confirms our understanding of the relationship between these

Table 4.2 *Carrying cost and total inventory cost for various lot sizes at East Orange Nursery*

Lot size (Q)	Annual ordering costs* (B)	Units of average inventory (Q/2)	Value of average inventory (PQ/2)	Annual carrying costs (C = KPQ/2)	Annual inventory costs (A = B + C)
72,000	$ 224	36,000	$25,200	$4536	$4760
36,000	448	18,000	12,600	2268	2716
24,000	672	12,000	8,400	1512	2184
16,000	1008	8,000	5,600	1008	2016
12,000	1344	6,000	4,200	756	2100
8,000	2016	4,000	2,800	504	2520

*From Table 4.1

Figure 4.3 *Graphical representation of inventory costs for East Orange Nursery*

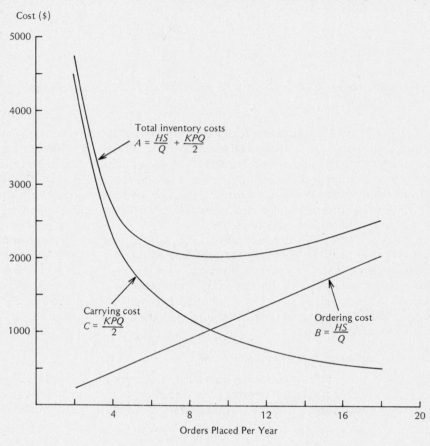

costs and lot size. As the number of orders placed per year increases (that is, lot size decreases), annual ordering cost will increase and annual carrying cost will decrease. Total inventory cost will decrease, reach a minimum point, and then increase. The graph reveals that a lot size of 16,000 vases yields the lowest total inventory cost. This result is consistent with the tabular analysis presented in Tables 4.1 and 4.2. It is important to realize that Figure 4.3 is nothing more than a graphical representation of the three inventory cost equations.

Derivation of EOQ

The formula for total cost is

$$A = \frac{HS}{Q} + \frac{KPQ}{2}$$

We want to determine what value of Q will give A its minimum value. Referring to Figure 4.3, we note that the total cost curve has its minimum value at the point where carrying cost equals ordering cost. This fact gives us a method of deriving the EOQ formula.[1] We can let ordering cost equal carrying cost and solve for Q.

$$\frac{HS}{Q} = \frac{KPQ}{2}$$

$$Q^2 = \frac{2HS}{KP}$$

$$Q = \sqrt{\frac{2HS}{KP}}$$

We can now use the EOQ formula to solve directly for the optimal lot size for the East Orange Nursery.

$$Q = \sqrt{\frac{(2)(144,000)(\$112)}{(.18)(.70)}}$$

$$= \sqrt{256,000,000} = 16,000$$

Ms. Baughman can minimize total inventory cost by ordering in lot sizes of 16,000 units. The result is identical to the solution found by tabular and graphical methods. Solving directly for the EOQ eliminates the trial and error associated with other methods. It is by far the best approach.

The data used in the EOQ calculations are generally management's best estimates of what the actual values will be. Therefore, the optimal EOQ cannot be taken as an exact figure. It is often necessary to round off to the nearest appropriate order quantity, such as a dozen, a ton, or a truckload. Fortunately, determination of lot size is not highly sensitive to small errors in the input data. Practice has shown that although a calculated Q may not be 100% accurate, it is much more accurate than a subjective estimate of the proper lot size.

[1]Some readers may be interested in the calculus derivation of the EOQ formula. Using calculus, we obtain the value of Q that yields the minimum total cost by setting the first derivative of A with respect to Q equal to zero. This equation will locate all values of Q that correspond to points where the slope of the total-cost curve is zero. Note in Figure 4.3 that the slope of the total-cost curve is zero at its minimum value.

$$\frac{dA}{dQ} = -\frac{HS}{Q^2} + \frac{KP}{2} = 0$$

$$Q^2 = \frac{2HS}{KP}$$

$$Q = \sqrt{\frac{2HS}{KP}}$$

Alternative derivation of EOQ

In the foregoing example, we derived a formula that solved directly for the optimal value of the lot size. We were then able to calculate the optimal days' supply per order, the optimal number of orders per year, and the maximum and average inventory value. For some managerial purposes, it may be helpful to solve directly for one of these quantities. As an example, we will solve for the optimal number of orders per year. To do so, we must let

$$N = \text{the number of orders placed per year}$$

$$\text{Ordering cost} = \begin{array}{c}\text{Orders} \\ \text{per year}\end{array} \times \begin{array}{c}\text{Cost per} \\ \text{order}\end{array}$$

$$B = N \qquad \times S \qquad = NS$$

$$\text{Carrying cost} = \begin{array}{c}\text{Average} \\ \text{inventory} \\ \text{value}\end{array} \times \begin{array}{c}\text{Percentage} \\ \text{cost}\end{array}$$

$$C = \frac{HP}{2N} \qquad \times K \qquad = \frac{HPK}{2N}$$

Setting ordering cost equal to carrying cost, we obtain

$$NS = \frac{HPK}{2N}$$

$$N = \sqrt{\frac{HPK}{2S}}$$

For the East Orange Nursery, the optimal value of N can be obtained as follows:

$$N = \sqrt{\frac{(144,000)(.7)(.18)}{(2)(112)}} = \sqrt{81} = 9$$

This means that the company can minimize inventory cost by ordering 9 times per year. The result is consistent with our previous calculations.

Alternative derivations are important, because quantities may sometimes be expressed in terms other than those used in the two EOQ derivations. For example, some firms typically express inventory cost in terms of dollars per unit rather than as a percentage of average inventory. Others may express annual merchandise requirements in terms of dollars per year rather than units per year. Analysts often derive a specific EOQ formula for a specific inventory situation. Their formula will use the terms, concepts, and units normally associated with that situation.

Sample problem 4.1   *BISHOFF SUBURBAN UTILITIES*

The Bishoff Company uses fuel oil to generate electricity for a small suburban community. The value of fuel oil consumed annually (E) is $1,200,000. Price of the fuel oil (P) is $.30 per gallon. Ordering cost (S) is $200 per order, and carrying cost (J) is $.04 per gallon per year. Using the symbols given, derive an expression for annual ordering cost and annual carrying cost. Solve for Q, the optimal order quantity expressed in gallons per order.

SOLUTION

$$\text{Ordering cost} = \frac{ES}{PQ} \qquad \text{Carrying cost} = \frac{JQ}{2}$$

$$\frac{ES}{PQ} = \frac{JQ}{2}$$

$$Q = \sqrt{\frac{2ES}{JP}} = \sqrt{\frac{(2)(1,200,000)(200)}{(.04)(.30)}} = 200,000 \text{ gallons per order}$$

Use of EOQ in more complex situations

In the first part of this chapter, we discussed the most basic type of inventory situation. We assumed that the rate of demand was constant, that inventory was replenished by receiving an entire order at one time, that the time of receipt of a shipment could be predicted precisely, and that the unit cost did not change with the size of the order (there were no quantity discounts). In the following sections, we will upgrade the EOQ analysis by illustrating its usefulness in situations that do not meet all of the requirements of the simple EOQ model just outlined. In order to illustrate different situations, we will make several modifications to the East Orange Nursery problem. We will consider these variations one at a time. Thus, *each modification will apply only to the section in which it is used for illustrative purposes.*

Dividing carrying cost into component parts

In deriving the simple EOQ model, we stated that carrying cost was generally considered to be a percentage of average inventory. In some cases, we can improve the EOQ model by separating carrying cost into its component parts. In other words, the equation for carrying cost might have separate terms for interest cost, warehouse cost, record-keeping cost, and so on. In order to illustrate this, we will slightly modify the East Orange Nursery problem so that carrying cost is composed of two parts: an interest cost and a warehouse or storage fee. In the original statement of the East Orange Nursery problem, the company was assumed to have excess warehouse space, and consequently there was no storage cost associated with the inventory of vases. Let us now assume that the company has no permanent warehouse space. Each year, it signs an annual lease agreement for portable buildings to hold the inventory of vases. Since this is an annual lease agreement, the company must have enough storage space to satisfy the maximum level of inventory. Cost of storage space to the company is $.049 per item per year. In discussing the concept of storage cost, we will let

W = Storage cost expressed as dollars per item per year

We can now determine carrying cost as follows:

$$\text{Carrying cost} = \text{Interest cost} + \text{Storage cost}$$

$$C = \frac{KPQ}{2} + QW$$

$$C = \frac{KPQ}{2} + \frac{2QW}{2} = \frac{Q}{2}(KP + 2W)$$

Ordering cost remains HS/Q. We can determine the new optimal lot size by again setting carrying cost equal to ordering cost and solving for Q.

$$\frac{HS}{Q} = \frac{Q}{2}(KP + 2W)$$

$$Q = \sqrt{\frac{2HS}{KP + 2W}}$$

For the East Orange Nursery problem,

$$Q = \sqrt{\frac{(2)(144{,}000)(\$112)}{(.18)(.70) + (2)(.049)}} = 12{,}000$$

The new optimal lot size is 12,000 vases. Since the company uses 144,000 vases a year, it should now reorder 12 times per year. This calculation confirms our judgment about the relationship between lot size and inventory cost. We added a warehouse cost, which increased the cost of carrying inventory. As carrying cost becomes more expensive, the tendency is to try to reduce it by ordering in smaller lot sizes. A basic reason for splitting the carrying cost into two elements is that one of the components of carrying cost varies directly with the average inventory level, while the second varies with the maximum inventory level. In situations such as this, we can improve the accuracy of the model by dividing total carrying cost into its component parts.

Quantity discounts

In many industries, it is common practice for a supplier to give price discounts on purchase orders for large quantities. A company is often faced with the question of whether or not to increase the lot size in order to take advantage of the price discount. One procedure in analyzing this type of problem is to calculate an optimal lot size for each price range. If the calculated EOQ is below the minimum quantity necessary for a given price, then the best place to "take the price" is the lowest quantity at which that price can be obtained. After the best lot size for each price range is determined, total cost (including the purchase cost of the inventory, which now varies with the order size) should be calculated for each of these lot sizes. The best alternative is the lot size that yields the lowest total cost.

As an example, consider the East Orange Nursery case. Let us assume that the supplier of vases will give a 21% discount for lot sizes of 17,000 to 99,999 and a 23% discount on lot sizes of 100,000 or more. As shown in Table 4.3, this results in prices of $.553 and $.539 respectively. The appropriate lot size for each price is obtained from the EOQ formulas as follows:

For a price of $.70,

$$Q = \sqrt{\frac{(2)(144{,}000)(\$112)}{(.18)(.70)}} = \sqrt{256{,}000{,}000} = 16{,}000$$

For a price of $.553,

$$Q = \sqrt{\frac{(2)(144{,}000)(\$112)}{(.18)(.553)}} = \sqrt{324{,}050{,}633} \approx 18{,}000$$

For a price of $.539,

$$Q = \sqrt{\frac{(2)(144{,}000)(\$112)}{(.18)(.539)}} = \sqrt{332{,}467{,}533} \approx 18{,}230$$

Table 4.3 *Quantity discount prices for vases in the East Orange Nursery problem*

Lot size	Discount	New price
0–16,999	None	$.700
17,000–99,999	21%	.553
100,000 or more	23%	.539

Ms. Baughman should compare the total costs of the three alternative lot sizes available to East Orange Nursery. The lot sizes of 16,000 and 18,000 can be used directly; they are appropriate lot sizes for the price discount allowed by the manufacturer. In order to obtain a price of $.539, however, East Orange must increase the lot size to 100,000 units. Thus, the three relevant lot sizes are 16,000, 18,000 and 100,000. Table 4.4 compares the total costs for these three lot sizes. The lowest total cost is obtained with a lot size of 18,000. East Orange Nursery should take advantage of the first price discount and purchase 18,000 vases per order.

Note that in Table 4.4 carrying cost does not equal ordering cost for a lot size of 100,000 units. At a price of $.539, Ms. Baughman would prefer to order 18,230 units rather that 100,000 units, but she would have to order 100,000 units to obtain the reduced price. Thus, 100,000 units are a "forced" or constrained optimum. In such cases, ordering cost does not necessarily equal carrying cost.

These calculations illustrate the *sensitivity* of EOQ to a change in the price of inventory. When the price decreased by 23%, EOQ increased by only 14%, from 16,000 units to 18,230 units. In general, a change in one of the independent variables, such as price or demand, will cause a proportionally smaller change in EOQ. This is important to the manager, because any error or lack of precision in measuring one of these variables causes less than a proportional change in EOQ.

Gradual receipt of inventory

Our previous analysis assumed that the company replenishes its inventory by receiving an entire order all at one time. In many cases, this is a valid assumption. Outside suppliers normally deliver a complete order,

Table 4.4 *Comparison of total inventory costs for various price discounts at East Orange Nursery*

	Lot size		
	16,000	18,000	100,000
Price (P)	$ .70	$ .553	$ .539
Orders per year (N)	9	8	1.44
Average inventory (units)	8,000	9,000	50,000
Average inventory ($)	$ 5,600	$ 4,977	$26,950
Ordering cost (HS/Q)	$ 1,008	$ 896	$ 161
Carrying cost (KPQ/2)	1,008	896	4,851
Materials cost (PH)	100,800	79,632	77,616
Total cost	$102,816	$81,424	$82,628

Figure 4.4 *Inventory with receipt over a period of time*

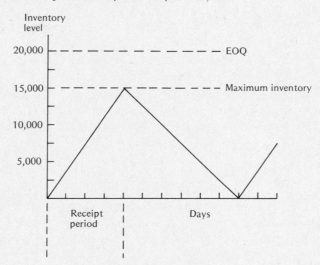

although in some industries it is customary to receive several partial shipments over a period of time. The "complete shipment" assumption is less likely to hold true when the inventory is manufactured by the firm using or selling the product. It may take several days or even weeks for the firm to produce an optimal lot size of a product that it sells to consumers. Instead of arriving all at once, inventory will build up over a period of time. Sales will be made during this same period of time. For this reason, the level of inventory will never be as large as the lot size. Figure 4.4 is a graphical representation of this type of inventory situation.

To illustrate this concept, let us modify the East Orange Nursery problem. The company's supplier of vases will now deliver the vases at a rate of 720 per day. Ms. Baughman would like to derive an EOQ that would minimize inventory cost under this new receipt policy. In deriving the new EOQ, we will need two new variables. Let

U = Use (or sales) rate expressed as items per day

R = Receipt rate expressed as items per day

The major change is that maximum inventory will be less than the lot size, because sales and receipts are occurring simultaneously. Many items will have already been sold by the time the last item of a particular order is received. Since carrying cost is dependent on the value of average inventory, our first step should be to determine the value of average inventory.

The number of days required to receive an entire order (the receipt period) is equal to the number of units ordered divided by the receipt rate, or

$$\text{Days to receive order} = \frac{Q}{R}$$

Sales are being made during the period of time when a lot is being received. The number of items sold during this period is equal to the length of the receipt period (Q/R) multiplied by the daily usage or sales rate. Thus,

$$\text{Usage during the receipt period} = \frac{QU}{R}$$

The maximum level of inventory occurs when the last item is received. Prior to this time, QU/R units have been sold. Thus, maximum inventory is equal to the amount ordered less the quantity sold during the receipt period, or

$$\text{Maximum inventory} = Q - \left(\frac{QU}{R}\right) = Q\left(1 - \frac{U}{R}\right)$$

Since average inventory is half of maximum inventory,

$$\text{Average inventory} = \frac{Q}{2}\left(1 - \frac{U}{R}\right)$$

We may now solve for the EOQ exactly as we did before.

$$\text{Ordering cost} = \text{Orders per year} \times \text{Cost per order}$$

$$B = \frac{H}{Q} \times S = \frac{HS}{Q}$$

$$\text{Carrying cost} = \text{Average inventory value} \times \text{Carrying cost percentage}$$

$$C = \frac{PQ}{2}\left(1 - \frac{U}{R}\right) \times K = \frac{KPQ}{2}\left(1 - \frac{U}{R}\right)$$

Setting ordering cost equal to carrying cost, we obtain

$$\frac{HS}{Q} = \frac{KPQ}{2}\left(1 - \frac{U}{R}\right)$$

$$Q = \sqrt{\frac{2HS}{KP(1 - U/R)}}$$

For the East Orange Nursery problem,

$$Q = \sqrt{\frac{(2)(144,000)(112)}{(.18)(.70)(1-400/720)}} = \sqrt{576,000,000} = 24,000$$

The lot size that will minimize total inventory cost is now 24,000, which means that the company should order 6 times a year. Substituting into the foregoing equations, we find that annual ordering cost still equals annual carrying cost, each having a value of $672. The total cost of $1344 is less than the cost of $2016 when the entire shipment was received at once. This is logical, because both average inventory and number of orders placed per year are smaller than when the entire shipment of vases was received at one time.

EOQ concepts in production

The concepts used in minimizing inventory cost can also be quite helpful in analyzing certain production processes. There are two basic types of production systems. Oil refineries, can manufacturing plants, and mass-production industries with production lines are examples of *continuous production*. General machine shops, photography studios, and paint manufacturers are examples of *intermittent* or *batch production*. In a batch process, general purpose machines are used to produce a given amount of a product and then converted to manufacture a second product. For example, a paint manufacturer may set up its equipment to manufacture a batch of red paint. Some time later, the company will stop manufacturing red paint and reset the equipment to manufacture a batch of white or blue paint. EOQ concepts can be quite helpful in determining the proper batch size in intermittent production systems.

A major objective of the production manager is to manufacture in batches or lot sizes that will minimize cost. As was the case in inventory analysis, this involves two types of cost. *The setup cost is similar to ordering cost* and is incurred each time production facilities are reassigned to a new product. In the paint example, setup cost would involve cleaning and resetting machinery as well as initial quality control tests which must be performed on the new product. Total annual setup cost will increase as the number of setups increases. In other words, total setup cost for a few large batches will be less than the total setup cost for many small batches.

One method of decreasing setup cost is to make large lot sizes or batches. Doing so will increase the firm's inventory or carrying cost, however. If a company makes a large batch of red paint, it must hold the paint in inventory until customers purchase it. During this holding period, the company will incur the cost of carrying stock in inventory. It is the task of the production manager to balance these two types of costs and choose a lot size that will minimize the total cost.

The methods used in solving problems related to production lot size are identical to the methods used in inventory analysis. The analyst need only substitute setup cost for ordering cost. We will not repeat the discussion here. Sample Problem 4.2 and several exercises at the end of the chapter illustrate the technique of solving for the proper production lot size.

Sample problem 4.2   DELOTTA MANUFACTURING COMPANY

Delotta Manufacturing Company produces a particular type of window in production lots. Sales are made during the production runs. Production rate (R) is 50 units per day, and sales rate (U) is 30 units per day. Estimated annual sales volume (H) is 6000 units. Cost of carrying the inventory (J) is $2 per window per year, and setup cost is $150 per setup. Using the symbols given, derive expressions for maximum inventory, setup cost, and carrying cost. Solve for N, the optimal number of setups to make in one year.

SOLUTION

$$\text{Maximum inventory} = \frac{H}{N} - \frac{HU}{NR} = \frac{H}{N}\left(1 - \frac{U}{R}\right)$$

$$\text{Setup cost} = NS \qquad \text{Carrying cost} = \frac{JH}{2N}\left(1 - \frac{U}{R}\right)$$

$$N = \sqrt{\frac{JH}{2S}\left(1 - \frac{U}{R}\right)} = \sqrt{\frac{(2)(6000)}{(2)(150)}\left(1 - \frac{30}{50}\right)} = 4$$

Illustrative example: PATTERSON AUTO SUPPLY

Patterson Auto Supply is a locally owned wholesale distributor of automobile parts. It is located in a New England metropolitan area of approximately half a million people. The company sells primarily to service stations, independent garages, and other small repair shops. Patterson Auto Supply remains open 24 hours a day. Most of its customers are not large enough to maintain inventory of expensive parts, and they buy from Patterson on an "as needed" basis.

Mr. Bill Clarke has recently become general manager of the Patterson company. He is concerned with the company's ordering and inventory policy for radiators. The previous manager had used EOQ analysis to determine that the optimal lot size of radiators was 360. This is a 60-day supply, since the company averages 6 sales per day. Radiators are ordered from a nearby distributor, and a shipment is delivered 35 days after an order is placed. The company's reorder policy is to place a new order when the inventory falls to 210 units. Thus, the new order should arrive just as the present supply is being exhausted.

On many occasions, existing inventory is depleted before the new shipment arrives. During this stockout period, the company loses potential profit because it cannot supply the radiators requested. Mr. Clarke feels the problem is more serious than the simple loss of sales. He knows that when he is out of stock, his customers must go elsewhere to purchase a radiator. He is afraid that some of these customers will switch their business permanently to another distributor.

A possible solution to the stockout problem is to reorder earlier so that the new shipment will arrive before the inventory is depleted. Mr. Clarke feels that this procedure would give him a safety margin of inventory and eliminate or reduce stockout cost.

He knows, however, that reordering earlier will increase his inventory carrying cost. He must search for a solution that will balance stockout and inventory carrying costs.

Inventory problems with uncertainty

In the first part of this chapter, we were concerned with determining the optimal lot size by minimizing the sum of ordering and carrying costs. We assumed that the rate of inventory usage was uniform over time and that the time of receipt of a shipment of inventory could be predicted with certainty. We were not concerned with stockouts, and we gave little attention to the question of when to reorder inventory. We will discuss these topics in the sections that follow.

The decision of when to reorder

The absence of certainty introduces several new elements into inventory management. Since we cannot predict the rate of demand and time of inventory replenishment with certainty, the possibility of a shortage, or stockout, exists. The cost associated with stockouts must be considered in a total analysis of the inventory situation. Our decision about when to order new inventory will affect both stockout cost and inventory carrying cost.

Lead time and the reorder point

The *reorder point* is the condition that tells a company it is time to reorder inventory. *Lead time* is the amount of time that elapses between placement of an order and receipt of the new inventory. Under conditions of certainty, we can determine the reorder point easily by multiplying the lead time by the daily usage. Patterson Auto Parts averages 6 sales a day. Suppose it is known that the firm sells exactly 6 radiators a

Figure 4.5 *Relationship of EOQ, reorder point, and lead time under conditions of certainty*

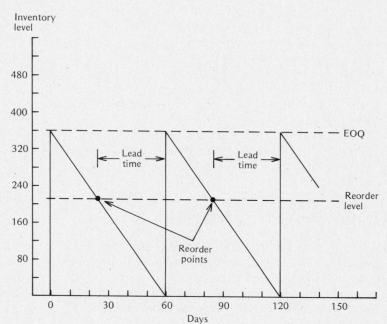

day and that lead time is always exactly 35 days. Under these conditions, the firm would reorder whenever inventory dropped to a level of 210 units. Figure 4.5 illustrates the relationships between EOQ, reorder level, and lead time for conditions of certainty.

Unfortunately, neither demand nor lead time can be predicted with certainty. Quite often, actual usage of inventory will exceed planned usage or the lead time will be longer than expected. These two conditions are illustrated in Figure 4.6. In the first example, the rate of usage increased after a new lot had been ordered, resulting in a depletion of inventory before the new shipment arrived. The firm has no inventory between points (or times) *a* and *b*.

Any potential sales during this period will be lost, and the customer will presumably purchase the item elsewhere. In the second example in Figure 4.6, new stock was scheduled to arrive at point *c* but was delayed until point *d*. This resulted in a stockout from time *c* to time *d*.

Stockout costs

When a business cannot supply an item that it normally carries in stock, a stockout occurs and the firm incurs *stockout* or *shortage costs*. We can

Figure 4.6 *Illustration of stockouts resulting from increased demand and late arrival of a shipment of inventory*

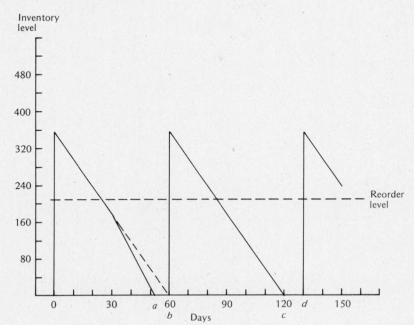

use Patterson Auto Supply to illustrate the concept of stockout cost. If a customer requests a radiator and it is not available at Patterson Auto Supply, the customer will probably purchase the item elsewhere. The loss of profit is a stockout cost. Furthermore, Patterson's failure to supply an item may cause the customer to trade elsewhere in the future. This loss of future business is also a stockout cost.

Stockout costs also crop up in manufacturing organizations. A production facility or assembly line may have to be shut down because the supply of a raw material has run out or because a spare part needed for repair is not in the storeroom. The costs associated with these situations should be considered stockout costs. Unfortunately, shortage costs are often quite difficult to measure or quantify. They must be considered, however, because they may amount to a significant portion of the firm's total cost.

Safety stock

Organizations can reduce stockout cost by carrying a safety stock. A *safety stock* is an inventory maintained to help prevent the undesirable effects of unexpected events depleting regular inventory. Assume that

Figure 4.7 *Inventory at Patterson Auto Supply, with certainty and safety stock*

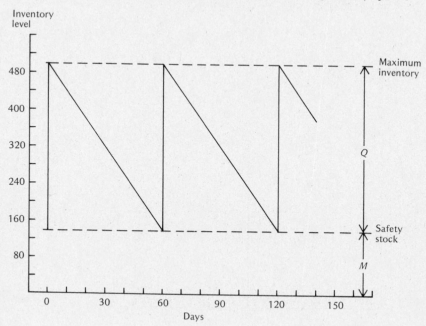

Patterson Auto Supply carries a safety stock of 140 units. The inventory is then portrayed as shown in Figure 4.7. Maximum inventory is now $Q + M$, where M is the safety stock. Under expected conditions, the inventory level will vary between a minimum of M units and a maximum of $Q + M$ units.

Figure 4.8 illustrates how a safety stock protects against the two stockout conditions illustrated in Figure 4.6. An increase in the rate of use after the reorder point depleted the safety stock to point M_1. Likewise, an increase in lead time necessitating a delay in delivery caused the level of inventory to drop to point M_2. In both cases, the company used its safety stock to prevent an undesirable stockout. Obviously, a firm cannot carry enough safety stock to guard against *all* unexpected events. Carrying safety stock costs money, and the firm must balance this additional cost against savings obtained by reducing the frequency of stockouts.

Two items in Figure 4.8 need clarification. Use of safety stock is affected only by an increase in demand *after* the reorder point. The company would presumably detect any increase in usage that occurred before placement of an order and would place the order earlier. In the example shown in Figure 4.8, the increase in rate of demand occurred

Figure 4.8 *Use of safety stock to protect against stockouts*

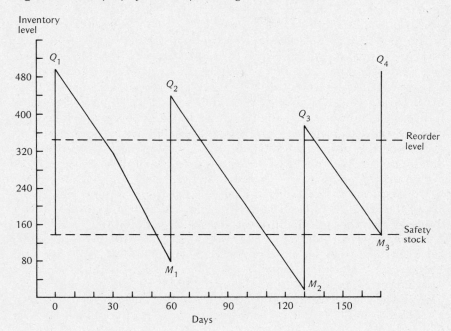

after the order was placed, so there was no chance to adjust the size of the order. Second, when the order is delivered at M_1, the level of inventory increases only by the amount of the EOQ. The level of inventory therefore rises to point Q_2, which is lower (by the amount of safety stock consumed) than the maximum inventory level illustrated by point Q_1.

Determining the proper level of safety stock[2]

Determining the proper amount of safety stock a firm should carry is a matter of balancing, or trading off, two contrasting types of costs. If the amount of safety stock is increased, the probability of running out of stock decreases, which reduces annual stockout cost. Conversely, an increase in the amount of safety stock will increase total inventory carrying cost. Good inventory management calls for the level of safety

---

[2]In this text, we determine EOQ and the proper level of safety stock independently. This approach must be considered as an approximating method, because stockouts vary with EOQ and safety stock. More sophisticated inventory models consider the interacting effects of EOQ, safety stock, and stockouts, but these models and the data they use are still approximations and still subject to inaccuracies. Our approach is a simple and practical way to become familiar with the important concepts of inventory analysis.

stock that minimizes the sum of these two costs. This value is dependent on the cost of carrying stock, the cost of a stockout, and the probability that a stockout will occur.

The first step in determining the optimal level of safety stock is to estimate annual stockout cost for various levels of safety stock. We will use Patterson Auto Supply to illustrate this calculation, and we will assume a constant lead time of 35 days. A stockout can occur only because of an increase in the rate of demand after the reorder point. It has been determined that the optimal lot size is 360, the average use rate is 6 radiators per day, and lead time is 35 days. We now wish to determine the proper safety stock to carry. Mr. Clarke first needs to determine, for various levels of safety stock, the probability of a stockout occurring before a new shipment arrives. Table 4.5 gives the number of requests for radiators during 100 reorder periods in the past. Using this data, Mr. Clarke can assign probability values to the various usage levels. These probability values are also shown in Table 4.5.

Average use during the reorder period is 210 units. With no safety stock, the company would reorder when the inventory level drops to 210 units. A stockout would occur only when demand during the reorder period exceeded 210 radiators (240, 270, or 300 units, for example). If Mr. Clarke wanted to prevent these stockouts, he could carry a safety stock of 30, 60, or 90 radiators. In order to accomplish this, he would increase the reorder point to a level of either 240, 270, or 300 units.

Let us determine the effect of each of these acts on total annual stockout cost. These calculations are illustrated in Table 4.6. We will assume that the cost to the company of running out of stock is $20 for each unit requested. With *no safety stock*, the company would reorder at an inventory level of 210 units. A stockout would occur only if requests for radiators exceeded this amount. If actual demand was for 240 radiators, then a shortage of 30 units would occur. We obtain the

Table 4.5 *Probabilities of various demands during the reorder period at Patterson Auto Supply*

Demand during reorder periods	Number of periods	Probability
150	20	.20
180	15	.15
210	30	.30
240	20	.20
270	10	.10
300	5	.05
	100	1.00

Table 4.6 *Determination of shortage cost for various levels of safety stock*

Safety stock	Reorder point	Demand	Probability of stockout	Number short	EASC* ($)
0	210	240	.20	30	720
		270	.10	60	720
		300	.05	90	540
					1980
30	240	270	.10	30	360
		300	.05	60	360
					720
60	270	300	.05	30	180
					180
90	300	Never out of stock			0

*Expected annual stockout cost (EASC) = Number short × Probability of occurrence of that demand × Per-unit stockout cost ($20) × Number of orders per year (6)

expected annual cost of this shortage (for this stock action) by multiplying together the number short (30), the probability of occurrence of this shortage (.20), the per-unit stockout cost ($20), and the number of reorder periods per year (6). For no safety stock and a demand of 240, the expected annual stockout cost is $720. The corresponding expected stockout costs for demands of 270 and 300 are $720 and $540 respectively. Total expected stockout cost for this stock action is $1980.

If Patterson Auto Supply carries a *safety stock of 30 units,* the reorder point will be 240 and stockouts will occur only if the level of demand is 270 or 300. As shown in Table 4.6, the expected annual stockout cost for this stock action is $720. Likewise, the annual stockout cost when the company carries a *safety stock of 60 units* is $180. The company can avoid all stockout cost by carrying a *safety stock of 90 units.*

For the Patterson company, the carrying cost of the inventory in safety stock is $10 per item per year. The annual costs of carrying the various levels of safety stock are shown in Table 4.7. This table also gives the total of carrying costs and stockout costs for the four alternatives investigated. Table 4.7 shows that the policy of carrying a safety stock of 60 radiators is the optimal inventory policy. Thus, Mr. Clarke should adopt a policy of reordering when inventory falls to 270 units.

Sample problem 4.3   HELEN'S ICE CREAM

Helen's Ice Cream Company has determined that the optimal lot size of strawberry ice cream is 1500 gallons. The company orders this quantity 12 times a year. Sales average 50 gallons a day and normal lead time is 12 days. Carrying cost is $5 per gallon per year. The magnitude of this cost results primarily from refrigeration. The company estimates stockout cost to be $4 per gallon. For the reorder period, the probabilities of selling 500, 600, 700, and 800 gallons are .4, .3, .2, and .1 respectively. What level of safety stock should the company carry to minimize the sum of carrying cost and stockout cost?

SOLUTION

Safety stock	Demand	Probability of stockout	Stockout costs ($)	Carrying costs ($)	Total costs ($)
0	700	.2	960		
	800	.1	960		
			1920	0	1920
100	800	.1	480	500	980
200	——— Never out of stock ———			1000	1000

The optimal policy is to carry 100 gallons of safety stock.

Service level approach to inventory management

We have indicated that it is difficult to determine the exact value of the per-unit cost of being out of stock. In a retail establishment, the direct cost of a lost sale can be determined, but the cost resulting from future loss of sales and customer good will is difficult to estimate. The problem is even more complex for wholesale establishments and manufacturing industries. For this reason, many companies adopt a service-level approach to inventory management.

Table 4.7 *Evaluation of alternative safety stock policies for Patterson Auto Supply*

Safety stock	Reorder point	Stockout cost	Cost of carrying safety stock*	Total cost
0	210	$1980	$ 0	$1980
30	240	720	300	1020
60	270	180	600	780
90	300	0	900	900

*Based on a carrying cost of $10 per unit per year

Defining the service level

The value of an inventory *service level* is the probability that the company will not experience a stockout during a reorder period. For example, suppose a company adopted a service level of 90%. This means that the company will be able to satisfy all demand during 90% of the inventory cycles. During 10% of the reorder periods, it will run out of stock before the new shipment arrives. Obviously, a service level of 90% will require more safety stock than a service level of 70%. It will consequently result in a higher carrying cost. Conversely, the 90% service level will entail a lower stockout cost. Thus, the service-level concept provides management with another method of balancing these two contrasting costs.

In some cases, tradition, necessity, or legal requirements call for a particular service level. For example, the inventory of blood in a hospital must be maintained at a sufficiently high level to meet emergencies as they occur. In most cases, however, determination of a proper service level is a subjective judgment made by management. In other words, managers set the service level where they feel it should be. But in making this determination managers should be aware of the carrying cost associated with alternative service levels. This information is best provided in a table or figure known as a service-level cost curve.

Carrying cost for a particular service level

In order to illustrate the service-level approach to inventory management, we will use the example of Lefty's, Inc., a wholesale sporting goods distributor. In discussing this example, we will refer to the *normal probability distribution* and to the *standard deviation* of this distribution. Readers who want to review these topics should turn to the appropriate section in Chapter 14.

Lefty's is concerned with its inventory of golf bags. Inventory lead time for a shipment of golf bags is 6 weeks. Inventory carrying cost is $8 per bag per year. A study of sales history indicates that during past reorder periods, sales have averaged 300 units with a standard deviation of 40 units. Lefty is convinced that demand during the reorder period can be approximated by the normal distribution. He wants to maintain a service level of 90%, requiring the level of the inventory at the beginning of the reorder period to be large enough so that stockouts occur only 10% of the time. In other words, Lefty must determine what level of demand will be exceeded in only 10% of the reorder periods.

Figure 4.9 is a graphical representation of the demand distribution for past reorder periods. The shaded area of the curve represents the 10% of the reorder periods that Lefty is willing to be out of stock. The question, of course, is what level of inventory is represented by point M in Figure 4.9. The area between the mean of 300 and point M

Figure 4.9 *Demand during past reorder periods at Lefty's, Inc.*

contains 40% of the total area under the curve. From Table A in the Appendix, we know that point *M* is 1.28 standard deviation units to the right of the mean. Thus, point *M* represents a safety stock level of 51.

$$\text{Safety stock} = 1.28 \times 40 = 51$$

The reorder point can be determined as follows:

$$\text{Reorder point} = 300 + 51 = 351$$

If the company reorders when the stock level falls to 351 units, it will experience a stockout during only 10% of the reorder periods. The carrying cost of the golf bags is $8 per item per year. The cost of carrying the 51 units of safety stock associated with this level is $408 per year.

Sample problem 4.4   DAVID'S ICE CREAM

David's Ice Cream maintains a service level of 80% for blackberry ice cream. During past reorder periods, demand has averaged 60 gallons with a standard deviation of 10 gallons. Carrying cost is $5 per gallon per year. Determine the additional cost that would result from raising the service level to 98%.

SOLUTION

Service level	"Z" value*	Safety stock	Carrying cost
98%	2.05	20.5	$102.50
80%	.84	8.4	42.00
			$ 60.50

*Z value is the number of standard deviation units represented by the required safety stock.

Table 4.8 *Cost of various service-level policies for Lefty's, Inc.*

Service level (%)	Standard deviations	Safety stock	Cost
50.0	.00	0	$ 0
60.0	.25	10	80
70.0	.52	21	168
80.0	.84	34	272
90.0	1.28	51	408
95.0	1.65	66	528
99.0	2.33	93	744
99.9	3.09	124	992

The service-level cost curve

A manager should be aware of the cost of carrying the safety stock associated with various service levels. Table 4.8 gives the cost of various service levels for Lefty's, Inc. These data are best displayed in a service-level cost curve like the one shown in Figure 4.10. It is evident that the relationship between carrying cost and service level is not linear. In fact, *it becomes more and more costly to obtain a given or constant increase in the service level.* A curve of this type should help a manager determine where to make the trade-off between additional stockout cost and additional inventory carrying cost.

Reordering practices

A firm's inventory system must provide some means of signaling the manager when it is time to reorder inventory. Inventory control systems usually fall into one of two types. One method is to observe the level of inventory and to reorder when this level drops to a certain point. The second method is to reorder stock at preestablished intervals, at which time the manager observes the level of inventory to see how many units to order at that particular time.

Perpetual inventory systems

If the reorder point is based on the level of inventory, the company must have some method of constantly monitoring the quantity of inventory on hand. Such systems are *perpetual inventory systems.* Many companies now have electronic inventory systems that monitor the current level of inventory in stock. In systems of this type, an order is placed when the inventory drops to a predetermined level known as the *reorder point.* Since the inventory is always at the same level when the

Figure 4.10 *Service-level cost curve for Lefty's, Inc.*

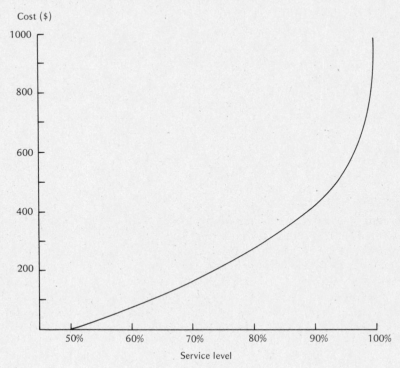

new order is placed, the order quantity is always the same. For this reason, this type of system is frequently referred to as a *fixed order-quantity system.*

Periodic inventory systems

Periodic systems are based on a review of the inventory level at predetermined time intervals. For some items, this review may take place once a week. For other items, the review may occur quarterly or even annually. At every review, it is determined how much (if any) inventory should be ordered. The size of the order will vary with the inventory level. For this reason, these systems are often referred to as *variable order-quantity systems.*

This approach offers the obvious advantage of eliminating the need to constantly monitor the level of inventory. The disadvantage is that it usually requires a larger safety stock to protect against stockouts. No one observes the level of inventory until the end of a fixed time interval. Thus, the safety stock must guard against variation in demand during the order interval as well as variation in demand during the reorder period.

Symbols used in inventory analysis

We have used a number of different symbols in this chapter on inventory analysis. For convenient reference, these symbols are listed here. Pay careful attention to the units that are used with each symbol. (Two symbols may be used for the same quantity when this quantity has been expressed in different units within the chapter.)

A = Total inventory cost, the annual sum of ordering cost and carrying cost

B = Total yearly ordering cost

C = Total yearly carrying cost

D = Monetary value of the inventory in an economic order quantity

E = Monetary value of the annual inventory requirement

H = Annual inventory requirement expressed in units of inventory

J = Cost of carrying inventory expressed as dollars per unit per year

K = Cost of carrying inventory expressed as a percent of the average inventory value

M = Level of safety stock expressed in units of inventory

N = Number of orders (or setups) placed per year

P = Value (price) of a unit of inventory

Q = Order quantity

R = Receipt (or production) rate expressed as units per period of time

S = Per-lot ordering (or setup) cost expressed as dollars per order

T = Inventory tax expressed as a percent of maximum inventory value

U = Use or sales rate expressed as units per period of time

W = Storage cost expressed as dollars per item per year

X = Number of days' supply per order

Problems and exercises

1. Explain the following terms:

carrying cost	intermittent production
ordering cost	continuous production
lot size	reorder point
EOQ	stockout

receipt rate

use rate

setup cost

lead time

safety stock

service level

perpetual inventory system

periodic inventory system

INSTRUCTIONS FOR PROBLEMS 2–5

For each problem, calculate annual ordering cost, annual carrying cost, and total annual inventory cost for selected lot sizes. Construct a graph showing the relationship between each of these values and orders per year. Use the tabular method to determine the optimal EOQ.

2. The Wolcott Company sells electric travel irons. Annual inventory requirement is 6400 units. Price is $10 per iron. The company estimates ordering cost to be $100 per order and carrying cost to be 20% of average inventory value.

3. The Dexter Company has annual sales of 1800 novelty bedspreads. Each inventory item has a value of $40. Ordering cost is $600 per order. Carrying cost is 15% of average inventory value.

4. The annual inventory requirement at the Gallatin Company is 36,000 units. Price is $2 per unit. Ordering cost is $100 per order. Carrying cost is 10% of average inventory value.

5. The Campbell Company sells large industrial machines that have an inventory value of $2000. The company expects to order 200 machines during the next year. Ordering cost is $400, and carrying cost is estimated to be 20% of the value of average inventory.

INSTRUCTIONS FOR PROBLEMS 6–11

Solve for the values specified, using the formulas derived in the textbook.

6. Consider problem 2. Solve for Q, the optimal lot size at the Wolcott Company.

7. Consider problem 3. Solve for Q, the optimal lot size at the Dexter Company.

8. Consider problem 4. Use the formula derived in your textbook to solve for N, the optimal number of times per year for the Gallatin Company to place an order.

9. Consider problem 5. Use the formula derived in your textbook to solve for N, the optimal number of times per year for the Campbell Company to place an order.

10. The Dallas Company manufactures paper punches. Manufacturing cost is $10 per item. Setup cost is $500 per setup. The company produces 20,000 units annually at a rate of 300 units per day. The company sells punches at a rate of 60 units per day. Carrying cost is 10% of average inventory value. Solve for Q, the optimal production lot size.

11. The Crawford Company manufactures large industrial dryers. Expected annual demand is 100 units at a rate of 1 every 3 days. Setup cost is $5000.

The company can manufacture 2 units every 3 days at a cost of $1000 per unit. Carrying cost is 20% of average inventory. Solve for Q, the optimal production lot size.

INSTRUCTIONS FOR PROBLEMS 12–22

In each of the following problems, derive an expression for annual ordering cost and annual carrying cost. Use the symbols given in each problem, and do not make up new symbols. Derive an expression to solve directly for the quantity in question. Substitute the proper numerical quantities into this expression and solve for the optimal value.

12. The Rush Company sells desk lamps. Price (P) is $20 per lamp. Carrying cost (J) is $4 per lamp per year. Ordering cost (S) is $100 per order. The total annual inventory requirement (H) is 1800 units. Solve for Q, the optimal number of lamps to order at one time.

13. The Ingham Company sells charcoal. The inventory value of annual sales (E) is $1,960,000. Carrying cost (K) is 20% of average inventory value. Ordering cost (S) is $1000 per order. Solve for N, the optimal number of times per year to place an order.

14. The McLane Company uses $10,000 of inventory ($E$) each year. Ordering cost (S) is $40 per order. Carrying cost (K) is 20% of average inventory value. Solve for D, the dollar value of an optimal lot size of inventory.

15. The Duane Company operates 360 days a year. Its annual sales volume (H) is 4050 units. Ordering cost (S) is $50 per order. Carrying cost (J) is $2 per item per year. Solve for X, the optimal number of days' supply per order.

16. The Taney Company has an annual inventory requirement (H) of 5000 units. Ordering cost (S) is $250 per order. Price of the inventory (P) is $12 per unit. Inventory carrying cost (K) is 20% of average inventory. The company also has a warehouse cost (W) of $.60 per unit, based on maximum inventory. Solve for N, the optimal number of times per year to place an order.

17. The Woodbury Company sells frozen figurines. The value of annual inventory (E) is $128,000. Ordering cost ($S$) is $100 per order. The cost of the inventory (P) is $8 per item. Carrying cost (J) is $3 per item per year, based on average inventory. Refrigeration cost (W) is $1 per item per year, based on maximum inventory. Solve for Q, the optimal number of units per order.

18. Annual inventory requirement (H) at the Forward Company is 200,000 units. Ordering cost (S) is $1000 per order. Basic carrying cost (J) is $20 per unit, based on average inventory. Price (P) is $100 per unit. Warehouse cost (W) is $10 per unit, based on maximum inventory. Inventory tax (T) is 30% of maximum inventory value. Solve for Q, the optimal number of units per order.

19. The Spencer Company manufactures lawn swings in production lots. Expected yearly demand (H) is 30,000 units, which are sold at a rate (U) of

100 per day. Carrying cost (J) is $5 per item per year, based on average inventory. The units can be produced at a rate (R) of 300 units per day. Setup cost (S) is $500 per setup. Solve for N, the optimal number of setups per year.

20. The Bibb Company manufactures $800,000 worth of material (E) yearly. The cost of a production setup (S) is $10,000. Inventory costs (K) are 20% of average inventory. The production rate (R) is $8000 per day, and the sales rate (U) is $4000 per day. Solve for D, the optimal dollar value of a lot size.

21. The Walker Company manufactures $18,000 worth of material (E) yearly at a rate (R) of $100 per day. The use rate (U) is $80 per day. Setup cost ($S$) is $100 per setup. The inventory has a value (P) of $1 per item. Carrying cost (W) is $1 per item per year, based on maximum inventory. Solve for Q, the optimal number of units per lot.

22. The Corwin Company annually produces 27,000 shirts (H), which have an inventory value (P) of $6 each. The production rate (R) is 400 units per day, and the sales rate (U) is 100 units per day. The cost of setting up for production (S) is $1000. Inventory cost ($K$) is 15% of average inventory. There is also a warehouse cost (W) of $.55 per shirt, based on maximum inventory. Solve for Q, the optimal number of units for a production run.

INSTRUCTIONS FOR PROBLEMS 23–27
In each problem, use the proper EOQ formula to answer the question asked.

23. The Guthrie Company buys 16,200 chairs a year at a price of $20 per chair. The company presently orders in lot sizes of 900. It has been offered a 19% discount to order in lots of 950 or more. Should the company take the discount, and if so, what is the proper lot size? Ordering cost is $100 per order, and carrying cost is 20% of average inventory.

24. The Cobb Company purchases 40,000 specialty radios each year. The high ordering cost of $5000 results from the manufacturer's setup expenses. Carrying cost is 10% of average inventory. The price of the radios is $40 in quantities of 1 to 12,499; $36 in quantities of 12,500 to 19,999; and $32 in quantities of 20,000 or more. What is the minimum-cost order quantity?

25. The Thomas Company purchases 9000 travel bags a year at a price of $5 each. Ordering cost is $90 per order. Inventory cost is 20% of average inventory. Warehouse cost is $.50 per item, based on maximum inventory. The firm has been offered a 38% discount on lot sizes of 3000 or more. What is the optimum EOQ?

26. Annual sales volume at the Dix Company is 20,000 units, or 80 units per day for the 250 working days in the year. After inventory is ordered, it is received at a rate of 400 units per day until a complete order is delivered. Ordering cost is $640 per order. Carrying cost is 20% of average inventory. The cost of the merchandise is $10 per unit. The supplier to the company has offered a 20% discount if the firm will accept an entire lot at once rather

than partial deliveries of 400 units daily. Should the Dix Company accept this new offer from the supplier?

27. The Fessenden Company sells 10,000 units annually at a rate of 40 per day for the 250 working days in the year. When an order is placed, the company receives shipments of 80 units per day until the entire lot is delivered. Ordering cost is $1000 per order. Inventory is valued at $100 per unit. Carrying cost is 40%, based on average inventory value. The company has been offered a 4% discount to order in lots of 5000 or more. Should the company take the discount? Show total cost, ordering cost, and carrying cost for the two alternative lot sizes.

INSTRUCTIONS FOR PROBLEMS 28–31

For each problem, determine annual stockout cost, safety stock carrying cost, and the optimal number of units of safety stock.

28. The Boutwell Company orders inventory 4 times a year. Lead time for reordering a shipment of inventory is 10 days. Demand averages 4 units per day. The company estimates stockout cost to be $100 per item. Inventory carrying cost is $60 per item per year. During the past 160 reorder periods, demand has been distributed as follows:

Demand	30	35	40	45	50
Occurrences	16	32	64	32	16

The objective is to minimize cost. Should the company carry 0, 5, or 10 units of safety stock?

29. Demand at the Bristow Company averages 20 units per day, 360 days per year. The company orders 6 times per year in lot sizes of 1200. Lead time is 30 days. Carrying cost is estimated to be $15 per item per year. Stockout cost is $10 per item. Demand during past reorder periods is as follows:

Demand	500	550	600	650	700	750
Occurrences	15	15	35	20	10	5

Should the company carry 0, 50, 100, or 150 units of safety stock?

30. Lead time for reordering inventory at the Morrill Company is 20 days. Average usage is 15 units per day. During 100 past reorder periods, demands of 260, 280, 300, 320, 340, and 360 have occurred 20, 25, 20, 15, 10, and 10 times respectively. The company orders inventory twice a year in lot sizes of 2700 units. Carrying cost is $4 per item per year. Estimated stockout cost is $25 per item per stockout. In order to minimize costs, should the company carry 0, 20, 40, or 60 units of safety stock?

31. The Windom Company reorders inventory 6 times per year. Lead time is 6 days. Demand averages 5 units per day. Carrying cost is $100 per item per year. The company estimates shortage costs to be $100 per item. During the

past 200 reorder periods, demands of 25, 30, 35, and 40 have occurred 60, 90, 40, and 10 times respectively. Should the company maintain 0, 5, or 10 units of safety stock?

INSTRUCTIONS FOR PROBLEMS 32-35

Each problem is concerned with the service-level approach to inventory management. Assume normally distributed demand, and answer the questions asked.

32. The Folger Company is considering changing the service level from 85% to 95% on one of its product lines. During past reorder periods, demand for this product has averaged 200 units with a standard deviation of 40 units. How much additional carrying cost would result from the proposed change in inventory policy? The company orders in lot sizes of 800. Carrying cost is $10 per item per year.

33. The Gresham Company is considering service levels of 80%, 90%, and 99% for one of its major product lines. Lead time for this product is 40 days. Carrying cost is $80 per item per year. During past reorder periods, demand has averaged 40 units with a standard deviation of 8 units. Determine the cost of carrying the safety stock associated with each of the service levels under consideration.

34. The Manning Company sells dictionaries for $20 each. Cost of carrying the dictionaries in stock is $3 per book per year. The company orders 6 times a year in lot sizes of 2000. Demand during past reorder periods has averaged 1000 units with a standard deviation of 140. Draw a service-level cost curve for this product.

35. During past reorder periods, demand for desk lamps at the Fairchild Company has averaged 80 units with a standard deviation of 12. Cost of carrying inventory is $8 per unit per year. Draw a service-level cost curve for desk lamps at the Fairchild Company.

Supplementary readings

Agee, M. H., R. E. Taylor, and P. E. Torgenson. *Quantitative Analysis for Management Decisions*. Englewood Cliffs, N.J.: Prentice-Hall, 1976.

Budnick, F. S., R. Mojena, and T. E. Vollman. *Principles of Operations Research for Management*. Homewood, Ill.: Irwin, 1977.

Buffa, E. S., and W. Taubert. *Production–Inventory Systems: Planning and Control*. Homewood, Ill.: Irwin, 1972.

Hartley, R. V. *Operations Research: A Managerial Emphasis*. Pacific Palisades, Calif.: Goodyear, 1976.

Johnson, R. H., and P. R. Winn. *Quantitative Methods for Management*. Boston: Houghton Mifflin, 1976.

Levin, R. I., and C. A. Kirkpatrick. *Quantitative Approaches to Management,* 2nd ed. New York: McGraw-Hill, 1975.

Shamblin, J. E., and G. T. Stevens. *Operations Research: A Fundamental Approach.* New York: McGraw-Hill, 1974.

Starr, M. K., and D. W. Miller. *Inventory Control: Theory and Practice.* Englewood Cliffs, N.J.: Prentice-Hall, 1962.

Vollman, T. E. *Operations Management.* Reading, Mass.: Addison-Wesley, 1973.

Chapter 5

Introduction to linear programming

Illustrative example: **THE BELL METAL COMPANY**

Mr. Ford is owner and operator of the Bell Metal Company, a small metalworking company that manufactures brass lamps for home use. Because demand was low in the past, Bell Metal has been able to satisfy demand by simply filling requests on order. Recently, however, demand increased dramatically, and the firm is having difficulty filling all orders. For this reason, Mr. Ford decided that he must use a systematic procedure to help him utilize the firm's resources in a way which will optimize their value.

Bell Metal Company manufactures only two types of lamps. The first lamp is known as a China Sea lamp and is manufactured after a nautical oriental design. The second lamp is known as the Matanzas Bay lamp and is designed after artifacts left by the early Spanish settlers of Florida. Mr. Ford has determined each lamp's contribution to profit by subtracting variable costs used in manufacturing and marketing the product from the selling price of the lamp. By this method, he has determined that the contribution to profit of the China Sea lamp is $60 per lamp and that the contribution to profit of the Matanzas Bay lamp is $30 per lamp.

Each China Sea lamp produced requires 2 pounds of brass in the production process, and each Matanzas Bay lamp requires 4 pounds of brass. During the next production period, the company's brass supply is limited to 320 pounds. The company's milling machines are involved in production of the lamps, and only 180 hours of milling machine time are available during the next production period. Each China Sea lamp requires 3 hours of milling machine time and each Matanzas Bay lamp requires 1 hour of milling machine time. An additional limitation is that each China Sea lamp requires two special oriental lamp shades that must be imported from Hong Kong. At present, federal trade restrictions limit imports to 100 shades for each production period.

Linear programming is a method of analyzing a variety of problems similar to that faced by Mr. Ford at the Bell Metal Company. Basically, it is a mathematical technique used to help managers properly utilize scarce resources. It is the most widely used quantitative technique.

Areas of application include marketing, finance, ecology, and education. For example, linear programming is used to decide how to allocate advertising dollars to various media. In finance, linear programming is used in asset management of banks and in portfolio selection. The technique has been used to determine the combination of pollution control methods that will cost the least and maintain an acceptable emission level. Universities have also used linear programming to determine the proper allocation of their resources.

We will illustrate linear programming by showing how it can help Mr. Ford, the president of the Bell Metal Company. Utilizing linear programming in a simple example is the best way to learn the technique. The Bell Metal example is only a learning device, and we could probably solve Mr. Ford's problem with pencil, paper, and intuition. The power and value of linear programming lie in assisting managers who are confronted with far more complicated problems.

Elements of a linear programming problem

Linear programming can be used on a wide variety of problems, but there are many problems for which linear programming is not an appropriate tool of analysis. A problem must meet a certain set of requirements or specifications before we can analyze it by the method of linear programming. We begin, therefore, by discussing those elements common to every linear programming problem. If a particular problem does not meet all of these specifications, then linear programming is not an appropriate tool for the analyst to use.

1. *The decision maker must have an objective that she or he wishes to achieve. This objective must relate to an item such as profit or cost, which the decision maker wishes to maximize or minimize.*

In most of our elementary examples, the objective will be to minimize cost of production or to maximize the contribution to profit. We could have chosen some other objective, such as to maximize total volume of output or to minimize downtime on the milling machines.

2. *There must be processes or decision variables that the decision maker can operate at different levels.*

This is the most fundamental aspect of linear programming problems. It is also a concept that many of us have difficulty understanding. Perhaps the easiest way to understand this concept is to imagine that we have been assigned to solve Mr. Ford's problem. What Mr. Ford wants to know is how many China Sea lamps to produce and how many

Matanzas Bay lamps to produce. Our answer must be that he should produce a certain number of China Sea lamps and a certain number of Matanzas Bay lamps. We must, therefore, have two decision variables.

Decision variables are the controllable elements or alternatives specified by the model as being available to the decision maker. In our example we would let

X_1 = Number of China Sea lamps produced and sold

X_2 = Number of Matanzas Bay lamps produced and sold

Thus, if X_1 has a value of 30 and X_2 has a value of 40, the firm produced and sold 30 China Sea lamps and 40 Matanzas Bay lamps.

It might be helpful to think of a decision variable as a process, that is, a set of events that happen as a unit. Thus, when the firm manufactures 1 China Sea lamp (X_1 = 1), it consumes 2 pounds of its brass supply, uses 3 hours of the total machine time available, reduces the inventory of available lamp shades by 2, and contributes $60 toward the profit of the firm. Likewise, when X_2 = 40, the firm produces 40 Matanzas Bay lamps, consumes 160 pounds of brass, uses 40 hours of machine time, and contributes $1200 to profit.

3. *The actions of the decision maker must be constrained; that is, the decision variables must be operated at levels that do not violate the limitations placed on the decision maker.*

We all realize that our actions are limited or constrained by circumstances that may be beyond our control. We might prefer to take our vacation on the French Riviera, but because of our financial limitations, we settle for a week at the state campgrounds. We might like to use our vacation money to install a tennis court in our backyard. We find, however, that we are limited in space and there is not enough room for a tennis court in the backyard. Or we have a yard big enough for a tennis court, but zoning restrictions prevent the construction of tennis courts in our neighborhood.

In the Bell Metal problem, the *constraints* facing the decision maker are limits on the supply of necessary resources. Mr. Ford is faced with three limitations. During the next production period, the firm can use a maximum of 320 pounds of brass, 180 hours of milling machine time, and 100 oriental lamp shades.

Every linear programming problem also has the requirement that all variables have a value greater than or equal to zero. In other words, no process can be operated at a negative level. These constraints are referred to as the *nonnegativity constraints*, and they are implicit in every linear programming problem.

A statement of the level of operation of each decision variable is known as a *decision set* or *production plan*. Thus, X_1 = 40 and X_2 = 10 constitute a decision set for the Bell Metal problem. Likewise, $X_1 = 30$ and $X_2 = 50$ constitute a decision set for the same problem. Any decision set or production plan that satisfies all of a problem's constraints is known as a *solution* to the linear programming problem. Mathematicians often make a distinction between a *solution* and a *feasible solution* in linear programming. If we make this distinction, a solution is a production plan that satisfies the stated managerial constraints. A feasible solution also satisfies the nonnegativity constraints. Since the nonnegativity constraints are a part of every linear programming problem, we know that the decision maker is looking for the feasible solution that best satisfies his or her objectives.

4. *The decision variables must be interrelated, and we must be able to express this relationship in terms of linear mathematical equations or inequalities.*

After reading the discussion of the first three requirements of every linear programming problem, we now become aware of the interdependence of the decision variables at Bell Metal Company. In this case, contribution to profit is directly related to the production of each type of lamp. Production of lamps is also directly related to the use of resources. For example, producing one China Sea lamp requires 2 pounds of brass, 3 hours of milling machine time, and 2 oriental lamp shades.

It is also true that the production of China Sea lamps and the production of Matanzas Bay lamps are interrelated. Note that if we are producing 40 China Sea lamps and 60 Matanzas Bay lamps, we are consuming all of the brass available $[(2 \times 40) + (4 \times 60) = 320]$. In order to obtain brass to produce additional China Sea lamps, it would be necessary to reduce production of Matanzas Bay lamps.

In a linear programming problem, the relationship between the variables must be a *linear relationship*. Perhaps the easiest way to describe a linear relationship is to say that two variables are linearly related if this relationship can be expressed as a straight line on a graph. Another characteristic of linear relationships between two variables is that a change in one variable causes a proportional change in the other. A linear relationship may exist among more than two variables. In such cases, the relationship is additive (for example, $Z = 3X + 4Y$), and no such relationships as X^2, Y^3, or XY may be used.

In Chapter 1, we discussed road maps and other models. We learned that in order to be useful, a model must in some sense simplify and abstract from reality. There are many real situations that may not exactly meet all four specifications for linear programming, but they may be modeled in a format that *does* meet these specifications. Linear programming may be a very useful tool of analysis for such situations.

Formulating the linear programming problem

To formulate a linear programming problem simply means to translate a real problem into a standardized format consisting of mathematical equations and inequalities. Formulating the problem is often the most difficult part of analyzing problems in business and economics. Formulation is crucial, however, if we are to apply developed analytical techniques to aid us in the analysis of managerial problems. The textbook author in quantitative methods is faced with a "chicken and egg" dilemma in introducing problem formulation. We cannot learn solution techniques until we have learned how to correctly formulate a problem. Conversely, the formulation process becomes much more understandable when we have solved a basic linear programming problem. Our approach will be to formulate a simple problem and then move to graphical representations and solution techniques. In Chapter 6, we will return to problem formulation and concern ourselves with more complicated examples.

Consider the following formulation:

$$\text{Max } Z = 60X_1 + 30X_2$$

s.t.
$$2X_1 + 4X_2 \leqslant 320 \quad \text{(brass supply)}$$
$$3X_1 + 1X_2 \leqslant 180 \quad \text{(machine time)}$$
$$2X_1 + 0X_2 \leqslant 100 \quad \text{(lamp shades)}$$
$$X_1, X_2 \geqslant 0$$

This problem is an example of a standard linear programming formulation. It happens to be a simple problem, that of the Bell Metal Company, but it is typical of all linear programming formulations. Each linear programming problem consists of only two parts. The first part is a mathematical equation that represents the objective to be maximized or minimized. It is referred to as the *objective function*. The second part is a set of mathematical expressions that represent the limitations placed on the decision maker. These mathematical restrictions can be either equations or inequalities. Taken as a group, they are referred to as the *constraint set*, and collectively they define the decision maker's sphere of discretion. The s.t. used in the formulation is an abbreviation for "subject to." It indicates that the decision maker's actions are restricted by the limitations that follow.

Objective functions

The *objective function* of a linear programming problem is simply a mathematical statement expressing the relationship between the item that the decision maker wishes to optimize and the level of operation of the decision variables in the problem. The objective function statement is generally preceded by the word maximize or minimize, depending on whether the item under consideration is to be maximized or minimized. The objective function introduces a new variable into the problem. We will refer to this variable as Z. Z is the value of the variable being optimized. Thus, if Z = $2000 in the Bell Metal problem, the production processes in use are contributing $2000 to the profit of the firm. Of course, Z = $3000 would be preferable to Z = $2000, because Mr. Ford would rather have a solution that contributes $3000 to profit than one that contributes $2000.

Note that some decision variables contribute nothing to the achievement of the decision maker's objective. In a standard linear programming formulation, we include these variables in the objective function with a zero coefficient. If Bell Metal had a third process, X_3, that contributed nothing to profit, the objective function should be Max Z = $60X_1 + 30X_2 + 0X_3$.

A logical question is: "Why would we have a process that contributes no profit?" Many problems have processes that contribute no direct profit but are necessary for the operation of processes that do contribute profit. In fact, some of these "enabling processes" may have a negative effect on profit. Some analysts would argue that advertising is a negatively contributing process but is necessary to production and selling processes that do contribute to the profit of the firm.

Constraints

The constraints of a linear programming problem are mathematical statements of the limitations placed on the decision maker. The constraint section of a standard linear programming formulation is generally preceded by the words "subject to," or often just the letters "s.t.," which imply that the decision maker's choice of action is restricted by the constraints that follow. In the case of resource limitations, the constraints relate the amount of a particular resource consumed to the amount of that resource available. One constraint must be formulated for each resource. In the case of Bell Metal, we have three constraints plus the nonnegativity constraints that are part of every linear programming problem.

In each of the resource constraints, the mathematical expression on the left side of the inequality sign represents the amount of a resource consumed by a particular linear programming solution. The number on the right side of the inequality sign tells us how much of that resource is available. In the case of Bell Metal, the inequality signs all mean "less than or equal to," and they tell us that the amount of resource consumed by a particular solution must be less than or equal to the amount of resource available. Let us first consider the brass constraint, $2X_1 + 4X_2 \leq 320$. This is a mathematical statement that the amount of brass consumed by a particular solution $(2X_1 + 4X_2)$ must be less than or equal to the 320 pounds available for use. The solution $X_1 = 40$ and $X_2 = 30$ satisfies the brass restriction, because the 200 pounds of brass consumed by this solution *are* less than or equal to the amount available. The production plan $X_1 = 50$ and $X_2 = 60$ does not satisfy the brass constraint, because the 340 pounds of brass this plan calls for are greater than the 320 pounds available.

Formulation of the machine time constraint is similar to that of the brass supply constraint. The quantity on the left $(3X_1 + 1X_2)$ represents the amount of machine time used by a particular solution. The quantity on the right (180) represents the total number of hours available during the next period. The less-than-or-equal-to sign tells us that we cannot choose a production plan that will consume more machine time than is available.

Again, we should note that some processes do not consume or use any of a particular resource. In the case of Bell Metal, the process X_2 (production of 1 Matanzas Bay lamp) does not consume any oriental lamp shades. In such cases, the process should be included in the constraint with a zero coefficient. Thus, the lamp shade constraint should be written as $2X_1 + 0X_2 \leq 100$.

Sample problem 5.1   THE BURNS COMPANY

The Burns Company produces aluminum frying pans and aluminum casserole dishes. Each frying pan and each casserole dish require 10 ounces of aluminum. The firm's daily aluminum supply is limited to 140 ounces. Each frying pan requires 20 minutes on the casting machine, and each casserole dish requires 40 minutes on the casting machine. The casting machine is available for 400 minutes daily. Each frying pan requires an insulated handle, and only 12 of these are available each day. Each casserole dish requires two special "pick up" handles, and only 16 of these are available daily. Each frying pan contributes $3 to profit, and each casserole dish contributes $4 to profit. Demand is good, and the firm can sell all it can produce. Formulate the Burns Company problem as a linear programming.problem. The objective is to find a daily production schedule that maximizes contribution to profit.

SOLUTION
Let X_1 represent the number of frying pans produced per day, X_2 the number of casserole dishes produced per day, and Z the total contribution to profit. The formulation is

$$\text{Max } Z = 3X_1 + 4X_2$$

s.t. $\qquad\qquad 10X_1 + 10X_2 \leq 140 \qquad$ (aluminum supply)

$$20X_1 + 40X_2 \leqslant 400 \quad \text{(casting time)}$$
$$X_1 + 0X_2 \leqslant 12 \quad \text{(frying pan handles)}$$
$$0X_1 + 2X_2 \leqslant 16 \quad \text{(casserole handles)}$$
$$X_1, X_2 \geqslant 0$$

Constraints with $\geqslant$ and $=$ signs

In addition to the less-than-or-equal-to constraints, many linear programming problems contain greater-than-or-equal-to constraints and equality constraints. In the case of Bell Metal, let us assume that Mr. Ford had a labor agreement specifying that he would use at least 100 hours of machine time during the next production period. The constraint would be formulated with a greater-than-or-equal-to sign as $3X_1 + 1X_2 \geqslant 100$. For a solution to satisfy this constraint, the amount of machine time consumed may be more than, but *must* be at least equal to, 100 hours. Thus, the solution $X_1 = 30$ and $X_2 = 40$ would satisfy the constraint, whereas the decision set $X_1 = 20$ and $X_2 = 30$ would not, because the 90 hours this second plan calls for are less than the 100 hours required.

In some cases, the amount of resources used must exactly equal the amount available. These equality constraints are formulated with equals signs. In order for a solution to satisfy an equality constraint, the amount of resource consumed must exactly equal the amount available. We will discuss graphical representations and solution techniques for problems with these types of constraints in Chapter 6.

Graphical representation and solution of linear programming problems

Linear programming problems with only two variables can be represented graphically, and simple problems can be solved graphically. More important, however, we can use graphical representations to help us illustrate and understand mathematical techniques of solving linear programming problems. We shall use the Bell Metal Company to illustrate how linear programming problems can be described and solved graphically.

Graphing the constraint set

The first step in graphically describing a linear programming problem is to graph the constraints of the problem. In graphing a problem, we need to consider only the first quadrant, which is the section of the graph above the X_1 axis and to the right of the X_2 axis. The nonnegativity constraints implicit in every linear programming problem exclude all other sections of the graph. Let us first consider the brass constraint, $2X_1 + 4X_2 \leq 320$. If we overlook for a moment the fact that this relationship is an inequality and assume it is an equality instead, we can graph the relationship as a straight line. Since any two points define a straight line, we can graph an equality by selecting two points that satisfy the equation and connecting them with a straight line. The easiest method of finding two solutions is first to let $X_1 = 0$ and solve for X_2 and then to let $X_2 = 0$ and solve for X_1. Using this procedure, we find that one solution to the brass equality is $X_1 = 0$ and $X_2 = 80$ and that a second solution is $X_1 = 160$ and $X_2 = 0$. These two points are shown as points A and B respectively in Figure 5.1.

The brass constraint is an inequality rather than an equality, and any solution to the linear programming problem that consumes 320 pounds of brass or less satisfies the constraint. Accordingly, any solution represented by a point on *or* to the left of the line AB satisfies the constraint. Any point to the right of AB does not satisfy the brass constraint. We have shaded the area to the left of AB in Figure 5.1 to indicate that production plans represented by the coordinates of any points in this area satisfy the brass constraint.

Figure 5.2 is a similar graphical representation of the constraint on available milling machine time, $3X_1 + 1X_2 \leq 180$. The line CD represents the equality $3X_1 + 1X_2 = 180$. The shaded area indicates that any

Figure 5.1 *Graphical representation of brass supply constraint*

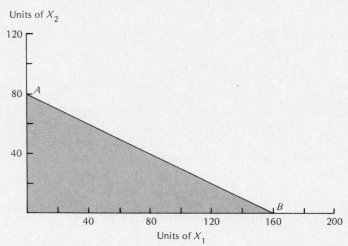

Figure 5.2 *Graphical representation of machine time constraint*

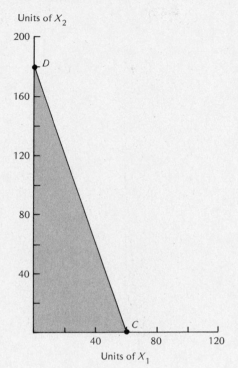

point on the line or to the left of it satisfies the machine time limitation; that is, the number of hours used must be less than or equal to 180. There is a tendency to automatically shade the portion of the graph to the left and below the constraint line. In some problems, the correct area may lie on the opposite side of the constraint line. To be sure that we know which side of the line to shade, we should always choose one point and see if it satisfies the constraint.

Figure 5.3 is a graphical representation of the lamp shade constraint, $2X_1 + 0X_2 \leq 100$. Note that all points on or to the left of the line representing the equality $X_1 = 50$ satisfy the constraint. This constraint is unbounded in the X_2 direction, which means that as long as $X_1 \leq 50$, X_2 can be infinitely large without violating the lamp shade constraint.

Figure 5.4 superimposes all of the problem's constraints on one graph. In order for a point to be a solution, *it must satisfy all of the constraints*. The production plans represented by the coordinates of the points in the shaded area are the only plans that satisfy all three

Figure 5.3 *Graphical representation of lamp shade constraint*

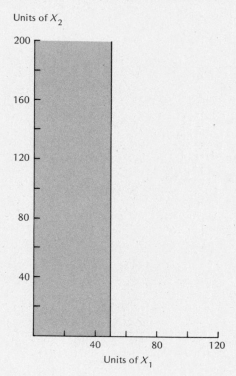

constraints. Thus, the polygon *DEFGH* represents the *set of feasible solutions* to this problem. As a check, note that the solution $X_1 = 20$ and $X_2 = 40$ (point *T*) satisfies all constraints. The point $X_1 = 20$ and $X_2 = 100$ (point *U*) satisfies the milling machine time and lamp shade constraints, but it does not satisfy the brass constraint. It is, therefore, not a solution. The point $X_1 = 100$ and $X_2 = 60$ (point *W*) is not a solution; it violates all three of the constraints.

Determining the optimal solution

We make decisions with reference to our objective function. The set of feasible solutions must therefore be "referenced," "oriented," or "rotated" to coincide with the objective of the decision maker. We determine our *objective function reference plane* by arbitrarily choosing any objective function value, finding two points that satisfy this objective value, and then connecting the points with a straight line. Assume that we arbitrarily choose a value of $1200 so that the objective function

Figure 5.4 *Graphical representation of Bell Metal Company's constraints*

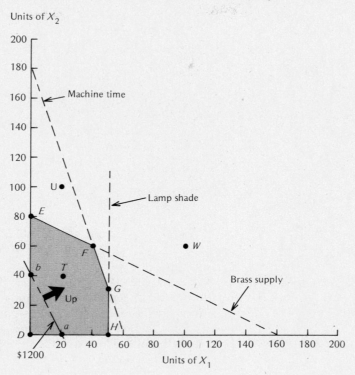

becomes $1200 = 60X_1 + 30X_2$. The solution $X_1 = 20$ and $X_2 = 0$ satisfies this objective function equation, as does the solution $X_1 = 0$ and $X_2 = 40$. These solutions are represented by the points a and b respectively in Figure 5.4.

It may be helpful to rotate the set of feasible solutions so that the line ab is horizontal. We have done so in Figure 5.5. This rotation ensures that solutions represented by points that are "higher" in the vertical direction will have objective function values greater than the objective function values of solutions represented by lower points. Hence, the solution with the "largest" objective function value is represented by the highest point in the rotated set of feasible solutions. In a maximization problem, *this is the optimal solution*. For the Bell Metal problem, this highest point is point F in Figure 5.5.

In choosing an objective function value, we selected the $1200 figure arbitrarily. Selecting another value would have resulted in a line parallel to ab and would have achieved the same rotation. To illustrate, let us

Figure 5.5 *Rotated graph of the Bell Metal problem*

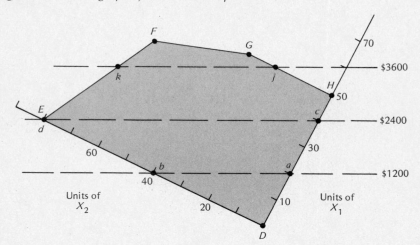

select an objective function value of $2400. The solution $X_1 = 40$ and $X_2 = 0$ has an objective function value of $2400, as does the solution $X_1 = 0$ and $X_2 = 80$. These solutions are represented as points c and d in Figure 5.5. The line cd is horizontal in our new orientation and, of course, parallel to the line ab. Additional lines derived from different objective function values also plot as horizontal lines on the rotated set of feasible solutions.

Rather than actually rotating the graph as shown in Figure 5.5, we can plot the $1200 line on the unrotated graph. This is shown in Figure 5.4. The line ab and similar parallel lines are called *isoprofit lines,* because each point on the line represents a solution with the same objective function value. The arrow drawn perpendicular to ab represents "up," and solutions "higher" in this direction have larger objective function values than do "lower" points. In Figure 5.4, the highest point in the "up" direction is again point F. Both methods always yield the same optimal answer to any given linear programming problem.

Sample problem 5.2   THE BURNS COMPANY (Continued)

Consider the Burns Company problem given in Sample Problem 5.1. Graph each constraint and then shade the set of feasible solutions. Plot an isoprofit line for $24. Draw an arrow showing "up" in relation to the objective function reference plane. State the values in the optimal solution.

SOLUTION

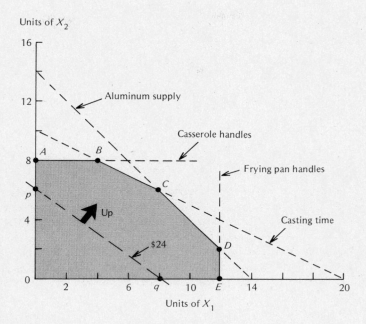

Optimal solution: $X_1 = 8$ and $X_2 = 6$

Sets, convex sets, and extreme points

A graphical portrayal of a linear programming problem illustrates several concepts with which we should be familiar. The polygon *DEFGH* in Figure 5.4 is known as the *set of feasible solutions* to the linear programming problem. It contains the points that represent all feasible solutions to our problem. In other words, any solution that does not violate any of the managerial constraints is represented by a point in the set of feasible solutions. Conversely, solutions represented by any point outside the set of feasible solutions violate at least one managerial constraint and therefore cannot be put into operation by the decision maker.

In every linear programming problem, the set of feasible solutions is always a particular type of set known as a *convex set*. In lay terms, a two-dimensional set is a convex set if a straight line joining any two points within the set does not go outside of the set. The first set shown in Figure 5.6 is convex. If we pick any two points and connect them

Figure 5.6 *Graphical representation of convex and nonconvex sets*

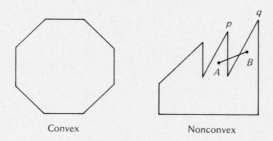

Convex   Nonconvex

with a straight line, we can see that this line will not go outside of the set. The second set in Figure 5.6 is not a convex set. If we connect points *A* and *B* with a straight line, part of this line goes outside of the set, as shown.

The corner points of the convex set are known as *extreme points*. Extreme points represent a particular type of solution known as a *basic solution*. In a basic solution, the number of variables with nonzero values is equal to or less than the number of constraints in the linear programming problem. It can be proved mathematically that if a linear programming problem has only one optimal solution, then that unique optimal solution will be a basic solution. If there are two or more equally optimal solutions, then at least two of these solutions must be basic solutions. Thus, no solution can be better than the best basic solution.

All linear programming problems contain a finite number of extreme points. Theoretically, therefore, another method of finding an optimal solution to a linear programming problem would be to evaluate the solutions represented by each of the extreme points. The optimal solution would be the extreme point that best achieved our objective. The difficulty is that almost any real problem contains so many extreme points that it is impossible to evaluate them all. For this reason, more efficient methods of solution have been developed. In a later section, we will discuss the simplex method, a procedure for determining the optimal solution by systematically evaluating only a small percentage of the total number of extreme points.

For illustrative purposes, we have evaluated the five extreme points of the Bell Metal problem. The results of these calculations are shown in Table 5.1. It should come as no surprise that point *F*, the highest point on the rotated graph, represents the solution that best satisfies Mr. Ford's objective of maximizing the contribution to profit.

Table 5.1 *Evaluation of extreme points*

Extreme point	Solution		Objective function (Z)
	X_1	X_2	
D	0	0	$ 0
E	0	80	2400
F	40	60	4200
G	50	30	3900
H	50	0	3000

Iterative optimizing techniques

There are two reasons why it is important to learn how to solve linear programming problems. First, it is the only way that we can fully appreciate the benefits of linear programming. A knowledge of solution techniques will help us recognize managerial situations wherein linear programming would be a valuable tool of analysis.

A second important reason for learning how to solve linear programming problems is that linear programming solution techniques are excellent examples of the iterative optimizing method, a technique that many of us use in solving day-to-day problems. Basically, when we apply *iterative optimizing techniques*, we move from step to step, improving our situation at each stage of the process, until we reach what we feel is an optimal solution.

The analysis that follows is painfully simple, but clear understanding of iterative optimizing procedures greatly enhances our ability to learn the more difficult material that follows.

Visualize yourself at the base of Schupp's Mountain, a large mountain in Arizona. The thick mountain growth is interrupted by many trails and paths, which crisscross and intersect at thousands of points on the large mountain. An interesting feature of these paths is that they all continue in the same direction until they intersect or join another path. Thus, if a path leads up the mountain, it will continue to go upward at the same angle until it intersects another path. Likewise, any path that leads down the mountain will continue to do so until it intersects another path.

Let us assume that we want to use the paths to reach the top of the mountain. If we have several paths to choose from, we will probably choose that path that leads most directly up the mountain: the path that ascends at the most rapid rate. We will continue to follow this path until we reach a crossroads. We have a new decision to make at this point, because we now have several new paths from which to choose. Again, it is likely that we will choose the path that ascends the mountain at the steepest angle. We will continue, proceeding from crossroad to cross-road, until we finally reach an intersection where all paths lead in a downward direction. If we know that the mountain has only one peak (a convex mountain) and that at least one path passes over that peak, then when we reach a point where all paths lead downward, we can be sure that we have reached the top of Schupp's Mountain.

The graphical representation of the Bell Metal problem shown in Figure 5.5 serves as a simple example of the type of mountain we want to climb. Suppose we start at point D. We can move along the path toward point H, or we can choose to move toward point E. The path leading toward point H has the steepest rate of ascent, so we travel to point H. At point H, the path of steepest ascent leads to point G and then to point F. At point F, all paths lead downward. Since this is a convex set, there is only one point from which all paths lead downward, and point F represents the highest point on the mountain.

It may help you to bear this simple analysis in mind during the discussion of the simplex method that follows.

The simplex method

The simplex method is a computational procedure — an *algorithm* — for solving linear programming problems. It is an iterative optimizing technique. To iterate means to repeat. Thus, the *simplex method* repeats the process of mathematically moving from extreme point to extreme point until an optimal solution is reached. The process is very similar to climbing Schupp's Mountain (see the previous section).

In the simplex process, we must first find an initial basic solution (extreme point). We then proceed to an adjacent extreme point. We continue moving from point to point until we reach an optimal solution. For a maximization problem, the simplex procedure always moves in the direction of steepest ascent, thus ensuring that the value of the objective function improves with each new solution. Fortunately, the convex property of every linear programming problem ensures that there is only one "peak" in the set of feasible solutions. Thus, we know that we have reached the optimal solution when the only direction to travel is downward, that is, when all adjacent extreme points have objective functions values less than the one being evaluated.

In the following sections, we will examine the simplex process. Our goal should be to go beyond the mechanical steps that eventually lead to a solution. We should try to understand the process itself, including the logic and economic significance of each step we take. Figure 5.7 is a

Figure 5.7 *Schematic representation of the simplex process*

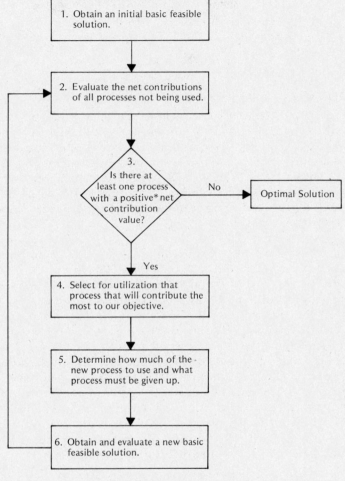

For minimization problems, we are seeking a negative net contribution value.

schematic representation of the simplex process. You should refer to this flow diagram as we discuss the various steps in the simplex process. At step 6, we cycle back to step 2, and we continue to do so until we reach an optimal solution and exit from the cycle by answering "no" to the question asked in step 3.

Since the simplex technique is mathematical, it will be helpful to restate the mathematical formulation of the Bell Metal problem.

$$\text{Max } Z = 60X_1 + 30X_2$$

s.t.
$$2X_1 + 4X_2 \leqslant 320 \quad \text{(brass supply)}$$
$$3X_1 + 1X_2 \leqslant 180 \quad \text{(machine time)}$$
$$2X_1 + 0X_2 \leqslant 100 \quad \text{(lamp shades)}$$
$$X_1, X_2 \geqslant 0$$

Step 1: Obtaining an initial solution

The first step in the simplex process is to obtain an initial solution that satisfies all the managerial constraints of the problem. The simplex process is a mathematical process and requires that all constraints be expressed as equations. Therefore, we must convert all inequalities into equalities. For convenience, we will subdivide step 1 into two parts. First, we will discuss the conversion of inequalities to equalities. Second, we will discuss the procedure for obtaining an initial solution to the set of equality constraints.

Conversion of inequalities to equalities In the case of Bell Metal, let us first consider the brass constraint, $2X_1 + 4X_2 \leqslant 320$. In our discussion of constraints, we noted that the value on the left side of the inequality sign represents the amount of brass a particular solution uses, while the quantity on the right side of the inequality sign represents the total amount of brass available during the next production period. Let us create a new variable S_1 to represent the quantity of brass that remains unused at the end of the next production period. If S_1 has a value of 50 in a given solution, this implies that 50 of the 320 units of brass are not consumed by that particular solution. If $S_1 = 0$ in another solution, all available brass is being used. It must be true that the amount of brass used ($2X_1 + 4X_2$) plus the amount of brass not used (S_1) equals the total amount of brass available (320 units). By introducing the variable S_1, we have converted the brass inequality into the equality

$$2X_1 + 4X_2 + S_1 = 320$$

We can likewise convert the milling machine time constraint to an equality by creating a new variable S_2 to represent the amount of milling machine time that is available but is not used. Again, it must be true that the amount of machine time consumed by a solution ($3X_1 + 1X_2$) plus the amount of time not consumed (S_2) must equal the total amount of machine time available (180 hours). Thus,

$$3X_1 + 1X_2 + S_2 = 180$$

Finally, we can create a variable S_3 to represent the quantity of oriental lamp shades available but not used. And it must be true that

$$2X_1 + 0X_2 + S_3 = 100$$

The variables S_1, S_2, and S_3 are referred to as slack variables. *Slack variables* represent the quantity of a resource not used by a particular solution, and they are necessary to convert the constraint inequalities to equalities. These slack variables should be thought of as decision variables. The variable S_1, for example, is a process that consumes one unit of brass. It contributes nothing to profit and therefore has a zero coefficient in the objective function. The process S_1 consumes no milling time and uses no lamp shades, so it should have a zero coefficient in each of these constraints.

The process S_2 represents the act of reserving one hour of milling machine time for nonuse. It does not contribute to the firm's profit, nor does it consume any brass or lamp shades. The coefficient of the process S_2 should therefore be zero in the objective function, the brass constraint, and the lamp shade constraint.

The process S_3 uses one available lamp shade, contributes no profit to the firm, and does not consume any brass or milling machine time. It therefore has a unit coefficient (1) in the lamp shade constraint and a zero coefficient in the objective function, the brass constraint, and the machine time constraint.

We can now rewrite our linear programming problem as follows:

$$\text{Max } Z = 60X_1 + 30X_2 + 0S_1 + 0S_2 + 0S_3$$

s.t.
$$2X_1 + 4X_2 + 1S_1 + 0S_2 + 0S_3 = 320 \quad \text{(brass supply)}$$
$$3X_1 + 1X_2 + 0S_1 + 1S_2 + 0S_3 = 180 \quad \text{(machine time)}$$
$$2X_1 + 0X_2 + 0S_1 + 0S_2 + 1S_3 = 100 \quad \text{(lamp shades)}$$
$$X_1, X_2, S_1, S_2, S_3 \geq 0$$

As we proceed with the simplex method, it will be helpful to place certain information in a separate table known as a *simplex tableau*. This tableau is designed to assist us in handling the data we will need for a simplex solution. Table 5.2 shows the part of the tableau that contains the objective function and the constraints. The objective function coefficients are listed in a row immediately above the row of letters identifying the processes. Thus, from the top row, we can read the objective function as $Z = 60X_1 + 30X_2 + 0S_1 + 0S_2 + 0S_3$. For convenience, we have identified the objective function row as the 0 row.

Table 5.2 *Constraints and objective function added to the simplex tableau*

0		60	30	0	0	0
Row	Quantity vector	X_1	X_2	S_1	S_2	S_3
I	320	2	4	1	0	0
II	180	3	1	0	1	0
III	100	2	0	0	0	1

The three constraints are represented by the three rows beneath the identifying letters. These are labeled with roman numerals I, II, and III respectively. Note, however, that the numbers that identify how much of a resource is available (formerly the right-hand side of the equations) have been moved to the left side of the tableau. The reason for this will become clear when we move to the solution section of the tableau. The first constraint row in the tableau represents the brass constraint, $2X_1 + 4X_2 + 1S_1 + 0S_2 + 0S_3 = 320$. The second row represents the machine time constraint, $3X_1 + 1X_2 + 0S_1 + 1S_2 + 0S_3 = 180$, and the third row represents the lamp shade constraint, $2X_1 + 0X_2 + 0S_1 + 0S_2 + 1S_3 = 100$.

The column that contains the numbers representing the amounts of resource available is known as the *"Quantity vector"* column. The remaining columns presently in the tableau are referred to as *process vectors*, and they are numerical representations of the decision variables. For example, consider the columns

$$
\begin{array}{ccc}
60 & & 0 \\
X_1 & & S_1 \\
2 & \text{and} & 1 \\
3 & & 0 \\
2 & & 0
\end{array}
$$

The first column indicates that process X_1, when operated at a unit level, contributes \$60 to profit, consumes 2 pounds of brass, 3 hours of milling machine time, and 2 oriental lamp shades. The second column indicates that process S_1, when operated at a unit level, contributes nothing to profit. It consumes 1 pound of brass but uses no milling machine time and does not require any lamp shades. We will add more information to the simplex tableau as we develop it in our discussion of the simplex method.

Obtaining a solution to the equality constraints After converting the inequalities to equalities, we are in a position to obtain an initial solution to our linear programming problem. Finding a solution now appears more difficult, because a solution must now satisfy all of our equality constraints. Fortunately, however, we only need concern ourselves with basic solutions. As we mentioned earlier, *basic solutions* are the solutions represented by the extreme points of the convex set of feasible solutions. We know that an optimal solution is represented by an extreme point, so if we find the optimal basic solution to a problem, we can be assured that this solution is optimal for the problem.

In mathematical terms, a solution is *basic* if the number of decision variables that have positive values (values greater than zero) is equal to or less than the number of constraint equations. There are three constraints in the Bell Metal problem, so a basic solution would have no more than three decision variables with positive values, while the remaining two decision variables must be operated at a zero level. Thus, the solution $X_1 = 40$, $X_2 = 60$, $S_1 = 0$, $S_2 = 0$, and $S_3 = 20$ is a basic solution, but the solution $X_1 = 30$, $X_2 = 50$, $S_1 = 60$, $S_2 = 40$, and $S_3 = 40$ is not basic, because it contains five decision variables that are being operated at a positive level.

The easiest way to obtain an initial solution to a problem with only less-than-or-equal-to constraints is to set the real variables equal to zero and then solve the constraint equations for the values of the slack variables. When we let X_1 equal zero and X_2 equal zero, our constraint equations may be written as follows:

$$2(0) + 4(0) + 1S_1 + 0S_2 + 0S_3 = 320$$
$$3(0) + 1(0) + 0S_1 + 1S_2 + 0S_3 = 180$$
$$2(0) + 0(0) + 0S_1 + 0S_2 + 1S_3 = 100$$

We can remove any term that has either a zero value or a zero coefficient, because any value multiplied by zero is equal to zero. Therefore, our equations will reduce to

$$1S_1 = 320$$
$$1S_2 = 180$$
$$1S_3 = 100$$

It is obvious that a basic solution to our problem is $X_1 = 0$, $X_2 = 0$, $S_1 = 320$, $S_2 = 180$, and $S_3 = 100$.

With a little practice, you will find the procedure of obtaining the initial solution obvious and simple. In the learning process, however, it is helpful to actually substitute the solution values into the constraints and prove to yourself that a given solution does satisfy each and every constraint equality.

Each solution, of course, has its associated objective function value. We calculate the objective function values by substituting the solution values into the objective function equation and solving for Z. For this first solution, the contribution to profit is $0. A solution that contributes nothing to profit will probably be considered a very unsatisfactory solution to a profit-maximizing problem. Remember, however, that we are looking for a starting point — a place at which to begin. We have found that starting point.

We now have an *initial solution*, and we must add this information to our initial simplex tableau. In every initial solution, one variable always has a value equal to each element in the quantity column. In the case of Bell Metal, S_1 is equal to 320, S_2 is equal to 180, and S_3 is equal to 100. We add this information to the simplex tableau by adding a "Solution vector" column to the left of the "Quantity vector" column, as shown in Table 5.3. This solution vector is obtained by ensuring that there is a

Table 5.3 *Simplex tableau expanded to include initial basic solution*

0				60	30	0	0	0
Row	Price vector	Solution vector	Quantity vector	X_1	X_2	S_1	S_2	S_3
I	0	S_1	320	2	4	1	0	0
II	0	S_2	180	3	1	0	1	0
III	0	S_3	100	2	0	0	0	1

row-by-row correspondence between the letter designation of a particular variable and its value in a particular solution. The fact that S_1 and 320 are in the same row implies that the value of S_1 is 320. Likewise, the row-by-row correspondence implies that S_2 has a value of 180 and that S_3 equals 100.

All variables that do not appear in the solution vector of the tableau have a value of zero. In other words, the decision maker is not using these particular processes while the solution represented by the table is in operation. From the simplex tableau, we should be able to read the complete initial solution as

$$X_1 = 0, X_2 = 0, S_1 = 320, S_2 = 180, \text{ and } S_3 = 100$$

Note that we have also added a second new column, the "Price vector" column. The *price vector* is a restatement of the contribution to profit of the variables in the basic solution. There is a row-by-row correspondence between a variable and its objective function coefficient. This column is basically a convenience column. It will help us make calculations in future steps of the simplex method.

Before proceeding, we should realize that the solution $X_1 = 0$, $X_2 = 0$, $S_1 = 320$, $S_2 = 180$, and $S_3 = 100$ corresponds to point D in Figure 5.5. We have started at the bottom of the mountain. In step 2 of the simplex method, we calculate the rates of ascent of paths leading to adjacent extreme points.

Sample problem 5.3   THE BURNS COMPANY (Continued)

Consider the Burns Company problem given in Sample Problems 5.1 and 5.2. Convert the inequalities to equations. Obtain an initial solution, and put this information into a simplex tableau.

SOLUTION

$$\text{Max } Z = 3X_1 + 4X_2 + 0S_1 + 0S_2 + 0S_3 + 0S_4$$

s.t.
$$10X_1 + 10X_2 + S_1 + 0S_2 + 0S_3 + 0S_4 = 140$$

$$20X_1 + 40X_2 + 0S_1 + S_2 + 0S_3 + 0S_4 = 400$$
$$X_1 + 0X_2 + 0S_1 + 0S_2 + S_3 + 0S_4 = 12$$
$$0X_1 + 2X_2 + 0S_1 + 0S_2 + 0S_3 + S_4 = 16$$
$$X_1, X_2, S_1, S_2, S_3, S_4 \geqslant 0$$

Initial Solution: $Z = 0$, $X_1 = 0$, $X_2 = 0$, $S_1 = 140$, $S_2 = 400$, $S_3 = 12$, and $S_4 = 16$

0				3	4	0	0	0	0
Row	Price vector	Solution vector	Quantity vector	X_1	X_2	S_1	S_2	S_3	S_4
I	0	S_1	140	10	10	1	0	0	0
II	0	S_2	400	20	40	0	1	0	0
III	0	S_3	12	1	0	0	0	1	0
IV	0	S_4	16	0	2	0	0	0	1

Step 2: Evaluating the net contributions of unused processes

The second step in the simplex process is to evaluate the net contribution of processes that are not being used. In simple terms, this tells us to determine, for each process not being used, how much the objective function would increase or decrease if 1 unit of this process were utilized.

We know, for example, that producing 1 China Sea lamp contributes $60 to the profit of the firm. In calculating net contribution, however, we must also consider the opportunity cost involved in the production of 1 China Sea lamp. This opportunity cost will offset or subtract from the $60 contribution to profit.

Opportunity costs arise from the forgone opportunities that have to be sacrificed in order to produce 1 unit of a particular process. Consider a business firm operating at full capacity. In order to produce more chairs, a firm might have to produce fewer tables, and the profit forgone in producing fewer tables must be considered as an opportunity cost of producing more chairs. Another example is a farmer who has all of her or his land in cultivation. In order to produce an acre of corn worth $1000, the farmer would have to give up an acre of peas worth $800. This $800 must be attributed to the cost of corn as an opportunity cost. Even if a firm is not operating at full capacity, it must give up slack time in order to increase output of another one of its processes. The rate of trade off between production possibilities is known as the *technical rate of substitution*. If, for example, a firm must give up 3 chairs in order to produce 1 table, then the technical rate of substitution between chairs and tables is 3:1.

The technical rates of substitution can be found in the simplex tableau. In Table 5.3, the 2 that appears in the X_1 column and the S_1 row tells us that the technical rate of substitution between S_1 and X_1 is 2:1. For each unit of X_1 produced, we must give up 2 units of S_1. We can easily verify this by considering the first constraint equation, $2X_1 + 4X_2 + 1S_1 + 0S_2 + 0S_3 = 320$. The initial solution is $X_1 = 0$, $X_2 = 0$, $S_1 = 320$, $S_2 = 180$, and $S_3 = 100$. Let us keep everything constant except X_1 and S_1 and assume that we increase X_1 by 1 unit (from 0 to 1). We can solve for S_1.

$$S_1 = 320 - 2X_1 - 4X_2 - 0S_2 \quad - 0S_3$$
$$S_1 = 320 - 2(1) - 4(0) - 0(180) - 0(100) = 318$$

In order to increase the value of X_1 by 1 unit, we must decrease S_1 by 2 units (320 to 318). The technical rate of substitution between the two variables is therefore 2:1.

The *zero technical rate of substitution* between X_2 and S_3 implies that processes X_2 and S_3 are independent and do not utilize common resources. Thus, production of additional units of X_2 does not affect the amount of S_3 that can be utilized. The technical rate of substitution between a process and itself is always 1:1. The 1 that appears in the S_1 column and the S_1 row indicates this unit rate of substitution. We would have to give up 1 unit of S_1 in order to produce an additional unit of S_1. Occasionally, we find a *negative technical rate of substitution* between two products. This means that in order to produce more of one process, we must also produce more of the other process. Products that have negative technical rates of substitution are known as *complementary* products. Pork and bacon are complementary products in that the production of more of one implies the production of more of the other.

We can calculate the opportunity cost involved in producing an extra unit of a particular process by obtaining the total value that must be given up in order to produce 1 extra unit of that process. For example, consider process X_1 of the Bell Metal problem. In order to produce 1 unit of process X_1, the technical rates of substitution tell us that we must give up 2 units of S_1 worth $0 per unit, 3 units of S_2 worth $0 per unit, and 2 units of S_3 worth $0 per unit. The opportunity cost of producing 1 unit of X_1 is therefore

$$OC = 2(\$0) + 3(\$0) + 2(\$0) = \$0$$

Likewise, the opportunity cost of X_2 is

$$OC = 4(\$0) + 1(\$0) + 0(\$0) = \$0$$

A word of caution is in order at this point. All of the processes we are presently using have zero profit contributions, which makes this analysis seem meaningless. In future iterations of this problem, however, many of the processes we remove will have positive levels of profit contribution. The significance of this analysis will then be more apparent. In addition, more complex problems have initial solutions wherein the profit contributions are positive or negative. In these cases, we must be very careful to calculate the opportunity cost of each process correctly.

We calculate the net contribution of each process by taking the objective function coefficient and subtracting from it the opportunity cost associated with the process. The net contribution of a process is often referred to as the marginal contribution, because it is the amount by which the objective function would increase if 1 unit of this process were utilized. In the Bell Metal case, X_1 has a marginal contribution of $60, calculated as follows:

$$\$60 - [2(\$0) + 3(\$0) + 2(\$0)] = \$60$$

X_2 has a marginal contribution value of $30, calculated as follows:

$$\$30 - [4(\$0) + 1(\$0) + 0(\$0)] = \$30$$

S_1, S_2, and S_3 all have marginal contribution values of $0. We can verify this by subtracting the opportunity costs of these processes from their objective function coefficients. It might help to remember that the net contribution value of processes in the basic solution is always zero.

The net contributions of each process are needed in the simplex method and should be added to our simplex tableau. We do this by adding an additional row to the simplex tableau, as shown in Table 5.4. This row is labeled NC, which stands for "net contribution." The net contribution of process X_1 is $60, so we place this value at the intersection of the NC row and the X_1 column. Likewise, we place the net contributions of X_2, S_1, S_2, and S_3 in their respective columns of the NC row.

The value in the "Quantity vector" column of the NC row requires special attention. This number represents the contribution to profit value of the present solution multiplied by a negative one (-1). In other

Table 5.4 *Initial simplex table (complete)*

0				60	30	0	0	0
Row	Price vector	Solution vector	Quantity vector	X_1	X_2	S_1	S_2	S_3
I	0	S_1	320	2	4	1	0	0
II	0	S_2	180	3	1	0	1	0
III	0	S_3	100	2	0	0	0	1
NC		$-Z$	-0	60	30	0	0	0

words, *the negative of this number is the present value of the objective function*. The reason for using the negative of Z is to simplify our calculations as we proceed from iteration to iteration in the simplex process.

We can calculate the value of the objective function of the present solution by substituting the solution values into the objective function equation.

$$Z = 60X_1 + 30X_2 + 0S_1 \quad + 0S_2 \quad + 0S_3$$
$$Z = 60(0) + 30(0) + 0(320) + 0(180) + 0(100) = 0$$

The negative of zero is zero, so we insert a zero in the simplex tableau. The negative sign is for emphasis, a reminder that the value inserted and used is the negative of the actual objective function value.

Step 3: Testing for optimality

Step 3 in the simplex process asks the question: "Can we better achieve our objective by utilizing a process that we are not now using?" If the answer is "no," then we have found the optimal solution and can exit from our decision process confident that we have found the solution that best achieves our objective. If the answer is "yes," we move to step 4.

Observing the NC row of Table 5.4, we note that two processes in the Bell Metal problem, X_1 and X_2, do have positive net contribution values. Since the Bell Metal problem is a maximizing problem, the positive net contribution values tell us that we do not have an optimal solution, and we move to step 4. If, in a maximization problem, all net contribution values are zero or negative, we are "at the top of the mountain," because all adjacent extreme points have objective function values less than or equal to the one currently being considered.

Step 4: Selecting the process to begin utilizing

Step 4 is perhaps the easiest step in the simplex process. In a maximizing problem, we simply select the process with the largest net contribution value.[1] We will utilize this process in our next solution. In the Bell Metal problem, X_1 has the largest net contribution value, so we select it. It will be helpful to *circle the selected column*, as shown in Table 5.5.

Step 5: Determining how much to use and what to give up

Step 4 tells us to begin utilizing process X_1. We know that each unit of X_1 utilized contributes $60 to the profit of the firm. We would therefore

---

[1] If there is a tie, we may select either process.

Table 5.5 *Initial simplex tableau, showing process to be entered and process to be removed*

0				60	30	0	0	0	
Row	Price vector	Solution vector	Quantity vector	X_1	X_2	S_1	S_2	S_3	Entrance test ratio
I	0	S_1	320	2	4	1	0	0	160
II	0	S_2	180	3	1	0	1	0	60
III	0	S_3	100	2	0	0	0	1	50
NC		$-Z$	-0	60	30	0	0	0	

like to utilize as much of this process as possible. We know from our discussion of technical rates of substitution that each unit of X_1 produced requires a reduction in our utilization of other processes. Specifically, production of 1 unit of X_1 requires us to give up 2 units of S_1, 3 units of S_2, and 2 units of S_3. Remember that no process, including the slack processes, can be operated at a negative level. At present, $S_1 = 320$. Since the technical rate of substitution between S_1 and X_1 is 2:1, the production of 160 units (320 ÷ 2) of X_1 would require us to give up 320 units of S_1. This would reduce the value of S_1 to zero. Any further increase in X_1 would require S_1 to take on a negative value, which would violate our nonnegativity constraints.

Now let us consider the S_2 row. In the present solution, $S_2 = 180$. The technical rate of substitution between S_2 and X_1 is 3:1. Utilization of 60 units (180 ÷ 3) of X_1 would reduce the value of S_2 to zero. Any further increase in the value of X_1 would cause S_2 to become negative, which is not permitted. Likewise, the S_3 row tells us that the maximum amount of X_1 that can be utilized is 50 units. Utilization of more than 50 units of X_1 would require S_3 to be negative, which would violate our nonnegativity constraints.

To summarize, utilization of more than 160 units of X_1 would require S_1 to be negative; utilization of more than 60 units of X_1 would require S_2 to be negative; and utilization of more than 50 units of X_1 would require S_3 to be negative. Since neither S_1, S_2, nor S_3 can be negative, the maximum amount of X_1 that can be utilized is 50 units, the smallest of these values. Therefore, in the next solution, X_1 will enter with a value of 50 and S_3 will be removed from the solution. In our simplex tableau, we should *circle the S_3 row* to indicate that S_3 is being removed from our basic solution. This is illustrated in Table 5.5.

A *negative technical rate of substitution* indicates that utilization of more of the entering process requires utilization of more of the complementary process. A *zero technical rate of substitution* indicates that the two processes are independent. Therefore, zero and negative rates of substitution are never limiting factors in determining how much of an entering process to utilize.

An easy rule-of-thumb method of determining which process to remove is as follows. Divide each element of the "Quantity vector" column by the corresponding element in the circled column. These ratios are called *entrance test ratios* and are shown in the last column in Table 5.5. In making this calculation, we ignore the elements in the NC row, because the NC row does not represent a process that can be removed. The row containing the smallest positive ratio indicates the process to be removed. We should circle that row, as shown in Table 5.5. A tie for the smallest positive entrance test ratio would indicate degeneracy, a special problem discussed in the next chapter. Generally, we may break the tie by arbitrary selection. (The "Entrance test ratio" column in Table 5.5 is for illustrative purposes only. This column is not normally a part of the simplex tableau.)

Step 6: Developing the new solution

The next step in the simplex process is to develop the new solution. The computational procedure described in this section generates the second and subsequent tableaus of our problem. In leading up to this step, we have attempted to explain the significance and rationale for this computational procedure. We will also add a step 6A for verifying the new solution, which should contribute further to the significance of this section.

Before proceeding, we should note that the 0 row at the top of the tableau (60   30   0   0   0) and the row of letters immediately below the 0 row are table headings and do not change from iteration to iteration. The following instructions do not apply to these table headings. The "Price vector" column is a convenience column and should be filled in after the rest of the tableau is completed. Consequently, the following instructions also do not apply to the quantities listed in the "Price vector" column.

In Table 5.5, we have already circled the X_1 column and the S_3 row, indicating that X_1 is the process to be entered and S_3 the process to be removed. Our first act in setting up a new tableau is to create a new row to replace the circled row in the old tableau. The S_3 in the solution vector of row III should be replaced by X_1, indicating that X_1 is replacing S_3 in the new tableau. We can calculate all values in the new row III by dividing each element in the old row III by the element that is in both the circled column and the circled row. This doubly circled element at the intersection of the circled row and the circled column is called the *pivot element*. In our example, the elements of the old row III

Table 5.6 *Second simplex tableau, showing replacement for circled row*

0				60	30	0	0	0
Row	Price vector	Solution vector	Quantity vector	X_1	X_2	S_1	S_2	S_3
I	0	S_1						
II	0	S_2						
III	60	X_1	50	1	0	0	0	½
NC		$-Z$						

are 100 2 0 0 1. Dividing these numbers by the value of the pivot element (2), gives us the new row III, which is 50 1 0 0 0 ½. The new row III, including the X_1 in the solution vector, is shown in Table 5.6.

Our second act in setting up the new tableau is to calculate the new values of the remaining rows by the following formula:

$$\text{ERR} - [(\text{CERR} \div \text{PE}) \times \text{CECR}] = \text{ENR}$$

where

ERR = Elements of the row to be replaced (that is, the outgoing row)

CERR = Circled element in the row to be replaced

PE = Pivot element (doubly circled)

CECR = Corresponding elements of the circled row

ENR = Elements of the new row (that is, the incoming row)

These calculations for row I, row II, and row NC of the new simplex tableau are shown in Table 5.7, and the results of these calculations appear in Table 5.8. Remember that this formula is used for each row except the circled row. The calculations have already been made for the circled row, and the results are shown in Table 5.6. This row is also included in Table 5.8.

In performing these calculations, we proceed one row at a time. In the formula, the elements of the row to be replaced (ERR) are the elements in the original simplex tableau of the row we are operating on. Thus, in going from Table 5.5 to Table 5.8, we might first solve for the new elements in row I. The ERR are taken from row I of Table 5.5; they are 320 2 4 1 0 0. The circled element in the row to be replaced (CERR) also refers to the original tableau shown in Table 5.5. In the case of row I, the CERR is 2. The pivot element (PE) is always the element at the intersection of the circled row and the circled column in the old

Table 5.7 *Calculations for moving from tableau 1 to tableau 2 in the simplex process*

	ERR	−	[(CERR ÷ PE)	×	CECR]	=	ENR
Row I	320	−	$2 \div 2$	×	100	=	220
	2	−	$2 \div 2$	×	2	=	0
	4	−	$2 \div 2$	×	0	=	4
	1	−	$2 \div 2$	×	0	=	1
	0	−	$2 \div 2$	×	0	=	0
	0	−	$2 \div 2$	×	1	=	−1
Row II	180	−	$3 \div 2$	×	100	=	30
	3	−	$3 \div 2$	×	2	=	0
	1	−	$3 \div 2$	×	0	=	1
	0	−	$3 \div 2$	×	0	=	0
	1	−	$3 \div 2$	×	0	=	1
	0	−	$3 \div 2$	×	1	=	$-\frac{3}{2}$
Row NC	−0	−	$60 \div 2$	×	100	=	−3000
	60	−	$60 \div 2$	×	2	=	0
	30	−	$60 \div 2$	×	0	=	30
	0	−	$60 \div 2$	×	0	=	0
	0	−	$60 \div 2$	×	0	=	0
	0	−	$60 \div 2$	×	1	=	−30

solution. In our case, this value is 2, again taken from Table 5.5. Likewise, the corresponding elements of the circled row (CECR) are taken from the tableau representing the old solution. From Table 5.5, we can read these CECR as 100 2 0 0 0 1.

After making these calculations for row I and entering the results in Table 5.8, we proceed to make the same calculations for row II and the NC row. This should complete our movement from the first tableau to the second tableau. Our second solution, therefore, is represented by Table 5.8.

Table 5.8 *Second simplex tableau (completed)*

0				60	30	0	0	0
Row	Price vector	Solution vector	Quantity vector	X_1	X_2	S_1	S_2	S_3
I	0	S_1	220	0	4	1	0	−1
II	0	S_2	30	0	1	0	1	$-\frac{3}{2}$
III	60	X_1	50	1	0	0	0	$\frac{1}{2}$
NC		−Z	−3000	0	30	0	0	−30

Exhibit 5.1 *SUMMARY OF STEPS 4, 5, AND 6 OF THE SIMPLEX METHOD*

1. Select the process to begin utilizing. Choose the process column with the largest net contribution value (the smallest net contribution value for a minimization problem). Circle that column.
2. Select the process to stop utilizing. Calculate an entrance test ratio for each row except the NC row by dividing the element in the "Quantity vector" column by the corresponding element in the circled column. The smallest positive ratio indicates the process to be removed. Circle that row.
3. Define the doubly circled element as the pivot element.
4. Calculate the elements of the new row that is replacing the circled row. In the solution vector, replace the letter representing the process being removed with the letter representing the process entering. Calculate the new numerical elements of this row by dividing each of the elements in the old row by the pivot element.
5. Calculate the elements of the remaining rows, the rows that are replacing the noncircled rows. The identifying letters in the solution vector do not change. Calculate the new numerical elements by the formula

$$ERR - [(CERR \div PE) \times CECR] = ENR$$

where

ERR = Elements of the row to be replaced

$CERR$ = Circled element in the row to be replaced

PE = Pivot element (doubly circled)

$CECR$ = Corresponding elements of the circled row

ENR = Elements of the new row

6. Fill in the "Price vector" column with the objective function coefficients of the processes identified in the new solution vector.

Exhibit 5.1 presents a summary of steps 4, 5, and 6 of the simplex process. This should be quite helpful as we move from iteration to iteration in the simplex process. Remember that the information presented in Exhibit 5.1 is mechanical and means little unless we appreciate the rationale underlying the technique.

Step 6A: Analyzing and verifying the new tableau

Table 5.8 represents a new basic feasible solution. Our decision process tells us to return to step 2 and proceed with another iteration. Before doing so, however, we should analyze and verify the information in the second simplex tableau. This analysis and verification will not be necessary after each iteration. It is a learning step that we should perform only until we thoroughly understand the information in each simplex tableau.

A convenient way of analyzing the information in a simplex tableau is to answer the series of questions given in Exhibit 5.2 and applied here to the problem at hand.

1. *What is the solution given in Table 5.8?*

    The correspondence between the elements in the "Solution vector" and the "Quantity vector" columns in Table 5.8 tells us that in this solution, $S_1 = 220$, $S_2 = 30$, $X_1 = 50$, and $Z = 3000$ ($-Z = -3000$). Since X_2 and S_3 do not appear in the solution vector, we know that $X_2 = 0$ and $S_3 = 0$.

2. *Is the objective function value of $3000, which is found in Table 5.8, consistent with the value of Z obtained from the objective function equation?*

    Yes. Our objective function equation is

    $$Z = 60X_1 + 30X_2 + 0S_1 + 0S_2 + 0S_3$$

    Substituting the solution values of X_1, X_2, S_1, S_2, and S_3 into the objective function equation, we obtain

    $$Z = 60(50) + 30(0) + 0(220) + 0(30) + 0(0) = 3000$$

3. *Does this solution satisfy all of the original constraint equations?*

    Yes. Substituting the solution values into the original constraint equations, we obtain the following equalities:

    $$2X_1 + 4X_2 + 1S_1 + 0S_2 + 0S_3 = 320$$
    $$2(50) + 4(0) + 1(220) + 0(30) + 0(0) = 320$$
    $$3X_1 + 1X_2 + 0S_1 + 1S_2 + 0S_3 = 180$$
    $$3(50) + 1(0) + 0(220) + 1(30) + 0(0) = 180$$
    $$2X_1 + 0X_2 + 0S_1 + 0S_2 + 1S_3 = 100$$
    $$2(50) + 0(0) + 0(220) + 0(30) + 1(0) = 100$$

4. *Did the objective function increase by the amount expected from tableau 1 to tableau 2?*

    Yes. The increase in the objective function value was $3000. This was expected, because we added 50 units of X_1. From Table 5.5, we knew that the net contribution of X_1 was $60 per unit. Our expected increase was therefore 60×50 units, or $3000.

5. *Are the net contribution values shown in Table 5.8 consistent with the technical rates of substitution given in the same table?*

    Yes. For example, we may calculate the net contribution values of

X_2 and S_3 as follows:

$$\text{For } X_2: \quad 30 - [4(0) + 1(0) + 0(60)] = 30$$
$$\text{For } S_3: \quad 0 - [-1(0) - 1.5(0) + .5(60)] = -30$$

Subsequent iterations

The schematic of our simplex process tells us to return to step 2 and repeat the procedure until we reach an optimal solution. The tableaus generated by this procedure are given in Table 5.9. It took four tableaus to solve the problem by the simplex method. The objective function increased at each iteration until we reached an optimal solution in the fourth tableau. We know the last tableau is optimal because all of the net contribution values are zero or negative.

We should compare the solutions in Table 5.9 with the corner points in Figure 5.5. Remember that we started at point D. The solution in the second tableau is $X_1 = 50$ and $X_2 = 0$, which corresponds to point H in Figure 5.5. Likewise, the solutions in the third and fourth tableaus correspond to points G and F. Thus, via the simplex method, we mathematically "climbed the mountain" by moving from extreme point to adjacent extreme point until we reached an optimal solution.

The optimal solution

The fourth tableau in Table 5.9 tells us that the optimal solution to the Bell Metal problem is

$$X_1 = 40, X_2 = 60, S_1 = 0, S_2 = 0, S_3 = 20, \text{ and } Z = \$4200$$

In step 6A of the simplex method, we noted that it would be quite helpful to analyze and verify the tableau by answering a series of

Exhibit 5.2 *QUESTIONS FOR ANALYZING AND VERIFYING A SIMPLEX TABLEAU*

1. What is the solution given in the tableau? That is, what is the value of each variable and the value of the objective function?
2. Is the objective function value found in the tableau consistent with the value obtained from the objective function equation?
3. Does the solution satisfy all of the original constraint equations?
4. Did the value of the objective function increase (or decrease) by the amount expected from the prior tableau?
5. Are the net contribution values in the tableau consistent with the technical rates of substitution given in the same table?

Table 5.9 *Second, third, and fourth (final) simplex tableaus for the Bell Metal problem*

0				60	30	0	0	0
Row	Price vector	Solution vector	Quantity vector	X_1	X_2	S_1	S_2	S_3
Second tableau								
I	0	S_1	220	0	4	1	0	−1
II	0	S_2	30	0	1	0	1	−$\frac{3}{2}$
III	60	X_1	50	1	0	0	0	$\frac{1}{2}$
NC		−Z	−3000	0	30	0	0	−30
Third tableau								
I	0	S_1	100	0	0	1	−4	5
II	30	X_2	30	0	1	0	1	−$\frac{3}{2}$
III	60	X_1	50	1	0	0	0	$\frac{1}{2}$
NC		−Z	−3900	0	0	0	−30	15
Fourth (final) tableau								
I	0	S_3	20	0	0	$\frac{1}{5}$	−$\frac{4}{5}$	1
II	30	X_2	60	0	1	$\frac{3}{10}$	−$\frac{2}{10}$	0
III	60	X_1	40	1	0	−$\frac{1}{10}$	$\frac{4}{10}$	0
NC		−Z	−4200	0	0	−3	−18	0

questions. The final tableau should be verified, though we will not repeat that analysis here.

One final act remains, and that is to translate the mathematical statement of the optimal solution into a verbal statement of the optimal solution. The $X_1 = 40$ and $X_2 = 60$ tells Mr. Ford that his optimal action is to schedule the production of 40 China Sea lamps and 60 Matanzas Bay lamps. The $S_1 = 0$ and $S_2 = 0$ tells him that this production schedule calls for all the available brass supply (no slack) and consumes all the available milling machine time (no slack). The $S_3 = 20$ indicates 20 units of slack in the lamp shade constraint. Even though 100 lamp shades are available for import, the firm will only utilize 80 in the optimal production schedule. Finally, $Z = \$4200$ tells Mr. Ford that this production schedule will contribute $4200 to the firm's profit. It is optimal — he can do no better with the resources presently available.

Sample problem 5.4   THE BURNS COMPANY (Continued)

Consider the Burns Company problem given in Sample Problems 5.1, 5.2, and 5.3. Set up the initial simplex tableau, and then solve the problem.

SOLUTION

		0			3	4	0	0	0	0
	Row	Price vector	Solution vector	Quantity vector	X_1	X_2	S_1	S_2	S_3	S_4
Initial	I	0	S_1	140	10	10	1	0	0	0
tableau	II	0	S_2	400	20	40	0	1	0	0
	III	0	S_3	12	1	0	0	0	1	0
	IV	0	S_4	16	0	2	0	0	0	1
	NC	$-Z$		-0	3	4	0	0	0	0
Second	I	0	S_1	60	10	0	1	0	0	-5
tableau	II	0	S_2	80	20	0	0	1	0	-20
	III	0	S_3	12	1	0	0	0	1	0
	IV	4	X_2	8	0	1	0	0	0	$\frac{1}{2}$
	NC	$-Z$		-32	3	0	0	0	0	-2
Third	I	0	S_1	20	0	0	1	$-\frac{1}{2}$	0	5
tableau	II	3	X_1	4	1	0	0	$\frac{1}{20}$	0	-1
	III	0	S_3	8	0	0	0	$-\frac{1}{20}$	1	1
	IV	4	X_2	8	0	1	0	0	0	$\frac{1}{2}$
	NC	$-Z$		-44	0	0	0	$-\frac{3}{20}$	0	1
Fourth	I	0	S_4	4	0	0	$\frac{1}{5}$	$-\frac{1}{10}$	0	1
(final)	II	3	X_1	8	1	0	$\frac{1}{5}$	$-\frac{1}{20}$	0	0
tableau	III	0	S_3	4	0	0	$-\frac{1}{5}$	$\frac{1}{20}$	1	0
	IV	4	X_2	6	0	1	$-\frac{1}{10}$	$\frac{1}{20}$	0	0
	NC	$-Z$		-48	0	0	$-\frac{1}{5}$	$-\frac{1}{20}$	0	0

The optimal solution tells us to manufacture 8 frying pans ($X_1 = 8$) and 6 casserole dishes ($X_2 = 6$) daily. The contribution to profit will be \$48 ($-Z = -48$). There are 4 frying pan handles ($S_3 = 4$) and 4 casserole handles ($S_4 = 4$) that are available for use but not needed.

Sample problem 5.5 THE BURNS COMPANY (Continued)

Consider the third tableau of the Burns Company problem given in Sample Problem 5.4. Analyze and verify this tableau by answering the questions given in Exhibit 5.2.

SOLUTION
1. The solution in the third tableau is $Z = 44$, $X_1 = 4$, $X_2 = 8$, $S_1 = 20$, $S_2 = 0$, $S_3 = 8$, and $S_4 = 0$.
2. $Z = 3(4) + 4(8) + 0(20) + 0(0) + 0(8) + 0(0) = 44$

3. $10(4) + 10(8) + 1(20) + 0(0) + 0(8) + 0(0) = 140$ (constraint 1)
   $20(4) + 40(8) + 0(20) + 1(0) + 0(8) + 0(0) = 400$ (constraint 2)
    $1(4) + 0(8) + 0(20) + 0(0) + 1(8) + 0(0) = 12$ (constraint 3)
    $0(4) + 2(8) + 0(20) + 0(0) + 0(8) + 1(0) = 16$ (constraint 4)

4. Increase expected: \$3 per unit times 4 units = \$12
   Actual increase: \$44 − \$32 = \$12

5. For X_1: $3 - [0(0) + 1(3) + 0(0) + 0(4)] = 0$
   For S_2: $0 - [-\frac{1}{2}(0) + \frac{1}{20}(3) - \frac{1}{20}(0) + 0(4)] = -\frac{3}{20}$
   For S_4: $0 - [5(0) - 1(3) + 1(0) + \frac{1}{2}(4)] = 1$

Problems and exercises

1. Explain the following terms:

decision variable	inequality
process variable	slack variable
decision set	iteration
production plan	tableau
solution	process vector
basic solution	solution vector
optimal solution	price vector
feasible solution	quantity vector
linear relationship	opportunity cost
objective function	complementary processes
constraint set	independent processes
isoprofit line	net contribution
convex set	entrance test ratio
extreme points	pivot element
algorithm	technical rate of substitution

FORMULATION EXERCISES. INSTRUCTIONS FOR PROBLEMS 2–8

Formulate the following problems as linear programming problems. Use the appropriate inequality sign. Label the constraints. Do not convert the inequalities to equations, and do not attempt to solve these problems.

2. The Coleman Company produces tables and chairs and can sell all it can produce. Each table contributes \$6 to the profit of the firm, and each chair contributes \$5. Production of each table requires 100 minutes in the company's assembly center and 200 minutes in the company's finishing center. Production of each chair requires 140 minutes in the assembly center and 120 minutes in the finishing center. The company's assembly center is available only 2000 minutes a day and its finishing center is available only 1680 minutes a day. The objective is to maximize profit contribution to the firm.

3. The Rusk Company produces desks and bookcases. Demand for these products is excellent. Each desk sold contributes $42 to profit, and each bookcase sold contributes $36 to profit. The company's monthly supply of hardwood is limited to 27,000 board feet of usable lumber per month. The company's supply of pine is limited to 83,000 usable board feet per month. Each desk requires 20 board feet each of pine and hardwood. Each bookcase requires 8 board feet of hardwood and 32 board feet of pine. The objective is to maximize profit contribution to the firm.

4. The Morton Company has two products, X_1 and X_2. The profit contribution of X_1 is $2 per unit, and the profit contribution of X_2 is $2 per unit. The company has three machine centers that daily make available 20, 24, and 18 hours respectively. The time requirements of the two products in the three machine centers are as follows, in hours per unit:

Product	Center 1	Center 2	Center 3
X_1	1	3	3
X_2	2	2	1

The objective is to maximize profit contribution. The company can sell all it can produce.

5. The Wilson Company manufactures two types of bathroom tile. Square-cut tile may be made by either of two processes (X_1 or X_2). Hexagonal-cut tile may be made by any of three processes (X_3, X_4, or X_5). All five processes require use of the company's blenders, forming machines, and baking ovens. These pieces of equipment are available 100, 80, and 120 hours a week respectively. Processes X_1, X_2, X_3, X_4, and X_5 utilize .5, .4, .4, .5, and .6 hours of blending time respectively. Processes X_1 and X_2 require .5 hours each on the forming machines. Processes X_3, X_4, and X_5 require .7 hours each on the forming machines. For the baking ovens, X_1 requires .5 hours, X_2 requires .4 hours, X_3 requires .8 hours, X_4 requires .7 hours, and X_5 requires .3 hours. The company believes it can sell all it can produce. Each unit of square-cut tile (X_1 and X_2) contributes $120 to profit, and each unit of hexagonal-cut tile (X_3, X_4, and X_5) contributes $150 to profit. The objective is to maximize profit contribution.

6. The Houston Company has three processes for converting liquid xenthane and zethum into two types of perfume known as "Engagement" and "Honeymoon." Process 1 utilizes 6 gallons of xenthane and 4 gallons of zethum to produce 5 gallons each of Engagement and Honeymoon perfume. Process 2 utilizes 5 gallons each of xenthane and zethum to produce 7 gallons of Engagement and 3 gallons of Honeymoon. Process 3 utilizes 3 gallons of xenthane and 7 gallons of zethum to produce 2 gallons of

Engagement and 8 gallons of Honeymoon. Demand for both types of perfume is excellent. Engagement perfume sells for $10 a gallon, and Honeymoon perfume sells for $8 a gallon. Xenthane costs $3 a gallon, and supply during the next production period is limited to 1400 gallons. Zethum costs $2 a gallon, and supply during the next production period is limited to 1600 gallons. The cost of raw materials is the only cost affecting profit contribution, and the objective is to maximize profit contribution.

7. The Meredith Company uses four machine centers (stamping, forming, assembling, and painting) to produce four products, X_1, X_2, X_3, and X_4. The company believes it can sell all of these products that it can produce. The profit contributions of these products are $20, $25, $15, and $30 respectively. The total weekly availability of the stamping center is 100 hours. The weekly availabilities of the forming, assembling, and painting centers are 320, 600, and 400 hours respectively. The number of hours that each process requires in each center is shown in the following table. The objective is to maximize profit contribution.

Center	Process			
	X_1	X_2	X_3	X_4
Stamping	1	1	1	1
Forming	4	2	5	4
Assembly	6	6	8	8
Painting	4	5	5	4

8. The Wallace Company produces chairs, lamps, and tables. Each chair produced requires 6 minutes in machine center A, 5 minutes in machine center B, and 8 minutes in machine center C. Each lamp produced requires 5, 4, and 5 minutes in machine centers A, B, and C respectively. Likewise, each table produced requires 6, 4, and 6 minutes in machine centers A, B, and C respectively. The company has a daily availability of 2400 minutes in center A, 2000 minutes in center B, and 3000 minutes in center C. The company can sell all it can produce. Since the company is not sure of the profit contributions of the various products, it decides that its objective is to maximize total volume of output.

GRAPHICAL EXERCISES. INSTRUCTIONS FOR PROBLEMS 9–19
Graph the following linear programming problems. Shade the set of feasible solutions. Draw an appropriate objective function reference plane (iso-profit line). State the optimal values of all variables, including the value of the optimal objective function.

9. Max $Z = 10X_1 + 10X_2$

    s.t. $8X_1 + 12X_2 \leqslant 96$

        $10X_1 + 5X_2 \leqslant 80$

              $X_1, X_2 \geqslant 0$

10. Max $Z = 5X_1 + 6X_2$

    s.t. $100X_1 + 200X_2 \leqslant 2000$

        $140X_1 + 120X_2 \leqslant 1680$

              $X_1, X_2 \geqslant 0$

11. In problem 10, change the objective function to

    Max $Z = 3X_1 + 2X_2$.

12. Max $Z = 2X_1 + 2X_2$

    s.t. $X_1 + 2X_2 \leqslant 20$

        $3X_1 + 2X_2 \leqslant 24$

        $3X_1 + 1X_2 \leqslant 18$

           $X_1, X_2 \geqslant 0$

13. In problem 12, change the objective function to

    Max $Z = 18X_1 + 2X_2$.

14. In problem 12, change the objective function to

    Max $Z = 2X_1 + 0X_2$.

15. Max $Z = 2X_1 + 1X_2$

    s.t. $1X_1 + 1X_2 \leqslant 12$

        $0X_1 + 1X_2 \leqslant 9$

        $1X_1 + 0X_2 \leqslant 7$

           $X_1, X_2 \geqslant 0$

16. Max $Z = 3X_1 + 3X_2$

    s.t. $0X_1 + 1X_2 \leqslant 60$

        $2X_1 + 3X_2 \leqslant 240$

        $2X_1 + 1X_2 \leqslant 160$

        $1X_1 + 0X_2 \leqslant 70$

           $X_1, X_2 \geqslant 0$

17. Max $Z = 4X_1 + 5X_2$

    s.t. $X_1 + 0X_2 \leqslant 10$

        $0X_1 + 1X_2 \leqslant 8$

        $X_1 + 2X_2 \leqslant 20$

           $X_1, X_2 \geqslant 0$

18. Max $Z = 5X_1 + 4X_2$

    s.t. $2X_1 + 3X_2 \leqslant 6$

        $2X_1 + 1X_2 \leqslant 4$

           $X_1, X_2 \geqslant 0$

19. Max $Z = 5X_1 + 6X_2$

    s.t. $1X_1 + 2X_2 \leqslant 20$

        $7X_1 + 6X_2 \leqslant 84$

           $X_1, X_2 \geqslant 0$

SIMPLEX EXERCISES. INSTRUCTIONS FOR PROBLEMS 20–31

Add the appropriate slack variables, construct a simplex tableau, and then solve the problem by using the simplex method.

20. Solve problem 9 by the simplex method. Compare the solution of each tableau with the extreme points obtained in the graphical representation.

21. Solve problem 12 by the simplex method. Compare the solution of each tableau with the extreme points obtained in the graphical representation.

22. Solve problem 16 by the simplex method. Compare the solution of each tableau with the extreme points obtained in the graphical representation.

23. Max $Z = 12X_1 + 10X_2 + 8X_3$
    s.t. $8X_1 + 6X_2 + 10X_3 \le 360$
    $8X_1 + 10X_2 + 12X_3 \le 360$
    $10X_1 + 8X_2 + 6X_3 \le 360$
    $X_1, X_2, X_3 \ge 0$

24. Max $Z = 7X_1 + 5X_2 + 8X_3$
    s.t. $2X_1 + 4X_2 + 2X_3 \le 100$
    $5X_1 + 2X_2 + 10X_3 \le 300$
    $X_1, X_2, X_3 \ge 0$

25. Solve problem 15 by the simplex method.

26. Solve problem 17 by the simplex method.

27. Solve problem 18 by the simplex method.

28. Solve problem 19 by the simplex method.

29. Max $Z = 20X_1 + 25X_2 + 15X_3 + 30X_4$
    s.t. $1X_1 + 1X_2 + 1X_3 + 1X_4 \le 100$
    $4X_1 + 2X_2 + 5X_3 + 4X_4 \le 320$
    $6X_1 + 6X_2 + 8X_3 + 8X_4 \le 600$
    $4X_1 + 5X_2 + 5X_3 + 4X_4 \le 400$
    $X_1, X_2, X_3, X_4 \ge 0$

30. Max $Z = 9X_1 + 6X_2 + 11X_3 + 8X_4$
    s.t. $1X_1 + 1X_2 + 1X_3 + 1X_4 \le 480$
    $4X_1 + 8X_2 + 2X_3 + 5X_4 \le 2400$
    $4X_1 + 2X_2 + 5X_3 + 5X_4 \le 2000$
    $6X_1 + 4X_2 + 8X_3 + 4X_4 \le 3000$
    $X_1, X_2, X_3, X_4 \ge 0$

31. Max $Z = 9X_1 + 6X_2 + 8X_3$
    s.t. $6X_1 + 5X_2 + 6X_3 \le 2400$
    $5X_1 + 4X_2 + 4X_3 \le 2000$
    $8X_1 + 5X_2 + 6X_3 \le 3000$
    $X_1, X_2, X_3 \ge 0$

Supplementary readings

Anderson, D. R., D. J. Sweeney, and T. A. Williams. *An Introduction to Management Science.* St. Paul, Minn.: West, 1976.

Bierman, H., C. P. Bonini, and W. H. Hausman. *Quantitative Analysis for Business Decisions.* Homewood, Ill.: Irwin, 1977.

Dorfman, R., P. A. Samuelson, and R. M. Solow. *Linear Programming and Economic Analysis.* New York: McGraw-Hill, 1958.

Gass, S. I. *Linear Programming: Methods and Applications.* New York: McGraw-Hill, 1964.

Hadley, G. W. *Linear Programming.* Reading, Mass.: Addison-Wesley, 1962.

Hartley, R. V. *Operations Research: A Managerial Emphasis.* Pacific Palisades, Calif.: Goodyear, 1976.

Hughes, A. J., and D. E. Grawoig. *Linear Programming: An Emphasis on Decision Making.* Reading, Mass.: Addison-Wesley, 1973.

Lapin, L. L. *Quantitative Methods for Business Decisions.* New York: Harcourt Brace Jovanovich, 1976.

Levin, R. I., and C. A. Kirkpatrick. *Quantitative Approaches to Management,* 2nd ed. New York: McGraw-Hill, 1975.

Chapter 6

Linear programming: more complex analysis

Illustrative example: WERBELL FARMS, INC.

Dr Mary Tomlinson has recently accepted the position of director of food control at Werbell Farms, Inc., a large poultry farm in Pennsylvania. Mr. Werbell, the owner of Werbell Farms, has asked Dr. Tomlinson to reduce the cost of food fed to the chickens in pen 38. In the past, Werbell Farms has used two types of chicken feed, "Arlington" brand and "Bellemeade" brand. Each of these feeds provides the chickens with the nutrients for healthy growth. Dr. Tomlinson wonders, however, if using a mixture of Arlington and Bellemeade brands would not be better than using either one exclusively.

There are three nutritional elements that are essential to the health of chickens. We shall simply refer to these as elements A, B, and C. Dr. Tomlinson has determined that, for these chickens, the minimum daily requirement of element A is 12 units and the minimum daily requirement of element B is 36 units. (These are minimum requirements, and an excess of nutrients A and/or B is not harmful.) The daily requirement of nutrient C is 24 units. Dr. Tomlinson hopes to settle on a mixture that will provide the chickens with exactly 24 units of nutrient C, because she believes that either a deficiency *or* an excess of nutrient C is harmful.

A pound of Arlington brand chicken feed costs $5 and contains 2 units of nutritional element A, 2 units of element B, and 2 units of element C. Likewise, the manufacturers of Bellemeade brand certify that each pound of their chicken feed contains 1 unit of nutritional element A, 9 units of element B, and 3 units of element C. Bellemeade brand sells for $4 a pound.

Dr. Tomlinson recently heard of the success Bell Metal has had with linear programming. She hopes that this technique will be helpful to her in determining what mix of Arlington brand and Bellemeade brand will minimize daily food cost and still provide the chickens in pen 38 with all the nutritional elements they require.

The problem faced by Dr. Tomlinson at Werbell Farms is very similar to the problem faced by Mr. Ford at the Bell Metal Company. There are, however, two major differences. First, the problem at Werbell Farms is a minimization problem. In other words, Dr. Tomlinson wants to minimize cost, whereas Mr. Ford wanted to maximize contribution to profit. Second, Dr. Tomlinson's problem introduces greater-than-or-equal-to ($\geq$) and equal-to ($=$) constraints, which we did not deal with in Chapter 5.

Analysis of more complex problems

In Chapter 5, we were concerned with simple maximization problems that had only less-than-or-equal-to constraints. Minimization objective functions, equality constraints, and greater-than-or-equal-to constraints require some modifications and extensions of the procedures we have discussed. It is time that we learned how to formulate, graph, and solve linear programming problems that have equality or greater-than-or-equal-to constraints.

We will discuss the simplex method of solution as it relates to these types of problems. Most analysis of these problems is similar to the analysis of problems discussed in Chapter 5, so we will emphasize only the differences.

Formulating the problem

As director of food control at Werbell Farms, Dr. Tomlinson must decide how many pounds of Arlington brand and how many pounds of Bellemeade brand to include in the daily chicken feed mix. There are two processes available. She should let

X_1 = Number of pounds of Arlington brand included in the daily mix

X_2 = Number of pounds of Bellemeade brand included in the daily mix

Suppose we let the variable Z represent the cost of the feed mix to the firm. The *objective function* of the problem is

$$\text{Min } Z = 5X_1 + 4X_2$$

There are three constraints in the Werbell Farms problem. We know that the amount of nutrient A available for the chickens must be greater than or equal to the amount needed. We calculate the amount of nutrient A available by multiplying the amount of nutrient A in a pound of Arlington brand by the number of pounds of Arlington brand used and then adding this to the number of units of nutrient A in a pound of Bellemeade brand multiplied by the number of pounds of Bellemeade brand used. This total amount must be greater than or equal to the 12 units the chickens must have. Thus,

$$2X_1 + 1X_2 \geq 12 \qquad \text{(nutrient A)}$$

Likewise, we formulate the constraint for nutritional element B as follows:

$$2X_1 + 9X_2 \geqslant 36 \qquad \text{(nutrient B)}$$

The third constraint differs from the first two in that it is an equality constraint. Dr. Tomlinson wants the amount of nutrient C in any decision set to exactly equal the amount of nutrient C required. Accordingly, we formulate this constraint with an equals sign.

$$2X_1 + 3X_2 = 24 \qquad \text{(nutrient C)}$$

As in all linear programming problems, no process can be operated at a negative level. Each problem must have nonnegativity constraints; therefore, the complete formulation of the Werbell Farms problem is

$$\text{Min } Z = 5X_1 + 4X_2$$

s.t.
$$2X_1 + 1X_2 \geqslant 12 \qquad \text{(nutrient A)}$$
$$2X_1 + 9X_2 \geqslant 36 \qquad \text{(nutrient B)}$$
$$2X_1 + 3X_2 = 24 \qquad \text{(nutrient C)}$$
$$X_1, X_2 \geqslant 0$$

Sample problem 6.1 THE JONES COMPANY

The Jones Company manufactures four types of electronic tubes known as type A, type B, type C, and type D tubes. Regardless of type, each tube produced requires 1 hour of labor. The firm's daily labor supply is limited to 200 hours. Each type A tube requires 8 minutes on the filament tester machine. Type B tubes require 2 minutes and type C tubes require 7 minutes on this same machine. Type D tubes do not use this machine. The filament testing machine is available for 8 hours (480 minutes) each day. A government contract requires that the Jones Company produce and ship at least 100 tubes daily for special "space electronic equipment." This equipment can use either type A or type B tubes, but not type C or type D tubes. Type C and type D tubes are complementary products; that is, when one is installed (replaced) the other must also be replaced. The Jones Company can sell all it can produce. The contribution to profit of types A, B, C, and D tubes are $8, $8, $6, and $30 respectively. Formulate this problem as a linear programming problem. The objective is to find the solution that maximizes contribution to profit.

SOLUTION

Let Z represent the total contribution to profit, and let X_1, X_2, X_3, and X_4 be the number of type A, B, C, and D tubes produced respectively. The contract requirement constraint demands that the sum of the type A tubes and the type

B tubes produced be 100 or more. They may be all type A, or all type B, or any combination thereof. The complementary product constraint tells us that the number of type C tubes must exactly equal the number of type D tubes. Thus, $X_3 = X_4$, or $X_3 - X_4 = 0$. The formulation therefore becomes:

$$\text{Max } Z = 8X_1 + 8X_2 + 6X_3 + 30X_4$$

s.t.
$$X_1 + X_2 + X_3 + X_4 \leqslant 200 \quad \text{(labor supply)}$$
$$8X_1 + 2X_2 + 7X_3 + 0X_4 \leqslant 480 \quad \text{(testing machine)}$$
$$X_1 + X_2 + 0X_3 + 0X_4 \geqslant 100 \quad \text{(contract requirement)}$$
$$0X_1 + 0X_2 + 1X_3 - 1X_4 = 0 \quad \text{(complementary product)}$$
$$X_1, X_2, X_3, X_4 \geqslant 0$$

Graphical representation and solution

Graphing a minimization problem is very similar to graphing a maximization problem, and the greater-than-or-equal-to constraints offer no particular difficulty. The equality constraints, however, require special attention. The easiest way to graphically illustrate an equality constraint is to begin by graphing the problem with the equality constraints omitted. Thus, we would first graph the problem

$$\text{Min } Z = 5X_1 + 4X_2$$

s.t.
$$2X_1 + 1X_2 \geqslant 12 \quad \text{(nutrient A)}$$
$$2X_1 + 9X_2 \geqslant 36 \quad \text{(nutrient B)}$$
$$\text{(Nutrient C constraint is omitted.)}$$
$$X_1, X_2 \geqslant 0$$

The graph of these constraints is shown in Figure 6.1. The shaded area indicates that points above and to the right of *ECH* represent feasible solutions to the constraints we have formulated, that is, to the problem with the nutrient C constraint omitted. An isocost line for $20 has been included in Figure 6.1. Since this is a minimization problem, we want to move in the "down" direction until we find the lowest or least-cost point that satisfies both constraints. This is point C in Figure 6.1, where $X_1 = 4.5$ and $X_2 = 3$.

Let us now graph the Werbell Farms problem with the nutrient C equality constraint included. The line *AB* in Figure 6.2 represents the nutrient C constraint, $2X_1 + 3X_2 = 24$. Since this constraint is an equality, only points on the line *AB* satisfy the constraint. Therefore, the only solutions to the Werbell Farms problem are the points that are both on line *AB* and in the shaded area of Figure 6.2. These are the points that are on the line segment *FG* in Figure 6.2. The optimal solution is at point *F*, where $X_1 = 3$ and $X_2 = 6$.

Figure 6.1 *Werbell Farms problem with nutrient C constraint removed*

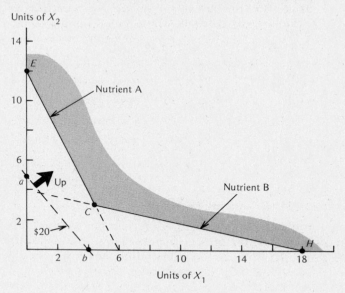

Figure 6.2 *Werbell Farms problem with nutrient C constraint added*

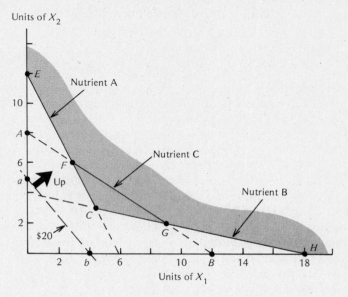

Sample problem 6.2   *WILSON FARMS*

Ms. Wilson, the owner of Wilson Farms, has correctly formulated her feed mix problem as follows:

$$\text{Min } Z = 5X_1 + 5X_2$$

s.t.
$$12X_1 + 8X_2 \geqslant 96 \quad \text{(nutrient A)}$$
$$4X_1 + 8X_2 \geqslant 48 \quad \text{(nutrient B)}$$
$$10X_1 + 0X_2 \geqslant 20 \quad \text{(nutrient C)}$$
$$X_1, X_2 \geqslant 0$$

Graph the problem; shade the feasible area; draw an isocost line of $30; and state the optimal values of X_1, X_2, and the objective function.

SOLUTION

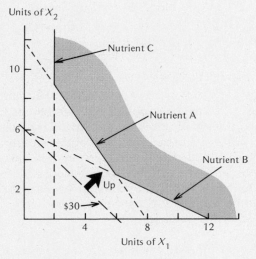

Optimal values: $X_1 = 6$, $X_2 = 3$, $Z = 45$.

The simplex method for minimization problems

The procedure for utilizing the simplex method for problems with minimizing objective functions is similar to the method we used in Chapter 5. The only real changes are in steps 3 and 4, which are concerned with testing a solution for optimality and selecting the process to enter a new solution. The addition of greater-than-or-equal-to and/or equality constraints to either a maximization or a minimization problem make the determination of an initial solution more difficult. Otherwise, their addition does not alter the steps of the simplex method.

The two new types of constraints require the introduction of new concepts into the simplex method. For this reason, we will review the simplex method, emphasizing the differences brought about by adding greater-than-or-equal-to and equality constraints, and by changing from a maximizing to a minimizing objective function. Before proceeding, we should review the steps of the simplex method shown in Figure 5.7. The steps of the simplex method are always the same. Only the method of implementing the steps changes. We will utilize the Werbell Farms problem to illustrate the process, so it will be helpful to repeat the mathematical formulation of that problem.

$$\text{Min } Z = 5X_1 + 4X_2$$

s.t.
$$2X_1 + 1X_2 \geqslant 12 \quad \text{(nutrient A)}$$
$$2X_1 + 9X_2 \geqslant 36 \quad \text{(nutrient B)}$$
$$2X_1 + 3X_2 = 24 \quad \text{(nutrient C)}$$
$$X_1, X_2 \geqslant 0$$

Step 1: Obtaining an initial solution

The first step is to obtain an initial solution that satisfies all of the managerial constraints of the problem. We remember from Chapter 5 that the simplex process requires us to convert inequality constraints into equations. For convenience, we will again subdivide step 1 into two parts. First, we will discuss the conversion of inequality constraints into equations. Second, we will discuss the procedure for obtaining an initial solution to the set of equality constraints. Because of the greater-than-or-equal-to and equality constraints, step 1 here differs significantly from the analysis in Chapter 5.

Conversion of inequalities into equalities In the case of Werbell Farms, first consider the nutrient A constraint, $2X_1 + 1X_2 \geqslant 12$. The value on the left side of the inequality ($2X_1 + 1X_2$) represents the amount of nutrient a particular solution provides, while the quantity on the right side of the inequality (12) represents the minimum amount of nutrient A required in the chickens' daily diet. We can now create a new variable, T_1 to represent the amount of nutrient A provided in excess of the minimum daily requirement. Thus, the actual amount of nutrient A provided daily ($2X_1 + 1X_2$), minus the daily excess above the minimum (T_1), must equal the minimum daily requirement of nutrient A. Therefore,

$$2X_1 + 1X_2 - T_1 = 12 \quad \text{(nutrient A)}$$

We can convert the nutrient B constraint into an equality constraint by creating a new variable, T_2, to represent the amount of nutrient B provided in excess of the daily minimum requirement. Therefore,

$$2X_1 + 9X_2 - T_2 = 36 \quad \text{(nutrient B)}$$

The third constraint in the Werbell Farms problem is already an equality constraint, so we do not have to make any changes in it.

The variables T_1 and T_2 are *surplus variables*, sometimes referred to as *negative slack variables*. They generally represent an excess above minimum requirements and are used to convert greater-than-or-equal-to inequalities into equations. As with slack variables, their objective function coefficients are zero.

We can now write our linear programming problem as follows:

$$\text{Min } Z = 5X_1 + 4X_2 + 0T_1 + 0T_2$$

s.t.
$$2X_1 + 1X_2 - 1T_1 + 0T_2 = 12 \quad \text{(nutrient A)}$$
$$2X_1 + 9X_2 + 0T_1 - 1T_2 = 36 \quad \text{(nutrient B)}$$
$$2X_1 + 3X_2 + 0T_1 + 0T_2 = 24 \quad \text{(nutrient C)}$$
$$X_1, X_2, T_1, T_2 \geqslant 0$$

Obtaining a solution to the equality constraints In Chapter 5, we obtained an initial basic solution to the constraint equations by setting the real variables equal to zero and solving for the values of the slack variables. Let us try this procedure again.

$$2(0) + 1(0) - 1T_1 + 0T_2 = 12 \quad \text{(nutrient A)}$$
$$2(0) + 9(0) + 0T_1 - 1T_2 = 36 \quad \text{(nutrient B)}$$
$$2(0) + 3(0) + 0T_1 + 0T_2 = 24 \quad \text{(nutrient C)}$$

We can again remove any term that has either a zero value or a zero coefficient, because any value multiplied by zero is equal to zero. The equations reduce to

$$-1T_1 \qquad = 12$$
$$-1T_2 = 36$$

It is apparent that the solution $X_1 = 0$, $X_2 = 0$, $T_1 = -12$, and $T_2 = -36$ is not an initial solution to our problem. The statements $T_1 = -12$ and $T_2 = -36$ violate our nonnegativity constraints. In addition, the values do not satisfy the nutrient C equality.

We can prevent this problem by introducing a new type of variable known as an *artificial variable*. Artificial variables are added to every constraint that was originally a greater-than-or-equal-to or an equality constraint. Since our problem has two greater-than-or-equal-to constraints and one equality constraint, we will add three artificial variables, designated as A_1, A_2, and A_3. The sole purpose of introducing these variables is to obtain an initial solution. After we add the artificial variables, our constraint equations become

$$2X_1 + 1X_2 - 1T_1 + 0T_2 + 1A_1 + 0A_2 + 0A_3 = 12 \qquad \text{(nutrient A)}$$
$$2X_1 + 9X_2 + 0T_1 - 1T_2 + 0A_1 + 1A_2 + 0A_3 = 36 \qquad \text{(nutrient B)}$$
$$2X_1 + 3X_2 + 0T_1 + 0T_2 + 0A_1 + 0A_2 + 1A_3 = 24 \qquad \text{(nutrient C)}$$

Since we are looking for a basic solution, we know that only three (the number of equations) variables will have positive values and that the other variables must be arbitrarily set equal to zero. In obtaining an initial basic solution, a good rule of thumb to follow is: *Set all real variables and all surplus (negative slack) variables equal to zero, and solve for the values of the remaining positive slack and artificial variables.* Following this procedure, we obtain

$$2(0) + 1(0) - 1(0) + 0(0) + 1A_1 + 0A_2 + 0A_3 = 12$$
$$2(0) + 9(0) + 0(0) - 1(0) + 0A_1 + 1A_2 + 0A_3 = 36$$
$$2(0) + 3(0) + 0(0) + 0(0) + 0A_1 + 0A_2 + 1A_3 = 24$$

If we remove all terms that are equal to zero, our equations reduce to

$$1A_1 \qquad\qquad = 12$$
$$1A_2 \qquad = 36$$
$$1A_3 = 24$$

We now have our initial basic feasible solution to our problem: $X_1 = 0$, $X_2 = 0$, $T_1 = 0$, $T_2 = 0$, $A_1 = 12$, $A_2 = 36$, and $A_3 = 24$. Up to this point, we have not discussed the objective function coefficients of the artificial variables. As we have said, the sole purpose of introducing the artificial variables is to obtain an initial basic solution. Since these variables have no real significance, we must ensure that they do not appear in the optimal solution. We can accomplish this by assigning the artificial variables an objective function coefficient that makes them highly undesirable variables. Assume that we are trying to minimize cost. If one unit of A costs us $1,000,000, it is very unlikely that A would appear in a minimum-cost solution. Thus, we prevent artificial variables from appearing in a final solution of a minimization problem by assigning them a very large objective function coefficient. In a maximization problem, we assign artificial variables a very negative objective function coefficient (such as −$1,000,000).

How large should these coefficients be? There is no definite answer to this question. Many textbooks avoid the question by assigning the artificial variables an objective function coefficient of M or $-M$ and then stating that M is "a very large number." For this reason, the process of removing artificial variables is often referred to as the *Big M method*. Students generally find it easier to assign an actual numerical value. A good rule of thumb is to assign a value 100 times larger than the largest objective function coefficient. In order to simplify calculations, however, we will use a smaller number in our sample problem.

In the Werbell Farms problem, we will assign each artificial variable an objective function coefficient of 10. The objective function then becomes

$$\text{Min } Z = 5X_1 + 4X_2 + 0T_1 + 0T_2 + 10A_1 + 10A_2 + 10A_3$$

We calculate the objective function value of the initial solution by substituting the values of the initial solution into the objective function equation.

$$Z = 5(0) + 4(0) + 0(0) + 0(0) + 10(12) + 10(36) + 10(24) = 720$$

Since this is a minimization problem, we are starting with a large positive objective function value. We will attempt to reduce this value at each iteration of the simplex process.

Again, it will be helpful to put this information in a simplex tableau. The constraints, objective function, and initial solution to the Werbell Farms problem are shown as the first tableau in Table 6.1.

Step 2: Evaluating the net contributions of unused processes

The second step in the simplex process is to evaluate the net contribution of processes that are not being used. The procedure used in this section is identical to the procedure used in Chapter 5. The initial solutions of the problems discussed there, however, were composed entirely of slack variables. Since slack variables have zero profit contributions, the analysis seemed trivial. The initial solutions of the problems discussed in this chapter contain artificial variables. For this reason, the calculations for the initial net contribution values are slightly more complicated.

In the Werbell Farms problem, let us first calculate the *opportunity cost* arising from the production of 1 additional unit of X_2. Table 6.1 tells us that the technical rates of substitution between X_2 and A_1, A_2, and A_3 are 1, 9, and 3 respectively. Thus, to produce 1 additional unit of X_2 we must give up 1 unit of A_1, 9 units of A_2, and 3 units of A_3. A_1, A_2, and A_3 all have a profit contribution of \$10. We can calculate the opportunity cost (OC) of X_2 as follows:

$$OC = 1(\$10) + 9(\$10) + 3(\$10) = \$130$$

We can calculate the *net contribution* of each process by subtracting the opportunity cost associated with the process from the corresponding

Table 6.1 The Werbell Farms problem

0 Row	Price vector	Solution vector	Quantity vector	X_1 (5)	X_2 (4)	T_1 (0)	T_2 (0)	A_1 (10)	A_2 (10)	A_3 (10)
First (initial) tableau										
I	10	A_1	12	2	1	-1	0	1	0	0
II	10	A_2	36	2	9	0	-1	0	1	0
III	10	A_3	24	2	3	0	0	0	0	1
NC		$-Z$	-720	-55	-126	10	10	0	0	0
Second tableau										
I	10	A_1	8	$16/9$	0	-1	$1/9$	1	$-1/9$	0
II	4	X_2	4	$2/9$	1	0	$-1/9$	0	$1/9$	0
III	10	A_3	12	$12/9$	0	0	$3/9$	0	$-3/9$	1
NC		$-Z$	-216	-27	0	10	-4	0	14	0
Third tableau										
I	5	X_1	$9/2$	1	0	$-9/16$	$1/16$	$9/16$	$-1/16$	0
II	4	X_2	3	0	1	$2/16$	$-2/16$	$-2/16$	$2/16$	0
III	10	A_3	6	0	0	$12/16$	$4/16$	$-12/16$	$-4/16$	1
NC		$-Z$	$-189/2$	0	0	$-83/16$	$-37/16$	$243/16$	$197/16$	0
Fourth tableau										
I	5	X_1	9	1	0	0	$3/12$	0	$-3/12$	$9/12$
II	4	X_2	2	0	1	0	$-2/12$	0	$2/12$	$-2/12$
III	0	T_1	8	0	0	1	$4/12$	-1	$-4/12$	$16/12$
NC		$-Z$	-53	0	0	0	$-7/12$	10	$127/12$	$83/12$
Fifth (final) tableau										
I	5	X_1	3	1	0	$-3/4$	0	$3/4$	0	$-1/4$
II	4	X_2	6	0	1	$2/4$	0	$-2/4$	0	$2/4$
III	0	T_2	24	0	0	3	1	-3	-1	4
NC		$-Z$	-39	0	0	$7/4$	0	$33/4$	10	$37/4$

objective function coefficient. In the Werbell Farms case, X_2 has a net contribution (NC) of $-\$126$, which is calculated as follows:

$$NC = \$4 - [1(\$10) + 9(\$10) + 3(\$10)] = -\$126$$

Likewise, the net contribution values of X_1, T_1, and T_2 can be calculated as follows:

$$\text{For } X_1: \quad NC = \$5 - [2(\$10) + 2(\$10) + 2(\$10)] = -\$55$$
$$\text{For } T_1: \quad NC = \$0 - [-1(\$10) + 0(\$10) + 0(\$10)] = \$10$$
$$\text{For } T_2: \quad NC = \$0 - [0(\$10) - 1(\$10) + 0(\$10)] = \$10$$

These values have been entered in the initial tableau shown in Table 6.1.

Step 3: Testing for optimality

Step 3 asks us the question: "Can we better achieve our objective by utilizing a process that we are not now using?" For a *minimization problem*, we can answer "yes" to this question if one or more of the processes have a negative net contribution value. Processes X_1 and X_2 both have negative net contribution values, so our answer to the question is "yes," and we move to step 4 of the simplex process. If all of the net contribution values had been zero or positive, this would indicate that we had obtained an optimal solution to our minimization problem. We would then have stopped our decision process.

Step 4: Selecting the process to begin utilizing

In a minimization problem, we simply select the process with the most negative net contribution value. In the Werbell Farms problem, X_2 has the most negative net contribution value, so we select it. We will utilize this process in our next solution.

Step 5: Determining how much to use and what to give up

The procedure used here is identical to the method described in Chapter 5. In tableau 1, our entrance test ratios are 12, 4, and 8. Since 4 is the smallest positive ratio, we know that 4 units of X_2 will be included in our next solution and that A_2 will be removed from the solution in the next tableau.

Step 6: Developing the new solution

Again, the procedure used here is identical to the method described in Chapter 5. For convenience, however, the five tableaus required for the Werbell Farms problem are given in Table 6.1.

Optimal solution

The optimal solution to the Werbell Farms problem is given in the fifth tableau of Table 6.1. In that tableau, there are no negative net contribution values. In a minimization problem, this indicates that we have reached an optimal solution. In this case, our optimal solution is $X_1 = 3$, $X_2 = 6$, $T_2 = 24$, and $Z = 39$ ($-Z = -39$). T_1, A_1, A_2, and A_3 all equal zero.

Our final step is to translate the mathematical statement of the optimal solution into a verbal solution. The $X_1 = 3$ and $X_2 = 6$ tell Dr. Tomlinson that her optimal action is to mix 3 pounds of Arlington brand and 6 pounds of Bellemeade brand chicken feed. The $T_2 = 24$ tells her that an excess of 24 units of nutrient B will be provided daily to the chickens. The $T_1 = 0$ indicates that this daily mix provides exactly the amount of nutrient A required. Since A_1, A_2, and A_3 are artificial variables, we expect them to have a value of zero in the final solution. If they were not zero, we would suspect that we had incorrectly formulated the problem. (This situation is discussed later in the chapter under the heading "a problem with no real solution.") Finally, the $Z = 39$ indicates that the mix of 3 pounds of Arlington brand and 6 pounds of Bellemeade brand will cost \$39 per day. It is optimal — the least-cost mixture that satisfies all of the nutrient requirements.

Sample problem 6.3   THE JONES COMPANY (Continued)

Consider the Jones Company problem given in Sample Problem 6.1. Convert the inequalities into equalities by adding the necessary slack variables (S_i) and surplus variables (T_i). Add any artificial variables necessary to obtain an initial basic solution. State the values of all variables in this solution. Solve using the simplex method.

SOLUTION

$$\text{Max } Z = 8X_1 + 8X_2 + 6X_3 + 30X_4 + 0S_1 + 0S_2 + 0T_1 - 100A_1 - 100A_2$$

s.t.
$$1X_1 + 1X_2 + 1X_3 + 1X_4 + 1S_1 + 0S_2 + 0T_1 + 0A_1 + 0A_2 = 200$$
$$8X_1 + 2X_2 + 7X_3 + 0X_4 + 0S_1 + 1S_2 + 0T_1 + 0A_1 + 0A_2 = 480$$
$$1X_1 + 1X_2 + 0X_3 + 0X_4 + 0S_1 + 0S_2 - 1T_1 + 1A_1 + 0A_2 = 100$$
$$0X_1 + 0X_2 + 1X_3 - 1X_4 + 0S_1 + 0S_2 + 0T_1 + 0A_1 + 1A_2 = \ \ \ 0$$
$$X_1, X_2, X_3, X_4, S_1, S_2, T_1, A_1, A_2 \geqslant \ \ \ 0$$

Initial solution: $S_1 = 200$, $S_2 = 480$, $A_1 = 100$, $A_2 = 0$, $Z = -10,000$

The first tableau and the final (fifth) tableau are as follows:

0	Price	Solution	Quantity	8	8	6	30	0	0	0	−100	−100
Row	vector	vector	vector	X_1	X_2	X_3	X_4	S_1	S_2	T_1	A_1	A_2
First (initial) tableau												
I	0	S_1	200	1	1	1	1	1	0	0	0	0
II	0	S_2	480	8	2	7	0	0	1	0	0	0
III	−100	A_1	100	1	1	0	0	0	0	−1	1	0
IV	−100	A_2	0	0	0	1	−1	0	0	0	0	1
NC		−Z	10,000	108	108	106	−70	0	0	−100	0	0
Fifth (final) tableau												
I	0	S_1	20	$-12/7$	0	0	0	1	$-2/7$	$3/7$	$-3/7$	1
II	30	X_4	40	$6/7$	0	0	1	0	$1/7$	$2/7$	$-2/7$	−1
III	8	X_2	100	1	1	0	0	0	0	−1	1	0
IV	6	X_3	40	$6/7$	0	1	0	0	$1/7$	$2/7$	$-2/7$	0
NC		−Z	−2240	$-216/7$	0	0	0	0	$-36/7$	$-16/7$	$-684/7$	−70

Linear programming problems with special characteristics

Occasionally, we encounter a linear programming problem with a special characteristic, such as many optimal solutions, no solution at all, a solution with an infinite objective function, or a problem referred to as degeneracy. Since each of these characteristics may have significant meaning for the managerial analyst, we will discuss a problem of each type.

A problem with multiple optimal solutions

Consider the problem

$$\text{Max } Z = 3X_1 + 2X_2$$

s.t.

$$1X_1 + 0X_2 \leqslant 6 \quad \text{(constraint 1)}$$
$$0X_1 + 1X_2 \leqslant 9 \quad \text{(constraint 2)}$$
$$6X_1 + 4X_2 \leqslant 48 \quad \text{(constraint 3)}$$
$$X_1, X_2 \geqslant 0$$

The graph of this problem appears in Figure 6.3. The area in the graph bounded by the polygon $OABCD$ represents the set of feasible solutions. Suppose we choose an objective function value of $12 and plot an objective function reference plane. Note that the reference plane is parallel to the line segment BC. Thus, when the graph is rotated to make the reference plane horizontal, the line segment BC will also be horizontal. Consequently, every point on the line segment BC has the same optimal objective function value. In this particular case, every point on the line segment BC represents a solution that has an objective

Figure 6.3 *Graphical representation of a problem with multiple optimal solutions*

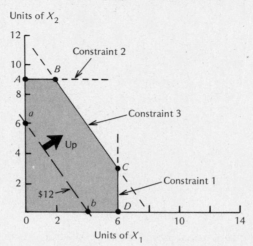

function value of $24. If we plotted an isoprofit line of $24, it would fall on top of the line segment BC. Since every point on BC represents an optimal solution, the problem has an infinite number of optimal solutions. It can be proven that if a linear programming problem has two optimal solutions, then it has an infinite number of optimal solutions.

In the simplex method, multiple optimal solutions are indicated when a nonbasic variable has a zero net contribution value in an optimal tableau. Table 6.2 gives the third tableau of the foregoing problem. The solution in this tableau is $Z = 24$, $X_1 = 6$, $X_2 = 3$, $S_1 = 0$, $S_2 = 6$, and $S_3 = 0$. There are no processes with positive net contribution values; this indicates that this is an optimal solution. Note, however, that the process S_1 is not being utilized in the present tableau. S_1 has a net contribution value of zero. This tells us that if we brought S_1 into the solution, the objective function would neither increase or decrease. In fact, if we actually utilized S_1 and performed another iteration, we would obtain a solution of $Z = 24$, $X_1 = 2$, $X_2 = 9$, $S_1 = 4$,

Table 6.2 *Simplex tableau indicating multiple optimal solutions*

0 Row	Price vector	Solution vector	Quantity vector	3 X_1	2 X_2	0 S_1	0 S_2	0 S_3
I	3	X_1	6	1	0	1	0	0
II	0	S_2	6	0	0	$3/2$	1	$-1/4$
III	2	X_2	3	0	1	$-3/2$	0	$1/4$
NC		$-Z$	-24	0	0	0	0	$-1/2$

$S_2 = 0$, and $S_3 = 0$. Since both of these solutions have the same objective function value, they are "equally optimal."

A problem with no real solution

Consider the problem

$$\text{Max } Z = X_1 + 2X_2$$

s.t.
$$X_1 + X_2 \leq 8 \quad \text{(constraint 1)}$$
$$4X_1 + 3X_2 \geq 36 \quad \text{(constraint 2)}$$
$$X_1, X_2 \geq 0$$

The two constraints of this problem are graphed in Figure 6.4. The area that satisfies the first constraint lies below and to the left of the line AB. The area of the graph that satisfies the second constraint lies above and to the right of the line CD. There is no point that will satisfy both of the constraints. The problem is *nonfeasible*; it has no real solution.

Although the problem has no real solution, we can obtain a solution with artificial variables. When we attempt to obtain an optimal solution by the simplex method, however, we are unable to drive the artificial variables out of the solution. Table 6.3 gives the "final" iteration for the foregoing problem. It appears to be an optimal solution, because there are no positive net contribution values. However, closer inspection reveals that A_1, an artificial variable, is in the solution (has a value other than zero). Whenever an apparent optimal solution contains an artificial

Figure 6.4 *Graphical representation of a problem with no real solution*

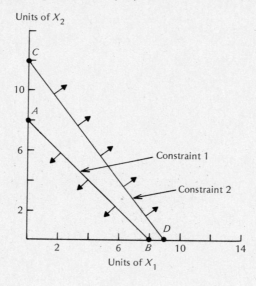

Table 6.3 *Simplex tableau indicating a problem with no real solution*

0	Price vector	Solution vector	Quantity vector	1 X_1	2 X_2	0 S_1	0 T_1	−10 A_1
Row								
I	1	X_1	8	1	1	1	0	0
II	−10	A_1	4	0	−1	−4	−1	1
NC		$-Z$	32	0	−9	−49	−10	0

variable, this generally indicates a problem with no real solution. Occasionally, though, we will reach this situation because we have not assigned a large enough value for the objective function coefficients of the artificial variables.

A problem with an infinite objective function value

Consider the problem

$$\text{Max } Z = X_1 + X_2$$

s.t.

$$3X_1 + 2X_2 \geqslant 24 \quad \text{(constraint 1)}$$
$$-X_1 + 3X_2 \leqslant 3 \quad \text{(constraint 2)}$$
$$X_1, X_2 \geqslant 0$$

The graph of this problem appears in Figure 6.5. The set of feasible solutions is the area to the right of the line segment *AB* and below the

Figure 6.5 *Graphical representation of a problem with an infinite objective function value*

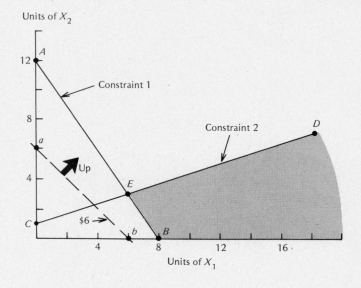

Table 6.4 *Simplex tableau indicating a problem with an infinite objective function value*

0 Row	Price vector	Solution vector	Quantity vector	1 X_1	1 X_2	0 T_1	0 S_1	-10 A_1
I	1	X_1	6	1	0	$-3/11$	$-2/11$	$3/11$
II	1	X_2	3	0	1	$-1/11$	$3/11$	$1/11$
		$-Z$	-9	0	0	$4/11$	$-1/11$	$-114/11$

line segment *ED*. The objective function reference plane for $6 is also plotted in Figure 6.5. If we rotate the graph so that the objective function reference plane is horizontal, then the area of feasible solutions extends upward to infinity. Since this is a maximization problem, the value of the objective function may be made infinitely large. Problems of this type are referred to as *unbounded problems*. We are unaware of any real, applied problem that has infinite returns. Thus, an unbounded solution always represents a problem that has been incorrectly formulated.

In the simplex method, an unbounded solution is indicated when there are *no positive values in the process vector of the process selected to enter the solution*. The third tableau of the foregoing problem is given in Table 6.4. The process T_1 has the largest positive net contribution value, so T_1 should be brought into the solution. At this point in the simplex method, we normally calculate entrance test ratios by dividing each element of the quantity vector by the corresponding element of the entering process vector. The minimum nonnegative ratio indicates the process to be removed from the solution. In Table 6.4, there are no nonnegative entrance test ratios. This indicates an unbounded solution.

A problem of degeneracy

Consider the problem

$$\text{Max } Z = 60X_1 + 30X_2$$

s.t.
$$2X_1 + 4X_2 \leqslant 320$$
$$3X_1 + 1X_2 \leqslant 180$$
$$2X_1 + 0X_2 \leqslant 100$$
$$0X_1 + 1X_2 \geqslant 30$$
$$X_1, X_2 \geqslant 0$$

We obtained this problem by adding one constraint to the Bell Metal problem discussed in Chapter 5. The second and third tableaus of this

Table 6.5 *A simplex problem with degeneracy*

0	Price vector	Solution vector	Quantity vector	60 X_1	30 X_2	0 S_1	0 S_2	0 S_3	0 T_1	-10 A_1
Second tableau										
I	0	S_1	220	0	4	1	0	-1	0	0
II	0	S_2	30	0	1	0	1	-3/2	0	0
III	60	X_1	50	1	0	0	0	1/2	0	0
IV	-10	A_1	30	0	1	0	0	0	-1	1
NC		-Z	-2700	0	40	0	0	-30	-10	0
Third tableau										
I	0	S_1	100	0	0	1	-4	5	0	0
II	30	X_2	30	0	1	0	1	-3/2	0	0
III	60	X_1	50	1	0	0	0	1/2	0	0
IV	-10	A_1	0	0	0	0	-1	3/2	-1	1
NC		-Z	-3900	0	0	0	-40	30	-10	0

problem are given in Table 6.5. In the second tableau, process X_2 has the largest net contribution value and is selected to enter the solution in the next tableau. Our next step in the simplex method is to calculate the entrance test ratios to determine which process to remove. When we make this calculation, however, we discover that there is a tie between S_2 and A_1 for the minimum positive ratio. For the moment, let us assume that we can choose either S_2 or A_1 arbitrarily. Since S_2 is "higher" in the solution vector (if we read down the column we come to S_2 before A_1), we decide to remove S_2. In going from the second to the third tableau, we therefore select process X_2 to enter and process S_2 to remove.

In the third tableau, note that not only was S_2 removed, but the value of A_1 was reduced to zero. In effect, we have entered one process and removed two processes. At this point, the number of processes with positive (nonnegative and nonzero) values is less than the number of constraints. This condition is known as degeneracy. We stated previously that a basic solution never has more variables with positive values than the number of constraints to the problem. When a basic solution has fewer variables with positive values than the number of constraints, it is known as a *degenerate basic solution*.

Let us again refer to the third tableau in Table 6.5. At this point, S_3 has a positive net contribution value, indicating that this process should be brought into the solution and utilized. Our minimum positive entrance test ratio is zero (0 divided by 3/2). This indicates that zero amount of S_3 should be brought into the solution to replace A_1. We can calculate the increase in the objective function value from tableau to tableau by multiplying the net contribution value of the entering process by the amount of this process to be utilized in the next tableau. Since the new process (S_3) is to be brought in at the zero level, the increase in the objective function value is zero.

In the case of degeneracy, the objective function value may not increase at each iteration. It is possible to perform several iterations of a problem and discover that a particular iteration may be identical to a previous iteration; the seventh tableau, for instance, may be identical to the third tableau. This "cycling" possibility would seem to make degeneracy an interesting problem. But the problem is actually of little concern to managerial analysts. With great ingenuity, theorists have constructed linear programming problems that will cycle, but as far as we know, no real problem has ever cycled, even when the process to be removed is selected arbitrarily. Nevertheless, procedures have been developed for selecting the process to be removed, so as to insure that cycling does not occur. We will not discuss these methods here, but they are built into almost every linear programming computer routine.

Degeneracy has nothing to do with choosing which process to enter into the solution. In a maximizing problem, if there is a tie between two processes for the most positive net contribution value, selecting either process arbitrarily will cause no problems.

Illustrative example: JENNINGS FOUNDRY, INC.

Jennings Foundry, Inc., is a small metalworking company located in southern Illinois. During the past few years, the company has limited its production to four types of metal fondue pots. These pots are simply referred to by the company as types A, B, C, and D fondue pots. Demand for fondue pots is excellent at the present time, and forecasts indicate an even larger demand in the future. For this reason, the company is considering expanding its production facilities.

Ms. Mary Ann Jones, a recent industrial engineering graduate, has just joined the company as chief of production. She has determined that there are four major operations in the production of fondue pots. First, sheets of metal are run through the firm's stamping machines, where the parts for the fondue pots are stamped out. These parts are then routed to a forming room, where they are shaped to meet specifications. The formed parts are then taken to an assembly room, where the various metal parts are welded together to form the complete fondue pot. Finally, the assembled fondue pots are taken to the paint shop, where a decorative coat of fireproof enamel is sprayed on each item.

The contributions to profit of types A, B, C, and D fondue pots are $9, $6, $11, and $8 respectively. Ms. Jones has also determined that each of the four types of fondue pots requires 1 minute of stamping time. In addition, A fondue pots require 4 minutes of forming time, 4 minutes of assembly time, and 6 minutes of painting time. Type B fondue pots require 8 minutes of forming time, 2 minutes of assembly time, and 4 minutes of painting time. Type C fondue pots require 2 minutes of forming time, 5 minutes of assembly time, and 8 minutes of painting time. Type D fondue pots require 5 minutes of both forming and assembly time and 4 minutes of painting time. The company has only one stamping machine, and its daily availability is limited to 480 minutes. Although the company has multiple forming, assembly, and painting centers, the total daily availabilities of these centers are limited to 2400, 2000, and 3000 minutes respectively.

Ms. Jones is aware that she could use a management science technique such as linear programming to assist her in determining an optimal production schedule. Since the company is considering expansion, however, she is more concerned with the company's resources than with its production processes. She remembers that one of her college courses discussed the dual linear programming problem and that the emphasis in the dual problem was on the productive resources of the firm. She therefore returns to her college textbook to learn more about the dual linear programming problem.

The dual linear programming problem

The problem format that we have been using is known as the *primal problem*. The format that we shall now discuss is known as the *dual problem*. The dual linear programming problem is simply another way of looking at the problem we are considering. Which problem to use depends on what the analyst wants to see. The primal problem highlights certain features, while the dual emphasizes others. As we shall show, the dual problem is quite helpful when we are investigating the effects of changes in the value of parameters of the problem. This type of analysis, known as sensitivity or postoptimality analysis, is discussed later in the chapter.

Let us first formulate and then solve Ms. Jones' problem as a primal linear programming problem. Suppose we let

X_1 = Number of type A fondue pots produced daily

X_2 = Number of type B fondue pots produced daily

X_3 = Number of type C fondue pots produced daily

X_4 = Number of type D fondue pots produced daily

Table 6.6 *Initial and final tableaus of the primal problem for Jennings Foundry, Inc.*

0 Row	Price vector	Solution vector	Quantity vector	9 X_1	6 X_2	11 X_3	8 X_4	0 S_1	0 S_2	0 S_3	0 S_4
Initial tableau											
I	0	S_1	480	1	1	1	1	1	0	0	0
II	0	S_2	2400	4	8	2	5	0	1	0	0
III	0	S_3	2000	4	2	5	5	0	0	1	0
IV	0	S_4	3000	6	4	8	4	0	0	0	1
NC		$-Z$	0	9	6	11	8	0	0	0	0
Final tableau											
I	9	X_1	400	1	3	0	0	5	0	-1	0
II	0	S_2	610	0	$6/4$	0	0	$-42/4$	1	$2/4$	$3/4$
III	8	X_4	10	0	$-2/4$	0	1	$-2/4$	0	$2/4$	$-1/4$
IV	11	X_3	70	0	$-6/4$	1	0	$-14/4$	0	$2/4$	$1/4$
NC		$-Z$	-4450	0	$-2/4$	0	0	$-10/4$	0	$-2/4$	$-3/4$

If we assume that Ms. Jones wants to maximize daily contribution to profit, the primal formulation becomes

$$\text{Max } Z = 9X_1 + 6X_2 + 11X_3 + 8X_4$$

s.t.
$$X_1 + X_2 + X_3 + X_4 \leqslant 480 \quad \text{(stamping time)}$$
$$4X_1 + 8X_2 + 2X_3 + 5X_4 \leqslant 2400 \quad \text{(forming time)}$$
$$4X_1 + 2X_2 + 5X_3 + 5X_4 \leqslant 2000 \quad \text{(assembly time)}$$
$$6X_1 + 4X_2 + 8X_3 + 4X_4 \leqslant 3000 \quad \text{(painting time)}$$
$$X_1, X_2, X_3, X_4 \geqslant 0$$

In order to solve this problem by the simplex method, we must add slack variables. Table 6.6 gives the initial and final tableaus of the Jennings Foundry primal problem. From the final tableau, we know that the optimal solution is $Z = \$4450$, $X_1 = 400$, $X_2 = 0$, $X_3 = 70$, $X_4 = 10$, $S_1 = 0$, $S_2 = 610$, $S_3 = 0$, and $S_4 = 0$. Our verbal translation is that in order to optimize daily profit contribution, Ms. Jones should schedule production of 400 type A fondue pots, no type B fondue pots, 70 type C fondue pots, and 10 type D fondue pots. The $S_2 = 610$ tells us that there will be 610 minutes of slack time in the forming center. The $Z = 4450$ indicates that this production schedule would result in a daily contribution to profit of $\$4450$.

Formulating the dual problem

In Chapter 5, we stated that opportunity cost arises from the opportunities that must be sacrificed in order to produce one unit of a particular process. The concept of opportunity cost also applies to the production resources of the firm. Let us assume that we want to sell 1 minute of stamping time. This reduction in productive capacity would cause output to decline and consequently reduce the daily profit contribution value. The decrease in profit contribution caused by a decrease of 1 unit of a productive resource is the opportunity cost of that resource.

In the primal problem, Ms. Jones' objective was to maximize the profit contribution to the firm. It would be just as logical for Ms. Jones to try to arrange production so as to *minimize the total opportunity cost* of the resources. With this in mind, let us define four new variables as follows:

Y_1 = Opportunity cost associated with one unit of stamping time

Y_2 = Opportunity cost associated with one unit of forming time

Y_3 = Opportunity cost associated with one unit of assembly time

Y_4 = Opportunity cost associated with one unit of painting time

We obtain the total opportunity cost for any resource by multiplying the opportunity cost per unit by the total amount of resource available. Total opportunity cost for the firm is the sum of the opportunity costs for all resources. The daily availabilities of stamping, forming, assembly, and painting centers are 480, 2400, 2000, and 3000 units respectively. Suppose we let Z represent the value of the *dual objective function*. Since we are minimizing opportunity costs, formulation of the dual objective function becomes

$$\text{Min } Z = 480\,Y_1 + 2400\,Y_2 + 2000\,Y_3 + 3000\,Y_4$$

Note that these objective function coefficients are the constants on the right-hand side of the primal problem.

Perhaps the easiest way to discuss the *dual constraints* is to first state the rules for formulating the dual constraints and then to discuss the economic significance of what we have done. *The dual constraint coefficients are formed by transposing the constraint coefficients of the primal problem.* The first column of the primal problem constraints becomes the first row of the dual problem constraints; the second column of the primal problem constraints becomes the second row of the dual problem constraints; etc. Table 6.7 illustrates this transposition for the Jennings Foundry problem. To complete the dual constraint equations, we must concern ourselves with the sense of the inequality and the constants on the right-hand side. The sense of the inequality is reversed from the primal problem to the dual problem. In the Jennings Foundry example, all of our constraints were of the less-than-or-equal-to type. In the dual problem, therefore, all constraints will be greater-than-or-equal-to constraints. The objective function coefficients of the primal

Table 6.7 *Constraint coefficients of the primal and dual problems for Jennings Foundry, Inc.*

Primal				Dual			
Before transposition				After transposition			
1	1	1	1	1	4	4	6
4	8	2	5	1	8	2	4
4	2	5	5	1	2	5	8
6	4	8	4	1	5	5	4

problem become the constants on the right-hand side of the dual problem. Thus, in the Jennings Foundry problem, the objective function coefficients of the primal (9, 6, 11, and 8) become the constants on the right-hand side of the four dual constraints. As in all linear programming problems, the decision variables must be nonnegative. Thus, our dual formulation becomes

$$\text{Min } Z = 480Y_1 + 2400Y_2 + 2000Y_3 + 3000Y_4$$

s.t.
$$1Y_1 + 4Y_2 + 4Y_3 + 6Y_4 \geqslant 9 \quad \text{(type A fondue pots)}$$
$$1Y_1 + 8Y_2 + 2Y_3 + 4Y_4 \geqslant 6 \quad \text{(type B fondue pots)}$$
$$1Y_1 + 2Y_2 + 5Y_3 + 8Y_4 \geqslant 11 \quad \text{(type C fondue pots)}$$
$$1Y_1 + 5Y_2 + 5Y_3 + 4Y_4 \geqslant 8 \quad \text{(type D fondue pots)}$$
$$Y_1, Y_2, Y_3, Y_4 \geqslant 0$$

Note that we have now labeled our four dual constraints to conform with the four productive processes of the Jennings Foundry problem. The following interpretation of these constraints should help us understand the relationship between the primal and dual linear programming problems.

In each of the constraints in the dual formulation, the quantity on the left-hand side of the inequality sign represents the total opportunity cost of the resources consumed by a particular process. The right-hand side represents the contribution to profit of that same process. For example, the first constraint tells us that utilizing 1 unit of process X_1 consumes 1 unit of stamping time with an opportunity cost of $\$Y_1$ per unit, 4 units of forming time with an opportunity cost of $\$Y_2$ per unit, 4 units of assembly time with an opportunity cost of $\$Y_3$ per unit, and 6 units of painting time with an opportunity cost of $\$Y_4$ per unit. Thus, the total opportunity cost of resources consumed by 1 unit of X_1 is $1Y_1 + 4Y_2 + 4Y_3 + 6Y_4$. The 9 on the right-hand side of the inequality sign tells us that utilizing 1 unit of resource X_1 will contribute $\$9$ to the profit of the firm.

The inequality sign in each constraint tells us that the opportunity cost of production is going to be either greater than or equal to the profit contribution of that particular process. For example, the first dual constraint tells us that the production schedule must be arranged such that the production of 1 type A fondue pot consumes resources with a total opportunity cost either greater than or equal to the $9 profit contribution. (In practice the firm will produce type A fondue pots if opportunity cost equals profit contribution. If opportunity cost exceeds profit contribution, none of this process will be utilized.) The dual problem formulation does not allow for the opportunity cost of production to be less than the profit contribution. This seems confusing, but remember that these costs are opportunity costs, not accounting costs, and that the value of a resource is determined by the profit it can produce. From an economic standpoint, the profit contribution of a process cannot exceed the opportunity cost that, in effect, was generated by this process.

Before proceeding, let us review what we have said about *the relationship between the primal and dual problems.* Each linear programming primal problem has a corresponding dual problem. If the primal problem is a maximization problem, then the dual is a minimization problem. Conversely, if the primal is a minimization problem, then the dual is a maximization problem. The objective function coefficients of the primal problem are the constants on the right-hand side of the dual problem. The constants on the right-hand side of the primal problem are the objective function coefficients of the dual problem. We obtain the coefficients of the constraints in the dual problem by transposing the constraint coefficients of the primal problem. If the constraints in the primal are less-than-or-equal-to ($\leqslant$) constraints, then the constraints in the dual are greater-than-or-equal-to ($\geqslant$) constraints. If the primal constraints are $\geqslant$, then the dual constraints are $\leqslant$. Finally, the dual of the dual is the primal.

Sample problem 6.4   THE FOWLER COMPANY

Jim Fowler, owner of the Fowler Company, has correctly formulated his production problem as follows:

$$\text{Max } Z = 32X_1 + 40X_2 + 48X_3$$

s.t.
$$1X_1 + 1X_2 + 1X_3 \leqslant 180 \quad \text{(machine center 1)}$$
$$4X_1 + 2X_2 + 5X_3 \leqslant 280 \quad \text{(machine center 2)}$$
$$2X_1 + 5X_2 + 5X_3 \leqslant 380 \quad \text{(machine center 3)}$$
$$X_1, X_2, X_3 \geqslant 0$$

Let Y_1, Y_2, and Y_3 be the opportunity costs associated with machine centers 1, 2, and 3 respectively. Formulate the dual linear programming problem.

SOLUTION

$$\text{Min } Z = 180Y_1 + 280Y_2 + 380Y_3$$

s.t.

$$1Y_1 + 4Y_2 + 2Y_3 \geq 32 \qquad \text{(process 1)}$$

$$1Y_1 + 2Y_2 + 5Y_3 \geq 40 \qquad \text{(process 2)}$$

$$1Y_1 + 5Y_2 + 5Y_3 \geq 48 \qquad \text{(process 3)}$$

$$Y_1, Y_2, Y_3 \geq 0$$

Solving the dual problem

We can solve the dual linear programming problem by the standard simplex method. In order to solve the dual of the Jennings Foundry problem, we first have to add a surplus variable and an artificial variable to each constraint. The surplus variables we add to our four constraints represent the amount by which the opportunity cost of producing the respective product exceeds the profit contribution of that product. Applying the simplex method, we then obtain an optimal solution of $Z = 4450$, $Y_1 = {}^{10}\!/\!4$ or 2.50, $Y_2 = 0$, $Y_3 = \frac{2}{4}$ or .50, $Y_4 = \frac{3}{4}$ or .75, and T_2 (surplus in constraint 2) $= .50$. The first and final tableaus of this problem are given in Table 6.8.

The verbal translation is that the minimum total opportunity cost is $4450. The Y_1 value of 2.50 tells us that the opportunity cost of 1 unit of stamping time is $2.50. In other words, if the daily availability of stamping time were reduced from 480 minutes to 479 minutes, the total daily profit contribution would decrease by $2.50. The Y_3 value of $.50 tells us that the assembly center has an opportunity cost of $.50. Reducing the daily availability of the assembly center from 2000 minutes to 1999 minutes would reduce total daily profit contribution from $4450 to $4449.50. Likewise, the Y_4 value of $.75 indicates that the opportunity cost of the painting center is $.75 per unit.

The $Y_2 = 0$ indicates that the opportunity cost of the forming center is zero. This implies that reducing the daily availability of the forming center from 2400 minutes to 2399 minutes would not affect the daily profit contribution to the firm. If we refer to the optimal solution of the primal, we can see that the optimal production schedule did not utilize all of the available forming time. Since there is slack forming time, reducing the total availability of forming time by 1 unit would not cause a decrease in production or reduce profit contribution. In the present solution, therefore, the opportunity cost of this resource should be zero.

Table 6.8 The dual of the Jennings Foundry problem

0	Price vector	Solution vector	Quantity vector	480	2400	2000	3000	0	0	0	0	1000	1000	1000	1000
Row				Y_1	Y_2	Y_3	Y_4	T_1	T_2	T_3	T_4	A_1	A_2	A_3	A_4
Initial tableau															
I	1000	A_1	9	1	4	4	6	−1	0	0	0	1	0	0	0
II	1000	A_2	6	1	8	2	4	0	−1	0	0	0	1	0	0
III	1000	A_3	11	1	2	5	8	0	0	−1	0	0	0	1	0
IV	1000	A_4	8	1	5	5	4	0	0	0	−1	0	0	0	1
NC		−Z	−34,000	−3520	−16,600	−14,000	−19,000	1000	1000	1000	1000	0	0	0	0
Final tableau															
I	0	T_2	2/4	0	−6/4	0	0	−3	1	6/4	2/4	3	−1	−6/4	−2/4
II	480	Y_1	10/4	1	42/4	0	0	−5	0	14/4	2/4	5	0	−14/4	−2/4
III	3000	Y_4	3/4	0	−3/4	0	1	0	0	−1/4	1/4	0	0	1/4	−1/4
IV	2000	Y_3	2/4	0	−2/4	1	0	1	0	−2/4	−2/4	−1	0	2/4	2/4
NC		−Z	−4450	0	610	0	0	400	0	70	10	600	1000	930	990

The solution of the dual problem can also be found in the final tableau of the primal problem. Let us again refer to the final tableau of the Jennings Foundry primal problem in Table 6.6. The optimal objective function value of the primal is identical to the optimal objective function value of the dual. This will always be true. The dual objective function represents opportunity cost — the loss in profit contribution caused by a decrease in resources. If we give up all of our resources, we will also give up all of our profit contribution. It is logical, therefore, that in the optimal solution, total profit contribution equals total opportunity cost.

The negative of the value of the dual variables is found in the NC row of the slack-variable columns of the optimal primal tableau. From Table 6.6 or Table 6.9 (final iteration), we find that the values in the NC row for S_1, S_2, S_3, and S_4 are $-1\frac{0}{4}$, 0, $-\frac{1}{2}$, and $-\frac{3}{4}$ respectively. This tells us that the values of the corresponding dual variables are 2.50, 0, .50, and .75. The negative of the dual surplus variables is found in the NC row of the original-variable columns in the final tableau of the primal problem. From Table 6.6 (final iteration), we find that the values in the NC row for X_1, X_2, X_3, and X_4 are 0, $-\frac{1}{2}$, 0, and 0. Thus, we know that the surplus variables in the first, third, and fourth dual constraints have a value of zero. The dual surplus variable in the second constraint has a value of .50.

The solution values for the surplus variables again show us that the opportunity costs of producing fondue pots A, C, and D equal their profit contributions. These pots should be included in the optimal production schedule. Production of fondue pot B should be avoided; the opportunity cost of producing this product exceeds its profit contribution by .50.

Sample problem 6.5   THE FOWLER COMPANY (Continued)

The following table is the final (optimal) tableau of the primal Fowler Company problem given in Sample Problem 6.4. State the optimal value of the variables in the dual.

0 Row	Price vector	Solution vector	Quantity vector	32 X_1	40 X_2	48 X_3	0 S_1	0 S_2	0 S_3
I	0	S_1	80	0	0	$-\frac{9}{16}$	1	$-\frac{3}{16}$	$-\frac{2}{16}$
II	32	X_1	40	1	0	$\frac{15}{16}$	0	$\frac{5}{16}$	$-\frac{2}{16}$
III	40	X_2	60	0	1	$\frac{10}{16}$	0	$-\frac{2}{16}$	$\frac{4}{16}$
NC		$-Z$	-3680	0	0	-7	0	-5	-6

SOLUTION

$Z = 3680$, $Y_1 = 0$, $Y_2 = 5$, $Y_3 = 6$, $T_1 = 0$, $T_2 = 0$, and $T_3 = 7$

Sensitivity and postoptimality analysis

It would be unusual for a managerial analyst such as Ms. Jones to be satisfied with a simple statement of the optimal solution to a linear programming problem. She would probably also want to ask, "What happens if something changes?" This change could result from an action the decision maker takes or an action beyond the decision maker's control.

The analyst might be trying to determine what happens if more of a limited resource becomes available, or if a new process is added to the system. Furthermore, certain parameters, such as prices, cannot be controlled perfectly by the decision maker. In the terminology of Chapter 2, we are using a model that assumes certainty in an environment of risk. For this reason, the manager should want to know how much some input values can change without causing difficulties in implementing the calculated optimal solution.

Analysis of the effect of change in one or more parameters is called *sensitivity* or *postoptimality analysis*. Many practitioners of management science consider it the most important aspect of linear programming. Our discussion is only an introduction, and many more complex procedures of sensitivity analysis are available to the analyst.

Evaluating new production processes

The dual problem is often helpful to the managerial analyst in evaluating new production processes. For example, assume that an engineer at Jennings Foundry has proposed that the company introduce a new type of fondue pot, which we will call type E. The design engineer has determined that production of 1 unit of this new fondue pot will require 1 minute of stamping time, 2 minutes of forming time, 6 minutes of assembly time, and 12 minutes of painting time. The firm's cost accountant has determined that this process, when operated at a unit level, contributes $13 to the profit of the firm. Ms. Jones must decide whether or not to allocate funds for the development of this new fondue pot.

If we added this new process to our primal problem, we would simultaneously add the following constraint to our dual problem:

$$1Y_1 + 2Y_2 + 6Y_3 + 12Y_4 \geq 13 \qquad \text{(type E fondue pot)}$$

A new process will not be a valuable addition unless the associated dual constraint is violated; that is, it will not be used unless the value of resources consumed is less than the profit contribution. Substituting our optimal dual variables into the constraint, we obtain

$$1(\$2.50) + 2(\$0) + 6(\$.50) + 12(\$.75) \geq \$13$$
$$\$14.50 \geq \$13$$

Since the constraint is not violated, we know that type E fondue pots are not profitable to Jennings Foundry at the present time.

At first, it seems strange to say that this process is not profitable when the cost accountant has determined that it has a profit contribution value of $13. Remember, however, that we are concerned with economic or opportunity cost, whereas the $13 is an accounting profit. The situation is analogous to an example mentioned earlier. An acre of peas may be worth $800. But if we have only one acre of land, and if we have to give up an acre of corn worth $1000 to produce the acre of peas, then the acre of peas actually costs us $200.

Sensitivity of present process parameters

The optimal solution to the primal Jennings Foundry problem does not call for the production of any type B fondue pots; that is, $X_2 = 0$. There are two ways to make this a profitable process: increasing the price or reducing the cost of production. First, let us see how much price would have to increase. The associated dual constraint for X_2 is

$$1Y_1 + 8Y_2 + 2Y_3 + 4Y_4 \geq 6.00 + g$$

In this expression, g is the change in price, or profit contribution. If we substitute in the value of the optimal dual variables, we obtain

$$1(2.50) + 8(0) + 2(.50) + 4(.75) \geq 6.00 + g$$
$$6.50 \geq 6.00 + g$$

This indicates that g would have to have a value of more than .50 in order to violate the constraint. Thus, if the price of X_2 is increased by more than .50, X_2 will become a profitable process and the optimal solution will change.

A second possibility for making type B fondue pots profitable would be to reduce the per-unit consumption of one of the firm's resources. Type B fondue pots (X_2) presently require 4 minutes of painting time. Let us see how much this would have to be reduced. The associated dual constraint is

$$1Y_1 + 8Y_2 + 2Y_3 + (4 - h)Y_4 \geq 6.00$$

The value of h is the required reduction in painting time. Substituting the optimal dual variables, we obtain

$$1(2.50) + 8(0) + 2(.50) + (4 - h)(.75) \geq 6.00$$
$$-.75h \geq -.50$$
$$h \leq .67$$

If h has a value greater than .67, X_2 will become profitable and the optimal solution will change. Thus, type B fondue pots will become profitable if the time in the painting center can be reduced to less than 3.33 minutes.

Economic evaluation of resources

We defined our dual variables Y_1, Y_2, Y_3, and Y_4 to be the opportunity costs associated with the four production resources of the firm — the stamping, forming, assembly, and painting centers. The fact that Y_1 has a value of 2.50 indicates that the opportunity cost of 1 minute of stamping center time is $2.50. The economic interpretation is that if 1 less minute of stamping time was available, production would decrease and the resultant loss in profit contribution would be $2.50.

Conversely, if 1 more unit of stamping time becomes available, production increases and the resultant gain in profit contribution is $2.50. So, the $2.50 represents not only the opportunity cost of the resource, but also the *marginal contribution* of the resource. That is, if 1 more unit is obtained at the same cost as prior units, then total contribution to profit increases by $2.50. We know that we should never pay more for a resource than it is worth to the firm. Therefore, the maximum we would pay for an additional unit of stamping time is $2.50.

The Y_3 value of .50 and the Y_4 value of .75 indicate that an additional unit of assembly time would contribute $.50 and an additional unit of painting time would contribute $.75. Y_2 has a value of 0.0. Thus, the marginal value of an additional unit of forming time is $0. This indicates that we would pay nothing for an additional unit of forming time. This is logical. The optimum production schedule utilizes only 1790 minutes of the 2400 minutes of forming time available. Obviously, we would not pay a premium for additional time in the forming center.

We should be able to attribute the total contribution of a firm to the various productive resources of that firm. In other words, the total profit contribution of the firm should be the sum of the contributions made by each resource. We can obtain the contribution made by any resource by multiplying the marginal contribution of that resource by the units available for use. For the stamping center, there are 480 units being used and each unit contributes $2.50. The contribution of the stamping center is 480 multiplied by $2.50, which equals $1200. For the Jennings Foundry problem, we can see that the total profit contribution of $4450 is equal to the sum of the contributions of each resource.

Resource	Unit value	Units available	Contribution
Stamping	$2.50	480	$1200
Forming	.00	2400	0
Assembly	.50	2000	1000
Painting	.75	3000	2250
			$4450

The optimal values of the dual variables are often referred to as *shadow prices*. Remember that the value of the shadow prices and the corresponding resource evaluation are for this solution only. For example, we know that for this optimal solution, the stamping center has a marginal contribution of $2.50. As we purchase more and more stamping time, however, we may eventually reach a point where an additional unit of stamping time no longer contributes $2.50. This is because one of the other resources will cause a production bottleneck. At that point, further expansion of the stamping center will add less than $2.50 to the profit contribution of the firm. Thus, the marginal values obtained from the dual variables only hold true within a certain range. This range is easier to determine by using the primal problem, so it is covered in the following section.

Sample problem 6.6   THE FOWLER COMPANY (Continued)

Consider the Fowler Company problem given in Sample Problems 6.4 and 6.5. Use the dual problem and the optimal dual values to answer the following questions.

1. Use the dual values to attribute total profit contribution to the 3 machine centers of the firm.
2. A proposed new process, when operated at a unit level, consumes 3 units (hours) in each of the firm's machine centers. In order for this process to be profitable, how large must the objective function coefficient be?
3. At the present time, process X_3 is not being manufactured. One unit of process X_3 consumes 5 units of time in machine center 2. If X_3 is to be profitable, its utilization of time in machine center 2 must be reduced to at least what value?
4. Would you pay a premium of $5.50 for 1 more hour of time in machine center 2?

SOLUTIONS

1.

Machine center	Unit value	Units available	Contribution
1	$0	180	$ 0
2	5	280	1400
3	6	380	2280
			3680

2. The associated dual constraint is

$$3Y_1 + 3Y_2 + 3Y_3 \geq P$$
$$3(0) + 3(5) + 3(6) \geq P$$
$$33 \geq P$$

The constraint must be violated; therefore, P must be ≥ 33.

3. Let S be the required time in machine center 2. Since the constraint must be violated,

$$1Y_1 + SY_2 + 5Y_3 \leqslant 48$$
$$1(0) + S(5) + 5(6) \leqslant 48$$
$$5S \leqslant 18$$
$$S \leqslant 3.6$$

4. No; its marginal value is only $5.00.

Sensitivity analysis using the primal problem

As we stated earlier, the primal and the dual are simply two alternative ways of viewing the same problem. Thus, any sensitivity analysis performed with the dual problem can also be performed with the primal. In the following sections, we will use the primal problem to perform selected types of sensitivity analysis. For convenience, the final tableau of the Jennings Foundry problem is repeated as Table 6.9.

Shadow prices

We can use the primal problem to determine the shadow prices or marginal values of the four resources, the stamping, forming, assembly, and painting centers. For any process, such as X_1, the quantity in the NC (net contribution) row represents the amount the objective function would change if 1 unit of that process were brought into the solution. For example, the $-10/4$ in the NC row of column S_1 indicates that if we utilize 1 unit of S_1, profit will decrease by $10/4$, or $2.50.

The variable S_1 represents the amount of slack time in the stamping center. Forcing S_1 to have a value of 1 is equivalent to reducing the availability of stamping time by 1 unit. In other words, giving up 1 unit of stamping time is equivalent to increasing S_1 (slack time) by 1 unit. This will decrease the objective function by $2.50. Thus, 1 unit of the first resource (stamping time) must be worth $2.50. The analysis also works in the opposite direction. If we could get S_1 to equal a negative 1, it would be equivalent to adding an additional unit of stamping time. This increase in resource availability would increase the objective function by $2.50; that is $-1 \times -$2.50$.

The same reasoning applies to the other slack variables. An extra unit of S_3 would decrease the objective by $.50. This is equivalent to losing a unit of assembly time. Thus, a unit of assembly time must be worth $.50. Likewise, the marginal value of a unit of forming time is zero, and

Table 6.9 *Final tableau for the Jennings Foundry problem*

Original problem

Max $Z = 9X_1 + 6X_2 + 11X_3 + 8X_4$

s.t.

$$X_1 + X_2 + X_3 + X_4 \leqslant 480 \qquad \text{(stamping time)}$$
$$4X_1 + 8X_2 + 2X_3 + 5X_4 \leqslant 2400 \qquad \text{(forming time)}$$
$$4X_1 + 2X_2 + 5X_3 + 5X_4 \leqslant 2000 \qquad \text{(assembly time)}$$
$$6X_1 + 4X_2 + 8X_3 + 4X_4 \leqslant 3000 \qquad \text{(painting time)}$$
$$X_1, X_2, X_3, X_4 \geqslant 0$$

Final tableau

0 Row	Price vector	Solution vector	Quantity vector	9 X_1	6 X_2	11 X_3	8 X_4	0 S_1	0 S_2	0 S_3	0 S_4
I	9	X_1	400	1	3	0	0	5	0	-1	0
II	0	S_2	610	0	$6/4$	0	0	$-42/4$	1	$2/4$	$3/4$
III	8	X_4	10	0	$-2/4$	0	1	$-2/4$	0	$2/4$	$-1/4$
IV	11	X_3	70	0	$-6/4$	1	0	$-14/4$	0	$2/4$	$1/4$
NC		$-Z$	-4450	0	$-2/4$	0	0	$-10/4$	0	$-2/4$	$-3/4$

the marginal value of a unit of painting time is $.75. These are the same values we obtained when we used the dual problem for sensitivity analysis.

Right-hand-side ranging

The marginal contribution values of the resources are valid only for a given range of resource availability. For example, the marginal value of a unit of painting time is $.75. As more and more (or less and less) painting time becomes available, however, we may reach a point where an additional unit of painting time is no longer worth $.75. It may be quite important to the decision maker to know how many additional units of this resource can be added (or subtracted) before the $.75 value changes. Determining this range of applicability is easiest using the primal problem, and it is often referred to as *right-hand-side ranging*.

We will use the painting center at Jennings Foundry to illustrate right-hand-side ranging. The marginal contribution of each additional unit of painting time is $.75. We wish to learn how many additional units we can add (or subtract) before this value will change. Reducing the number of available units of painting time is equivalent to introducing S_4 into the solution. Thus, we treat the situation as though S_4 were entering the solution and another iteration were being performed. It is necessary to determine how much S_4 may be entered into solution before one of the basic variables is driven to a zero value.

In the simplex method, we create entrance test ratios by dividing the element in the "Quantity vector" column by the corresponding element in the entering process column. If S_4 is the entering process, the entrance test ratios are as follows:

$$400 \div 0 = \text{undefined}$$
$$610 \div \tfrac{3}{4} = 813.3$$
$$10 \div -\tfrac{1}{4} = -40$$
$$70 \div \tfrac{1}{4} = 280$$

The smallest positive ratio indicates how much S_4 may enter and consequently how much resource can be removed before the marginal value of that resource changes. In this example, 280 is the smallest positive ratio. Thus, each unit of painting time removed, up to 280 units, will subtract $.75 from the objective function value. Since there were originally 3000 minutes of painting time available, the resource evaluation is valid down to 2720 minutes of resource availability.

The decision maker may also want to know how many units of resource can be added before the shadow price will change. Adding painting time is the same as introducing negative S_4. Thus, the largest negative ratio (the one closest to zero) indicates how much resource can be added before the value changes. In our example, the largest negative ratio is -40. Thus, the range of applicability of the $.75 value is 2720 to 3040, that is, $(3000 - 280)$ to $(3000 + 40)$.

If there are no finite negative entrance test ratios, then each additional unit will add the same amount to the objective function, regardless of the number of units added. If there are no finite positive ratios, then each unit of resource subtracted will reduce the objective function value by the same amount.

As a second example, consider the 2000 units of assembly time. The shadow price of an additional unit of assembly time is $\tfrac{2}{4}$ or $.50. Subtracting an additional unit of assembly time is equivalent to adding a unit of S_3. The entrance test ratios are

$$400 \div -1 = -400$$
$$610 \div \tfrac{2}{4} = 1220$$
$$10 \div \tfrac{2}{4} = 20$$
$$70 \div \tfrac{2}{4} = 140$$

The minimum positive and largest negative ratios are 20 and -400 respectively. Thus, the marginal value of $.50 per unit is valid over the range 1980 to 2400, that is, $(2000 - 20)$ to $(2000 + 400)$. The data for all four resources are given in Table 6.10.

Table 6.10 *Right-hand-side range values for the Jennings Foundry problem*

	Amount	Contribution	Change limits		Range limits	
Resource	available	value	Lower	Upper	Lower	Upper
Stamping	480	$2.50	80	20	400	500
Forming	2400	.00	610	none	1790	∞
Assembly	2000	.50	20	400	1980	2400
Painting	3000	.75	280	40	2720	3040

Sample problem 6.7 THE FOWLER COMPANY (Continued)

In Sample Problem 6.6, the marginal contribution values of machine centers 1, 2, and 3 were found to be $0, $5, and $6 respectively. Determine the range of applicability of these values. In other words, perform right-hand-side ranging on the Fowler Company problem.

SOLUTION

The entrance test ratios for S_1, S_2, and S_3 are as follows:

$$S_1 = 80.0, \text{ undefined, undefined}$$
$$S_2 = -426.7, 128, -480$$
$$S_3 = -640, -320, 240$$

The ranges are as follows:

Machine center 1: $(180-80)$ to $(180 + \infty) = 100$ to ∞

Machine center 2: $(280-128)$ to $(280 + 426.7) = 152$ to 706.7

Machine center 3: $(380-240)$ to $(380 + 320) = 140$ to 700

Objective function coefficients

A topic we have not yet covered in this chapter is the sensitivity of the solution to changes in objective function coefficients of basic variables, that is, processes that are being used in a particular solution. For example, the objective function coefficient of X_1 is now $9. It may be helpful to know how much this value could increase or decrease before the present optimal solution changes.

If X_1 is to be replaced so that the present optimal solution changes, it must be replaced by a variable that is nonbasic in the present solution. Thus, we create a set of *exit ratios* by dividing each of the elements in the NC row of each nonbasic process by the corresponding element in the X_1 row. The smallest positive ratio indicates how much the objective function coefficient can increase before the solution changes. The largest negative ratio indicates how much the coefficient can decrease before the solution changes.

For X_1, the four exit ratios are as follows:

$$-2/4 \div 3 = -1/6$$
$$-10/4 \div 5 = -1/2$$
$$-2/4 \div -1 = 1/2$$
$$-3/4 \div 0 = \text{undefined}$$

The smallest positive ratio, $1/2$, indicates that the objective function coefficient of X_1 can increase by as much as $1/2$ before the solution changes. The largest negative ratio, $-1/6$, indicates that the coefficient of X_1 can decrease by as much as $1/6$ before the solution changes. Thus, the range of profitability for X_1 is $8\frac{5}{6}$ to $9\frac{1}{2}$, that is, $(9 - 1/6)$ to $(9 + 1/2)$.

We can perform the same analysis on the other basic variables. As a second example, consider X_4. The exit ratios are

$$-2/4 \div -2/4 = 1$$
$$-10/4 \div -2/4 = 5$$
$$-2/4 \div 2/4 = -1$$
$$-3/4 \div -1/4 = 3$$

The largest negative and minimum positive ratios are -1 and $+1$ respectively. Thus, the range of profitability for X_4 is 7 to 9, that is, $(8 - 1)$ to $(8 + 1)$. The intervals of feasibility for all basic variables are given in Table 6.11.

Sample problem 6.8   THE FOWLER COMPANY (Continued)

Consider the Fowler Company problem given in Sample Problem 6.5. For each basic variable in the optimal solution, find an interval for the objective function coefficient such that the present solution remains optimal.

SOLUTION

The exit ratios are as follows:

$$X_1 = -7.5, -16, 48$$
$$X_2 = -11.2, 40, -24$$

The intervals are as follows:

$$X_1: \quad (32 - 7.5) \text{ to } (32 + 48) = 24.5 \text{ to } 80$$
$$X_2: \quad (40 - 11.2) \text{ to } (40 + 40) = 38.8 \text{ to } 80$$

Table 6.11 *Sensitivity of objective function coefficients in the Jennings Foundry problem*

Basic variable	Objective function coefficient	Change limits		Range limits	
		Lower	*Upper*	*Lower*	*Upper*
X_1	9	$-\frac{1}{6}$	$\frac{1}{2}$	$^{53}/_6$	$^{57}/_6$
X_4	8	-1	1	7	9
X_3	11	-1	$\frac{1}{3}$	10	$^{34}/_3$

Other types of linear programming problem formulations

Before concluding this second chapter on linear programming, we will introduce several different types of problems that are amenable to analysis by linear programming. The purpose of this section is to sharpen our skill at problem formulation and to increase our awareness of areas wherein linear programming may be a helpful tool of analysis.

Variations in objective functions

Most of the linear programming illustrations that we have used assumed that the decision maker wished to maximize profit contribution or to minimize cost. There are, however, situations wherein the decision maker may wish to pursue other objectives, such as maximizing volume of output or minimizing idle time in a machine center. There are also situations wherein the decision maker's primary concern is to balance two somewhat conflicting goals.

In order to discuss and illustrate these types of situations, we will introduce a small problem that is very similar to the Jennings Foundry problem. Let us assume that there are only three processes, X_1 (a new, type H fondue pot), X_2 (a new, type J fondue pot), and X_3 (a new, type K fondue pot). We shall also assume that there are only three resource centers (forming, assembly, and painting). Ms. Jones is still the decision maker, and we shall begin by assuming that she still wishes to *maximize profit contribution*. The objective function coefficients of X_1, X_2, and X_3 are \$9, \$6, and \$8 respectively. The problem formulation is

$$\text{Max } Z = 9X_1 + 6X_2 + 8X_3$$

s.t.
$$6X_1 + 5X_2 + 6X_3 \leq 2400 \quad \text{(forming time)}$$
$$5X_1 + 4X_2 + 4X_3 \leq 2000 \quad \text{(assembly time)}$$
$$8X_1 + 5X_2 + 6X_3 \leq 3000 \quad \text{(painting time)}$$
$$X_1, X_2, X_3 \geq 0$$

After we add the appropriate slack variables, the formulation is

$$\text{Max } Z = 9X_1 + 6X_2 + 8X_3 + 0S_1 + 0S_2 + 0S_3$$

s.t.
$$6X_1 + 5X_2 + 6X_3 + 1S_1 + 0S_2 + 0S_3 = 2400$$
$$5X_1 + 4X_2 + 4X_3 + 0S_1 + 1S_2 + 0S_3 = 2000$$
$$8X_1 + 5X_2 + 6X_3 + 0S_1 + 0S_2 + 1S_3 = 3000$$
$$X_1, X_2, X_3, S_1, S_2, S_3 \geqslant 0$$

The problem as formulated here can be solved by the simplex method. The optimal solution is $Z = \$3500$, $X_1 = 300$, $X_2 = 0$, $X_3 = 100$, $S_1 = 0$, $S_2 = 100$, and $S_3 = 0$. In order to maximize contribution to profit, Ms. Jones should schedule production of 300 units of X_1 and 100 units of X_3. This will result in a profit contribution of \$3500. Total volume of production will be 400 ($X_1 = 300$ and $X_3 = 100$) and total slack time will be 100 minutes ($S_2 = 100$).

Instead of maximizing profit contribution,.the decision maker may wish to *maximize total volume of output*. If the goal is to maximize units of production, we can simply assign a unit (1) objective function coefficient to X_1, X_2, and X_3. The objective function becomes

$$\text{Max } Z = 1X_1 + 1X_2 + 1X_3 + 0S_1 + 0S_2 + 0S_3$$

The constraints have not changed. With this new objective function, however, we obtain a new optimal solution: $Z = 480$, $X_1 = 0$, $X_2 = 480$, $X_3 = 0$, $S_1 = 0$, $S_2 = 80$, and $S_3 = 600$. Total production has increased from 400 units in the previous problem formulation to 480 units in this formulation. The company, of course, has paid a price for this increase in production. Total profit contribution is down from \$3500 to \$2880. We have switched our production plan from a high-consumption–high-profit solution to a low-consumption–low-profit solution. The low consumption per unit of output allows for the higher total volume of output.

Another alternative would be to *minimze the amount of idle time in the various machine centers*. We know that S_1 represents the slack time in the forming center, S_2 the slack time in the assembly center, and S_3 the slack time in the painting center. If our objective is to minimize slack time, we can formulate the objective function as follows:

$$\text{Min } Z = 0X_1 + 0X_2 + 0X_3 + 1S_1 + 1S_2 + 1S_3$$

This objective function considers neither profit nor units of production. Instead, the idea is to schedule operations in such a way as to utilize as much of our resources as possible. With this objective function, the optimal solution is $Z = 20$, $X_1 = 300$, $X_2 = 120$, $X_3 = 0$, $S_1 = 0$, $S_2 = 20$, and $S_3 = 0$. Total production in this solution is 420 units, which is less than the 480 units of production in the previous solution. Rearrangement of the production schedule, however, has reduced total

Table 6.12 *Comparison of optimal solutions for various objective function criteria*

| | Criteria | | |
	Maximizing profit contribution	Maximizing units of production	Minimizing slack time
Problem variables			
Profit contribution	$3500	$2880	$3420
X_1	300	0	300
X_2	0	480	120
X_3	100	0	0
S_1	0	0	0
S_2	100	80	20
S_3	0	600	0
Total production	400	480	420
Total slack	100	680	20

slack time from 680 minutes to 20 minutes. It has also reduced profit contribution from $3500 to $3420.

Table 6.12 compares the three optimal solutions obtained by varying the objective function from maximizing profit contribution to maximizing units of production to minimizing slack time.

On some occasions, a decision maker may wish to achieve two or more somewhat conflicting goals. In many cases, it is not possible to exactly achieve both of these goals at the same time. One alternative to simultaneous achievement would be to minimize a function of the deviations from the two goals. We analyze problems of this type by a special type of linear programming known as goal programming. *Goal programming* is capable of handling problems that have multiple goals or objectives. The procedure allows the decision maker to rank the goals so that low-priority goals are considered only after goals with higher priorities have been satisfied to the fullest extent possible. The first part of Chapter 8 is devoted to goal programming.

Blending problems

Let us assume that we operate a sidewalk refreshment stand where we sell two types of fruit punches to pedestrians. We mix two brands of commercial punches to form the two new "homemade" punches that we sell to the customer. Because the commercial brands are used for blending purposes only, we refer to them as blending agent 1 and blending agent 2. We refer to the two new blends that we sell to the consumer as fruit punch 1 and fruit punch 2.

It will be helpful to introduce *doubly subscripted variables*. These variables are quite common in many types of mathematical models. In our fruit punch example, we will need four of the doubly subscripted variables. We define them as follows:

X_{11} = Amount of blending agent 1 used for fruit punch 1

X_{12} = Amount of blending agent 1 used for fruit punch 2

X_{21} = Amount of blending agent 2 used for fruit punch 1

X_{22} = Amount of blending agent 2 used for fruit punch 2

It is important to recognize and read the subscripts as double sub-scripts. Thus, X_{12} should be read "X-one, two" rather than "X-twelve."

In our simple example, the only costs and revenues we are concerned with are the costs of the blending agents and the selling prices of the fruit punches. If we can buy blending agent 1 for $.60 a gallon and sell fruit punch 1 for $.90 a gallon, then the contribution to profit of 1 gallon of blending agent 1 used to make fruit punch 1 is $.30. (We are assuming no loss of punch in the mixing process.) In other words, X_{11} has an objective function coefficient of $.30. Likewise, if fruit punch 2 sells for $1.30 a gallon, then 1 gallon of X_{12} contributes $.70 to the profit of our sidewalk operation. If blending agent 2 costs $.40 per gallon, then X_{21} and X_{22} have profit contributions of $.50 and $.90 respectively. If our objective is to maximize profit, we can state the objective function as follows:

$$\text{Max } Z = .30X_{11} + .70X_{12} + .50X_{21} + .90X_{22}$$

Problems such as this are characterized by a particular type of con-straint known as a *blending constraint*. These constraints require a specific type of relationship between two or more inputs and/or outputs in a mixing or blending process. For example, let us assume that taste considerations require fruit punch 1 to contain at least twice as much blending agent 1 as blending agent 2. This constraint may be written

$$\frac{X_{11}}{X_{21}} \geqslant 2$$

$$X_{11} \geqslant 2X_{21}$$

$$X_{11} - 2X_{21} \geqslant 0$$

Since X_{12} and X_{22} are not involved, this first blending constraint may be written as

$$1X_{11} + 0X_{12} - 2X_{21} + 0X_{22} \geqslant 0 \qquad \text{(first blending constraint)}$$

There are two additional blending constraints to our problem. Let us assume that blending agent 1 consists of 15% of a particular type of ingredient, such as grape juice. Blending agent 2 consists of 35% of this same ingredient. There is a requirement that fruit punch 1 contain at least 20% of this same ingredient. The total volume of fruit punch 1 can be expressed as $X_{11} + X_{21}$. The amount of grape juice in fruit punch 1 can be expressed as $.15X_{11} + .35X_{21}$. If fruit punch 1 must contain at least 20% grape juice, we can formulate our second blending constraint as follows:

$$\frac{.15X_{11} + .35X_{21}}{X_{11} + X_{21}} \geq .20$$

$$.15X_{11} + .35X_{21} \geq .20X_{11} + .20X_{21}$$

$$-.05X_{11} + .15X_{21} \geq 0$$

Again, since X_{12} and X_{22} are not involved, the constraint may be formulated as

$$-.05X_{11} + 0X_{12} + .15X_{21} + 0X_{22} \geq 0 \quad \text{(second blending constraint)}$$

For the third blending constraint, let us assume that the first blending agent is a diet punch that contains only .3% of sweetener. The second blending agent contains 4% of this same ingredient. We hope that fruit punch 2 can contain less than 1% of this ingredient so that we can sell it as a diet punch. We formulate this constraint as follows:

$$\frac{.003X_{12} + .04X_{22}}{X_{12} + X_{22}} \leq .01$$

$$-.007X_{12} + .03X_{22} \leq 0$$

$$0X_{11} - .007X_{12} + 0X_{21} + .03X_{22} \leq 0 \quad \text{(third blending constraint)}$$

To complete our problem, let us assume that there are three additional constraints. The first two require us to produce at least 5 gallons of each type of fruit punch. These may be formulated as follows:

$$1X_{11} + 0X_{12} + 1X_{21} + 0X_{22} \geq 5 \quad \text{(fruit punch 1 minimum)}$$

$$0X_{11} + 1X_{12} + 0X_{21} + 1X_{22} \geq 5 \quad \text{(fruit punch 2 minimum)}$$

The last constraint is necessary because the supply of blending agent 1 is limited to 25 gallons per day. It is formulated as follows:

$$1X_{11} + 1X_{12} + 0X_{21} + 0X_{22} \leq 25 \quad \text{(supply of blending agent 1)}$$

Since our objective is to maximize profit, the total problem may be formulated as

$$\text{Max } Z = .30X_{11} + .70X_{12} + .50X_{21} + .90X_{22}$$

s.t.

$$
\begin{aligned}
1X_{11} + \quad\; 0X_{12} - \quad\; 2X_{21} + \quad\; 0X_{22} &\geq 0 \\
-.05X_{11} + \quad\; 0X_{12} + .15X_{21} + \quad\; 0X_{22} &\geq 0 \\
0X_{11} - .007X_{12} + \quad\; 0X_{21} + .03X_{22} &\leq 0 \\
1X_{11} + \quad\; 0X_{12} + \quad\; 1X_{21} + \quad\; 0X_{22} &\geq 5 \\
0X_{11} + \quad\; 1X_{12} + \quad\; 0X_{21} + \quad\; 1X_{22} &\geq 5 \\
1X_{11} + \quad\; 1X_{12} + \quad\; 0X_{21} + \quad\; 0X_{22} &\leq 25 \\
X_{ij} &\geq 0, \text{ for all } i, j
\end{aligned}
$$

The optimal solution to this problem is $Z = \$21.55$, $X_{11} = 3.33$, $X_{12} = 21.67$, $X_{21} = 1.67$, and $X_{22} = 5.06$. This means that we will produce 5 gallons of fruit punch 1 by mixing 3.33 gallons of mixing agent 1 and 1.67 gallons of mixing agent 2. We will also produce 26.73 gallons of fruit punch 2 by mixing 21.67 gallons of blending agent 1 and 5.06 gallons of blending agent 2. This solution will satisfy all of the blending constraints and will yield a daily profit contribution of $21.55. We can do no better.

Dynamic or time-staged problems

The word "dynamic" is generally used to describe models that encompass several time periods. Almost all of the linear programming illustrations we have used could be extended to include several time periods. Consider the Baur Company, a firm with two production processes and three limited resources, which we will again refer to as forming time, assembly time, and painting time. The first process, a type M fondue pot, utilizes 8, 6, and 4 minutes respectively of forming, assembly, and painting time. The second process, a type N fondue pot, utilizes 4, 9, and 3 minutes respectively of forming, assembly, and painting time. It is our intention to extend the planning horizon over four production periods, the months of January, February, March, and April. So it is again convenient to use doubly subscripted variables:

$X_{11} =$ Units of process 1 produced in period 1

$X_{21} =$ Units of process 2 produced in period 1

$X_{12} =$ Units of process 1 produced in period 2

$X_{22} =$ Units of process 2 produced in period 2

$X_{13} =$ Units of process 1 produced in period 3

$X_{23} =$ Units of process 2 produced in period 3

$X_{14} =$ Units of process 1 produced in period 4

$X_{24} =$ Units of process 2 produced in period 4

During the first and second production periods, processes 1 and 2 have profit contributions of $17 and $14 respectively. During these same periods, the forming, assembly, and painting centers are available for 32,000, 40,000, and 15,000 hours respectively. The production constraints for the first two periods may be written as follows:

$$8X_{11} + 4X_{21} \leqslant 32,000 \quad \text{(forming, period 1)}$$
$$6X_{11} + 9X_{21} \leqslant 40,000 \quad \text{(assembly, period 1)}$$
$$4X_{11} + 3X_{21} \leqslant 15,000 \quad \text{(painting, period 1)}$$
$$8X_{12} + 4X_{22} \leqslant 32,000 \quad \text{(forming, period 2)}$$
$$6X_{12} + 9X_{22} \leqslant 40,000 \quad \text{(assembly, period 2)}$$
$$4X_{12} + 3X_{22} \leqslant 15,000 \quad \text{(painting, period 2)}$$

Several changes are expected at the beginning of the third production period. An expansion in the painting center should allow this center to be available for 25,000 minutes during each of the third and fourth periods. In addition, expected changes in the cost of raw materials will change the profit contributions of both processes during the third and fourth periods. It is expected that process 1 will have a profit contribution of $15 and that process 2 will have a profit contribution of $16 during these last two periods. The production constraints for these two periods can be formulated as follows:

$$8X_{13} + 4X_{23} \leq 32,000 \qquad \text{(forming, period 3)}$$
$$6X_{13} + 9X_{23} \leq 40,000 \qquad \text{(assembly, period 3)}$$
$$4X_{13} + 3X_{23} \leq 25,000 \qquad \text{(painting, period 3)}$$
$$8X_{14} + 4X_{24} \leq 32,000 \qquad \text{(forming, period 4)}$$
$$6X_{14} + 9X_{24} \leq 40,000 \qquad \text{(assembly, period 4)}$$
$$4X_{14} + 3X_{24} \leq 25,000 \qquad \text{(painting, period 4)}$$

Dynamic formulations are generally characterized by *interrelationship constraints*, which are used to tie one production period to another. The most common interrelationship constraint deals with inventory and states that ending inventory is equal to beginning inventory plus production less sales. In order to formulate the interrelationship constraints, we must introduce variables to represent the amount of inventory being held at the end of a production period. We shall introduce the following new variables:

I_{11} = Inventory of product 1 at the end of period 1

I_{21} = Inventory of product 2 at the end of period 1

I_{12} = Inventory of product 1 at the end of period 2

I_{22} = Inventory of product 2 at the end of period 2

I_{13} = Inventory of product 1 at the end of period 3

I_{23} = Inventory of product 2 at the end of period 3

I_{14} = Inventory of product 1 at the end of period 4

I_{24} = Inventory of product 2 at the end of period 4

Let us assume that there are 1000 units of each product in inventory at the beginning of the first production period. Contract sales for the two products for the next four production periods are as follows:

	Period 1	Period 2	Period 3	Period 4
Product 1	1800	1800	1800	1800
Product 2	2500	2000	3000	1000

In general, interrelationship constraints can be formulated as follows:

Ending inventory = Beginning inventory + Production − Sales

or

Production + Beginning inventory − Ending inventory = Sales

Since beginning inventory is 1000 units for both products, the interrelationship constraints for the two products for the first two time periods can be formulated as follows:

$$X_{11} + 1000 - I_{11} = 1800$$
$$X_{11} - I_{11} = 800 \qquad \text{(product 1, periods 0–1)}$$
$$X_{21} + 1000 - I_{21} = 2500$$
$$X_{21} - I_{21} = 1500 \qquad \text{(product 2, periods 0–1)}$$

In succeeding time periods, ending inventory in one period will be beginning inventory in the next period. The remaining interrelationship constraints can therefore be formulated as follows:

$$X_{12} + I_{11} - I_{12} = 1800 \qquad \text{(product 1, periods 1–2)}$$
$$X_{22} + I_{21} - I_{22} = 2000 \qquad \text{(product 2, periods 1–2)}$$
$$X_{13} + I_{12} - I_{13} = 1800 \qquad \text{(product 1, periods 2–3)}$$
$$X_{23} + I_{22} - I_{23} = 3000 \qquad \text{(product 2, periods 2–3)}$$
$$X_{14} + I_{13} - I_{14} = 1800 \qquad \text{(product 1, periods 3–4)}$$
$$X_{24} + I_{23} - I_{24} = 1000 \qquad \text{(product 2, periods 3–4)}$$

Finally, each dynamic formulation usually has several constraints of a type known as *initializing* or *specifying constraints*. These constraints define a particular variable to be equal to (or perhaps greater than or less than) a specific value. For example, suppose that the inventory for both products at the end of period 4 has to be no less than 1000. These constraints may be formulated as follows:

$$I_{14} \geq 1000 \qquad \text{(inventory, product 1, period 4)}$$
$$I_{24} \geq 1000 \qquad \text{(inventory, product 2, period 4)}$$

Because of repairs that must be made in some of the production operations, it will not be possible to produce product 1 in period 3, nor will it be possible to produce product 2 in period 4. These specifying constraints may be formulated as follows:

$$X_{13} = 0 \qquad \text{(product 1, period 3)}$$
$$X_{24} = 0 \qquad \text{(product 2, period 4)}$$

Earlier, we stated that process 1 contributes $17 to profit in the first and second production periods and $15 in the third and fourth periods.

Likewise, process 2 contributes $14 in the first two periods and $16 in the last two periods. Let us assume that the cost of holding inventory is $1 per unit per period. Therefore, each variable representing ending inventory has an objective function coefficient of $-1. The objective function can therefore be written as follows:

Max $Z =$
$$17X_{11} + 14X_{21} + 17X_{12} + 14X_{22} + 15X_{13} + 16X_{23} + 15X_{14} + 16X_{24}$$
$$- 1I_{11} - 1I_{21} - 1I_{12} - 1I_{22} - 1I_{13} - 1I_{23} - 1I_{14} - 1I_{24}$$

This problem has 16 variables (not counting slack, surplus, and artificial variables) and 24 constraints. Most real dynamic or time-staged problems have many more variables and constraints. Efficient linear programming computer programs used on modern electronic computers can efficiently solve problems with thousands of variables and more than 5000 constraints. If a problem fits the linear programming model, the greatest difficulty is almost always in formulating the problem rather than in finding an answer to the problem once it is formulated.

As a matter of interest, the optimal solution to the foregoing problem is to schedule production as follows:

	Period 1	*Period 2*	*Period 3*	*Period 4*
Product 1	2567	1833	0	2800
Product 2	1500	2556	4444	0

And the resultant ending inventory values are as follows:

	Period 1	*Period 2*	*Period 3*	*Period 4*
Product 1	1767	1800	0	1000
Product 2	0	556	2000	1000

Problems and exercises

1. Explain the following terms:

equality constraint	primal problem
surplus variable	dual problem
big M method	sensitivity analysis
artificial variable	double subscript
unbounded solution	dynamic problem
multiple optimal solutions	blending constraint
shadow price	right-hand-side ranging
degenerate solution	

GRAPHICAL EXERCISES. INSTRUCTIONS FOR PROBLEMS 2–16

Graph the following linear programming problems. Shade the set of feasible solutions. Draw an appropriate objective function reference plane (iso-revenue line). Problems 2–7 should yield unique optimal solutions. For these problems, state the optimal values of all variables, including the optimal objective function value. For Problems 8–16, state whether the solution is nonfeasible, is unbounded, or has multiple optimal solutions.

2. Min $Z = 3X_1 + 4X_2$

   s.t. $4X_1 + 2X_2 \geqslant 32$

   $1X_1 + 3X_2 \geqslant 18$

   $X_1, X_2 \geqslant 0$

3. Min $Z = 1X_1 + 2X_2$

   s.t. $5X_1 + 20X_2 \geqslant 100$

   $15X_1 + 10X_2 \geqslant 150$

   $32X_1 + 8X_2 \geqslant 160$

   $X_1, X_2 \geqslant 0$

4. In problem 3, change the objective function to Min $Z = 2X_1 + 1X_2$.

5. Min $Z = 1X_1 + 1X_2$

   s.t. $5X_1 + 1X_2 \geqslant 20$

   $2X_1 + 3X_2 \geqslant 30$

   $3X_1 + 2X_2 = 30$

   $X_1, X_2 \geqslant 0$

6. Min $Z = 3X_1 + 2X_2$

   s.t. $1X_1 + 0X_2 \geqslant 5$

   $0X_1 + 1X_2 \geqslant 2$

   $1X_1 + 1X_2 \geqslant 10$

   $1X_1 + 1X_2 \leqslant 15$

   $X_1, X_2 \geqslant 0$

7. In Problem 6, add the constraint $X_1 + 3X_2 = 18$.

8. Max $Z = 5X_1 + 5X_2$

   s.t. $X_1 + 2X_2 \leqslant 20$

   $X_1 + X_2 \leqslant 12$

   $2X_1 + X_2 \leqslant 20$

   $X_1, X_2 \geqslant 0$

9. Max $Z = 210X_1 + 350X_2$

   s.t. $3X_1 + 5X_2 \leqslant 25$

   $-3X_1 + 5X_2 \leqslant 15$

   $1X_1 + 0X_2 \geqslant 5$

   $X_1, X_2 \geqslant 0$

10. In problem 5, change the objective function to Min $Z = 6X_1 + 4X_2$.

11. Max $Z = 0X_1 + 1X_2$

    s.t. $10X_1 + 0X_2 \leqslant 150$

    $X_1 - X_2 \leqslant 5$

    $X_1, X_2 \geqslant 0$

12. In problem 9, *remove* the constraint $3X_1 + 5X_2 \leqslant 25$.

13. Min $Z = X_1 - X_2$

    s.t. $4X_1 + X_2 \geqslant 20$

    $1X_1 + 4X_2 \geqslant 20$

    $X_1, X_2 \geqslant 0$

14. Max $Z = 6X_1 + 12X_2$
    s.t. $8X_1 + 5X_2 \leqslant 40$
    $6X_1 + 9X_2 \geqslant 90$
    $X_1, X_2 \geqslant 0$

15. Min $Z = 1X_1 + 1X_2$
    s.t. $3X_1 + 2X_2 = 30$
    $0X_1 + 1X_2 \leqslant 5$
    $1X_1 + 2X_2 = 18$
    $X_1, X_2 \geqslant 0$

16. Max $Z = 1X_1 + 1X_2$
    s.t. $1X_1 + 0X_2 \geqslant 6$
    $0X_1 + 1X_2 \leqslant 4$
    $X_1 - X_2 \leqslant 0$
    $X_1, X_2 \geqslant 0$

SIMPLEX EXERCISES. INSTRUCTIONS FOR PROBLEMS 17–30
Add the appropriate slack, surplus, and artificial variables. Use a value of 10 (plus or minus as appropriate) for the objective function coefficient of artificial variables. Solve the problem using the simplex method. Problems 17–22 should yield unique optimal solutions. For Problems 23–30, state if the problem is degenerate, is unbounded, has multiple optimal solutions, or has no feasible solution. In some cases, degeneracy may appear before the final solution.

17. Max $Z = X_1 + 2X_2$
    s.t. $X_1 + X_2 \leqslant 10$
    $3X_1 + X_2 = 12$
    $X_1, X_2 \geqslant 0$

18. Min $Z = 2X_1 + 2X_2$
    s.t. $X_1 + 2X_2 = 6$
    $X_1 + 0X_2 \geqslant 4$
    $X_1, X_2 \geqslant 0$

19. Min $Z = 4X_1 + 3X_2$
    s.t. $2X_1 + 1X_2 \geqslant 16$
    $1X_1 + 3X_2 \geqslant 18$
    $X_1, X_2 \geqslant 0$

20. Min $Z = X_1 + X_2$
    s.t. $2X_1 + 3X_2 \geqslant 15$
    $0X_1 + 1X_2 \geqslant 2$
    $2X_1 + 1X_2 = 10$
    $X_1, X_2 \geqslant 0$

21. Min $Z = 2X_1 + 1X_2 + 3X_3$
    s.t. $2X_1 + 3X_2 + 2X_3 \geqslant 30$
    $4X_1 + 1X_2 + 1X_3 \geqslant 20$
    $2X_1 + 2X_2 + 2X_3 \geqslant 20$
    $X_1, X_2, X_3 \geqslant 0$

22. Min $Z = 2X_1 + 1X_2 + 8X_3$
    s.t. $1X_1 + 1X_2 + 1X_3 = 6$
    $2X_1 + 4X_2 + 1X_3 = 20$
    $2X_1 + 1X_2 + 0X_3 \geqslant 5$
    $X_1, X_2, X_3 \geqslant 0$

23. Max $Z = 1X_1 + 1X_2$
    s.t. $2X_1 + 1X_2 \leqslant 10$
    $1X_1 + 3X_2 \leqslant 15$
    $0X_1 + 1X_2 \leqslant 4$
    $X_1, X_2, \geqslant 0$

24. Max $Z = 1X_1 + 1.5X_2$
    s.t. $2X_1 + 4X_2 \leqslant 20$
    $2X_1 + 6X_2 \leqslant 22$
    $2X_1 + 8X_2 \leqslant 24$
    $X_1, X_2 \geqslant 0$

25. Max $Z = 2X_1 + 1X_2$

 s.t. $10X_1 + 0X_2 \leqslant 150$

 $1X_1 - 1X_2 \leqslant 5$

 $X_1, X_2 \geqslant 0$

26. Solve problem 12 by the simplex method.

27. Max $Z = 5X_1 + 10X_2$

 s.t. $1X_1 + 1X_2 \leqslant 12$

 $1X_1 + 2X_2 \leqslant 20$

 $X_1, X_2 \geqslant 0$

28. Solve problem 8 by the simplex method.

29. Solve problem 14 by the simplex method.

30. Max $Z = 5X_1 + 5X_2$

 s.t. $X_1 + 2X_2 = 10$

 $2X_1 + X_2 = 30$

 $X_1, X_2 \geqslant 0$

DUAL EXERCISES. INSTRUCTIONS FOR PROBLEMS 31 and 32

In each problem, use the variables indicated and write the dual problem.

31. Use the variables Y_1, Y_2, and Y_3. Write the dual to problem 8. Do not attempt to solve the problem.

32. Use the variables Y_1, Y_2, and Y_3. Write the dual to problem 24. Do not attempt to solve the problem.

DUAL EXERCISES. INSTRUCTIONS FOR PROBLEMS 33-35

The primal problem formulation and the final (optimal) tableau of the primal problem are given. In each problem, do the following:

 a. Write the dual problem.
 b. State the value of each dual variable.
 c. State the value of the dual objective function.
 d. Verify that total contribution is the sum of the contributions of the individual resources.
 e. Determine how much the price of X_2 would have to increase before this process became profitable.
 f. Would we utilize a proposed new process that has a profit contribution of $2 and consumes 1 unit of each productive resource? Would we utilize the process if it had a profit contribution of .95 and used 1 unit of the first and third resources only?

33. Max $Z = 2X_1 + 1X_2 + 2.5X_3$

 s.t. $2X_1 + 2X_2 + 3X_3 \leqslant 29$ (labor)

 $4X_1 + 1X_2 + 1X_3 \leqslant 20$ (machine time)

 $2X_1 + 2X_2 + 2X_3 \leqslant 20$ (raw material)

 $X_1, X_2, X_3 \geqslant 0$

0 Row	Price vector	Solution vector	Quantity vector	2 X_1	1 X_2	2.5 X_3	0 S_1	0 S_2	0 S_3
I	2.5	X_3	9	0	0	1	1	0	−1
II	0	S_2	7	0	−3	0	3	1	−5
III	2	X_1	1	1	1	0	−1	0	$3/2$
NC		−Z	−24.50	0	−1	0	−$1/2$	0	−$1/2$

34. Max $Z = 5X_1 + 4X_2 + 10X_3 + 8X_4$

s.t. $1X_1 + 1X_2 + 1X_3 + 1X_4 \leqslant 120$ (labor)

$1X_1 + 2X_2 + 4X_3 + 4X_4 \leqslant 420$ (material A)

$2X_1 + 4X_2 + 2X_3 + 4X_4 \leqslant 380$ (material B)

$4X_1 + 5X_2 + 5X_3 + 2X_4 \leqslant 400$ (material C)

$X_1, X_2, X_3, X_4 \geqslant 0$

0 Row	Price vector	Solution vector	Quantity vector	5 X_1	4 X_2	10 X_3	8 X_4	0 S_1	0 S_2	0 S_3	0 S_4
Final tableau											
I	5	X_1	20	1	$6/9$	0	0	$12/9$	−$3/9$	0	0
II	8	X_4	60	0	−$2/9$	0	1	$11/9$	$1/9$	0	−$3/9$
III	0	S_3	20	0	$22/9$	0	0	−$40/9$	−$2/9$	1	$6/9$
IV	10	X_3	40	0	$5/9$	1	0	−$14/9$	$2/9$	0	$3/9$
NC		−Z	−980	0	−$28/9$	0	0	−$8/9$	−$13/9$	0	−$6/9$

35. Max $Z = 2X_1 + 3X_2 + 1X_3$

s.t. $2X_1 + 2X_2 + 6X_3 \leqslant 30$ (labor)

$2X_1 + 3X_2 + 4X_3 \leqslant 36$ (material)

$3X_1 + 4X_2 + 6X_3 \leqslant 49$ (machine time)

$X_1, X_2, X_3 \geqslant 0$

0 Row	Price vector	Solution vector	Quantity vector	2 X_1	3 X_2	1 X_3	0 S_1	0 S_2	0 S_3
I	0	S_1	4	0	0	2	1	2	−2
II	3	X_2	10	0	1	0	0	3	−2
III	2	X_1	3	1	0	2	0	−4	+3
NC		−Z	−36	0	0	−3	0	−1	0

RIGHT-HAND-SIDE RANGING. INSTRUCTIONS FOR PROBLEMS 36–38

Each of the following problems is concerned with establishing ranges of applicability for the marginal values, or shadow prices, of the productive resources. Answer each question as asked.

36. Consider problem 33.
    a. How much labor power can be added before the present contribution of $.50 will change? How much can be subtracted?
    b. The present shadow prices of machine time and raw material are $.00 and $.50 respectively. Over what range of resource availability are these values applicable?
37. Consider problem 34.
    a. Over what range of resource availability are the marginal contributions of materials A, B, and C applicable?
    b. How much labor could be added before the shadow price would change?
38. Consider problem 35. Determine the interval, or range of applicability, of the present shadow prices of labor, material, and machine time.

INSTRUCTIONS FOR PROBLEMS 39–41
The following problems are concerned with the sensitivity of the optimal solution to changes in the objective function coefficients.
39. In problem 33, give an interval for the objective function coefficients X_1, X_2, and X_3 such that the optimal solution does not change.
40. In problem 34, give an interval for the objective function coefficients of X_1, X_2, and X_3 such that the optimal solution does not change.
41. In problem 35, determine an interval for the objective function coefficients of all real variables such that the optimal solution does not change.

FORMULATION EXERCISES. INSTRUCTIONS FOR PROBLEMS 42–54
Formulate the following problems as linear programming problems. Use the appropriate equality or inequality sign. Label the constraints. Do not use slack or artificial variables, and do not attempt to solve these problems.
42. The Washington Company purchases two chemical mixtures (which they call mixture A and mixture B) and then extracts the chemicals xenthane and zethum from the mixtures. Chemical mixture A costs $4 per unit (100 gallons). The company can extract 2 gallons of xenthane and 1 gallon of zethum from 100 gallons of mixture A. Mixture B costs $3 per unit (100 gallons). The company can extract 1 gallon of xenthane and 3 gallons of zethum from 100 gallons of mixture B. During the next period, the company will need 16 gallons of xenthane and 18 gallons of zethum. The company wishes to minimize the cost of raw materials. What quantities of mixture A and mixture B should the Washington Company purchase in order to minimize cost and still have at least the required amount of xenthane and zethum?
43. In order to feed Albert the Alligator (the company mascot) the Adams Company mixes dog food and hog feed. A pound of the dog food used contains 5 units of vitamins, 15 units of protein, and 32 units of fat. It costs

$1 a pound. The hog feed purchased by the company costs $2 a pound, and each pound contains 20 units of vitamins, 10 units of protein, and 8 units of fat. Albert's minimum daily requirements are 100 units of vitamins, 150 units of protein, and 160 units of fat. What quantities of dog food and hog feed should be mixed daily in order to minimize cost and still keep Albert healthy?

44. In problem 43, assume that instead of concerning itself with cost, the company wants a mix that will give Albert as little feed as possible and still meet all of his minimum daily requirements.

45. In problem 43, assume that instead of concerning itself with cost, the company wants a mix that will exactly meet all requirements or exceed them by as small an amount as possible.

46. The Jefferson Company is considering purchasing a number of radio spot commercials. A morning spot costs $20 and is estimated to reach 200 teen-agers, 400 homemakers, and 200 retired people. An afternoon spot costs $10 and is estimated to reach 300 teen-agers, 100 homemakers, and 200 retired people. An evening commercial costs $30 and is expected to reach 200 teen-agers, 100 homemakers, and 20 retired people. What advertising mix should the Jefferson Company use if it wants its commercials to be heard daily by at least 3000 teen-agers, 2000 homemakers, and 200 retired people? The company wants the least-cost mix that will satisfy these constraints.

47. The Madison Company produces two types of cough syrup (type Y and type Z) from three different drugs (A, B, and C). The company purchases drugs A, B, and C for $10, $12, and $14 per gallon respectively. The selling prices of syrups Y and Z are $25 and $30 per gallon respectively. Syrup Y must be at least 60% drug A. Syrup Y must also contain at least twice as much of drug A as of drug B. Syrup Z must contain exactly the same amount of drug B as of drug C. In addition, the amount of drug A in syrup Z must be 30% or less. Trade restrictions prevent the company from purchasing more than 150 gallons of any drug or more than 300 gallons of all drugs. The company wishes to maximize contribution to profit. Demand is excellent.

48. The Monroe Chemical Company uses a common production process to convert two chemicals, chemical A and chemical B, to two different drugs, drug Y and drug Z. The company has 10,000 hours of production process time available during the next production period. Each gallon of drug Y produced requires 5 hours of production process time, and each gallon of drug Z requires 7 hours of production process time. There are blending requirements. Drug Y must be at least 10% chemical A. Drug Z must contain at least twice as much chemical B as chemical A. The company can sell all it can produce. The company buys chemical A for $11 a gallon and chemical B for $13 a gallon; it sells drug Y for $25 a gallon and drug Z for $30 a gallon. The object is to maximize profit contribution.

49. Assume that in problem 48 there is a national shortage of chemical A. The company would like to minimize the use of chemical A and at the same time

assure itself of a net contribution to profit of $10,000 during the next production period. Modify problem 48 to accomplish this objective.

50. Consider problem 2 in Chapter 5. The company would like to plan a three-period production schedule to meet a projected demand of 10, 8, and 12 tables and 6, 8, and 10 chairs in the next three periods. The firm has an initial inventory of 5 tables and 5 chairs. It wants to have an inventory of at least 4 tables and 2 chairs at the end of the third period. The company's assembly center is available for 2000, 3000, and 1500 minutes in the three periods. The availability of the company's finishing center is limited to 1680, 1200, and 2400 units in the three periods. Any inventory held at the end of a period costs the firm $.30 per unit. No chairs can be produced in the second period. All other factors remain the same.

51. The Jackson Company has two processes to convert lumber into plywood. Process X_1 utilizes 1 board foot of lumber and produces .6 board foot of grade A plywood, .3 board foot of grade B plywood, and .1 board foot of scrap. Process X_2 utilizes 1 board foot of lumber and produces .4 board foot of grade A plywood, .4 board foot of grade B plywood, and .2 board foot of scrap. The only direct cost associated with these processes is the cost of lumber, which is $1 per board foot. The company has two more processes to convert plywood into boxes. Process X_3 produces 1 "big box" and requires 8 board feet of grade A plywood and 5 board feet of grade B plywood. Process X_4 produces 1 "little box" and requires 2 board feet of grade A plywood and 3 board feet of grade B plywood. Process X_3 contributes $30 to profit, and process X_4 contributes $10 to profit. (*Note:* This assumes that the cost of lumber has been charged to processes X_1 and X_2.) The company would like to maximize net profit, but it realizes that only 100,000 board feet of lumber are available during the next period. The company can sell all of the little boxes it can produce, but it must limit production of big boxes to 5000 or less. The objective is to maximize profit contribution.

52. The Van Buren Lumber Company converts pine and spruce into two different grades of plywood. The company presently has two processes (X_1 and X_2) available for the conversion process. When operated at a unit level, process X_1 requires 7000 board feet of spruce and 2000 board feet of pine to produce 4000 board feet of grade A plywood, 3000 board feet of grade B plywood, and 2000 board feet of scrap. (Assume that scrap has no value.) Process X_2 requires 5000 board feet of spruce and 5000 board feet of pine to produce 3000 board feet of grade A plywood, 6000 board feet of grade B plywood, and 1000 board feet of scrap. Process X_1 has a net contribution of $150 per unit, and process X_2 has a net contribution of $200 per unit. During the next production period, the supply of spruce is limited to 150,000 board feet and the supply of pine is limited to 250,000 board feet. The company can sell all of the plywood it produces and has a definite commitment for 25,000 board feet of grade A plywood. The objective is to maximize contribution to profit.

53. In problem 52, the Van Buren Company has just learned that it can sell its scrap wood. A cabinet maker will purchase any type of scrap wood for $30 per 1000 board feet. The cabinet maker will purchase any quantity up to 50,000 board feet, but he will accept no more than 50,000 board feet during the production period. No other market for scrap wood is known. Reformulate the problem to maximize profit contribution.

54. The Harrison Florist Company uses cardboard to produce artificial flowers. The company buys cardboard in units of 1 square yard and stamps (cuts) each unit into one of three different patterns. Pattern 1 (X_1) produces 70 roses and 20 carnations. Pattern 2 (X_2) produces 60 roses and 60 carnations. Pattern 3 (X_3) produces 23 roses and 117 carnations. The only controllable cost in these stamping processes is the cost of the cardboard, which is $10 per square yard. The company sells two types of floral arrangements. Arrangement 1 (X_4) requires 8 roses and 4 carnations. Arrangement 2 (X_5) requires 3 roses and 12 carnations. Arrangement 1 (X_4) has a net contribution of $7 and arrangement 2 ($X_5$) has a net contribution of $5. (*Note:* Net contribution includes all controllable costs and revenues *except the cost of cardboard*.) The company must produce all the flowers it uses in the floral arrangements. Cardboard supply is limited to 1000 units. The company has agreed to sell at least 40 units of floral arrangement 1 (X_4), and it knows that it cannot sell more than 200 units of floral arrangement 1 (X_4) during the coming period. The objective is to maximize contribution to profit.

Supplementary readings

Bell, C. E. *Quantitative Methods for Administration*. Homewood, Ill.: Irwin, 1977.

Bierman, H., C. P. Bonini, and W. H. Hausman. *Quantitative Analysis for Business Decisions*. Homewood, Ill.: Irwin, 1977.

Budnick, F. S., R. Mojena, and T. E. Vollman. *Principles of Operations Research for Management*. Homewood, Ill.: Irwin, 1977.

Eck, R. D. *Operations Research for Business*. Belmont, Calif.: Wadsworth, 1976.

Hadley, G. W. *Linear Programming*. Reading, Mass.: Addison-Wesley, 1962.

Hartley, R. V. *Operations Research: A Managerial Emphasis*. Pacific Palisades, Calif.: Goodyear, 1976.

Hillier, F. S., and G. J. Lieberman. *Introduction to Operations Research*. San Francisco: Holden-Day, 1974.

Hughes, A. J., and D. E. Grawoig. *Linear Programming: An Emphasis on Decision Making*. Reading, Mass.: Addison-Wesley, 1973.

Shamblin, J. E., and G. T. Stevens. *Operations Research: A Fundamental Approach*. New York: McGraw-Hill, 1974.

Chapter 7

Linear programming: transportation and assignment methods

Illustrative example: KAPPA TILE COMPANY

Mr. H. D. Johnson is president and majority stockholder of the Kappa Tile Company, a large manufacturer of high-quality bathroom and patio tile. Mr. Johnson purchased the company approximately 20 years ago. At that time, the company had only one manufacturing plant, which was located in a small town in Tennessee. Kappa Tile Company has grown rapidly during the past 20 years. It is now one of the top five manufacturers of bathroom tile in the United States. Its Tennessee plant has quadrupled in size, and it has built two large new plants, one in Texas and one in the Midwestern area of the United States.

The company is concerned with a logistics problem that involves its major product line, white bathroom tile. This product accounts for 37% of the company's total sales volume. It is produced at all three of Kappa's manufacturing locations. The company's total volume of bathroom tile is sold to four major distributors located throughout the central part of the United States. The monthly requirements of the four distributors are 1500, 2000, 2500, and 3500 units. Each of the four distributors can be supplied from any of the company's manufacturing plants. There are production limitations, however, in that the Tennessee plant (plant 1), the Southwest plant (plant 2), and the Midwest plant (plant 3) are limited to monthly production of 3000, 2750, and 3750 units respectively.

The Kappa Company must pay shipping costs on all tile, and Mr. Johnson believes that the company can save money by better allocating plant production. He has asked the chief accountant for an estimate of the per-unit shipping cost from each manufacturing plant to each distributor. These costs in dollars are as follows:

		Distributors			
		1	2	3	4
	1	$15	$18	$22	$26
Plants	2	21	25	16	23
	3	14	19	20	24

After receiving the cost data, Mr. Johnson discussed his logistics problem with the chief engineer. He knows that the firm has been quite successful in utilizing managerial decision techniques such as linear programming to reduce production costs and hopes that a similar tool of analysis will help him reduce distribution costs.

Many applied problems have special mathematical structures that allow us to solve them by utilizing procedures that are computationally more efficient than the standard simplex method. These include finding the shortest or longest route through a network, assigning labor power to specified tasks, and analyzing an equipment replacement problem. The logistics problem at the Kappa Tile Company can be solved by the *transportation method,* one of the most useful and well-known special-purpose algorithms. In this analysis, we shall first set up the Kappa Tile problem as a standard linear programming problem. We shall then investigate the special properties that allow us to analyze it and similar problems by the transportation method. We can then proceed to analyze the problem with the assistance of the transportation method.

Standard linear programming formulation of a transportation problem

Figure 7.1 is a schematic representation of the Kappa Tile problem, that of finding the least-cost method of getting production from plants to distributors. Mr. Johnson has twelve alternatives from which to choose. For convenience, he decides to use doubly subscripted variables as follows:

X_{11} = Number of units shipped from plant 1 to warehouse 1

X_{12} = Number of units shipped from plant 1 to warehouse 2

In general,

X_{ij} = Number of units shipped from plant i to warehouse j

Objective function

Mr. Johnson's objective is to minimize total transportation cost. We obtain total transportation cost by multiplying the amount shipped over each route by the per-unit shipping cost for that route and summing these costs for all routes. Thus, the objective function is

$$\text{Min } Z = 15X_{11} + 18X_{12} + 22X_{13} + 26X_{14} + 21X_{21} + 25X_{22} + 16X_{23}$$
$$+ 23X_{24} + 14X_{31} + 19X_{32} + 20X_{33} + 24X_{34}$$

Figure 7.1 *Schematic representation of the transportation problem at Kappa Tile Company*

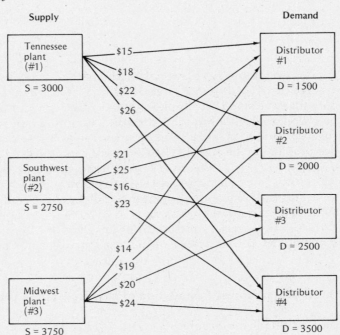

Demand constraints

Mr. Johnson is concerned with two types of constraints. There are four demand constraints, which state that the amount requested by each distributor must be shipped to that distributor. Likewise, there are three supply constraints, which state that the amount shipped from a particular plant cannot exceed available production capacity at that plant.

Let us first consider the *demand constraints.* Distributor 1 has asked for 1500 units of white bathroom tile. Mr. Johnson has a choice of shipping from plant 1, plant 2, plant 3, or some combination thereof. His only restriction is that the amount shipped from plant 1 to distributor 1, plus the amount shipped from plant 2 to distributor 1, plus the amount shipped from plant 3 to distributor 1 must equal 1500 units. Mathematically stated,

$$X_{11} + X_{21} + X_{31} = 1500 \qquad \text{(demand by distributor 1)}.$$

Likewise, the amounts shipped from the various plants to distributors

2, 3, and 4 must be 2000, 2500, and 3500 units respectively. Thus, the three remaining demand constraints are formulated as follows:

$$X_{12} + X_{22} + X_{32} = 2000 \quad \text{(demand by distributor 2)}$$
$$X_{13} + X_{23} + X_{33} = 2500 \quad \text{(demand by distributor 3)}$$
$$X_{14} + X_{24} + X_{34} = 3500 \quad \text{(demand by distributor 4)}$$

Supply constraints

The three *supply constraints* state that the amount shipped from a manufacturing plant cannot exceed capacity. Note that in this problem, the amount requested by the four distributors exactly equals the total production capacity of the three manufacturing plants. Thus, the entire capacity of each plant will be utilized, and we can formulate our supply constraints as equality constraints. Doing so will simplify our computation.

First, let us consider plant 1. The amount shipped from plant 1 to distributor 1, plus the amount shipped from plant 1 to distributor 2, plus the amount shipped from plant 1 to distributor 3, plus the amount shipped from plant 1 to distributor 4 must equal 3000 units. Mathematically formulated,

$$X_{11} + X_{12} + X_{13} + X_{14} = 3000 \quad \text{(supply by plant 1)}$$

Likewise, the supply constraints for plants 2 and 3 are formulated as follows:

$$X_{21} + X_{22} + X_{23} + X_{24} = 2750 \quad \text{(supply by plant 2)}$$
$$X_{31} + X_{32} + X_{33} + X_{34} = 3750 \quad \text{(supply by plant 3)}$$

This problem, like all linear programming problems, has nonnegativity constraints. All X's must be nonnegative.

It would be helpful to restate our linear programming problem and put it into standard form, as shown in Table 7.1. Obviously, we could solve this problem by the standard simplex method. This would result in the following unique optimal solution: $Z = \$181,750$, $X_{11} = 1000$, $X_{12} = 2000$, $X_{23} = 2500$, $X_{24} = 250$, $X_{31} = 500$, and $X_{34} = 3250$.

It is interesting to note that the Kappa Tile problem has one *redundant constraint*. In other words, one constraint is unnecessary, because it is simply a combination of the other six. *This is true for any problem that can be solved by the transportation method.* When solving the Kappa Tile problem by the simplex method, we could drop any one of the seven constraints and still obtain the same unique optimal solution.

Table 7.1 *Mathematical statement of the Kappa Tile Company problem*

Min $Z = 15X_{11} + 18X_{12} + 22X_{13} + 26X_{14} + 21X_{21} + 25X_{22} + 16X_{23} + 23X_{24} + 14X_{31} + 19X_{32} + 20X_{33} + 24X_{34}$

s.t.

$$1X_{11} + 1X_{12} + 1X_{13} + 1X_{14} = 3000$$
$$1X_{21} + 1X_{22} + 1X_{23} + 1X_{24} = 2750$$
$$X_{31} + X_{32} + X_{33} + X_{34} = 3750$$
$$X_{11} + X_{21} + X_{31} = 1500$$
$$X_{12} + X_{22} + X_{32} = 2000$$
$$X_{13} + X_{23} + X_{33} = 2500$$
$$X_{14} + X_{24} + X_{34} = 3500$$
$$X_{ij} \geqslant 0$$

Note: All terms with zero coefficients have been omitted.

Sample problem 7.1   ALPHA AERONAUTICAL PRODUCTS (AAP)

The Alpha Aeronautical Products Company (AAP) uses a certain chemical in its manufacturing process. The product is mined at three locations and shipped to the company's three manufacturing plants. Next month, the company expects to have 250 tons available at mine 1, 225 tons at mine 2, and 425 tons at mine 3. The monthly requirements at plants 1, 2, and 3 are 200, 300, and 400 tons respectively. Per-ton shipping costs are given in the following table.

	Plant 1	Plant 2	Plant 3
Mine 1	$6	$8	$5
Mine 2	9	2	4
Mine 3	4	7	6

The problem is to get available supply to the proper manufacturing locations while minimizing shipping costs. Formulate this as a standard linear programming problem. Let X_{ij} be the amount of chemical shipped from mine i to plant j.

SOLUTION

$$\text{Min } Z = 6X_{11} + 8X_{12} + 5X_{13} + 9X_{21} + 2X_{22} + 4X_{23} + 4X_{31} + 7X_{32} + 6X_{33}$$

$$
\begin{aligned}
\text{s.t.} \quad X_{11} + X_{12} + X_{13} &= 250 \\
X_{21} + X_{22} + X_{23} &= 225 \\
X_{31} + X_{32} + X_{33} &= 425 \\
X_{11} + X_{21} + X_{31} &= 200 \\
X_{12} + X_{22} + X_{32} &= 300 \\
X_{13} + X_{23} + X_{33} &= 400 \\
X_{ij} &\geq 0
\end{aligned}
$$

Simplifying features of the transportation problem

There is a much easier way of obtaining an optimal solution to Mr. Johnson's problem at Kappa Tile. Since this is a transportation problem, it can be solved by a special simplex algorithm known as the *transportation method*. It is important to know what characteristics, or special structures, a problem must have before it can be solved by the transportation method.

Structure of a transportation problem

We will define a *transportation problem* to be a linear programming problem that can be solved by the transportation method. Every transportation problem has the following set of characteristics.[1]

1. All constraints must be equality constraints.
2. The sum of the supplies must equal the sum of the demands.
3. Each coefficient in the constraint matrix must be either 1, -1, or 0.
4. Each column of the constraint matrix, except for the supply-and-demand quantity column on the right-hand side of the equality sign, must have exactly two nonzero elements.

From Table 7.1, it is easy to verify that the Kappa Tile problem meets all four requirements. It is therefore a transportation problem and can be analyzed with the assistance of the transportation method.

The transportation table

The special structure of a transportation problem allows us to present the relevant data in a concise format known as a *transportation table*. This table serves as a convenient framework for displaying and reviewing data concerned with each iteration of the transportation method. It is analogous to the simplex tableau we used in Chapter 6. Figure 7.2 is a standard transportation table constructed especially for the Kappa Tile problem. The following rules for formulating a transportation table are general, however, and can be used to construct any transportation table.

1. The transportation table contains one row for each source of supply and one column for each demand point.
2. The supply availabilities of each supply point are given in an "Availability" column to the right of the main body of the table. (In the case of Kappa Tile, the capacities of plants 1, 2, and 3 are 3000, 2750, and 3750 respectively.)
3. The demand requirements of each of the demand points are given in a "Requirements" row below the main body of the table. (In the case of Kappa Tile, distributors 1, 2, 3, and 4 have demand requirements of 1500, 2000, 2500, and 3500 respectively.) Taken together, the supply availabilities and demand requirements are often called *rim values* or *rim requirements* of a transportation problem.
4. There should always be a one-to-one correspondence between the squares or cells in the main body of the table and the decision

---

[1] Few real problems exactly meet all of these specifications. Many problems, however, are readily transformed into transportation problems and solved by the transportation method. We will discuss this procedure later in the chapter.

Figure 7.2 *The transportation table for the Kappa Tile Company problem*

Supply \ Demand		Distributors				Availability
		1	2	3	4	
Plants	1	15 X_{11}*	18 X_{12}	22 X_{13}	26 X_{14}	3000
	2	21 X_{21}	25 X_{22}	16 X_{23}	23 X_{24}	2750
	3	14 X_{31}	19 X_{32}	20 X_{33}	24 X_{34}	3750
Requirements		1500	2000	2500	3500	9500

*X_{ij} not usually included in table

variables of the standard linear programming problem. (The Kappa Tile Company problem has 12 decision variables. In Figure 7.2, we have 12 cells, and each of these 12 cells relates directly to a decision variable. For illustrative purposes, we have inserted the symbolic representations of the decision variables, such as X_{13}, into the cells of the transportation table.)

5. The "boxed-in" value in the upper right-hand corner of each table cell is the objective function coefficient of the relevant decision variable. (In the case of Kappa Tile, the 15 in cell (1-1) tells us it costs $15 to ship one unit of tile from plant 1 to distributor 1.) To obtain the value of the objective function, all we need to do is multiply the value of a cell by the per-unit cost of the cell and sum for all cells.

We should note the correspondence between the constraints in the standard linear programming format, as given in Table 7.1, and the rows and columns in the transportation table, as shown in Figure 7.2. The first row in Figure 7.2 is the first supply constraint. The second row is the second supply constraint, and the third row is the supply constraint for plant 3. Likewise, the first column is the first demand constraint, and the second, third, and fourth columns are the demand constraints for the second, third, and fourth distributors. Thus, the objective function and all seven constraints are neatly compressed into the transportation table.

The transportation simplex algorithm

The procedure discussed in the following sections is usually referred to as the *transportation method.* We should remember, however, that it is nothing more than a simplified version of the simplex procedure discussed in Chapter 5. The transportation method is an iterative optimizing technique. It utilizes the same six basic steps that we encountered in our discussion of the simplex method in Chapters 5 and 6. As we shall see, the special mathematical structure of a transportation problem greatly simplifies each of these six steps. Before proceeding, however, we should review the flow diagram of the simplex process shown in Figure 5.7.

Step 1: Obtaining an initial solution

The first step in the transportation method is to find an initial solution that satisfies all of the constraint equations. In the standard simplex procedure, this requires the use of slack variables and artificial variables. In the transportation method, we can utilize the transportation table and perform this step directly without adding any artificial variables.

There are many methods of finding an initial solution. The *northwest corner method* of finding an initial solution is often used, because it is simple, logical, and systematic. It consists of the following five steps.

1. Begin in the upper left-hand cell (the northwest corner) of the main body of the transportation table. Insert into this cell the largest value that exceeds neither the supply constraint nor the demand constraint.
2. If the supply constraint is satisfied, move to step 3. If the supply constraint is not satisfied, move one cell to the right in the same row. Insert into that cell the largest value that exceeds neither the supply for that row nor the demand for that column. Remember that in determining whether or not demand or supply is exceeded, you must consider all cell values previously entered in that row or column. If supply is still not exhausted, repeat this step until the supply constraint is satisfied.
3. When the supply for a particular row is satisfied, move down to the next cell in the same column. Insert into this cell the largest value that exceeds neither the supply for that row nor the unfilled demand for that column. Remember that in determining whether demand is exceeded, you must consider all values previously entered in that column.
4. Return to step 2 and repeat steps 2 and 3 until all rim requirements have been satisfied.

5. Determine the objective function value of the solution by multiplying the value in each cell by the objective function coefficient, and then sum for all cells. Note that step 5 is not mandatory, because we can apply the transportation method without knowing the initial objective function value. It is helpful, however, to determine how much cost improvement is obtained at each iteration.

Let us use the northwest corner method to obtain an initial solution to the Kappa Tile problem. Figure 7.3 gives this initial solution. We began with cell (1-1) and inserted a value of 1500 units. This is the maximum value that we could enter, because any larger value would have exceeded the demand requirements for column 1.

Since the 1500 units did not exhaust the supply requirements of row 1, we moved to cell (1-2). Again, the largest value we could enter into this cell is 1500, because any larger number would have exceeded the supply availability for row 1. When the supply availability of row 1 was exhausted, we moved down to cell (2-2). The largest value that we could enter here is 500; any larger value would have exceeded the demand requirements for that column.

Next, we moved to cell (2-3) and entered 2250 units. Again, this is the largest value that we could enter without exceeding supply availability of 2750 for the row. Proceeding in the same manner, we determine that the proper value for cell (3-3) is 250 and that the value for cell (3-4) is 3500.

Figure 7.3 *Initial solution to the Kappa Tile problem*

Supply \ Demand		Distributors				
		1	2	3	4	Availability
Plants	1	15 1500	18 1500	22	26	3000
	2	21	25 500	16 2250	23	2750
	3	14	19	20 250	24 3500	3750
Requirements		1500	2000	2500	3500	9500

O.F. = 1500(15) + 1500(18) + 500(25) + 2250(16) + 250(20) + 3500(24)
    = 22,500 + 27,000 + 12,500 + 36,000 + 5000 + 84,000 = 187,000

As in Chapter 6, it is important to give a verbal "translation" of the solution we have represented in our transportation table. The value of 1500 that we have entered into cell (1-1) indicates that the decision variable X_{11} has a value of 1500 in the initial solution. This means that if this initial solution were actually put into operation, the Kappa Tile Company would be shipping 1500 units from plant 1 to distributor 1. The value of 1500 in cell (1-2) indicates that the additional 1500 units of production at plant 1 would be shipped to distributor 2. By the same reasoning, we know that in this solution, the company is shipping 500 units from plant 2 to distributor 2; 2250 units from plant 2 to distributor 3; 250 units from plant 3 to distributor 3; and 3500 units from plant 3 to distributor 4. We should verify that when this solution is applied each distributor receives the correct amount of bathroom tile and the correct amount of tile is shipped from each manufacturing location.

The objective of Kappa Tile Company is to minimize the cost of shipping merchandise from plant to distributor. We obtain the cost of this initial solution by multiplying the amount shipped over each route by the per-unit cost of shipping over that route and then summing for all routes used. These calculations are shown at the bottom of Figure 7.3, where the cost of this solution is found to be $187,000.

In Figure 7.3, there are a number of cells to which no value was assigned. These cells are referred to as *unused squares, cells,* or *routes.* They represent routes that are not being used in that particular solution. In other words, no units are shipped over a route represented by an unused square. In any solution, the number of used squares should be one less than the number of supply points plus the number of demand points. That is, the *number of used squares should be equal to the number of rows plus the number of columns minus one.* Wherever a solution has less than this number of used squares, a condition of *degeneracy* exists, which causes problems in the transportation method. Later in this chapter, we shall show how to handle the degeneracy problem. For the moment, we shall limit ourselves to testing each solution for degeneracy.

You may wonder why the number of used squares is limited to the number of rows plus the number of columns minus one. Each row in the transportation table represents a supply constraint, and each column represents a demand constraint. Thus, the number of rows plus the number of columns is equal to the number of supply and demand constraints in the standard linear programming formulation, illustrated in Table 7.1. Remember, however, that every situation that meets the definition of a transportation problem has one redundant constraint. The number of relevant constraints is therefore one less than the total number of rows and columns in the transportation table. In finding an optimal solution, we do not have to consider solutions wherein the number of used cells is greater than the number of rows plus the number of columns minus one.

The northwest corner procedure is only one method of obtaining an initial solution. Other available procedures often yield a solution that is closer to the optimal solution, so less computational work is required to obtain the optimal solution. One such procedure is the *Vogel approximation method*,[2] which is especially helpful in solving large transportation problems.

In many real situations, a company may wish to improve on a solution that is presently in operation. In such cases, the solution presently being used may be a good initial solution. Finally, the reader should realize that judgment and intuition often provide an initial solution that is close to optimal.

Step 2: Evaluating the net contribution of unused routes

The second step in the transportation method is to evaluate the net contribution of routes that are not being used. In simple terms, we are to determine, for each unused cell in the transportation table, how much the objective function would increase or decrease if one unit of material were shipped over this route.

Two alternative procedures are commonly used for evaluating the unused routes. We will discuss the stepping stone method in this section, because it is generally considered the easiest to visualize and comprehend. Later in this chapter, we shall discuss the modified distribution or dual evaluation method.

The purpose of the *stepping stone method* is to determine what would happen to total cost if one unit of material were shipped over a route that is presently not being used. In order to illustrate this procedure, let us consider the unused cell (1-3) in Figure 7.4(a).

The addition of one unit to (1-3) would mean that the Kappa Tile Company is shipping 3001 units from plant 1. This is not possible, of course, because the capacity of plant 1 is 3000 units. To compensate, we have to decrease shipments by one unit to either distributor 1 or distributor 2. Let us assume that we reduce the shipment to distributor 2 (cell 1-2). This change means that distributor 2 is not receiving the full order of 2000 units. To compensate, we must add another unit to route (2-2). This adjustment takes care of the demand to distributor 2, but we now have plant 2 shipping one more unit than its capacity of 2750 units. We take care of this by reducing the shipment over route (2-3) by one unit. Fortunately, the last adjustment not only brings shipments from

---

[2]A discussion of the Vogel approximation method appears in Ross H. Johnson and Paul R. Winn, *Quantitative Methods for Management,* Houghton Mifflin, Boston, 1976, pp. 263–265.

Figure 7.4 *Evaluation of unused routes in the initial solution of the Kappa Tile problem*

(a) Evaluation of route (1-3)

Supply \ Demand (Distributors)	1	2	3	4	Availability
Plants 1	1500 [15]	1500 [18] (−1)	[22] (+1)	[26]	3000
Plants 2	[21]	500 [25] (+1)	2250 [16] (−1)	[23]	2750
Plants 3	[14]	[19]	250 [20]	3500 [24]	3750
Requirements	1500	2000	2500	3500	9500

Net contribution (1-3) = +22 – 18 + 25 – 16 = +13

(b) Evaluation of route (3-1)

Supply \ Demand (Distributors)	1	2	3	4	Availability
Plants 1	1500 [15] (−1)	1500 [18] (+1)	[22]	[26]	3000
Plants 2	[21]	500 [25] (−1)	2250 [16] (+1)	[23]	2750
Plants 3	[14] (+1)	[19]	250 [20] (−1)	3500 [24]	3750
Requirements	1500	2000	2500	3500	9500

Net contribution (3-1) = +14 – 20 + 16 –25 + 18 – 15 = –12

plant 2 back to capacity, but also reduces the shipment to distributor 3 to the required 2500 units. This completes our chain of adjustments.

Before proceeding, refer to Figure 7.4(a) to be sure you understand the adjustments that were made. The object of this chain of adjustments is to see what happens to total cost when an additional unit is added to cell (1-3). The addition of one unit over route (1-3) added $22 to total cost. At the same time, however, we subtracted one unit from route (1-2) for a saving of $18, added a unit to route (2-2) at a cost of $25, and subtracted a unit from route (2-3) for a saving of $16. Thus, the net contribution of adding one unit to route (1-3) is a cost increase of $13, which is calculated as follows:

$$\$22 - \$18 + \$25 - \$16 = \$13$$

This calculation tells us that if we actually added one unit to route (1-3), we would add $13 to total cost, which is not desirable. Before making any decisions on route adjustments, we want to determine the net contribution of all unused cells. Later, we will discuss additional examples of this cell evaluation calculation. Before doing so, however, let us formulate a set of rules to use in evaluating routes.

The following procedure is used to evaluate the net contribution of unused cells in the transportation table.

1. Beginning with the unused cell to be evaluated, trace a closed path from this cell via other used cells back to the original unused cell that you are evaluating. In a correctly formulated problem, only one closed path exists for any unused cell in any particular solution. The closed path may skip over either used or unused cells. Turns (or corners) on the closed path may be made only on used squares. In other words, except for the route being evaluated, no units may be added to or subtracted from an unused cell.
2. On the closed path, assign a plus (+) to each route to which a unit is being added and a minus (−) to each route from which a unit is being subtracted. Do this by beginning with a plus (+) in the route being evaluated and then alternately placing a minus (−) and a plus (+) on each corner of the closed path.
3. Determine the net contribution of this chain of adjustments by adding the per-unit costs of all routes containing a plus sign and subtracting the per-unit costs of all routes containing a minus sign. The resulting net contribution may be either positive, negative, or zero — indicating an increase, a decrease, or no change in total cost.

In order to illustrate these rules, let us consider route (3-1) in the initial solution to the Kappa Tile problem. The evaluation of this route is illustrated in Figure 7.4(b). The closed path is no longer a simple

Figure 7.5 *Transportation table of the Kappa Tile initial solution, showing net contribution values of unused routes*

Supply \ Demand		Distributors				Availability
		1	2	3	4	
Plants	1	15 / 1500	18 / 1500	22 / (+13)	26 / (+13)	3000
	2	21 / (−1)	25 / 500	16 / 2250	23 / (+3)	2750
	3	14 / (−12)	19 / (−10)	20 / 250	24 / 3500	3750
Requirements		1500	2000	2500	3500	9500

O.F. = 1500(15) + 1500(18) + 500(25) + 2250(16) + 250(20) + 3500(24)
     = 22,500 + 27,000 + 12,500 + 36,000 + 5000 + 84,000 = 187,000

square, but a zig-zag path that requires three additions and three subtractions. The net contribution can be determined as follows:

$$+14 - 20 + 16 - 25 + 18 - 15 = -12$$

Thus, the addition of one unit to this cell would reduce total cost by $12.

Figure 7.5 gives the net contribution values for all unused routes. These values have been circled to distinguish them from the quantity values in the used routes.

Before moving to step 3 of the simplex method, we should consider two additional and more complex examples of route evaluation. Consider the solution to the transportation problem given in Figure 7.6. In Figure 7.6(a), the closed path necessary to evaluate route (2-4) is shown. Note that this crossover pattern is not only permissible, but is often necessary to evaluate a particular route. With large tables, the closed path may resemble a large and complicated crossover pattern.

In Figure 7.6(b), the closed path necessary to evaluate route (3-1) is shown. This path illustrates that it is sometimes necessary to skip a used square in the evaluation process. In this particular example, we skipped over route (4-2) in constructing our closed path.

Step 3: Testing for optimality

In step 3, we should ask the question: "Can the objective function be improved by utilizing any route that we are presently not using?" If the

Figure 7.6 *Additional examples of cell evaluation*

(a) Evaluation of cell (2-4) — "crossover closed path"

Supply \ Demand		Distributors 1	Distributors 2	Distributors 3	Distributors 4	Availability
Plants	1	‎ 3	100 ⊕+1 8	2	400 ⊖−1 8	500
	2	150 ⊖−1 2	4	7	⊕+1 9	150
	3	8	6	350 10	3	350
	4	250 ⊕+1 6	300 ⊖−1 5	200 7	4	750
Requirements		400	400	550	400	1750

Net contribution = + 9 − 8 + 8 − 5 + 6 − 2 = + 8

(b) Evaluation of cell (3-1)—"skipping a used cell"

Supply \ Demand		Distributors 1	Distributors 2	Distributors 3	Distributors 4	Availability
Plants	1	3	100 8	2	400 8	500
	2	150 2	4	7	9	150
	3	⊕+1 8	6	350 ⊖−1 10	3	350
	4	250 ⊖−1 6	300 5	200 ⊕+1 7	4	750
Requirements		400	400	550	400	1750

Net contribution = + 8 − 6 + 7 − 10 = −1

answer is "no," we have found the optimal solution. If there *is* an unused route that will improve the objective function value, we should continue the transportation method and move to step 4. For a minimization problem, all unused routes with negative net contribution values represent potential cost reductions, while unused routes with positive values represent potential cost increases. For a minimization problem, then, the solution is optimal if all net contribution values are positive.

For a maximization problem, the solution is optimal if all net contribution values are negative.

Note from Figure 7.5 that in the Kappa Tile Company problem, there are three routes, X_{21}, X_{31}, and X_{32}, that have negative net contribution values. The solution is therefore not an optimal solution.

Step 4: Selecting the route to begin utilizing

Step 4 is the easiest step in the transportation method. In a minimization problem, we simply select the route with the smallest (most negative) net contribution value. If a tie exists for the smallest value, we may select either route. In a maximization problem, we select the route with the largest net contribution value. The Kappa Tile Company problem is a minimization problem. From Figure 7.5, we know that route (3-1) has the smallest net contribution value, so we select this route to utilize at the next iteration.

Sample problem 7.2   AAP (Continued)

Consider the AAP problem given in Sample Problem 7.1. Construct a transportation table for this problem, use the northwest corner method to obtain an initial solution, and then use the stepping stone method to evaluate the net contribution of unused routes. What is the objective function value of this initial solution?

SOLUTION

Demand / Supply		Manufacturing locations			Availability
		1	2	3	
Mines	1	6 200	8 50	5 (−2)	250
	2	9 (+9)	2 225	4 (+3)	225
	3	4 (−1)	7 25	6 400	425
Requirements		200	300	400	900

O.F. = 200(6) + 50(8) + 225(2) + 25(7) + 400(6)
  = 1200 + 400 + 450 + 175 + 2400 = 4625

Step 5: Determining the amount to ship over the selected route

At this point in the Kappa Tile problem, we have decided to begin utilizing route (3-1). We must now decide how many units to ship over this route. Each unit shipped over this route will reduce total cost by $12, so we would like to utilize this route to the fullest extent possible. In Figure 7.4(b), we constructed a closed path to evaluate the net contribution of cell (3-1). In this closed path, we added to cells (3-1), (2-3), and (1-2), which are called *positive corners,* and we subtracted from cells (3-3), (2-2), and (1-1), which are called *negative corners.* The maximum quantity that can be assigned to route (3-1) is equal to the value of the negative corner of the closed path that has the smallest value. This must be true, because any larger amount would cause some cell value to be negative, which is not allowed. In Figure 7.4(b), the negative corners have values of 250, 500, and 1500 respectively. The smallest of these is 250, and therefore 250 is the maximum number of units that can, at the next iteration, be shipped over route (3-1).

Step 6: Developing the new solution

In the standard simplex method, development of the new solution was an involved mathematical process. In the transportation method, the procedure is much simpler. First, values of routes not on the relevant closed path are carried forward "as is" from one iteration to the next. This is true for used and unused routes. For the Kappa Tile problem, these values have been carried forward to Figure 7.7(a), which gives the second solution. Second, 250 units are added to each positive corner of the relevant closed path, and 250 units are subtracted from each negative corner. The value 250 was previously determined to be the correct amount to ship over the new route (3-1).

In the initial solution, the positive corners of the closed path had values of 0, 2250, and 1500 respectively. After we add 250 units to each, the new values are 250, 2500, and 1750 respectively. The negative corners of the closed path had values of 250, 500, and 1500 respectively. After we subtract 250 units from each of these cells, the new values are 0, 250, and 1250 units respectively. These values have also been entered in Figure 7.7(a).

The objective function of the second solution is obtained as before, by multiplying the units shipped over each route by the per-unit cost of that route and then summing for all routes. The calculation of the objective function value of the second solution is shown in Figure 7.7(a). The value of $184,000 is an improvement of $3000 over the cost of the initial solution.

Step 6A: Analyzing and verifying the new table

Figure 7.7(a) represents a new solution to the Kappa Tile problem. We know that we should now return to step 2. Before doing so, we should

Figure 7.7 *Second and third (final) iterations of the Kappa Tile problem*

(a) Second iteration

Supply \ Demand		Distributors				Availability
		1	2	3	4	
Plants	1	15 1250	18 1750	22 (+13)	26 (+1)	3000
	2	21 (−1)	25 250	16 2500	23 (−9)	2750
	3	14 250	19 (+2)	20 (+12)	24 3500	3750
Requirements		1500	2000	2500	3500	9500

O.F. = 1250(15) + 1750(18) + 250(25) + 2500(16) + 250(14) + 3500(24)
    = 18,750 + 31,500 + 6250 + 40,000 + 3500 + 84,000 = 184,000

(b) Third (final) iteration

Supply \ Demand		Distributors				Availability
		1	2	3	4	
Plants	1	15 1000	18 2000	22 (+4)	26 (+1)	3000
	2	21 (+8)	25 (+9)	16 2500	23 250	2750
	3	14 500	19 (+2)	20 (+3)	24 3250	3750
Requirements		1500	2000	2500	3500	9500

O.F. = 1000(15) + 2000(18) + 2500(16) + 250(23) + 500(14) + 3250(24)
    = 15,000 + 36,000 + 40,000 + 5750 + 7000 + 78,000 = 181,750

Exhibit 7.1   QUESTIONS USED TO ANALYZE AND VERIFY A TRANSPORTATION
TABLE

1. What is the solution given in the table; that is, how much is being shipped
   from each source to each destination, and what is the cost of this shipping
   plan?
2. Does this solution satisfy all supply availabilities and demand requirements?
3. Did the objective function value increase (or decrease) by the amount
   expected from the previous table?
4. Are the correct number of cells being used?

analyze and verify the information in the second transportation table.
(Like step 6A for the simplex tableau, this step is not necessary after
each iteration. Again, it is a learning step that we should perform only
until we believe we understand all the information in each transportation table.) A convenient way of performing this step is to answer the
following series of questions, which are applied here to the Kappa Tile
problem and listed for easy reference in Exhibit 7.1.

1. *What is the solution given in the table?*
   If Kappa Tile used the solution given in Figure 7.7(a), plant 1
   would ship 1250 units to distributor 1 and 1750 units to distributor 2.
   Plant 2 would ship 250 units to distributor 2 and 2500 units to
   distributor 3. Plant 3 would ship 250 units to distributor 1 and 3500
   units to distributor 4. Total transportation cost of this shipping plan
   is $184,000.
2. *Does this solution satisfy all supply availabilities and demand
   requirements?*
   Yes. This solution calls for 3000, 2750, and 3750 units to be shipped
   from plants 1, 2, and 3 respectively, which are the appropriate
   capacities at these plants. Likewise, this solution satisfies the four
   distributor demand requirements of 1500, 2000, 2500, and 3500 units.
3. *Did the objective function value decrease by the amount expected from
   the first to the second solution?*
   Yes. In the initial solution, total cost was $187,000. The net contri-
   bution value of route (3-1) is −$12. Since we added 250 units to this
   route, we would expect total cost to decrease by $3000, from $187,000
   to $184,000. This is exactly what happened. This calculation serves as
   a convenient check on other calculations as we proceed from iteration to iteration.
4. *Are the correct number of cells being used?*
   Yes. Our transportation table contains three rows and four columns. The number of used cells should therefore be six. The solution
   in Figure 7.7(a) does have six used squares. (If this were not true, a

condition of degeneracy would exist, and we would have to follow special procedures discussed later in the chapter.)

Subsequent iterations

We should now return to step 2 and repeat the procedure until we reach an optimal solution. In Figure 7.7(a), there are two cells with negative net contribution values. Since route (2-4) has the most negative net contribution, we utilize it and perform another iteration. The results appear in Figure 7.7(b). This is an optimal solution; every unused route has a positive net contribution value.

The solution shown in Figure 7.7(b) tells Mr. Johnson that he should ship 1000 units from plant 1 to distributor 1 and 2000 units from plant 1 to distributor 2. Plant 2 should ship 2500 units to distributor 3 and 250 units to distributor 4. Plant 3 should ship 500 units to distributor 1 and 3250 units to distributor 4. From a standpoint of total transportation cost, this is an optimal routing plan. Mr. Johnson can do no better.

Sample problem 7.3   AAP (Continued)

Consider the AAP example given in Sample Problems 7.1 and 7.2. Use the transportation method to solve for the least-cost routing plan.

SOLUTION

(a) Second iteration

Supply \ Demand		1	2	3	Availability
		Manufacturing locations			
Mines	1	200 [6]	(+2) [8]	50 [5]	250
	2	(+7) [9]	225 [2]	(+3) [4]	225
	3	(−3) [4]	75 [7]	350 [6]	425
Requirements		200	300	400	900

O.F. = 200(6) + 50(5) + 225(2) + 75(7) + 350(6) = 4525

(b) Third (final) iteration

Supply \ Demand		Manufacturing locations			Availability
		1	2	3	
Mines	1	6 (+3)	8 (+2)	5 250	250
	2	9 (+10)	2 225	4 (+3)	225
	3	4 200	7 75	6 150	425
Requirements		200	300	400	900

O.F. = 250(5) + 225(2) + 200(4) + 75(7) + 150(6) = 3925

The unbalanced transportation problem

Earlier in this chapter, we listed a number of criteria that a problem must meet before it can be solved by the transportation method. While few real problems meet all of these specifications exactly, many problems can be easily transformed into transportation problems. We can analyze these problems with the aid of the transportation simplex algorithm. In the following sections, we will discuss the simplest and most useful of these transformations: the conversion of an *unbalanced problem*, wherein supply does not equal demand, into a *balanced problem*, wherein supply equals demand. This one conversion makes it possible to solve many real problems using the transportation method. Although we will not discuss them here, there are many other, generally more complex transformations that allow us to analyze even more varied problems with the assistance of the transportation method.

Supply exceeds demand

Let us slightly modify the Kappa Tile Company problem so that supply exceeds demand. Suppose the available capacity at plant 1 is increased to 3500 and the capacity at plant 2 is increased from 2750 to 3250. The capacity of plant 3 and all distributor requirements remain the same. Total supply is now 10,500 units, while total demand is only 9500 units. We have excess capacity of 1000 units. To balance this type of problem, we create a fictitious or *dummy demand* of 1000 units. This modification

Figure 7.8 *Transportation table for the unbalanced problem wherein supply exceeds demand*

Supply \ Demand		Distributors					Availability
		1	2	3	4	5	
Plants	1	15	18	22	26	0	
		500	2000			1000	3500
	2	21	25	16	23	0	
				2500	750		3250
	3	14	19	20	24	0	
		1000			2750		3750
Requirements		1500	2000	2500	3500	1000	10,500

O.F. = 500(15) + 2000(18) + 1000(0) + 2500(16) + 750(23) + 1000(14) + 2750(24)
     = 7500 + 36,000 +   0   + 40,000 + 17,250 + 14,000 + 66,000 = 180,750

allows the problem to fit the definition of a transportation problem. This *dummy distributor* will theoretically receive 1000 units of bathroom tile, though these 1000 units will never actually be produced or shipped. The per-unit cost of getting material to this dummy distributor is therefore zero.

Figure 7.8 is a transportation table for this modified problem. Note that a fifth column has been added to handle the dummy distributor. This column adds three new cells to the transportation table. Earlier, we stated that each cell corresponds to a decision variable in the standard linear programming formulation. With excess supply, the supply constraints of the Kappa Tile problem are properly formulated as less-than-or-equal-to constraints, because it is no longer necessary for a plant to ship its entire supply. The new cells, (1-5), (2-5), and (3-5), correspond to the slack variables we need to convert the supply constraints from inequalities into equalities. Like slack variables, they have objective function coefficients of zero.

The problem can now be solved exactly as we solved the original Kappa Tile Company problem. The solution given in Figure 7.8 is the optimal solution to the modified problem. The 1000 units in cell (1-5) are theoretically the amount shipped from plant 1 to the dummy distributor. These 1000 units in cell (1-5) actually tell us that we should allocate our excess capacity to plant 1. The optimal shipping policy is to ship 500 units from plant 1 to distributor 1; 2000 units from plant 1 to distributor 2; 2500 units from plant 2 to distributor 3; 750 units from plant 2 to distributor 4; 1000 units from plant 3 to distributor 1; and 2750 units from plant 3 to distributor 4. There will be 1000 units of excess capacity at plant 1. The cost of this new routing is $180,750.

Demand exceeds supply

If demand exceeds supply, we simply create a *dummy supply* by adding an additional row to our transportation table and then solve the problem by the same procedure we used in previous sections. You may find the concept of a dummy supply more difficult to visualize than the concept of a dummy demand. Remember, however, that this procedure will allocate available supply at minimum cost. The distributor who runs short must purchase from an outside source or perhaps go without supply.

The modified distribution (MODI) method

In step 2 of the transportation method, we used the stepping stone method to determine the net contribution of shipping routes that were not being used in a particular solution. A second method of evaluating routes is referred to as the *modified distribution* (MODI) or *dual evaluation method*. The MODI method is a more efficient procedure for calculating the net contribution values of unused routes. As the term "dual evaluation" implies, the MODI method is based on the dual linear programming problem discussed in Chapter 6. It is not necessary to understand this relationship in order to use the MODI method effectively. For the interested reader, the relationship between the MODI method and dual linear programming is explained later in this chapter.

Route evaluation using the MODI method

Figure 7.9 illustrates the procedures we use in the MODI method. Note that a new column has been added to the left of the table and a new row above the table. We will let V_1, V_2, and V_3 be the new row values and W_1, W_2, W_3, and W_4 be the new column values. In general, we will use the following terminology:

V_i = Value assigned to row i

W_j = Value assigned to column j

In the MODI method, we make extensive use of the cost factors associated with each cell, that is, the cost of shipping one unit over a given route. As in previous tables, this value appears in the upper

Figure 7.9 *Transportation table for a MODI solution*

Supply \ Demand			Distributors				Availability
		$W_1=$ 1	$W_2=$ 2	$W_3=$ 3	$W_4=$ 4		
$V_1=$	1	15 \ 1500	18 \ 1500	22	26		3000
$V_2=$	2	21	25 \ 500	16 \ 2250	23		2750
$V_3=$	3	14	19	20 \ 250	24 \ 3500		3750
Requirements		1500	2000	2500	3500		9500

right-hand corner of each cell. It is helpful to use the following symbolic notation:

C_{ij} = Per-unit cost of shipping over route ij

The key to using the MODI method is to utilize the used routes to solve for each V_i and W_j value and then use these values to calculate the net contributions of the unused cells. We will illustrate this procedure by again utilizing the initial solution to the original Kappa Tile problem. In this problem, total supply is equal to total demand. The solution, which we obtained by the northwest corner method, has been entered into Figure 7.9.

For every used cell, the following relationship is true:

$$V_i + W_j = C_{ij}$$

In Figure 7.9, we have six used squares, so the following six relationships must be true:

1. $V_1 + W_1 = 15$
2. $V_1 + W_2 = 18$
3. $V_2 + W_2 = 25$
4. $V_2 + W_3 = 16$
5. $V_3 + W_3 = 20$
6. $V_3 + W_4 = 24$

Since every transportation table contains one redundant constraint, we can choose one of these values arbitrarily. For simplicity, we will choose V_1 and set it equal to zero. From equations 1 and 2, we can solve for the values of W_1 and W_2, which are 15 and 18 respectively. We can then use the value of W_2 in equation 3 to obtain the value of V_2: $V_2 = 25 - 18 = 7$. We can use this value in equation 4 to determine the value of W_3. We proceed, equation by equation, until we have obtained the values of all V_i and W_j. The proper V_i and W_j values are

$$\begin{array}{ll}
V_1 = 0 & W_1 = 15 \\
V_2 = 7 & W_2 = 18 \\
V_3 = 11 & W_3 = 9 \\
& W_4 = 13
\end{array}$$

We should note two things about the MODI method. First, one value was assigned arbitrarily in the equations we worked with. It then became a trivial process to solve for the remaining values. Fortunately, this will always be the case. Second, all of the values in the present solution are positive numbers. But remember that a V_i or W_j value may be positive, negative, or zero.

We can now easily obtain the *net contribution of the unused routes* from the expression:

$$NC = C_{ij} - V_i - W_j$$

These calculations are given in Table 7.2. The net contribution values obtained by the MODI method are identical to the values we obtained using the stepping stone method.

Does it seem as if we invoked some type of magic in arbitrarily selecting V_1 and assigning it a value of zero? Such is not the case. If we chose a different variable the V_i's and W_j's would probably take on different values, but the net contribution values would remain the same. Arbitrarily assign W_3 a value of 20. The values of V_1, V_2, V_3, W_1, W_2, and W_4 will be -11, -4, 0, 26, 29, and 24 respectively. Using these values in our net contribution formula results in the same values as those given in Figure 7.5.

Table 7.2 *Utilizing the MODI method to calculate route improvement factors for unused routes*

Route	C_{ij}	$-V_i$	$-W_j$	$=$	NC
1-3	22	0	9	=	13
1-4	26	0	13	=	13
2-1	21	7	15	=	−1
2-4	23	7	13	=	+3
3-1	14	11	15	=	−12
3-2	19	11	18	=	−10
$V_1 = 0$		$V_3 = 11$		$W_1 = 15$	$W_3 = 9$
$V_2 = 7$				$W_2 = 18$	$W_4 = 13$

Sample problem 7.4   AAP (Continued)

Consider the second iteration of the AAP example given in Sample Problem 7.3. For the solution given, let $V_2 = 0$ and solve for the remaining V_i and W_j. Determine the net contribution values of unused routes. Repeat the analysis after letting $W_3 = 10$.

SOLUTION

$$
\begin{aligned}
V_1 \quad &+ W_1 && = 6 \\
V_1 \quad & && + W_3 = 5 \\
V_2 \quad & \quad + W_2 && = 2 \\
V_3 \quad & \quad + W_2 && = 7 \\
V_3 \quad & && + W_3 = 6
\end{aligned}
$$

If $V_2 = 0$, then $V_1 = 4$, $V_3 = 5$, $W_1 = 2$, $W_2 = 2$, and $W_3 = 1$.

Route	C_{ij}	−	V_i	−	W_j	=	NC
1-2	8	−	4	−	2	=	2
2-1	9	−	0	−	2	=	7
2-3	4	−	0	−	1	=	3
3-1	4	−	5	−	2	=	−3

If $W_3 = 10$, then $V_1 = -5$, $V_2 = -9$, $V_3 = -4$, $W_1 = 11$, and $W_2 = 11$. Net contribution values remain unchanged.

Subsequent iterations

After evaluating the unused routes, we proceed as before to move from iteration to iteration until we reach an optimal solution. A word of caution should be interjected here. The routes that are used will change from iteration to iteration. The only relationships utilized in determining the V_i and W_j values are those that correspond to the used routes. Thus, the appropriate set of relationships will be different for each solution. Likewise, the values of V_i and W_j will usually change with each new iteration.

Simplifying the MODI method

The MODI method is even less complicated than the foregoing discussion indicates, because it is not necessary to write out the relevant relationships among the V_i's, W_j's, and C_{ij}'s. All we have to do is add the V_i column and the W_j row to the transportation table.

Figure 7.10(a) illustrates this for the first iteration of the Kappa Tile Company problem. Note that we have arbitrarily assigned V_1 a value of zero. For every used route, $V_i + W_j$ must equal C_{ij}. From Figure 7.10(a), we know that $V_1 + W_1$ must equal 15 and that $V_1 + W_2$ must equal 18.

Figure 7.10 *Illustration of the simplified MODI method*

(a) Solving for W_1 and W_2

		$W_1 = 15$ 1	$W_2 = 18$ 2	$W_3 =$ 3	$W_4 =$ 4	
$V_1 = 0$	1	15 / 1500	18 / 1500	22	26	3000
$V_2 =$	2	21	25 / 500	16 / 2250	23	2750
$V_3 =$	3	14	19	20 / 250	24 / 3500	3750
		1500	2000	2500	3500	9500

(b) Solving for V_2 and W_3

		$W_1 = 15$ 1	$W_2 = 18$ 2	$W_3 = 9$ 3	$W_4 =$ 4	
$V_1 = 0$	1	15 / 1500	18 / 1500	22	26	3000
$V_2 = 7$	2	21	25 / 500	16 / 2250	23	2750
$V_3 =$	3	14	19	20 / 250	24 / 3500	3750
		1500	2000	2500	3500	9500

(c) Table with net contribution values shown

		$W_1 = 15$ 1	$W_2 = 18$ 2	$W_3 = 9$ 3	$W_4 = 13$ 4	
$V_1 = 0$	1	15 / 1500	18 / 1500	22 (+13)	26 (+13)	3000
$V_2 = 7$	2	21 (−1)	25 / 500	16 / 2250	23 (+3)	2750
$V_3 = 11$	3	14 (−12)	19 (−10)	20 / 250	24 / 3500	3750
		1500	2000	2500	3500	9500

Therefore, $W_1 = 15$ and $W_2 = 18$. These values have also been entered in Figure 7.10(a).

Since route (2-2) is a used route, we can use the value W_2 to solve for the value of V_2. We know that $V_2 + W_2 = 25$; therefore, $V_2 = 7$. This value is shown in Figure 7.10(b). Once we obtain the value of V_2, we may use it to determine the value of W_3, which is also shown in Figure 7.10(b). We continue this procedure until we have obtained the values for all V_i and W_j. These values have been entered in the appropriate places in Figure 7.10(c).

Once we have obtained the value of these variables, it is a simple matter to determine the net contribution value of the unused routes. For each unused route, net contribution is equal to the per-unit route cost minus the V_i value in the same row minus the W_j value in the same column. Thus, for route (3-1), the net contribution is $14 - 11 - 15 = -12$. Again we should verify that these net contribution values are the same as we obtained before by the stepping stone method. We might also want to verify that we would have obtained the same net contribution values if we had assigned an arbitrary value to a different variable.

Sample problem 7.5   AAP (Continued)

Consider the AAP example given in Sample Problems 7.1, 7.2, and 7.3. Assume that the requirements of plants 1, 2, and 3 have increased to 300, 400, and 500 respectively. Assume that the delivered cost of purchases made from an outside market is the same for all plants. Begin with the solution shown in the first table. Solve for the least-cost route, using the simplified MODI method. Analyze and verify the final table by answering the questions asked in Exhibit 7.1 on page 253.

First table

S \ D		$W_1 = -3$	$W_2 = 0$	$W_3 = -4$	
		1	2	3	
$V_1 = 9$	1	6 50	8 (−1)	5 200	250
$V_2 = 2$	2	9 (+10)	2 225	4 (+6)	225
$V_3 = 7$	3	4 250	7 175	6 (+3)	425
$V_4 = 4$	4	0 (−1)	0 (−4)	0 300	300
		300	400	500	1200

O.F. = 3975

Second table

D / S		$W_1 = -3$ 1	$W_2 = 0$ 2	$W_3 = 0$ 3	
$V_1 = 5$	1	6 (+4)	8 (+3)	5 250	250
$V_2 = 2$	2	9 (+10)	2 225	4 (+2)	225
$V_3 = 7$	3	4 300	7 125	6 (−1)	425
$V_4 = 0$	4	0 (+3)	0 50	0 250	300
		300	400	500	1200

O.F. = 3775

Third table

D / S		$W_1 = -2$ 1	$W_2 = 0$ 2	$W_3 = 0$ 3	
$V_1 = 5$	1	6 (+3)	8 (+3)	5 250	250
$V_2 = 2$	2	9 (+9)	2 225	4 (+2)	225
$V_3 = 6$	3	4 300	7 (+1)	6 125	425
$V_4 = 0$	4	0 (+2)	0 175	0 125	300
		300	400	500	1200

O.F. = 3650

SOLUTION

1. Mine 1 ships 250 units to plant 3. Mine 2 ships 225 units to plant 2. Mine 3 ships 300 units to plant 1 and 125 units to plant 3. Plants 2 and 3 must purchase 175 and 125 units respectively on the outside market.
2. Yes. Dummy must supply 300 units.
3. Yes. 3775 − (1)(125) = 3650.
4. Yes. There are 4 + 3 − 1 = 6 used routes.

The MODI method and the dual linear programming problem

The MODI method is directly related to the dual linear programming problem. In fact, the relationships used to determine the values of V_i and W_j and the net contributions of unused routes are constraints to the dual linear programming problem. The standard linear programming formulation of the Kappa Tile Company problem is given in Table 7.1. Suppose we let the variables V_1, V_2, and V_3 be the dual variables associated with the three supply constraints and W_1, W_2, W_3, and W_4 be the dual variables associated with the four demand constraints. Using these variables, we can formulate the dual problem. The dual constraints to this problem are given in Table 7.3. Since the original primal constraints were equalities rather than inequalities, the dual variables given in Table 7.3 are unrestricted in sign; they can be positive, negative, or zero.

As illustrated in Table 7.3, there are 12 dual constraints associated with the Kappa Tile problem. Six of these are associated with used routes in the original northwest corner solution to the Kappa Tile problem. These are the six relationships that we previously used to solve for the initial values of V_i and W_j. Six of the dual constraints in Table 7.3 are associated with unused routes in the original Kappa Tile solution. These are the relationships that we used in Table 7.2 to calculate the net contribution factors of the unused routes.

In Chapter 6, we learned two facts about dual constraints that allow us to use them in this way. First, for processes being used in a particular solution, the associated dual constraint always holds as a strict equality. Thus, for every route being used in a particular solution, the sum of the dual variables equals the per-unit route cost; that is, $V_i + W_j = C_{ij}$.

Table 7.3 *Dual constraints for the Kappa Tile Company problem*

Route				Dual constraint				
1-1*	V_1			$+W_1$				$\leqslant 15$
1-2*	V_1				$+W_2$			$\leqslant 18$
1-3	V_1					$+W_3$		$\leqslant 22$
1-4	V_1						$+W_4$	$\leqslant 26$
2-1		V_2		$+W_1$				$\leqslant 21$
2-2*		V_2			$+W_2$			$\leqslant 25$
2-3*		V_2				$+W_3$		$\leqslant 16$
2-4		V_2					$+W_4$	$\leqslant 23$
3-1			V_3	$+W_1$				$\leqslant 14$
3-2			V_3		$+W_2$			$\leqslant 19$
3-3*			V_3			$+W_3$		$\leqslant 20$
3-4*			V_3				$+W_4$	$\leqslant 24$

*Routes used in the original northwest corner solution to the Kappa Tile problem.

Figure 7.11 *Degeneracy in the initial solution and its resolution*

Supply \ Demand	Demand points				Availability
	1	2	3	4	
1	8 150	12 50	18	15 0*	200
2	14	11 200	17 100	9	300
3	13	10	19	16 325	325
Requirements	150	250	100	325	825

*Usable zero assigned to route (1-4)

Second, for processes not being used in a particular solution, the net contribution of any such process is the numerical difference between the right-hand and left-hand sides of the dual constraint. Thus, for every unused route, we can obtain the net contribution by subtracting the sum of the dual variable values from the per-unit cost of the route; that is,

$$NC = C_{ij} - V_i - W_j$$

Degeneracy in the transportation method

Consider the solution to the transportation problem given in Figure 7.11. Try to evaluate the net contribution of the unused route (3-1). Note that it cannot be evaluated by either the stepping stone method or the MODI method. This is because the solution given in Figure 7.11 is a *degenerate solution*. We have indicated that the number of used cells in any solution must be equal to the number of rows plus the number of columns minus one. If the number of used cells is less than this rule requires, then degeneracy exists, and we must use special procedures to resolve the degeneracy.

Occasionally a solution will have more used cells than are required. This happens only when we develop an initial solution, and there is always at least one initial solution in which this condition does not exist. Accordingly, if we should develop an initial solution with this condition, we simply find a new initial solution.

Degeneracy in an initial solution

Let us again consider the transportation problem given in Figure 7.11. Since there are three rows and four columns, the solution should have six used squares. Instead, it has only five. The solution is therefore degenerate and cannot be evaluated by standard methods. In this case, we can resolve the degeneracy by assigning a *usable zero* to one of the previously unused routes.[3] Assignment of this usable zero converts an unused route to a used route and allows us to use the cell in the evaluation process. It may be helpful to think of assigning a usable zero as shipping an empty truck over a particular route.

When degeneracy exists in the initial solution, there is no "one right cell" to which the usable zero should be assigned. The analyst has a great deal of flexibility in choosing the proper cell. Generally, there is more than one cell location that will resolve the degeneracy problem. In fact, the degeneracy can be resolved by adding the usable zero to any cell that cannot presently be evaluated. In Figure 7.11, we have added the usable zero to route (1-4). The problem now has the proper number of used routes and can be solved by the standard transportation method.

When moving from iteration to iteration, it is necessary to make a chain of adjustments along the closed path. Occasionally, the usable zero will be on a negative corner of the closed path. This means that the maximum amount that can be added to the new route is also usable zero. The net effect is to shift the usable zero from one cell to another. Continuing this procedure will eventually resolve the degeneracy and lead to an optimal solution.

In Figure 7.11, only one usable zero was required to resolve the degeneracy. In some problems, more than one usable zero is required to make the number of used routes equal to the number of rows plus the number of columns minus one.

Degeneracy in subsequent iterations

Consider the solution to the transportation problem given in Figure 7.12(a). The net contribution values of all unused routes are also given in the table. Route (3-3) has the most negative net contribution value

---

[3]The usable zero method is similar to the epsilon method described in other textbooks. In that method, a very small positive value is added to an appropriate unused cell (or cells). This resolves the degeneracy problem and allows all cells to be evaluated. When this value is no longer needed, it is dropped from the solution. The Greek letter epsilon (ϵ) and the English letter d are two of the symbols often used to represent the amount added to the unused cell.

Figure 7.12 *Degeneracy in subsequent iterations and its resolution*

(a) Nondegenerate, nonoptional solution

Supply \ Demand		Demand points				Availability
		1	2	3	4	
Supply points	1	13 \ 100	14 \ 200	8 \ 150	17 \ (+2)	450
	2	17 \ (+1)	20 \ (+3)	11 \ 100	18 \ 150	250
	3	17 \ (+1)	18 \ (+1)	10 \ (−1)	18 \ 100	100
Requirements		100	200	250	250	800

(b) Subsequent iteration, which is degenerate

Supply \ Demand		Demand points				Availability
		1	2	3	4	
Supply points	1	13 \ 100	14 \ 200	8 \ 150	17	450
	2	17	20	11 \ −	18 \ 250	250
	3	17	18	10 \ 100	18 \ −	100
Requirements		100	200	250	250	800

and should be utilized at the next iteration. The proper chain of adjustments is to add 100 units to cells (3-3) and (2-4) and to subtract 100 units from cells (2-3) and (3-4). The results of this action are shown in Figure 7.12(b).

In Figure 7.12(b), the quantities shipped on both routes (2-3) and (3-4) were reduced to zero. The resulting solution is degenerate. The remedy is to again assign a usable zero to an unused route. In this case, the usable zero is assigned to a cell that had a value (was a used route) in the previous solution. In our example, the usable zero may be assigned to either cell (2-3) or cell (3-4). We should verify that assigning a usable zero to either of these cells allows all routes to be evaluated.

In some cases, more than two routes will be reduced to zero on a given iteration. In these cases, we add enough usable zeros to satisfy the requirement that the number of used routes equal the number of rows plus the number of columns minus one. Addition of these usable zeros will resolve the degeneracy, and we can solve the problem by the standard transportation method.

Generality and significance of the transportation problem

Transportation problems are important because a large number of firms have distribution problems that can be analyzed with the aid of the transportation method. But even more important is the fact that we can solve other types of large problems by using the transportation method. There are many real problems with more than 1000 variables and hundreds of constraints. Large cost savings will accrue if we can use an efficient algorithm, such as the transportation method, to analyze these problems. In fact, some problems may be so large that the only practical approach is to find an appropriate simplified algorithm.

Illustrative example: KAPPA TILE COMPANY REVISITED

Mr. Johnson has been encouraging Kappa Tile's four distributors to install new inventory control systems, and they will make the conversion next month if Kappa Tile provides the technical assistance. Mr. Johnson has selected four engineers from his tile plants and intends to assign them to the distribution sites.

Mr. Johnson must decide which engineer should be assigned to which distributor. The cost of a given engineer assisting a given distributor varies according to differences in the complexity of the distributors' operations, the backgrounds of the engineers, and the distances between the engineers' homes and the distribution sites. The costs of assigning particular engineers to particular distributors are as follows:

	Distributors			
	1	2	3	4
Engineers 1	$1100	$ 800	$1000	$700
2	600	500	300	800
3	400	800	1000	900
4	1100	1000	500	700

Mr. Johnson has a solution that appears to represent a least-cost set of assignments. He has difficulty, however, in assuring himself that it is the best possible arrangement. He wonders if there is a special form of linear programming, such as the transportation method, that he could use to solve for the least-cost assignment.

The assignment problem

We can formulate the revisited problem at Kappa Tile as a standard transportation problem by treating the four engineers as supply sources with an availability of one unit each. The distributors are viewed as destinations or demand points. Each destination has a demand for a single unit, that is, one engineer. Before creating a transportation table, it will be helpful to examine the mathematical structure of the problem.

Standard linear programming formulation

We can develop a mathematical formulation of this problem by using the following symbolic notation:

$X_{11} = 1$ if engineer 1 is assigned to distributor 1

$X_{11} = 0$ if engineer 1 is not assigned to distributor 1

In general,

$X_{ij} = 1$ if engineer i is assigned to distributor j

$X_{ij} = 0$ if engineer i is not assigned to distributor j

The complete linear programming formulation is given in Table 7.4. The four supply constraints indicate that each engineer must be assigned to one of the four distributors. For example, engineer 1 must be assigned to either distributor 1, distributor 2, distributor 3, or distributor 4. That is,

$$X_{11} + X_{12} + X_{13} + X_{14} = 1$$

In this relationship, one of the variables must have a value of one while the other variables must have a value of zero.

The four demand constraints indicate that the demand by any distributor must be satisfied by the assignment of one and only one engineer to that distributor. For example, either engineer 1, engineer 2, engineer 3, or engineer 4 must be assigned to distributor 1. That is,

$$X_{11} + X_{21} + X_{31} + X_{41} = 1$$

The objective function given in Table 7.4 indicates that Mr. Johnson's goal is to provide the technical assistance at minimum cost.

Table 7.4 *Mathematical statement of the Kappa Tile assignment problem*

$$Z = 11X_{11} + 8X_{12} + 10X_{13} + 7X_{14} + 6X_{21} + 5X_{22} + 3X_{23} + 8X_{24} + 4X_{31} + 8X_{32} + 10X_{33} + 9X_{34} + 11X_{41} + 10X_{42} + 5X_{43} + 7X_{44}$$

$$X_{11} + X_{12} + X_{13} + X_{14} = 1$$
$$X_{21} + X_{22} + X_{23} + X_{24} = 1$$
$$X_{31} + X_{32} + X_{33} + X_{34} = 1$$
$$X_{41} + X_{42} + X_{43} + X_{44} = 1$$
$$X_{11} + X_{21} + X_{31} + X_{41} = 1$$
$$X_{12} + X_{22} + X_{32} + X_{42} = 1$$
$$X_{13} + X_{23} + X_{33} + X_{43} = 1$$
$$X_{14} + X_{24} + X_{34} + X_{44} = 1$$
$$X_{ij} \geq 0$$

Notes: Objective function coefficients are in terms of $100. All terms with zero coefficients have been omitted.

Figure 7.13 *Transportation formulation of Kappa Tile's assignment problem (costs in hundreds of dollars)*

Supply \ Demand		Distributors 1	2	3	4	Availability
Engineers	1	11 — 1	8	10	7	1
	2	6	5 — 1	3	8	1
	3	4	8	10 — 1	9	1
	4	11	10	5	7 — 1	1
Requirements		1	1	1	1	4

Note: The initial solution was developed by use of the northwest corner method.

Solution as a transportation problem

The mathematical formulation of this problem reveals that it exhibits all the characteristics that define a transportation problem, so it can be solved by the transportation method. The transportation formulation for the revisited Kappa Tile problem is given in Figure 7.13. The engineers are treated as sources and the distributors as destinations. An initial solution, developed by the northwest corner method, is included in the table.

Note that there is a single entry, or used route, in each row and column in Figure 7.13. This, of course, is required by our stipulation that an engineer assist one and only one distributor and that a distributor receive the assistance of one and only one engineer. In a problem with four rows and four columns, there will be exactly four used routes. The number of rows plus the number of columns minus one is equal to seven, so the initial solution is degenerate. It is impossible to evaluate the unused routes unless we insert three usable zeros into three appropriate cells in the transportation table.

Once we have assigned the usable zeros, we can solve the problem by straightforward application of the transportation method. The existence of degeneracy, however, tends to extend the calculations and reduce the efficiency of the transportation method. As the size of a problem increases, the associated computational burden increases dramatically. The special structure of the assignment problem allows us to use an alternative solution method that can substantially reduce the required computational effort.

The assignment method

Assume that Mr. Johnson has encountered the degeneracy that arose in solving his assignment problem via the transportation method and has decided to see if he can develop a simpler solution process. He is encouraged by the apparently simple structure of the problem.

Characteristics of an assignment problem

The allocation problem at Kappa Tile has all of the characteristics of a transportation problem. As such, it may be solved by the transportation method. However, it also has two characteristics that make it a special type of transportation problem. Any transportation problem that meets the following two specifications is known as an *assignment problem* and can be solved by a procedure known as the *assignment method.*

1. The number of sources or supply points is equal to the number of destinations or demand points.
2. The amount supplied by each source and the amount required by each demand point are both equal to one unit.

Rationale of the assignment method

It is obvious to Mr. Johnson that there are three assignment procedures that will guarantee an optimal, or least-cost, assignment. If any of these procedures results in a solution that can actually be put into operation, Mr. Johnson's problem is solved. The three procedures are as follows:

1. Since four assignments must be made, choose the four least-cost cells in Figure 7.13 and assign one unit to each cell. This results in the assignment of engineer 2 to distributor 2, engineer 2 to distributor 3, engineer 3 to distributor 1, and engineer 4 to distributor 3. This solution has a cost of $1700, and no solution can have a lower cost. Unfortunately, it is not a feasible solution, because engineer 2 has been assigned to two different distributors.
2. An optimal solution would also be obtained if each distributor were supplied by the least-cost engineer, which we can accomplish by assigning one unit to the least-cost cell in each column. For Kappa Tile, this results in a total cost of $1900. This is not a feasible solution, however, because engineer 2 is assigned to both distributor 2 and distributor 3.
3. An alternative to procedure 2 would be to send each engineer to his or her least-cost destination, that is, to assign one unit to the least-cost cell in each row. For Kappa Tile, this solution has a cost of $1900.

It is not feasible, however, since engineer 2 and engineer 4 are both assigned to distributor 3.

Since we can find no feasible solution meeting our criteria, it may be helpful to adjust the cost matrix into a form wherein such a solution would exist and could be easily located. A key observation provides the means to make these adjustments. If the same number is subtracted from every entry in the same row or in the same column, the basic structure of the problem will not be changed.

Using this observation, we can develop an efficient method of solving assignment problems. This approach is based on reducing the cost matrix to a point where we can locate a solution using only cells whose costs have been adjusted to zero. If the adjustments are made in a way that precludes negative table entries, such a solution meets the optimality criteria and must be the best solution. It will be optimal in both the reduced table and the original table.

Steps in the assignment method

We apply the following steps to the cost tables of an assignment problem in order to locate an optimal solution.

1. Subtract the smallest cost in each row from all costs appearing in that row. This will ensure a zero entry in each row of the table. If a solution using only zero assignments can now be made, it is the optimal solution. If not, go on to step 2.
2. Subtract the smallest cost in each column of the *reduced cost matrix* from all costs appearing in the same column. There will now be at least one zero entry in each row and each column in the table. If a solution using only zero assignments is available, an optimal solution has been found. If not, go on to step 3.
3. Cover all zero entries in the reduced table with as few vertical and horizontal lines as possible. Subtract the smallest uncovered table entry from all uncovered entries and add it to entries where the covering lines intersect. A solution using only zero assignments is optimal. If no such solution exists, repeat this step until you obtain an optimal solution.

In applying these steps, it may be difficult to establish whether an all-zero solution is available. Cover all zero entries in the table with the minimum number of vertical and horizontal lines. If the required number of lines is equal to the number of rows or columns in the table, an all-zero assignment is possible.

The set of lines used to cover all zero entries in a table does not have to be unique. For example, all zeros in a particular table may be covered by two horizontal lines and one vertical line *or* by one horizontal line and two vertical lines. You will soon become aware of other alternative covering patterns. Likewise, the optimal solution to an assignment problem does not have to be unique. As in any linear programming problem, there may be alternative optimal solutions.

In some cases, it is difficult to determine just what combination of lines represents the minimum. A helpful decision rule is to locate a row or column with a single zero entry and draw a line through this zero. In determining whether the line should be vertical or horizontal, try to draw the line in a way that allows it to cover other zero entries. This is particularly true if the zero is the only one appearing in another row or column.

Application to the Kappa Tile problem

Let us illustrate the solution procedure by applying it to the Kappa Tile problem. The cost table for this assignment problem is given in Figure 7.14. To facilitate computation, all costs have been divided by 100.

At step 1, the smallest cost in each row is subtracted from the other cost elements in the same row. Thus, we subtract 7 from row 1, 3 from row 2, 4 from row 3, and 5 from row 4. The results are shown in Figure 7.14(b). An all-zero assignment is not possible. There is no zero in column 2.

The second step is to subtract the minimum value in each column of Figure 7.14(b) from all entries in the corresponding column. The only adjustment possible in this case is to subtract one unit from each value in column 2. The result is shown in Figure 7.14(c). All zeros in Figure 7.14(c) can be covered by three lines, so an all-zero adjusted-cost solution does not exist.

In step 2, we covered all zero entries with the minimum number of lines, which was three, in order to see if an all-zero assignment was possible. The same three lines can be used as the covering lines in step 3. The smallest uncovered value in Figure 7.14(c) is the one in row 2, column 2. Step 3 indicates that we should subtract this number from all uncovered numbers and add it to the two locations where covering lines intersect: row 1, column 3 and row 3, column 3. The results appear in Figure 7.14(d).

A little experimentation reveals that four lines are now needed to cover all zeros in the new table. An all-zero assignment is possible. The solution that makes use of four zero cost cells in Figure 7.14(d) is summarized in Table 7.5. This is the least-cost solution to Mr. Johnson's problem. The actual cost of this set of assignments is $2100.

Opportunity costs and the assignment method

The concept of opportunity cost was introduced in Chapter 3. The reduced-cost tables used in the preceding analysis are actually opportunity-cost tables. When the smallest number, $700, was subtracted from the four assignments available for engineer 1, the reduced assignment

Figure 7.14 *Solution of assignment problem*

(a) Original assignment table

Distributions

		1	2	3	4
	1	11	8	10	7
Engineers	2	6	5	3	8
	3	4	8	10	9
	4	11	10	5	7

(b) Reduced assignment table after step 1

Distributions

		1	2	3	4
	1	4	1	3	0
Engineers	2	3	2	0	5
	3	0	4	6	5
	4	6	5	0	2

(c) Reduced assignment table after step 2

Distributions

		1	2	3	4
	1	4	0	3	0
Engineers	2	3	1	0	5
	3	0	3	6	5
	4	6	4	0	2

(d) Reduced assignment table after step 3

Distributions

		1	2	3	4
	1	4	0	4	0
Engineers	2	2	0	0	4
	3	0	3	7	5
	4	5	3	0	1

costs of $400, $100, $300, and $0 in Figure 7.14(b) represented opportunity costs of all possible assignments. If engineer 1 is assigned to distributor 4, there is no opportunity cost; that is, he is assigned to his least-cost distributor. If he is assigned to distributor 1, the company incurs an opportunity cost of $400.

Figure 7.14(d) represents a table that takes into account opportunity cost of both the engineers and the distributors. It has been adjusted to a format where a zero opportunity-cost solution exists. This must be an optimal solution.

Table 7.5 *Least-cost solution for the Kappa Tile assignment problem*

Assigned engineer	Distributor	Adjusted cost [Figure 7.14(d)]	Original cost [Figure 7.14(a)]
1	4	0	7
2	2	0	5
3	1	0	4
4	3	0	5
Total cost		0	21

Sample problem 7.6 THE HILL COMPANY

The Hill Company has three different production jobs to complete next week. Three multipurpose machines, each with somewhat different characteristics, are available. The estimated costs of completing each job on each of the three machines are shown in the following matrix.

		Machines		
		A	B	C
	1	150	190	230
Jobs	2	170	220	210
	3	190	160	150

Time constraints preclude the use of one machine on more than one job. Use the assignment method to determine the least-cost production schedule.

SOLUTION

Step 1: Subtracting the minimum cost in each row from all entries in that row yields

		Machines		
		A	B	C
	1	0	40	80
Jobs	2	0	50	40
	3	40	10	0

Step 2: Since an all-zero assignment is not possible, subtract the minimum adjusted cost in each column from each cost in that column. Cover all zeros with as few lines as possible.

		Machines		
		A	B	C
	1	0	30	80
Jobs	2	0	40	40
	3	40	0	0

Step 3: Since all zeros in this table may be covered by only two lines, an all-zero assignment is still not possible. Now subtract the least-cost entry not covered by a line, $30, from all entries not covered by a line, and add it to all locations where overlaying lines intersect.

		Machines		
		A	B	C
	1	0	0	50
Jobs	2	0	10	10
	3	70	0	0

Step 4: At least three lines are required to cover all zero entries in the table, so an all-zero assignment is possible.

Assignment: 1 to B (190)
2 to A (170)
3 to C (150)
$ 510 (minimum cost)

Extensions of the assignment method

The range of application of the assignment method may be extended in much the same way as the area of application of the transportation method was increased. Problems in which the number of assignees and assignments are not equal can be adjusted for solution by the assignment method. The procedure is identical to that suggested for the unbalanced transportation problem. We add dummy rows or columns with zero assignment costs as needed to develop a table wherein the number of sources is equal to the number of destinations.

Problems and exercises

1. Explain the following terms:
   transportation method
   supply constraint
   demand constraint
   transportation table
   rim values
   northwest corner method
   used route
   unused cell
   degeneracy
   assignment problem
   stepping stone method
   MODI method
   positive corners
   negative corners
   balanced problem
   unbalanced problem
   dummy demand
   usable zero
   assignment method
   reduced-cost matrix

LINEAR PROGRAMMING FORMULATIONS. INSTRUCTIONS FOR PROBLEMS 2–5

Formulate each of the following problems as a standard linear programming problem. Use doubly subscripted variables. Label each constraint as either supply or demand. Check to see if the problem meets the specifications of a transportation problem.

2. The Ewig Company has two manufacturing plants and three distributors. Plant 1 can produce 400 units per period, and plant 2 can produce 500 units per period. The requirements of distributors 1, 2, and 3 are 225, 325, and 350 units respectively. Shipping costs from plant 1 to distributors 1, 2, and 3 are $25, $18, and $20. The corresponding costs from plant 2 are $21, $30, and $24. The objective is to find the least-cost way of shipping from plants to distributors.

3. The McKennon Company mines a certain chemical at three different locations and ships it for processing to three different manufacturing locations. Ore availabilities are 18 tons, 21 tons, and 26 tons at mines 1, 2, and 3 respectively. Requirements at plants 1, 2, and 3 are 20, 20, and 25 tons respectively. The objective is to find a routing plan that minimizes shipping cost. Shipping costs from mine to plant are as follows:

		Plants		
		1	2	3
	1	$4	$7	$5
Mines	2	8	5	7
	3	6	5	6

4. The Stuart Company has three manufacturing plants and three warehouses. The costs of shipping from plant 1 to warehouses 1, 2, and 3 are $40, $50, and $60 respectively. The corresponding costs for plant 2 are $65, $70, and $45, and they are $60, $55, and $75 for plant 3. The objective is to find the least-cost shipping plan that will properly route inventory from plants to warehouses. Unit availabilities of inventory at the three plants and unit requirements at the three warehouses are as follows:

Plants	1	2	3	Warehouses	1	2	3
Availability	100	40	60	Requirements	70	50	80

5. The Thompson Company employs a two-step operation in the production of cardboard boxes. The paper for the boxes is made at two locations and then shipped to one of four box plants for conversion into cardboard boxes. Next week, mill 1 can produce 2250 tons of paper, and mill 2 can produce 4600 tons of paper. The requirements at box factories 1, 2, 3, and 4 are 1850, 1350, 2000, and 1650 tons respectively. The objective is to find the least-cost

method of getting the paper from the two mills to the required box plants. Shipping costs are as follows:

		Box plants			
		1	2	3	4
Mills	1	$5.00	$8.00	$6.00	$7.50
	2	8.50	5.50	6.00	7.00

TRANSPORTATION TABLES AND INITIAL SOLUTIONS. INSTRUCTIONS FOR PROBLEMS 6–10

For each of the following problems, set up a transportation table and solve for an initial solution by the northwest corner method. Problems 6 and 7 are balanced transportation problems. Problems 8, 9, and 10 are unbalanced problems, so either a dummy supply or a dummy demand must be added.

6. The Usher Company manufactures game tables in four locations and sells to four major customers. In the next production period, plants 1, 2, 3, and 4 will produce 25, 15, 45, and 25 tables respectively. The demand requirements of customers 1, 2, 3, and 4 are 20, 10, 40, and 40 respectively. The per-unit profit depends on a number of items such as plant production cost, shipping cost, and prevailing prices at various plants. The company's accountant has determined the per-unit profit of shipping a table from each given plant to each given customer. This information is as follows:

		Customers			
		1	2	3	4
Plants	1	$70	$20	$10	$40
	2	20	60	30	20
	3	30	40	50	20
	4	50	40	30	50

The objective is to find a shipping plan that will maximize contribution to profit.

7. The Harlan Company wishes to minimize shipping costs from its three plants to its five distributors. The per-unit costs of shipping from plant 1 to distributors 1, 2, 3, 4, and 5 are $2, $5, $8, $7, and $6 respectively. The costs of shipping from plant 2 to distributors 1, 2, 3, 4, and 5 are $5, $8, $3, $7, and $4 respectively. The corresponding costs from plant 3 are $9, $6, $5, $5, and $6 respectively. The production capacities of the three plants and the demand requirements of the five distributors are as follows:

| Plants | 1 | 2 | 3 |
| Capacities | 325 | 325 | 350 |

| Distributors | 1 | 2 | 3 | 4 | 5 |
| Requirements | 100 | 300 | 150 | 250 | 200 |

8. The Delano Company wishes to find the best way of allocating the capacity at its three mining locations to its three manufacturing locations. The costs of shipping a ton of ore from each mining location to each manufacturing location are as follows:

		Plants		
		1	2	3
	1	$3	$10	$2
Mines	2	4	11	8
	3	8	11	4

Since the company produces different products at different locations, a ton of ore is worth $12 at plant 1, $16 at plant 2, and $11 at plant 3. During the next period, the capacities at mines 1, 2, and 3 are 20, 30, and 20 tons respectively. The requirements at the three plants are 15, 25, and 18 tons respectively. Find a shipping plan to maximize contribution to profit.

9. The Chandler Company ships from two plants to three distributors. The per-unit costs of shipping from plant 1 to distributors 1, 2, and 3 are $25, $55, and $35 respectively. The corresponding costs of shipping from plant 2 are $60, $30, and $0. The objective is to find a shipping plan that will satisfy requirements at minimum cost. The plant availabilities and demand requirements are as follows:

Plants	1	2	Distributors	1	2	3
Availabilities	30	50	Requirements	23	32	18

10. The Kirkwood Company ships from two plants to three distributors. The per-unit costs of shipping from plant 1 to distributors 1, 2, and 3 are $50, $90, and $70 respectively. The corresponding costs from plant 2 are $85, $35, and $80 respectively. The objective is to allocate available supply at minimum cost. The plant availabilities and demand requirements are as follows:

Plants	1	2	Distributors	1	2	3
Availabilities	55	55	Requirements	30	40	60

SOLUTIONS BY THE STEPPING STONE METHOD. INSTRUCTIONS FOR PROBLEMS 11–15
Solve each of the following problems by the stepping stone method. Problems 11, 12, and 13 should take no more than three iterations.

11. Solve problem 6. Begin with the solution $X_{13} = 25$, $X_{21} = 15$, $X_{32} = 10$, $X_{33} = 15$, $X_{34} = 20$, $X_{41} = 5$, and $X_{44} = 20$.

12. Solve problem 7. Begin with the solution $X_{11} = 100$, $X_{12} = 225$, $X_{22} = 75$, $X_{23} = 150$, $X_{24} = 100$, $X_{34} = 150$, and $X_{35} = 200$.

13. Solve problem 9. Begin with the solution $X_{11} = 23$, $X_{12} = 7$, $X_{22} = 25$, $X_{23} = 18$, and $X_{24} = 7$.

14. Solve problem 8 using the stepping stone method. Begin with an appropriate starting solution.

15. Solve problem 10 using the stepping stone method. Begin with an appropriate starting solution.

INSTRUCTIONS FOR PROBLEMS 16–21

Use the MODI method in each of the following problems. Use V_i and W_j for the appropriate row and column values.

16. Construct a transportation table for problem 2. Assume that the initial solution is $X_{11} = 225$, $X_{12} = 175$, $X_{22} = 150$, and $X_{23} = 350$. Let $V_1 = 0$ and then solve for the remaining V_i and W_j values. Use the results to evaluate the net contribution of the unused routes.

17. Solve problem 16. Begin by letting $W_2 = 28$.

18. Construct a transportation table for problem 3. Assume that the initial solution is $X_{11} = 18$, $X_{21} = 2$, $X_{22} = 19$, $X_{32} = 1$, and $X_{33} = 25$. Let $V_1 = 0$ and then solve for the remaining V_i and W_j values. Use the results to evaluate the net contribution of the unused routes.

19. Solve problem 18. Begin by letting $W_3 = 12$.

20. Construct a transportation table for problem 5. Assume that the initial solution is $X_{11} = 1850$, $X_{12} = 400$, $X_{22} = 950$, $X_{23} = 2000$, and $X_{24} = 1650$. Let $V_2 = 0$ and then solve for the remaining V_i and W_j values. Use the results to evaluate the net contribution values of the unused routes.

21. Solve problem 20. Begin by letting $W_2 = 0$.

SOLUTIONS BY THE SIMPLIFIED MODI METHOD. INSTRUCTIONS FOR PROBLEMS 22–25

Construct a transportation table and then solve each of the following problems by the simplified MODI method. Problems 22 and 23 should take no more than three iterations.

22. Solve problem 2. Begin with the solution $X_{11} = 225$, $X_{12} = 175$, $X_{22} = 150$, and $X_{23} = 350$.

23. Solve problem 3. Begin with the solution $X_{11} = 18$, $X_{21} = 2$, $X_{22} = 19$, $X_{32} = 1$, and $X_{33} = 25$.

24. Solve problem 4. Begin with an appropriate initial solution.

25. Solve problem 5. Begin with an appropriate initial solution.

RESOLUTION OF DEGENERACY. INSTRUCTIONS FOR PROBLEMS 26–28

For each of the following problems, set up a transportation table, begin with the solution given, and then solve for an optimal solution. In each problem, you will encounter a degenerate solution.

26. The Lamar Company has two plants with supply availabilities of 50 and 55 units respectively. The requirements at warehouses 1, 2, 3, and 4 are 30, 20, 30, and 25 units respectively. The company would like to minimize total

shipping costs. Begin with a solution of $X_{11} = 30$, $X_{12} = 20$, $X_{23} = 30$, and $X_{24} = 25$. Per-unit costs of shipping from each plant to each warehouse are as follows:

		Warehouses			
		1	2	3	4
Plants	1	$3	$5	$7	$6
	2	5	4	2	6

27. The Vilas Company has two plants and three warehouses. The costs of shipping from plant 1 to warehouses 1, 2, and 3 are $3, $4, and $6 respectively. The corresponding costs for plant 2 are $5, $4, and $9. Availabilities are 50 tons at plant 1 and 45 tons at plant 2. Requirements are 20, 45, and 30 tons at warehouses 1, 2, and 3 respectively. The objective is to find a least-cost shipping plan. Begin with a solution of $X_{11} = 20$, $X_{12} = 30$, $X_{22} = 15$, and $X_{23} = 30$.

28. The Noble Company wants to find the least-cost way of shipping from its two plants to its four warehouses. Begin with a solution of $X_{11} = 30$, $X_{12} = 20$, $X_{13} = 15$, $X_{23} = 20$, and $X_{24} = 40$. The data for the Noble Company are as follows:

Plants	1	2	Warehouses	1	2	3	4
Availabilities	65	60	Requirements	30	20	35	40

		Cost to ship to warehouses			
		1	2	3	4
Plants	1	$2	$6	$5	$3
	2	6	4	8	7

ASSIGNMENT PROBLEMS. INSTRUCTIONS FOR PROBLEMS 29–34

Solve each of the following problems by the assignment method.

29. Determine the optimal assignment of the management teams to the four projects.

		Projects			
		A	B	C	D
Teams	1	19	10	16	20
	2	14	12	9	16
	3	12	15	11	13
	4	18	10	14	17

30. In problem 29, change the cost of assignments 3-A, 3-C, 3-D and 4-A to 18, 13, 11, and 14 respectively.

31. Given the following data, determine the least-cost allocation of the available machines to the five jobs.

		Jobs				
		A	B	C	D	E
	1	25	29	31	42	37
	2	22	19	35	18	26
Machines	3	39	38	26	20	33
	4	34	27	28	40	32
	5	24	42	36	23	45

32. In problem 31, change the cost of assignments 3-C and 3-D to 20 and 26 respectively.

33. In problem 29, project D has been canceled. Determine the least-cost allocation of the four teams to the three projects. No cost will be incurred for the unassigned team.

34. In problem 31, job E has been canceled. Determine which of the five machines should be used to complete the four jobs.

Supplementary readings

Cook, T. M., and R. A. Russell. *Introduction to Management Science*. Englewood Cliffs, N.J.: Prentice-Hall, 1977.

Hartley, R. V. *Operations Research: A Managerial Emphasis*. Pacific Palisades, Calif.: Goodyear, 1976.

Hughes, A. J., and D. E. Grawoig. *Linear Programming: An Emphasis on Decision Making*. Reading, Mass.: Addison-Wesley, 1973.

Johnson, R. H., and P. R. Winn. *Quantitative Methods for Management*. Boston: Houghton Mifflin, 1976.

Lapin, L. L. *Quantitative Methods for Business Decisions*. New York: Harcourt Brace Jovanovich, 1976.

Levin, R. I., and C. A. Kirkpatrick. *Quantitative Approaches to Management*, 2nd ed. New York: McGraw-Hill, 1975.

Shamblin, J. E., and G. T. Stevens. *Operations Research: A Fundamental Approach*. New York: McGraw-Hill, 1974.

Turban, E., and J. R. Meredith. *Fundamentals of Management Science*. Dallas, Texas: Business Publications, 1977.

Wagner, H. M. *Principles of Management Science*. Englewood Cliffs, N.J.: Prentice-Hall, 1975.

Chapter 8

Additional programming models: goal, integer, and dynamic programming

Goal programming

Illustrative example: KIEFER INDUSTRIES

Kiefer Industries specializes in manufacturing novelty and souvenir items sold at baseball parks and football stadiums. Some items are mass-produced for general consumption. Most items, however, are produced for a customer and carry the name or emblem of the team the buyer represents. These items are purchased in lot sizes, and the contract specifies that the Kiefer Company must produce exactly the amount ordered. No items may be held in inventory.

The company recently received an order for 13,000 embroidered cloth handbags. The purchaser will accept either of two styles: "Western American" or "Roaring Twenties." The handbags must be produced and shipped during the next production period. The company's design engineer estimates that each Western American handbag will require 2 minutes of cutting time and 2 minutes of stitching time. Each Roaring Twenties handbag will require 1 minute of cutting time and 3 minutes of stitching time. Each Western American handbag sells for $3. Variable costs are $1.40 per item. Thus, each item has a net profit contribution of $1.60. A Roaring Twenties handbag sells for $4 with variable costs of $2.80. This bag has a net profit contribution of $1.20. During the next production period, the company has available 20,000 minutes of cutting time and 36,000 minutes of stitching time.

The production superintendent used linear programming to schedule production of handbags in a way that would maximize profit contribution. This schedule has been presented to Mr. Galla, the company president. Mr. Galla customarily approves production schedules in a routine fashion. Recently, however, he has been concerned that the mathematical programming routine used by the production department considers only a single objective. He realizes that very few decisions are characterized by a single objective. More often, the situation encompasses many goals and subgoals. Mr. Galla wonders if this fact could be incorporated into the model the production department uses.

Standard linear programming models assume that the decision maker strives to optimize a single objective, such as profit maximization or cost minimization. Many decision situations, however, cannot be properly characterized by using a single objective function. Quite often, the decision maker will have many goals and subgoals. Some of these will be complementary; others will be conflicting. The decision maker will strive to fulfill some goals to the fullest extent possible and will accept a satisfactory level of achievement of other goals.

Goal programming is a special type of linear programming that can be used to analyze decision situations involving single or multiple goals. In goal programming, all of the decision maker's objectives, or goals, can be considered in the function or functions to be optimized. The procedure is to minimize deviations from these stated goals. Goal programming also allows for ranking of objectives by absolute priority. Low-priority goals are considered only after higher-priority goals are satisfied to the fullest extent possible.

Since goal programming is a special type of linear programming, all the assumptions of the linear programming model apply to the goal programming model. Likewise, the simplex method of linear programming is the basis of the goal programming algorithm. The primary difference between the two is that the goal programming model attempts to minimize deviations from stated goals. Thus, these goals must be stated in the constraint section of the formulation, and variables must be introduced to represent the deviations from these goals. These deviational variables must appear in the objective function and in the appropriate goal constraint of the problem formulation.

In the following sections, we will illustrate goal programming using Kiefer Industries as the basis of our discussion. We begin with a simple linear programming profit-maximizing solution. Then we introduce the concepts of programming to single and multiple goals.

Profit-maximizing linear programming formulation

Before proceeding with our analysis, it would be helpful to formulate and solve the Kiefer Industries problem as a standard linear programming problem. In this formulation, we will use the following variables.

X_1 = Number of Western American handbags produced
X_2 = Number of Roaring Twenties handbags produced

The objective is to maximize profit contribution, subject to the constraints on cutting and stitching times. A third constraint must be formulated, because, according to contract specifications, exactly 13,000 handbags must be made. The standard linear programming formulation is

$$\text{Max } Z = 1.60X_1 + 1.20X_2$$

s.t.
$$2X_1 + 1X_2 \leqslant 20,000 \quad \text{(cutting time)}$$
$$2X_1 + 3X_2 \leqslant 36,000 \quad \text{(stitching time)}$$
$$X_1 + X_2 = 13,000 \quad \text{(contract quantity)}$$
$$X_1, X_2 \geqslant 0$$

We must add two slack variables and one artificial variable to put the relationships in a form suitable for solution by the simplex method. In the following equations, we have used a negative 10 for the penalty coefficient of the artificial variable in the objective function.

$$\text{Max } Z = 1.60X_1 + 1.20X_2 + 0S_1 + 0S_2 - 10A_1$$

s.t.
$$2X_1 + 1X_2 + 1S_1 + 0S_2 + 0A_1 = 20,000$$
$$2X_1 + 3X_2 + 0S_1 + 1S_2 + 0A_1 = 36,000$$
$$1X_1 + 1X_2 + 0S_1 + 0S_2 + 1A_1 = 13,000$$
$$X_1, X_2, S_1, S_2, A_1 \geqslant 0$$

The problem can be solved by the simplex method. The optimal solution is $X_1 = 7000$, $X_2 = 6000$, and $Z = \$18,400$. Hence, if the sole objective is to maximize profit contribution, production should be scheduled so as to make 7000 Western American handbags and 6000 Roaring Twenties handbags. This would result in a profit contribution of $18,400. Total revenue would be $45,000.

Programming to a single goal

We will begin our discussion by illustrating the most basic concept of goal programming, programming to a single goal. Once we understand this principle, we can consider the concepts involved in programming to multiple goals. The following discussion and examples should clarify the difference between programming to a goal and optimizing an objective function. Basically, the difference is that we optimize an objective function by finding a feasible solution that will make the value of the objective function as large or small as possible. We program to a goal by finding a solution that, as nearly as possible, exactly achieves a specific value, such as sales of 1000 units or revenue of $50,000.

Statement of the problem

Assume that Mr. Galla at Kiefer Industries decides that the firm should not strive for maximum profit contribution. He feels that during this period, it is more important for the firm to have a satisfactory dollar volume of sales. He believes that $50,000 constitutes a satisfactory sales volume and should therefore be considered the "target sales volume." He realizes that the company may not be able to exactly achieve this goal. In such cases, however, he would like to come as close as possible to achieving the goal. In other words, he would like to minimize the deviation from the stated goal.

Mathematical formulation

In order to state this goal mathematically, we must introduce two new variables. These variables are referred to as *deviational variables* because they represent deviations from the stated goal.

U_1 = Amount of underachievement of the stated goal

E_1 = Amount of excess or overachievement of the stated goal

The target revenue goal may now be mathematically stated as

$$3X_1 + 4X_2 + U_1 - E_1 = 50,000 \qquad \text{(target revenue)}$$

This relationship should be written into the linear programming problem as a constraint. The new objective is to minimize the sum of the values of the deviational variables U_1 and E_1. This has the effect of minimizing the deviation from the stated goal. Mathematically, therefore, *the objective function is*

$$\text{Min } Z = U_1 + E_1$$

The new constraint set consists of the original linear programming constraints augmented by the new goal of a satisfactory revenue. The constraints may be written as follows:

$$
\begin{aligned}
2X_1 + 1X_2 & \leqslant 20,000 && \text{(cutting time)} \\
2X_1 + 3X_2 & \leqslant 36,000 && \text{(stitching time)} \\
X_1 + X_2 & = 13,000 && \text{(contract quantity)} \\
3X_1 + 4X_2 + U_1 - E_1 & = 50,000 && \text{(target revenue)}
\end{aligned}
$$

After adding the appropriate artificial and slack variables, we can place the problem in a simplex tableau as shown in Table 8.1. The artificial variable in the contract constraint has been given an objective function penalty coefficient of a positive 10. No artificial variable is needed in the revenue constraint, because U_1 can be used as a slack variable.

Solution by the simplex method

The problem can be solved by the simplex method. The tableaus generated are given in Table 8.1. The optimal solution is $X_1 = 3000$, $X_2 = 10,000$, $S_1 = 4000$, $U_1 = 1000$, and $Z = 1000$.

Table 8.1 *Simplex solution for a problem with a single goal*

0 Row	Price vector	Solution vector	Quantity vector	0.00 X_1	0.00 X_2	0.00 S_1	0.00 S_2	1.00 U_1	1.00 E_1	10.00 A_1
Initial tableau										
I	0.00	S_1	20,000	2.00	1.00	1.00	0.00	0.00	0.00	0.00
II	0.00	S_2	36,000	2.00	3.00	0.00	1.00	0.00	0.00	0.00
III	10.00	A_1	13,000	1.00	1.00	0.00	0.00	0.00	0.00	1.00
IV	1.00	U_1	50,000	3.00	4.00	0.00	0.00	1.00	−1.00	0.00
NC		−Z	−180,000	−13.00	−14.00	0.00	0.00	0.00	2.00	0.00
Second tableau										
I	0.00	S_1	8,000	1.33	0.00	1.00	−.33	0.00	0.00	0.00
II	0.00	X_2	12,000	.67	1.00	0.00	.33	0.00	0.00	0.00
III	10.00	A_1	1,000	.33	0.00	0.00	−.33	0.00	0.00	1.00
IV	1.00	U_1	2,000	.33	0.00	0.00	−1.33	1.00	−1.00	0.00
NC		−Z	−12,000	−3.67	0.00	0.00	4.67	0.00	2.00	0.00
Third (final) tableau										
I	0.00	S_1	4,000	0.00	0.00	1.00	1.00	0.00	0.00	−4.00
II	0.00	X_2	10,000	0.00	1.00	0.00	1.00	0.00	0.00	−2.00
III	0.00	X_1	3,000	1.00	0.00	0.00	−1.00	0.00	0.00	3.00
IV	1.00	U_1	1,000	0.00	0.00	0.00	−1.00	1.00	−1.00	−1.00
NC		−Z	−1,000	0.00	0.00	0.00	1.00	0.00	2.00	11.00

The optimal solution indicates that the firm should produce 3000 Western American handbags and 10,000 Roaring Twenties handbags. The objective function has a value of 1000, indicating that the best we can do is come within $1000 of target revenue. This may be verified in two ways. The optimal value of U_1 is 1000, which indicates that we were $1000 under the stated goal. We obtain total revenue by multiplying the units of each type of handbag produced by its selling price and summing for the two products. Thus, 3000(3) + 10,000(4) = 49,000.

Distinguishing between underachievement and overachievement

The problem formulation we considered in the previous section contained a variable (U_1) that represented underachievement and a variable (E_1) that represented overachievement. The presence of these variables in the objective function indicates that the decision maker is striving for exact achievement of the goal — to minimize the total deviation, whether it be in the positive or the negative direction. In any solution, either U_1 or E_1 must be zero, because a single solution cannot deviate in both directions from a stated goal.

In many situations, the decision maker may be anxious to avoid underachievement of a particular goal but willing to accept overachievement. In such cases, E_1 would be eliminated from the objective function and the model would seek to minimize only U_1, underachievement of the goal. Underachievement may be acceptable in other situations, wherein the objective is to minimize overachievement. In these situations, U_1 would be eliminated from the objective function and the model would seek to minimize E_1, overachievement of the goal.

Goal programming with weighted deviational variables

In the foregoing sections, we introduced the concept of programming to a goal by minimizing the sum of the deviations from that goal. In many cases, preventing one type of deviation may be more important to the decision maker than preventing another type of deviation. An extension of our analysis is to weigh the deviational variables in the objective function according to the importance the decision maker places on them.[1] As we shall show, this technique also allows the decision maker to incorporate several goals into a single objective function.

The constraint set

Assume that in a subsequent production period, Kiefer Industries signs a contract to produce 16,000 handbags. This represents an increase of 3000 handbags over the previous period. In fact, production of this many units in a given period may require the use of overtime in the cutting department, the stitching department, or both departments. Overtime costs the company $.18 per minute in the cutting department and $.30 per minute in the stitching department. We can allow for overtime in the cutting department by writing the cutting time constraint as follows:

$$2X_1 + 1X_2 + U_1 - E_1 = 20,000 \qquad \text{(cutting constraint)}$$

The variable U_1 represents underachievement, or underutilization of the 20,000 minutes of cutting time available. It is similar to the slack variables used in less-than-or-equal-to constraints. The variable E_1 represents overutilization of cutting time; that is, it is the amount of overtime that must be used in the cutting department.

Overtime in the stitching department can be handled in a like manner. We can write the constraint as follows:

$$2X_1 + 3X_2 + U_2 - E_2 = 36,000 \qquad \text{(stitching constraint)}$$

The variable U_2 is analogous to a slack variable and represents underutilization of the 36,000 minutes of stitching time available. The amount of necessary overtime in the stitching department is represented by the variable E_2.

[1]Technically, failure to assign weights other than 1 in the previous example implies that the deviations are of equal importance to the decision maker.

We must ensure that the production quota of 16,000 is met exactly, without any deviation. Accordingly, we use no deviational variables in the production contract constraint, but formulate it as a strict equality constraint as follows:

$$X_1 + X_2 = 16,000 \qquad \text{(contract constraint)}$$

To simplify this example, we have not placed a limit on the amount of overtime that can be used. In most problems, constraints must be formulated to limit the use of overtime.

The objective function

Mr. Galla would like to minimize the cost of the overtime used in the cutting and stitching departments at Kiefer Industries. The cost of overtime in the cutting department is $.18 a minute, and the cost of overtime in the stitching department is $.30 a minute. Thus, other things being equal, Mr. Galla would prefer to use overtime in the cutting department rather than in the stitching department. He can accomplish this by assigning weights to the deviational variables in the objective function. These weights should reflect the relative magnitude of the decision maker's preference. In this example, the decision maker's preference is accurately reflected by the cost of overtime in the two departments. Thus, the objective function can be written as

$$\text{Min } Z = .18E_1 + .30E_2$$

Mr. Galla is not concerned about underutilization of resources. Presumably, no cost is associated with slack time. The two variables representing underutilization do not appear in the objective function. This, of course, is the same as assigning them a zero coefficient in the objective function. In other examples, variables representing both underutilization and overutilization may be assigned weights in the objective function.

Solving a problem with a weighted objective function

The appropriate linear programming formulation for this problem is

$$\text{Min } Z = .18E_1 + .30E_2$$
$$\begin{aligned}
\text{s.t.} \quad & 2X_1 + 1X_2 + U_1 - E_1 = 20,000 \qquad \text{(cutting constraint)} \\
& 2X_1 + 3X_2 + U_2 - E_2 = 36,000 \qquad \text{(stitching constraint)} \\
& X_1 + X_2 = 16,000 \qquad \text{(contract constraint)} \\
& X_i, U_i, E_i \geq 0, \text{ for all } i
\end{aligned}$$

The problem can be solved by the simplex method. The initial and final tableaus are given in Table 8.2. The optimal solution is $X_1 = 12,000$, $X_2 = 4000$, $E_1 = 8000$, and $Z = \$1440$. The Kiefer Company should produce the 16,000 handbags by utilizing 8000 minutes of

Table 8.2 *Programming to a goal with weighted variables*

0 Row	Price vector	Solution vector	Quantity vector	0.00 X_1	0.00 X_2	0.00 U_1	.18 E_1	0.00 U_2	.30 E_2	10.00 A_1
Initial tableau										
I	0.00	U_1	20,000	2.00	1.00	1.00	−1.00	0.00	0.00	0.00
II	0.00	U_2	36,000	2.00	3.00	0.00	0.00	1.00	−1.00	0.00
III	10.00	A_1	16,000	1.00	1.00	0.00	0.00	0.00	0.00	1.00
NC		−Z	−160,000	−10.00	−10.00	0.00	.18	0.00	.30	0.00
Fourth (final) tableau										
I	0.00	X_1	12,000	1.00	0.00	0.00	0.00	−1.00	1.00	3.00
II	0.00	X_2	4,000	0.00	1.00	0.00	0.00	1.00	−1.00	−2.00
III	.18	E_1	8,000	0.00	0.00	−1.00	1.00	−1.00	1.00	4.00
NC		−Z	−1,440	0.00	0.00	.18	0.00	.18	.12	9.28

overtime in the cutting department. The cost of this overtime is $1440. This is the optimal solution. It produces the 16,000 handbags at minimum overtime cost.

Programming to multiple goals with ordinal priority

In the previous sections, we discussed the concept of programming to goals and illustrated how deviations from these goals could be weighted according to the preferences of the decision maker. We now want to program to two or more separate goals. We will also assume that the decision maker can assign a priority to the goals. This is an *absolute priority* in the sense that the goal with the highest priority will be satisfied to the fullest extent possible before the next-priority goal is considered.

Formulating the constraints

Assume that Mr. Galla at Kiefer Industries has established two goals for the next production period. His first-priority goal is to ensure that revenue equals or exceeds $55,000. His second-priority goal is to produce the 16,000 handbags with a minimum overtime cost in the two production departments. We may therefore formulate the constraints to the problem as follows:

$$2X_1 + X_2 + U_1 - E_1 = 20,000 \quad \text{(cutting time)}$$
$$2X_1 + 3X_2 + U_2 - E_2 = 36,000 \quad \text{(stitching time)}$$
$$1X_1 + 1X_2 = 16,000 \quad \text{(contract production)}$$
$$3X_1 + 4X_2 + U_3 - E_3 = 55,000 \quad \text{(target revenue)}$$
$$X_i, U_i, E_i \geq 0, \quad \text{for all } i.$$

The first two constraints allow for both underutilization and overtime in the cutting and stitching departments. The third constraint indicates that production must exactly equal 16,000 units. The fourth constraint allows for both underachievement and overachievement of the target revenue goal of $55,000.

Multiple objective functions

In goal programming, if ordinal goals exist, we formulate an objective function for each goal. In this example, the *first priority* is to strive for a total revenue of at least $55,000. In other words, Mr. Galla wants to minimize underachievement of the revenue goal, which we represent mathematically as follows:[2]

$$[P_1] \quad \text{is} \quad \text{Min } Z_1 = 1U_3$$

In this relationship, E_3 has a zero coefficient, because overachievement of the goal is satisfactory. Thus, no objective function penalty coefficient is assigned to overachievement.

The *second priority* is to minimize the overtime cost in the two production centers, or

$$[P_2] \quad \text{is} \quad \text{Min } Z_2 = .18E_1 + .30E_2$$

The initial tableau

The initial tableau for this problem is given in Table 8.3. This tableau closely resembles the simplex tableaus of Chapters 5 and 6. In this tableau, however, there are two "Price vector" columns and two net contribution (NC) rows. One "Price vector" column and one NC row correspond to the first-priority objective. The second "Price vector" column and the second NC row correspond to the second-priority objective. The table is arranged so that the "Price vector" column and NC row associated with the highest-priority objective function are located on the outer part or rim of the tableau. Lower-priority items are located successively inward toward the center of the tableau.

The solution in the initial tableau of Table 8.3 is $U_1 = 20,000$, $U_2 = 36,000$, $A_1 = 16,000$, and $U_3 = 55,000$. The objective function value for priority one is 215,000, which we obtain by multiplying the value of each variable by its objective function coefficient and summing for all variables in the solution. Thus,

$$Z_1 = 20,000(\$0) + 36,000(\$0) + 16,000(\$10) + 55,000(\$1) = \$215,000$$

In this example, the artificial variable A_1 has an objective function penalty coefficient of $10.

For each priority, the net contribution values are determined exactly

[2]The symbol $[P_i]$ is used to indicate the objective function with priority i.

Table 8.3 *An example of the goal programming algorithm*

Row	Price vector	Price vector	Solution vector	Quantity vector	X_1	X_2	U_1	E_1	U_2	E_2	U_3	E_3	A_1
0 [P_1]					0.00	0.00	0.00	.00	0.00	.00	1.00	.00	10.00
0 [P_2]					0.00	0.00	0.00	.18	0.00	.30	.00	0.00	10.00
Initial Tableau													
I	0	0.00	U_1	20,000	2.00	1.00	1.00	−1.00	0.00	0.00	0.00	0.00	0.00
II	0	0.00	U_2	36,000	2.00	3.00	0.00	0.00	1.00	−1.00	0.00	0.00	0.00
III	10.00	10.00	A_1	16,000	1.00	1.00	0.00	0.00	0.00	0.00	0.00	0.00	1.00
IV	1.00	0.00	U_3	55,000	3.00	4.00	0.00	0.00	0.00	0.00	1.00	−1.00	0.00
NC_2			$-Z_2$	−160,000	−10.00	−10.00	0.00	.18	0.00	.30	0.00	0.00	0.00
NC_1			$-Z_1$	−215,000	−13.00	−14.00	0.00	0.00	0.00	0.00	0.00	1.00	0.00
Fourth tableau													
I	0	0	U_1	4,000	1.00	0.00	1.00	−1.00	0.00	0.00	0.00	0.00	−1.00
II	0	0	X_2	16,000	1.00	1.00	0.00	0.00	0.00	0.00	0.00	0.00	1.00
III	0	0	E_3	9,000	1.00	0.00	0.00	0.00	0.00	0.00	−1.00	1.00	4.00
IV	0	.30	E_2	12,000	1.00	0.00	0.00	0.00	1.00	−1.00	0.00	0.00	3.00
NC_2			$-Z_2$	−3,600	−.30	0.00	0.00	.18	.30	0.00	0.00	0.00	9.10
NC_1			$-Z_1$	0	0.00	0.00	0.00	0.00	0.00	0.00	1.00	0.00	10.00
Fifth tableau													
I	0	0	X_1	4,000	1.00	0.00	1.00	−1.00	0.00	0.00	0.00	0.00	−1.00
II	0	0	X_2	12,000	0.00	1.00	−1.00	1.00	0.00	0.00	0.00	0.00	2.00
III	0	0	E_3	5,000	0.00	0.00	−1.00	1.00	0.00	0.00	−1.00	1.00	5.00
IV	0	.30	E_2	8,000	0.00	0.00	−1.00	1.00	1.00	−1.00	1.00	0.00	4.00
NC_2			$-Z_2$	−2,400	0.00	0.00	.30	−.12	.30	0.00	0.00	0.00	8.80
NC_1			$-Z_1$	0	0.00	0.00	0.00	0.00	0.00	0.00	1.00	0.00	10.00
Sixth (final) tableau													
I	0	0	X_1	9,000	1.00	0.00	0.00	0.00	0.00	0.00	−1.00	1.00	4.00
II	0	0	X_2	7,000	0.00	1.00	0.00	0.00	0.00	0.00	1.00	−1.00	−3.00
III	0	.18	E_1	5,000	0.00	0.00	−1.00	1.00	0.00	0.00	−1.00	1.00	5.00
IV	0	.30	E_2	3,000	0.00	0.00	0.00	0.00	−1.00	1.00	1.00	−1.00	−1.00
NC_2			$-Z_2$	−1,800	0.00	0.00	.18	0.00	.30	0.00	−.12	.12	9.40
NC_1			$-Z_1$	0	0.00	0.00	0.00	0.00	0.00	0.00	1.00	0.00	10.00

as in the standard simplex method. As an example, consider the variable X_2. In priority one, it has a zero objective function coefficient. For each unit of X_2 entered into the solution, we must give up 1 unit of U_1, 3 units of U_2, 1 unit of A_1 and 4 units of U_3. In the first-priority objective function, these variables have coefficients of 0, 0, 10, and 1 respectively. Thus, the net contribution value of X_2 for the priority-one NC row is

$$NC_1 = 0 - [1(0) + 3(0) + 1(10) + 4(1)] = -14$$

Likewise, the priority-two objective function coefficients for X_2, U_1, U_2, A_1, and U_3 are 0, 0, 0, 10, and 0 respectively. Thus, the priority-two net contribution factor for X_2 is

$$NC_2 = 0 - [1(0) + 3(0) + 1(10) + 4(0)] = -10$$

The goal programming simplex algorithm is very similar to the standard linear programming simplex algorithm. It first seeks the solution that best achieves the highest-priority objective. Once the priority-one objective is satisfied to the fullest extent possible, the algorithm moves toward satisfying the priority-two objective. Each lower objective is then considered on a priority basis. The algorithm ensures that no sacrifice is ever made on a higher-priority goal in order to better satisfy a lower-priority goal. In other words, every improvement made on a lower-priority goal must be made without decreasing the degree of satisfaction of all higher-priority goals. We will use the Kiefer Industries example to illustrate the algorithm.

The goal programming algorithm

The first step in the goal programming routine is to decide which variable to enter into the solution. Since this is a minimization problem, we select the variable that has the most negative value in the NC_1 row. In the first tableau this is X_2, which has a net contribution value of -14. From this point on, the new tableau is generated by exactly the same procedure that we used in the standard simplex method. The same process is used for the third and fourth tableaus. At each iteration, we enter the variable with the most negative coefficient in the NC_1 row.

In the fourth tableau, all elements in the NC_1 row are either positive or zero. This indicates that the priority-one objective has been satisfied to the fullest extent possible, and we may now turn our attention to the priority-two objective. The next variable to enter the solution should be the one with the most negative value in the NC_2 row. *No variable can be chosen to enter the solution, however, unless it has a zero net contribution value for all higher-priority goals.* This simply means that we cannot enter a variable that would reduce the degree of satisfaction of an objective considered more important by the decision maker. Thus, the variable we choose to enter is the one with the most negative net contribution value for the priority under consideration and with a zero net contribution value for all higher-priority goals. In the fourth tableau, this is variable X_1. This variable has a net contribution value of $-.30$ for the priority-two goal and a net contribution value of zero for the priority-one goal. Thus, 1 unit of X_1 would decrease overtime cost by \$.30 and would have no effect on the degree of satisfaction of the revenue goal.

In the sixth tableau in Table 8.3, U_3 is the only variable with a negative net contribution value for the priority-two objective. It cannot be entered into the solution, because it does not have a zero value in all higher-priority NC rows. Thus, tableau six represents the optimal solution to the goal programming problem. This optimal solution is $X_1 = 9000$, $X_2 = 7000$, $E_1 = 5000$, $E_2 = 3000$, $Z_1 = 0$, and $Z_2 = 1800$.

Sample problem 8.1   *THE WARRINGTON RESEARCH FOUNDATION*

The Warrington Research Foundation is determining how to allocate $300,000 to three research foundations. The Alpha Foundation is known to use 40% of its income for pure research, 30% for applied research, and 30% for administrative overhead. The Beta Foundation allocates 50% to pure research, 10% to applied research, and 40% to administrative overhead. The corresponding figures at the Gamma Foundation are 20%, 60%, and 20%. The Warrington Foundation's first priority is to keep total administrative cost to less than $75,000. Its second priority is to allocate $150,000 each to pure and applied research. It knows this goal is not completely attainable. Any dollar shortage in funds for pure research is twice as undesirable as the same dollar shortage in funds for applied research. As its third priority, the foundation would like to minimize the amount given to Gamma Foundation, which has received large contributions from other sources. Let X_1, X_2, and X_3 be the amounts given to Alpha, Beta, and Gamma Foundations respectively. Formulate this as a goal programming problem.

SOLUTION

$$[P_1] \quad \text{Min } Z_1 = E_1$$
$$[P_2] \quad \text{Min } Z_2 = 2U_3 + 1U_2$$
$$[P_3] \quad \text{Min } Z_3 = X_3$$

s.t.
$$X_1 + X_2 + X_3 = 300{,}000 \qquad \text{(total funds)}$$
$$.3X_1 + .4X_2 + .2X_3 + U_1 - E_1 = 75{,}000 \qquad \text{(administrative cost)}$$
$$.3X_1 + .1X_2 + .6X_3 + U_2 - E_2 = 150{,}000 \qquad \text{(applied research)}$$
$$.4X_1 + .5X_2 + .2X_3 + U_3 - E_3 = 150{,}000 \qquad \text{(pure research)}$$
$$X_i, U_i, E_i \geqslant \qquad 0, \quad \text{for all } i$$

A review of the solution process

It would be helpful to review the solution process of this goal programming problem. The priority-one goal was to ensure that total revenue is at least $55,000. The algorithm first sought to achieve this objective to the fullest extent possible. The solution given in tableau 4 does satisfy this objective. The 16,000 Roaring Twenties handbags ($X_2 = 16{,}000$) generated a net revenue of $64,000. This solution is obtained, however, by using 12,000 minutes of overtime ($E_2 = 12{,}000$) in the stitching department. This overtime cost to the firm is $3600.

The algorithm then proceeded to minimize the cost of overtime. In the process, care was taken to ensure that a revenue of at least $55,000 was maintained in all solutions. The optimal solution is given in the sixth tableau. It calls for the production of 9000 Western American handbags and 7000 Roaring Twenties handbags. This requires the use of 5000 minutes of overtime in the cutting department and 3000 minutes of overtime in the stitching department. Total cost of overtime has been reduced to $1800, and the solution generates exactly $55,000 of total revenue.

Integer programming

Illustrative example: PIB'S LITTLE GOLF CLUB

PIB's Little Golf Club is a miniature golf course located in a New England resort area. Ms. Ola Alvarez is owner and operator of PIB's. She plans to advertise during the summer resort season and has budgeted $71 a week for this purpose. This budget will be spent to show "promotional putting minifilms" at two movie theaters. Ms. Alvarez would like to allocate her expenditures between the two theaters so as to reach the largest possible number of viewers.

Minifilms shown at the downtown theater are 4 minutes in length. Each showing costs $12 and is expected to be seen by an average audience of 200 people. The downtown theater can only sell 13 minutes of commercial time a week to PIB's. Minifilms shown at the drive-in theater are 2 minutes in length. The cost of each presentation is $16. Each minifilm is expected to be seen by 300 people. During the next several months, the drive-in theater has a maximum of 7 minutes of commercial time a week available for sale to PIB's.

Ms. Alvarez was formerly chief production engineer for a large manufacturer of home ice cream freezers. In that capacity, she used linear programming to determine weekly production schedules. She has applied her knowledge of linear programming to the present problem. The optimal linear programming solution is to run 1.25 films a week at the downtown theater and 3.5 films a week at the drive-in theater.

Unfortunately, it is not possible to show part of a film. At the freezer plant, Ms. Alvarez was dealing with such large numbers that relatively little was lost by "dropping the fractions" and using only the integer parts of the answer. Dropping the fractions in this example would result in showing 1 film per week in the downtown theater and 3 films per week in the drive-in theater. Ms. Alvarez wonders, however, if this is really the proper course of action.

Integer programming, like goal programming, can be considered a special type of linear programming. Actually, integer linear programming models are nonlinear models. They would be linear except for the fact that some or all of the variables are constrained to have integer values. Ms. Alvarez' problem, simple as it is, requires integer values.

She cannot purchase 1.25 or 3.5 commercials. She must purchase either a whole commercial or none at all.

A possible solution for Ms. Alvarez is to use only the integer parts of the answers. This would call for the purchase of 1 minifilm per week at the downtown theater and 3 films per week at the drive-in theater. As we shall see, this is not the optimal integer solution. A second possibility is to round the answers to the nearest integer value. In many cases, however, the solution obtained by rounding will not satisfy all of the constraints. And even if the rounded solution is feasible, there is no guarantee that it is the optimal integer solution. Thus, we must use a special procedure to ensure that we do have the optimal integer solution.

Many procedures can be used to solve integer programming problems. Most algorithms in use today fall into a broad category known as *branch-and-bound* techniques. A second general approach is to introduce a series of secondary constraints, or *cutting planes*, that successively reduce the feasible region until an optimal integer solution is obtained. Regardless of the procedure used, the computational burden for solving an integer programming problem is much greater than for solving a standard linear programming problem of similar size.

This chapter emphasizes the secondary-constraint approach to the solution of integer programming problems. Recent research has indicated that branch-and-bound methods are more efficient on high-speed computers than are algorithms that use the secondary-constraint approach. However, we have chosen the cutting-plane approach, because it best illustrates the concepts of integer programming.

Basic representation of an integer programming problem

Before proceeding with solution techniques, we must put the integer programming problem into a standard mathematical format. A graphical representation will also help us understand the mathematical solution techniques that follow.

Standard mathematical formulation

The standard integer programming formulation is almost identical to the standard linear programming format. The only difference is the inclusion of a statement that some, or all, of the variables must be integer-valued. Problems that require all of the original variables to be integers are referred to as *pure-integer problems*. In many situations, only some of the variables must have integer values. These are known as *mixed-integer problems*. The formulation of the PIB's Little Golf Club problem follows. The variable X_1 represents the number of minifilms to be shown per week at the downtown theater. The variable X_2 represents the number of minifilms to be shown each week at the drive-in theater.

$$\text{Max } Z = 2X_1 + 3X_2 \quad \text{(hundreds of viewers)}$$

s.t.
$$12X_1 + 16X_2 \leqslant 71 \quad \text{(budget)}$$
$$4X_1 + 0X_2 \leqslant 13 \quad \text{(downtown)}$$
$$0X_1 + 2X_2 \leqslant 7 \quad \text{(drive-in)}$$
$$X_1, X_2 \geqslant 0$$
$$X_1 \text{ and } X_2 \text{ are integers}$$

All-integer constraints and objective function

Some integer programming algorithms require that all coefficients in the constraints and objective function be integer-valued. The right-hand side of each constraint must also be integer-valued. For the constraints, this can be accomplished by multiplying every value in the constraint by the least common denominator. As an example, consider the constraint

$$\tfrac{1}{2}X_3 + \tfrac{2}{3}X_4 \leqslant \tfrac{25}{4}$$

The least common denominator is 12, and the equivalent integer-valued constraint is $6X_3 + 8X_4 \leqslant 75$.

The objective function can be treated in the same manner. For example, the objective function $Z = \tfrac{2}{3}X_5$ can be changed to $3Z = 2X_5$. Remember that the calculated optimal solution is for $3Z$. We must divide by 3 to obtain the optimal value of the original objective function.

Graphing the integer programming problem

The graphical representation of the PIB problem is given in Figure 8.1. It is similar to a standard linear programming graphical representation, but there is one major difference. If integer answers were not required, the feasible region would be represented by the entire shaded area in Figure 8.1. Since integer answers are required, however, the only feasible areas are represented by the integer dots within the shaded area.

The isoprofit line for an objective function value of 6 is given in Figure 8.1. By moving in the direction of increasing viewers, we see that the optimal noninteger solution is at point A, where $X_1 = 1.25$ and $X_2 = 3.5$. The optimal integer solution is at point B, where $X_1 = 3$, $X_2 = 2$, and $Z = 1200$. Thus, the procedure of using only the integer parts of the optimal noninteger answer would have yielded incorrect results. This can be easily verified for the PIB problem. The integer parts of the

Figure 8.1 *Graphical representation of the PIB problem*

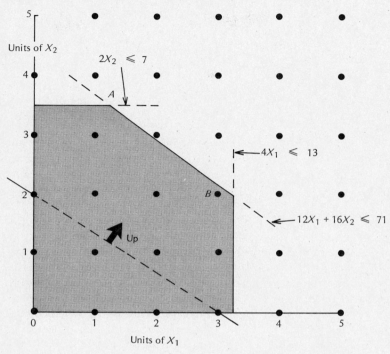

optimal noninteger answer are $X_1 = 1$ and $X_2 = 3$. This yields an objective function value of $Z = 2(1) + 3(3) = 11 = 1100$ viewers.

These calculations confirm Ms. Alvarez' fear that taking the integer parts of the optimal noninteger answer may not lead to the proper course of action.

The cutting-plane approach

The rationale underlying the cutting-plane approach is simple. We begin with an optimal solution to the noninteger linear programming problem. If the optimal solution happens by chance to be an integer solution, then our problem is solved. In most situations, the optimal linear programming solution is not integer-valued. In these cases, we add a series of secondary constraints to the linear programming problem. Each secondary constraint forms a cutting plane that reduces the size of the set of feasible solutions.

A cutting plane only "cuts away" noninteger solutions; that is, no

Table 8.4 *Linear programming solution to the PIB problem*

0 Row	Price vector	Solution vector	Quantity vector	2 X_1	3 X_2	0 S_1	0 S_2	0 S_3
Initial tableau								
I	0	S_1	71	12	16	1	0	0
II	0	S_2	13	4	0	0	1	0
III	0	S_3	7	0	2	0	0	1
NC		$-Z$	0	2	3	0	0	0
Third (final) tableau								
I	2	X_1	$5/4$	1	0	$1/12$	0	$-2/3$
II	0	S_2	8	0	0	$-1/3$	1	$8/3$
III	3	X_2	$7/2$	0	1	0	0	$1/2$
NC		$-Z$	-13	0	0	$-1/6$	0	$-1/6$

Note: Z is in hundreds of viewers.

integer solution is lost by applying a cutting plane. After each cut, an optimal solution is found for the new set of feasible solutions. Since no integer values are cut away, this procedure must eventually lead to the optimal integer answer.

Table 8.4 gives the initial and final tableaus that result from solving the noninteger PIB problem by the simplex method. The optimal noninteger solution, as shown in the final tableau of Table 8.4, is $X_1 = 1.25$, $X_2 = 3.5$, and $Z = 13$.

Congruence and fractional parts

Each cutting plane will be formed from the fractional parts of a row in the simplex tableau. In order to determine the fractional part of a number, it is necessary to understand the concept of congruence. Two numbers are said to be *congruent* if the difference between them is an integer. Thus, $8/3$ is congruent to $2/3$, because the difference is the integer 2. Likewise, $-10/3$ is congruent to $2/3$, because the difference between them is the integer -4; that is, $(-10/3) - (+2/3) = -4$.

We will consider the *fractional part* of a number X to be the smallest nonnegative number that is congruent to X. Thus, if $X = 5/3$, the fractional part of X is $2/3$. If $X = -7/5$, the fractional part of X is $3/5$, because $-7/5$ minus $+3/5$ equals -2. The fractional part of any integer is zero. The fractional part of $1/4$ is $1/4$. The fractional part of $-1/4$ is $3/4$.

The first secondary constraint

The first secondary constraint for the PIB problem should be formed from the final simplex tableau in Table 8.4. We form this constraint by using the fractional parts of one of the rows in the tableau. The row we use must be associated with a variable in the final solution that is required to have an integer value. Consider the final tableau of Table 8.4. The variables X_1 and X_2 are both required to have integer values, but the variable S_2 may take on any positive value. Thus, either row I or row III may be used to form the secondary constraint. In practice, the variable with the largest fractional part in the final solution is usually chosen. In our example, X_1 has a fractional part of $\frac{1}{4}$ and X_2 has a fractional part of $\frac{1}{2}$, so we choose row III, which is associated with X_2.

We form the new constraint by adding together the fractional parts of each variable in the selected row, subtracting a surplus variable, and setting them equal to the fractional part of the values in the "Quantity vector" column. We will use row III in the final tableau of Table 8.4 as an example. The only variable in this row that has a fractional part is S_3. Its fractional part is $\frac{1}{2}$. All other variables have integer coefficients and thus zero fractional parts. The right-hand-side value (in the "Quantity vector" column) is $\frac{7}{2}$ and therefore has a fractional part of $\frac{1}{2}$. Thus, the new constraint is

$$0X_1 + 0X_2 + 0S_1 + 0S_2 + .5S_3 - T_1 = .5 \quad \text{or}$$
$$.5S_3 - T_1 = .5$$

This constraint should now be added to the final tableau, and a new optimal solution should be determined.

Graphically representing the cutting plane

The new constraint formed from row III is

$$.5S_3 - T_1 = .5$$

Since T_1 is a surplus variable,

$$.5S_3 \geq .5$$

In the original linear programming formulation, the third constraint was

$$2X_2 + S_3 = 7$$

Since S_3 must now be greater than or equal to 1, this implies that

$$2X_2 \leq 6$$

A graphical representation of the PIB problem with this constraint added is shown in Figure 8.2. Three items should be noted. (1) The new cutting plane reduced the size of the set of feasible solutions. (2) Among the points eliminated was the optimal noninteger solution to the original problem. (3) In the reduction process, no integer-valued feasible solutions were removed. This will be the case with each cutting plane.

Figure 8.2 *Graphical representation of the first cutting plane in the PIB problem*

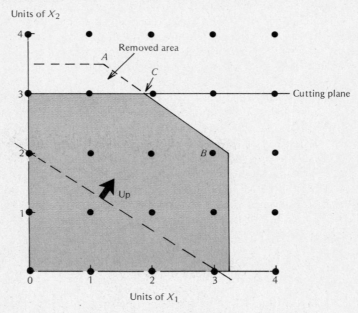

The optimal noninteger solution to the new problem can be obtained from the graph in Figure 8.2. It is at point C, where $X_1 = {}^{23}\!/_{12}$ and $X_2 = 3.0$.

Mathematically determining the new optimal solution

The new constraint should be multiplied by a -1, yielding the constraint

$$-.5S_3 + T_1 = -.5$$

We must add this constraint to the final tableau of Table 8.4, and doing so results in the initial tableau given in Table 8.5. The only change that has been made is to add a T_1 row and a T_1 column.[3]

---

[3]The reader should be aware that some of the procedures used in this section are different from the standard simplex procedures discussed in Chapter 5. For example, it is now permissible for a variable to have a negative value. Also, the dual simplex method first selects the variable to be removed and then selects the variable to enter. This is the opposite of the standard simplex method. These changes result from the different natures of the simplex and dual simplex methods. The simplex method begins with a suboptimal feasible solution and moves toward an optimal feasible solution. In this situation, the addition of a constraint makes the present solution nonfeasible; that is, it does not satisfy all of the constraints. The dual simplex method is used to regain feasibility.

Table 8.5 *Obtaining an optimal solution with one secondary constraint*

0 Row	Price vector	Solution vector	Quantity vector	2 X_1	3 X_2	0 S_1	0 S_2	0 S_3	0 T_1
Initial tableau									
I	2	X_1	$5/4$	1	0	$1/12$	0	$-2/3$	0
II	0	S_2	8	0	0	$-1/3$	1	$8/3$	0
III	3	X_2	$7/2$	0	1	0	0	$1/2$	0
IV	0	T_1	$-1/2$	0	0	0	0	$-1/2$	1
NC		$-Z$	-13	0	0	$-1/6$	0	$-1/6$	0
Second (final) tableau									
I	2	X_1	$23/12$	1	0	$1/12$	0	0	$-4/3$
II	0	S_2	$16/3$	0	0	$-1/3$	1	0	$16/3$
III	3	X_2	3	0	1	0	0	0	1
IV	0	S_3	1	0	0	0	0	1	-2
NC		$-Z$	$-77/6$	0	0	$-1/6$	0	0	$-1/3$

We obtain the new optimal solution by applying a technique known as the *dual simplex method*. For a maximization problem, the procedure is as follows:

1. First *select the variable to be removed* from the solution. This is the variable with the most negative value in the "Quantity vector" column. Circle this row.
2. Form a set of entrance test ratios by dividing every element in the NC row by the corresponding element in the "leaving" or circled row. *Select the variable with the minimum positive ratio to enter the solution.* Circle this column.
3. Use the standard simplex procedure to derive the next tableau. *If all values in the "Quantity vector" column are positive, an optimal solution has been obtained.* If one or more values are negative, we must return to step 1 and perform another iteration.

The tableau generated by using this procedure is given in Table 8.5. The optimal linear programming solution, with the first cutting plane attached, is given in the final tableau of Table 8.5. This solution is $X_1 = 23/12$, $X_2 = 3$, and $Z = 77/6$.

Subsequent cutting planes

The first secondary constraint did not result in an integer solution. Additional cutting planes must be utilized. In the optimal solution in Table 8.5, X_1 is the variable with the largest fractional part. The new constraint will therefore be formed from row I. Using the same procedure as in the preceding section, we find that the new constraint is

$$\tfrac{1}{12}S_1 + \tfrac{2}{3}T_1 - T_2 = \tfrac{11}{12}$$

This constraint should be multiplied by a -1 and added to the simplex tableau. The new tableau is given in Table 8.6. We can then use the dual simplex method to obtain a new optimal solution. The final tableau of Table 8.6 is the optimal solution to the linear programming problem with two secondary constraints added. In this solution, $X_1 = \tfrac{13}{4}$ and $X_2 = \tfrac{15}{8}$. This obviously does not meet the integer requirements, so an additional cutting plane must be used.

The third and final secondary constraint is formed from row III of the final tableau in Table 8.6. The new tableau and its solution by the dual simplex method are given in Table 8.7. The optimal solution is $X_1 = 3$ and $X_2 = 2$. This is an integer solution. The objective function has a value of 12. Ms. Alvarez should show 3 commercials per week at the downtown theater and 2 commercials per week at the drive-in theater. This will provide an average viewing audience of 1200.

Table 8.6 *The solution with two secondary constraints*

0	Price	Solution	Quantity	2	3	0	0	0	0	0
Row	vector	vector	vector	X_1	X_2	S_1	S_2	S_3	T_1	T_2
Initial tableau										
I	2	X_1	$\tfrac{23}{12}$	1	0	$\tfrac{1}{12}$	0	0	$-\tfrac{4}{3}$	0
II	0	S_2	$\tfrac{16}{3}$	0	0	$-\tfrac{1}{3}$	1	0	$\tfrac{16}{3}$	0
III	3	X_2	3	0	1	0	0	0	1	0
IV	0	S_3	1	0	0	0	0	1	-2	0
V	0	T_2	$-\tfrac{11}{12}$	0	0	$-\tfrac{1}{12}$	0	0	$-\tfrac{2}{3}$	1
NC		$-Z$	$-\tfrac{77}{6}$	0	0	$-\tfrac{1}{6}$	0	0	$-\tfrac{1}{3}$	0
Second tableau										
I	2	X_1	$\tfrac{45}{12}$	1	0	$\tfrac{3}{12}$	0	0	0	-2
II	0	S_2	-2	0	0	-1	1	0	0	8
III	3	X_2	$\tfrac{13}{8}$	0	1	$-\tfrac{1}{8}$	0	0	0	$\tfrac{3}{2}$
IV	0	S_3	$\tfrac{45}{12}$	0	0	$\tfrac{1}{4}$	0	1	0	-3
V	0	T_1	$\tfrac{33}{24}$	0	0	$\tfrac{3}{24}$	0	0	1	$-\tfrac{3}{2}$
NC		$-Z$	$-\tfrac{99}{8}$	0	0	$-\tfrac{1}{8}$	0	0	0	$-\tfrac{1}{2}$
Third (final) tableau										
I	2	X_1	$\tfrac{13}{4}$	1	0	0	$\tfrac{3}{12}$	0	0	0
II	0	S_1	2	0	0	1	-1	0	0	-8
III	3	X_2	$\tfrac{15}{8}$	0	1	0	$-\tfrac{1}{8}$	0	0	$\tfrac{1}{2}$
IV	0	S_3	$\tfrac{39}{12}$	0	0	0	$\tfrac{1}{4}$	1	0	-1
V	0	T_1	$\tfrac{27}{24}$	0	0	0	$\tfrac{3}{24}$	0	1	$-\tfrac{1}{2}$
NC		$-Z$	$-\tfrac{97}{8}$	0	0	0	$-\tfrac{1}{8}$	0	0	$-\tfrac{3}{2}$

Table 8.7 *Optimal solution to the PIB problem with three cutting planes*

0 Row	Price vector	Solution vector	Quantity vector	2 X_1	3 X_2	0 S_1	0 S_2	0 S_3	0 T_1	0 T_2	0 T_3
Initial tableau											
I	2	X_1	$13/4$	1	0	0	$3/12$	0	0	0	0
II	0	S_1	2	0	0	1	-1	0	0	-8	0
III	3	X_2	$15/8$	0	1	0	$-1/8$	0	0	$1/2$	0
IV	0	S_3	$39/12$	0	0	0	$1/4$	1	0	-1	0
V	0	T_1	$27/24$	0	0	0	$3/24$	0	1	$-1/2$	0
VI	0	T_3	$-7/8$	0	0	0	$-7/8$	0	0	$-1/2$	1
NC		$-Z$	$-97/8$	0	0	0	$-1/8$	0	0	$-3/2$	0
Second (final) tableau											
I	2	X_1	3	1	0	0	0	0	0	$-1/7$	$2/7$
II	0	S_1	3	0	0	1	0	0	0	$-52/7$	$-8/7$
III	3	X_2	2	0	1	0	0	0	0	$4/7$	$-1/7$
IV	0	S_3	3	0	0	0	0	1	0	$-8/7$	$2/7$
V	0	T_1	1	0	0	0	0	0	1	$-4/7$	$1/7$
VI	0	S_2	1	0	0	0	1	0	0	$+4/7$	$-8/7$
NC		$-Z$	-12	0	0	0	0	0	0	$-107/7$	$-1/7$

A review of the cutting-plane approach

Figure 8.3 provides a graphical review of the cutting plane, or secondary-constraint, approach to integer programming. The example used is the problem at PIB's Little Golf Club.

The first step in the solution process was to find an optimal solution to the noninteger programming problem. This appears at point J in Figure 8.3(a), where $X_1 = 1.25$ and $X_2 = 3.5$. The first cutting plane was determined to be $X_2 \leq 3$. The portion of the feasible region removed by this cut is the shaded area of Figure 8.3(b). The optimal solution to the reduced set is at point K, where $X_1 = 23/12$ and $X_2 = 3.0$.

The second cutting plane reduced the feasible region even further, leaving the new optimal solution at $X_1 = 13/4$ and $X_2 = 15/8$, which is shown at point M in Figure 8.3(c). Figure 8.3(d) shows the effect of all three cuts on the original linear programming problem. The optimal solution is at point R, where $X_1 = 3$ and $X_2 = 2$.

Figure 8.3(d) also points out how conceptually simple the cutting-plane approach is. In this two-dimensional example, all that was required was to connect the outermost integers of the original feasible set with straight lines. This formed the new set $PQRST$. Since every extreme point of this new set is an integer, the optimal solution must be an integer. All of this, of course, was accomplished without removing any integer values from the original set of feasible solutions.

Figure 8.3 *Graphical review of the cutting-plane method (removed area shaded)*

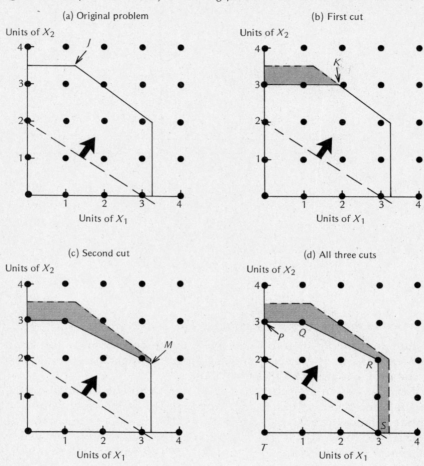

Branch-and-bound algorithms

All bounded integer programming problems have a finite number of possible solutions. One method of finding the optimal solution is to evaluate all possible solutions and find the one that provides the optimal value. In most cases, however, the number of possible solutions is so large that it is nearly impossible to explicitly enumerate them all. What we need is a way to evaluate a manageable number of possible solutions and implicitly enumerate the other possibilities. The *branch-and-bound approach* is one means of obtaining a solution by implicit enumeration.

The branch-and-bound technique obtains an optimal solution by a series of systematic steps. Assume that we have a minimization problem. The first step is to establish an upper bound or limit on the objective function. The upper bound is usually established by determining the solution value for any easily located feasible solution. It should be possible to find a solution with an objective function value equal to or smaller than this limit.

The second step is to divide or partition the solution set into several subsets. A lower bound, or minimum possible objective function value, is established for each subset. For purposes of computational efficiency, we usually establish the lower bounds without regard to whether they are feasible. Any subset with a lower bound larger than the upper bound is immediately eliminated from further consideration, because such a subset cannot possibly contain the optimal solution.

In the process of locating lower bounds for the subsets, we may locate one or more additional feasible solutions. The upper bound is adjusted to the level of the smallest objective value associated with a feasible solution. This adjustment may allow us to eliminate additional subsets. The normal procedure is to then select the remaining subset, if any, with the smallest nonfeasible lower bound for further partitioning. Lower bounds are again established for these subsets. This process is continued until the upper bound is equal to the smallest lower bound. At this point, all subsets except the one containing the optimal solution have been eliminated from consideration, and the optimal solution within this subset has been located. This must be the optimal solution, and we have located it without enumerating all possible solutions.

Computer programs for the branch-and-bound method are available. These programs are generally considered more efficient than programs that use the cutting-plane method. None of these programs, however, are computationally efficient compared with noninteger programming routines. It appears that the most important determinant of computational time is the number of variables constrained to integer values. Thus, analysts should formulate their problems with as few integer-valued variables as possible. In some cases, the variables in an integer programming problem may be constrained to be either 0 or 1. With binary variables, integer programming algorithms are more efficient but still fall far short of the efficiency obtained with the simplex method.

Some specific integer programming formulations

It is easy to imagine situations wherein the optimal practical answer must be integer valued. Examples include production scheduling, media selection, and special types of resource allocation problems.

Formulation of these problems is straightforward. Quite often, all we must do is stipulate that certain variables must have integer values. In many of these cases, however, a very good approximation to the optimal integer solution can be obtained by standard linear programming methods. These problems are not, therefore, the primary reason for our interest in integer programming.

Integer variables, particularly binary integer variables, extend the range of problems that are amenable to solution by mathematical programming techniques. A wide variety of problems fail to conform exactly to one or more of the characteristics required for linear programming solutions. In some instances, the judicious use of integer variables eliminates these difficulties and allows the formulation of a problem that can be handled by integer linear programming methods. This approach has its greatest use in situations dealing with setup costs, batch sizes, equipment selection, and capital budgeting. In the following sections, we will discuss several categories of integer programming problems and the techniques that can be used in their formulation.

The "go or no go" problem

This category contains some of the most important managerial decisions that can be formulated as integer programming problems. It is best illustrated by a capital budgeting problem. Assume that a firm has a limited supply of money to allocate among competing capital projects. If work is begun on a project, that project must be completely finished; hence the term "go or no go." Conventional formulation of this problem, letting X_1 represent the amount of money invested in project 1, will not work, because project 1 must be fully funded or rejected. We can avoid this difficulty by using X_1 as a binary variable that is equal to 1 if the investment is made and equal to 0 if the investment is not made. Consider the following example.

$$\text{Max } Z = 10X_1 + 12X_2 + 8X_3 + 14X_4$$

$$\text{s.t.} \quad 2X_1 + 3X_2 + 2X_3 + 4X_4 \leq 8$$

$$5X_1 + 2X_2 + 4X_3 + 3X_4 \leq 10$$

$$X_1, X_2, X_3, X_4 \geq 0$$

$$X_1, X_2, X_3, X_4 \text{ are integer-valued}$$

In this example, assume that X_1, X_2, X_3, and X_4 all represent different capital budgeting projects. The following stipulations can be added to the problem to ensure that each of these variables has a value of either 0 or 1.

$$X_1 \leq 1 \qquad X_3 \leq 1$$

$$X_2 \leq 1 \qquad X_4 \leq 1$$

We can easily formulate several extensions of this problem. First, assume that only three of the four projects can be completed. This can be accomplished by adding the constraint

$$X_1 + X_2 + X_3 + X_4 \leqslant 3$$

In some instances, we will want to select only one project from a group of similar projects. For example, assume that X_1 and X_2 are similar projects and that we do not want to select both of them. Thus,

$$X_1 + X_2 \leqslant 1$$

We may also have the reverse situation. For example, assume that X_2 and X_3 are complementary projects and one is of no value without the other. This may be stated as follows:

$$X_2 = X_3 \quad \text{or}$$
$$X_2 - X_3 = 0$$

A lot-size problem

In some situations, one of two *alternative constraints* must hold. For example, consider the following production scheduling problem.

$$\text{Max } Z = 7X_1 + 9X_2$$

s.t.
$$10X_1 + 12X_2 \leqslant 10,000$$
$$15X_1 + 10X_2 \leqslant 12,000$$
$$X_1, X_2 \geqslant \quad 0$$

This formulation is not adequate if the variable X_2 represents a process that, if produced, must be made in lots of 100 or more. Thus, one of the two following constraints must hold.

$$X_2 = 0 \quad \text{or}$$
$$X_2 \geqslant 100$$

Assume that the variable M represents a very large number such that the relationship $X_2 \leqslant M$ is certainly true. In our example, M could equal 2000. The "either/or" condition can be satisfied by the stipulations

$$X_2 \leqslant MX_3$$
$$X_2 \geqslant 100X_3$$
$$X_3 \leqslant \quad 1$$
$$X_3 \geqslant \quad 0 \quad \text{and integer-valued}$$

In this example, X_3 is a new variable, often called a *control variable*, that must be either 0 or 1. If X_3 has a value of 0, then X_2 must be 0 in order to satisfy the first relationship. If X_3 has a value of 1, then X_2 must have a value of 100 or more. Since X_3 must be either 0 or 1, it must be true that X_2 has a value of 0 (no production) or a value of 100 or more. The complete formulation can be written as follows:

$$\text{Max } Z = 7X_1 + 9X_2 + 0X_3$$

s.t.
$$10X_1 + 12X_2 \leqslant 10{,}000$$
$$15X_1 + 10X_2 \leqslant 12{,}000$$
$$X_2 - MX_3 \leqslant 0$$
$$X_2 - 100X_3 \geqslant 0$$
$$X_3 \leqslant 1$$
$$X_1, X_2, X_3 \geqslant 0$$
$$X_3 \text{ is integer-valued}$$

A fixed-charge problem

It is quite common in industrial situations to incur a setup cost or fixed charge in order to perform a given activity. Problems of this type constitute a special category of the alternative-constraint problems we have just discussed. Consider the following production scheduling example.

$$\text{Max } Z = 3X_1 + 4X_2$$

s.t.
$$2X_1 + 3X_2 \leqslant 90$$
$$5X_1 + 4X_2 \leqslant 120$$
$$X_1, X_2 \geqslant 0$$

Assume that a setup must be performed in order to make any amount of X_2. The variable X_3 will represent this setup. It will have a value of 1 if the setup is performed and a value of 0 if no setup is made. In other words,

$$\text{If } X_2 = 0, \quad \text{then } X_3 = 0$$
$$\text{If } X_2 > 0, \quad \text{then } X_3 = 1$$

The variable X_3 must be constrained to be either 0 or 1.

$$X_3 \leqslant 1$$
$$X_3 \text{ is integer-valued}$$

It is necessary to ensure that X_3 is 0 when X_2 is 0 and that X_3 is 1 when X_2 is greater than 0. In order to accomplish this, we select a large number M that exceeds the maximum possible value of X_2. If we let M equal 1000, the following constraint will serve our purpose.

$$X_2 \leq 1000X_3$$

If X_3 is 0, then X_2 must be 0. If X_3 is 1, then X_2 may take on any value in the feasible range of 0 to 1000.

If the variable X_3 represents a setup, the objective function coefficient of X_3 is the cost associated with the setup. In our example, assume that it costs $50 to set up for the production of process X_2. The new objective function is

$$\text{Max } Z = 3X_1 + 4X_2 - 50X_3$$

The cost coefficient in the objective function ensures that a setup will not be made unless enough X_2 can be produced to offset the setup cost. The complete formulation is as follows:

$$\text{Max } Z = 3X_1 + 4X_2 - 50X_3$$

s.t.
$$
\begin{aligned}
2X_1 + 3X_2 &\leq 90 \\
5X_1 + 4X_2 &\leq 120 \\
X_2 - 1000X_3 &\leq 0 \\
X_3 &\leq 1 \\
X_1, X_2, X_3 &\geq 0 \\
X_3 \text{ is integer-valued}
\end{aligned}
$$

Sample problem 8.2 *BECKER SUPERMARKET*

The Becker Company must purchase 50,000 light bulbs for holiday season displays in their supermarkets. The company has received bids from three suppliers. The Red Company will supply bulbs for 3 cents apiece. The minimum order from this company is 20,000 and the maximum order is 30,000. The Blue Company will supply bulbs for 5 cents apiece. The minimum order is 10,000, and the Blue Company will supply any amount above 10,000. The Green Company will supply any quantity from 0 to 30,000 for $200 plus 1 cent a bulb. The company has decided that it should purchase from not more than two suppliers. Formulate this as an integer programming problem. The objective is to minimize the cost of purchasing the necessary bulbs.

SOLUTION

$X_1 =$ Number of bulbs purchased from the Red Company

$X_2 =$ Number of bulbs purchased from the Blue Company

$X_3 =$ Number of bulbs purchased from the Green Company

$X_4 = 1$, if purchase is made from Red; zero, if otherwise

$X_5 = 1$, if purchase is made from Blue; zero, if otherwise

$X_6 = 1$, if purchase is made from Green; zero, if otherwise

$$\text{Min } Z = .03X_1 + .05X_2 + .01X_3 + 200X_6$$

s.t. $\qquad X_1 + X_2 + X_3 \geq 50{,}000$

$$X_1 \leq 30{,}000 \ X_4$$

$$X_1 \geq 20{,}000 \ X_4$$

$$X_2 \leq MX_5 \qquad (M \text{ is a very large number.})$$
$$X_2 \geq 10{,}000 \ X_5$$

$$X_3 \leq 30{,}000$$

$$X_3 \leq MX_6$$

$$X_1 + X_2 + X_3 \leq 2$$

$$X_4 \leq 1 \qquad X_5 \leq 1 \qquad X_6 \leq 1$$

$$X_i \geq 0, \text{ for all } i$$

$$X_i \text{ is integer-valued for all } i$$

Approximations to integer programming solutions

In the PIB example, we indicated that Ms. Alvarez was formerly chief production engineer for a manufacturer of home ice cream freezers. In that capacity, she used linear programming to determine weekly production schedules. This company manufactures three-quart freezers that contribute $3 to profit, four-quart freezers that contribute $4 to profit, and five-quart freezers that contribute $5 to profit.

For a particular week, a standard linear programming solution indicated that the optimal production schedule was to produce 843.2 three-quart freezers, 677.4 four-quart freezers, and 950.6 five-quart freezers. If a part or fraction of a freezer could be produced and sold, this would result in a total profit contribution of $9,992.20; that is,

$$843.2(\$3) + 677.4(\$4) + 950.6(\$5) = \$9{,}992.20$$

The procedure used at the freezer plant is to "drop the fraction" and use the integer parts of the solution. Thus, the company would schedule production of 843 three-quart freezers, 677 four-quart freezers, and 950 five-quart freezers. This results in a profit contribution of $9,987.00; that is,

$$843(\$3) + 677(\$4) + 950(\$5) = \$9,987$$

There is no assurance that this solution is the optimal integer solution. It is known, however, that the objective function value of the optimal integer solution cannot be greater than $9,992.20. Thus, the maximum loss that might be incurred by using the integer-parts approximation is $5.20, the difference between $9,992.20 and $9,987. The extra computational cost of obtaining the optimal integer solution would certainly exceed $5.20. In this case, the best procedure is to use the integer-parts approximation.

The computational effort and cost associated with integer programming are great. Before seeking an optimal integer answer, we should estimate the possible savings we may realize by using this method instead of an integer-parts approximation. In some cases, the possible saving will be very large. For other problems, it may not be worth the cost.

Dynamic programming

Illustrative example: *JANICE ADAMS*

Janice Adams is a young, hard-working, and popular member of the United States Senate. She is considering running for national office in the next election year. In order to better assess her probability of winning, she decides to make a trip across the country to "test the political wind." She feels that discussions in four cities should be sufficient, provided that each city is in a different time zone in the continental United States.

John Smith has been asked to prepare the itinerary for Janice Adams. He knows that the trip must begin in Washington, D.C., but this city cannot be one of the survey cities. Mr. Smith is not sure which cities Senator Adams should visit in the four time zones. He decides to select three cities in each zone and let the senator choose among them. In each time zone, he makes a preliminary selection of one city from the Sun Belt, one from the Heartland, and one close to the Canadian border. He presents these tentative selections to Senator Adams, along with the traveling times between them.

Senator Adams must make the final decision about which cities to visit, and she has one personal characteristic that does not enhance her political career.

She does not like to travel. She therefore decides to choose the route from time zone to time zone that will minimize her total travel time.

Dynamic programming, unlike the first two topics we discussed in this chapter, cannot be considered as a special type of linear programming. One feature that distinguishes it from linear programming is that a standard solution technique does not exist. Instead, dynamic programming is a general approach or procedure for problem solving. This procedure is especially applicable for a class or category of problems wherein the decision maker must make a series of interrelated decisions.

Dynamic programming represents a distinct departure from more traditional methods of problem solving and is a powerful, but basic, decision-making strategy. This strategy is based on the "divide and conquer" philosophy. When facing a complex problem, it may be possible to subdivide the problem into a series of smaller problems in such a way that solution of the smaller problems leads to solution of the overall problem.

Characteristics of a dynamic programming problem

A problem that can be solved by dynamic programming can always be divided into a series of *stages.* Figure 8.4 illustrates Janice Adams' problem. In this example, each time zone can be considered a stage. In other examples, stages may be time periods, decision points in a continuous production operation, or simply sequential steps in the decision process. In dynamic programming, a decision must be made at each stage of the problem.

At each stage in the decision-making process, there are a number of *states.* In our example, there are three states per stage. At a given stage, the traveler may be in a Canadian border city, a Heartland city, or a Sun Belt city. In other examples, states may refer to the amount of inventory on hand, the state of the economy, or the number of trucks in a service depot. In general, a state represents the condition of the system at a particular stage of the decision process.

In every dynamic programming problem, there is an optimal policy for each state and stage in the decision-making process. Calculation of these optimal strategies represents the solution of the smaller problems into which the overall problem has been divided. The optimal policy is independent of the prior decisions that led to a particular stage and state. For example, in Janice Adams' problem, there is an optimal policy

Figure 8.4 *Travel times for Janice Adams' problem*

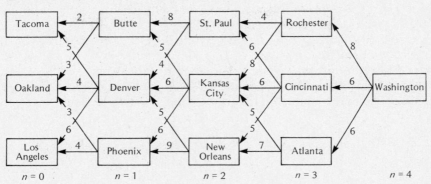

for reaching the West Coast from St. Paul. This optimal policy is independent of the routes used in traveling from Washington to St. Paul.

Solving a dynamic programming problem

We will use Janice Adams' problem to illustrate the dynamic programming solution process. There are five stages to this decision situation. Since a decision is generally not made at the last stage, this stage is given the number 0. Other stages are numbered sequentially in a backward direction. Thus, a stage number of 2 implies that there are two stages remaining in the decision process. There are three states in each stage of this problem. The traveling time between states is given in Figure 8.4. When no arrow is drawn between two states, travel between them is impossible; that is, it is a nonfeasible route.

Illustrating the backward algorithm

We usually solve dynamic programming problems by working backward from stage to stage. This represents one of the significant distinguishing features of dynamic programming problems. The traditional approach to Janice Adams' problem would be to start at the beginning: to first attempt to decide whether she should go from Washington to Rochester, or from Washington to Cincinnati, or from Washington to Atlanta. This is a relatively complex decision, because it is necessary to consider all options available on subsequent legs of the journey.

We can pose a much smaller and simpler problem by assuming that Senator Adams is in Butte in stage 1 and must decide if she should go to

Tacoma or to Oakland. The dynamic programming strategy is to solve a number of problems of this type and eventually obtain a solution to the larger, overall routing problem.

Creating a dynamic programming worksheet, illustrated in Table 8.8, is a convenient way of recording the information we need to work our way back through the dynamic programming problem. We begin by determining the optimal decision for each state in stage 1. Suppose Senator Adams is in stage 1 at Butte. She has two choices: to go to

Table 8.8 *Dynamic programming worksheet for Janice Adams' problem*

	Present state	New state	Time	Future time	Total time
Stage 1	Butte	Tacoma	2	0	2*
		Oakland	3	0	3
	Denver	Tacoma	5	0	5
		Oakland	4	0	4*
		Los Angeles	6	0	6
	Phoenix	Oakland	3	0	3*
		Los Angeles	4	0	4
Stage 2	St. Paul	Butte	8	2	10
		Denver	4	4	8*
	Kansas City	Butte	5	2	7*
		Denver	6	4	10
		Phoenix	6	3	9
	New Orleans	Denver	5	4	9*
		Phoenix	9	3	12
Stage 3	Rochester	St. Paul	4	8	12*
		Kansas City	8	7	15
	Cincinnati	St. Paul	6	8	14
		Kansas City	6	7	13*
		New Orleans	5	9	14
	Atlanta	Kansas City	5	7	12*
		New Orleans	7	9	16
Stage 4	Washington	Rochester	8	12	20
		Cincinnati	6	13	19
		Atlanta	6	12	18*

*Minimum travel time

Tacoma or to go to Oakland. These routes have traveling times of 2 hours and 3 hours respectively. This information is shown in the dynamic programming worksheet. Since both Tacoma and Oakland represent a possible final destination, there is no additional or future time to consider. Thus, total travel time from Butte to the west coast is 2 hours if the senator decides to go to Tacoma and 3 if she goes to Oakland. Since she wants to minimize travel time, she will choose Tacoma. This optimal choice is indicated by an asterisk in the dynamic programming worksheet.

If Senator Adams is in Denver, she has three choices. She can go to Tacoma, Oakland, or Los Angeles. Of the three, the route to Oakland offers the minimum travel time. An asterisk is placed by this route in the "Total time" column. The same procedure is followed for the possibility of being in Phoenix in stage 1.

In stage 2, Senator Adams could be in St. Paul, Kansas City, or New Orleans. Consider the possibility of being in Kansas City. There are three routes to take. She can go to Butte, Denver, or Phoenix. If she goes to Denver, there is a travel time of 6, as shown in Table 8.8. This is not the whole story, however, because once she reaches Denver, she must continue to the West Coast. From previous calculations, we know the optimal travel time from Denver is 4 hours. This is shown in stage 1 in Table 8.8, and we must add it to the 6 to obtain a total travel time of 10 hours. Similar calculations can be made for going to the West Coast via Butte or Phoenix, yielding travel times of 7 hours and 9 hours respectively. Of the three travel times, 7 hours is the minimum. Thus, Senator Adams would proceed from Kansas City to Butte and then to Tacoma. An asterisk is placed next to the Butte alternative.

Similar calculations can be made for the other cities in stage 2. At St. Paul, the minimum time of 8 hours is obtained by going to Denver and then to Oakland. At New Orleans, the optimal routing is to Denver and then Oakland, which has a travel time of 9 hours.

At stage 3, we follow the same procedure as in the first two stages. For each city, we always utilize the information we obtained from previous stages. These calculations indicate that the minimum travel times from Rochester, Cincinnati, and Atlanta are 12 hours, 13 hours, and 12 hours respectively. These values are marked with asterisks in the dynamic programming worksheet.

There is only one city in stage 4. Travel time from Washington to Rochester is 8 hours, to Cincinnati is 6, and to Atlanta is 6. When these times are added to future optimal travel times, they yield total times to the West Coast of 20, 19, and 18 hours.

We now know that the minimum travel time from Washington to the West Coast is 18 hours. To find the optimal route, it is necessary to work upwards from stage to stage in the dynamic programming worksheet.

From Washington, Senator Adams should proceed to Atlanta (as indicated by the asterisk). In stage 3, we know that from Atlanta the proper destination is Kansas City. In stage 2, the optimal route is from Kansas City to Butte. Finally, when Senator Adams reaches Butte, she can minimize travel time to the West Coast by going to Tacoma. Thus, the route from Washington to the West Coast that offers the minimum travel time is to Atlanta, to Kansas City, to Butte, and to Tacoma. It has a travel time of 18 hours. It is optimal, and the senator can do no better.

Summary of the dynamic programming process

The technique we have just illustrated is typical of dynamic programming problems. The procedure is to move backward, stage by stage. We find an optimal policy for each state in a stage, and we continue this procedure until we find an optimal policy for the initial or starting stage.

In a small problem, such as this example, it may not be evident that the dynamic programming routine is more efficient than simply enumerating all possible alternatives. Note, however, that the dynamic programming procedure in this problem required only 24 additions. There are 41 distinct routes that Senator Adams could have traveled. Each of these routes requires four additions to find the time required for a given route. Thus, 164 additions would have been required for complete enumeration. The dynamic programming routine reduced the number of additions required from 164 to 24. The magnitude of this saving increases geometrically as the number of stages and states increases.

Utilizing computational matrices

The dynamic programming worksheet illustrated in Table 8.8 is fine for pedagogical purposes. Often, however, it is better to summarize the necessary computational information in a series of computational matrices. The matrices for Janice Adams' problem are given in Table 8.9.

Consider the matrix given for stage 1. There is *a row for each possible state* in this stage. For convenience, we have designated Canadian border cities as state 1, Heartland cities as state 2, and Sun Belt cities as state 3. There is *a column for each possible decision* that Senator Adams can make. In this example, the decision is whether to exit via state 1, state 2, or state 3. In other words, she can choose to travel to Tacoma (T, state 1), Oakland (O, state 2), or Los Angeles (LA, state 3). The number shown in the body of the matrix represents the travel time from a particular state in stage 1 (Rocky Mountain time zone) to a particular state in stage 0 (Pacific time zone). The letters NF in a matrix cell indicate that it is not feasible to travel between the row and column states. The last two columns represent the optimal decision and the

Table 8.9 *Computational matrices for the Janice Adams problem*

Stage 1
$(n = 1)$

Entering state	Decision: exit state			Optimal	
	1 (T)	2 (O)	3 (LA)	Distance	Route
1 (B)	(2 + 0) 2	(3 + 0) 3	NF	2	1 (T)
2 (D)	(5 + 0) 5	(4 + 0) 4	(6 + 0) 6	4	2 (O)
3 (P)	NF	(3 + 0) 3	(4 + 0) 4	3	2 (O)

Stage 2
$(n = 2)$

Entering state	Decision: exit state			Optimal	
	1 (B)	2 (D)	3 (P)	Distance	Route
1 (SP)	(8 + 2) 10	(4 + 4) 8	NF	8	2 (D)
2 (KC)	(5 + 2) 7	(6 + 4) 10	(6 + 3) 9	7	1 (B)
3 (NO)	NF	(5 + 4) 9	(9 + 3) 12	9	2 (D)

Stage 3
$(n = 3)$

Entering state	Decision: exit state			Optimal	
	1 (SP)	2 (KC)	3 (NO)	Distance	Route
1 (R)	(4 + 8) 12	(8 + 7) 15	NF	12	1 (SP)
2 (C)	(6 + 8) 14	(6 + 7) 13	(5 + 9) 14	13	2 (KC)
3 (A)	NF	(5 + 7) 12	(7 + 9) 16	12	2 (KC)

Stage 4
$(n = 4)$

Entering state	Decision: exit state			Optimal	
	1 (R)	2 (C)	3 (A)	Distance	Route
2 (W)	(8 + 12) 20	(6 + 13) 19	(6 + 12) 18	18	3 (A)

travel time associated with this decision. For example, in state 2 (Denver), the minimum travel time is 4 hours, which is associated with traveling to state 2 on the West Coast.

The matrix for stage 2 is similar to the matrix for stage 1. The travel time figures are determined by adding together the time from a particular state in stage 2 to a particular state in stage 1 and the optimal time from that state to the West Coast. For example, consider the route from Kansas City to Denver, route 2-2. The time from Kansas City to Denver is 6 hours. From the previous matrix, we know that the optimal time from Denver to the West Coast is 4 hours. Thus, the appropriate entry is 10. Note that in column 2, a time of 4 hours is added to every row. This is because 4 hours is the optimal time from Denver, regardless of the route traveled to Denver. The last two columns are again used to show the optimal time and destination for each state.

We treat the matrix for stage 3 just like we did the matrices for stages 1 and 2. In this case, the entering states are Rochester, Cincinnati, and Atlanta. The exit states are St. Paul, Kansas City, and New Orleans.

There is only one possible state in stage 4. Thus, this matrix has only one row. It shows a travel time of 20 hours if the choice is Rochester, 19 if the choice is Cincinnati, and 18 if the choice is Atlanta. Of course, 18 hours is the minimum, and the proper selection is Atlanta.

In order to determine the complete routing, it is necessary to work upward through the four computational matrices. At stage 4, the proper decision is to go to state 3 in stage 3 (Atlanta). In the table for stage 3, if we are in Atlanta, the proper choice is state 2 (Kansas City). We proceed from matrix to matrix to find the optimal routing of Washington to Atlanta to Kansas City to Butte to Tacoma.

The use of computational matrices may seem cumbersome. With a little practice, however, you will discover that they greatly simplify the computational burden associated with dynamic programming. They will be used in the sections that follow, and you should use them when you do the exercises at the end of the chapter.

Illustrating dynamic programming with an allocation example

Janice Adams' problem was used for pedagogical purposes. It is a good example to illustrate the basic characteristics of dynamic programming. The following problem is a more realistic example, and it also illustrates the flexibility of the dynamic programming process.

The problem

Assume that Rick Martin, an investor, has $60,000 to allocate among four possible investment alternatives. He may invest all, none, or part

Table 8.10 *Estimated returns* from investing various amounts in competing capital projects*

Amount invested	Project			
	A	B	C	D
0	0	0	0	0
$10,000	15	6	10	5
20,000	20	17	18	12
30,000	24	24	24	19
40,000	27	26	28	25
50,000	30	27	30	30
60,000	32	28	32	35

*Returns in thousands of dollars. Each value represents the return over and above the amount invested.

of the $60,000 in each alternative. He is, however, restricted to investing in units of $10,000. The expected return from an investment depends on the amount of money allocated to it. This information is given in Table 8.10. Mr. Martin would like to allocate his money so as to maximize his total return.

The computational matrices

In this example, there are four decisions to be made: how much to invest in projects A, B, C, and D. Each of these decisions should represent a stage in the dynamic programming process. Investment in project D represents stage 1, project C will be stage 2, project B will be stage 3, and project A will be stage 4.

At each stage, the various states are represented by the amount of money available to invest in that project. As an example, consider the matrix for stage 2 shown in Table 8.11. We may enter this stage with any amount of money from $0 to $60,000 (in units of $10,000). Thus, there are seven rows in the matrix, representing the seven possible entering states.

The columns of the matrix represent the choices available to the decision maker. This can be expressed in several ways. One method is to have a column for each possible investment amount, $0 to $60,000. Using this method, the amount available to the next stage equals the amount available at this stage less the amount invested at this stage. A second method is to have a column for each possible exit state. Thus, if we enter with $60,000 and exit with $40,000, we know that we have spent $20,000 at this stage. We have chosen to use the first method — to have a column for each possible amount that can be invested at a particular stage. This choice follows the procedure used in most of the

Table 8.11 *Computational matrices for an allocation problem*

Stage 1
(n = 1)

Entering state	Decision: amount invested in project D							Optimal	
	0	10	20	30	40	50	60	Return	Decision
0	(0+0) 0	NF	NF	NF	NF	NF	NF	0	0
10	(0+0) 0	(5+0) 5	NF	NF	NF	NF	NF	5	10
20	(0+0) 0	(5+0) 5	(12+0) 12	NF	NF	NF	NF	12	20
30	(0+0) 0	(5+0) 5	(12+0) 12	(19+0) 19	NF	NF	NF	19	30
40	(0+0) 0	(5+0) 5	(12+0) 12	(19+0) 19	(25+0) 25	NF	NF	25	40
50	(0+0) 0	(5+0) 5	(12+0) 12	(19+0) 19	(25+0) 25	(30+0) 30	NF	30	50
60	(0+0) 0	(5+0) 5	(12+0) 12	(19+0) 19	(25+0) 25	(30+0) 30	(35+0) 35	35	60

Stage 2
(n = 2)

Entering state	Decision: amount invested in project C							Optimal	
	0	10	20	30	40	50	60	Return	Decision
0	(0+0) 0	NF	NF	NF	NF	NF	NF	0	0
10	(0+5) 5	(10+0) 10	NF	NF	NF	NF	NF	10	10
20	(0+12) 12	(10+5) 15	(18+0) 18	NF	NF	NF	NF	18	20
30	(0+19) 19	(10+12) 22	(18+5) 23	(24+0) 24	NF	NF	NF	24	30
40	(0+25) 25	(10+19) 29	(18+12) 30	(24+5) 29	(28+0) 28	NF	NF	30	20
50	(0+30) 30	(10+25) 35	(18+19) 37	(24+12) 36	(28+5) 33	(30+0) 30	NF	37	20
60	(0+35) 35	(10+30) 40	(18+25) 43	(24+19) 43	(28+12) 40	(30+5) 35	(32+0) 32	43	20 or 30

Table 8.11 (*cont.*)

Stage 3
(*n* = 3)

Entering state	Decision: amount invested in project B							Optimal	
	0	10	20	30	40	50	60	Return	Decision
0	(0+0) 0	NF	NF	NF	NF	NF	NF	0	0
10	(0+10) 10	(6+0) 6	NF	NF	NF	NF	NF	10	0
20	(0+18) 18	(6+10) 16	(17+0) 17	NF	NF	NF	NF	18	0
30	(0+24) 24	(6+18) 24	(17+10) 27	(24+0) 24	NF	NF	NF	27	20
40	(0+30) 30	(6+24) 30	(17+18) 35	(24+10) 34	(26+0) 26	NF	NF	35	20
50	(0+37) 37	(6+30) 36	(17+24) 41	(24+18) 42	(26+10) 36	(27+0) 27	NF	42	30
60	(0+43) 43	(6+37) 43	(17+30) 47	(24+24) 48	(26+18) 44	(27+10) 37	(28+0) 28	48	30

Stage 4
(*n* = 4)

Entering state	Decision: amount invested in project A							Optimal	
	0	10	20	30	40	50	60	Return	Decision
60	(0+48) 48	(15+42) 57	(20+35) 55	(24+27) 51	(27+18) 45	(30+10) 40	(32+0) 32	57	10

literature on dynamic programming. It may also simplify certain types of problems.

The values in the body of the matrix give the expected return for a particular decision at a given stage and state. They represent the return over and above the amount invested.

The solution process

The computational matrices for this problem are given in Table 8.11. We begin at stage 1. Remember that dynamic programming uses a backward algorithm. At stage 1, we are concerned with project D, the last project to be allocated money. We may enter this stage with any amount of money from $0 to $60,000. This is reflected by the seven rows representing the seven possible entering states. In theory, we can invest any amount of money less than or equal to the amount we have available at this stage. In practice, of course, we will want to invest whatever we enter this stage with, because this is our last investment opportunity. Since it is impossible to invest more money than we have available, there are a number of nonfeasible cells in the computational matrix. These are labeled NF.

At stage 2, the decision is how much money to invest in project C. Prior to entering this stage, we could have spent all, none, or part of the $60,000 on prior investments. Thus, we can enter this stage at any state. We can also invest any amount as long as we do not invest more money than is available. For example, if we enter with $20,000, we can invest $20,000, $10,000, or nothing. We cannot, however, enter with $20,000 and invest $30,000. The nonfeasible alternatives are again labeled NF in the matrix.

The values in the matrix represent the return from a given investment in this project plus the optimal return for the exit state. Assume that we enter with $50,000 and invest $20,000. This means that we will enter the next stage (stage 1) with $30,000. The $20,000 expended on project C returns $18,000. From the stage 1 matrix, the optimal return with $30,000 is $19,000. Thus, the total return from entering stage 2 at $50,000 and investing $20,000 is $37,000. The last two columns indicate the value of the optimal decision and the corresponding amount invested at this stage. As an example, if we enter with $40,000, the optimal action is to invest $20,000 and exit with $20,000. This has a return of $30,000.

We continue working backward through stage 3 to stage 4. There is only one row in this table, because we must enter this initial stage with $60,000. The optimal investment is $10,000, which indicates that we should exit this stage with $50,000. We would therefore enter stage 3 (project B) with $50,000. Working backward through the computational matrices, we find that the optimal decision is to spend $30,000 on project B in stage 3 (exit with $20,000) and $20,000 on project C. No money is invested in project D. This pattern of allocation of funds yields an expected return of $57,000. It is optimal.

This allocation problem illustrates a second dynamic programming formulation. A critical aspect of solving problems with dynamic programming is the ability to distinguish among the stages and states in the problem. Unfortunately, the only way to develop this ability is to practice. Due to the unique approach underlying dynamic programming, it may be difficult to recognize an appropriate formulation for a problem. Without practice, it is also difficult to appreciate the range of applicability of the dynamic programming process.

Problems and exercises

1. Explain the following terms:

integer programming	goal programming
branch-and-bound	deviational variables
cutting plane	priority goals
secondary constraint	dynamic programming
pure-integer problem	stage
mixed-integer problem	state
congruence	backward algorithm
fractional parts	computational matrix

   INSTRUCTIONS FOR PROBLEMS 2–6
   Formulate each problem as a goal programming problem. Show all deviational variables. Formulate objective functions by priority.

2. The Metcalf Company produces two types of calculators for home use. Type A requires 2 hours of production time and contributes $2 to profit. Type B requires 1 hour of production time and contributes $3 to profit. The company is limited to 120 hours per month of production time. Total sales of the two products cannot exceed 100 units per month. The first priority is to achieve a profit contribution of at least $240, and the second priority is to minimize underutilization of production time.

3. A director of a typing pool must allocate a number of letters between two typists. Typist A can type 8 letters per hour and typist B can type 6 letters per hour. Overtime must be paid for more than 7 hours of work on a given day. Overtime pay for typist A is $4 per hour for the first 2 hours and $8 per hour for additional hours. Overtime pay for typist B is $4.50 per hour regardless of the hours worked. The first priority is to achieve the day's goal of 140 letters, and the second priority is to minimize the amount of overtime paid.

4. The Straus Company manufactures two types of fondue pots, brass and silver. Each brass pot requires 4 minutes in machine center 1 and 2 minutes in machine center 2. Each silver pot requires 6 minutes in machine center 1 and 8 minutes in machine center 2. During the next production period, the firm has 2000 minutes available in machine center 1 and 5000 minutes available in machine center 2. Brass pots sell for $10 and contribute $4 to profit. Silver pots sell for $7 and contribute $3 to profit. The decision maker's priorities are as follows:

   $[P_1]$ Manufacture at least 400 brass fondue pots.

   $[P_2]$ Manufacture at least 600 total fondue pots.

   $[P_3]$ Obtain a total revenue of at least $5000.

[P_4] Obtain a target profit contribution of exactly $1800.

[P_5] Minimize underutilization of machine centers 1 and 2. Reducing idle time in machine center 1 is twice as important as reducing idle time in machine center 2.

5. The Nagel Company is trying to allocate commercial time among three radio stations. In any given week, the company cannot exceed its budget of $120. Each minute of commercial time on station 1 costs $2 and is expected to be heard by 2000 people. Commercial minutes in stations 2 and 3 cost $3 and $4 and are expected to be heard by 4000 and 1000 listeners respectively. Management's first priority is to reach at least 80,000 listeners per week. The second priority is to air 30 minutes of commercial time per week. Deviations on the low side are twice as unattractive as deviations on the high side. The final priority is to minimize the use of commercial time on radio station 3.

6. The Wilson Company sells two types of gas-powered sidewalk snow removers. The company can only order once a year and must sell out of inventory during the entire cold-weather season. Coolbaugh brand removers contribute $18 to profit and require 8 cubic feet of inventory space. Toohey brand removers contribute $12 to profit and require 6 cubic feet of inventory space. The company has 10,000 cubic feet of inventory space available. Additional inventory space is available in the basement, but this space is undesirable and the firm prefers to use as little of it as possible. Let X_1 and X_2 be the amounts of Coolbaugh and Toohey equipment purchased. Formulate this as a goal programming problem wherein the objectives, in order of priority, are

[P_1] Achieve a profit contribution of at least $24,000.

[P_2] Meet the sales goals of selling exactly 600 Coolbaughs and 1000 Tooheys. Variation from the goal of selling 1000 Tooheys is considered to be twice as costly as variation from the Coolbaugh sales goal.

[P_3] Minimize the amount of inventory space used in excess of 10,000 cubic feet.

INSTRUCTIONS FOR PROBLEMS 7–9
Solve each of the following goal programming problems.

7. [P_1] Min $Z_1 = U_3$

[P_2] Min $Z_2 = U_1$

s.t. $2X_1 + 1X_2 + U_1 \qquad = 120$

$\qquad X_1 + \ X_2 + U_2 \qquad = 100$

$2X_1 + 3X_2 + U_3 - E_3 = 240$

$\qquad\qquad X_i, U_i, E_i \ \geqslant \ 0, \quad \text{for all } i$

8. $[P_1]$ Min $Z_1 = U_3$

   $[P_2]$ Min $Z_2 = 2U_2 + E_2$

   $[P_3]$ Min $Z_3 = X_3$

   s.t. $2X_1 + 3X_2 + 4X_3 + U_1 \qquad = 120$

   $\qquad X_1 + \ X_2 + \ X_3 + U_2 - E_2 = \ 30$

   $\qquad 3X_1 + 4X_2 + 1X_3 + U_3 - E_3 = \ 80$

   $\qquad\qquad\qquad\qquad X_i, \ U_i, \ E_i \ \geqslant \ 0, \quad \text{for all } i$

9. $[P_1]$ Min $Z_1 = U_2$

   $[P_2]$ Min $Z_2 = U_3$

   s.t. $X_1 + \ X_2 + U_1 \qquad = \ 90$

   $\qquad 5X_1 + 4X_2 + U_2 \qquad = 400$

   $\qquad\qquad X_2 + U_3 - E_3 = \ 70$

   $\qquad\qquad X_i, \ U_i, \ E_i \geqslant \ 0, \quad \text{for all } i$

INSTRUCTIONS FOR PROBLEMS 10–15

Formulate each of the following problems as integer programming problems. Do not solve these problems.

10. The Davis Company is trying to determine how to allocate $100,000 among four proposed capital projects. Project 1 requires $20,000, Project 2 requires $30,000, Project 3 requires $50,000, and Project 4 requires $25,000. There is also a space limitation of 27,000 square feet. Projects 1 through 4 require 12,000, 5,000, 18,000, and 10,000 square feet respectively. Discounted cash return for Project 1 is $5000, for Project 2 is $7000, for Project 3 is $10,000, and for Project 4 is $4000. There is an additional requirement that no more than three projects be undertaken. The object is to choose the projects that will maximize discounted cash return.

11. The projects officer for the Doak Company is assigning projects to a senior engineer. The planning time is a 20-day period. There are five projects to choose from. Their expected completion times are 3, 8, 5, 4, and 10 days respectively. The project values are $7, $17, $11, $9, and $21 respectively. At least three projects must be completed. If project 1 is chosen, then project 2 must also be chosen. Project 3 and project 4 are similar, and they should not both be chosen. The objective is to select the projects that will maximize value return to the company.

12. The Redfield Company manufactures three products: chairs, big tables, and little tables. Each chair requires 2 hours in the assembly room and 4 hours in the painting center. Each big table requires 4 hours in assembly and 2 hours in painting. The corresponding values for little tables are 3 hours and

2 hours. The company has available 180 hours of assembly time and 200 hours of painting time. Contribution to profit is $8 for each chair, $10 for each big table, and $7 for each little table. There is a requirement that at least 50 tables (big and/or little) be produced or no tables be produced. The objective is to maximize profit contribution.

13. The Alexander Company manufactures three products. Products 1, 2, and 3 contribute $7, $18, and $4 respectively to profit. The company has 10,000 units of labor available, and products 1, 2, and 3 require 8, 12, and 10 units respectively. There is an additional requirement that *either* 500 units of product 1 *or* 500 units of product 2 must be made. The objective is to maximize profit contribution.

14. The Hoover Company manufactures desks and lamps. Each desk contributes $10 to profit, and each lamp contributes $8 to profit. Each desk requires 3 hours of manufacturing time and 2 hours of assembly time. Each lamp requires 2 hours of manufacturing time and 1 hour of assembly time. A setup requires 60 hours of manufacturing time if any desks are manufactured. A setup for lamps requires 100 hours of manufacturing time. There are no variable costs associated with these setups. During the next production period, the company has available 3000 hours of manufacturing time and 1000 hours of assembly time. The objective is to maximize profit contribution.

15. The Whiting Company manufactures four types of cough syrup, which contribute $7, $8, $9, and $6 respectively to profit. There is a setup cost of $400 associated with each of the first two cough syrups. There is no setup cost for the third and fourth cough syrups. During the next production period, the company has 8000 hours of production time available. Each gallon of cough syrup 1 requires 2.3 hours of production time. The corresponding values for products 2, 3, and 4 are 4.2 hours, 2.7 hours, and 3.0 hours. Setups do not consume production time. The objective is to maximize profit contribution.

INSTRUCTIONS FOR PROBLEMS 16–19
Graph each of the following problems. Use the simplex method to determine the optimal noninteger solution. Apply the cutting-plane method to solve for the optimal integer answer.

16. Max $Z = 2X_1 + 1X_2$

    s.t. $26X_1 + 52X_2 \leqslant 169$

            $10X_1 \leqslant 45$

            $X_1, X_2 \geqslant 0$

         X_1 and X_2 are integers

17. Max $Z = X_1 + 2X_2$

    s.t. $X_1 + X_2 \leqslant 8$

            $2X_2 \leqslant 15$

           $X_1, X_2 \geqslant 0$

        X_1 and X_2 are integers

18. Max $Z = 4X_1 + 3X_2$

    s.t. $4X_1 + 4X_2 \leqslant 17$

           $2X_1 + 0X_2 \leqslant 7$

              $X_1, X_2 \geqslant 0$

          X_1 and X_2 are integers

19. Max $Z = 2X_1 + 3X_2$

    s.t. $2X_1 + 2X_2 \leqslant 9$

           $1X_1 + 2X_2 \leqslant 6$

              $X_1, X_2 \geqslant 0$

          X_1 and X_2 are integers

INSTRUCTIONS FOR PROBLEMS 20–26

Use computational matrices and solve the following problems by dynamic programming.

20. Consider Janice Adams' problem, as shown in Figure 8.4. Another traveler wants to begin in Cincinnati and travel to Hawaii using the minimum-time route. Travel times to Hawaii from Tacoma, Oakland, and Los Angeles are 10, 12, and 14 respectively. What route should this traveler choose?

21. Consider Janice Adams' problem, as shown in Figure 8.4. Another traveler wants to begin in Rochester and travel to Manila. Travel times to Manila from Tacoma, Oakland, and Los Angeles are 9, 8, and 10 respectively. What route should this traveler choose in order to minimize travel time?

22. The LaMont Company manufactures large industrial equipment. The company has projected sales of 3 units in each of the months of January, February, March, and April. Beginning inventory in January (ending inventory in December) is 2 units. The company desires that ending inventory in April also be 2 units. Demand for any month may be satisfied from beginning inventory or that month's production. Ending inventory in any month is limited to 5 units, and production during any month is limited to 5 units. There is a $10,000 holding cost for any unit left in inventory at the end of a month. Production cost depends on the number of units manufactured in a month as follows:

Units/month	0	1	2	3	4	5
Cost ($000)	0	80	100	120	130	140

Determine the optimal production schedule for the months of January, February, March, and April. (*Hint:* The stages can be the monthly production decisions. The states can be the amount of inventory on hand.)

23. The Chapin Company manufactures large machinery. The company has contracted for sales of 2 units in July, 2 units in August, 2 units in September, 4 units in October, and 3 units in November. The company has 1 unit in inventory at the beginning of July and wishes to have 2 units at the end of November. Demand during any month can be satisfied by that month's production or from beginning inventory. There is a setup cost of

$50,000 during each month that 1 or more units are produced. Cost per unit is $20,000. (For example, production of 2 units in a single month would cost $90,000.) There is also a holding charge of $10,000 for each unit in inventory at the end of a month. Maximum production during any month is 4 units. Maximum inventory that can be carried from month to month is 3 units. Determine a least-cost production schedule for the months of July, August, September, October, and November. (*Hint:* The stages can be the monthly production decisions. The states can be the amount of inventory on hand.)

24. A merchant would like to maximize the value of a package that cannot exceed 9 pounds. He can fill the package with items of type A, B, or C or any combination thereof. Type A items weigh 3 pounds and have a value of $4. Type B items weigh 2 pounds and have a value of $3. Type C items weigh 1 pound and have a value of $1. How many of each item should the merchant put in the package? (*Hint:* Treat this as an allocation problem. Allocate the 9 pounds to items A, B, and C.)

25. The Roper Company has decided to add five new salespeople to its sales staff. A new salesperson can be assigned to project A, B, or C. The following table shows the expected profit return for each project, depending on the number of new salespeople assigned to that project. What is the optimal allocation of these five new salespeople?

| | Profit ($000) | | |
Salesperson	A	B	C
0	30	45	25
1	45	60	35
2	60	65	55
3	70	70	65
4	75	75	75
5	80	75	80

26. Use dynamic programming to solve problem 17. (*Hint:* Allocate 8 units between X_1 and X_2.)

Supplementary readings

Budnick, F. S., R. Mojena, and T. E. Vollman. *Principles of Operations Research for Management.* Homewood, Ill.: Irwin, 1977.

Eck, R. D. *Operations Research for Business.* Belmont, Calif.: Wadsworth, 1976.

Hadley, G. W. *Linear Programming.* Reading, Mass.: Addison-Wesley, 1962.

Hartley, R. V. *Operations Research: A Managerial Emphasis.* Pacific Palisades, Calif.: Goodyear, 1976.

Hillier, F. S., and G. J. Lieberman. *Introduction to Operations Research*. San Francisco: Holden-Day, 1974.

Hughes, A. J., and D. E. Grawoig. *Linear Programming: An Emphasis on Decision Making*. Reading, Mass.: Addison-Wesley, 1973.

Lee, S. M., and L. J. Moore. *Introduction to Decision Science*. New York: Petrocelli/Charter, 1975.

Shamblin, J. E., and G. T. Stevens. *Operations Research: A Fundamental Approach*. New York: McGraw-Hill, 1974.

Wagner, H. M. *Principles of Management Science*. Englewood Cliffs, N.J.: Prentice-Hall, 1975.

Chapter 9
Network models: PERT and CPM

Illustrative example: THE JASS COMPANY

The JASS (J. A. Sampson & Son) Company is a medium-sized firm in the motor carrier industry. The vice president of consumer services has recently presented the company's executive committee with a proposal for a new service. The committee members like the proposal. They feel, however, that before funds are allocated for development, a market research study should be carried out to gauge consumer acceptance of the service.

Ms. Sampson, the company president, has hired Dr. Zee as director of the company's market research department. He will organize the market research project. Ms. Sampson has asked Dr. Zee to expedite completion of the study. She believes that the success of the new service is at least partially dependent on introducing the service before competitors introduce a similar service.

Dr. Zee knows that the market research study will be composed of a number of interrelated activities. It will be his job to define these activities and to schedule them effectively in order to complete the study as quickly as possible.

The first step in the market research study will be for Dr. Zee and his staff to perform a preliminary study of the project, which should take 4 days. Once the preliminary study is completed, two additional activities can begin. One member of the staff will be assigned the task of preparing the experimental research design, which should take 10 days. At the same time, another staff member will undertake formal location studies to determine where to conduct the consumer survey. This should take 7 days. Once this location study is finished, physical arrangements for data collection can be made. It should take 8 days to complete these arrangements. It will take 7 days to arrange for the printing of the data collection forms, but this work cannot begin until after work is completed on the experimental design.

Dr. Zee knows that his staff will have to interview, select, and train field workers, which he estimates will take 12 days. This work cannot begin, however, until after work on the location studies and the experimental design is completed. The field survey work will take 5 days to complete. It cannot begin until the data collection forms have been printed, the physical arrangements for data collection made, and the field workers selected and trained. When the field work is completed, it should take the staff an additional 4 days to analyze the data and prepare the market research report.

There are many administrative situations wherein a manager must plan, organize, and control a project that consists of a number of different but interrelated activities. Network analysis can aid a manager in planning and controlling such a project. The two best-known network models are PERT, which stands for Program Evaluation and Review Technique, and CPM, which stands for Critical Path Method. These two models were developed independently in the late 1950s. The original versions of these models contained important differences. Revision of both models has made them so similar that, except for historical purposes, it is not important to distinguish between them. We use the term PERT instead of CPM simply because it is used more often in management science literature. The reader should be aware, however, that the same concepts apply to most network models.

PERT allows the manager to plan the program in advance and to estimate the expected completion time of the entire project. It indicates activities that might cause "bottlenecks." It reveals which activities are the most likely candidates for modification if the project completion time needs to be shortened. As a control device, PERT allows the manager to compare actual and planned progress of each activity. It "red flags" those activities that are behind schedule and may cause a delay in the total project.

Obtaining the PERT network

When completed, the PERT network should be a planned schedule of how the project should proceed. To obtain this plan, we must define the component parts of the project and determine the earliest time when each component part can be started. These component parts are referred to as *activities*. We must also calculate the latest time when any activity can be started without delaying the total project. Finally, we must determine the slack time for each activity, that is, the amount of time that the completion of any activity can be delayed without delaying the total project.

Information requirements of PERT

Dr. Zee knows that in order to use PERT on a particular project, he must have three pieces of information. To use PERT, we must have:

1. A definition of each activity or component of the project.
2. An estimate of how much time will be required to perform each activity. This estimate is known as the *expected performance time*. Later in the chapter, we will introduce uncertainty and variable expected performance estimates. For the moment, however, we will assume one estimate of performance time.

3. A determination of what activities must be completed before work can begin on the activity under consideration. Most activities will have *prerequisite activities,* and an activity cannot begin until all prerequisite activities have been completed.

Dr. Zee has reviewed his consumer service problem and compiled the necessary information. This information is given in Table 9.1. Each activity has been assigned a letter. This symbol is a shorthand method of identifying each activity. In future analysis and tables, we will often identify an activity only by its symbol. Table 9.1 contains an activity I that we have not discussed. In network problems, it is often helpful to add an "ending" activity. This activity has all other activities as prerequisites. It helps to ensure that we will not mistakenly end the project before all activities have been completed.

Each activity in Table 9.1 has a performance time, and most of the activities have prerequisite activities indicated. The performance time is the best estimate of how long it will take to complete that activity. In our example, activity performance times are given in days, but any appropriate unit of time is acceptable. The prerequisite activities specify which activities must be completed before a particular activity can begin. As an example, note that activity F has activity C as a prerequisite. This means that preparation of the data collection forms (activity F) cannot begin until the research design (activity C) has been completed. Activity E has both activity B and activity C as prerequisites. This means that activities B and C must both be completed before activity E can begin.

Schematic representation

Figure 9.1 is a schematic representation of the PERT network for the JASS Company problem. There are numerous ways to diagram a net-

Table 9.1 *Activities, prerequisites, and performance times for the JASS Company problem*

Symbol	Description	Performance time	Prerequisite activities
A	Formulate and study the problem	4	none
B	Perform location studies	7	A
C	Prepare a research design	10	A
D	Make arrangements for data collection	8	B
E	Select and train field workers	12	B, C
F	Prepare data collection forms	7	C
G	Conduct the field survey	5	D, E, F
H	Analyze data and prepare the report	4	G
I	End of project	0	H

Figure 9.1 *Schematic representation of the JASS Company problem*

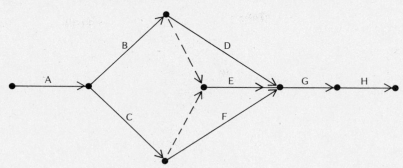

work. Later in this chapter, we will discuss several of these methods. At this point, however, Figure 9.1 should help you understand the material that follows. The two dotted lines in the diagram show prerequisite relationships only. The top dotted line indicates that activity B must precede activity E. The lower dotted line indicates that activity C is a prerequisite for activity E.

Calculating the earliest expected times

Table 9.2 is a PERT worksheet that we will use in analyzing the JASS Company problem. Similar worksheets can be made for any problem to be analyzed by PERT. This worksheet lists each activity by symbol and gives its expected performance time and its required prerequisite activities. It also allows room for calculating and recording the earliest expected time, the latest allowable time, and the expected slack time. As we proceed with our analysis, we will use partial worksheets to simplify our explanations. While PERT worksheets are quite helpful for explanatory purposes, those familiar with network analysis may find it more convenient to analyze problems directly from a schematic diagram. Larger problems are almost always solved by electronic computer. Efficient network routines are available for almost all types of electronic computers.

The first step in calculating the earliest expected time is to assume that each activity with no prerequisite starts on the first day of the project. Activity A, the preliminary study in the JASS Company problem, is the only activity with no prerequisites. We therefore enter a 1 as the earliest starting time for activity A. This is shown in Table 9.3. Since it takes 4 days to complete activity A, we know that it should be finished at the end of the fourth day. We therefore enter a 4 as the earliest finishing time, or completion date, for activity A.

We now move to activity B. Activity B cannot begin until activity A is complete. If activity A is scheduled to finish *at the end of day 4*, then the

Table 9.2 *PERT worksheet for the JASS Company problem*

Symbol	Performance time	Prerequisite activities	Earliest time		Latest time		Slack
			Start	Finish	Start	Finish	
A	4	none	____	____	____	____	____
B	7	A	____	____	____	____	____
C	10	A	____	____	____	____	____
D	8	B	____	____	____	____	____
E	12	B, C	____	____	____	____	____
F	7	C	____	____	____	____	____
G	5	D, E, F	____	____	____	____	____
H	4	G	____	____	____	____	____
I	0	H	____	____	____	____	____

earliest activity B can start is *the beginning of day 5*. If it takes 7 days to perform activity B, then it should be completed at the end of day 11. An 11 is therefore entered in Table 9.3. *Special caution should be taken here.* Activity B starts at the *beginning* of day 5 and proceeds for *7 days* (days 5, 6, 7, 8, 9, 10, and 11). It should therefore be finished at the *end* of day 11.

Activity C also cannot begin until A is finished. Since A finishes at the end of day 4, C will also begin at the beginning of day 5. Activity C

Table 9.3 *Partial PERT worksheet for the JASS Company problem, showing earliest times for activities A, B, C, D, and E*

Symbol	Performance time	Prerequisite activities	Earliest time	
			Start	Finish
A	4	none	1	4
B	7	A	5	11
C	10	A	5	14
D	8	B	12	19
E	12	B, C	15	26

Table 9.4 *PERT worksheet for the JASS Company problem, showing earliest times for all activities*

Symbol	Performance time	Prerequisite activities	Earliest time Start	Finish
A	4	none	1	4
B	7	A	5	11
C	10	A	5	14
D	8	B	12	19
E	12	B, C	15	26
F	7	C	15	21
G	5	D, E, F	27	31
H	4	G	32	35
I	0	H	36	

has an expected performance time of 10 days and should be completed at the end of day 14. We enter the 5 and the 14 in Table 9.3 as the earliest starting and finshing times for activity C. Activity D has activity B as a prerequisite. In Table 9.3, we have indicated that activity B should be completed at the end of day 11. Activity D, therefore, cannot start until the beginning of day 12 and should be completed at the end of day 19. These values are also entered in Table 9.3.

Activity E is slightly different, because activities B and C are both prerequisites for activity E. In other words, E cannot begin until *both* B and C are finished. B is expected to be finished on day 11, and C's expected completion time is the end of day 14. Thus, both B and C will be finished at the end of day 14, and activity E can start at the beginning of day 15. Since it takes 12 days to complete, E should be finished at the end of day 26. Before proceeding to Table 9.4, review the calculations we have made thus far to be sure you understand the procedures used. You should then have little difficulty in calculating the remaining earliest starting and finishing times.

Table 9.4 is an extension of Table 9.3. It has been expanded to include all activities. Activity F must wait for C, so it begins on day 15 and finishes on day 21. G must wait for D, E, and F. Of the three, the completion time of E (day 26) is the latest. G, therefore, begins on day 27 and finishes on day 31. H can start at the beginning of day 32 and should finish at the end of day 35. Activity I is the ending activity, indicating that all real activities have been performed and the total project has been completed. The starting time of day 36 for activity I indicates that, if everything goes as scheduled, the project should be completed by the end of day 35. In other words, we are ready to move on to something else at the beginning of day 36.

Sample problem 9.1   *HENNESSEY CONSTRUCTION COMPANY*

The following table describes a network problem of the Hennessey Construction Company. Determine the earliest expected time for each activity.

SOLUTION
The solution is given at the far right of the table.

Symbol	Description	Performance time	Prerequisite activities	Earliest times Start	Finish
A	Prepare building foundations	4	none	1	4
B	Erect building frame	5	A	5	9
C	Complete brickwork	8	B	10	17
D	Do initial plumbing work	5	A	5	9
E	Do initial electrical work	5	B	10	14
F	Complete interior work	8	C, E	18	25
G	Install kitchen appliances	3	D, E	15	17
H	Install bathroom fixtures	4	D	10	13
I	Complete roofing	6	C	18	23
J	Paint	5	F, G, H, I	26	30
K	End of project	0	J	31	—

Calculating the latest allowable times

The latest allowable time is the latest time when an activity can begin and still not interfere with the scheduled completion time of the total project. Determining the latest time at which an activity can start is necessary for control purposes. It is also helpful in determining the critical path, which is a major element of network analysis.

Activity H is the last real activity to be completed. It is obvious that this activity must be completed by the end of day 35 if the total project is to be completed in 35 days. Since it takes 4 days to complete activity H, the latest that this activity can start is the beginning of day 32 (work will be done over days 32, 33, 34, and 35). These values are entered in the appropriate place on the worksheet, as shown in Table 9.5. Activity H has activity G as a prerequisite. If the latest that H can start is the beginning of day 32, then the latest that G can be completed is the end of day 31 and, consequently, the latest that G can begin (since it has a 5-day performance time) is the beginning of day 27. Activity G differs from H in that it has three prerequisites: activities D, E, and F. Since G must start on day 27, activities D, E, and F must all be completed by the end of day 26. These values should be entered as the appropriate latest finishing dates, as shown in Table 9.5.

Table 9.5 *Partial PERT worksheet for calculating latest allowable times for the JASS Company problem*

Symbol	Performance time	Prerequisite activities	Earliest time		Latest time	
			Start	Finish	Start	Finish
C	10	A	5	14	—	19
D	8	B	12	19	—	26
E	12	B, C	15	26	—	26
F	7	C	15	21	20	26
G	5	D, E, F	27	31	27	31
H	4	G	32	35	32	35
I	0	H	36	—	36	—

Proceeding in a backward and upward direction, we note that activity F must start on day 20 and, consequently, activity C must be completed by the end of day 19. At this point, we should stop and review the calculations we have made and recorded in Table 9.5. For any activity, there is a tendency to calculate the latest starting date as soon as we have entered its latest finishing date in the worksheet. In other words, the tendency is to go ahead and calculate starting dates of day 10, day 19, and day 15 for activities C, D, and E respectively. This should not be done. As we shall show, day 10 is not the correct latest starting time for activity C. The correct procedure is to move backward up the column for latest starting time one activity at a time. After a latest starting date is entered, the latest finishing date for all prerequisites can be entered. But we should never move more than one step at a time up the column for latest starts.

Table 9.6 illustrates this procedure. Activity E must start at the beginning of day 15, which means that activities B and C must both be completed by the end of day 14. These values are entered in Table 9.6.

Table 9.6 *Partial PERT worksheet illustrating conflicting late finishing times for an activity*

Symbol	Performance time	Prerequisite activities	Earliest time		Latest time	
			Start	Finish	Start	Finish
B	7	A	5	11	—	14
C	10	A	5	14	—	~~19~~, 14
D	8	B	12	19	—	26
E	12	B, C	15	26	15	26
F	7	C	15	21	20	26

Note, however, that activity C now has two latest finishing times, day 14 and day 19. In such cases, the earliest of the two or more finishing times is the controlling time. We simply cross out and ignore the latest time(s), as 19 has been crossed out in Table 9.6. Table 9.7 illustrates the results of calculating all the latest allowable starting and finishing times.

Slack time

Slack time for any activity is the amount of time by which completion of that activity can be delayed without affecting the completion time of the total project. The completion of an activity may be delayed because it did not start on time, because it took longer to perform than had been expected, or because of some combination of the two. We can therefore think of *slack time* for a given activity as the length of time by which the starting of that activity can be delayed or the amount of time by which performance time can be extended without delaying the scheduled completion time of the total project.

We determine slack time for any activity by subtracting the earliest finishing time from the latest finishing time. The results of this calculation for the JASS Company problem are given in Table 9.7. The 5 days of slack for activity F indicate that a delay of 5 or fewer days in preparing the data collection forms would not affect the 35-day completion date of the total project. Similarly, the zero slack time listed for activity C indicates that any delay in preparing the research design would delay the 35-day completion date.

Significance of the critical path

Activities that have zero slack time are referred to as *critical activities*, and the sequence (path) of critical activities is known as the *critical path*. In the JASS Company problem, activities A, C, E, G, and H are critical activities, and the sequence A-C-E-G-H-I is the critical path. The critical activities and the critical path are the basis of network analysis. The following discussion highlights the significance of the critical items.

An increase in the performance time of any critical activity increases the completion time of the total project by an equal length of time. Thus, delays in the performance of critical items should be avoided. A noncritical item can be delayed up to the limit of its slack time without delaying the total project. We shall show later, however, that it is not necessarily true that two noncritical items can *both* be extended to the limits of their slack time. In the JASS Company problem, assume that on day 16 a staff member was ill for a day. This would cause Dr. Zee to delay activity D, activity E, or activity F. Since activity E is a critical activity, he should choose to delay either D or E.

Table 9.7 *Complete PERT worksheet for the JASS Company problem*

Symbol	Performance time	Prerequisite activities	Earliest time		Latest time		Slack
			Start	*Finish*	*Start*	*Finish*	
A	4	none	1	4	1	4,~~7~~	0
B	7	A	5	11	8	14,~~18~~	3
C	10	A	5	14	5	~~19~~,14	0
D	8	B	12	19	19	26	7
E	12	B, C	15	26	15	26	0
F	7	C	15	21	20	26	5
G	5	D, E, F	27	31	27	31	0
H	4	G	32	35	32	35	0
I	0	H	36	—	36	—	—

If it becomes necessary to reduce the total project time by reducing the performance time of an activity (by working overtime on the activity, for instance), this time reduction must be performed on a critical activity. Reducing the performance time of a noncritical item cannot reduce the time needed to complete the total project. Activity B in the JASS Company problem, the location study, is a noncritical item. If the performance time of this activity were reduced (for example, from 7 to 4 days), it would not affect the scheduled 35-day completion time of the total project.

Decreasing the performance time of a critical item may reduce the total project time by an equal amount. In general, reduction of the performance time of a critical item will yield a day-for-day reduction in project time, unless and until another item becomes critical. Unfortunately, it may be necessary to recalculate the network to determine how cuts in the performance time of critical items affect the total project time.

In this example, we calculated the latest allowable times by working backward from the estimated completion date of 35 days. Some analysts work backward from a *project-due date*. For example, suppose Ms. Sampson had asked Dr. Zee to complete the project in 40 days. Forty would be the project-due date and we could use this in calculating latest allowable times. All activities would have some slack, and the critical path would simply be the longest path in the network. In future examples, we will continue to work backward from the earliest expected completion date. The assumption that it is desirable to complete the project as soon as possible makes the project-due date coincide with the earliest completion date.

Sample problem 9.2 *HENNESSEY CONSTRUCTION COMPANY (Continued)*

Consider the Hennessey Construction Company problem given in Sample Problem 9.1. Determine the latest allowable time and the slack time for each activity.

SOLUTION

Symbol	Performance time	Prerequisite activities	Earliest time Start	Earliest time Finish	Latest time Start	Latest time Finish	Slack
A	4	none	1	4	1	16,4	0
B	5	A	5	9	5	12,9	0
C	8	B	10	17	10	19,17	0
D	5	A	5	9	17	21,22	12
E	5	B	10	14	13	22,17	3
F	8	C, E	18	25	18	25	0
G	3	D, E	15	17	23	25	8
H	4	D	10	13	22	25	12
I	6	C	18	23	20	25	2
J	5	F, G, H, I	26	30	26	30	0
K	0	J	31	—	31	—	0

PERT networks as continuous time functions

Our PERT worksheets have assumed that an activity would be completed at the end of a particular day and that the next activity would start at the beginning of the next day. In PERT analysis, it is helpful to assume that time is a *continuous function;* that is, we work on a "continuous clock."

Most of us have operated a stop watch. We know that the first minute begins when the clock reads 0:00. The first minute ends and the second minute begins when the clock reads 1:00. In network models, day 1 starts at time 0 and ends at time 1. Day 2 starts at time 1 and ends at time 2, etc. In other words, an activity finishing at time 7 will finish at the end of day 7, which is also the beginning of day 8. Likewise, an activity starting on day 9 will begin at time 8, which is the end of day 8 *and* the beginning of day 9.

It may be helpful to illustrate this on a graph. Figure 9.2 illustrates consecutive activities with performance times of 7, 4, and 6 days respectively. The length of the arrow indicates the performance time. The first activity, X, begins at time 0 and ends at time 7. The second activity, Y, begins at time 7 (the end of the seventh day and the beginning of the eighth day) and continues through time 11. We should

Figure 9.2 *Graphical representation of activities, using a continuous time function*

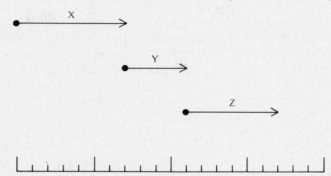

verify from the graph that this does span a period of 4 days. The third activity, Z, begins at time 11 and is completed at time 17.

The material that follows requires the use of this continuous time function. It would be helpful for us to go back and rework the JASS Company problem using the continuous clock. The only changes are in the starting times. Activity A now starts at time 0. Activities B and C start as soon as A is finished, which is at time 4. A PERT worksheet for the JASS Company problem using a continuous time function is given in Table 9.8. If we compare Tables 9.7 and 9.8, we note that the only difference is that the starting times of Table 9.7 have been reduced by a value of 1. We will use a continuous time function in the remainder of this chapter.

Table 9.8 *PERT worksheet for the JASS Company problem, using a continuous time function*

| Symbol | Performance time | Prerequisite activities | Earliest time | | Latest time | | Slack |
			Start	Finish	Start	Finish	
A	4	none	0	4	0	4	0
B	7	A	4	11	7	14	3
C	10	A	4	14	4	14	0
D	8	B	11	19	18	26	7
E	12	B, C	14	26	14	26	0
F	7	C	14	21	19	26	5
G	5	D, E, F	26	31	26	31	0
H	4	G	31	35	31	35	0
I	0	H	35	—	35	—	0

Arrow diagrams

A graphical representation of the JASS Company problem is given in Figure 9.3. This type of representation, known as an arrow diagram, is quite helpful in planning and controlling projects. Many analysts consider the arrow diagram the major tool of analysis and do not use the PERT worksheets we have discussed. Fiqure 9.3 differs slightly from Figure 9.1. The following sections explain the reason for this.

Activities

The arrow diagram is actually a representation of the "Earliest time" columns given in Table 9.8. *The earliest starting time* for each activity *is represented by a dot. The earliest finishing time* for each activity *is represented by an arrowhead.* The performance time is therefore represented by the horizontal length of the arrow (from dot to arrowhead). We construct the arrow diagram by locating a dot for each activity at its earliest starting time, as listed in Table 9.8. If several activities have the same starting time, the dots are located one above the other. There is no rule of thumb to tell us which dot goes above the other. Some analysts try to make the critical path a straight line. Generally, however, the arrangement that leads to the least complicated figure is the best.

For each activity, an arrow is drawn from the dot representing the earliest starting time toward the starting dot of each activity that has this activity as a prerequisite. For example, E is a prerequisite for G, so we draw an arrow from the dot representing the earliest starting time of E toward the dot representing the earliest starting time of G. We place

Figure 9.3 *Arrow diagram of the JASS Company problem*

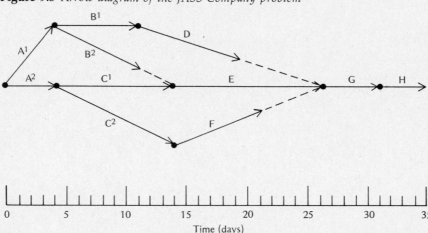

an arrowhead at this second dot, indicating that it also represents the earliest finishing time for activity E.

Activity A is a prerequisite for both activity B and activity C. Two arrows are therefore drawn from A, one toward the dot that represents the starting time of B and one toward the dot that represents the starting time of C. An arrowhead is placed at each of these dots. On Figure 9.3, we have labeled these arrows A^1 and A^2, indicating that activity A is represented by more than one arrow. This "double arrow" procedure is cumbersome, and several alternative methods are in use. One method is to have only one solid arrow per activity and to make the remaining arrows dotted lines. This procedure causes confusion if dotted lines are also used to represent slack time. A second alternative method utilizes dummy activities. This method also has advantages and limitations. It is the most commonly used method, however, and we will discuss it later in the chapter when we talk about standard PERT terminology.

Slack time

Activity B in Figure 9.3 represents another concept that requires special attention. Activity B is a prerequisite for both activities D and E. We therefore draw two arrows, one toward the dot representing the earliest starting time for D and one toward the dot representing the earliest starting time for E. Since the earliest finishing time for B is at time 11, we place arrowheads on both arrows at time 11 in the arrow diagrams. Since E does not start until time 14, a dotted line is used to connect the earliest finishing time (arrowhead) for activity B and the earliest starting time (dot) for activity E.

Slack times are represented by dotted lines. For example, the 7 days of slack time for activity D are represented by the dotted line segment between the finish of D and the beginning of G.

In many instances, there will be two or more paths from the earliest starting time for an activity to the end of the total project. In such cases, the amount of slack time for an activity is equal to the total amount of dotted line segments on the path that contains the *least* amount of dotted-line time. In Figure 9.3, there are two dotted lines between the start of B and the end of the project. The first is the 7-day dotted line between D and G on path B^1-D-G-H. The second is the 3-day dotted line between B^2 and E on path B^2-E-G-H. Slack time is always represented by the smallest of these possibilities. In this case, the smallest is the dotted line between the earliest finishing time for activity B and the earliest starting time for activity E.

In some cases, it is necessary to add together two or more dotted line segments to obtain the amount of slack on a given path. A good example of this appears in Sample Problem 9.3. The path D^1-G-J contains 5 days of slack between D^1 and G and 8 days of slack between G and J. This path has 13 days of slack. The path D^2-H-J has 12 days of slack. Slack time for activity D is the smaller of these two: 12 days.

Critical items contain a path to the project completion point that has no slack time and thus no dotted lines. As an example, consider activity C in Figure 9.3. There are two paths from the start of C to the project completion point: C^1-E-G-H and C^2-F-G-H. We can think of the first path as containing a dotted line of zero length. Thus, slack time for this activity is zero.

Multiple beginning activities

The networks we have discussed so far had only one beginning activity; that is, there was only one activity that had no prerequisites. Obviously, many real networks have several activities that can begin on the first day of the project. Consider the network shown in Figure 9.4. Activities A, B, and C all begin on the date the project starts. These activities can be represented by three arrows, one above the other, as shown in Figure 9.4(a). A second procedure is to draw all beginning activities from a common starting point, as shown in Figure 9.4(b). This method can become very cumbersome if there are many beginning activities, but it does emphasize the common starting time.

An arrow diagram is quite helpful in both project planning and project control. It is a simple, easily understandable, and direct method

Figure 9.4 *Arrow diagrams of network with multiple beginning activities*

(a) Representation using parallel activities

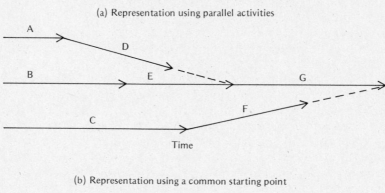

(b) Representation using a common starting point

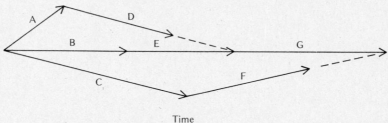

of displaying the interrelationships of activities in a complex project. It calls attention to those activities that are critical to the project completion time. It enables the analyst to quickly study the effect of any changes made in the network, and it reveals potential bottlenecks that might result from these changes. The arrow diagram is also a control device for the project manager. It allows the manager to compare planned progress with actual progress. And it is helpful to the person who must make necessary adjustments in the network.

Sample problem 9.3 HENNESSEY CONSTRUCTION COMPANY (Continued)

Consider the Hennessey Construction Company problem given in Sample Problems 9.1 and 9.2. Convert the earliest starting times into a continuous time function beginning at time zero. Draw an arrow diagram of the network.

SOLUTION
The new earliest starting times are A = 0, B = 4, C = 9, D = 4, E = 9, F = 17, G = 14, H = 9, I = 17, J = 25, and K = 30.

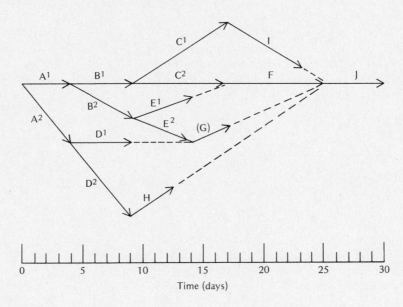

Probability concepts in PERT

Thus far in this chapter, we have assumed that a single estimate of performance time was made for each activity. The PERT methodology actually calls for three estimates of the performance time for each activity. This allows for the uncertainty inherent in almost every performance estimate. It also gives the project director a method of estimating the probability of completing the entire project on certain specified dates.

Time estimates in PERT

The three estimates required are a most optimistic (shortest) time, a most pessimistic (longest) time, and a most likely time. The most *optimistic time* is an estimate of the minimum time required to complete an activity. This shortest performance time will be obtained only if everything goes right. The probability of having such good fortune should be only 1 chance in 100. The most *pessimistic time* is an estimate of the maximum time required to complete an activity. This longest performance time will occur only if everything goes wrong. Again, the probability of having such bad luck should be only 1 chance in 100. Although this estimate reflects extremely bad luck, it should not be influenced by possible catastrophic events such as fire or earthquakes, unless these are natural and inherent risks in the activity.

The *most likely time* is an estimate of the normal time required to complete an activity. It is an estimate of the result that would occur most often if the activity were repeated a large number of times.

PERT assumes that the probability distribution associated with activity times is best approximated by the beta distribution. The mean of this distribution is referred to as the expected time and can be approximated by the formula

$$t = \frac{a + 4m + b}{6}$$

In this formula, a is the most optimistic time estimate, b is the most pessimistic time estimate, and m is the most likely time estimate. Thus, the formula allows us to combine the three time estimates into a single time estimate.

Expected times are the values that we should use as activity performance times in our PERT worksheets and arrow diagrams. It is often asked why expected times are better than normal times as estimates of performance. One reason is that follow-up studies of actual projects have indicated that accuracy is better when expected times are used. The second reason is that using expected times forces the decision maker to introduce uncertainty into the estimate. This allows us to determine the probability of completing projects by certain specified dates.

Table 9.9 gives the most optimistic, most likely, most pessimistic, and expected time estimates for the activities in the JASS Company

Table 9.9 *Performance estimates and standard deviations of activities of the JASS Company problem*

Symbol	Most optimistic time (a)	Most likely time (m)	Most pessimistic time (b)	Expected time (t)	Standard deviation (σ)
A	3	4	5	4	.33
B	4	6	14	7	1.67
C	4	11	12	10	1.33
D	6	8	10	8	.67
E	8	10	24	12	2.67
F	5	7	9	7	.67
G	4	5	6	5	.33
H	3	4	5	4	.33
I	0	0	0	0	—

problem. We can verify in Table 9.9 that we have been using the expected time estimates in our analysis of the JASS Company problem.

Probabilities of specified project completion times

The three time estimates we have just discussed can be used to provide a measure of the degree of variability in the expected performance times of an activity. They can be used to estimate a *standard deviation*, or measure of variability, for each activity. We can use the standard deviations of the activities to calculate the standard deviation of the critical path. For the beta distribution, the standard deviation, σ (sigma), can be approximated by the formula

$$\sigma = \frac{b - a}{6}$$

As an example, the standard deviation of activity B in the JASS Company problem is

$$\frac{14 - 4}{6} = 1.67$$

The standard deviation for activity G is

$$\frac{6 - 4}{6} = .33$$

All of the standard deviations for the activities in the JASS Company problem have been entered in Table 9.9.

The *standard deviation of a path* is equal to the square root of the sum of the squares of the standard deviations of activities that make up the path. Suppose we have an activity M that is a prerequisite for an activity N. M has a standard deviation of 3, and N has a standard deviation of 4. The standard deviation of the path M-N can be determined as follows:

$$\sigma_{M-N} = \sqrt{\sigma_M^2 + \sigma_N^2}$$

$$\sigma_{M-N} = \sqrt{3^2 + 4^2} = \sqrt{25} = 5$$

Suppose we have three activities, P, Q, and R, which have standard deviations of 1.5, 2.0, and 3.5 respectively. The standard deviations of the path P-Q-R would be:

$$\sigma_{P-Q-R} = \sqrt{\sigma_P^2 + \sigma_Q^2 + \sigma_R^2}$$

$$\sigma_{P-Q-R} = \sqrt{1.5^2 + 2.0^2 + 3.5^2} = \sqrt{2.25 + 4.00 + 12.25}$$

$$\sigma_{P-Q-R} = \sqrt{18.50} = 4.3$$

The critical path in the JASS Company problem is A-C-E-G-H-I. These activities have standard deviations of .33, 1.33, 2.67, .33, .33, and 0 respectively. The standard deviation of the critical path is therefore

$$\sigma_{cp} = \sqrt{.33^2 + 1.33^2 + 2.67^2 + .33^2 + .33^2}$$

$$\sigma_{cp} = \sqrt{9.2245} = 3.04$$

For projects with a large number of activities the distribution of completion times can be approximated by the normal curve. Most readers are familiar with the normal statistical distribution. Those who are not may want to read the section of Chapter 14 on the normal distribution. Areas under the standardized normal curve are given in Table A in the Appendix.

In the JASS Company problem, suppose Ms. Sampson asks Dr. Zee for an estimated probability of completing the project in 39 days or less.[1] The curve shown in Figure 9.5 is a pictorial representation of the problem. We have previously determined that the expected completion time of the project is 35 days. Thus, 35 is the mean of the distribution. The number of standard deviation units between 35 and 39 can be determined as follows:

$$\frac{39 - 35}{3.04} = 1.32$$

If we look up 1.32 in Table A in the Appendix, we discover that 40.66% of the area under the curve lies between 35 and 39. Since an additional 50% of the area under the curve lies to the left of 35, a total of 90.66% of

---

[1]This analysis actually computes the probability of completing the activities in the critical path in 39 days or less. A weakness of the analysis is that it fails to consider noncritical activities.

Figure 9.5 *Pictorial representation of completing in 39 days or less*

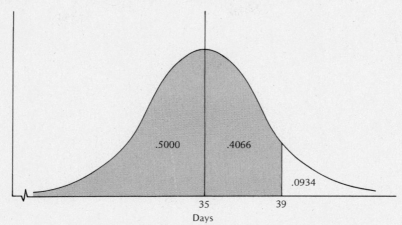

the area under the curve is less than 39. The probability of completing the project in 39 days or less is therefore .9066.

Suppose that Ms. Sampson had asked for the probability of completing the project in 29 days or less, as illustrated in Figure 9.6. The number of standard deviation units between 29 and 35 is 1.97; that is,

$$\frac{35 - 29}{3.04} = 1.97$$

If we look up 1.97 in Table A in the Appendix, we find that 47.56% of the area under the curve lies between 29 and 35. Since an additional

Figure 9.6 *Probability of completing in 29 days or less*

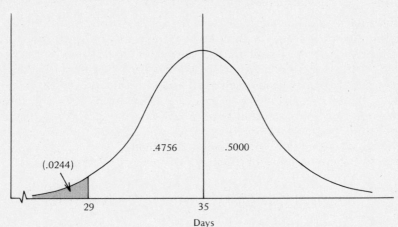

Figure 9.7 *Probability completion curve for the JASS Company problem*

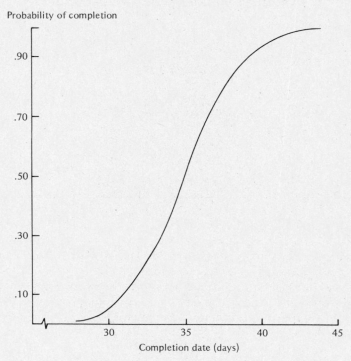

50% of the area under the curve is above 35, 97.56% of the area under the curve lies above 29 and 2.44% of the area under the curve lies below 29. The probability of completion in 29 days or less is therefore .0244.

Probability completion curves

Many projects are put out for bids with a stipulation that the work be completed within a specified period of time. This type of contract often calls for a penalty payment by the contractor if the work is not completed by the due date. It may also award a premium for early completion of the project. In cases such as these, a *probability completion curve* may be quite helpful to the managerial analyst. This is a graphical representation of the probability of completing the project[2] on specified dates. The probability completion curve for the JASS Company problem is given in Figure 9.7. It provides the analyst with a good, quick synopis of the likelihood of finishing the project at certain times.

---

[2]We should again caution that the curve actually describes the probability of completing the activities on the critical path.

Sample problem 9.4   *THE 231 COMPANY*

The following table gives the most optimistic, most likely, and most pessimistic time estimates (in days) for the activities of the 231 Company. For each activity, verify that the expected times and standard deviations shown in the table are correct. A, B, and D are the critical activities. Determine (1) the standard deviation of the critical path, (2) the probability of completing the project in 154 days or less, and (3) the probability of completing the project in 133 days or less.

Symbol	Most optimistic time (a)	Most likely time (m)	Most pessimistic time (b)	Expected time (t)	Standard deviation (σ)
A	24	30	36	30	2
B	46	58	82	60	6
C	28	40	52	40	4
D	39	51	57	50	3
E	20	20	20	20	0

SOLUTION

1.
$$\sigma_{cp} = \sqrt{2^2 + 6^2 + 3^2} = \sqrt{4 + 36 + 9} = \sqrt{49} = 7$$

2. Most likely completion time is 140 weeks (30 + 60 + 50).

$$\frac{154 - 140}{7} = 2 \text{ standard deviation units}$$

From Table A: .4773 + .5000 = .9773

3. $\dfrac{140 - 133}{7} = 1$ standard deviation unit

From Table A: .3413 + .5000 = .8413; (1 − .8413) = .1587

Standard PERT terminology

In developing this chapter, we have used "poetic license" in order to simplify the material for learning purposes. At this point, however, we should go back and ensure that we understand proper PERT terminology.

Events and activities

PERT is basically concerned with two concepts: events and activities. An *event* is an accomplishment or happening that occurs at a specific and recognizable instant in time. In the JASS Company problem, examples of events are the beginning of the preparation of the research design and the completion of the field study. An *activity* is the work required to complete a specified task. This definition conforms to the concept of an activity as we have been using it. In the JASS Company problem, performing location studies and preparing the research design are both activities.

In PERT network diagrams, events are drawn as circles called *nodes*. These nodes are assigned numbers for identification purposes. Each node represents a particular "point in time." Node 1, for example, might represent a point in time when some particular work started. Node 2 might represent the point in time when this same work was completed. Node 2 might also represent the beginning of a different piece of work.

Activities are represented by arrows connecting the nodes. Thus, an activity that has node 1 as its starting event and node 2 as its ending event would be represented by an arrow from node 1 to node 2. This arrow represents the time required to accomplish the actual work. In PERT terminology, activities are generally referred to by their starting and ending event or node numbers rather than by symbols (such as the A, B, and C we have been using). In Figure 9.8, several simple networks are described in PERT terminology. We should note that several different activities can have either the same starting or the same finishing events.

Several PERT networks are shown in Figure 9.9. *A time scale is not needed,* because PERT networks are not usually drawn to scale. Instead, the performance time of each activity is given on the diagram. *The critical path is always the longest path* through the network. The earliest expected time (TE) and the latest allowable time (TL) of each event can be determined by simple addition and subtraction. These values are given for each node. Slack time for each event is the difference between the earliest expected time and the latest allowable time.

Dummy activities

The network shown in Figure 9.9(c) is, of course, the JASS Company problem. Let us now refer to the activities by node numbers. Activity E becomes activity 5-7. Activity F becomes activity 6-7, and activity G becomes activity 7-8. A difficulty arises with those activities that are represented by two arrows on the diagram. Activity A is now referred to as activity 1-2 *and* activity 1-3. The dual names for this activity are likely to cause confusion.

We can eliminate this problem by introducing dummy activities. *Dummy activities* are assumed to have a zero performance time, and

Figure 9.8 *Simple networks described in proper PERT terminology*

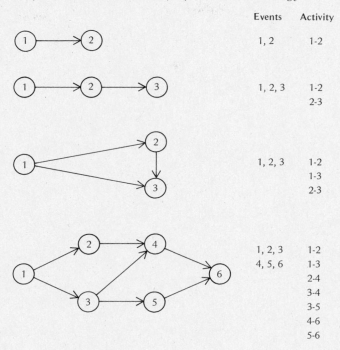

	Events	Activity
	1, 2	1-2
	1, 2, 3	1-2
		2-3
	1, 2, 3	1-2
		1-3
		2-3
	1, 2, 3	1-2
	4, 5, 6	1-3
		2-4
		3-4
		3-5
		4-6
		5-6

they are used for the sole purpose of illustrating prerequisite relationships. A dummy activity is usually represented by a dotted line in a PERT diagram. Figure 9.10 illustrates how the JASS Company problem can be drawn using dummy activities. For explanatory purposes, we have used both the node identification system and the symbol identification system for the activities of the JASS Company problem. Two dummy activities are needed. The activity 3-4 has a performance time of 0. It is used only to ensure that activity B (2-3) will be completed before activity E (4-6) begins. If 3-4 is a prerequisite for E (4-6) and if B (2-3) is a prerequisite for 3-4, then B (2-3) must precede E (4-6). Likewise, activity 5-4 ensures that C (2-5) is a prerequisite for E (4-6).

Adding dummy activities eliminates the need of using two arrows for one activity. This advantage is at least partially offset by the need for extra activities. Most analysts (and most computer routines) use the dummy activities. Many students, however, find that they can understand the process better by using the multiple-arrow method at first. The choice of method is a decision that really should be made by the person performing the work.

Figure 9.9 *Simple PERT networks*

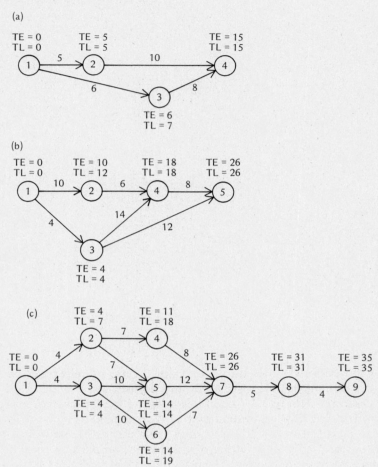

Figure 9.10 *Arrow diagram for the JASS Company problem, using dummy activities*

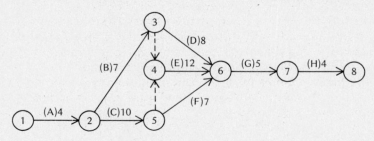

Sample problem 9.5 HENNESSEY CONSTRUCTION COMPANY (Continued)

Consider the Hennessey Construction Company problem given in Sample Problems 9.1 and 9.2. Draw an arrow diagram using dummy activities.

SOLUTION

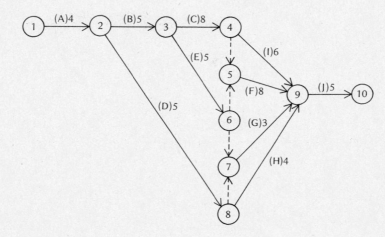

Extensions of basic network analysis

The network analysis we have discussed has been primarily concerned with planning, scheduling, and controlling time. Network analysis can be extended to aid in the solution of other managerial problems. We will discuss two of these extensions in this section.

Scheduling with limited resources

Standard network procedures assume that an activity should begin as soon as all prerequisite activities are completed. This guideline does not consider the amount of resources available to the project director or the amount of resources required by the various activities. In some cases, more efficient use of resources can be achieved by delaying the start of an activity past the earliest possible starting time. For example, consider the network model shown in Figure 9.11.

The network shown in Figure 9.11 represents the earliest possible time schedule. It is drawn to a time scale in days. The number of workers (such as welders) required for each activity is given in the diagram. We can determine the total number of workers required each day by summing the number of workers working on each activity scheduled for that day. These totals are shown at the bottom of Figure

Figure 9.11 *Schematic of project, showing daily labor power requirements*

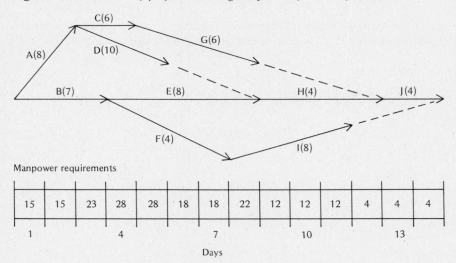

Manpower requirements

15	15	23	28	28	18	18	22	12	12	12	4	4	4

Days

9.11. This network schedule results in a very uneven use of labor. On day 4, 28 workers are required, while only 4 workers are required on day 13. It is often advantageous to balance the workload so that approximately the same number of workers are required each day.

On many projects, resource leveling can be obtained by delaying the start of one or more noncritical activities. In some cases, it is permissible to split an activity into two or more component parts. For example, the first half of an activity requiring 4 days might be accomplished on days 4 and 5, and the second half might be performed on days 9 and 10.

Management scientists and practitioners have developed a number of heuristic or "rule of thumb" programs to solve problems of this type. Heuristic programs do not guarantee an optimal solution, but they usually generate a usable or satisfactory solution. The arrow diagram given in Figure 9.12 is a solution obtained by trial and error. Labor usage varies from day to day, but the magnitude of the variation is much smaller than in the original network illustrated in Figure 9.11.

An uneven rate of resource usage can present major problems to a project manager. The procedure we have discussed does not generally lead to a perfectly balanced project. In many instances, however, a modest amount of resource leveling leads to a large reduction in costs. It is often worth the effort. In performing the analysis, remember that delaying the start of a noncritical item could increase the probability of delaying the project completion date. Once again, we must trade one advantage for another.

Figure 9.12 *Project after resource leveling*

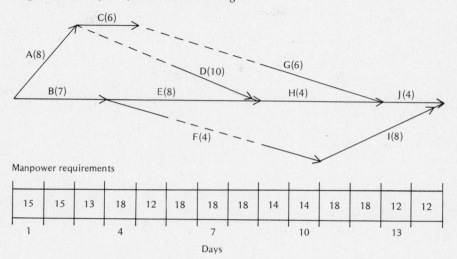

Manpower requirements

15	15	13	18	12	18	18	18	14	14	18	18	12	12

1   4   7   10   13

Days

Networks and project crashing

A second extension of network analysis is project crashing. The object of crash-cost models is to determine the minimum-cost method of reducing total project completion time. In this analysis, two time estimates and two cost estimates are made for each activity in the network. The *normal estimate of time* is similar to the most likely time estimate, which we discussed before. The *crash estimate* is the minimum estimate of the time that would be required to complete the activity, regardless of the costs involved. *Normal cost* is associated with completing the activity in normal time, and *crash cost* is the cost involved in performing the activity in crash time. It is assumed that the relationships between crash and normal estimates are linear. For example, if it costs an extra $180 to reduce an activity performance time by 6 days, we assume that it costs $30 per day for each of the 6 days.

As an example, consider the network shown in Figure 9.13(a). The first number represents the normal estimate of time, and the second number represents the crash estimate of time. Using the normal estimate of time, we find that the critical path is A-D-F and the expected completion time is 48 days. It is our task to find the most economical way of reducing this 48-day project completion time. (A word of caution before proceeding. Only critical items are candidates for time reduction, since reducing the performance time of noncritical activities does not affect the project completion time. In the process of crashing, the critical path is likely to change. In many cases, there will be two or

Figure 9.13 *Schematic illustration of crashing a project*

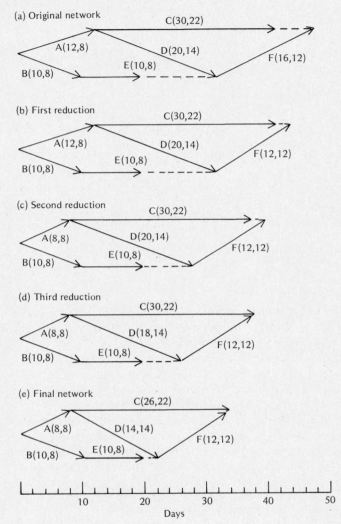

(a) Original network

C(30,22)

A(12,8)   D(20,14)

B(10,8)   E(10,8)   F(16,12)

(b) First reduction

C(30,22)

A(12,8)   D(20,14)

B(10,8)   E(10,8)   F(12,12)

(c) Second reduction

C(30,22)

A(8,8)   D(20,14)

B(10,8)   E(10,8)   F(12,12)

(d) Third reduction

C(30,22)

A(8,8)   D(18,14)

B(10,8)   E(10,8)   F(12,12)

(e) Final network

C(26,22)

A(8,8)   D(14,14)

B(10,8)   E(10,8)   F(12,12)

10   20   30   40   50

Days

more critical paths through a network. Thus, project crashing can quickly become a complex operation. Computer programs are available, and using them is often the only practical method of crashing real projects.)

Project crashing is generally done on a stepwise or iterative basis. We will use this method to illustrate the process of crashing the network shown in Figure 9.13(a).

Table 9.10 *Crashing a project*

	Time		Cost		Cost to reduce one day
Activity	Normal	Crash	Normal	Crash	
A	12	8	$ 20,000	$ 24,000	$1000
B	10	8	10,000	16,000	3000
C	30	22	40,000	64,000	3000
D	20	14	18,000	30,000	2000
E	10	8	22,000	27,000	2500
F	16	12	8,000	10,000	500
			$118,000	$171,000	

Iteration 1 Table 9.10 gives both crash and normal estimates for all activities. The right-hand column tells us how much additional cost we must incur to reduce completion time by 1 day. Since we want the most for our money, we will first crash the critical activity that has the lowest per-unit crash cost. We must choose among the critical activities A, D, and F, which have per-unit crash costs of $1000, $2000, and $500 respectively. Since activity F has the lowest per-unit crash cost, we select it and reduce its performance time from 16 to 12 days for an additional cost of $2000. The new network is shown in Figure 9.13(b).

Iteration 2 In Figure 9.13(b), the critical path is still A-D-F. We have already reduced activity F to its lowest time limit, so only activities A and D are candidates for crashing. Of these, A has the lower per-unit crash cost and is therefore selected. The new network is shown in Figure 9.13(c). Project completion time has been shortened by 4 days, but the firm had to spend $4000 to obtain the reduction in time.

Iteration 3 In Figure 9.13(c), activity D is the only critical item for which the performance time can be reduced by crashing. Note, however, that a reduction of more than 2 days will cause a new path to become critical. At this iteration, therefore, the maximum reduction that can be made on activity D is 2 days. This will result in an additional cost of $4000. The new network is shown in Figure 9.13(d). Total project completion time is now 38 days.

Iteration 4 The network shown in Figure 9.13(d) has two critical paths, A-D-F and A-C. Further reduction in project completion time will require simultaneous crashing of activity C and activity D. The per-day crash cost will be $5000.

Table 9.11 *Costs involved in crashing a project*

Iteration	Per-day cost reduction	Days reduced	Activities crashed	New completion time	Added cost	New project cost
0				48		$118,000
1	$ 500	4	F	44	$ 2,000	120,000
2	1000	4	A	40	4,000	124,000
3	2000	2	D	38	4,000	128,000
4	5000	4	C, D	34	20,000	148,000
					$30,000	

Figure 9.13(e) shows the new network with the performance times of activities A, D, and F reduced to the fullest extent possible. All activities on the critical path are now crashed to their minimum performance time. No further reduction of the project completion time is possible. The minimum performance time of the total project is 34 days.

Table 9.11 summarizes the steps we have taken in crashing the project from its original anticipated completion time of 48 days to the minimum possible time of 34 days. This reduction was obtained by incurring an additional cost of $30,000. Note that the daily, or incremental, cost of crashing the project became greater at each iteration. In other words, it becomes increasingly more expensive to obtain a 1-day reduction in project completion time. When time is very important, there is a temptation to crash each activity to its minimum performance time. As shown in Table 9.10, this would lead to a total cost of $171,000. The minimum completion time would still be 34 days, the same result we obtained by systematic crashing at a cost of only $148,000. We saved $23,000 by using the process of selective crashing.

Networks and linear programming

By this time, you may have realized that linear programming can be used to analyze network models. As an example, let us formulate the JASS Company problem as a linear programming problem. We will need a variable for the earliest starting time of each activity. For convenience, we can let X_1 represent the earliest starting time of activity A and X_2 the earliest starting time of activity B. We can use X_3 for the earliest starting time of C, X_4 for D, X_5 for E, X_6 for F, X_7 for G, X_8 for H, and X_9 for I.

The objective of this problem is to determine the earliest completion time for the entire project. Activity I represents the end of the project; when I starts, all other activities are finished. Our objective, therefore, is to make X_9, the starting time of I, as small as possible. Mathematically our *objective function* is

$$\text{Min } Z = X_9$$

The *constraints* are easily formulated. First, we know that activity A cannot start before time 0. Therefore,

$$X_1 \geqslant 0 \quad \text{(activity A starting time)}$$

Activities B and C must wait until activity A is completed. Since the performance time of A is 4 days, the completion time of A is $X_1 + 4$. We know that X_2 (the earliest starting time of B) and X_3 (the earliest starting time of C) must be greater than or equal to the completion time of A. Therefore, these constraints may be formulated as

$$X_2 - X_1 \geqslant 4 \quad \text{(activity B starting time)}$$
$$X_3 - X_1 \geqslant 4 \quad \text{(activity C starting time)}$$

Similarly, the earliest starting time of activity D (X_4) must be greater than or equal to the completion time of activity B ($X_2 + 7$).

$$X_4 - X_2 \geqslant 7 \quad \text{(activity D starting time)}$$

Activities that have more than one prerequisite must have one constraint formulated for each prerequisite. The use of dummy activities would not change the number of constraints. Activity E has both activity B and activity C as prerequisites. Thus, the earliest starting time of E (X_5) must be greater than or equal to the completion times of both B ($X_2 + 7$) and C ($X_3 + 10$). A separate constraint must be formulated for each of these relationships.

$$X_5 - X_2 \geqslant 7 \quad \text{(first activity E starting time)}$$
$$X_5 - X_3 \geqslant 10 \quad \text{(second activity E starting time)}$$

The remaining constraints may be formulated as follows:

$$X_6 - X_3 \geqslant 10 \quad \text{(activity F starting time)}$$
$$X_7 - X_4 \geqslant 8 \quad \text{(first activity G starting time)}$$
$$X_7 - X_5 \geqslant 12 \quad \text{(second activity G starting time)}$$
$$X_7 - X_6 \geqslant 7 \quad \text{(third activity G starting time)}$$
$$X_8 - X_7 \geqslant 5 \quad \text{(activity H starting time)}$$
$$X_9 - X_8 \geqslant 4 \quad \text{(activity I starting time)}$$
$$X_i \geqslant 0, \quad \text{for all } i$$

Linear programming is not normally used as a method of analyzing simple network models. However, this formulation illustrates the power of linear programming as a managerial tool. It also serves as an example of the interrelationship of many quantitative managerial tools.

Although we shall not prove it here, it is interesting to note that the dual of the foregoing problem, with one simple adjustment, has the special structure of a linear programming transportation problem.

Comparison of CPM and PERT

In this chapter, we have taken the approach that there is a body of network principles that have emerged from the original and independent developments of PERT and CPM. These network principles are common to CPM, PERT, and similar techniques that have been developed. Because of these similarities, it may be better to use the general term *network analysis,* rather than the more specific terms PERT and CPM. You may be interested in how and why CPM and PERT were originally developed. You should also be aware of the major differences between the original version of CPM and the original version of PERT.

PERT was developed in 1958 by the Special Projects Office of the United States Navy working in conjunction with the consulting firm of Booz, Allen, and Hamilton. At that time, the navy was faced with the challenge of producing the Polaris submarine in record time. PERT was developed to assist the navy in meeting this challenge. Since time was a very important factor in the Polaris program, PERT was originally developed to plan and control the time aspect of the project.

CPM grew out of a research effort begun jointly in 1957 by Du Pont and Remington Rand. This research team was primarily concerned with how best to reduce the time required to perform tasks such as construction work and plant maintenance. In other words, the originators of CPM were interested in determining an optimal tradeoff of cost and time.

Because of this difference in purpose, the original versions of CPM and PERT differ in two important ways. First, CPM assumes that activity performance times are deterministic; that is, there is no uncertainty involved. The "three-time-estimate" approach (pessimistic, most likely, and optimistic) that we used in this chapter was a part of the original version of PERT, but not a part of the original version of CPM. CPM places dual emphasis on time and cost. The normal and crash estimates of time and cost that we discussed were part of the original version of CPM. A major objective of CPM is to determine which tradeoffs should be made in order to complete the total project on a scheduled date at minimum cost.

Many extensions of the CPM–PERT methodology have been made. These include PERT-II, PERT-III, PERT-IV, PERT/COST, SPAR (Scheduled Program for Allocating Resources), and RAMPS (Resource Allocation of Multi-Project Scheduling). All of these, however, utilize basic networking principles. Depending on the type of project, some of these techniques may have advantages over others. A skilled specialist will be aware of the variations. For most of our purposes, it is sufficient to know the basic elements of network analysis and to appreciate how they can be used in managerial analysis.

Summary

In this chapter, we considered network analysis, a quantitative technique widely used in managerial analysis. We departed in several ways from the more conventional method of presenting this material. In the first part of the chapter, we presented basic network analysis, rather than specifically describing either PERT or CPM. We believe these general principles are more important to the manager than specific knowledge of CPM or PERT. Toward the end of the chapter, however, we tried to clarify these specifics for those who must know the language of network analysis.

This chapter also departed from the conventional presentation in other ways. The PERT worksheet, the discrete (as opposed to continuous) time function, the symbolic designation of activities, and the arrow diagrams drawn to scale are not normally used in network presentations. They were included in this chapter to simplify the presentation and allow the reader to better appreciate the many uses of network analysis.

Problems and exercises

1. Explain the following terms:

earliest time	expected time
latest allowable time	continuous function
activity	standard deviation
critical activity	event
prerequisite activity	node
critical path	dummy activity
slack time	normal cost
project-due date	crash cost
optimistic time	PERT
pessimistic time	CPM
most likely time	network model

INSTRUCTIONS FOR PROBLEMS 2–5

The following tables give a brief description of the activities of projects that **several** individuals face. Construct a PERT worksheet for each activity.

Calculate the earliest times, latest allowable times, and slack times for each activity.

2. Going on vacation

Symbol	Description	Performance time	Prerequisite activities
A	Plan with spouse	5	none
B	Obtain travel folders	10	A
C	Obtain vacation loan	13	A
D	Decide on mode of travel	6	A
E	Arrange for home care	4	A
F	Obtain reservations	5	B, D
G	Buy tickets	2	C, F
H	Leave on trip (end of project)	0	E, G

3. Hiring personnel

Symbol	Description	Performance time	Prerequisite activities
A	Prepare job description	5	none
B	Advertise job	15	A
C	Make preparations for interviews	6	A
D	Invite candidates for interviews	3	B
E	Conduct interviews	5	C, D
F	Give proficiency tests	6	B
G	Make final selection	2	E, F
H	Make offer (end of project)	0	G

4. Building a house

Symbol	Description	Performance time	Prerequisite activities
A	Clear land	8	none
B	Install driveway	4	A
C	Install rough plumbing	6	A
D	Do landscaping	20	B
E	Construct basement	5	C
F	Erect walls	9	B, E
G	Install initial wiring	4	E
H	Install inside plumbing	6	E
I	Construct roof	7	F
J	Lay carpets	2	I
K	Paint	3	G, H, I
L	Move in (end of project)	0	D, J, K

5. Preparing a group report for business policy

Symbol	Description	Performance time	Prerequisite activities
A	Perform initial study	5	none
B	Prepare marketing plan	8	A
C	Prepare financial plan	3	A
D	Hire typist	7	A
E	Integrate marketing and finance	3	B, C
F	Write report	5	E
G	Prepare appendix	2	E
H	Prepare tables and figures	4	E
I	Type	3	D, F, G
J	Bind	2	H, I
K	Hand in report (end of project)	0	J

INSTRUCTIONS FOR PROBLEMS 6–9

Draw an arrow diagram for each of the following problems. Draw the diagram to an appropriate time scale. Use a dotted line to represent slack time.

6. Construct an arrow diagram for problem 2.
7. Construct an arrow diagram for problem 3.
8. Construct an arrow diagram for problem 4.
9. Construct an arrow diagram for problem 5.

INSTRUCTIONS FOR PROBLEMS 10–12

In each of the following problems, determine the expected performance time and standard deviation of each activity, the critical path, the expected project completion time, and the standard deviation of the critical path.

10.

Symbol	Prerequisite activities	Most optimistic time	Most likely time	Most pessimistic time
A	none	20	41	56
B	A	26	32	38
C	A	40	61	88
D	B, C	30	30	30

What is the probability of completing the entire project in 124 days? in 154 days? in 132 days? in 128 days?

11.

Symbol	Prerequisite activities	Most optimistic time	Most likely time	Most pessimistic time
A	none	5	8	11
B	A	4	10	16
C	A	5	6	13
D	B	1	3	11
E	B, C	6	12	18
F	D, E	2	2	2

What is the probability of completing the entire project in 27 days? in 30 days? in 34 days? in 36 days?

12.

Symbol	Prerequisite activities	Most optimistic time	Most likely time	Most pessimistic time
A	none	42	60	78
B	A	42	60	78
C	A	20	30	52
D	B, C	9	18	27
E	C, D	0	0	0

What is the probability of completing the entire project in 156 days? in 138 days? in 129 days? in 147 days?

INSTRUCTIONS FOR PROBLEMS 13 AND 14
Draw the appropriate probability completion curve.
13. Draw a probability completion curve for problem 10.
14. Draw a probability completion curve for problem 12.

INSTRUCTIONS FOR PROBLEMS 15–20
Draw the arrow diagrams for the following problems. Determine the critical path. Calculate the earliest, latest, and slack times for all events. Use the node numbering system.

15.

Activity	Performance time
1-2	5
2-3	8
2-4	7
2-5	5
3-5	2
4-6	9
5-7	6
6-7	3

16.

Activity	Performance time
1-2	5
1-3	10
1-4	20
2-3	4
3-4	8

17.

Activity	Performance time
1-2	7
1-3	12
2-4	9
2-6	17
3-4	8
3-5	3
4-6	10
5-6	11
5-7	20
5-8	30
6-7	6
7-8	9
7-9	14
8-10	9
9-10	10

18.

Activity	Performance time	Prerequisite activities
A	14	none
B	12	A
C	16	B
D	7	B
E	35	B
F	20	C
G	15	C
H	24	C
I	8	F, G
J	10	E, H, I
K	0	D, J

19. Redraw the arrow diagram for problem 4 using the node numbering and dummy activity method.
20. Redraw the arrow diagram for problem 5 using the node numbering and dummy activity method.

INSTRUCTIONS FOR PROBLEMS 21–25

Consider each of the following arrow diagrams. Give the earliest scheduled time, the latest allowable time, and the slack time for each activity. State the critical path of each network.

21.

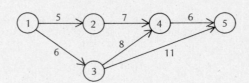

22.

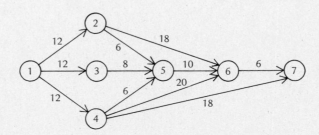

23.

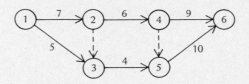

24.

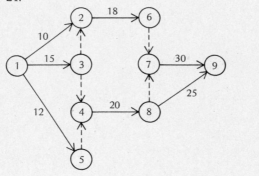

25.

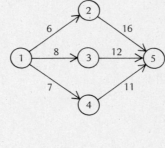

INSTRUCTIONS FOR PROBLEMS 26–28

For each problem, the performance time and labor requirements are given for each activity. First draw an arrow diagram corresponding to the earliest possible schedule. Adjust the network to obtain the least possible variation in daily labor requirements. In making the adjustments, do not extend performance time of the entire project. Assume that no activity can be split into two component parts.

26.

Activity	Performance time	Prerequisite activities	Labor required
A	8	—	3
B	8	—	2
C	9	—	5
D	3	A	3
E	6	B	6
F	2	C	3
G	7	D, E, F	2
H	6	C	8
I	0	G, H	0

27.

Activity	Performance time	Prerequisite activities	Labor required
A	9	—	3
B	10	—	7
C	2	A	7
D	4	C	4
E	8	B	5
F	5	B	6
G	3	F	3
H	6	E	6
I	0	D, H, G	0

28.

Activity	Performance time	Prerequisite activities	Labor required
A	4	—	12
B	6	—	8
C	5	A	3
D	6	B	16
E	5	B	2
F	4	C	6
G	3	C	7
H	4	D	4
I	4	E	14
J	4	G, H	10
K	0	F, J, I	0

INSTRUCTIONS FOR PROBLEMS 29–31

Draw a network diagram for each problem, using normal times for each activity. State the cost of this network. Crash the project to its minimum completion time. At each step, show the number of days' reduction, the cost of reducing on a per-day basis, the new completion time, and the new cost.

29.

Activity	Prerequisite activities	Time		Cost	
		Normal	Crash	Normal	Crash
A	—	6	4	$ 400	$ 500
B	—	15	12	2000	3200
C	—	12	6	1200	3000
D	A	10	6	2000	4000
E	C	8	6	1000	1500
F	D	6	4	800	1000
G	B	15	12	900	1200
H	E	18	12	600	1200
I	F, G, H	0	0	—	—

30.

Activity	Prerequisite activities	Time		Cost	
		Normal	Crash	Normal	Crash
A	—	40	35	$12,000	$16,000
B	A	20	10	300	600
C	A	30	15	500	800
D	B, C	50	40	600	1,000
E	C	30	25	1,000	2,000
F	D, E	0	0	—	—

31.

Activity	Prerequisite activities	Time		Cost	
		Normal	Crash	Normal	Crash
A	—	10	10	$ 5,000	$ 5,000
B	A	16	11	8,000	10,500
C	A	12	9	10,000	14,500
D	B	6	3	3,000	6,000
E	C	5	4	4,000	6,000
F	D, E	9	6	6,000	6,900

INSTRUCTIONS FOR PROBLEMS 32 AND 33
Formulate each problem as a linear programming problem. Set up the objective function and all appropriate constraints. Do not add slack, surplus, or artificial variables.

32. Formulate problem 2 as a linear programming problem.
33. Formulate problem 3 as a linear programming problem.

Supplementary readings

Budnick, F. S., R. Mojena, and T. E. Vollman. *Principles of Operations Research for Management.* Homewood, Ill.: Irwin, 1977.

Carlson, P. B. *Quantitative Methods for Managers.* New York: Harper & Row, 1967.

Hartley, R. V. *Operations Research: A Managerial Emphasis.* Pacific Palisades, Calif.: Goodyear, 1976.

Hillier, F. S., and G. J. Lieberman. *Introduction to Operations Research.* San Francisco: Holden-Day, 1974.

Levin, R. I., and C. A. Kirkpatrick. *Planning and Control with PERT/CPM.* New York: McGraw-Hill, 1966.

Levy, F. K., G. L. Thompson, and J. P. Weist. "The ABC's of the Critical Path Method." *Harvard Business Review,* 41 (September–October 1963), 98–108.

Miller, R. W. "How to Plan and Control with PERT." *Harvard Business Review,* 40 (March–April 1962), 93–104.

Moder, J. J., and C. R. Phillips. *Project Management with CPM and PERT.* New York: Van Nostrand, 1970.

Turban, E., and J. R. Meredith. *Fundamentals of Management Science.* Dallas, Texas: Business Publications, 1977.

Wiest, J. D., and F. K. Levy. *A Management Guide to PERT/CPM.* Englewood Cliffs, N.J.: Prentice-Hall, 1969.

Chapter 10
Queuing models

Illustrative example: ENGLISH CHEMICAL COMPANY

Susan English, president of the English Chemical Company, is concerned about the operation of the firm's scientific supply room. English employs a large number of chemists who conduct tests on samples submitted by customers. Once or twice a day, each chemist must go to the supply room and requisition materials. The supply room staff fills requisitions one at a time while the chemists wait in line. On several occasions, Ms. English has observed a number of chemists waiting in line to draw supplies. Since the average cost of a chemist is $16 per hour, she believes the operation of the supply room should be reviewed.

Mr. Blackwell, the supply room supervisor, stated that waiting lines could be reduced by increasing the supply room staff. He believes, however, that this would not be economical. The direct cost of operating the facility is $72 per hour. The staff is currently idle between 15% and 20% of the time. Adding to staff would increase unutilized time. Supply room records indicate that an average of 10 chemists arrive each hour and that the supply room can handle an average of 12 customers per hour. The time required to fill a requisition varies, because some chemists call for a single item while others request a number of chemicals and supplies.

The periodic congestion results from variation in the number of chemists arriving during a given hour and from variation in the length of time required to fill a requisition. During a particular hour, only 6 or 7 chemists may arrive for supplies. The next hour might see the arrival of 15 or more chemists, including several with extensive requisitions. During such periods, waiting lines develop.

Ms. English and Mr. Blackwell decided that the magnitude of the costs justify a detailed study of the supply room. They have asked Beverly Lyford, an industrial engineer, to look into the problem and submit her recommendations. She immediately identified the situation as a queuing or waiting-line problem and suspected that one of the existing queuing models would be useful in her study.

Everywhere one looks, queues or waiting lines abound. People wait in line at banks and supermarkets. Trucks line up for loading. Packages await delivery in post offices. Production systems consist of numerous queues of materials or subassemblies waiting for the next stage in the production process. Proper management of these queues is an important aspect of many organizations. Fortunately, reasonable decisions on queuing problems can often be made by relying on the past experience of the decision maker. Many queuing situations, however, require more complex analysis. We can perform this analysis by using mathematical models or by a procedure known as computer simulation. This chapter is concerned with mathematical queuing models. Simulation topics are covered in Chapter 11.

The approach we follow in this chapter is to establish a standard frame of reference for queuing systems and to present certain models that can be used in the analysis of these systems. These models are presented without reference to their underlying mathematical derivations. Attention is focused on the understanding we can achieve by studying a limited number of the more easily applied models.

Characteristics of queuing problems and systems

The basic queuing problem faced by English Chemical is to determine the optimal balance between the cost of letting customers wait for service and the cost of providing this service. Providing additional service personnel would reduce the cost of chemists waiting in line but increase the cost of service. Ideally, the company would like to provide just enough service so that the sum of service cost and waiting cost is minimized.

When arrivals are uniformly spaced in time and all customers have exactly the same service requirement, the problem is simple. Service capacity is set equal to service demand so that customers never have to wait in line and the service facility is never idle. Each customer arrives just as the facility finishes serving the previous customer. Unfortunately, this simple case rarely appears in a real situation.

In queuing analysis, the time between one arrival at the queue and the next arrival is known as an *interarrival time*. The time that an individual requires to obtain service from the system is known as a *service time*. In the English Chemical example, suppose one chemist arrives at 10:23 A.M. and the next chemist arrives at 10:31 A.M. The interarrival time is 8 minutes. If the second chemist requires 3 minutes to place and receive an order, then this service time is 3 minutes. Time spent waiting to be served is not included in service time.

The complicating feature of queuing systems is variation in service

Figure 10.1 *Components of a queuing system*

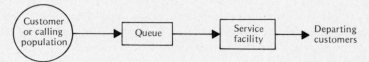

and interrarrival times. Periodically, this variation leads to system congestion, and customers must wait in line. This occurs even when service capacity is appreciably greater than demand and the service facility is idle a large part of the time.

Before studying a specific queuing model, it will be helpful to define the components of a queuing system. Its basic structure consists of the three elements shown in Figure 10.1. The *calling population* consists of the customers who may request service. On arriving at the service facility, a customer joins a *queue*, or waiting line, which is the second element of the system. The third component is the *service facility* that provides customers with the desired service.

When the facility is free, the customer enters for service. When service is completed, the customer either leaves the system or returns to the calling population. In the English Chemical example, the chemists are the calling population and the supply room is the service facility. In order to completely specify the structure of a given queuing system, we must make several assumptions about each of its three components.

The calling population

A major characteristic of the calling population is the manner and frequency with which customers "call" or arrive for service. This is referred to as the *arrival process*. Since it is virtually certain that the number of arrivals will vary from one time period to the next, it is necessary to describe the arrival process in probabilistic terms. We can do this in two ways.

One method of describing the arrival process is through a probability distribution of interarrival times. A second method is to describe the arrival rate — to choose a time interval and describe the number of arrivals and their spacing within that time interval. Either of these distributions may be described empirically. For example, Ms. Lyford may actually observe a large number of arrivals at the supply room, and she could obtain the interarrival distribution by recording the interarrival times. She could obtain the arrival distribution by dividing the day into small time periods and recording the number of arrivals in each period.

Extensive experience with operating systems has shown that the

Poisson probability distribution provides a good description of the pattern of customer arrivals and that the exponential probability distribution adequately describes many sets of interarrival times[1]. When this is true, it simplifies the queuing analysis and allows us to use mathematical models that assume a Poisson arrival distribution. All of the queuing problems discussed in this chapter, including the English Chemical Company example, are assumed to have a Poisson arrival process. Despite the operating success of the Poisson model, the user should statistically test the distribution to ensure that it adequately conforms to the assumptions of the model.

Another specification we must make about the calling population is whether it is *infinite* or *finite* in number. In this chapter, we assume that arrivals come from an infinite source. Real queuing systems do not have infinite sources, but most populations are large enough for this assumption to be valid. Actually, the assumption of an infinite population is related to the size of the population and the capacity of the system. If the source of the callers is large relative to the average number of units in the system, then the system has characteristics similar to those of systems that draw from an infinite population. If the calling population is infinite, then the arrival pattern is independent of the number of units in the system.

Any other conditions that may alter the rate at which customers join the queue must be specified. For example, an arrival may refuse to join the queue if there is an excessively long waiting line. Such a customer may plan to return for service at a later time or seek service elsewhere. This action is referred to as *balking*. Joining the queue but leaving before being served is known as *reneging*.

The queue

When more than one customer is waiting, it is necessary to establish a decision rule or *queue discipline* to determine which customer will be served next. The list of possible queue disciplines is virtually endless and includes rules of varying degrees of complexity. A *first-come-first-served* discipline exists, or is often approximated, in such actual situations as the English Chemical Company example. All queuing formulas and models used in this book assume a first-come-first-served discipline.

Other possible disciplines include priorities based on length of service time, magnitude of waiting cost, promised delivery or due date, customer rank, and degree of emergency. In some cases, the order of

---

[1]Mathematically, if the arrivals occur in accordance with a Poisson process, then the interarrival times *must* follow an exponential distribution. These are two different ways of describing the same process.

service may be random. Restaurant patrons with dinner reservations are often seated before customers who are waiting in line without reservations. In a hospital emergency room, the most seriously ill patients may be treated first. At a family-night church supper, a special rule such as "children go to the head of the line" may apply.

The maximum length of the queue, if any, must also be specified, and the conditions that may lead a discouraged customer to leave the queue before receiving service must be clearly detailed.

The service facility

To describe the service facility, we must describe both the physical structure and the ability of the facility to provide service. The physical structure of the service facility must be completely defined. A simple structure consists of a single server, while more complex systems contain many servers. Servers may be arranged to allow the processing of more than one customer at a time or in a series of stages wherein each server provides part of the overall service requirement. In a complex system, such as an automobile assembly plant, each stage may consist of parallel channels.

Three basic service configurations are illustrated in Figure 10.2. Figure 10.2(a) represents a *single-channel* or single-server queue. Customers line up before a single server, receive service, and leave the system (exit). Figure 10.2(b) illustrates a *multiple-channel* queue. This system has three servers, but there is still only one waiting line. Systems of this type are referred to as *parallel-service* systems, because more than one customer can be served at a time.

Figure 10.2(c) illustrates a single-channel queue with multiple stages. Each stage, or phase, is a part of the total service process. Queuing systems with multiple stages are sometimes referred to as *series processors*.

We can specify the ability to provide service by describing service times or the rate of service completions. In most systems, service time varies from customer to customer. As with interarrival times, it is necessary to describe service times in probabilistic terms. We can obtain a distribution of service times empirically. In the English Chemical Company example, Ms. Lyford could obtain a distribution of service times by actually observing a large number of chemists receiving supplies and recording the service time of each.

Analysis has indicated that in some situations, service times can be adequately approximated by an exponential distribution, or, equivalently, that service completions follow a Poisson probability distribution. When the assumption of exponential service time can be combined with the assumption of a Poisson arrival, several easily applied queuing formulas are available. These models assume that arrival rates

Figure 10.2 *Three basic types of queuing systems*

Key:

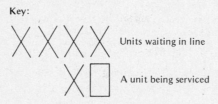

X X X X   Units waiting in line

X ☐   A unit being serviced

(a) A single channel queue

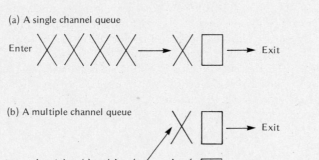

Enter X X X X ⟶ X ☐ ⟶ Exit

(b) A multiple channel queue

Enter X X X X X ☐ ⟶ Exit

X ☐ ⟶ Exit

X ☐ ⟶ Exit

(c) A single channel, multiple stage queue

Enter X X X X ⟶ X ☐ ⟶ X ☐ ⟶ X ☐ ⟶ Exit

follow a Poisson distribution and that service times are exponentially distributed. Such models are referred to as "Poisson arrival, exponential service" models, or simply "Poisson/exponential" models.

Probability distributions used in queuing analysis

In this chapter, we have repeatedly stated that many real queuing problems can be adequately represented by a Poisson arrival distribution and an exponential service-time distribution. With one exception, the constant service-time model, all models used in this chapter assume these distributions. A brief discussion of these distributions should increase our appreciation of the models and their applications.

The Poisson arrival distribution

If a Poisson distribution is used to describe an arrival process, it is assumed that the arrivals are randomly distributed through time. In particular, the probability that an arrival will occur during a specific, short time period is equal to the probability that an arrival will occur during any other time period of the same length. The Poisson process is memoryless; that is, the probability of an arrival occurring in the next instant of time is independent of recent arrival history. The probability of an arrival is the same if 5 arrivals occurred in the previous minute or if no arrivals occurred during this period.

The probability of a given number of Poisson arrivals in a specific time period depends only on the average arrival rate. The probability that a Poisson process will generate a given number of arrivals during a time period is given by the formula

$$P(x) = \frac{\lambda^x e^{-\lambda}}{x!}$$

The symbols used in this formula are as follows:

x = Given number of arrivals during a specific time period

$P(x)$ = Probability of x number of arrivals occurring

λ = Average or mean number of arrivals occurring during a specific time period

e = A mathematical constant equal to 2.718 . . .

We can gain an initial appreciation for the Poisson process and its inherent variability by examining an arrival distribution. In the English Chemical Company example, the arrival of chemists at the supply room follows a Poisson distribution with a mean arrival rate of 10 chemists per hour. This distribution is given in Table 10.1. It is taken from Table C in the Appendix. Readers unfamiliar with this material may want to review the section in Chapter 14 on the Poisson distribution. This section also explains the use of Table C in the Appendix.

Note that substantial variation exists in the arrival pattern. Although the mean arrival rate is 10 per hour, the probability of 5 arrivals in one hour is .0378 while the probability of 15 arrivals in an hour is .0347. In fact, the probability of obtaining 5 or fewer arrivals in an hour is .0671. The probability of obtaining 15 or more arrivals in a given hour is

Table 10.1 *Poisson distribution with a mean arrival rate of 10 per hour*

Arrival per hour (x)	Probability of occurrence P(x)
3 or fewer	.0104
4	.0189
5	.0378
6	.0631
7	.0901
8	.1126
9	.1251
10	.1251
11	.1137
12	.0948
13	.0729
14	.0521
15	.0347
16	.0217
17	.0128
18 or more	.0142
	1.0000

.0834. With this type of variability, it is evident that system congestion will develop unless service capacity is substantially greater than the arrival rate.

Exponential service-time distribution

An exponential service-time distribution implies that service completion times are independent of service duration times. Once a customer begins service, the probability that service will be completed during the next instant of time is fixed and independent of how long service has been under way. A customer who has been served for 10 minutes has the same probability of completing service in the next minute as a customer who just began to be served.

The assumptions made here are identical to those made for the Poisson arrival process, because the two distributions provide two ways of describing the same thing. If the pattern of arrivals follows a Poisson distribution, the distribution of time between arrivals is exponential. If the distribution of service times is exponential, a Poisson distribution describes the pattern of service completions during periods when the server is busy. Overall departures from the service facility *cannot* be assumed to be Poisson distributed, because the probability of a departure when the server is idle is zero.

The general form of an exponential distribution is shown in Figure 10.3. Mathematically, the distribution can be described by the relationship

$$f(t) = \mu e^{-\mu t}$$

The following symbols are used in this relationship.

t = Service time

$f(t)$ = Probability density of the service time t

μ = Mean service rate

The distribution is continuous. We must obtain the probability that a service completion time will be within a given range by computing the area under the curve between the indicated limits.

We can gain an appreciation for the variation inherent in the exponential distribution by examining selected completion-time probabilities. Consider the example of the supply room at the English Chemical Company. Service times are exponentially distributed. The mean service rate is 12 customers per hour. Thus, the mean service time is $\frac{1}{12}$ of an hour, or 5 minutes. The probabilities of a given service time falling within several selected ranges are shown in Table 10.2.

We should note several things about the probabilities listed in Table 10-2. It is more likely that a given service time will be closer to zero than

Figure 10.3 *Exponential service-time distribution*

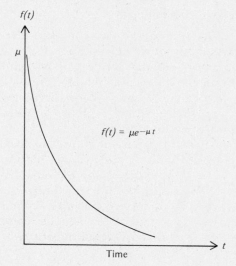

Table 10.2 *Selected exponential service-time probabilities for a mean service rate of 12 customers per hour*

Elapsed service time in minutes (t)	Probability
1 or fewer	.181
1 to 2	.149
2 to 5	.302
5 to 10	.233
10 to 15	.086
15 to 20	.031
20 to 25	.011
25 to 30	.005
30 or more	.002
	1.0000

to any other time. The probability that service will take 1 minute or less is .181, while the probability that it will take less than the mean of 5 minutes is .632. A significant number of service times must therefore be substantially larger than the mean of 5 minutes. The probability of an elapsed time of between 10 and 15 minutes is .086. There is a small probability, .002, that service will require more than 30 minutes.

For an exponential distribution to approximate service times, a large portion of the arrivals must require little service while others must demand extensive attention. Such conditions appear to exist at the English Chemical Company, where many arrivals request a single item and others call for a long list of supplies. Some operating systems exhibit these characteristics, but we should apply a statistical test to service data before we utilize a queuing model that assumes exponential service times.

The traffic intensity factor

Many queuing models assume that the average service rate is greater than the average or mean arrival rate, and indeed, difficulties may arise if this condition is not met. In the English Chemical Company example, assume that an average of 10 chemists arrive per hour, but only an average of 6 can be served in an hour. The waiting line would continue to grow longer and longer unless some chemists refused to join the line or left after they joined the line. Thus, unless balking or reneging are allowed, the mean service rate μ must be greater than the mean arrival rate λ, or λ/μ must be less than 1.

The relationship λ/μ is known as the traffic intensity factor. It is represented by the symbol ρ, such that

$$\rho = \frac{\lambda}{\mu}$$

The traffic intensity factor is a measure of the "busyness" of the queuing system. A value close to zero indicates a large service capacity relative to the number of those desiring service. We would expect very little waiting time and a lot of idle time in the service facility. As the value of the traffic intensity factor increases toward 1, we should expect more waiting time and less idle time.

Analysis using queuing models

Queuing models are descriptive in the sense that they do not directly solve the decision maker's central problem of interest. They cannot be solved, in the sense of linear programming models, to determine the service capacity that provides the optimal balance between waiting cost and service cost. Rather, queuing models provide information about a system's operating characteristics that is used in a separate economic evaluation of the servicing problem. Information of particular interest includes the average length of the waiting line, the average customer waiting time, the fraction of time that the service facility is idle, and so on.

Single-channel Poisson/exponential model

We will use the English Chemical Company to illustrate the single-channel Poisson/exponential model. After collecting and evaluating data on arrivals and service times at the English Chemical Company's supply room, Beverly Lyford is convinced that the arrival pattern is adequately described by a Poisson distribution with a mean arrival rate of 10 customers per hour. Service times are exponentially distributed with a mean time of $1/12$ of an hour, or 5 minutes. She believes that the calling population can be regarded as infinite. A large number of chemists are employed, and the number in the service system has virtually no effect on the arrival rate. She has also observed that operating conditions meet all other assumptions of the most readily applied Poisson/exponential queuing model. These conditions include:

1. Single-service channel
2. First-come, first-served queue discipline
3. No customer balking or reneging
4. A mean arrival rate less than the mean service rate (that is, the traffic intensity factor, λ/μ, is less than 1)

These assumptions result in a queuing model that yields readily to mathematical analysis. The equations used in the following sections have been derived for use in determining system operating characteristics.

Notation and symbols used

The following notation and symbols will be needed in the sections to come. We will use the same symbolic representation throughout the chapter. (For convenience, the symbols most often used in this chapter are summarized at the end of the chapter.)

n = State of the system; that is, the number of customers in the system, including those in line and those being served

P_0 = Probability that the server is idle or that the system is in state zero (no one being served or in line)

P_n = Probability that the system is in state n

λ = Mean or average arrival rate expressed as number of customers per time period

μ = Mean or average service rate expressed as customers per time period

L = Expected number of customers in the system, including those in line and those being served

L_q = Expected number of customers in the queue

W = Expected customer time in the system, including time spent in the line and time spent being served

W_q = Expected customer time in the queue

Expected number in the system

In the English Chemical Company example, the mean arrival rate and the mean service rate had the values

$$\lambda = 10 \text{ arrivals per hour}$$
$$\mu = 12 \text{ services per hour}$$

We may use the following relationships to determine the expected number in the system.

$$L = \frac{\lambda}{\mu - \lambda}$$

$$L = \frac{10}{12 - 10} = 5.0$$

$$L_q = \frac{\lambda^2}{\mu(\mu - \lambda)}$$

$$L_q = \frac{100}{12(2)} = \frac{100}{24} = 4.17$$

These formulas tell us that, on the average, we would expect to find 4.17 chemists waiting in line to receive supplies. The average number in the system, including those in line and those being served, is 5.0.

Average waiting time

$$W = \frac{1}{\mu - \lambda}$$

$$W = \frac{1}{12 - 10} = \frac{1}{2} \text{ hour, or 30 minutes}$$

$$W_q = \frac{\lambda}{\mu(\mu - \lambda)}$$

$$W_q = \frac{10}{12(2)} = \frac{10}{24} \text{ hour, or 25 minutes.}$$

The average time that a chemist spends waiting in line is 25 minutes. The average time spent in the entire system is 30 minutes. This is logical, because the average time spent in the system should equal the average time spent in line plus the average service time.

State of the system

$$P_0 = 1 - \frac{\lambda}{\mu}$$

$$P_0 = 1 - \frac{10}{12} = 1 - .83 = .17$$

$$P_1 = \frac{\lambda}{\mu} P_0$$

$$P_1 = (.83)(.17) = .14$$

$$P_2 = \left(\frac{\lambda}{\mu}\right)^2 P_0$$

$$P_2 = (.83)^2(.17) = .12$$

The probability of having no chemist in the system is .17. The probability of having 1 chemist in the system (1 being served, none waiting) is .14. Likewise, the probability of having 2 chemists in the system is .12. We may use either of the following two equivalent formulas to determine the probability of the system being in any given state n.

$$P_n = \left(\frac{\lambda}{\mu}\right)^n P_0$$

$$P_n = \left(\frac{\lambda}{\mu}\right)^n \left(1 - \frac{\lambda}{\mu}\right)$$

For example, we can determine the probability of 5 chemists being in the system as follows:

$$P_5 = \left(\frac{10}{12}\right)^5 \left(1 - \frac{10}{12}\right) = .067$$

Relationships among operating characteristics

If the service rate is independent of the state of the system, the expected time a customer spends in the facility (W) is equal to the expected time spent in line (W_q) plus the expected time being served ($1/\mu$). Thus,

$$W = W_q + \frac{1}{\mu}$$

It is also true that the expected number in the system (L) equals the expected time in the system (W) multiplied by the mean arrival rate (λ).

$$L = \lambda W$$

Thus, if the mean arrival rate is 10 per hour and the expected time spent in the system is ½ hour, the expected number in the system is 5.

Instead of considering the complete facility, we can apply this relationship to the waiting line. Thus,

$$L_q = \lambda W_q$$

These relationships are useful in problem solving, because the value of any one of the four quantities L, L_q, W, and W_q is all we need to know to determine the remaining three. This is particularly true for queuing models wherein direct calculation of one or more of the quantities is difficult.

Utilizing the results of the formulas

Ms. Lyford has used the foregoing equations to assist in analyzing the supply room problem. Initially she used them to estimate several operating characteristics of the existing system. She determined that, on the average, there will be 5 chemists in the service system and that each will average 30 minutes in the system. The predicted probability that the service facility will be idle is .17. These computed characteristics agree closely with conditions Ms. Lyford observed at the supply room and strengthen her conviction that the model is a good approximation of the actual situation.

The model relationships can be used to predict the effect of altering service capacity. Table 10.3 shows the impact of a number of different levels of service capacity on the expected number of chemists in the system, the expected time spent in the system, and the probability that

Table 10.3 *Computed values of L, W, and P_0 for selected service rates* in the English Chemical Company example*

Service rate (μ)	Probability that server is idle (P_0)	Expected number of customers in system (L)	Expected hours in system (W)
10.1	.010	100.00	10.00
10.5	.048	20.00	2.00
11.0	.091	10.00	1.00
12.0	.167	5.00	.50
13.0	.231	3.33	.33
14.0	.286	2.50	.25
15.0	.333	2.00	.20
16.0	.375	1.67	.17
17.0	.412	1.43	.14
18.0	.444	1.25	.12
19.0	.474	1.11	.11
20.0	.500	1.00	.10

*Mean arrival rate is 10 per hour.

the service facility is idle. The same arrival rate, 10 customers per hour, was used in all cases.

Ms. Lyford is interested in these results. She observes that a reduction in the service rate from 12 to 10.5 customers per hour sharply increases (from 5 to 20) the average number of customers in the system. Even after the reduction in capacity, the service facility is still idle about 5% of the time.

Any attempt to minimize idle service time will result in extremely large average waiting times. This relationship will tend to hold in a wide range of queuing systems characterized by substantial variation in arrivals and service times. The decision maker must consciously plan for a considerable amount of excess capacity in order to avoid long waiting times. Excessive concern about periods of idle service time may prevent the decision maker from reaching a satisfactory balance between waiting cost and service cost.

Also of interest is the rate at which expected waiting times and queue lengths increase as the service rate approaches the arrival rate. This is illustrated in Figure 10.4, which shows the general form of the relationship between traffic intensity (the arrival rate divided by the service rate) and the expected number of customers in the system. This has important implications for the system designer or operator.

In heavily loaded systems, wherein traffic intensity is close to 1, small changes in either the arrival rate or the service rate have an appreciable

Figure 10.4 *Relationship between traffic intensity and the expected number of customers in the system*

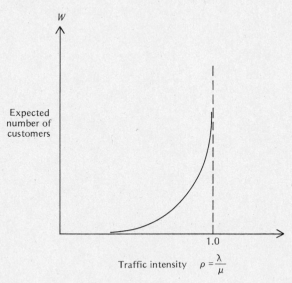

impact on the number of customers in the system. The data listed in Table 10.3 show that if service capacity is increased from 10.1 to 10.5 customers per hour (a 4.0% increase), the predicted reduction in the expected number of customers in the system is from 100 to 20 (an 80% reduction). On the other hand, if a system already has a substantial amount of excess capacity, large increases in service capacity are required to obtain a large absolute reduction in waiting time. In our example, increasing the service rate from 15 to 20 chemists per hour only resulted in reducing the average number of customers in the system by 1.

Sample problem 10.1   THE BROWNING COMPANY

The Browning Company operates a single-server maintenance storeroom where electrical repairpersons check out needed spare parts and equipment. Repairpersons arrive randomly at a rate of 8 per hour, or 1 every 7½ minutes. The service rate is 10 per hour. Arrivals are Poisson distributed, and service completion times follow the exponential model. Determine the following information for this storeroom.

W = Average time spent in the system

W_q = Average time spent in the queue

L = Expected number of repairpersons in the system

L_q = Average length of the waiting line

P_0 = Probability of no one being served

P_3 = Probability of 2 repairpersons in line and 1 being served

SOLUTION

$$W = \frac{1}{\mu - \lambda} = \frac{1}{10 - 8} = \frac{1}{2} \text{ hour, or 30 minutes}$$

$$W_q = \frac{\lambda}{\mu(\mu - \lambda)} = \frac{8}{10(10 - 8)} = \frac{8}{20} \text{ hour, or 24 minutes}$$

$$L = \frac{\lambda}{\mu - \lambda} = \frac{8}{2} = 4$$

$$L_q = \frac{\lambda^2}{\mu(\mu - \lambda)} = \frac{64}{10(10 - 8)} = \frac{64}{20} = 3.2$$

$$P_0 = 1 - \frac{\lambda}{\mu} = 1 - \frac{8}{10} = .20$$

$$P_3 = \left(\frac{\lambda}{\mu}\right)^3 P_0 = (.8)^3(.2) = .1024$$

Economic analysis

Knowledge of the operating characteristics of the queue should be quite helpful to the manager responsible for its operation. Normally, however, a complete analysis cannot be made until the data on operating characteristics are combined with economic data.

In the next two sections, we will consider two different forms of the English Chemical Company example. The discrete case may more closely approximate queuing situations with which you are familiar. The continuous case also has a wide range of applicability and should give us a better insight into the economic relationships associated with queuing analysis.

A discrete problem

In the English Chemical Company example, assume that the service rate may be varied by changing the size of the supply room staff. At present, there are three helpers on duty in the supply room. These helpers are employed at a cost of $12 per hour. Ms. Lyford's data indicate that employing a fourth helper would increase the mean service rate to 14 chemists per hour. Employing the fifth and sixth helpers would further increase the service rate to 16 and 18 chemists per hour respectively. Ms. Lyford wants to know which of these alternatives will result in the lowest total cost to the company.

Note that Ms. Lyford is not adding additional servers to supply the

Table 10.4 *Economic considerations in varying the number of helpers in the English Chemical Company example*

Number of helpers	Cost of helpers	Service cost (J)	Service rate (μ)	Average number in system (L)	Waiting cost (K)	Expected total cost (T)
3	$36.00	$ 72.00	12	5.00	$80.00	$152.00
4	48.00	84.00	14	2.50	40.00	124.00
5	60.00	96.00	16	1.67	26.67	122.67
6	72.00	108.00	18	1.25	20.00	128.00

chemists. This would violate our assumption of a single-channel queue. Instead, she is adding additional staff to make the single server more efficient.

Ms. Lyford's first step in the analysis is to find the average hourly cost of the present system, that is, the cost of operating the supply room and the cost of the chemists waiting in line. The cost of operating the supply room is now $72 per hour. Her analysis indicates that, at present, the average number of chemists in the system at any time is 5. (This calculation was illustrated in the section on operating characteristics.) Since the average cost of the chemists is $16 per hour, the average cost of waiting is (5 × $16) or $80 per hour.[2] Thus, the total cost of waiting and serving is ($72 + $80) or $152 per hour. It is this cost that Ms. Lyford would like to reduce by adding additional helpers to the supply room staff.

Assume that 1 additional helper is added. Serving cost would increase by $12 to $84 per hour. The mean service rate would increase to 14 per hour. The average number of chemists in the system could be calculated as follows:

$$L = \frac{\lambda}{\mu - \lambda} = \frac{10}{14 - 10} = \frac{10}{4} = 2.5$$

The chemists cost $16 per hour. The average cost of waiting is now (2.5 × $16) or $40 per hour. Thus, adding a single helper would increase the cost of service from $72 to $84 per hour but would reduce the average cost of waiting from $80 to $40 per hour. Total cost would be reduced to $124 per hour. This is an obvious improvement over the present total cost of $152 per hour.

This analysis can be repeated for Ms. Lyford's other two alternatives of using 5 helpers and using 6 helpers. The data for all four alternatives are given in Table 10.4. The choice of using 5 helpers appears to be the

[2]This value can also be obtained by multiplying together the average time spent in line (½ hour), the average arrival rate (10 per hour), and the cost of waiting ($16 per hour).

most attractive. It results in a service cost of $96 per hour, a waiting cost of $26.67 per hour, and a total cost of $122.67 per hour. From a cost standpoint, it is the best of the alternatives Ms. Lyford investigated.

Sample problem 10.2   THE BROWNING COMPANY (Continued)

Consider the Browning Company example given in Sample Problem 10.1. The cost of waiting is $9 per hour. The company is considering giving the stock clerk a helper, which would increase the service rate to 12 per hour. The cost of the helper is $6 per hour. Will the reduced waiting cost justify the cost of the helper?

SOLUTION
Previously, $L = 4$. Average waiting cost was $4 \times \$9 = \$36$. With the helper,

$$L = \frac{\lambda}{\mu - \lambda} = \frac{8}{12 - 8} = 2$$

The average hourly waiting cost is ($2 \times \$9$) or $18. The helper should be hired. This expenditure of $6 per hour saves the company $18 in waiting cost. The net result is a saving of $12 per hour.

The continuous case

Ms. Lyford could have analyzed her problem by using a slightly different procedure. She still wants to determine what service capacity will offer the optimal balance between the cost of providing service and the cost of chemists waiting for service. Thus, the general cost relationship to be minimized is

$$T = J + K$$

The following symbols are used in this relationship.

T = Expected total cost of waiting and serving

J = Service cost

K = Waiting cost

Service cost will be a function of service capacity. In the case of the English Chemical Company, Ms. Lyford has found that service cost varies directly with supply room capacity for service rates of between 10 and 20 customers per hour. The cost of operating the facility is $6 per hour for each unit of service capacity. The existing facility, with its service rate of 12 customers per hour, costs $72 per hour of operation. The service rate may be increased to 13 chemists per hour by increasing operating costs by $6 per hour to $78 per hour. The increase in capacity is obtained by increasing supply room staff. In general, the hourly cost of operating the service facility is equal to the mean service rate μ multiplied by C_1, the cost per unit of service capacity per hour. Thus,

$$J = C_1\mu$$

We can compute expected waiting cost per hour in several ways. In the previous example, we multiplied the average number in the system by the waiting cost per person per hour. A second and equivalent alternative is to multiply the expected number of customers per hour, represented by the arrival rate λ, by the expected waiting cost per customer. We determine expected waiting cost per customer by multiplying expected waiting time, W, by the cost of an hour of customer waiting time, C_2. For example, if each customer expects to wait ½ hour and the cost of this wait is $16 per hour, then the expected waiting cost per customer is ($16 × ½) or $8. If 10 customers arrive per hour, then waiting cost per hour is $80, the waiting cost per customer ($8) multiplied by the number of customers per hour (10).

In our example,

$$K = \lambda C_2 W$$

Since expected total cost is the sum of waiting cost and service cost, then

$$T = C_1\mu + \lambda C_2 W$$

At the English Chemical Company, C_1, the cost per hour per unit of service capacity, is $6, and C_2, the hourly cost of chemists, is $16. Substituting these values in the equation for expected total cost yields

$$T = 6\mu + 16\lambda W$$

Since W is equal to $1/(\mu - \lambda)$, or in our example $1/(\mu - 10)$, it is convenient to reduce the equation to

$$T = 6\mu + \frac{160}{\mu - 10}$$

Expected total cost for the English Chemical Company's supply room has been expressed as a function of its service rate. The general form[3] of the English Chemical Company's optimization problem is shown in Figure 10.5. As service capacity increases, there is an increase in service cost and a decrease in expected waiting cost. The decision maker must select the service capacity that yields the best balance between these

---

[3]In this example, service cost was found to be linearly related to service rate. In general, this will not be true. For a given range, however, a linear assumption may serve as a good approximation to many real systems.

Figure 10.5 *Cost relationships for the English Chemical Company*

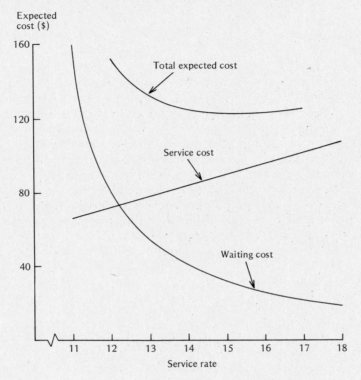

Table 10.5 *Economic data for various service rates in the English Chemical Company example*

Service rate (μ)	Service cost* (J)	Expected waiting time, in hours (W)	Waiting cost** (K)	Expected total cost (T)
11	$ 66.00	1	$160.00	$226.00
12	72.00	½	80.00	152.00
13	78.00	⅓	53.34	131.34
14	84.00	¼	40.00	124.00
15	90.00	⅕	32.00	122.00
16	96.00	⅙	26.67	122.67
17	102.00	1/7	22.87	124.87
18	108.00	⅛	20.00	128.00

*Service cost is $6 times the mean service rate.
**Waiting cost is the expected waiting time multiplied by the arrival rate of 10 per hour multiplied by the waiting cost of $16 per hour.

opposing cost components. Expected cost for selected service rates have been computed and are shown in Table 10.5. The tabulated service rate of 15 customers per hour has the smallest expected cost. The hourly cost of $122 is $30 less than the expected cost of $152 associated with the existing service rate of 12. The indicated increase in capacity would result in substantial annual savings. This is achieved by increasing the idle time of the service facility from 16.7% to 33.3%, as shown in Table 10.3.

Further cost reductions may be obtained by experimenting with service rates close to 15 chemists per hour. The anticipated savings would be small, because there is little difference among the expected costs shown in Table 10.5 for service rates close to 15 customers per hour. We obtain the actual minimum cost by selecting a service rate equal to approximately 15.16. We can determine this by trial and error or by using differential calculus techniques.[4] Total expected cost for this service rate is $121.96.

In most real situations, the service rate is not a continuous variable; that is, only certain service rates may be feasible. In such cases, the selected rates in Table 10.5 would be limited to those that can actually be put into operation. The least-cost alternative would be selected from among those available. The assumption that the service rate is continuous serves several purposes. It should increase our comprehension of the relationships involved in queuing analysis. The results of this analysis also often provide a method of determining which feasible alternatives we should investigate.

Estimating the cost of waiting

In all the problems we have considered in this chapter, we assumed that an estimate of the cost of customers waiting for service was available. In practice, this estimate is often difficult to obtain.

In situations wherein customers are members of the organization providing service, we must not assume that the direct cost of the employee or the asset is the correct waiting cost. For example, an employee's hourly wage (including fringe benefits) is usually an inappropriate estimate of the cost of an hour of waiting time. The cost to the organization is rather the return that would have been generated if the employee had been actively engaged in his or her job. This may include the return that would have been generated by resources idled by the employee's absence.

---

[4]Readers familiar with calculus may want to verify that the first differential with respect to μ of the equation for expected total cost is

$$\frac{6\mu^2 - 120\mu + 440}{\mu^2 - 20\mu + 100}$$

Setting this equal to zero yields an optimal value of μ of 15.164.

The estimation problem becomes even more difficult when the customer is not a member of the organization operating the service facility. In these situations, the cost of waiting is largely intangible; if a customer is forced to wait, she or he may refuse to return to the service system. Future service demands are lost. While it may be possible to estimate the revenues or benefits forgone when a customer is lost, the probability of the customer not returning is a function of the amount of waiting time and is difficult to assess.

In operating systems, this difficulty frequently results in the organization largely ignoring the existence of intangible waiting cost or, at best, arbitrarily establishing a service policy that is viewed as "reasonable." Such a policy will probably result in understaffing the service facility, because the direct and measurable cost of increasing service capacity usually outweighs the uncertain waiting cost. This may be particularly serious, as indicated by Figure 10.4, if it leads to the selection of a service rate that is very close to the demand for service. To avoid this pitfall, every effort should be made to quantify waiting cost and bring it directly into the analysis.

Sample problem 10.3   *GOLDMAN AND ASSOCIATES*

The engineering design firm of Goldman and Associates is replacing its scientific computer, which is used to solve problems encountered in design projects. The list of alternatives has been narrowed to three computers. Computer A will cost $600 a day to lease and operate and can solve problems at the rate of 20 a day. Computers B and C have processing rates of 25 and 35 problems per day respectively, with daily costs of $750 and $1050. In all cases, computation times are exponentially distributed. Arrivals of problems at the computer center follow a Poisson distribution with a mean rate of 15 per day. Progress on a project is delayed until a problem is solved. The firm has estimated that the daily cost of delaying a project is $250. Determine which computer will yield the lowest overall operating cost.

SOLUTION

Compute the average number of problems in the system for each alternative.

$$L = \frac{\lambda}{\mu - \lambda} = \frac{15}{20 - 15} = 3 \qquad \text{(computer A)}$$

$$L = \frac{15}{25 - 15} = 1.5 \qquad \text{(computer B)}$$

$$L = \frac{15}{35 - 15} = .75 \qquad \text{(computer C)}$$

$$T = J + K = 600 + 3(250) = \$1350.00 \qquad \text{(computer A)}$$
$$T = 750 + 1.5(250) = \$1125.00 \qquad \text{(computer B)}$$
$$T = 1050 + .75(250) = \$1237.50 \qquad \text{(computer C)}$$

Select computer B.

Additional queuing models

While the relationships in the basic, single-channel, Poisson/exponential model are the most readily derived and applied, other queuing models are available and may be applied without great difficulty. We briefly discuss three of these in the following sections. They are closely related to the basic model in that each of them alters only one of the underlying assumptions. Despite the similarity among these assumptions, the modified models extend the range of problems that may be analyzed and offer additional insights into the complexities of queuing systems.

Poisson arrivals with constant service times

The assumption of an exponential service-time distribution often results in our misrepresenting the nature of service variation. Models are available that relax the exponential service-time assumptions. A case of special interest occurs when service time is constant; that is, all customers require the same length of time to be served. With this condition, the queuing relationships become

$$L_q = \frac{\rho^2}{2(1 - \rho)} = \frac{\lambda^2}{2\mu(\mu - \lambda)}$$
$$L = \rho + L_q$$
$$W_q = \frac{\lambda}{2\mu(\mu - \lambda)}$$
$$W = \frac{1}{\mu} + W_q$$
$$P_0 = 1 - \rho$$

Comparison of the equation for expected queue length for the exponential service-time model and the corresponding equation for the constant service-time model shows that expected queue length is exactly half as large in the latter case. The equations are identical except for the 2 in the denominator of the equation for constant service time.

For example, the expected queue at the English Chemical Company's supply room, with $\lambda = 10$ and $\mu = 12$, is

$$L_q = \frac{\lambda^2}{\mu(\mu - \lambda)} = \frac{(10)^2}{12(12 - 10)} = 4.17 \qquad \text{(exponential service)}$$

If service time is constant (that is, all variability in service times is eliminated), the relationship becomes

$$L_q = \frac{\lambda^2}{2\mu(\mu - \lambda)} = \frac{(10)^2}{2(12)(12 - 10)} = 2.085 \qquad \text{(constant service)}$$

While it is ordinarily impossible to eliminate all variation in service times, any steps taken to reduce variation will yield improvements in system performance.

Maximum queue length

We noted earlier that queuing models are complicated when the arrival rate depends on the state of the system. Such is the case when the probability that a customer arriving for service will join the queue is affected by the number of customers already in the system.

A special case that can be handled without serious difficulty is a single server, Poisson/exponential system wherein there is a maximum queue length. When the queue is filled, additional arrivals balk or are unable to join the queue. The effective arrival rate during such periods is zero. Given the maximum number of customers in the system, M, the following relationships apply.

$$L = \frac{\rho}{1 - \rho} - \frac{(M + 1)\rho^{M+1}}{1 - \rho^{M+1}}$$

$$W = \frac{1}{\mu(1 - \rho)} - \frac{M\rho^M}{\mu(1 - \rho^M)}$$

$$P_0 = \frac{1 - \rho}{1 - \rho^{M+1}}$$

$$P_n = P_0 \rho^n$$

Note that the arrival rate in this model may be greater than the service rate and that the expected waiting time, W, is for customers who actually join the queue. In addition, the general relationships between L, L_q, W, and W_q do not apply, because the effective arrival rate is not independent of the state of the system.

The maximum queue-length model may be used as a starting point in examining the effect of balking on the performance of a service system. If less than M customers are in the system, an arrival will always join the queue. If M customers are in the system, an arrival will balk or refuse to join the queue. We can compute the portion of the arrivals that the server will lose by determining the probability that the system will be in state $n = M$. This is equal to the probability that an arrival will balk.

For example, given an arrival rate of 14 and a service rate of 20 ($\rho = {}^{14}\!/_{20} = .7$), the probability of losing an arrival when there is no place for it to wait ($M = 1$) can be computed as follows:

$$P_0 = \frac{1 - \rho}{1 - \rho^{M+1}} = \frac{1 - .7}{1 - (.7)^2} = .588$$

$$P_1 = P_0\rho^1 = .588(.7) = .412$$

In this case, the server will be busy 41.2% of the time, and 41.2% of the arrivals will be lost. The effect of providing space for one customer to wait for service ($M = 2$) is determined as follows.

$$P_0 = \frac{1 - .7}{1 - (.7)^3} = .457$$

$$P_2 = P_0\rho^2 = .457(.7)^2 = .224$$

Provision of space for one customer to wait for service has reduced the percent of the arrivals lost from 41.2 to 22.4. Similar calculations show that 13.5% of the arrivals will be lost with $M = 3$. If M is 4, 5, or 6, then 8.7%, 5.7%, and 3.8% respectively of the arrivals will be lost. With $M = 10$, only 0.9% of the arrivals will balk. The maximum length of the queue can have a substantial effect on operation of the service system.

Sample problem 10.4   CONSOLIDATED SHIPYARDS

Consolidated Shipyards is considering construction of a new facility for major repairs on oil tankers. Initial plans call for a single dry dock that will be able to repair, on the average, 10 tankers a year. Repair times are exponentially distributed. It is anticipated that repair requests will be received at the rate of only 7 a year and will be Poisson distributed. In addition to the dry dock, a single berth will be provided for vessels waiting for repair. Because of the long time periods required, Consolidated has decided to assume that any request received when two oil tankers are at the facility, one being repaired and one waiting for repair, will be lost. The tanker will go to another dry dock. The company wishes to estimate what part of the time the dry dock will be idle and how frequently it will be unable to handle a repair request.

SOLUTION

$$\rho = \frac{\lambda}{\mu} = \frac{7}{10} = .7$$

$$M = 2$$

$$P_0 = \frac{1 - \rho}{1 - \rho^{M+1}} = \frac{1 - .7}{1 - (.7)^3} = \frac{.3}{.657} = .46$$

The dock will be idle 46% of the time.

$$P_n = P_0 \rho^n$$
$$P_1 = .46(.7)^1 = .32$$
$$P_2 = .46(.7)^2 = .22$$

There will be two tankers at the repair facility 22% of the time. The firm can anticipate that it will be unable to handle 22% of the repair requests it receives.

Multiple service channels

Frequently a queuing system consists of more than one server. Consider a situation wherein servers are arranged in parallel, as shown in Figure 10.2(b). A multiple-server model is available for situations wherein arrivals are Poisson distributed and servers may be represented by identical exponential service-time distributions. Customers form a single line and are admitted into the first available service channel on a first-come-first-served basis. Such a situation could be approximated by a facility that accepts catalog orders and maintains queue discipline by requiring customers to pick up a numbered tag used to indicate their order of arrival.

Consider a system that consists of 5 identical servers, each with a service rate of 8 per hour. The total service capacity of the system is 40 per hour. In these formulas, we let S represent the number of identical servers, each of which has a service rate of μ. Thus, the combined service capacity of the system is S multiplied by μ. The letter n represents the number of customers in the system. A complicating aspect of this model is that the service rate is a function of the number of customers in the system. When n is less than S, customers are being served at an average rate equal to $n\mu$. If n is equal to or greater than S, the service rate is equal to $S\mu$. If the combined service capacity is greater than the arrival rate $(S\mu > \lambda)$, the following relationships hold.

$$P_0 = \left[\sum_{n=0}^{S-1} \frac{\left(\frac{\lambda}{\mu}\right)^n}{n!} + \frac{\left(\frac{\lambda}{\mu}\right)^S}{S!} \left(\frac{1}{1 - \frac{\lambda}{S\mu}} \right) \right]^{-1}$$

$$L_q = \frac{P_0 \left(\frac{\lambda}{\mu}\right)^S \frac{\lambda}{S\mu}}{S! \left(1 - \frac{\lambda}{S\mu}\right)^2}$$

This model is particularly helpful as a means of gauging the benefits that can result from consolidating or pooling independent service facilities. For example, consider two independent single-server systems. Each has a Poisson arrival rate of 8 customers per hour and exponential service times. The service rate of each server is 10 customers per hour. Each single-server system will contain an average of 4 customers.

$$L = \frac{\lambda}{\mu - \lambda} = \frac{8}{10 - 8} = 4$$

The expected customer time in one of the systems is ½ hour.

$$W = \frac{1}{\mu - \lambda} = \frac{1}{10 - 8} = \frac{1}{2}$$

Between the two systems, the expected number of customers in the system is 8.

Now consider the result of combining the two servers into a single system $(S = 2)$. The arrival rate at the combined system is 16 customers per hour, and the service rate is 20 customers per hour.[5] Since arrivals are still Poisson distributed, the multiple-channel model, with $S = 2$, may be used to determine that

$$P_0 = \frac{1}{1 + \frac{16}{10} + \frac{1}{2} \left(\frac{16}{10}\right)^2 \frac{1}{1 - (16/20)}} = .111$$

$$L_q = \frac{.111 \left(\frac{16}{10}\right)^2 \left(\frac{16}{20}\right)}{2 \left(1 - \frac{16}{20}\right)^2} = \frac{.227}{.68} = 2.842$$

[5] Each individual server has a service rate of 10. Thus, $\mu = 10$ and $S\mu = 20$.

From the general relationships between L, L_q, W, and W_q, we can further determine that

$$W_q = \frac{L_q}{\lambda} = \frac{2.842}{16} = .178$$

$$W = W_q + \frac{1}{\mu} = .178 + \frac{1}{10} = .278$$

$$L = \lambda W = 16(.278) = 4.45$$

Pooling the two service facilities has resulted in reducing the expected number of customers waiting from 8 to 4.45 and reducing the expected time in a system for each customer from .5 to .278 hours. These significant and often surprising improvements have been realized by eliminating the occasions when one of the servers was swamped with customers while the other was idle.

Sample problem 10.5 GUTHRIE MACHINE PARTS

Machinists at Guthrie Machine Parts periodically need a wide range of special-purpose tools, which are stored at three locations on the plant floor. Each tool room is staffed by one clerk, who checks the tools in and out. Arrivals at each tool room are Poisson distributed with a mean of 15 employees per hour. Service times are exponentially distributed and average 3 minutes. (The service rate is 20 machinists per hour per clerk, $^{60}/_3 = 20$).

It has been proposed that the three tool rooms be consolidated into a single, centrally located facility staffed by the three clerks. Travel time—the time it takes for a machinist to walk to and from the work area to a tool room—would be increased by an average of 2 minutes. Each hour that a machinist spends away from the work area has been estimated to cost Guthrie $10 an hour. Service costs will not be reduced by the move to a single tool room. Evaluate the proposal.

SOLUTION

The proposal may be evaluated by comparing the expected time a machinist spends in a single-server system to the time he cr she would spend in the consolidated system. For each of the single-server systems ($\lambda = 15$, $\mu = 20$),

$$W = \frac{1}{\mu - \lambda} = \frac{1}{20 - 15} = .2 \text{ hour}$$

For the consolidated system ($\lambda = 45$, $\mu = 20$, $S = 3$),

$$P_0 = \frac{1}{1 + \frac{45}{20} + \frac{1}{2}\left(\frac{45}{20}\right)^2 + \frac{1}{6}\left(\frac{45}{20}\right)^3 \left[\frac{1}{1 - 45/60}\right]} = .0748$$

$$L_q = \frac{(.0748)\left(\frac{45}{20}\right)^3\left(\frac{45}{60}\right)}{6\left(1 - \frac{45}{60}\right)^2} = 1.704$$

From the general relationships,

$$W_q = \frac{L_q}{\lambda} = \frac{1.704}{45} = .038$$

$$W = W_q + \frac{1}{\mu} = .038 + \frac{1}{20} = .088 \text{ hour}$$

Consolidation of facilities reduces expected time in the system by $(.2 - .088)$ hour, which is .112 hour. The overall time reduction per machinist is .079 hour (.112 hour less the increased travel time of $\frac{2}{60}$ hour, or .033 hour). The tool rooms should be consolidated. The company will save $.79 on each trip to the tool room, or $35.55 per hour (45 arrivals per hour × $.79 per arrival).

Use of queuing models

The focus of the queuing problems in this chapter has been on adjusting the capacity of the service system to obtain an optimal balance between the cost of service and the cost of waiting. In practice, the decision maker may adjust any factor or combination of factors in the service system. It may be feasible to adjust the rate of demand or the variation in demand. Changes in queue discipline often yield significant improvement in performance at little cost. For example, serving the customer with the shortest processing time first will reduce expected waiting time in the system from the level experienced with a first-come-first-served discipline.

The models covered in the preceding sections represent an extremely small percentage of the available queuing models. Unfortunately, none of the models will adequately represent the conditions found in certain queuing systems. This is particularly true for complex, multiple-server systems wherein arrivals or departures are not randomly distributed. In such cases, we must use an alternative method of analysis. The next chapter will explain the use of simulation as an aid in the design of service systems.

Review of symbols and formulas used

For convenience, the symbols we used most often in this chapter are summarized here. The formulas for the single-channel, Poisson/exponential model are also given.

Symbols

λ = Mean arrival rate

μ = Mean service rate

ρ = Traffic intensity factor, $\dfrac{\lambda}{\mu}$

J = Cost of service expressed as dollars per time period

K = Expected waiting cost expressed as dollars per time period

L = Expected number of customers in the system, including those being served

L_q = Expected number of customers in the queue

n = State of the system

P_n = Probability that the system is in state n

T = Expected total cost per unit of time; that is, the sum of J and K

W = Expected customer time in the system, including time spent being served

W_q = Expected time a customer spends in the queue

x = Number of arrivals during a specific time period, in a Poisson distribution

$P(x)$ = The probability of x arrivals occurring during a specific time period

Formulas for the single-channel Poisson/exponential model

$$L = \frac{\lambda}{\mu - \lambda}$$

$$L_q = \frac{\lambda^2}{\mu(\mu - \lambda)}$$

$$W = \frac{1}{\mu - \lambda}$$

$$W_q = \frac{\lambda}{\mu(\mu - \lambda)}$$

$$P_n = \left(\frac{\lambda}{\mu}\right)^n \left(1 - \frac{\lambda}{\mu}\right) = \left(\frac{\lambda}{\mu}\right)^n P_0$$

Problems and exercises

1. Explain the following terms:

   queue

   calling population

   infinite population

   arrival process

   interarrival time

   service facility

   Poisson distribution

   exponential distribution

   service time

   Poisson/exponential model

   operating characteristics

   traffic intensity factor

   parallel servers

   series processors

   balking

   reneging

   queue discipline

   first-come-first-served

   state of the system

   expected total cost

   service cost

   waiting cost

   intangible waiting cost

   INSTRUCTIONS FOR PROBLEMS 2–4

   Use the Poisson tables in the Appendix to solve the following problems.

2. Assume a Poisson arrival process with an average arrival rate of 2 items per hour. Use the Poisson tables to establish the probability distribution for the number of arrivals per hour. Use this distribution to compute the expected number of arrivals per hour, and compare this value to the average arrival rate.

3. Use the Poisson tables to determine the probability that a Poisson arrival process with a mean arrival rate of 8 customers per hour will produce the following numbers of arrivals in 1 hour.

   a. Exactly 4

   b. Exactly 8

   c. Exactly 14

   d. 5 or fewer

   e. 10 or more

   f. More than 5 and fewer than 10

4. Repeat problem 3 with $\lambda = 5$.

   INSTRUCTIONS FOR PROBLEMS 5–27

   Unless otherwise specified, all of the following problems assume a first-come-first-served queue discipline, a single server, Poisson arrivals, and exponential service times.

5. Given that $\lambda = 4$ per hour and $\mu = 5$ per hour, compute:

   a. Expected number of items in queue, L_q

   b. Expected number of items in system, L

   c. Expected time in queue, W_q

   d. Expected time in system, W

   e. Probability that the server is idle, P_0

   f. Probability that there are 2, 3, or 4 customers in the system

6. Answer all parts of problem 5 with $\lambda = 18$ per day and $\mu = 20$ per day.

7. Answer all parts of problem 5 with $\lambda = 8$ per hour and $\mu = 10$ per hour. Note that the queuing systems in problems 5 and 7 have the same traffic intensity factor. How do you account for any differences in the operating characteristics computed in these two cases?

8. Customers arrive at a service facility at a mean rate of 8 per hour. Compute L, W, and P_0 for service rates of 8.1, 8.2, 8.5, 9, 10, 12, 16, and 20 per hour. Plot the relationship between L and μ, given that $\lambda = 8$.

9. Assume that the service rates specified in problem 8 represent the feasible service alternatives. Given waiting costs of $15 an hour and service costs of $20 per unit of capacity per hour (C_1), determine the least-cost alternative.

10. Given a service system with $\lambda = 5$ and $\mu = 10$, determine the probabilities that there will be 0, 1, 2, 3, 4, and 5 customers respectively in the system. What is the probability that there will be more than 5 customers in the system? fewer than 3 customers? Compute L and determine if it is consistent with the computed probabilities.

11. Repeat problem 10 with $\lambda = 8$ and $\mu = 10$.

12. The arrivals at a service facility are Poisson distributed with a mean rate of 10 per day. The cost of a customer waiting is $40 per day. Two different exponential-service mechanisms may be acquired. Mechanism A will cost $100 per day to operate and can serve an average of 12 customers. The daily cost of operating B is $200, and it serves customers at the rate of 15 per day. Which mechanism should be installed?

13. An existing service facility has a service rate of 75 units per period. Operating costs are $25,000 per period. Waiting costs are $400 per customer per period. It is anticipated that the arrival rate will increase to 70 during the next several periods. The system can be modified to allow an increase in the service rate. This is a costly process, however. Each additional unit of service capacity will increase cost by $1000 per period; that is, if capacity is increased to 80 units, operating cost will increase by $5000 to a total of $30,000. What adjustment, if any, should be made in the service rate? Assume that fractional service rates are not allowed.

14. In problem 13, assume that the arrival rate increases to 73 in subsequent periods. What action should be taken at this time?

15. Arrivals at a service facility occur at a mean rate of 16 per week. The cost of waiting is estimated to be $40 per week per customer. The service rate may be set at any level, but the weekly cost of operating the facility is $25 times the service rate. What (approximate) service rate will minimize total expected cost?

16. A tax consultant is able to solve client problems at a rate of 6 per hour. Arrivals are essentially Poisson distributed, despite efforts to schedule visits. The consultant wishes to determine the rate at which consultations should be scheduled. The consultant would like to have a client in the office at least 70% of the time *and* to make sure that clients do not have to wait

more than 30 minutes, on the average, before attention is given to their problems. Is this possible? If it is possible, what is the maximum scheduling rate that will allow both criteria to be met?

17. Assume that the tax consultant in problem 16 decides to schedule clients at the rate of 4 per hour. What is the probability that there will be more than three clients in the office? more than 5? What is the expected waiting time for a client who arrives and finds 5 people already waiting for consultation?

18. Compare the values of W, W_q, L, L_q, and P_0 for an exponential service-time system with the corresponding values for a single-channel system with constant service times. Use a service rate of 20 per hour for both systems. Make the comparison for arrival rates of 15 and 19 per hour.

19. A facility with an arrival rate of 12 customers per day experiences a cost of $100 for each day of customer waiting time. Service times are exponentially distributed with a service rate of 15 per day. What is the expected daily cost of waiting? How much would this be reduced if all variation in service time could be eliminated?

20. Assume that the two service mechanisms in problem 12 can be adjusted so that service times are constant. Assume that these adjustments increase the daily cost of operating mechanism A to $150, while mechanism B's daily cost increases to $250. Which of the four alternatives should be adopted?

21. A service facility has a Poisson arrival rate of 9 customers per hour. There is no room for customers to wait for service, and arrivals encountering a busy system are forced to balk. If service times are exponentially distributed and the rate of service is 10 per hour, what percent of the customers will be unable to join the system? What percent will be lost if room is provided for 1 customer to wait? if room is provided for 2 customers to wait? if room is provided for 3 customers to wait?

22. Given a maximum queue-length system with $M = 3$, $\lambda = 6$ per period, and $\mu = 8$ per period, compute L, W, P_0, P_1, P_2, and P_3. Compare these operating characteristics with those that would be obtained if there were no limit on queue length. Are the computed probabilities for the various states of the maximum queue-length system internally consistent? How do you determine this?

23. A recent increase in consumer complaints at Jersey Electric Authority has led to a decision to assign one person to receive the complaints. Complaints are phoned in at a rate of 20 per hour and are Poisson distributed. Calls can be handled at a rate of 40 per hour. Service times vary considerably and have been found to be exponentially distributed. Jersey Electric would like to make sure that no more than 5% of the calls receive busy signals. If the operator is busy, calls can be placed on a "hold" line. How many hold lines should be provided to ensure that the 5% target will be reached?

24. Given a Poisson arrival process with a mean rate of 7 per day, determine W, W_q, L, L_q and P_0 for a service system with two parallel channels. Each channel has a service rate of 4 per day.

25. Compare the values of W, W_q, L, and L_q for each of the following: a single-server system with a service rate of 30 per week; a parallel-server system with 2 identical servers, each with a service rate of 15 per week; and a parallel-server system with 3 identical servers, each with a service rate of 10 per week. In all cases, service times are exponentially distributed. Assume a Poisson arrival rate of 24 per week. How do you account for differences in the computed operating characteristics for the three systems? (*Note:* The values of P_0 for the three systems are .2, .1111, and .0562 respectively.)

26. Orders for a firm's products arrive at the rate of 200 a week. A clerk processes paperwork that must be completed before an order can be shipped. One clerk can process an average of 250 orders a week. The cost of delaying an average shipment for 1 week is $500. If a clerk costs $300 per week, how many clerks should be assigned to process the paperwork?

27. The mean arrival rate at each of two identical service systems is 21 per day. Both systems operate independently and have service rates of 30 customers per day. The cost of 1 day of waiting time is $50 per customer. Assume that it is possible to consolidate the two servers into a multiple-channel system. Determine the reduction in waiting cost that such a move would accomplish.

Supplementary readings

Budnick, F. S., R. Mojena, and T. E. Vollman. *Principles of Operations Research for Management.* Homewood, Ill.: Irwin, 1977.

Cooper, R. B. *Introduction to Queueing Theory.* New York: Macmillan, 1972.

Cox, D. R., and W. L. Smith. *Queues.* New York: Wiley, 1961.

Gross, D., and C. Harris. *Fundamentals of Queueing Theory.* New York: Wiley, 1974.

Hillier, F. S., and G. J. Lieberman. *Introduction to Operations Research.* San Francisco: Holden-Day, 1974.

Newell, G. F. *Applications of Queueing Theory.* London: Chapman and Hall, Ltd., 1971.

Saaty, T. L. *Elements of Queueing Theory with Applications.* New York: McGraw-Hill, 1961.

Shamblin, J. E., and G. T. Stevens. *Operations Research: A Fundamental Approach.* New York: McGraw-Hill, 1974.

Taha, H. A. *Operations Research: An Introduction.* New York: Macmillan, 1971.

Wagner, H. M. *Principles of Management Science.* Englewood Cliffs, N.J.: Prentice-Hall, 1975.

Chapter 11

Simulation

Illustrative example: *BILL'S CAR WASH*

Bill's Car Wash is a small establishment located on a heavily traveled, one-way street in a downtown metropolitan area. The physical layout of the facility, shown in Figure 11.1, places several constraints on operations. No more than one car may be washed at a time, and there is parking space for only two cars to wait for washing. "No Parking" and "No Standing" signs are posted along the street.

Bill's Car Wash has a policy of making sure that each customer leaves with a spotlessly clean car. This policy, in conjunction with a washing process consisting of a combination of automatic and manual operations, results in substantial variation in the time required to clean a car. The two factors that determine washing time are the size of the car and the amount of accumulated dirt and grime.

The owner of the business, Mr. Bill James, is aware that customers who arrive for service and find the parking spaces full invariably continue down the street to a larger washing facility with ample parking space. For some time, Mr. James has been thinking about altering his car wash in an attempt to capture some of the business he is losing to his competitor.

Mr. James has considered several alternatives, such as installing new, high-speed washing equipment and/or leasing the patio area immediately adjacent to his location. This space would provide room for two more cars to wait for service. The owner of Burger's Unlimited has expressed an interest in leasing the space to Mr. James, because his customers are rarely willing to brave the noise and exhaust fumes in order to use the picnic benches now located there.

Mr. James has been reluctant to make any changes, however, until he is confident that they will increase his profit position. He has decided to evaluate the effect of several of the more promising alternatives. Mr. James picked up the rudiments of simulation in one of his college courses. He suspects he can evaluate the alternatives through a simulation of his car wash business.

In past chapters, we have discussed a number of tools and techniques designed to assist the manager in the decision-making process. Almost

Figure 11.1 *Layout of Bill's Car Wash*

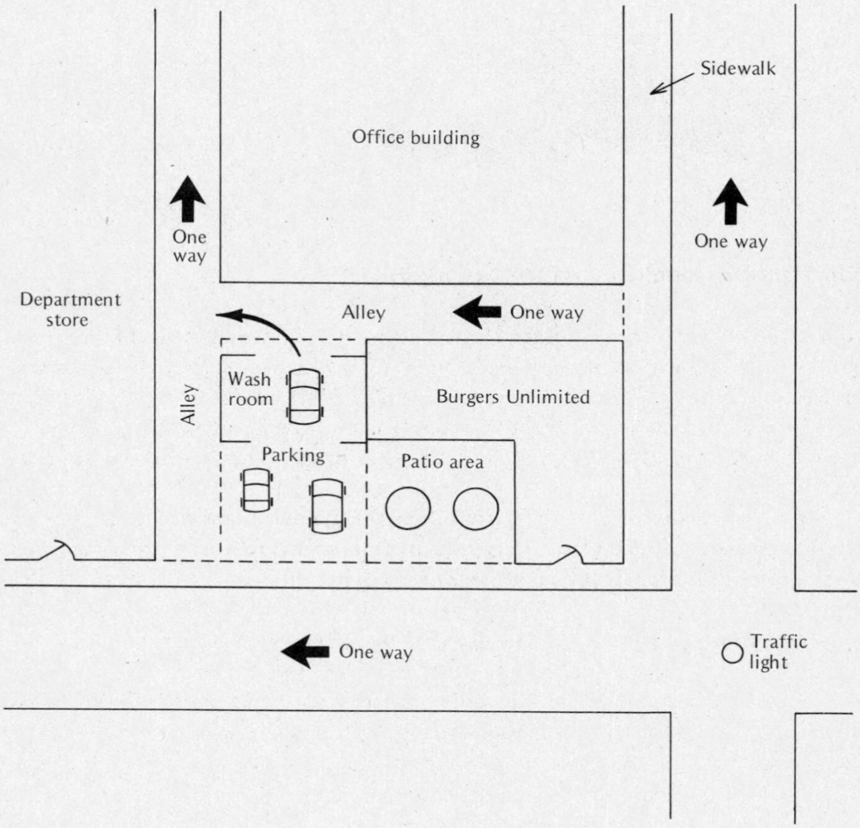

all of these can be categorized as *analytical techniques;* that is, they can be used to directly calculate optimal values for the mathematical model's decision variables. Frequently, however, situations arise that are too complex to be formulated in an analytical model. Or, once they are formulated, their complexity makes solution difficult or impossible. In such cases, experimentation with the actual system, or a model of the system, may be the only feasible method of analysis.

Queuing or waiting-line problems such as the one found at Bill's Car Wash represent a class of problems that are frequently analyzed with the aid of a simulation model. This is a result of the fact, noted in Chapter 10, that many complex queuing problems cannot be adequately handled by any of the available queuing models.

The simulation process

Simulation is an attempt to duplicate the operation of a system or activity without incurring the expense of building and/or operating the actual system or activity. It is an experimental method. The analyst first constructs a model of the problem or system of interest. Then, rather than solving the model in the traditional sense, the analyst operates or "runs" it under different sets of operating conditions. Output from these simulation runs is used to evaluate the relative merits of the proposed alternatives. In essence, simulation provides the manager with an experimental laboratory wherein a problem can be studied under carefully controlled conditions.

While simulation can be used to analyze complex problems, the rudiments of the method can be understood and applied by those with only limited mathematical backgrounds. Simulation has a number of additional advantages, which we will discuss later. They combine to make it one of the most widely applied management science techniques.

This chapter will focus on problems or systems with stochastic, or probabilistic, elements that can be analyzed by a form of simulation called Monte Carlo simulation. Most of these problems could be simulated using only paper and pencil. Most practical applied problems require the use of a computer.

Basically, there are five steps in the simulation process:

1. Formulate a model of the problem or system under consideration.
2. Specify a set of operating characteristics for the model.
3. Design and conduct a series of experiments to provide insight into the model's behavior under the specified conditions.
4. Analyze the results of model operation, and make inferences about how the actual system would behave under similar operating conditions.
5. Ordinarily, specify a different set of operating characteristics and rerun the model. Thus, we return to step 2. This procedure allows comparison of results under different operating conditions, which should assist us in selecting operating conditions for the real system.

Formulating the model

The first step in the simulation process is to formulate a model of the process or system under consideration. As always, the model is an abstraction from reality. It should be complex enough to include the essential features of the real system. While simulation usually allows the inclusion of more detail than a model intended for analytical solution, the model should be kept as simple as possible. Unnecessary detail merely increases the time and cost required to conduct the simulation and complicates the analysis of the output data.

In model construction, the analyst must clearly specify the components of the system and the relationships between these components. Doing so allows the analyst to break down the development of simulation models into segments, which simplifies their construction. The simulation is then conducted to forecast the results of the interaction between components of the real system.

Flow diagrams

It is always helpful to draw a schematic representation or flow diagram of the system under consideration. The diagram for Bill's Car Wash is shown in Figure 11.2. The first important event is the arrival of a car at

Figure 11.2 *Schematic representation of Bill's Car Wash*

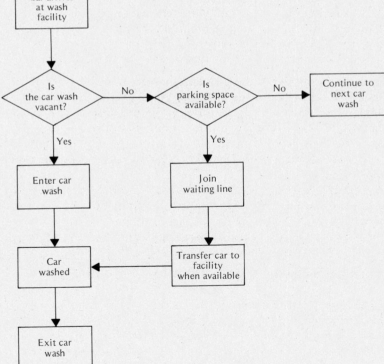

the washing facility. A question is then asked: "Is the car wash vacant?" If the answer is "yes," the car will proceed directly into the car wash. If the answer is "no," another question is asked: "Is parking space available?" If the answer to the second question is "no," the arrival *balks*, or refuses to join the waiting line. If the answer is "yes," the car joins the waiting line and waits for its turn in the facility. Once a car reaches the facility, it is washed and then exits the system.

The model shown in Figure 11.2 is quite simple, yet it incorporates the essential features of the problem Mr. James faces. It can be used as the basis for the steps that follow.

Specifying the operating characteristics

The flow diagram for Bill's Car Wash, Figure 11.2, indicates several operating characteristics that must be specified. Primary concerns include the way in which cars arrive for service, the number of parking spaces available for cars to wait for service, and the nature and duration of the service process itself.

The usual method of describing arrivals for a simulation model is to specify the probability distribution of *interarrival times* — the times between successive arrivals. Mr. James has his manager observe and record the times between a large number of successive arrivals. The relative frequency with which different interarrival times occurred was determined and used to establish the probability distribution given in Table 11.1.

Table 11.1 *Interarrival times for cars at Bill's Car Wash*

Interarrival time in minutes (T_i)	Probability (P_i)	Expected value $(T_i P_i)$
0	.06	0.00
1	.10	0.10
2	.13	0.26
3	.17	0.51
4	.15	0.60
5	.12	0.60
6	.10	0.60
7	.08	0.56
8	.05	0.40
9	.03	0.27
10	.01	0.10
	1.00	4.00

Expected interarrival time = 4.00 minutes

This distribution is an *empirical distribution*, because it was determined directly from the observed data. Interarrival times were found to vary between 0 and 10 minutes, with an average interval of 4 minutes. On the average, 15 cars will arrive each hour (60 minutes divided by the average interarrival time of 4 minutes).

Note that this discrete distribution resulted from our rounding each observed interarrival time to the nearest minute. Hence, an interarrival time of 0 implies that there were 30 seconds or less between successive arrivals. Care must be taken to ensure that the rounding assumption adopted will not bias the results of the simulation. Smaller time increments could be used, or the interarrival times could be represented by a continuous distribution. However, the general approach is the same in either case and is more readily illustrated with a discrete distribution.

Service time may be described by establishing the probability distribution for the amount of time a customer spends being served. Assume that Mr. James's manager also recorded the amount of elapsed time between the time a car began being washed and the time it left the system. This would have to be repeated for a large number of cars. The relative frequencies of the observed washing time, again rounded to the nearest minute, were used to establish the probability distributions given in Table 11.2.

Service times are given for two different types of cars. Type I cars are

Table 11.2 *Service times for type I and type II cars at Bill's Car Wash*

Service time in minutes (T_i)	Type I cars (45%)	
	Probability (P_i)	Expected value ($T_i P_i$)
2	.60	1.2
3	.40	1.2
	Expected service time = 2.4	

Service time	Type II cars (55%)	
	Probability	Expected value
4	.20	0.8
5	.40	2.0
6	.25	1.5
7	.10	0.7
8	.05	0.4
	Expected service time = 5.4	

compacts, and type II cars are full-sized models. Of course, the two distributions could be combined into a single distribution. The distinction was maintained, because Mr. James may want to examine washing and/or pricing policies wherein it would be helpful to distinguish between types of cars entering the facility.

The cars sampled included 45% compacts (type I) and 55% standard size cars (type II). The average service time for type I cars was 2.4 minutes, while type II cars required an average of 5.4 minutes of washing time. Overall, the average time required to wash a car is 4.05 minutes, that is, .45(2.4) + .55(5.4). Hence, demand exceeds capacity, and the car wash *must* lose some business. The average number of cars washed per hour during continuously busy periods is 14.8 (60 minutes divided by 4.05 minutes per car). This is slightly less than the average arrival rate of 15 cars per hour.

The initial simulation will be run with a waiting-line capacity of two cars. Cars will be washed on a first-come, first-served basis.

Validating the simulation model

Before drawing inferences about the performance of a real system under a range of operating conditions, we must make every effort to validate the accuracy of the model. This is one of the most difficult and challenging steps in the simulation process. If the model represents an existing system, one step that can be taken is to conduct a simulation under conditions approaching those found in the real world. The model's output can then be compared with data collected from the operating system. If the two are reasonably consistent, a degree of confidence in the model is established.

The Monte Carlo method

In order to run a simulation model, it is necessary to devise a method of generating the inputs on which the model will operate. In many cases, one or more of the inputs are random variables; that is, they can take on any one of a range of different values at a given time. This probabilistic variation is frequently the factor that prevents the use of an analytical solution procedure. In the case of Bill's Car Wash, interarrival time, type of arrival, and service time for a series of customers must be provided to the model.

The Monte Carlo method is a convenient means of generating a series of values for the variables of interest. The method utilizes random numbers to generate values for the random variables. These values must be consistent with their underlying probability distributions.

Table 11.3 *Two-digit random numbers*

33	24	52	87	13	31	14	53	65	35	02	76	07	62	93	67	23	93	42	16
50	72	85	56	18	51	49	20	94	53	06	43	09	07	51	70	88	54	35	75
13	19	79	96	61	23	74	91	76	35	17	84	97	48	48	80	77	34	90	29
82	20	86	44	47	63	04	98	43	77	32	33	63	46	79	66	60	33	70	97
59	91	72	29	60	07	04	83	73	28	70	95	41	55	44	20	07	28	93	97
30	88	20	80	29	98	80	68	52	80	55	91	46	92	56	92	57	78	33	63
24	95	12	56	03	08	83	06	15	20	62	57	59	41	90	31	90	56	73	29
02	38	21	96	23	78	87	31	54	77	30	14	18	10	08	79	38	98	35	86
15	41	99	86	67	63	04	76	94	56	06	97	79	66	68	03	21	95	38	21
38	51	58	80	61	85	21	26	52	81	45	33	21	56	21	88	83	65	29	48
12	08	04	33	62	78	49	42	61	53	15	22	03	98	17	69	41	82	45	92
85	23	36	43	13	37	21	50	09	12	96	91	17	31	62	90	86	94	58	31
92	55	01	88	68	65	65	08	96	72	94	86	06	29	28	30	66	52	76	36
79	27	84	90	59	40	21	83	87	79	88	93	63	34	10	54	73	56	35	67
59	80	13	96	77	11	15	89	47	74	28	61	22	45	41	66	88	09	96	62
11	26	06	05	73	01	49	45	69	31	61	47	39	71	66	12	28	67	52	16
97	54	15	28	63	60	82	89	02	91	10	73	20	47	08	55	52	99	90	86
39	47	73	11	96	60	18	56	00	98	72	17	68	62	06	10	66	60	90	25
71	14	64	64	28	82	47	36	87	75	48	60	37	90	15	80	54	43	61	93
16	59	96	95	85	66	88	02	37	08	88	98	85	02	90	02	13	60	60	96
77	87	27	72	76	79	15	68	23	57	46	80	88	57	41	10	33	15	47	86
78	15	18	02	65	23	14	08	54	97	62	61	13	23	43	01	23	29	77	62
40	37	69	32	79	84	37	50	76	78	23	54	60	23	72	17	56	86	67	11
83	43	17	25	54	99	29	15	13	96	64	94	50	87	51	76	82	18	73	00
28	71	96	61	27	84	81	27	99	64	34	53	34	21	74	53	95	01	11	35

Utilizing random numbers

The random-number concept can be clarified by discussing the structure of the two-digit random numbers provided in Table 11.3. Any one of the 100 possible combinations of digits, ranging from 01 to 100,[1] has exactly the same probability of appearing in a given location in the table. The numbers are arranged in random order. If a sequence of numbers is read from the table, every possible sequence has the same probability of occurring. The sequence 98, 33, 50, and 13 is just as likely to occur as 13, 13, 13, and 13. The probability that the fourth number in either of the sequences will be 13 is .01, and this probability is unaffected by the numbers obtained on the first three draws.

Selecting numbers from a table of two-digit random numbers gives

[1]In this textbook, we assume that when a double zero (00) appears in the table, it represents the number one hundred (100). Thus, the lowest number is 1 and the highest number is 100. Some textbooks assume that the lowest number in a two-digit table is zero (00) and the highest number is 99.

essentially the same result as drawing balls from a box containing 100 balls labeled from 01 to 100. (This assumes that the balls are replaced after each draw and that the contents are thoroughly mixed before the next draw.)

The Monte Carlo method is conceptually simple and may be introduced by a simple illustration. Assume that a coin is to be tossed to determine which of two players will take the first turn in a game. Given a fair coin and an unbiased flipping mechanism, each player has an equal chance of obtaining the first turn. A head is considered a "success" for player 1 while a tail is considered a success for player 2. The first player with five successes is awarded first turn in the game.

Rather than actually flipping a coin, we may select the first player by simulating tosses of the coin using the random numbers given in Table 11.3. The draw of a number from 01 to 50 could represent the toss of a head, while the numbers 51 to 00 could represent a tail. We should enter Table 11.3 at a random point and continue to select numbers according to a predetermined pattern. Suppose the first number selected was the 16 in the upper-right-hand corner of the table. Our predetermined pattern is to move straight down a chosen column. This generates the series of numbers 16, 75, 29, 97, etc. These numbers are entered in Table 11.4.

Table 11.4 also gives the events associated with the random numbers. The first number is 16 and the associated event is a head, which implies a success for player 1. Likewise, the 75 is associated with a tail and implies a success for player 2. The procedure is continued until one player has five successes.

The fundamental idea is to assign the random-number sequences such that the probability of drawing a number in a given sequence is exactly equal to the probability of the event with which the sequence is associated. The probability of drawing a number from 01 to 50 is .5.

Table 11.4 *Simulating a coin-tossing game*

Random number	Associated event	Winning player
16	head	1
75	tail	2
29	head	1
97	tail	2
97	tail	2
63	tail	2
29	head	1
86	tail	2

This is exactly equal to the probability of tossing the coin and getting a head. A few additional examples should clarify the procedure.

Consider simulating the draw of a single card from a deck of 52 well-shuffled playing cards. After each draw, the card is replaced and the deck reshuffled. The probability of drawing any particular suit is .25. Thus, the random numbers 01–25 could be used to represent drawing a spade. The sequences 26–50, 51–75, and 76–00 would then be associated with drawing a heart, diamond, or club respectively.

In some cases, it is necessary to skip certain random numbers that we generate. Suppose we want to simulate the repeated tossing of a single die. The sequence 01–10 could be associated with rolling a one. Likewise, the sequences 11–20, 21–30, 31–40, 41–50, and 51–60 could be associated with rolling a two, three, four, five, and six respectively. Whenever we draw a number greater than 60, we would simply ignore it and proceed to the next number.

Finally, we should realize that we may need random numbers with values larger than two-digit random numbers. Suppose we were simulating months of birth. We would need at least a three-digit random number. The sequence 01–31 would be assigned to January, 32–59 to February, all the way up to 335–365 for December. Larger random numbers can be obtained by combining two or more columns of Table 11.3.

Generating interarrival and service times

The procedure we have just described can be used to generate the inputs we need to simulate the car wash. In Table 11.5, a series of random numbers has been assigned to each possible interarrival time

Table 11.5 *Random-number assignments for interarrival times at Bill's Car Wash*

Interarrival time	Probability	Random numbers
0	.06	01–06
1	.10	07–16
2	.13	17–29
3	.17	30–46
4	.15	47–61
5	.12	62–73
6	.10	74–83
7	.08	84–91
8	.05	92–96
9	.03	97–99
10	.01	00
	1.00	

for car wash customers. The ratio of the number of random numbers assigned to a given event to the total number of random numbers assigned to the overall distribution of outcomes is equal to the probability of the given outcome occurring. In Table 11.5, the probability of an interarrival time of 3 minutes is .17. The random numbers 30–46 are assigned to represent an interarrival time of 3 minutes. There are 17 numbers from 30 to 46. This is 17% of the 100 numbers used in the overall assignment. Hence, the probability of drawing a number in this range is .17.

The random number sequence 36, 47, 82, and 13 would, according to Table 11.5, generate consecutive interarrival times of 3, 4, 6, and 1 minutes. This process may be continued indefinitely to generate as many inputs as we need to complete our simulation.

Before generating a service time for a given arrival, we must determine whether the arrival is a compact or a full-sized car. We will establish this through the use of random numbers. Since the probability of a type I arrival is .45, the random-number sequence 01–45 will represent this car type. The remaining numbers, 46–00, will represent a type II car. This information is given in Table 11.6.

A set of service times can also be generated using the Monte Carlo process. Table 11.7 shows assignments for the two service-time distributions. The probability that a type I car will require 2 minutes of washing time is .6. The probability of a service time of 3 minutes is .4. Hence, for type I cars, the random-number sequence 01–60 has been assigned to a washing time of 2 minutes. The remaining 40 numbers, 61–00, have been assigned to a washing time of 3 minutes.

Assume, for example, that a car has arrived for washing. The numbers 96 and 23 are drawn from consecutive locations in the random-number table. The first number is used to identify the car type. Since 96 falls in the 46–00 range, it is a type II car. The second number is used to determine the washing time by referring to the type II assignments in Table 11.7. The random number 23 determines that it will take 5 minutes to wash the car.

Utilizing theoretical distributions

In some cases, it is both possible and desirable to replace the empirical probabilty distribution used to describe a model's random variables

Table 11.6 *Random-number assignments for distinguishing between types of cars at Bill's Car Wash*

Car type	Probability	Random number
Compact (type I)	.45	01–45
Full-sized (type II)	.55	46–00

Table 11.7 *Random-number assignments for service times for type I and type II cars at Bill's Car Wash*

Service time	Type I (compact)	
	Probability	Random numbers
2	.60	01–60
3	.40	61–00

Service time	Type II (full-sized)	
	Probability	Random numbers
4	.20	01–20
5	.40	21–60
6	.25	61–85
7	.10	86–95
8	.05	96–00

with an appropriate theoretical distribution such as the normal or Poisson distribution. There are two major advantages in doing this. First, the theoretical distribution is often more representative of the underlying population from which the sample information for the empirical distribution was drawn. Second, it is often possible to develop a mathematical means of generating the values for the random variables.

An equation, derived from the cumulative probability function, is used to replace the procedure of looking up numbers in tables that characterized the Monte Carlo example. In the alternative approach, a random number is obtained and substituted into the developed equation or model to allow computation of a value of the random variable. This method is particularly efficient for simulations conducted on an electronic computer. Although we will not discuss it here, statistical "goodness of fit" tests are available to test the appropriateness of a particular theoretical distribution to a given situation.

Operating the model

At this point, most of the initial groundwork for the first simulation run is complete. We are now ready to generate the inputs and process them in accordance with the relationships specified in the model. The first run will be an attempt to simulate the existing car wash system.

A means of processing the inputs, recording the operating results, and keeping track of the system must be developed. In large simulation studies, this is accomplished through the use of a computer simulation model. For the car wash example, the simulation can be performed with a pencil and one or more simulation worksheets.

Input data

Random numbers were used to develop the interarrival times, car types, and service times given in Table 11.8 for 20 different customers. These will be treated as the initial simulated arrivals at Bill's Car Wash. The random numbers in column 2 were taken from the first column of Table 11.3. They are used in conjunction with the random-number assignments given in Table 11.5 to generate the interarrival times listed in column 3. The random numbers in columns 5 and 7 of Table 11.8 were taken from columns 2 and 3 of Table 11.3. They were used, with Tables 11.6 and 11.7, to determine the car types and service times set forth in columns 6 and 8 respectively.

The arrival times given in column 4 of Table 11.8 can be calculated from the interarrival times. Assume that the car wash begins operation at clock time 0. The interarrival time for the first customer or arrival will be interpreted as the elapsed time between the time when operation

Table 11.8 *Simulated arrrival and service times for Bill's Car Wash*

(1) Arrival number	(2) Random number	(3) Interarrival time	(4) Arrival time*	(5) Random number	(6) Type arrival	(7) Random number	(8) Service time
1	33	3	3	24	I	52	2
2	50	4	7	72	II	85	6
3	13	1	8	19	I	79	3
4	82	6	14	20	I	86	3
5	59	4	18	91	II	72	6
6	30	3	21	88	II	20	4
7	24	2	23	95	II	12	4
8	02	0	23	38	I	21	2
9	15	1	24	41	I	99	3
10	38	3	27	51	II	58	5
11	12	1	28	08	I	04	2
12	85	7	35	23	I	36	2
13	92	8	43	55	II	01	4
14	79	6	49	27	I	84	3
15	59	4	53	80	II	13	4
16	11	1	54	26	I	06	2
17	97	9	63	54	II	15	4
18	39	3	66	47	II	73	6
19	71	5	71	14	I	64	3
20	16	1	72	59	II	96	8

*Arrivals are assumed to occur at the end of a minute.

started and the time when the first arrival occurs. The generated interarrival time for the first customer is 3 minutes, so the first arrival occurs at time 3.

The interarrival time determined for the second arrival, 4 minutes, is added to the arrival time of the first customer to establish an arrival time of 7 for the second arrival. The interarrival times for customers 3 and 4 are 1 and 6 minutes and are used to establish arrival times of 8 and 14 for these customers. The arrival times of the remaining customers were determined by adding the interarrival time of each to the arrival time of the previous customer. Customers 7 and 8 both have the same arrival time, because the interarrival time generated for customer 8 was 0. Note that all arrivals are assumed to occur at the end of a minute.

Sample problem 11.1   THE URN GAME

A game consists of the random selection of one of two unlabeled urns, followed by the draw of a ball from the selected urn. A payoff is made on the basis of the color of the ball drawn. One urn contains 5 red, 2 white, and 3 blue balls. The second urn contains 4 red, 4 white, and 2 blue balls. Establish the necessary random-number assignments, and use them to simulate four plays of the game.

SOLUTION

Random-number assignments for urn selection

Urn	Probability	Random numbers
1	.5	01–50
2	.5	51–00

Random-number assignments for draw of ball

	Urn 1			Urn 2	
Color	Probability	Random numbers	Color	Probability	Random numbers
Red	.5	01–50	Red	.4	01–40
White	.2	51–70	White	.4	41–80
Blue	.3	71–00	Blue	.2	81–00

Draw the first 8 numbers from column 1 of Table 11.3. Group them into 4 pairs of 2-digit random numbers. The first number in each pair will be used to determine which urn is selected. The second number in each pair will determine the color of the ball drawn.

33, 50:   Urn 1, red ball
13, 82:   Urn 1, blue ball
59, 30:   Urn 2, red ball
24, 02:   Urn 1, red ball

The simulation worksheet

Table 11.8 specifies the exact arrival time and elapsed service time for each of the first 20 arrivals at the car wash. It supplies all the inputs required to conduct the simulation. The worksheet shown in Table 11.9 is known as a *simulation worksheet*, and it is used to keep track of the operation of the system. We shall discuss each column in the simulation worksheet and explain how the entries are calculated. Remember,

Table 11.9 *Simulation of 20 arrivals at Bill's Car Wash, with a maximum waiting line of 2 cars*

(1) Arrival number	(2) Arrival time	(3) Arrival type	(4) Service time	(5) Arrival state	(6) Join system?	(7) Start service*	(8) Complete service*	(9) Queue time	(10) Idle time
1	3	I	2	0	Yes	4	5	0	3
2	7	II	6	0	Yes	8	13	0	2
3	8	I	3	1	Yes	14	16	5	0
4	14	I	3	1	Yes	17	19	2	0
5	18	II	6	1	Yes	20	25	1	0
6	21	II	4	1	Yes	26	29	4	0
7	23	II	4	2	Yes	30	33	6	0
8	23	I	2	3	No	—	—	—	—
9	24	I	3	3	No	—	—	—	—
10	27	II	5	2	Yes	34	38	6	0
11	28	I	2	3	No	—	—	—	—
12	35	I	2	1	Yes	39	40	3	0
13	43	II	4	0	Yes	44	47	0	3
14	49	I	3	0	Yes	50	52	0	2
15	53	II	4	0	Yes	54	57	0	1
16	54	I	2	1	Yes	58	59	3	0
17	63	II	4	0	Yes	64	67	0	4
18	66	II	6	1	Yes	68	73	1	0
19	71	I	3	1	Yes	74	76	2	0
20	72	II	8	2	Yes	77	84	4	0

*Service is assumed to start at the beginnning of a minute and to be completed at the end of a minute.

however, that there is no standard format for this worksheet. The column arrangement must be designed specifically for the problem being simulated.

Columns 2, 3, and 4 contain information about the arrival time, arrival type, and service time of each car. This information is taken directly from Table 11.8. Column 5 in Table 11.9 gives the state of the system at the time of the new arrival. The *state of the system* is the number of automobiles in the system, including the car being washed and those waiting in line. We compute it by determining the number of service completion times that are greater than or equal to the arrival time under consideration. As an example, consider arrival 6 at time 21. From column 8, there is 1 service completion time greater than 21 (the 25 for arrival number 5). Thus, the arrival state for car 6 is 1. Likewise, the arrival state for car 8 is 3, because 3 prior arrivals (5, 6, and 7) have service completion times greater than 23, which is the arrival time for the eighth automobile.

Column 6 simply indicates whether the arriving car joins the system or proceeds to another car wash. If the arrival state is 2 or less, a "yes" is entered in column 6, indicating that the arrival decides to wait for service at Bill's Car Wash. If the arrival state is 3, both parking spots are being used. A "no" is entered in column 6, indicating that the arrival will not join the system.

Column 7 indicates at what time service will begin. If the arrival state is 0, service will start at the beginning of the minute after arrival. Car 1 arrives at the end of the third minute, for example, and service starts at the beginning of the fourth minute. If the state of the system is greater than 0, service begins immediately after the latest service completion time of prior arrivals. Car 6 arrives at time 21. The arrival state is 1. The latest service completion time of prior arrivals is 25. Thus, service begins at time 26.

Service completion time is shown in column 8. It is obtained by adding the service time to the time when service began. Remember that services start at the beginning of a minute and completions are made at the end of a minute. Thus, service begins for arrival 1 at the beginning of the fourth minute. Service time is 2 minutes, which means that service is completed at the end of the fifth minute.

Queue time is given in column 9. It represents the time that a particular car waits in line. It can be obtained from the "start service" and the "arrival time" of a particular entry. For example, car 3 arrives at the end of minute 8 (which is the beginning of minute 9), and service starts at the beginning of minute 14. There is a waiting time of 5 minutes: minutes 9, 10, 11, 12, and 13.

Column 10 refers to the amount of idle time experienced by the system from the preceding arrival to the present arrival. Idle time only occurs when the arrival state is 0. We obtain it by subtracting the departing time of the preceding arrival from the arrival time of the present arrival. Car 14 arrives at the end of minute 49. The preceding arrival completed service at the end of time 47. The system was empty, or idle, for 2 minutes.

Illustrating worksheet entries

Before turning to specific examples, we should note that it is necessary to keep track of time as we move through the simulation. For example, we must know and be able to specify what time customers arrive at the service facility, when service starts, and when it is completed. Instead of using the actual time of day, we use what is known as *clock time*. The process is similar to using a stop watch to time competitors in a one-mile run. The clock is set to 0 at the beginning of the simulation.

The car wash simulation will be conducted on a *variable time-increment* basis. In Table 11:9, there is one row entry for each arrival. Clock time is advanced to the time at which the next event of interest occurs. This "time interval of advancement" will vary from row to row. Later in the chapter, we will use a *fixed time increment*. In that example, each row entry will represent a uniform, or fixed, interval of advancement of the time clock.

Discussion of the entries for several selected arrivals should illustrate the use of the simulation worksheet. The first arrival occurs at the end of minute 3. Since the system is empty at that time, the car joins the system and immediately enters the working facility. Service starts at the beginning of minute 4. Elapsed service time for the car is 2 minutes, so service is completed at the end of minute 5. The car was washed during minutes 4 and 5. The first arrival did not have to wait in line, so a 0 queue (waiting-line) time is recorded in column 9. The service system was idle for 3 minutes just prior to the arrival of the first customer, so a 3 is entered in column 10.

The fourth arrival, which occurs at the end of clock time 14, encounters a somewhat different situation than that experienced by the first arrival. When the customer reaches the car wash, the third arrival is still in the system and will remain there until the end of minute 16. The appropriate entry, 1, is recorded as the arrival state, indicating that a customer was in the system when the fourth arrival occurred. This customer still joins the system, since both parking spaces are available, and waits until the beginning of minute 17 for service to begin. The queue time for customer 4 is 2 minutes: minutes 15 and 16. This is entered in column 9. Service time for this customer is 3 minutes, so service is completed at the end of minute 19. No idle time, recorded in column 10, occurred immediately prior to this arrival.

The experience of the eighth arrival is of particular interest. When this occurs at the end of minute 23, the fifth arrival is still being served and the sixth and seventh arrivals occupy the available parking spaces.

The system is full; it is in state 3. The eighth arrival will be unable to join the system. This is indicated in column 6. The congested state of the system is a direct result of the extended washing time required for the fifth arrival and the spacing of the arrivals that followed. This condition subsequently resulted in the loss of the eighth, ninth, and eleventh arrivals.

A schematic representation of the simulation of the first nine arrivals is shown in Figure 11.3, which represents an alternative, though more time-consuming, method of keeping track of system operation. The pictorial representation was constructed directly from the input data provided in Table 11.9 and may serve to clarify the simulation.

Predicting system performance

During the first 72 minutes of simulated time, 20 customers arrived at Bill's Car Wash and 3 of them were unable to join the system. Nevertheless, it would be very risky to infer that 3 customers will be lost every 72 minutes or that 15 percent of all arrivals will go to the competitor's

Figure 11.3 *Schematic representation of the first 26 minutes of simulated operation at Bill's Car Wash*

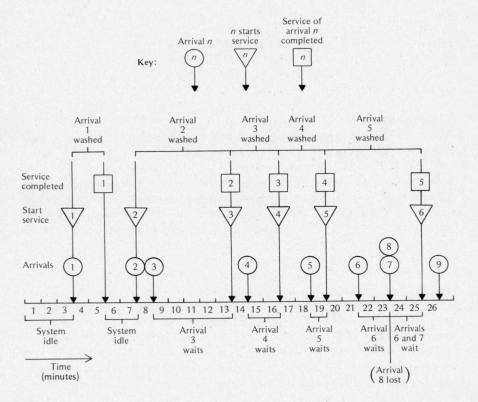

facility. The 72 minutes of simulated time represent a very small sample from the operation of the car wash. Inferences made on the basis of this output are subject to a large sampling error. An experimental design that allows sound inferences must be established. And in this area of simulation, a number of technical problems have not been fully resolved.

Decisions on the size of the sample (that is, the length of the simulation run or runs), the manner of sample selection, and the methods of statistical analysis are among the critical decisions that must be made. They are complicated by the serial correlation typically found in simulation output; that is, the state of the system at one time is not independent of earlier states of the system. In the case of Bill's Car Wash, it is likely that the probability of finding a certain number of cars in the system at a given time is affected by the number of cars in the system 5 minutes earlier. This correlation prevents direct application of statistical sampling procedures that assume the experimental observations to be statistically independent.

One popular way to circumvent this difficulty is to conduct a number of separate simulation runs. The performance measures generated by these runs are viewed as independent experimental observations. For example, assume 15 separate simulation runs of the car wash were conducted. The average number of customers lost in an hour could be computed for each run. Since these observations are independent, standard statistical techniques can be used to provide an overall estimate of the number of customers lost in an average hour of operation and to establish an estimate of the amount of sampling error present.

A disadvantage of this approach is created by the fact that the initial output from a simulation run may not represent typical system operation. Most simulation studies are characterized by two phases. Once started, the system takes some time to settle down, or stabilize. The *transient phase* refers to the time between when a system is started and when it reaches stability — the *steady state* phase. If the analyst is only interested in the behavior of the model after it reaches steady state, a common practice is to discard results from the transient phase to avoid biasing performance estimates. This procedure must be repeated on each run.

An alternative approach is to conduct one long simulation run and subdivide it into segments. If the length of the segments is long enough, the performance measures generated by one segment are independent of those drawn from adjoining segments. Although serial correlation is minimal in the car wash simulation, this approach was used in the analysis. Examination of the model and its related probability distributions indicates that the state of the system at a given time is essentially independent of the state of the system 1 hour or even ½ hour earlier.

Table 11.10 *Summary of selected performance measures for 15 consecutive 4-hour segments of simulated time at Bill's Car Wash*

Segment number	Number of arrivals	Number of arrivals lost	Percent of arrivals lost	System idle time	Average customer* queue time
1	66	11	17.7	20 minutes	3.60 minutes
2	56	3	5.4	29	2.55
3	59	5	8.5	13	3.26
4	55	3	5.5	33	2.44
5	61	7	11.5	29	3.28
6	60	9	15.0	12	4.94
7	62	3	4.8	27	2.14
8	63	8	12.7	30	3.15
9	61	7	11.5	10	3.98
10	57	9	15.8	31	2.96
11	63	9	14.3	25	2.76
12	57	5	8.8	47	2.67
13	59	5	8.5	33	1.61
14	58	4	6.9	35	2.41
15	67	8	11.9	28	2.22
Total	904	96	10.6	402	

*Average queue time is determined on the basis of customers who actually joined the system for service.

Summarizing performance data

One 60-hour simulation of the car wash system was conducted and divided into 15 four-hour segments. Performance measures for each of the segments are provided in Table 11.10. We can discover the variation inherent in system performance by examining the data for the percent of the arrivals who were unable to join the system and for the average customer queue time. Lost arrivals ranged from a high of 17.7% to a low of 4.8%, while the range for average queue time was from 4.94 to 1.61 minutes.

Based on the overall simulation, an estimated 10.6% of all arrivals will be unable to join the system, an average of 1.6 customers will be lost each hour, and the average customer who receives service will have to wait in line for 2.9 minutes.[2] These customers are lost, despite the existence of idle time in the system. This is a basic characteristic of queuing systems and a fundamental source of difficulty in system

[2]Standard statistical methods may be utilized to establish confidence intervals for these estimates. For example, the 90% confidence interval for the average number of customers lost per hour is from 1.32 to 1.88.

design. As noted earlier, we should compare the results of the simulation to actual operations to help evaluate the model.

Evaluating alternative systems

A simulation of each of the more promising system or solution alternatives of interest should be conducted and a means of evaluating their relative merits developed. The details of the approach used will vary from application to application and will have to be tailored to the specific situation. The analysis will usually include both tangible and intangible costs and/or returns.

Varying parameters of the model

Once the initial simulation run has been conducted, the operating characteristics of the model are ordinarily altered and the simulation repeated. In the case of Bill's Car Wash, we will investigate the effect of increasing the number of available parking spaces from 2 to 4.

Table 11.11 is a simulation worksheet that represents the results of the first 20 arrivals under the revised operating conditions. The arrival times, arrival types, and service times from Table 11.8 were again used as input. Hence, the second simulation was conducted under the same input or demand conditions as the initial simulation. This represents a significant advantage of Monte Carlo simulation. Since the exact sequence of random numbers or input values can be used, we can evaluate two or more system alternatives under identical demand conditions. It eliminates the possibility that performance differences may result from factors other than those specifically changed by the analyst. This allows the use of a smaller sample size to gain a given level of statistical significance in performance differences between two alternatives.

Of particular interest is the fact that only 1 of the first 20 arrivals was lost under our new operating characteristics. Both arrival 8 and arrival 9, who were lost in the initial simulation, were able to join the system. Arrival 11 was again unable to join the system, reaching the system at time 28 and finding arrival 6 being served and the 4 parking spaces filled by 4 other customers. This was accompanied by an increase in waiting time. The first 20 arrivals spent a total of 70 minutes waiting in the queue — more than double the total queue time of 37 minutes incurred in the first simulation. Despite these differences, the system was in the same state when customer 20 arrived.

Again, it is not possible to draw an accurate conclusion about the level of system performance on the basis of simulating only 20 arrivals.

Table 11.11 *Simulation of 20 arrivals at Bill's Car Wash, with a maximum waiting line of 4 cars*

Arrival number	Arrival time	Arrival type	Service time	Arrival state	Join system?	Start service*	Complete service*	Queue time	Idle time
1	3	I	2	0	Yes	4	5	0	3
2	7	II	6	0	Yes	8	13	0	2
3	8	I	3	1	Yes	14	16	5	0
4	14	I	3	1	Yes	17	19	2	0
5	18	II	6	1	Yes	20	25	1	0
6	21	II	4	1	Yes	26	29	4	0
7	23	II	4	2	Yes	30	33	6	0
8	23	I	2	3	Yes	34	35	10	0
9	24	I	3	4	Yes	36	38	11	0
10	27	II	5	4	Yes	39	43	11	0
11	28	I	2	5	No	—	—	—	—
12	35	I	2	3	Yes	44	45	8	0
13	43	II	4	2	Yes	46	49	2	0
14	49	I	3	1	Yes	50	52	0	0
15	53	II	4	0	Yes	54	57	0	1
16	54	I	2	1	Yes	58	59	3	0
17	63	II	4	0	Yes	64	67	0	4
18	66	II	6	1	Yes	68	73	1	0
19	71	I	3	1	Yes	74	76	2	0
20	72	II	8	2	Yes	77	84	4	0

*Service is assumed to start at the beginning of a minute and to be completed at the end of a minute.

A second 60-hour simulation run, also divided into 15 four-hour segments, was conducted. The number of customers lost during the 60 hours was reduced from the 96 (an average of 1.6 per hour) experienced in the first simulation to 47 (an average of approximately .8 per hour) in the second case. The addition of 2 parking spaces reduced the rate of customer loss from 10.6% to 5.2%. Average customer queue time more than doubled, however, going from 2.9 to 6.6 minutes per customer.

Comparing the alternatives

In the case of Bill's Car Wash, evaluation of the alternatives is quite simple. It is just a matter of determining if the revenue generated by washing additional cars will cover the cost of altering the service system.

Assume a charge of $3 for washing a car and an annual leasing cost for the 2 parking spaces that converts to a prorated cost of $.10 per hour of operation. Since the additional cars are washed by reducing the idle time of the service facility, the only direct expense incurred by washing another car is the cost of the water, cleaning agents, and miscellaneous materials expended. Mr. James has estimated this at an average of $.25 per car, so each additional car washed contributed $2.75 toward leasing expenses. Any income in excess of this expense contributes to profit. The additional parking spaces allow an average of approximately .8 more cars to be washed each hour and add about $2.10 to the expected hourly profit rate (.8 × 2.75 − .10 = 2.10). The number of parking spaces should be increased from 2 to 4. While the $2.10 increase in profit is an estimate subject to statistical error, the magnitude of the increase is sufficient to assure Mr. James of an increase in his profit position.

A potential difficulty that could invalidate these conclusions is the possible effect of the sharp increase in waiting time on customer decisions about whether to join the queue. Some customers who arrive at the car wash when there are already 3 cars in the system may decide to go to another car wash, even though a parking space is available. Such behavior would reduce the profitability of the increase in parking space. If Mr. James feels that this is possible, he should attempt to quantify its effect. This may prove to be a difficult undertaking.

Other changes in the operating characteristics, representing further system modifications contemplated by Mr. James, could be made and the simulation repeated. In some cases, it may be possible to avoid additional simulation runs. For example, acquisition of faster washing equipment that would increase operating cost by $5 an hour could be rejected on the basis of data already available. The present system loses an average of 1.6 cars an hour. If all these cars were washed, total revenue would only increase by $4.80 an hour — $.20 an hour less than the increase in operating cost. One potential difficulty in this decision should be noted. Installation of the new equipment would reduce waiting lines and waiting times. These changes might lead to an increase in demand or arrival rate sufficient to justify installation of the equipment.

Extending model complexity

If a measure of confidence in the validity of a model cannot be established, or if the analyst wishes to evaluate the impact of additional factors, it may be necessary to increase the complexity or detail of the model. In the case of Bill's Car Wash, equipment may periodically break down or the rate of customer arrivals may vary substantially from day to day or from hour to hour. If they significantly affect system operation, such factors should be included in the simulation model. These and other modifications can be accomplished without great difficulty. We could include the probability that an arrival will refuse to join the system, or balk, when waiting space is available by specifying the probability that a customer balks given the different possible queue lengths. We could provide for a customer reneging, or leaving the queue before receiving service, by making such behavior a function of the length of time the customer waits in the queue.

As we incorporate additional details into the simulation, we eventually reach a point of diminishing returns. This usually occurs when the increase in realism or accuracy of the model does not warrant the additional cost of conducting the simulation, and it is an ever-present danger in simulation modeling. The analyst must avoid building excessive details into the model. The cost of including each added detail should be weighed against the extent to which the model's realism is improved and against the benefits realized from the improvement.

Utilizing the computer in simulation studies

The analysis of Bill James's problem illustrates that simulation can be performed without the assistance of a computer. In reality, almost all managerial applications of simulation rely heavily on computers. The reason is simple. The speed of electronic computers allows us to compress years of operating history into a few minutes of computer time. It is unlikely that an operating manager will actually perform a computer simulation. He or she will probably explain the problem to a specialist, who will actually perform the computer simulation. Nevertheless, it is important to understand certain aspects of the computer process.

Many "canned programs" are available to computer programmers. These programs generally refer to a particular application of simulation, such as inventory control or queuing analysis. When these canned programs are available and applicable, all the user has to do is provide basic information about operating characteristics and decision rules. The program will then simulate the system and provide such data as average waiting time, maximum queue length, and so on.

Quite often, a particular situation will not fit a canned program. If the model is only moderately complex, the program may be written in a general-purpose language such as FORTRAN or PL/1. These languages have an important limitation in that almost all subroutines of the program must be written "from scratch." As a result, it is often expensive and time-consuming to write complex simulation programs in these languages. Simulation programs written in these languages may also be very inefficient and therefore expensive to run on a computer.

Several computer languages, such as SIMSCRIPT and GPSS, have been developed specifically for simulation studies. They contain statements and subroutines that the programmer can use directly, thus reducing programming workload. These languages are structured so that common simulation operations can be carried out easily and effectively. Special-purpose languages are commonly used in industry and government. In the future, almost all complex simulation studies will probably utilize one of these languages.

Other examples of simulation analysis

Simulation can be used and has been used in an enormous number of different situations. Its application to queuing problems has been demonstrated. Simulation can also be applied to inventory control, production scheduling, warehouse location, assembly-line balancing, portfolio analysis, executive training, and other situations. And it may be used in different ways, to describe a present system or to design a new system, for example. In this section, we will give brief examples of two additional areas of application.

Simulating an inventory problem

A company wishes to establish an inventory policy, that is, an order quantity and order point, for a particular product. The company is faced with both variation in demand and variation in the elapsed time between order placement and receipt of the order. Daily demand is distributed as shown in Table 11.12, while lead time varies from 1 to 6 days, according to the probability distribution given in Table 11.13. Carrying cost is $.50 per item per day. Stockout or loss-of-sale cost is $30 per unit. The cost of placing an order is $80. The company wishes to establish the inventory policy that will minimize the sum of inventory carrying cost, stockout cost, and ordering cost.

One approach to this problem is to establish a policy using the concepts we discussed in Chapters 3 and 4 — analysis of expected value

Table 11.12 *Demand distribution and associated random numbers for an inventory simulation*

Units of demand	Probability	Random numbers
8	.13	01–13
9	.19	14–32
10	.34	33–66
11	.23	67–89
12	.11	90–00
	1.00	

Table 11.13 *Distribution of delivery times and associated random numbers for an inventory simulation*

Days to delivery	Probability	Random numbers
1	.14	01–14
2	.34	15–48
3	.20	49–68
4	.12	69–80
5	.10	81–90
6	.10	91–00
	1.00	

and economic order quantity. An alternative procedure is to use simulation. A simulation solution can be obtained by experimenting with different order quantities and order points. The random-number assignments for generating the simulation inputs we need are specified in Tables 11.12 and 11.13. The actual Monte Carlo generation of input values for the random variables is shown in the simulation worksheet, Table 11.14.

The inventory analysis uses a fixed-increment method of moving the simulation through time. We advance clock time 1 day at a time rather than advancing it to the time of the next event of interest, as in the case of the variable-increment approach we used earlier. Selection of 1 day as the time increment necessitates the assumption that orders are always placed at the end of a day and that new shipments are available for use at the beginning of a day.

The company has decided to simulate first a policy wherein an order for 60 units is placed whenever inventory drops to 30 units. Beginning inventory is 60 units. At the end of day 3, inventory has dropped below the order point of 30 units and an order for 60 units is placed. The random number 54 was used to determine, with reference to Table 11.13, the lead time of 3 days for this order. The order is treated as being received 3 days later, at the end of day 6. It will be available for use on day 7; hence, a receipt of 60 units is entered for day 7. Before the order is received, inventory is exhausted and a stockout occurs. Lost sales of 2 units are experienced on day 6.

This process was continued for 40 days. For this period of operation, carrying cost was $480.50, stockout cost was $1410, and ordering cost was $480 for the 6 orders placed. This resulted in an average daily cost of $59.26. For decision-making purposes, it would be necessary to extend considerably the length of the simulation.

The simulation should be repeated under a number of different inventory policies and the cost of the alternatives compared. Based on

Table 11.14 *Simulation worksheet for an inventory problem*

Day	Receipts	Begin inventory	Random number	Demand	Ending inventory	Lost sales	Random number	Day to delivery
1		60	83	11	49			
2		49	70	11	38			
3		38	59	10	28*		54	3
4		28	12	8	20			
5		20	92	12	8			
6		8	46	10	0	2		
7	60	60	54	10	50			
8		50	04	8	42			
9		42	51	10	32			
10		32	99	12	20*		90	5
11		20	84	10	10			
12		10	81	11	0	1		
13		0	15	9	0	9		
14		0	36	10	0	10		
15		0	12	8	0	8		
16	60	60	54	10	50			
17		50	97	12	38			
18		38	00	12	26*		71	4
19		26	49	10	16			
20		16	44	10	6			
21		6	13	8	0	2		
22		0	23	9	0	9		
23	60	60	45	10	50			
24		50	54	10	40			
25		40	24	9	31			
26		31	50	10	21*		08	1
27		21	29	9	12			
28	60	72	61	10	62			
29		62	22	9	53			
30		53	47	10	43			
31		43	73	11	32			
32		32	18	9	23*		51	3
33		23	22	9	14			
34		14	38	10	4			
35		4	34	10	0	6		
36	60	60	54	10	50			
37		50	91	12	38			
38		38	42	10	28*		73	4
39		28	46	10	18			
40		18	30	9	9			
					961	47		

*Order point is reached.

the limited results of the first experiment, the company will probably conclude that stockout cost is excessive and will alter the initial policy in an attempt to reduce the stockout cost component. This could be accomplished by increasing the order point above 30 units, because it was originally set equal to the expected demand during lead time.[3] This will increase inventory carrying cost, but the increase will be more than offset by the resulting decrease in stockout costs.

Simulation of failure times

Hartman, Inc. has developed a new electronic system. It wishes to estimate the average length of repair-free operation time for a newly installed system. The system is assembled from three standard components. When one of these components fails, the system fails and must be repaired.

It would be too expensive and time-consuming to build and operate enough of the systems to develop an estimate based on actual operations. The company has collected extensive operating records on each of the components, and these records have been used to develop the

[3]The probability distributions given in Tables 11.12 and 11.13 can be used to compute the expected daily demand of 10 units and the expected lead time of 3 days. The expected demand during lead time is then 30 units (10×3).

Table 11.15 *Distribution of time to failure and associated random-number assignments for three electronic components*

Component A			Component B		
Time to failure	Probability	Random numbers	Time to failure	Probability	Random numbers
4 months	.10	01–10	2 months	.05	01–05
5	.20	11–30	3	.10	06–15
6	.30	31–60	4	.20	16–35
7	.20	61–80	5	.30	36–65
8	.15	81–95	6	.25	66–90
9	.05	96–00	7	.10	91–00

Component C		
Time to failure	Probability	Random numbers
6 months	.20	01–20
7	.30	21–50
8	.25	51–75
9	.15	76–90
10	.10	91–00

distributions of failure times given in Table 11.15. These distributions may be used to directly compute the probability distribution of failure times for the new system. A second alternative is to simulate the failure of a large number of the systems as a means of estimating the distribution of interest.

The random-number assignments needed to generate failure times for the three components are specified in Table 11.15. The simulation worksheet in Table 11.16 shows the simulation of 20 operating spans or failure times for 20 different systems. Three random numbers are used to determine the failure time for the three components in accordance with the assigned random-number sequences. In the first case, projected failure times of 6, 4, and 8 months are generated for components A, B, and C respectively. The earliest failure time, 4 months for component B, determines the failure time for the system. Based on the simulation of 20 systems, the average time to system failure is 4.6 months. The simulation should be extended to provide a more accurate estimate of operating time, based on the relative frequency of the simulated outcomes.

Table 11.16 *Simulation worksheet for failure time of an electronic system*

System	Random number	Month component A fails	Random number	Month component B fails	Random number	Month component C fails	Month system fails
1	33	6	24	4	52	8	4
2	50	6	72	6	85	9	6
3	13	5	19	4	79	9	4
4	82	8	20	4	86	9	4
5	59	6	91	7	72	8	6
6	30	5	88	6	20	6	5
7	24	5	95	7	12	6	5
8	02	4	38	5	21	7	4
9	15	5	41	5	99	10	5
10	38	6	51	5	58	8	5
11	12	5	08	3	04	6	3
12	85	8	23	4	36	7	4
13	92	8	55	5	01	6	5
14	79	7	27	4	84	9	4
15	59	6	80	6	13	6	6
16	11	5	26	4	06	6	4
17	97	9	54	5	15	6	5
18	39	6	47	5	73	8	5
19	71	7	14	3	64	8	3
20	16	5	59	5	96	10	5

Advantages and limitations of simulation

The widespread use of simulation in problem analysis reflects the significant number of advantages inherent in the simulation approach. While several of these have already been noted, we will expand on them in this section.

Simulation can be used to study large, complex problems containing stochastic, or probabilistic, elements. This is the primary reason for using simulation. Frequently, too, no alternative method of analysis is available, and it becomes a question of either using simulation or not using a model to study the problem. The only other alternative is to experiment with the actual system, which is often impractical or impossible. One major reason for the power of simulation is that it allows us to incorporate more details, and hence more realism, into the simulation model than a solvable analytical model could ordinarily handle.

Simulation provides an experimental laboratory for the analyst and the manager. It gives them the ability to predict, in a relatively short time, the performance of a proposed system under specified operating conditions. It also allows them to study the effect on an existing system of a change in a single variable or parameter. In the case of the second alternative simulated for Bill's Car Wash, Mr. James knew that any difference in system performance had to be due to the availability of 4 rather than 2 parking spaces. Nothing else had been changed. This is not possible in the actual system, because a variety of changes takes place at the same time, and it is difficult or impossible to isolate the effect of a given change. Simulation also allows the analyst to repeat the experiment with the same values for specified variables and parameters. This is also not possible in the actual system.

A further advantage of simulation is the simplicity of the basic approach. It is easy to comprehend. The results of the simulation are more easily understood by the managers who must adopt and apply them. When a solution has been developed by analytical methods, simulation can be used as a means of selling the proposed solution. Simulation also provides a means of checking the soundness of a proposed analytical solution and the validity of assumptions made in the course of its development.

Unfortunately, simulation has certain disadvantages beyond those ordinarily associated with model building, and we must weigh these drawbacks when we consider using it. Simulation models are "run"; they are not solved. The system alternative selected on the basis of a well-designed simulation study is nothing more than the best of the alternatives actually considered. There is no way of knowing, short of simulating virtually all possible systems, if the one selected is the best available. This is a fundamental disadvantage of model simulation as opposed to mathematical solution, which can ordinarily guarantee determination of the optimal solution to the model. The analyst must place considerable faith in the ability of those who select alternatives for consideration. Their experience and insight should permit them to include good systems, if not the optimal system, among their alternatives. As system complexity increases, however, this task becomes extremely difficult.

A second major disadvantage of simulation is the imprecise nature of its performance estimates. These estimates are subject to statistical error. Even in the best-designed experiments, it may be difficult or impossible to be certain which of the alternatives studied is the best one. Part of this difficulty results from the fact that appropriate and readily applied statistical methods for analyzing and comparing simulation outputs have not yet been fully developed.

Another significant disadvantage of this approach is the cost of developing the model and conducting the simulation. The cost of developing the computer program necessary for analysis of a complex system can be quite large. The cost of the computer time necessary to conduct the simulation may place a limit on the complexity of the model that can be utilized. Cost considerations may force the builder of the simulation model to make the same type of simplfying assumptions as those made in analytical models.

The disadvantages inherent in simulation imply that the analyst should view simulation as a substitute — not a replacement — for analytical methods. If a usable analytical technique is available, it should be used. The analyst must guard against what appears to be a natural tendency to rely too much on simulation as a vehicle of analysis. Simulation should only be used after careful study has indicated that a feasible analytical method is not available.

Problems and exercises

1. Explain the following terms:

simulation	random variable
analytical techniques	sampling error
queuing problem	simulation worksheet
flow diagram	clock time
balk	variable-increment method
stochastic	fixed-increment method
interarrival time	serial correlation
operating characteristics	transient phase
empirical distribution	steady state
model validation	canned programs
random number	Monte Carlo process

2. Daily demand for a product varies as follows:

Daily demand	Probability
5	.1
6	.2
7	.3
8	.2
9	.1
10	.1

Use the 50 random numbers in the third and fourth columns of Table 11.3 to generate a sequence of demands for a 50-day period. Determine the relative frequency with which the different daily demands occurred. Compare these frequencies with the foregoing distribution, and explain any differences you observe.

3. Previous delivery or lead times for a special product obtained from a supplier have been recorded. No trend is apparent in the data. Given the following frequency table, determine an empirical lead-time probability distribution.

Lead time	Frequency
3 days	13
4	21
5	9
6	7
Total	50

Use the 25 random numbers in the first column of Table 11.3 and the empirical distribution to generate 25 consecutive lead times. Compare the simulated lead times with the empirical distribution.

4. The first stage in a game consists of drawing a card from a well-shuffled deck of playing cards. If a red card is drawn, a fair coin is flipped. A head results in the player winning $10. The player loses $20 on a tail. If a spade is drawn, the player immediately wins $5. If a club is drawn, a ball is selected from an urn containing 25 red balls and 75 white balls. A red ball indicates a gain of $80, while a white results in no payoff. Compute directly the probability of each possible payoff and the expected value of a single play of the game. (*Note:* A tree diagram may assist you in this calculation.) Simulate 10 plays of the game. Compare the average payoff on your simulated plays with the expected value you computed. Explain any differences.

5. John, a gambler, is faced with deciding whether he should take part in a specific game of chance. A single die is rolled. If the die comes up 1, 2, or 3, he must draw 2 balls from box A. Each ball is marked with a payoff value. He receives the *highest* of the 2 indicated payoffs. If the die comes up 4, 5, or 6, he draws 2 balls from box B and receives the *lowest* of the 2 indicated payoffs. Assume that there is an extremely large number of balls in each box. The associated probabilities of drawing the various types of balls are given in the table.

Box A		Box B	
Payoff	*Probability*	*Payoff*	*Probability*
0	.20	0	.15
1	.20	1	.15
2	.20	2	.10
3	.10	3	.20
4	.10	4	.10
5	.10	5	.15
6	.10	6	.15

Set up a simulation designed to evaluate the probabilities of achieving different payoffs. Simulate 10 plays of the game. What was the average payoff on the 10 plays? Would you recommend that the gambler use this estimate to evaluate the game? Why?

6. Four friends are playing catch. When Ann has the ball, she makes 30% of her throws to Bob, 40% to Charlie, and 30% to Doris. Bob throws the ball to Ann 50% of the time and divides the remainder of his tosses evenly between Charlie and Doris. Charlie is Doris's little brother and must always throw the ball to Doris. The strategy used by Doris is slightly more complicated. If either Ann or Bob throws the ball to her, she immediately throws it back. When she receives a toss from Charlie, she splits her next throws equally between Ann and Bob. Set up a simulation designed to determine the relative frequency with which each player catches the ball. Clearly specify your random-number assignments, and simulate 30 tosses of the ball. Assume that Ann, the owner of the ball, makes the first throw.

7. Brown Manufacturing wishes to estimate the variation in time required to assemble a new product. The product consists of three subunits. Each subunit is assembled independently. The three units are then mounted on a housing and connected to form the finished product. Use the time estimates given in the table to estimate the distribution of assembly times, based on the simulation of the assembly of 50 units.

Subassembly 1		Subassembly 2	
Required time	*Probability*	*Required time*	*Probability*
10 minutes	.2	5 minutes	.3
11	.3	6	.5
12	.3	7	.2
13	.2		

Subassembly 3		Mount and connect	
Required time	*Probability*	*Required time*	*Probability*
15 minutes	.15	20 minutes	.10
16	.25	21	.20
17	.35	22	.30
18	.25	23	.20
		24	.15
		25	.05

8. The Internal Revenue Service is interested in improving the level of customer service provided in a large Eastern city. Recently, there has been a number of complaints about the length of time taxpayers have had to wait to use the department's consulting service. The consulting service is provided to answer taxpayers' questions about preparing their annual returns. The current practice is to provide service on a first-come, first-served basis. During a particularly heavy demand period, the taxpayers have had to wait an average of 20 minutes. The department is interested in determining if it would be feasible to cut average waiting time to 5 minutes. Feasibility will be determined by whether the department can afford to add the necessary number of consultants. Analysis of past records has yielded information about customer interarrival times and the time required to answer their particular questions. These data appear in the accompanying table.

Time between arrivals	Probability	Service time per customer	Probability
0 minutes	.05	5 minutes	.30
1	.10	10	.25
2	.15	15	.15
3	.20	20	.10
4	.20	30	.08
5	.15	40	.06
6	.10	50	.04
7	.05	60	.02

Develop a simulation model to determine the number of consultants required to provide the desired level of service. Simulate the arrival of 20 or more customers under 2 different staffing levels. Make sure that the number of consultants provided in each case is sufficient to meet demand. (*Hint:* Compute the expected demand for consulting time.) Compare the performances of the 2 systems. Are the results for the first 5 to 10 arrivals likely to be representative of ordinary operating conditions?

9. Simulate the inventory system described in the text for a period of 40 days, using a policy of placing an order for 60 units whenever inventory falls to or below 40 units. Use the same inputs generated in Table 11.14, and evaluate the attractiveness of this alternative proposal.

10. Mr. James has found that his existing equipment can be modified to increase the rate at which cars can be washed. The conversion will result in an increase of $2 per hour in operating cost. Simulate the operation of the modified facility, with the 2 existing parking spaces, for 4 hours. Compare the attractiveness of this alternative with the alternatives simulated in the text. The improved service times are shown in the accompanying table. Use all other data supplied in the text.

Type I cars		Type II cars	
Wash time	*Probability*	*Wash time*	*Probability*
2 minutes	.8	3 minutes	.20
3	.2	4	.40
		5	.25
		6	.10
		7	.05

11. A large chemical plant located on the Gulf Coast receives its raw materials by ship. All cargo is carried in company-owned vessels. Management has decided to construct its own port facilities and wants to determine how many berths should be provided for docking and unloading. The cost of operating 1 berth is estimated at $2000 per day, while the cost of a ship and crew waiting for 1 day is $2500. When a berth is not available, ships will anchor in the harbor and wait for an opening. The company's raw materials can be roughly separated into two major classes. Sixty percent of the ships carry class A material and can be unloaded in either 3 or 4 days. These two unloading times are equally likely. The remaining ships carry class B material, and unloading times are split evenly between 5 and 6 days. Operations have been fairly stable for the last few years and are expected to continue at roughly the same level. An analysis of historical records has provided the following information on interarrival times for the ships:

Days between arrivals	Probability
0	.2
1	.3
2	.3
3	.2

Determine through calculation of expected values the minimum number of berths that must be provided. Simulate the operation of the port, with two different unloading capacities, for 60 days. Compare the costs of operating under the two alternatives.

12. A company has decided to evaluate the inventory policy established for one of its key products. Daily demand varies in accordance with the probability distribution provided in problem 2. Lead time between order placement and order receipt is subject to variation. The lead times tabulated in problem 3 are for the supplier of this product. Inventory carrying cost for this product is $.25 per unit per day. Stockout cost is $50 per unit, and the cost of placing an order for a new shipment is $100. The current policy is to order 75 units whenever the inventory level drops to 35. Simulate this inventory policy for 50 days. Repeat the simulation with an order point of 50 units. Compare overall costs incurred with the two decision rules. Do you feel you can determine which is the better choice on the basis of your simulation? Assume an initial inventory of 75 units.

13. The Quickserve Company operates a facility with two servers. Based on past experience, Quickserve is aware that arrivals balk or refuse service when 2 customers are waiting in line or 4 customers are at the service facility. Each customer generates a revenue of $5. All customers who balk take their business elsewhere. The company wishes to evaluate the possibility of providing an additional server. The cost of providing a server for 1 hour is $25. Simulate the 2 systems for 2 hours. Discard the results of the first ½ hour of operation. Assume that the results of the 2 hours are representative of the system's long-run performance, and use them to evaluate the proposal. The following information on customer arrivals and service times is available:

Time between arrivals	Probability	Service time	Probability
0 minutes	.1	4 minutes	.2
1	.1	5	.6
2	.2	6	.2
3	.3		
4	.2		
5	.1		

14. Joe Flint manages two One Stop stores in Crescent City. One Stop accepts payment by cash or check and cashes checks. This policy creates a cash-flow problem on Sundays, when banks are closed. Mr. Flint prefers to keep as little cash as possible in his stores. A small initial cash balance on Sundays, however, subjects One Stop to the risk of running short of cash one or more times during the day. This forces the store to stop cashing checks. Mr. Flint wants to evaluate the policy of providing each store with an initial balance of $500. Cash balances at the stores will be checked at the end of each hour. If the balance at a store falls to $100 or less, cash may be transferred between stores. The transfer will be made only if one store has $300 or more on hand and will be designed to equalize the balances at the two stores. For example, if store A has $100 and store B has $500, $200 will be transferred from store B to store A. The probabilities for specific cash inflows and outflows are shown in the table. They apply to both stores.

Cash receipts per hour	Probability	Check cashing per hour	Probability
$100	.3	$ 0	.15
200	.4	100	.20
300	.3	200	.35
		300	.20
		400	.10

Simulate Mr. Flint's policy for 4 Sundays. He is interested in estimating the frequency of cash transfers as well as the average cash balance at the end of the day. The stores are open for 10 hours.

Supplementary readings

Eck, R. D. *Operations Research for Business.* Belmont, Calif.: Wadsworth, 1976.

Forrester, J. W. *Industrial Dynamics.* Cambridge, Mass.: M.I.T., 1961.

Hillier, F. S., and G. J. Lieberman. *Introduction to Operations Research.* San Francisco: Holden-Day, 1974.

Meier, R. G., W. T. Newell, and H. L. Pazer. *Simulation in Business and Economics.* Englewood Cliffs, N.J.: Prentice-Hall, 1969.

Naylor, T. H., J. L. Balintfy, D. S. Burdick, and K. Chu. *Computer Simulation Techniques.* New York: Wiley, 1966.

Reitman, J. *Computer Simulation Applications.* New York: Wiley, 1971.

Schmidt, J. W., and R. E. Taylor. *Simulation and Analysis of Industrial Systems.* Homewood, Ill.: Irwin, 1970.

Shamblin, J. E., and G. T. Stevens. *Operations Research: A Fundamental Approach.* New York: McGraw-Hill, 1974.

Shannon, R. E. *Systems Simulation: The Art and Science.* Englewood Cliffs, N.J.: Prentice-Hall, 1975.

Wagner, H. M. *Principles of Management Science.* Englewood Cliffs, N.J.: Prentice-Hall, 1975.

Chapter 12

Markov analysis

Illustrative example: WOODY'S PEST CONTROL

Woody's Pest Control is one of three exterminating firms that have served a Midwestern community for many years. Historically, Woody's has been the largest firm in the area, with 50% of the market. Bluejay River Exterminators serves 30% of the community's customers. The Rain Company is the smallest of the three organizations. In the past, the Rain Company has served 20% of the households who use a pest control service.

The Rain Company was recently purchased by a new management organization. The company has initiated marketing and service policies that seem to be attracting customers away from Woody's Pest Control and Bluejay River Exterminators. Ms. Woodward, owner of Woody's, is concerned about this apparent loss of customers. She employed a marketing research firm to investigate the extent of customer switching and to determine how serious the situation is.

The pest control services offered by the three companies are used on a quarterly basis by 10,000 households. The market research study indicates that during the first quarter (period 1), 5000 households purchased services from Woody's Pest Control, 3000 households used Bluejay River, and 2000 households contracted with the Rain Company. During the following quarter (period 2), Woody's retained 3500 of its customers. Of the remaining 1500 customers, 500 switched to Bluejay River and 1000 began using the services of the Rain Company. Bluejay River retained 2400 of its 3000 customers. The 600 who left were split equally between the other two companies; that is, 300 switched to Woody's and 300 went to the Rain Company. The Rain Company retained 1800 of its customers and lost 100 each to Woody's and Bluejay River.

The market research report presented to Ms. Woodward used Markov analysis to estimate the effect of present trends on future market shares. Ms. Woodward is unhappy with several conclusions reached in the report. She would like to know more about Markov analysis so that she can better understand the reasoning behind the unfavorable report.

Markov analysis is an analytical techique that utilizes the current state and movement of a variable to predict future states and movement of the same variable. The major managerial use of Markov analysis is in the area of marketing. It is used to analyze and predict buyer behavior in terms of market share, brand loyalty, and brand switching. It can also be used for other types of management problems. For example, it has been used to evaluate alternative maintenance policies, to analyze queuing systems, to determine optimal work assignments, and as an aid in inventory analysis.

Predicting market shares with Markov analysis

Ms. Woodward, of Woody's Pest Control, would like to utilize the market-share information gathered from two periods of operation to gain an insight into market-share conditions in future periods. She knows that four factors will interact to determine the distribution of customers in future sales periods. These are:

1. *Present market share*, the percentage of customers purchasing from each of the three companies
2. *Retention rate*, the tendency of a company's present customers to purchase from the same company in the next period
3. *Switching-out rate*, the tendency of a company's present customers to purchase from a different company in the next period
4. *Switching-in rate*, the tendency of a competitor's customers to purchase from our company in the next period

Flow of customers from period to period

The data on flow of customers are best summarized in matrices like those given in Table 12.1 and Table 12.2. Table 12.1 gives the flow of customers among firms from one period to a succeeding period. For convenience, we will let Woody's Pest Control be firm A, Bluejay River be firm B, and the Rain Company be firm C. *The rows of this matrix contain the following information:*

Row 1 indicates that of Woody's 5000 period 1 customers, 3500 remained with Woody in period 2; 500 switched to firm B (Bluejay River); and 1000 switched to firm C (the Rain Company).

Table 12.1 *Flow of customers in the Woody's Pest Control example*

| Firm | Period 1 customers | Supplying firm in period 2 | | |
		A	B	C
A	5000	3500	500	1000
B	3000	300	2400	300
C	2000	100	100	1800
Period 2 customers		3900	3000	3100

Table 12.2 *Matrix of transition probabilities for the Woody's Pest Control example*

	Retention and loss		
Firm	A	B	C
A	3500/5000 = .700	500/5000 = .100	1000/5000 = .200
B	300/3000 = .100	2400/3000 = .800	300/3000 = .100
C	100/2000 = .050	100/2000 = .050	1800/2000 = .900

Row 2 indicates that firm B, Bluejay River, retained 2400 of its original 3000 customers. The company lost 300 customers to firm A and 300 customers to firm B.

Row 3 indicates that firm C, the Rain Company, retained 1800 of its 2000 customers. The company lost 100 customers to firm A and 100 customers to firm B.

The columns of Table 12.1 supply the following information:

Column 1 indicates that firm A retained 3500 of its customers from the previous quarter. It attracted 300 new customers from firm B and 100 new customers from firm C. It therefore has 3900 customers in period 2, for a net loss of 1100 customers.

Column 2 indicates that firm B retained 2400 of its original customers. It gained 500 new customers from firm A and 100 new customers from firm B. Thus, there was no net gain or loss of customers for firm B.

Column 3 indicates that firm C has a net gain of 1100 customers. It gained 1000 new customers from firm A and 300 new customers from firm B. The company retained 1800 of its original 2000 customers.

Matrix of transition probabilities

The information given in Table 12.1 is more useful when placed into a matrix of *transition probabilities,* as shown in Table 12.2. This table is obtained by dividing the number of customers of a particular firm in one period by the number of customers in the preceding period. A given *row* in this table indicates the percentage of customers that a firm will retain from period to period and the percentage of customers that will be lost to competing firms. Each *column* indicates the percentage of customers a particular firm will retain and the percentage of a competitor's customers that the firm will gain in the subsequent period. In summary, *rows represent retention and loss; columns represent retention and gain.*

The matrix of transition probabilities also represents the likelihood or probability that a randomly selected customer will be loyal to a particular firm from period to period. For example, if we randomly select one of Woody's customers, there is a 70% chance that this customer will remain with Woody's in the subsequent period, a 10% chance that the household will switch to Bluejay River, and a 20% chance that the customer will switch to the Rain Company.

Calculating market shares for period 2

In the example of Woody's Pest Control Service, firm A had 5000 customers, or 50% of the market, in the initial period. Firm B had 30% of the market, and firm C had 20% of the market. We will use the matrix of transition probabilities to predict market share in the second period. We do this by multiplying the matrix of market shares by the matrix of transition probabilities.

$$
\begin{array}{c}
\text{Market share in period 1} \\
[.500 \quad .300 \quad .200]
\end{array}
\times
\begin{array}{c}
\text{Matrix of} \\
\text{transition} \\
\text{probabilities} \\
\begin{bmatrix}
.700 & .100 & .200 \\
.100 & .800 & .100 \\
.050 & .050 & .900
\end{bmatrix}
\end{array}
=
\begin{array}{c}
\text{Market share in period 2} \\
[.390 \quad .300 \quad .310]
\end{array}
$$

The explanation of this multiplication follows.

1. We obtain the *market share for firm A in period 2* by multiplying the market-share data for period 1 by column 1 in the matrix of transition probabilities. The following is an item-by-item explanation.

A's ability to retain its customers, multiplied by A's share of the market	$.700 \times .500 = .350$
A's ability to acquire customers from B, multiplied by B's share of the market	$.100 \times .300 = .030$
A's ability to acquire customers from C, multiplied by C's share of the market	$.050 \times .200 = \underline{.010}$
A's share of the market in period 2	$= .390$

2. We obtain the *market share for firm B in period 2* by multiplying the market-share data for period 1 by column 2 in the transition matrix. The following is an item-by-item explanation.

B's ability to acquire customers from A, multiplied by A's share of the market	$.100 \times .500 = .050$
B's ability to retain its customers, multiplied by B's share of the market	$.800 \times .300 = .240$
B's ability to acquire customers from C, multiplied by C's share of the market	$.050 \times .200 = \underline{.010}$
B's share of the market in period 2	$= .300$

3. We obtain the *market share for firm C in period* 2 by multiplying the market-share data for period 1 by column 3 in the transition matrix. Thus,

C's ability to acquire customers from A, multiplied by A's share of the market	$.200 \times .500 = .100$
C's ability to acquire customers from B, multiplied by B's share of the market	$.100 \times .300 = .030$
C's ability to retain its customers, multiplied by C's share of the market	$.900 \times .200 = \underline{.180}$
C's share of the market in period 2	$= .310$

Market shares in subsequent periods

The calculations just illustrated tell us what we already knew. In period 2, Woody's has 39% of the market, Bluejay River has 30% of the market, and the Rain Company has 31% of the market. We are interested in using the data we have collected to predict market shares for future periods.

We can obtain the market shares for each firm in the next quarter (period 3) by multiplying the market shares in period 2 by the matrix of transition probabilities. In period 2, the market shares for firms A, B, and C are .390, .300, and .310 respectively. Multiplying these market shares by the transition matrix yields new market shares of .319, .294, and .387 for period 3. These calculations are as follows:

$$
\begin{array}{c}
\text{Market share in period 2} \\
[.390 \quad .300 \quad .310]
\end{array}
\times
\begin{array}{c}
\text{Matrix of} \\
\text{transition} \\
\text{probabilities} \\
\begin{bmatrix} .700 & .100 & .200 \\ .100 & .800 & .100 \\ .050 & .050 & .900 \end{bmatrix}
\end{array}
=
\begin{array}{c}
\text{Market share in period 3} \\
[.319 \quad .294 \quad .387]
\end{array}
$$

For Firm A:	$(.700 \times .390) + (.100 \times .300) + (.050 \times .310) =$	$.319$
For Firm B:	$(.100 \times .390) + (.800 \times .300) + (.050 \times .310) =$	$.294$
For Firm C:	$(.200 \times .390) + (.100 \times .300) + (.900 \times .310) =$	$\underline{.387}$
		1.000

These data indicate that if present trends continue, Woody's will have 31.9% of the market in period 3, Bluejay River will have 29.4% of the market, and the Rain Company will have a market share of 38.7%. These market-share data and the matrix of transition probabilities can

Table 12.3 *Market-share data for periods 1–10 in the Woody's Pest Control example*

Period	Market share (%)		
	Firm A	*Firm* B	*Firm* C
1	50.0	30.0	20.0
2	39.0	30.0	31.0
3	31.9	29.4	38.7
4	27.2	28.6	44.2
5	24.1	27.9	48.0
6	22.1	27.1	50.8
7	20.7	26.4	52.9
8	19.8	25.8	54.4
9	19.1	25.4	55.5
10	18.7	25.0	56.3

be used to estimate the relative market shares in the following period. The calculations are as follows:

Market share in period 3 $\times$ Matrix of transition probabilities $=$ Market share in period 4

$$[.319 \quad .294 \quad .387] \times \begin{bmatrix} .700 & .100 & .200 \\ .100 & .800 & .100 \\ .050 & .050 & .900 \end{bmatrix} = [.272 \quad .286 \quad .442]$$

For Firm A: $(.700 \times .319) + (.100 \times .294) + (.050 \times .387) = .272$

For Firm B: $(.100 \times .319) + (.800 \times .294) + (.050 \times .387) = .286$

For Firm C: $(.200 \times .319) + (.100 \times .294) + (.900 \times .387) = .442$

Obviously, this process can be continued to find relative market shares in any future period.[1] The market-share data for periods 1–10 are given in Table 12.3. These data should concern Ms. Woodward, because they predict a steady decline in market share for Woody's Pest Control.

[1]Readers familiar with matrix algebra know that the market-share data for any period n can be determined by the following matrix equation:

Market share in period 1 $\times$ Matrix of transition probabilities $=$ Market share in period n

$$[.500 \quad .300 \quad .200] \times \begin{bmatrix} .700 & .100 & .200 \\ .100 & .800 & .100 \\ .050 & .050 & .900 \end{bmatrix}^n = [S_1 \quad S_2 \quad S_3]$$

In period 10, for example, it is estimated that Woody's share of the market will decline to 18.7% if present trends continue. In the same period, Bluejay River will have 25% of the market share, and the Rain Company will have 56.3%.

Sample problem 12.1   *TOM, DICK, AND HARRY*

Tom, Dick, and Harry rent automobile trailers. Their business establishments are located in different parts of the city. Trailers are generally rented early in the morning and returned late the same day. Tom, Dick, and Harry have an agreement that a trailer may be returned to any of their establishments, regardless of where the trailer was rented. On a particular day, Tom had 30% of the trailers, Dick had 50% of the trailers, and Harry had 20%. Past analysis indicates that 60% of Tom's customers return their trailers to him, while 10% go to Dick and 30% go to Harry. Dick retains 80% of his trailers, while losing 10% to Tom and 10% to Harry. Of those individuals who rent from Harry, 50% return their trailers to him, 30% return their trailers to Tom, and 20% return their trailers to Dick. Develop a matrix of transition probabilities. Assume that these probabilities will remain constant. Determine the percentage of trailers at the three locations for the next two days.

SOLUTION
For day 2:

$$[.300 \quad .500 \quad .200] \quad \times \quad \begin{bmatrix} .6 & .1 & .3 \\ .1 & .8 & .1 \\ .3 & .2 & .5 \end{bmatrix} \quad = \quad [.290 \quad .470 \quad .240]$$

For Tom: .300(.6) + .500(.1) + .200(.3) = .290
For Dick: .300(.1) + .500(.8) + .200(.2) = .470
For Harry: .300(.3) + .500(.1) + .200(.5) = .240

For day 3, the market shares are .293, .453, and .254.

Equilibrium conditions

From Table 12.3, we can see that Woody's (firm A's) share of the market declines from period to period, while the Rain Company's share steadily increases. From a managerial viewpoint, we would like to know if these changes will continue or if an equilibrium condition will be reached. An equilibrium condition, or a *steady-state condition*, is reached when the exchange of customers is such that the relative market shares do not change from period to period. If such a condition exists, it would be helpful to know the market shares of each firm at equilibrium.

Determining market shares at equilibrium

Figure 12.1 is a graphical representation of Woody's Pest Control's share of the market. The *change* in market share becomes smaller with each succeeding period. Eventually (theoretically after an infinite number of periods), this change will be so small that it can be considered to be zero. The same phenomenon will occur for the market shares of the other two companies. Thus, at equilibrium, market shares will not change from period to period.

At equilibrium, we can multiply the market-share matrix in one period by the matrix of transition probabilities and obtain the exact same market-share matrix for the following period. In the Woody's Pest Control example, we will let A, B, and C represent the market shares of firms A, B, and C respectively. Thus, at equilibrium, the following relationship must be true.

$$\underset{\substack{\text{Market share in}\\ \text{period } n}}{[A \quad B \quad C]} \times \underset{\substack{\text{Matrix of}\\ \text{transition}\\ \text{probabilities}}}{\begin{bmatrix} .700 & .100 & .200 \\ .100 & .800 & .100 \\ .050 & .050 & .900 \end{bmatrix}} = \underset{\substack{\text{Market share in}\\ \text{period } (n+1)}}{[A \quad B \quad C]}$$

In some future period (period $n + 1$), firm A's market share will be equal to 70% of its market share in the preceding period (period n) plus 10% of firm B's market share in the preceding period plus 5% of firm C's market share in the preceding period. Thus, at equilibrium,

$$A = .700A + .100B + .050C$$

The same relationships hold for firms B and C.

$$B = .100A + .800B + .050C$$
$$C = .200A + .100B + .900C$$

The sum of the market shares for the three firms must equal 1.0. Thus, the following equation must also be true.

$$A + B + C = 1.0$$

We now have four equations and only three unknowns. We can use three of these equations to solve for the equilibrium values of A, B, and C. In the solution process, we must use the last equation ($A + B + C = 1.0$) and any two of the other three. We cannot drop the last equation, because the solution $A = B = C = 0$ satisfies the first three equations

Figure 12.1 *Market share for Woody's Pest Control in periods 1 through 10*

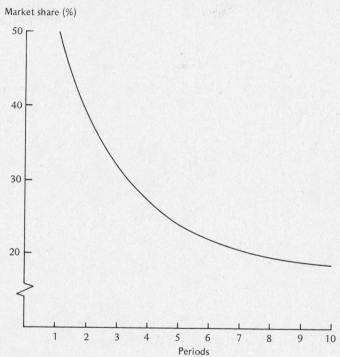

Market share (%)

Periods

but is not a feasible solution to our problem. For illustrative purposes, let us drop the first equation and use the following three relationships:

$$B = .100A + .800B + .050C$$
$$C = .200A + .100B + .900C$$
$$A + B + C = 1$$

These three equations can be rewritten as follows:

$$.100A - .200B + .050C = 0 \qquad [1]$$
$$.200A + .100B - .100C = 0 \qquad [2]$$
$$1.000A + 1.000B + 1.000C = 1 \qquad [3]$$

To solve them simultaneously, we first multiply equation 1 by −10 and add it to equation 3. This will give us a new equation that does not contain the variable A.

$$-A + 2B - 0.5C = 0$$
$$\underline{A + B + C = 1}$$
$$3B + 0.5C = 1 \qquad [4]$$

Then we obtain a similar result by multiplying equation 2 by -5.0 and adding it to equation 3.

$$-A - 0.5B + 0.5C = 0$$
$$\underline{A + \quad B + \quad C = 1}$$
$$0.5B + 1.5C = 1 \quad [5]$$

We now solve equations 4 and 5 to obtain the equilibrium values of B and C. This is accomplished by multiplying equation 4 by -3 and adding it to equation 5.

$$-9.0B - 1.5C = -3$$
$$\underline{.5B + 1.5C = \quad 1}$$
$$-8.5B \qquad = -2$$

Thus,

$$B = .2353$$

We now substitute the computed value of B into equation 4 to determine the value of C.

$$3(.2353) + 0.5C = 1$$
$$0.5C = .2941$$
$$C = .5882$$

And we substitute these values of B and C into equation 3 to solve for the equilibrium value of A.

$$A + B + C = 1$$
$$A = 1 - B - C$$
$$A = 1 - .2353 - .5882 = .1765$$

These calculations tell us that if the transition probabilities remain constant, equilibrium will be reached when firm A, Woody's Pest Control, has 17.65% of the market, Bluejay River has a market share of 23.53%, and the Rain Company's share of the market is 58.82%. In future periods, the market share for the three firms will remain constant from period to period, which can be tested by multiplying these market shares by the matrix of transition probabilities.[2]

Market share in period n

Matrix of transition probabilities

Market share in period $(n + 1)$

$$[.1765 \quad .2353 \quad .5882] \times \begin{bmatrix} .700 & .100 & .200 \\ .100 & .800 & .100 \\ .050 & .050 & .900 \end{bmatrix} = [.1765 \quad .2353 \quad .5882]$$

[2]In testing for equilibrium, be sure to make allowance for rounding errors.

Sample problem 12.2 TOM, DICK, AND HARRY (Continued)

Consider the Tom, Dick, and Harry problem given in Sample Problem 12.1. Set up four equations that could be used to determine equilibrium conditions. Select three equations and solve them simultaneously to determine the equilibrium market share for each.

SOLUTION

$$T = .6T + .1D + .3H$$
$$D = .1T + .8D + .2H$$
$$H = .3T + .1D + .5H$$
$$1 = T + D + H$$

Equilibrium market shares: Tom = .308, Dick = .423, and Harry = .269

(*Note:* The last equation must be used in the solution process. It can be combined with any two of the first three equations.)

Equilibrium conditions with zero market shares

When equilibrium was reached in the foregoing example, all firms shared in the total market. In other situations, one or more of the competitors may be driven completely out of the market. Consider the following matrix of transition probabilities.

	A	B	C
A	.700	.300	.000
B	.100	.900	.000
C	.100	.100	.800

In this example, firm A retains 70% of its customers and loses 30% to firm B. Firm B retains 90% of its customers and loses 10% to firm A. Firm C retains 80% of its customers and loses 10% to both A and B. The significant point is that C loses customers to both A and B but never gains any customers in return. Obviously, firm C must eventually lose all of its customers, and the entire market will be shared by A and B. Using the calculations we have illustrated, we can show that, at equilibrium, firm A will have 25% of the market and firm B will have a market share of 75%.

The following matrix of transition probabilities describes a situation wherein one firm would drive all other firms out of the market.

	A	B	C
A	1.00	.000	.000
B	.100	.700	.200
C	.100	.100	.800

In this example, A gains customers from both B and C but never loses a customer to either competitor. Obviously, if this situation continues, firm A will eventually capture 100% of the market.

Relationship of market shares and equilibrium conditions

To calculate equilibrium market conditions, we used only the matrix of transition probabilities and not the present, or initial, state of the market. We did not need initial market shares, because steady-state market conditions are independent of the initial market shares held by competing firms. In Markov analysis, this will always be true unless a particular market share is zero.

Applications to marketing strategy

In the example of Woody's Pest Control, Markov analysis indicated that Woody's share of the market will gradually decline from 50% of the market to an equilibrium or steady-state share of approximately 18% of the market. This, of course, is based on the assumption that transition probabilities remain constant from period to period.

This trend toward a low market share should be of great concern to Ms. Woodward. She would like to develop a marketing strategy that would reverse the trend and allow her company to maintain its favorable market position. The following discussion indicates how Markov analysis can be used to assist managers in evaluating various marketing strategies.

Retention strategy

The first alternative strategy that Ms. Woodward might employ is to attempt to retain a larger percentage of her own customers. This *retention strategy* might be implemented by providing better service or by discounting the price for customers who purchase in two successive periods. Assume that Woody's is able to raise its retention rate from 70% to 85% by reducing the loss of customers to firm C, the Rain Company. The new matrix of transition probabilities is as follows:

$$
\begin{array}{c c}
 & \begin{array}{ccc} A & B & C \end{array} \\
\begin{array}{c} A \\ B \\ C \end{array} &
\left[\begin{array}{ccc}
.850 & .100 & .050 \\
.100 & .800 & .100 \\
.050 & .050 & .900
\end{array} \right]
\end{array}
$$

At the new equilibrium, firm A has a market share of 31.6%, B has a market share of 26.3%, and C's market share is 42.1%. This strategy indicates a definite improvement for Woody's. It cannot be obtained without cost, however, and Ms. Woodward should analyze other possible strategies before implementing it.

Acquisitions strategy

A second possible strategy is for Woody's Pest Control to concentrate on taking customers away from the other two firms. This *acquisitions strategy* might be implemented by direct mail or other forms of advertising. Suppose that in a given period, Woody's (firm A) can obtain 15% of the customers who were purchasing from the other two firms in the preceding period. The new matrix of transition probabilities is as follows:

$$
\begin{array}{c}
 \\
A \\
B \\
C
\end{array}
\begin{array}{ccc}
A & B & C \\
\begin{bmatrix}
.700 & .100 & .200 \\
.150 & .750 & .100 \\
.150 & .050 & .800
\end{bmatrix}
\end{array}
$$

At equilibrium, firm A will have a market share of 33.3%, and the market shares for B and C will be 22.2% and 44.5% respectively.

The two alternative strategies result in market shares for Woody's Pest Control that are roughly equivalent: 31.6% for the retention strategy and 33.3% for the acquisitions strategy. In this case, the cost of implementing the two strategies will probably be the deciding factor. If there were major differences in the resulting market shares, it would be necessary to compare the benefits of the anticipated market shares with the relative costs of the strategies involved.

Assumptions underlying Markov analysis

In the preceding sections, we have made a number of assumptions about market conditions and the behavior of the competing firms. A major assumption we have not yet discussed is the assumption that we have been dealing with a first-order Markov process. After discussing this subject, we will review the assumptions underlying Markov processes.

First-order and higher-order Markov processes

Our analysis in this chapter has been concerned with what is known as a first-order Markov process. A *first-order process* assumes that the probability of the next event depends only on the outcome of the previous event. A *second-order Markov process* assumes that the probability of the next event depends on the two previous outcomes. Likewise, a *third-order process* assumes that an event, such as buyer behavior, depends on experience in the past three buying periods.

If we analyze Woody's Pest Control as a first-order process, we are assuming that a particular customer's probability of using an exterminator in one period depends only on the customer's experience during the previous period. There are many real examples wherein a consumer's behavior is not solely affected by the previous period. Buyer behavior is often at least partially related to a consumer's entire purchasing history, or at least two or three purchasing periods. These situations can be studied more realistically with second- or third-order processes.

We will limit ourselves to the study of first-order Markov processes for two reasons. First, studies have indicated that useful analysis can be made with first-order processes. This is particularly true if the matrix of transition probabilities tends to remain stable over time. Second, the mathematics involved in higher-order processes is burdensome and difficult.

Summary of assumptions

At this point, we should specify the assumptions we have made in this chapter about Markov analysis.

1. We have employed only first-order Markov models.
2. The matrix of transition probabilities remained constant from period to period.
3. The total market size remained constant from period to period.
4. Customers purchased at regular time intervals and purchased equal quantities on each buying occasion.
5. The number of competitors in the market remained constant. No new sellers entered into competition and none went out of business.
6. The buying population was relatively homogeneous so that the matrix of transition probabilities applied to all customers.

Mathematicians and management scientists have found ways to partially overcome the limitations imposed by these assumptions. Such improvements allow for more realistic use of Markov analysis. At the same time, however, they add greatly to the mathematical complexity and computational burden required.

Other uses of Markov analysis

Our discussion of Markov analysis has been concerned with problems in marketing, particularly in analyzing market shares of competing firms. Although this is the primary area of application of Markov analysis, its use is not limited to marketing. The following sections illustrate two additional ways in which Markov processes can be used in managerial analysis.

Queuing problems as Markov processes

Some queuing or waiting-line problems can be analyzed as Markov processes. Consider the Hunt Company, which operates a machine repair facility at one of its manufacturing locations. If a machine in the plant is operating ineffectively, it is brought to the repair facility for maintenance. Data on arrivals at the facility have been collected and are presented in Table 12.4. An analysis of service times indicates that the probability of a service completion during any one-hour period is .7, given that there is a unit to be serviced. There is no possibility of more than one service completion in any one-hour period.

It is assumed that arrivals occur at the beginning of a one-hour period and that service completions occur at the end of a one-hour period. If a queue was previously empty, service can be completed during the same period in which that unit arrived. The maximum queue length is two. Beyond this point, service is refused and machines are returned to their original location.

To formulate this as a Markov process, we will define a *state* as the number of units in the system in any given period. This includes the unit being served as well as those waiting in line. Thus, the maximum state of this system is 3: 1 unit being served and 2 waiting in line. Each element in the transition matrix represents the probability of going from a given state in one period to a given state in the next period. The calculations to determine the value of these elements are given in Table 12.5. The transition matrix is given in Table 12.6.

A sample calculation should help us better understand Tables 12.5 and 12.6. Consider the element T_{12}, which represents the probability of going from a state of 1 unit in the system to a state of 2 units in the system. This can occur in two ways. First, we can have 1 arrival and no service completions or departures $(1 + 1 - 0 = 2)$. We obtain the probability of this by multiplying the probability of 1 arrival (.2) by the probability of no service completion $(1 - .7 = .3)$. Thus, the probability of 1 arrival and no completion is .06.

Table 12.4 *Arrivals at a machine repair facility*

Number of arrivals in a one-hour period	Probability of occurrence
0	.6
1	.2
2	.2

Table 12.5 *Determining the value of the elements in a transition matrix for a queuing problem*

Element	Initial state	Arrivals	Services	Event	Element
		Event description		Probabilities	
T_{00}	0	0	0	.6(1) = .60	
	0	1	1	.2(.7) = .14	
				.74	.74
T_{01}	0	1	0	.2(.3) = .06	
		2	1	.2(.7) = .14	
				.20	.20
T_{02}	0	2	0	.2(.3) = .06	.06
T_{03}	0	not possible			.00
T_{10}	1	0	1	.6(.7) = .42	.42
T_{11}	1	0	0	.6(.3) = .18	
	1	1	1	.2(.7) = .14	
				.32	.32
T_{12}	1	1	0	.2(.3) = .06	
	1	2	1	.2(.7) = .14	
				.20	.20
T_{13}	1	2	0	.2(.3) = .06	.06
T_{20}	2	not possible			.00
T_{21}	2	0	1	.6(.7) = .42	.42
T_{22}	2	0	0	.6(.3) = .18	
	2	1, 2*	1	.4(.7) = .28	
				.46	.46
T_{23}	2	1, 2*	0	.4(.3) = .12	.12
T_{30}	3	not possible			.00
T_{31}	3	not possible			.00
T_{32}	3	0, 1, 2*	1	1(.7) = .7	.70
T_{33}	3	0, 1, 2*	0	1(.3) = .3	.30

*Queue capacity is 3. If additional units arrive, they are turned away.

Table 12.6 *Matrix of transition probabilities for a queuing problem*

State in period n	0	1	2	3
	State in period $(n + 1)$			
0	.74	.20	.06	.00
1	.42	.32	.20	.06
2	.00	.42	.46	.12
3	.00	.00	.70	.30

Alternatively, we can move from state 1 to state 2 by having 2 arrivals and 1 service completion $(1 + 2 - 1 = 2)$. The probability of this is .14 and is obtained by multiplying the probability of 2 arrivals (.2) by the probability of 1 departure (.7). T_{12}, the probability of moving from state 1 to state 2, is .20 (that is, $.06 + .14 = .20$).

The results of these calculations are given in Table 12.6. For example, the .42 in row 1, column 0 indicates that if the system is in state 1 in one period, the probability of it being in state 0 in the succeeding period is .42. The two elements in row 3 with a value of .00 indicate that it is impossible to move from state 3 to either state 0 or state 1. Likewise, the system cannot move from state 0 to state 3 or from state 2 to state 0.

Let P_0, P_1, P_2, and P_3 be the respective probabilities of 0, 1, 2, or 3 units being in the system. At equilibrium, the following relationship must be true.

$$[P_0 \quad P_1 \quad P_2 \quad P_3] \quad \times \quad \begin{bmatrix} .74 & .20 & .06 & .00 \\ .42 & .32 & .20 & .06 \\ .00 & .42 & .46 & .12 \\ .00 & .00 & .70 & .30 \end{bmatrix} = [P_0 \quad P_1 \quad P_2 \quad P_3]$$

The equilibrium values of P_0, P_1, P_2, and P_3 are .437, .270, .230, and .063 respectively. Thus, the likelihood of the service system being empty (no unit being served and no unit in the system) is .437. The probability of 1 unit being served but none in line is .270. The probability of 1 unit being served and one in line is .230. The probability of 3 units in the system is .063. The expected number of units in the system, including the unit being served, is

$$0(.437) + 1(.270) + 2(.230) + 3(.063) = .919$$

Markov processes should not replace the methods we discussed in Chapter 10 as the primary means of analyzing queuing problems. Instead, this technique should be considered as an additional tool of managerial analysis. Analyzing a queue as a Markov process may have advantages, particularly if the arrival or service distribution is unusual.

Optimal maintenance policies

Consider a manufacturing establishment that makes a quarterly inspection of its large chemical-process pumps. At each inspection, the pumps are classified into one of five states, depending on the extent of corrosion in the pump housing. The five states are as follows:

State 1: Excellent condition, like new
State 2: Good condition, little corrosion
State 3: Satisfactory condition, mild corrosion
State 4: Usable condition, extensive corrosion
State 5: Unusable condition

At present, the company utilizes a "one-state" maintenance policy, so named because one state, state 5, is designated as a repair state and all pumps found to be in this state are repaired. The cost of this repair is $500 per pump. The company is considering two alternative policies. It hopes to find a policy that will reduce total cost of pump repairs. The first policy, a two-state policy, designates both state 4 and state 5 as repair states. The second policy, a three-state policy, calls for repair of any pump that is in state 3, state 4, or state 5. The estimated average cost of repair is $200 for pumps in state 3 and $250 for pumps in state 4. It will still cost $500 to repair any pump that is in state 5.

Past experience indicates that a pump in state 1 in a given inspection period has a .6 probability of being in state 2, a .2 probability of being in state 3, a .1 probability of being in state 4, and a .1 probability of being in state 5 in the next inspection period. For a pump in state 2, the probability of remaining in state 2 during the next period is .3. The probabilities of going to states 3, 4, and 5 are .4, .2, and .1 respectively.

If a pump is in state 3 in one quarter, the probability of it remaining in that state for one quarter is .4. The probabilities of it moving to states 4 and 5 are .4 and .2 respectively. Pumps in state 4 in one quarter have a .5 probability of remaining in that state and a .5 probability of advancing to state 5. Since all pumps in state 5 are repaired, they will all be in state 1 in the succeeding quarter.

Our first step should be to determine the expected quarterly repair cost of the present maintenance policy. We accomplish this by determining, at equilibrium, the probability that a pump will need repair and multiplying that probability by the cost of repair. Then we can compare the cost of the present repair policy with the expected cost of the two-state and three-state policies.

The matrix of transition probabilities is shown in Table 12.7. Equilibrium conditions can be obtained by solving the following matrix equation:

$$[S_1 \ S_2 \ S_3 \ S_4 \ S_5] \times \begin{bmatrix} 0 & .6 & .2 & .1 & .1 \\ 0 & .3 & .4 & .2 & .1 \\ 0 & 0 & .4 & .4 & .2 \\ 0 & 0 & 0 & .5 & .5 \\ 1 & 0 & 0 & 0 & 0 \end{bmatrix} = [S_1 \ S_2 \ S_3 \ S_4 \ S_5]$$

The resulting equilibrium conditions are $S_1 = .199$, $S_2 = .170$, $S_3 = .180$, $S_4 = .252$, and $S_5 = .199$.

The present maintenance policy is a one-state policy, because only pumps in state 5 are repaired. The cost of this repair is $500. Thus, the expected maintenance cost per pump per period for a one-state policy (EMC_1) is

$$EMC_1 = \$500(.199) = \$99.50$$

Table 12.7 *Probability of moving among repair states in a maintenance problem*

State in period n	State in period (n + 1)				
	1	2	3	4	5
1	0	.6	.2	.1	.1
2	0	.3	.4	.2	.1
3	0	0	.4	.4	.2
4	0	0	0	.5	.5
5	1	0	0	0	0

We shall now investigate the expected cost of a two-state maintenance policy. The new matrix of transition probabilities is as follows:

$$\begin{array}{c c c c c c} & S_1 & S_2 & S_3 & S_4 & S_5 \\ S_1 & \begin{bmatrix} 0 & .6 & .2 & .1 & .1 \\ S_2 & 0 & .3 & .4 & .2 & .1 \\ S_3 & 0 & 0 & .4 & .4 & .2 \\ S_4 & 1 & 0 & 0 & 0 & 0 \\ S_5 & 1 & 0 & 0 & 0 & 0 \end{bmatrix} \end{array}$$

Row 4 in this matrix is different from Table 12.7, because pumps in
state 4 and state 5 are now repaired, and all of these pumps will be in
state 1 at the next inspection period. The new equilibrium conditions
are $S_1 = .266$, $S_2 = .228$, $S_3 = .241$, $S_4 = .168$, and $S_5 = .097$.

In the two-state policy, pumps in both state 4 and state 5 are repaired
at costs of $250 and $500 respectively. The expected maintenance cost
(EMC$_2$) of this policy is

$$\text{EMC}_2 = \$250(.168) + \$500(.097) = \$90.50$$

The procedure for evaluating the three-state policy is identical. The
new matrix of transition probabilities is as follows:

$$\begin{array}{c c c c c c} & S_1 & S_2 & S_3 & S_4 & S_5 \\ S_1 & \begin{bmatrix} 0 & .6 & .2 & .1 & .1 \\ S_2 & 0 & .3 & .4 & .2 & .1 \\ S_3 & 1 & 0 & 0 & 0 & 0 \\ S_4 & 1 & 0 & 0 & 0 & 0 \\ S_5 & 1 & 0 & 0 & 0 & 0 \end{bmatrix} \end{array}$$

The matrix is different, because now all pumps in states 3, 4, and 5 are
repaired. These pumps will be in state 1 during the next quarter. The
new equilibrium conditions are $S_1 = .350$, $S_2 = .300$, $S_3 = .190$, $S_4 =
.095$, and $S_5 = .065$.

Pumps in states 3, 4, and 5 are now repaired at costs of $200, $250, and $500. The expected maintenance cost (EMC_3) of this three-stage policy is

$$EMC_3 = \$200(.190) + \$250(.095) + \$500(.065) = \$94.25$$

The EMC's of the three alternative policies are $99.50, $90.50, and $94.25. It appears that the two-state policy is the minimum-cost maintenance policy. In the two-state policy, the probability of a pump having to be repaired is .265, that is (.168 + .097). This is greater than the .199 probability of repair for the one-stage policy. The cost savings result from the fact that many pumps are repaired at the lower cost of $250, compared to the state 5 repair cost of $500.

Sample problem 12.3   RALPH'S HOBBY SHOP

Ralph Walter operates a small hobby shop in his basement and is open for business only on Saturdays. Mr. Walter has the following reorder policy for one infrequently purchased item: "If ending inventory is 0 or 1, order 3 units. If ending inventory exceeds 1 unit, do not reorder." Items ordered at the close of business on Saturday will be ready for sale on the following Saturday. This policy ensures that beginning inventory will be either 2, 3, or 4 units.

The probabilities of daily demands of 0, 1, 2, and 3 units are .4, .3, .2, and .1 respectively. Determine the matrix of transition probabilities that shows the probability of going from opening inventory states in one week to corresponding states in the following week. For equilibrium conditions, determine the probabilities of beginning the day with 2, 3, and 4 units in stock.

SOLUTION

The transition matrix is as follows:

$$
\begin{array}{c}
\quad\quad 2 \quad\ 3 \quad\ 4 \\
\begin{array}{c} 2 \\ 3 \\ 4 \end{array}
\left[
\begin{array}{ccc}
.4 & .3 & .3 \\
.3 & .5 & .2 \\
.2 & .3 & .5
\end{array}
\right]
\end{array}
$$

The calculations to determine the probabilities of going from a beginning inventory of 3 in one week to beginning inventories of 2, 3, and 4 in the next week are given in the following table.

Demand	Ending inventory	Units ordered	Beginning inventory, week $(n + 1)$	Probability
0	3	0	3	.4
1	2	0	2	.3
2	1	3	4	.2
3	0	3	3	.1

The equilibrium probabilities are $P_2 = .297$, $P_3 = .375$, and $P_4 = .328$.

Alternative methods of analysis

In this section, we have illustrated how Markov analysis can be used to analyze a queuing problem or a maintenance (replacement) problem. We also indicated that it has other uses, such as inventory analysis. Each of these topics — replacement, inventory, and queuing analysis — are covered in other chapters of the book. A particular problem can often be analyzed with several different management science techniques. One management science tool may be superior to another in some cases, and the analyst must choose the most appropriate quantitative technique. And for some problems, two quantitative methods may provide more and better information than either one could if it were used alone.

Problems and exercises

1. Explain the following terms:

market share	retention strategy
retention rate	acquisitions strategy
switching-in rate	first-order process
transition probabilities	second-order process
steady state	third-order process
equilibrium	queue

INSTRUCTIONS FOR PROBLEMS 2–5

In each problem, a matrix of current market shares and a matrix of transition probabilities are given. Determine the market shares for the next two periods. In each problem, assume a first-order Markov process.

2.
A	B	C
(.4	.2	.4)

	A	B	C
A	.8	.1	.1
B	.1	.7	.2
C	.2	.2	.6

3.
A	B	C
(.3	.3	.4)

	A	B	C
A	.5	.3	.2
B	.1	.5	.4
C	.2	.2	.6

4.
A	B
(.4	.6)

	A	B
A	.5	.5
B	.3	.7

5.
A	B	C	D
(.2	.2	.3	.3)

	A	B	C	D
A	.7	.1	.1	.1
B	.1	.6	.2	.1
C	.1	.1	.6	.2
D	.1	.1	.2	.6

INSTRUCTIONS FOR PROBLEMS 6–9

In each problem, a matrix of transition probabilities is given. Determine the relative market shares at equilibrium or steady-state conditions. Check your results by multiplying the steady-state market shares by the transition matrix. Assume that all problems are first-order Markov processes.

6.

	A	B	C
A	.2	.3	.5
B	.3	.3	.4
C	.2	.4	.4

7.

	S_1	S_2	S_3
S_1	.75	.15	.10
S_2	.15	.70	.15
S_3	.15	.25	.60

8.

	S_1	S_2
S_1	.8	.2
S_2	.1	.9

9.

	S_1	S_2
S_1	.75	.25
S_2	.40	.60

INSTRUCTIONS FOR PROBLEMS 10–13

In each problem, a matrix of transition probabilities for a first-order Markov process is given. When equilibrium is reached, how many firms will have market shares greater than zero? (*Note:* Do not solve for actual steady-state market shares.)

10.

	A	B	C
A	.90	.10	.00
B	.00	.80	.20
C	.30	.00	.70

11.

	A	B	C
A	.75	.25	.00
B	.15	.85	.00
C	.35	.00	.65

12.

	A	B	C
A	.7	.3	.0
B	0.0	1.0	.0
C	.2	.2	.6

13.

	A	B
A	1.0	0
B	0	1.0

INSTRUCTIONS FOR PROBLEMS 14–24

Assume that the following problems can be characterized by a first-order Markov process.

14. Three service stations share a local market in which customers make weekly purchases. In week 1, stations A and B each had 40% of the market, while station C had 20% of the market. A market research firm has discovered the following weekly changes in purchasing habits. Station A retains 60% of its customers and loses 20% to B and 20% to C. Station B retains 50% of its customers and loses 20% to station A and 30% to station C. Station C retains 70% of its customers and loses 20% to B and 10% to A. What will each firm's share of the market be during the second week? What will the market shares be at equilibrium?

15. In the month of March, the Alpha, Beta, and Gamma Companies shared equally in a local market. From month to month, Alpha retains 60% of its

own customers, gains 15% of Beta's customers, and gains 30% of Gamma's customers. The Beta Company retains 70% of its own customers, gains 10% of Alpha's customers, and gains 20% of Gamma's customers. The Gamma Company retains 50% of its own customers, gains 30% of Alpha's customers, and gains 15% of Beta's customers. Determine market shares for the next month and for the time when steady-state conditions are reached.

16. Two cafeterias share a lunchtime business in an urban area. On Monday, cafeteria A had 60% of the business and cafeteria B had 40% of the business. Past research has shown that 50% of the customers who eat in cafeteria A on one day will return there the next day. The other 50% will move to cafeteria B. Cafeteria B will retain 70% of its customers from day to day, while losing 30% to cafeteria A. Determine the respective market shares for Tuesday and Wednesday. What will market shares be at equilibrium?

17. A boarding house serves breakfast to a large number of customers. On a given day, 50% of the patrons chose ham and 50% chose bacon. Experience indicates that 30% of those ordering ham on one day will reorder ham the next day, while 70% will switch to bacon. Of those eating bacon, 60% will stay with bacon the next day and 40% will switch to ham. For the next two days, determine the percentages of ham eaters and bacon eaters. What will these percentages be when steady-state conditions are reached?

18. The Red Company, the White Company, and the Blue Company share a local market. A market research company has estimated the following period-to-period changes in consumer loyalty:

The Red Company retained 60% of its customers and lost 20% to the White Company and 20% to the Blue Company.

The White Company retained 80% of its customers and lost 10% to Red and 10% to Blue.

The Blue Company retained 50% of its customers and lost 30% to Red and 20% to White.

The Blue Company is evaluating two new marketing strategies. The costs of the two strategies are approximately equal. Strategy A, a retention strategy, would allow the company to retain 70% of its customers, while losing 20% and 10% to Red and White respectively. Strategy B, an acquisitions strategy, would allow Blue to take 30% of Red's customers and 30% of White's customers. The increases would be obtained directly from customers whom Red and White originally retained from period to period. Evaluate the two alternative strategies.

19. The X, Y, and Z Companies share a local market, and each has one third. The matrix of transition probabilities is as follows:

$$
\begin{array}{c c}
 & \begin{array}{ccc} X & Y & Z \end{array} \\
\begin{array}{c} X \\ Y \\ Z \end{array} &
\begin{bmatrix}
.4 & .4 & .2 \\
.1 & .7 & .2 \\
.3 & .2 & .5
\end{bmatrix}
\end{array}
$$

At equilibrium, how much would X's share of the market increase if it could retain half of the customers it now loses to Y and Z?

20. The Foster Company inspects all the electronic tubes in its plant at the beginning of each month. Its present maintenance policy is to replace all tubes that are burned out and all tubes that have completed 3 months of useful life. Thus, when they are inspected, tubes may be in any one of four states:

State 1: Working, 1 month old
State 2: Working, 2 months old
State 3: Working, 3 months old
State 4: Burned out

New tubes have a 10% probability of burning out during their first month of operation. Tubes that are 1 month old at the beginning of a month have a 20% chance of burning out in the following month. Tubes that are 2 months old at the beginning of a month have a 30% chance of burning out during the following month. The cost of replacing a usable tube is $5, and the cost of replacing a burned-out tube is $50. Compare the cost of the present policy with the cost of replacing 2-month-old tubes and burned-out tubes.

21. The Gage Company makes a quarterly inspection of freezer coils in its ice cream plant. At each inspection, the coils are classified into one of four states as follows:

State 1: Excellent
State 2: Good
State 3: Average
State 4: Poor

The probabilities of moving among states in succeeding periods are as follows:

$$
\begin{array}{c@{\quad}cccc}
 & S_1 & S_2 & S_3 & S_4 \\
\begin{array}{c} S_1 \\ S_2 \\ S_3 \\ S_4 \end{array} &
\left[\begin{array}{cccc}
.2 & .4 & .2 & .2 \\
0 & .3 & .5 & .2 \\
0 & 0 & .6 & .4 \\
0 & 0 & 0 & 1
\end{array}\right]
\end{array}
$$

Coils that are replaced at the beginning of a period have a .8 probability of remaining in state 1 and a .2 probability of advancing to state 2 at the next inspection period. Compare the cost of replacing all coils in states 3 and 4 with a policy of replacing coils in state 4 only. Cost of replacement is $20 in state 3 and $50 in state 4. (*Note:* This matrix cannot be used as the matrix of transition probabilities. It must be modified in terms of the policy being evaluated.)

22. The Shaw Company has analyzed the waiting line at its small power-tool repair facility. Arrivals are assumed to occur at the beginning of a period,

and service completions occur at the end of a period. The maximum queue length is 3 (4 in the system), beyond which items are returned to their original population. The probabilities of 0, 1, 2, and 3 arrivals during any given period are .5, .3, .1, and .1 respectively. If 1 unit is waiting to be served, the probability of a service completion is 1.0. If more than 1 unit is ready to be served, the probability of 1 service completion is .5 and the probability of 2 service completions is .5. There is no possibility of more than 2 units being served in any single period. Determine the average queue length.

23. The Cortelyou College operates a morning, an afternoon, and an evening division. Data indicate that 70% of the students in the morning division will remain in that division for the next quarter, while 20% will switch to the afternoon division and 10% will move to the evening division. For students in the afternoon division, 50% will remain, while 25% will move to the morning division and the other 25% will switch to the evening division. Of the evening students, 60% will remain in that division from quarter to quarter. Of the remainder, half will switch to the morning division and half will go to the afternoon division. At equilibrium, what percentage of the students will be attending each division?

24. The MacVeagh Company has acquired data concerning the transition of its charge accounts from current to delinquent and vice versa. For current accounts, 80% will remain current next month, while 20% will become delinquent. For delinquent accounts, 50% will remain delinquent and 50% will become current in the next month. During January, 40% of the accounts were delinquent. Estimate the percentage of accounts that will be delinquent in February and March. What will this percentage be when equilibrium conditions are reached?

Supplementary readings

Anderson, D. R., D. J. Sweeney, and T. A. Williams. *An Introduction to Management Science*. St. Paul, Minn.: West, 1976.

Bell, C. E. *Quantitative Methods for Administration*. Homewood, Ill.: Irwin, 1977.

Bierman, H., C. P. Bonini, and W. H. Hausman. *Quantitative Analysis for Business Decisions*. Homewood, Ill.: Irwin, 1977.

Derman, C. *Finite State Markov Decision Processes*. New York: Academic, 1970.

Hillier, F. S., and G. J. Lieberman. *Introduction to Operations Research*. San Francisco: Holden-Day, 1974.

Howard, R. A. *Dynamic Probabilistic Systems*. 2 vols. New York: Wiley, 1971.

Jolson, M. A., and R. T. Hise. *Quantitative Techniques for Marketing Decisions*. New York: Macmillan, 1973.

Kemeny, J. G., and J. L. Snell. *Finite Markov Chains*. Princeton, N.J.: Van Nostrand, 1960.

Lapin, L. L. *Quantitative Methods for Business Decisions.* New York: Harcourt Brace Jovanovich, 1976.

Levin, R. I., and C. A. Kirkpatrick. *Quantitative Approaches to Management,* 2nd ed. New York: McGraw-Hill, 1975.

Shamblin, J. E., and G. T. Stevens. *Operations Research: A Fundamental Approach.* New York: McGraw-Hill, 1974.

Turban, E., and J. R. Meredith. *Fundamentals of Management Science.* Dallas, Texas: Business Publications, 1977.

Chapter 13

Game theory

Illustrative example: LAUVER'S GARAGE

Mr. Earl Lauver owns and operates a gasoline station and automobile repair shop in a small town in central Pennsylvania. Mr. Lauver's only competitor is Wilbur's Auto Service, which is located on the same highway at the other entrance to town. Both firms are well established in the community and have excellent reputations for providing quality service at reasonable prices. Lauver's Garage presently has about 55% of the town's business, compared to 45% for Wilbur's Auto Service. This difference is attributable to Lauver's slightly better business location.

A new local radio station is preparing to begin operations in the community. The sales manager of the station has recently talked with Mr. Lauver about advertising on the new station. He has offered Lauver's Garage a choice of three different advertising packages. For convenience, these are referred to as advertising strategies X_1, X_2, and X_3. Mr. Lauver is aware that the radio station has also offered a choice of three advertising packages to Wilbur Torrez, the manager of Wilbur's Auto Service. He also knows that his volume of business will be affected not only by the choice that he makes, but also by the decision made at Wilbur's.

Mr. Lauver has discussed the situation with Jane Heckendorn, who represents an advertising firm in a nearby city. This agency has estimated what will happen to Lauver's market share for each of the advertising strategies chosen by Mr. Lauver and his competitor. These estimates were based on experience with similar competitive situations.

Ms. Heckendorn estimates that if Mr. Lauver chooses advertising strategy X_1, his market share will increase by 3% if Wilbur's Auto Service chooses the first strategy, will decrease by 4% if Wilbur's chooses the second strategy, and will increase by 1% if Wilbur's chooses the third strategy. If Mr. Lauver chooses X_2, his market share will decrease by 3%, will not change, or will increase by 1%, depending on the choice of strategies by Wilbur's Auto Service. If Mr. Lauver's choice is X_3, his market share will increase by 4%, increase by 3%, or increase by 2%, depending on the choice of strategies by Wilbur's Auto Service.

In this situation, any increase in business by one firm must be gained at the expense of the other firm; that is, what one gains the other loses. Both firms know that all the information available to one firm is also available to the other. Each manager has the same goal: to choose the advertising strategy that will increase his own market share by the greatest amount.

Game theory is concerned with decision situations wherein one party is in conflict with another. Competitive situations arise in almost every facet of human activity—in parlor games, sports, military strategy, and business. In all of these situations, the results achieved depend on both our own action and that of our competitor. There are many features common to both simple games and complicated conflicts in business and industry. For this reason, knowledge of the theory of games should be helpful to the decision maker who continually faces competitive situations in business, industry, and government.

In the first part of the chapter, we will assume that the opponent is a competitor such as we find in checkers, football, or selling automobiles. Later in the chapter, we will be concerned with nonhostile opponents, such as nature "deciding" if it should rain on the Labor Day picnic.

Two-person, zero-sum game

We can think of the Lauver's Garage problem as a two-person, zero-sum game. This is the simplest type of game and therefore the easiest to describe and analyze. We limit ourselves to this type of game, because the mathematics of larger and more complex games is simply too cumbersome to include in a textbook at this level. While many business decisions resemble more complex games, the basic principles underlying competitive strategy are the same for all games, and knowledge of these principles should help us in real competitive situations.

Requirements of the two-person, zero-sum game

A competitive situation must have all of the following characteristics in order to be a *two-person, zero-sum game:*

1. There must be two and only two players. Each player can choose one of a finite set of strategies.
2. The term *zero-sum* implies that any gain by one competitor is exactly equal to the loss of the other competitor.
3. Each player has full knowledge of the strategies available to both competitors. The outcomes, or payoffs, associated with every possible combination of strategies are known to both players.
4. Both competitors are considered to be rational; that is, their only motivation is to maximize their own payoffs.

5. Bargaining is not allowed. Strategies are chosen simultaneously so that a competitor must select a strategy without knowing the choice made by the competitor. Since these games are strictly competitive, there can be no agreement that would be mutually advantageous.

No business situations exactly resemble two-person, zero-sum games. Many situations are close enough, however, so that the participants may utilize the principles and logic of this type of game. There are two competitors in the Lauver's Garage problem. One competitor's gain in market share is equal to the other's loss in market share. Both managers have full knowledge, and each is trying to maximize his own market share. There is no bargaining between parties. We can therefore treat this situation as a two-person, zero-sum game.

Standard representation of two-person, zero-sum games

The matrix given in Table 13.1 is for the Lauver's Garage problem. It is a standard representation of a two-person, zero-sum game. This representation is often referred to as a *payoff matrix* or *game matrix*. In this example, Lauver's Garage is considered player X and has three available strategies, X_1, X_2, and X_3. Wilbur's Auto Service is player Y, whose three available strategies are Y_1, Y_2, and Y_3. The matrix represents the net gain for player X and the net loss for player Y. In other words, a positive number indicates a gain by player X and a loss by player Y. A negative number indicates a loss by player X and a gain by player Y.

Consider the $+3$ at the intersection of the X_1 row and the Y_1 column. It indicates that if Lauver's Garage chooses strategy X_1 and Wilbur's Auto Service chooses strategy Y_1, the net result will be a 3% increase in market share for player X (Lauver's Garage). At the same time, player Y (Wilbur's Auto Service) will lose 3% of the community's business. As a second example, consider the -4 at the intersection of the X_1 row and the Y_2 column. This negative value indicates a loss of 4% for player X and a gain of 4% for player Y.

Table 13.1 *A standard game representation of the Lauver's Garage example*

		Player Y (Wilbur's Auto Service)		
		Y_1	Y_2	Y_3
Player X (Lauver's Garage)	X_1	3	−4	1
	X_2	−3	0	1
	X_3	4	3	2

Solution by dominance

A competitor will often have one alternative, or strategy, that dominates another strategy. *Dominance* occurs when one choice yields an equivalent or better payoff than another, regardless of the action taken by the competitor. Consider strategies X_2 and X_3 in the Lauver's Garage example. If player Y chooses Y_1, X will play X_3 over X_2 ($4 \geq -3$). If Y_2 is chosen, X_3 is still preferable to X_2 ($3 \geq 0$). If Y_3 is played, X_3 still has a better payoff than X_2 ($2 \geq 1$). Strategy X_3 dominates strategy X_2, because player X will prefer X_3 to X_2 regardless of the choice made by his opponent. It is interesting to note that strategy X_3 also dominates strategy X_1.

A competitor may have many strategies, none of which dominates any other. Consider player Y in our example. If player X chooses X_1, then Y_2 is preferable to Y_1 ($-4 \leq 3$), but if strategy X_2 is chosen, then Y_1 is preferable to Y_2 ($-3 \leq 0$). Neither of these two strategies dominates the other. By the same type of analysis, we can see that player Y has no strategy that dominates another strategy.

The concept of dominance can sometimes be used to solve simple games. A competitor will never select a dominated strategy, because equal or better results can always be obtained by selecting some other strategy. For this reason, *dominated strategies may be removed from the payoff matrix.* Let us again consider the payoff matrix for the Lauver's Garage example.

	Y_1	Y_2	Y_3
X_1	3	-4	1
X_2	-3	0	1
X_3	4	3	2

Since X_1 and X_2 are dominated strategies, they may be stricken from the payoff matrix, leaving the following reduced matrix.

	Y_1	Y_2	Y_3
X_3	4	3	2

Player X has only one relevant choice, which is to select X_3. Player Y now realizes that X will always choose X_3. He will optimize by choosing Y_3, the strategy that will minimize his loss in market share.

This "game analysis" of the Lauver's Garage problem tells us that Mr. Lauver should choose advertising strategy X_3 and that the manager of Wilbur's Auto Service should choose strategy Y_3. This will result in a 2% market gain for player X, Lauver's Garage. Wilbur's Auto Service is losing 2% of the market under these conditions, and it is tempting to believe that he should try another strategy. Remember, however, that if player X acts optimally, then the best Y can do is hold his loss of market share to 2%. Conversely, there is a tendency to believe that player X can do better than a 2% gain in market share. If Y acts optimally, however, 2% is the best X can do; the selection of any other strategy may result in a lower gain.

Sample problem 13.1 *FARMER'S FIRST BANK*

A rural Midwestern county is served by two commercial banks, Farmer's First Bank and Rancher's First Bank. Total deposits in the two banks are approximately equal. The state has recently passed a law that, for the first time, will allow banks to have branches within the county. Farmer's First Bank has decided on full-service branches. It has the capital to build a maximum of two of these branches. Market studies indicate that each of these branches will add $6 million of deposits to the bank. These deposits will be taken from Rancher's First Bank.

Rancher's First Bank has decided to expand with automated electronic tellers, rather than full-service branches. It has the capital to install a maximum of three of these tellers. It is estimated that each of these installations will add $4 million in deposits, which will be taken from Farmer's First Bank. Let Farmer's First Bank be player X and Rancher's First Bank be player Y. The manager of each bank would like to maximize total deposits. Formulate this as a two-person, zero-sum game.

SOLUTION

	Electronic Tellers			
	0	1	2	3
Branches	Y_1	Y_2	Y_3	Y_4
0 X_1	0	−4	−8	−12
1 X_2	6	2	−2	−6
2 X_3	12	8	4	0

Pure strategies, saddle points, and game value

Every game solution is composed of two parts: a statement of the strategies used by the competitors and a statement of the value of the game. In our example, there was a single best strategy for player X and a single best strategy for player Y. Regardless of the number of times the game is repeated, each player acts optimally by continuing to play his one best strategy. In games of this type, each player is said to have a *pure strategy*, one that is played on every occasion.

If a game is repeated a large number of times, the *value of the game* is the average amount won or lost by player X. When pure strategies exist,

X will win or lose the same amount each time the game is played. This value is known as a *saddle point*.[1] It is easily recognizable in a payoff matrix because it is the largest value in its column and the smallest value in its row. When a saddle point exists, each player will have a pure strategy represented by the row and column that contain the saddle point. Games of this type are said to be *strictly determined*.

It is easy to find the saddle point in the Lauver's Garage game. The $+2$ saddle-point value is the smallest value in row X_3 and the largest value in column Y_3. The strategies associated with a saddle point are said to be in equilibrium, because the row strategy is the best alternative against the column and the column strategy is the best choice against the row. In our example, X_3 is the best strategy against Y_3. Y_3 is also the best strategy against X_3. In other words, there is no tendency for either player to change to another strategy.

The saddle point as a minimax solution

The solution represented by the saddle point is known as a *minimax solution*. For each player, it minimizes the maximum possible loss (or maximizes the minimum possible gain). As an example, let us consider the Lauver's Garage example again.

	Y_1	Y_2	Y_3
X_1	3	-4	1
X_2	-3	0	1
X_3	4	3	2

If player X chooses X_1, then the worst that can happen (maximum possible loss) is for player Y to choose Y_2. In this case, player X will lose 4% of the market. If player X chooses X_2, then the worst that can happen is for competitor Y to play Y_1. In this case, X loses 3%. If X chooses X_3, then the worst that can happen (maximum loss) is actually a gain of 2% when Y chooses Y_3. Thus, the maximum losses for player X for strategies X_1, X_2, and X_3 are -4, -3, and $+2$ respectively. The minimum of these maximum losses is $+2$, which is therefore the minimax solution for player X.

This minimax solution represents the maximization of a security level, since player X, by choosing strategy X_3, can be assured of at least a gain of 2%. No other strategy offers this degree of security.

The saddle-point value also represents a minimax solution for player Y. For strategy Y_1, the worst that can happen to player Y is a loss of 4%. Likewise, the maximum possible losses for strategies Y_2 and Y_3 are 3% and 2% respectively. Consequently, the minimum of these three maxi-

---

[1]Technically, the saddle point refers to the row and column location of this value.

mum losses is 2%. It also represents a security level; by choosing Y_3, competitor Y can be assured of never losing more than 2% of the market.

In strictly determined games, the minimax solution is always the best choice if the other competitor chooses a minimax solution. This solution is sometimes referred to as an equilibrium solution. The position of a single player cannot be improved by moving away from the minimax solution, provided the other competitor maintains a minimax posture. In this example, the minimax solution is for X to play X_3 and for Y to play Y_3. The game value is a payoff of 2% to player X. If Y maintains strategy Y_3, then X cannot gain by shifting to X_1 or X_2. Likewise, if X maintains X_3, then player Y cannot gain by shifting to Y_1 or Y_2. Thus, there is a tendency for both players to maintain their equilibrium or minimax positions.

Not all games contain saddle points. We will discuss these nonstrictly determined games later in the chapter. Before doing so, let us briefly examine some other games in which saddle points exist.

Examples of strictly determined games

The following problems are examples of strictly determined games. In each example, the saddle point has been circled and a statement of the solution is given.

Example 1

	Y_1	Y_2
X_1	①	3
X_2	0	7

In this example, strategy Y_1 dominates strategy Y_2. Once it is determined that Y will play Y_1, X will maximize the game value by selecting X_1.

Example 2

	Y_1	Y_2
X_1	4	−2
X_2	5	②
X_3	−2	0

Strategy X_2 dominates both strategy X_1 and strategy X_3. After X's strategy is determined, Y will minimize her or his loss by selecting Y_2.

Example 3

	Y_1	Y_2	Y_3
X_1	3	−2	−3
X_2	2	1	1
X_3	0	0	2

In this example, strategy Y_2 dominates Y_1, but player X has no dominated strategy. This game can be solved by *iterative dominance*, a step-by-step reduction of the payoff matrix. Since Y_1 is dominated, it may be removed, yielding the following reduced matrix.

	Y_2	Y_3
X_1	-2	-3
X_2	1	1
X_3	0	2

Strategy X_2 dominates X_1 in the reduced matrix, which allows X_1 to be removed, yielding a second reduced matrix.

	Y_2	Y_3
X_2	①	1
X_3	0	2

Y_2 now dominates Y_3. Once it is determined that Y will play Y_2, then X will choose X_2.

Example 4

	Y_1	Y_2	Y_3
X_1	18	3	-6
X_2	14	⑨	20
X_3	0	6	24

This game illustrates a situation wherein there are no dominant strategies but a saddle point exists. The game is in equilibrium when strategies X_2 and Y_2 are chosen. When strategy X_2 is played, there is no tendency for Y to shift to Y_1 or Y_3. Likewise, when Y_2 is played, there is no tendency for player X to move to either strategy X_1 or strategy X_3.

In this example, we can easily locate the saddle point by determining the minimum value in each row and the maximum value in each column. A saddle point exists if the maximum of the row minimums is equal to the minimum of the column maximums. We will illustrate by using the foregoing example. First, we must find the minimum value in each row and the maximum value in each column.

	Y_1	Y_2	Y_3	Row minimum
X_1	18	3	-6	-6
X_2	14	9	20	9
X_3	0	6	24	0
Column maximum	18	9	24	

The minimum values in rows 1, 2, and 3 are -6, 9, and 0 respectively. The largest of these is 9. Likewise, the maximum values in columns 1, 2, and 3 are 18, 9, and 24 respectively. The smallest of these is 9. Thus, the maximum of the row minimums is equal to the minimum of the column maximums. A saddle point exists.

Example 5

	Y_1	Y_2	Y_3
X_1	−6	3	−5
X_2	⓪	4	⓪
X_3	−5	1	−6
X_4	⓪	2	⓪

Can a game have more than one saddle point? In this example, there are four saddle points at (X_2, Y_1), (X_2, Y_3), (X_4, Y_1), and (X_4, Y_3). Note, however, that all four saddle points have the same payoff value. Multiple saddle points can exist in zero-sum games. If they do occur, however, they will always have the same payoff value, so that the competitors will be indifferent among them. Each saddle point is the minimum value in a row and the maximum value in a column.

Sample problem 13.2   HOLMAN MANAGEMENT CONSULTANTS

Sue Leason, an analyst for HMC, is studying the following games. For each game, her task is to determine the best strategy for each player and the value of the game.

	Y_1	Y_2
X_1	−5	3
X_2	①	5

	Y_1	Y_2	Y_3
X_1	③	6	8
X_2	2	1	0

	Y_1	Y_2
X_1	−4	4
X_2	0	−1
X_3	①	2

	Y_1	Y_2	Y_3
X_1	−12	−10	10
X_2	12	−5	−6
X_3	6	③	9

SOLUTION

The saddle point in each game has been circled.

2 × 2 games with mixed strategies

The first step in analyzing a game should be to look for a saddle point. Unfortunately, there are many games wherein saddle points do not exist. In these situations, there are no pure strategies—no choices, that is, that the competitors will always make. If no pure strategy exists, then player X can optimize by playing each available strategy an appropriate percentage of the time. Likewise, player Y can optimize by playing each strategy an appropriate percentage of the time. This type of game plan is known as a *mixed strategy*. The next section is concerned with determining mixed strategies for 2×2 games, games wherein each player has only two alternatives.

Selection of mixed strategies

The game about to be described is a simple two-person, zero-sum game. There is no saddle point and, consequently, no pure strategies exist.

	Y_1	Y_2
X_1	3	−4
X_2	−3	0

Before proceeding, we should note that this game is the Lauver's Garage game with strategies X_3 and Y_3 removed. Suppose that each of the competitors now chooses from only two alternative advertising packages. This is a "weekly game" and both Lauver's Garage and Wilbur's Auto Service can vary their selections on a week-by-week basis. Neither firm now has a pure strategy. As a result, each firm will be shifting from one choice to another, hoping to somehow out-maneuver the other competitor.

If this game is repeated a large number of times, the best strategy for Mr. Lauver (player X) is to proportion his playing time between alternatives X_1 and X_2. His problem is to determine what percent of his time should be spent on each strategy in order to optimize his playing position. Wilbur's Auto Service (player Y) will be alternating between strategies Y_1 and Y_2. This player must also determine the proper percent of playing time to allocate to each of his two choices.

Suppose we let P represent the fraction of time that player X utilizes strategy X_1. The fraction of time that he utilizes X_2 would then be represented by $(1 - P)$. For example, if strategy X_1 was employed 30% of the time, P would be equal to .3 and $(1 - P)$ would be equal to .7. We can represent player Y's choices in the same way. If we let Q equal the fraction of time that strategy Y_1 is used, $(1 - Q)$ will represent the fraction of time that player Y chooses strategy Y_2. This is illustrated as follows:

	Q Y_1	$(1 - Q)$ Y_2
P X_1	3	−4
$(1 - P)$ X_2	−3	0

Player X would like to solve for the values of P and $(1 - P)$ that would optimize his playing position. Logically, competitor X wants to divide his time between X_1 and X_2 in such a way that his winnings will be the same, regardless of the strategy chosen by competitor Y. When player Y chooses Y_1, player X will have a probability of P of winning 3 points and a probability of $(1 - P)$ of losing 3 points. Thus, when strategy Y_1 is chosen, the average winnings by player X can be mathematically stated as follows:

X's average winnings when Y plays $Y_1 = 3P - 3(1 - P)$

If player Y selects strategy Y_2, then X will lose 4 points each time he plays strategy X_1, and he will exactly break even when X_2 is chosen. This can be stated mathematically as follows:

X's average winnings when Y plays $Y_2 = -4P + 0(1 - P)$

Player X wants to equalize his expected winnings, regardless of whether player Y is choosing Y_1 or Y_2. We can therefore set the average expected winnings equal to each other and solve for the optimal value of P and $(1 - P)$.

$$3P - 3(1 - P) = -4P + 0(1 - P)$$
$$3P - 3 + 3P = -4P$$
$$10P = 3$$
$$P = .3$$
$$1 - P = .7$$

This solution tells us that competitor X should divide his time between strategies X_1 and X_2 so that he plays X_1 30% of the time and X_2 70% of the time.

We can use the same approach to solve for player Y's optimal strategies. This player will want to divide his time between Y_1 and Y_2 in such a way that his expected winnings (or losses) will be the same, regardless of whether player X chooses strategy X_1 or strategy X_2. When X_1 is chosen, player Y will have a probability of Q of losing 3 points and a probability of $(1 - Q)$ of winning 4 points. Using this information, we can determine the expected average loss for Y when player X is playing X_1. (Remember that it is customary to describe a game in terms of X's winnings.) When X plays X_1, Y's average loss can be determined as follows:

Y's average loss when X plays $X_1 = 3Q - 4(1 - Q)$

Using this same reasoning, we can express Y's expected loss when player X is playing X_2 as follows:

Y's average loss when X plays $X_2 = -3Q + 0(1 - Q)$

We can now equate Y's expected losses when X plays strategy X_1 with his expected losses when X chooses strategy X_2.

$$3Q - 4(1 - Q) = -3Q + 0(1 - Q)$$
$$3Q - 4 + 4Q = -3Q$$
$$10Q = 4$$
$$Q = .4$$
$$1 - Q = .6$$

The solution indicates that Y's optimal strategy is a mixed strategy. He should divide his choices so that strategy Y_1 is played 40% of the time and Y_2 60% of the time.

Sample problem 13.3   HOLMAN MANAGEMENT CONSULTANTS (Continued)

The following is another game being considered by Ms. Leason at HMC. Determine the optimal mixed strategy for player X. Solve by assuming that competitor X's playing time will be allocated in such a way that the winnings will be the same, regardless of the strategy chosen by player Y. Let P represent the probability that X_1 is played, and let $(1 - P)$ represent the probability that X_2 is played.

	Y_1	Y_2
P X_1	9	3
$(1 - P)$ X_2	4	6

SOLUTION

$$9P + 4(1 - P) = 3P + 6(1 - P)$$
$$9P + 4 - 4P = 3P + 6 - 6P$$
$$8P = 2$$
$$P = \tfrac{2}{8}$$
$$1 - P = \tfrac{6}{8}$$

Alternative determination of mixed strategies

In the previous section, we showed how to determine the optimal mixed strategy for competitors in 2 × 2 games wherein no saddle point exists. That analysis was based on the logical assumption that player X wanted expected winnings to be the same, regardless of the strategy chosen by player Y. And we assumed that player Y acted in a similar manner.

There is a much simpler method of solving for the optimal strategy of a 2 × 2 game. We will illustrate this procedure by using the same game that we used in the previous section.

	Y_1	Y_2
X_1	3	−4
X_2	−3	0

The first step in this simplified method is to subtract the smallest number in each row from the largest number in the same row. We then subtract the smallest value in each column from the largest value in the same column.

	Y_1	Y_2	
X_1	3	−4	7
X_2	−3	0	3
	6	4	

The next step is to interchange the two numbers obtained in the row subtractions: 7 for 3 and 3 for 7. The same interchange is made for the two numbers obtained in the column subtraction. The sum of the column subtractions should always equal the sum of the row subtractions. In this example, $3 + 7 = 6 + 4 = 10$. This value is referred to as the *sum of the differences.* It is entered in the bottom-right-hand corner of the table, as shown in the following matrix. The asterisks in the matrix indicate that an appropriate reversal has been made for the row differences and the column differences.

	Y_1	Y_2	
X_1	3	−4	3*
X_2	−3	0	7*
	4*	6*	10

We can determine the fraction of time that player X should devote to strategies X_1 and X_2 by dividing the appropriate row differences (after the interchange) by the sum of the differences. Likewise, we determine the proper strategies for player Y by dividing the appropriate column differences by the sum of the differences.

For X_1: $P = \frac{3}{10} = .3$

For X_2: $(1 - P) = \frac{7}{10} = .7$

For Y_1: $Q = \frac{4}{10} = .4$

For Y_2: $(1 - Q) = \frac{6}{10} = .6$

The results of these calculations again tell us that competitor X

(Lauver's Garage) should divide his choices so that he plays X_1 on 30% of the occasions and X_2 on 70% of the occasions. The proper strategy for Wilbur's Auto Service is to select Y_1 40% of the time and Y_2 60% of the time. These are the same values that we obtained in the previous section.

Value of the game

When we discussed games with saddle points, we noted that a game solution was composed of two parts: a statement of the strategies employed by each player and a value of the game. For games with mixed strategies, the value of the game is the average winnings of player X over a large number of repetitions of game play.

To illustrate how to determine the value of the game, we will continue to use the 2×2 game example that we have been using. Before proceeding, however, we should note that the probabilities associated with player X's strategies are statistically independent of the probabilities associated with player Y's strategies. This is because the theory of games assumes that both competitors play independently and that each makes his decision without knowledge of the action taken by the other player. The game we are using as our example and the probabilities associated with each strategy are as follows:

		.4	.6
		Y_1	Y_2
.3	X_1	3	-4
.7	X_2	-3	0

Consider the payoff of 3 points,[2] which is at the intersection of the X_1 row and the Y_1 column in the payoff matrix. This payoff is obtained only when competitor X chooses alternative X_1 and competitor Y chooses alternative Y_1. Since the probabilities are independent, we can obtain the probability of this occurrence by multiplying the respective row and column probabilities, that is, $.4 \times .3 = .12$. This calculation is given in Table 13.2. Similar calculations can be made for the other cells in the payoff matrix. We determine the value of the game by multiplying the probability of occurrence of each payoff by the value of the payoff and then summing for all cells in the matrix. This calculation also appears in Table 13.2. The expected value of the game is -1.20.

If the game were repeated a large number of times, and if either or both players acted optimally, player Y would win an average of 1.2

---

[2] When the units to be gained or lost in a game, such as the market shares in the Lauver's Garage example, are not specified, units will be expressed as points.

Table 13.2 *Determining the value of the game for games with mixed strategies*

Cell	Payoff (E_{ij})	Probability (P_{ij})	$(E_{ij})(P_{ij})$
1, 1	3	$.3 \times .4 = .12$	.36
1, 2	−4	$.3 \times .6 = .18$	−.72
2, 1	−3	$.7 \times .4 = .28$	−.84
2, 2	0	$.7 \times .6 = \underline{.42}$	$\underline{.00}$
		1.00	−1.20

points per game and player X would lose an average of 1.2 points per game. It is, of course, impossible for Y to win exactly 1.2 points on any one game. The game value (G) refers to the average over many replays of the same game.

Earlier, we stated that player X wants to equalize expected winnings, regardless of whether player Y chooses strategy Y_1 or strategy Y_2. Thus, we can determine the expected value of the game by assuming that player Y chooses Y_1 exclusively or Y_2 exclusively. First, assume that competitor Y plays Y_1 on every occasion. We determine the game value by multiplying the payoff associated with each of X's strategies by the probability that this strategy will be used and then summing for all possible strategies. Thus, when player Y plays Y_1,

$$G = .3(3) + .7(-3) = -1.2$$

Likewise, when competitor Y plays Y_2,

$$G = .3(-4) + .7(0) = -1.2$$

We can make the same calculations by assuming that player Y is playing a mixed strategy and that competitor X is playing either strategy X_1 or strategy X_2 exclusively. Thus, when X plays X_1,

$$G = .4(3) + .6(-4) = -1.2$$

Likewise, when player X chooses X_2,

$$G = .4(-3) + .6(0) = -1.2$$

Applying mixed strategies

In the preceding analysis, we simply stated that each player should choose a particular alternative a given percent of the time. For example, in the game we have used for illustration, we know that X should choose X_1 30% of the time and X_2 70% of the time. We have said nothing about *what* 30% of the time X_1 should be played and *what* 70% of the time X_2 should be played. In order to act optimally, the mixed strategy must be applied without bias and in a way in which no discernible pattern develops. If a competitor can detect a playing pattern, then that player will adjust his strategy to capitalize on his knowledge of his opponent's future actions.

The proper method of avoiding a pattern of play is to make each selection randomly. The frequency with which a given alternative is chosen must be in agreement with the optimal mixed strategy. In our example, X_1 should be chosen 30% of the time and X_2 should be chosen 70% of the time. A table of random numbers, such as Table 11.3, can be quite useful in employing this mixed strategy. Suppose player X utilized a series of two-digit random numbers between 00 and 99. If the number selected was between 00 and 29, then X_1 would be played. If the number selected was between 30 and 99, then X_2 would be played. This procedure would provide randomness and ensure that no discernible pattern developed. It would also ensure that the percentages associated with the optimal mixed strategy were adhered to.

Sample problem 13.4   HOLMAN MANAGEMENT CONSULTANTS (Continued)

Use the simplified method to determine the optimal mixed strategies for player X and player Y. Determine the value of the game.

		Q Y_1	$(1 - Q)$ Y_2	
P	X_1	6	2	1*
$(1 - P)$	X_2	4	5	4*
		3*	2*	

SOLUTION

$P = \frac{1}{5}, (1 - P) = \frac{4}{5}, Q = \frac{3}{5}, (1 - Q) = \frac{2}{5}$

Value of the game

Cell	Payoff	Probability	Value
1, 1	6	$\frac{3}{25}$	$\frac{18}{25}$
2, 2	2	$\frac{2}{25}$	$\frac{4}{25}$
2, 1	4	$\frac{12}{25}$	$\frac{48}{25}$
2, 2	5	$\frac{8}{25}$	$\frac{40}{25}$
			$\frac{110}{25}$

Solution of larger games with mixed strategies

Our previous discussion of mixed strategies was concerned with games in which each player was limited to only two alternatives. In this section, we will consider games wherein one or both competitors have more than two choices. If a saddle point exists, we can easily determine the pure strategies and then the value of the game. For games with no saddle point, however, the methods by which we have determined mixed strategies in 2×2 games either are no longer applicable or must be used in combination with other procedures.

Reduction by dominance

The easiest way to solve a large game is to reduce it to a 2×2 game and then solve the reduced game. We can use the method of dominance to reduce many large games to 2×2 games. The following two examples illustrate the procedure.

Example 1

	Y_1	Y_2	Y_3	Y_4
X_1	0	1	4	5
X_2	3	4	2	2

For player Y, strategy Y_1 dominates strategy Y_2. Player Y will never choose Y_2, because regardless of the choice made by X, Y will prefer Y_1 to Y_2. Likewise, Y_3 dominates Y_4, and player Y will never choose strategy Y_4. Since they will never be used, strategies Y_2 and Y_4 may be removed from the payoff matrix. This has the effect of reducing the larger 2×4 game to the following 2×2 game.

	Y_1	Y_3
X_1	0	4
X_2	3	2

This game matrix can be solved using methods we discussed in previous sections. X's optimal strategy is to play X_1 20% of the time and X_2 80% of the time. Y's optimal strategy is to play Y_1 40% of the time and Y_3 60% of the time. The value of the game is 2.40.

Example 2

	Y_1	Y_2	Y_3
X_1	0	−4	0
X_2	−2	4	0
X_3	−1	−5	−2

This game can be reduced to a 2×2 game by iterative dominance. Strategy X_1 dominates X_3, yielding the following reduced matrix.

	Y_1	Y_2	Y_3
X_1	0	-4	0
X_2	-2	4	0

Strategy Y_1 now dominates Y_3, reducing the matrix to the following 2×2 game.

	Y_1	Y_2
X_1	0	-4
X_2	-2	4

The proper strategies are for X to play X_1 60% of the time and X_2 40% of the time. Player Y should play Y_1 80% of the time and Y_2 20% of the time. The value of the game is $-.80$.

In solving large games, we should always try to use dominance to reduce the size of the game before proceeding with more complicated methods of solution. If a game can be reduced in size, there is simply no reason to struggle with the calculations associated with the larger, unreduced game.

Graphical solutions

A game can be solved graphically if one of the two players is limited to a choice of only two strategies. Any number of strategies may be available to the second player. As an example, consider the following game.

	Y_1	Y_2	Y_3
X_1	1	7	13
X_2	9	0	-2

In this game, player X has two choices, X_1 and X_2. Suppose that player Y chooses strategy Y_1. Player X will win 1 point if X_1 is chosen and 9 points if X_2 is chosen. This is illustrated graphically in Figure 13.1. The "Strategy Y_1" line in this figure gives the game results when Y uses strategy Y_1 against any strategy X may choose, either pure or mixed. The two pure strategies of using X_1 or X_2 exclusively are represented by two X axes in the figure. Suppose X selects a mixed strategy of playing X_1 in 25% of the games and X_2 in the remaining 75%. This is indicated by point A in Figure 13.1. Player X's average winnings would be 7 points, as shown at point B. This can be verified as follows:

$$\text{For } X_1: \quad .25 \times 1 = \quad .25$$
$$\text{For } X_2: \quad .75 \times 9 = \underline{6.75}$$
$$7.00$$

Figure 13.1 *X's winnings if Y plays strategy Y₁*

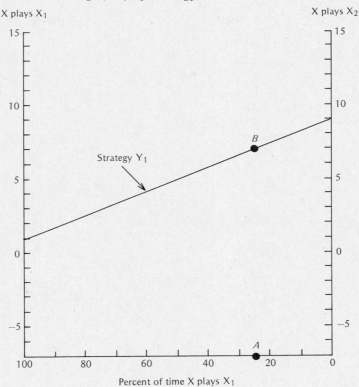

Figure 13.2 is a graphical representation of the complete game. It shows the results when Y uses any alternative, Y_1, Y_2, or Y_3, against any pure or mixed strategy that X might choose. These three alternatives are represented by the three lines connecting the two X axes. As is customary, the values in the graph represent the game in terms of points that X would win and Y would lose.

Assume that X employs a mixed strategy of playing X_1 80% of the time and X_2 20% of the time, as indicated by point S in Figure 13.2. From this figure, we see that X's average winnings will be 2.6 if Y uses Y_1, 5.6 if Y uses Y_2, and 10.0 if Y uses Y_3. Player Y wants to minimize X's winnings and will therefore choose Y_1 against this mixed strategy. Since point B represents X playing X_1 60% of the time, player Y will choose strategy Y_1 when X_1 is played between 60% and 100% of the time. Likewise, point C represents a situation wherein player X will play X_1 on 25% of the game repetitions. Thus, strategy Y_2 will be chosen when X_1 is played

Figure 13.2 *Graphical representation of the game in our example*

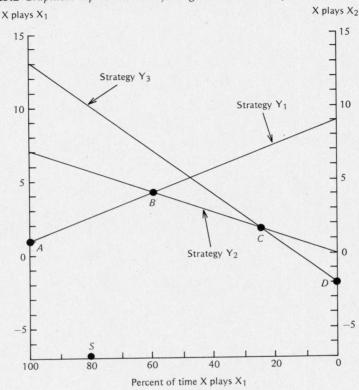

between 25% and 60% of the time. Alternative Y_3 will minimize X's winnings if X_1 is played on 25% or fewer of the game repetitions.

If Y acts optimally, the best X can do is represented by the path A-B-C-D in Figure 13.2. The game is graphed in terms of X's choice; that is, player X can move between axis 1 and axis 2. Player X wants to maximize the value of the game and will therefore choose to play the game at point B, the highest point on the path A-B-C-D.

We can learn several pieces of information from the graph in Figure 13.2. First, as noted, point B is 60% of the distance from the X_2 axis to the X_1 axis. Thus, X's optimal strategy is to play X_1 for 60% of the games and X_2 for 40% of the games. The value of the game can also be determined graphically. In this example, the game value is the value of point B, which is 4.2.

Note that point B represents the intersection of strategy Y_1 and strategy Y_2. Thus, the graphical procedure gives us another method of reducing a large game to a 2×2 game. Since choice Y_3 is not involved in the optimal strategy, the game can be reduced to the following 2×2 game.

	Y_1	Y_2
X_1	1	7
X_2	9	0

Solving this game by standard procedures for 2×2 games yields the following results, which are consistent with our graphical analysis. The value of the game is 4.2. Player X should play X_1 60% of the time and X_2 40% of the time. Competitor Y should play Y_1 46.7% of the time and Y_2 53.3% of the time.

The same type of graphical analysis can be used when player Y has two alternatives and player X has more than two alternatives. Figure 13.3 is a graphical representation of the following game.

	Y_1	Y_2
X_1	1	0
X_2	0	5
X_3	5	-5
X_4	4	-1

This game is graphed in terms of Y's choice. Since player Y always tries to minimize the value of the game, the relevant game path is E-F-G-H. The minimum point on this path is point G, which has a game value of 2.0. Y's optimal strategy is to play Y_1 on 60% of the occasions and Y_2 on 40% of the occasions.

Point G in Figure 13.3 is the intersection of the lines representing strategies X_2 and X_4. Thus, the game can be reduced to the following 2×2 game.

	Y_1	Y_2
X_2	0	5
X_4	4	-1

The value of the game is 2.0. X_2 and X_4 should both be played 50% of the time. Y_1 and Y_2 should be played 60% and 40% of the time respectively.

Solution of games by linear programming

Linear programming can be used to solve any two-person, zero-sum situation. Small games, wherein at least one player is limited to only two alternatives, can best be solved by the methods we have already

Figure 13.3 *Graphical representation of a game wherein Y has two choices*

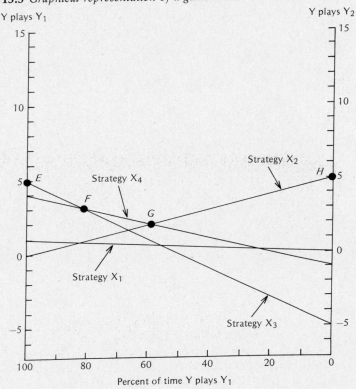

Y plays Y₁   Y plays Y₂

Percent of time Y plays Y_1

discussed in this chapter. Linear programming is therefore generally used only on games with the following characteristics:

1. Each competitor has three or more alternatives.
2. No saddle point exists.
3. Dominance cannot be used to reduce the game to a more manageable size.

As an example, consider the following game.

	Y_1	Y_2	Y_3
X_1	8	4	12
X_2	12	6	2
X_3	4	16	8

With more than two strategies, it is no longer convenient to let *P* represent the fraction of time that one strategy is played and $(1 - P)$ the fraction of time that the other strategy is played. We will let Y_1, Y_2, and Y_3 represent the proportions of time that competitor Y plays his three available strategies. Likewise, X_1, X_2, and X_3 are the proportions of time that player X chooses his respective strategies. The symbol G represents the value of the game. Assume that player X decides to play X_1 exclusively. The average payoff would depend on how player Y divided his time among his three available strategies. This average payoff can be expressed as follows:

Average payoff when X plays $X_1 = 8Y_1 + 4Y_2 + 12Y_3$

Player Y wants to minimize the expected average payoff (since the game matrix is expressed in terms of X's winnings). Player Y knows that if he acts optimally, he can always hold the average payoff to the game value or some lesser amount. If both players act optimally, the average payoff will be G, the game value. If Y acts optimally and X does not, the average payoff may be less than G. Thus, when competitor X plays X_1 and Y acts optimally,

$$8Y_1 + 4Y_2 + 12Y_3 \leq G$$

Likewise, when competitor X chooses X_2, and Y acts optimally,

$$12Y_1 + 6Y_2 + 2Y_3 \leq G$$

And when competitor X chooses X_3,

$$4Y_1 + 16Y_2 + 8Y_3 \leq G$$

The total proportion of time that Y spends playing each of the strategies must equal 1.0. Therefore,

$$Y_1 + Y_2 + Y_3 = 1.0$$

If we are to use linear programming, we must remove G from the right-hand side of the inequalities. We accomplish this by dividing each term in the relationships by G.

$$\frac{Y_1}{G} + \frac{Y_2}{G} + \frac{Y_3}{G} = \frac{1}{G}$$

$$\frac{8Y_1}{G} + \frac{4Y_2}{G} + \frac{12Y_3}{G} \leq 1$$

$$\frac{12Y_1}{G} + \frac{6Y_2}{G} + \frac{2Y_3}{G} \leq 1$$

$$\frac{4Y_1}{G} + \frac{16Y_2}{G} + \frac{8Y_3}{G} \leq 1$$

We can now remove G from the denominator of each expression by introducing three new variables, Y^*_1, Y^*_2, and Y^*_3, where $Y^*_i = Y_i/G$. Our procedure will be to solve the linear programming problem using these new variables, Y^*_1, Y^*_2, and Y^*_3. Once we obtain an optimal solution, we can work backwards to obtain the game value and the optimal mixed strategy for player Y. Let us restate the relationships that are now expressed in terms of the new variables.

$$Y^*_1 + Y^*_2 + Y^*_3 = \frac{1}{G}$$

$$8Y^*_1 + 4Y^*_2 + 12Y^*_3 \leqslant 1$$
$$12Y^*_1 + 6Y^*_2 + 2Y^*_3 \leqslant 1$$
$$4Y^*_1 + 16Y^*_2 + 8Y^*_3 \leqslant 1$$

Competitor Y wants to minimize G, the value of the game, which is the same as maximizing $1/G$. Thus, the linear programming objective function can be stated as follows:

$$\text{Max } Z = \frac{1}{G} = Y^*_1 + Y^*_2 + Y^*_3$$

We can add slack variables to form the following linear programming equality constraints.

$$8Y^*_1 + 4Y^*_2 + 12Y^*_3 + 1S_1 + 0S_2 + 0S_3 = 1$$
$$12Y^*_1 + 6Y^*_2 + 2Y^*_3 + 0S_1 + 1S_2 + 0S_3 = 1$$
$$4Y^*_1 + 16Y^*_2 + 8Y^*_3 + 0S_1 + 0S_2 + 1S_3 = 1$$
$$Y^*_i \geqslant 0, \ S_i \geqslant 0, \ i = 1, 2, 3$$

Table 13.3 gives the tableaus generated when the simplex method is used to solve this linear programming problem. The optimal solution is

$$Y^*_1 = \frac{1}{16}$$
$$Y^*_2 = \frac{1}{32}$$
$$Y^*_3 = \frac{1}{32}$$
$$1/G = \frac{1}{8}; \text{ therefore } G = 8.0$$

These values may now be converted back to the original Y_1, Y_2, and Y_3 values as follows:

$$Y_i = G \times Y^*_i$$
$$Y_1 = 8 \times \frac{1}{16} = \frac{1}{2}$$
$$Y_2 = 8 \times \frac{1}{32} = \frac{1}{4}$$
$$Y_3 = 8 \times \frac{1}{32} = \frac{1}{4}$$

Table 13.3 *Linear programming solution of a 3 × 3 game*

0 Row	Price vector	Solution vector	Quantity vector	1 Y^*_1	1 Y^*_2	1 Y^*_3	0 S_1	0 S_2	0 S_3
Initial tableau									
I	0	S_1	1	8.00	4.00	12.00	1.00	.00	.00
II	0	S_2	1	12.00	6.00	2.00	.00	1.00	.00
III	0	S_3	1	4.00	16.00	8.00	.00	.00	1.00
NC		$-Z$	0	1.00	1.00	1.00	.00	.00	.00
Second tableau									
I	0	S_1	$\frac{1}{3}$	.00	.00	10.67	1.00	$-.67$	.00
II	1	Y^*_1	$\frac{1}{12}$	1.00	.50	.17	.00	.08	.00
III	0	S_3	$\frac{1}{3}$	.00	14.00	7.33	.00	$-.33$	1.00
NC		$-Z$	$-\frac{1}{12}$	.00	.50	.83	.00	$-.08$	.00
Third tableau									
I	1	Y^*_3	$\frac{2}{64}$	.00	.00	1.00	.09	$-.06$	.00
II	1	Y^*_1	$\frac{5}{64}$	1.00	.50	.00	$-.02$	.09	.00
III	0	S_3	$\frac{28}{64}$	.00	14.00	.00	$-.69$	.13	1.00
NC		$-Z$	$-\frac{7}{64}$	.00	.50	.00	$-.08$	$-.03$	.00
Final tableau									
I	1	Y^*_3	$\frac{1}{32}$	.00	.00	1.00	.09	$-.06$	.00
II	1	Y^*_1	$\frac{2}{32}$	1.00	.00	.00	.01	.09	$-.04$
III	1	Y^*_2	$\frac{1}{32}$	.00	1.00	.00	$-.05$	.01	.07
NC		$-Z$	$-\frac{1}{8}$	.00	.00	.00	$-.05$	$-.04$	$-.04$

In this problem, player Y can minimize player X's average winnings by playing Y_1 50% of the time, Y_2 25% of the time, and Y_3 25% of the time. This is the optimal strategy for player Y.

We can determine the optimal mixed strategy for player X by solving the game from the viewpoint of competitor X. By acting optimally, competitor X can be assured of average winnings at least as large as G, the game value. Thus, the following relationships are true, depending on whether Y chooses Y_1, Y_2, or Y_3.

$$8X_1 + 12X_2 + 4X_3 \geq G$$
$$4X_1 + 6X_2 + 16X_3 \geq G$$
$$12X_1 + 2X_2 + 8X_3 \geq G$$

We may now introduce new variables X^*_1, X^*_2, and X^*_3 and make the same substitutions that we made in the analysis for determining player Y's strategies. This results in the linear programming formulation

$$\text{Min } Z = 1/G = X^*_1 + X^*_2 + X^*_3$$

s.t.
$$8X^*_1 + 12X^*_2 + 4X^*_3 \geqslant 1$$
$$4X^*_1 + 6X^*_2 + 16X^*_3 \geqslant 1$$
$$12X^*_1 + 2X^*_2 + 8X^*_3 \geqslant 1$$
$$X^*_1, X^*_2, X^*_3 \geqslant 0$$

The proper surplus variables can be added, and then the problem can be solved by the simplex method of linear programming. The optimal solution is

$$X^*_1 = {}^{15}\!/_{280}$$
$$X^*_2 = {}^{10}\!/_{280}$$
$$X^*_3 = {}^{10}\!/_{280}$$
$$1/G = {}^1\!/_8; \text{ therefore } G = 8.$$

The optimal mixed strategy for player X can then be calculated as follows:

$$X_1 = 8 \times {}^{15}\!/_{280} = {}^3\!/_7$$
$$X_2 = 8 \times {}^{10}\!/_{280} = {}^2\!/_7$$
$$X_3 = 8 \times {}^{10}\!/_{280} = {}^2\!/_7$$

Linear programming solutions for games with negative values

One special procedure is required when we use linear programming to solve a game such as the following:

	Y_1	Y_2	Y_3
X_1	6	−4	−14
X_2	−9	6	−4
X_3	1	−9	1

In this game, the game value G is negative. When a new variable such as $Y^*_1 = Y_1/G$, is created, it will also be negative. This presents a problem, because the simplex method requires all variables to be nonnegative. The problem can be resolved by creating a *nonnegative companion game*. We create this game by adding T units to every value in the payoff matrix, where T is the value of the smallest, or most negative, element in the matrix.[3] In our example, the −14 in row 1 and column 3 is the smallest element in the payoff matrix. Thus, T equals

---

[3]Technically, T may have to be larger than the smallest element to ensure that G is greater than zero. If G equals zero, then $Y^*_1 = Y_1/G$ would not be defined.

14. This value should be added to every element in the matrix, yielding the companion game

	Y_1	Y_2	Y_3
X_1	20	10	0
X_2	5	20	10
X_3	15	5	15

This game can now be solved by linear programming. The optimal strategies for both competitors are the same in the original game as they are in the companion game. The game value of the original game is equal to the game value of the companion game less the quantity T.

The following optimal results were obtained by using the simplex method to solve the companion game.

$$G = 11.5$$
$$X_1 = \tfrac{1}{10} \qquad X_2 = \tfrac{4}{10} \qquad X_3 = \tfrac{5}{10}$$
$$Y_1 = \tfrac{8}{20} \qquad Y_2 = \tfrac{7}{20} \qquad Y_3 = \tfrac{5}{20}$$

The value of the original game is 11.5 minus T units ($T = 14$), or -2.5. The optimal mixed strategy for player X and player Y is the same, as shown for the companion game.

Linear programming will solve games of any size, the only restriction being the capacity of the computing machinery. The reader may find the linear programming procedure time-consuming and tedious. With a little practice, and with the help of modern linear programming computer codes, the procedure becomes much simpler than it seems at first. Linear programming provides the best method of solving large games that do not have saddle points.

Nonzero-sum games

So far in this chapter, we have been concerned with zero-sum games, in which the gain to one competitor always equals the loss to the other. In nonzero-sum games, it is not necessarily true that one player's gain must exactly equal the other player's loss. In fact, it is possible that both may gain or both may lose. In nonzero-sum games, binding agreements between the parties may significantly affect the outcome of the game.

As an example, consider the game shown in Table 13.4. This game is similar to the Lauver's Garage example. In this case, however, each of the two firms is considering expanding its service facilities. The values given in the matrix are net profit changes. The first value represents the net change in profit for player X, and the second value represents the

Table 13.4 *Example of a nonzero-sum game*

	Do not expand Y_1	Expand Y_2
Do not expand X_1	0, 0	−10, +5
Expand X_2	+5, −10	−5, −5

net change in profit for player Y. The game is a nonzero-sum game, because a firm may incur a loss by spending money for expansion without gaining additional revenue. This loss by one firm does not result in an equivalent gain by the other.

The rationale for this game is as follows. If player X expands his facilities and player Y does not, X will take $10,000 of business away from Y. Since the expansion costs X $5000, the net result is a gain of $5000 for X and a loss of $10,000 for Y. The same is true if Y expands and X does not. If both expand, each will lose $5000, because neither competitor will gain any new business.

Assume that neither player decides to expand. The result is no change in net profit for either player. Note, however, that there is a great temptation for player X to expand because of the potential gain of $5000. Player Y is also tempted to expand. If both expand, however, both will lose $5000. Obviously, an agreement not to expand (which may be illegal), would benefit both parties.

The game shown in Table 13.4 can also be solved by dominance. For player X, strategy X_2 dominates strategy X_1, because no matter what Y does, X is better off playing X_2. Likewise, strategy Y_2 dominates strategy Y_1. The solution, by dominance, is for both players to expand. In reality, however, this is an unfavorable solution, and both players would be better off if neither expanded.

It is very difficult to formulate generalized decision rules for nonzero-sum games. Analysis can, however, provide a framework for considering similar real situations. It can identify obviously unwise moves and suggest choices that would seem to be profitable. From this standpoint, it should be helpful to the decision maker.

Games against nature

Decision making involves the selection of one act or strategy from among available alternative acts or strategies. Game theory is an analysis of decisions under conflict. The outcome of a given situation depends not only on the strategy a particular individual may choose, but also on the action taken by competitors. The first part of this chapter assumed that each competitor acted on the basis of self-interest. In *games against nature*, the opponent is assumed to be nonhostile, and the actions of this opponent cannot be predicted on the basis of self-interest.

In this type of game, the opponent's strategies are referred to as *states of nature*. This is a general term used in decision theory and refers to all factors beyond the control of the decision maker. For example, an individual selling concessions at a football game might find the weather rainy, overcast, or sunny. Since the weather is beyond the decision maker's control, it is referred to as a state of nature. Such other phenomena as consumer reaction to a new product and daily changes in the stock market are also considered states of nature, because they are beyond the control of the decision maker.

In this section, we also assume that no information is available about the probabilities of occurrence of the different states of nature. Thus, we are in an environment that decision theorists refer to as a state of *uncertainty*, or complete ignorance. Under uncertainty, the best we can do is establish a set of decision criteria to make the decisions consistent with the attitude and philosophy of the decision maker. Decision criteria also add an element of consistency to the decision-making process. (Chapters 2 and 3 treat decision making under conditions wherein probabilities of outcome can be assigned.)

An example of a game against nature

Fred's Green Frog Catering Company has received a contract to supply concessions for Saturday's "Homecoming" football game. Fred must choose one of three service policies. Strategy X_1 is oriented toward soft drinks and ice cream. Strategy X_2 favors hot dogs and coffee. Strategy X_3 contains "a little something for everybody." The success of any strategy depends on the state of nature that occurs: a rainy day, an overcast day, or a hot and sunny day. The payoffs associated with each service strategy and state of nature are given in Table 13.5. For example, strategy X_1 with rain would cause a loss of $70. The same strategy on a

Table 13.5 *Payoff matrix for Fred's Green Frog Catering Company*

	Rain S_1	Overcast S_2	Sunny S_3
Soft drinks and ice cream X_1	−70	20	530
Hot dogs and coffee X_2	300	150	60
A little of everything X_3	140	140	140

sunny day would yield a profit of $530. Probabilities of the various states of nature are not available.

The minimax criterion

The *minimax criterion* is often referred to as the *criterion of pessimism*. It states that an individual should minimize the loss (or, conversely, maximize the payoff) under the worst possible state of nature.[4] To utilize this criterion, the decision maker should find the worst possible payoff for each strategy. If Fred chooses X_1, for example, the worst possible state of nature is rain, which would result in a $70 loss. If he chooses X_2, the worst state of nature is sun, which would result in a $60 gain. The three available strategies, with their respective worst possible consequences are as follows:

Strategy	Payoff
X_1	−$70
X_2	$60
X_3	$140

The minimax criterion states that the strategy associated with the best of these values should be chosen. This is strategy X_3. It represents the minimum loss or maximum gain if the worst possible state of nature for a given strategy choice occurs.

Earlier, we talked about using the minimax solution in game theory. In strictly determined games, the minimax solution is the best solution for both competitors. In game theory, it is reasonable to assume that a competitor would try to place an opponent in the worst possible position. When the competitor is nature, however, there is no reason to assume that nature will be a hostile opponent. For this reason, the minimax criterion is considered pessimistic in a game against nature but reasonable in a game against a rational competitor.

The maximax criterion

Using the *maximax criterion*, the decision maker selects the alternative that will maximize the payoff (or, conversely, minimize the loss) under the best possible state of nature. For this reason, it is called the *criterion*

---

[4]This strategy is referred to as a minimax strategy, because it minimizes the maximum possible loss. It is also sometimes referred to as a *maximin strategy*, because it maximizes the minimum possible gain.

of optimism. The three alternatives and the highest payoffs associated with these alternatives are as follows:

Strategy	Payoff
X_1	$530
X_2	$300
X_3	$140

In this case, $530 is the best of the best, and the decision maker should select strategy X_1.

The LaPlace criterion

The *LaPlace criterion* states that when the probabilities of occurrence of various states of nature are unknown, they should be considered equal. Since there is no reason to believe that any one is more likely to occur than any other, they should all be treated equally.

In our example, there are three states of nature, so each should be assigned a weight of $\frac{1}{3}$. We determine the weighted value of each strategy by multiplying the payoff value for each state of nature by $\frac{1}{3}$ and then summing for all possible states. These calculations are as follows:

Strategy	Weighted payoff
X_1	$-70(\frac{1}{3}) + 20(\frac{1}{3}) + 530(\frac{1}{3}) = 160$
X_2	$300(\frac{1}{3}) + 150(\frac{1}{3}) + 60(\frac{1}{3}) = 170$
X_3	$140(\frac{1}{3}) + 140(\frac{1}{3}) + 140(\frac{1}{3}) = 140$

The strategy with the largest weighted value is X_2. A decision maker using the LaPlace criterion would therefore select alternative X_2.

The minimax regret criterion

In Chapter 2, we first introduced the concept of regret. A regret table expresses the difference between the best payoff for a given state of nature and the other payoffs which may be available. Consider the payoff table for Fred's catering company, shown in Table 13.5. If rain occurs, Fred's optimal strategy is X_2, and he would have no regret about selecting it. If he had chosen X_3, however, his payoff would be $140, which is $160 less than he could have made if he had acted optimally

Table 13.6 *Regret table*
for Fred's Green Frog
Catering Company

	S_1	S_2	S_3
X_1	370	130	0
X_2	0	0	470
X_3	160	10	390

and chosen X_2. Thus, he regrets his action by an amount of $160. In the regret table given in Table 13.6, this is shown at the intersection of the X_3 row and the S_1 column. If Fred had chosen X_1, he would have lost $70, which is $370 worse than the best possible payoff. We obtain the regret values for columns S_2 and S_3 similarly by subtracting every value in each column from the largest value in that column.

An individual using the minimax regret criterion determines the maximum regret value for each strategy and then selects the strategy that yields the minimum of these values. The maximum regret values for strategies X_1, X_2, and X_3 are as follows:

Strategy	Regret value
X_1	$370
X_2	$470
X_3	$390

The strategy associated with the minimum value is X_1, so it should be chosen.

Comparison of decision criteria

In our example, the maximax criterion and the minimax regret criterion resulted in the selection of strategy X_1. The minimax criterion led to X_3, and the LaPlace criterion led to X_2. It is not unusual for different criteria to result in the selection of different strategies.

The minimax and minimax regret criteria are considered conservative. In both cases, the attitude of the decision maker is pessimistic. Essentially, these criteria assume that nature is a hostile opponent and will, in effect, play against the decision maker. Under the maximax criterion, the mood is optimistic, assuming an intent by nature to cooperate. The assumption of some intent by nature raises serious questions about the original assumption of uncertainty (the assumption that, probabilities could not be specified).

In summary, no single criterion is accepted as the one best criterion. The proper criterion must be selected on the basis of the situation and the personality of the decision maker.

Sample problem 13.5   *SARAH'S SHOP*

In the following game matrix, X_1, X_2, and X_3 are the strategies available to Sarah. The four states of nature are S_1, S_2, S_3, and S_4. The probabilities associated with these states of nature are unknown. What strategy should she use when the decision criterion is minimax? maximax? LaPlace? minimax regret?

	S_1	S_2	S_3	S_4
X_1	30	70	0	100
X_2	80	200	10	10
X_3	20	50	100	150

SOLUTION

Minimax: X_3

Maximax: X_2

LaPlace: X_3

Minimax regret: X_1

Problems and exercises

1. Explain the following terms:
   zero-sum game
   nonzero-sum game
   two-person game
   payoff·matrix
   game matrix
   dominance
   iterative dominance
   pure strategy
   mixed strategy
   saddle point

   value of the game
   companion game
   state of nature
   minimax criterion
   maximax criterion
   LaPlace criterion
   minimax regret criterion
   decisions under conflict
   decisions under uncertainty

INSTRUCTIONS FOR PROBLEMS 2–5

Formulate each problem as a two-person game. Give a standard game matrix for each problem.

2. A game is played as follows. Player X selects one color from among red,

white, and yellow. Player Y selects one of three urns, a Grecian urn, a Persian urn, or an Oriental urn. A payoff is made from player Y to player X. One point is awarded for each ball of the color selected by X that appears in the urn selected by Y. The Grecian urn contains 0 red, 2 white, and 3 yellow balls. The Persian urn contains 4 red, 1 white, and 3 yellow balls. The Oriental urn contains 2 red balls, 4 white balls, and 1 yellow ball.

3. A game called "Rock, Scissors, and Paper" is played as follows. Two players simultaneously choose one of three strategies: rock, scissors, or paper. If both players choose the same strategy, no points are awarded to either player. If one player chooses scissors and the other paper, then the player choosing scissors gains 1 point and the player choosing paper loses 1 point. (This is because "scissors cut paper.") If scissors and rock are the competing strategies, then the person choosing rock gains 1 point and the person choosing scissors loses 1 point. (This is because "rock breaks scissors.") Finally, since "paper covers rock," a person choosing paper would win 1 point while a person choosing rock would lose 1 point.

4. A game called "Tuesday Night Football" is played as follows. An offensive player chooses one of three strategies: run, pass, or draw. A defensive player simultaneously chooses one of three strategies: standard, blitz, or deep coverage. If the offensive player chooses draw, the gain will be 2 yards against standard, 18 yards against blitz, and 6 yards against deep coverage. If the offense chooses pass, the results are a gain of 8 yards against standard, a loss of 8 yards against blitz, and no gain or loss against deep coverage. If the offense chooses run, the gain is 3 against standard, 0 against blitz, and 7 against deep coverage. Let the offense be player X and the defense be player Y.

5. Triple River City is divided into three major sections by the joining of 3 rivers, as shown in the accompanying figure.

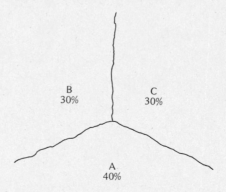

Of the city's residents, 40% live in section A, 30% in section B, and 30% in section C. At present, Triple River City has no ice skating rinks. Two companies, X and Y, have plans to build rinks in the city. Company X will build two rinks, one each in two of the town's three sections. Company Y will build only one rink. Each company knows that if there are two rinks in a given section of town, the two rinks will split that section's business. If there is only one rink in a section of town, that rink will receive all of that section's business. If there is no rink built in a particular section, the business from that section will be split equally among the city's three rinks. Each company would like to locate its rinks or rink in an area that would maximize its market share. Formulate this situation as a game from company X's point of view.

INSTRUCTIONS FOR PROBLEMS 6–9
Each of the following games contains a pure strategy for both players. Determine these strategies and the value of the game.

6.

	Y_1	Y_2	Y_3
X_1	0	4	−1
X_2	3	−1	−2
X_3	9	7	6

7.

	Y_1	Y_2	Y_3
X_1	0	2	4
X_2	4	3	4
X_3	7	3	2

8.

	Y_1	Y_2	Y_3
X_1	3	−2	0
X_2	5	2	−3
X_3	2	7	1

9.

	Y_1	Y_2	Y_3	Y_4
X_1	13	7	12	7
X_2	4	3	8	5
X_3	12	7	13	7

INSTRUCTIONS FOR PROBLEMS 10–12
Solve for the optimal mixed strategies of both players. Use the method of letting a player's expected winnings against one of the opponent's strategies equal that player's expected winnings against the other strategy.

10.

	Y_1	Y_2
X_1	4	6
X_2	8	3

11.

	Y_1	Y_2
X_1	4	−5
X_2	0	3

12.

	Y_1	Y_2
X_1	80	30
X_2	60	100

INSTRUCTIONS FOR PROBLEMS 13–16
Use the alternative, or simplified, method to determine the optimal mixed strategy for each player. Determine the value of the game.

13.

	Y_1	Y_2
X_1	5	−2
X_2	−3	0

14.

	Y_1	Y_2
X_1	3	5
X_2	4	2

15.

	Y_1	Y_2
X_1	50	100
X_2	80	30

16.

	Y_1	Y_2
X_1	500	-700
X_2	-100	700

INSTRUCTIONS FOR PROBLEMS 17–19

Use the method of dominance to reduce each of the following games to a 2 × 2 game.

17.

	Y_1	Y_2	Y_3	Y_4
X_1	0	4	1	-5
X_2	-3	3	2	-4
X_3	5	-1	-3	3

18.

	Y_1	Y_2	Y_3
X_1	4	8	3
X_2	2	10	2
X_3	0	3	6

19.

	Y_1	Y_2	Y_3
X_1	100	20	90
X_2	20	70	80
X_3	90	10	80

INSTRUCTIONS FOR PROBLEMS 20–24

Solve each of the following games. Some have pure strategies; others have mixed strategies. All 2 × 3 games can be reduced to at least 2 × 2 games by dominance.

20.

	Y_1	Y_2
X_1	14	20
X_2	16	12

21.

	Y_1	Y_2
X_1	8	6
X_2	10	-2

22.

	Y_1	Y_2	Y_3
X_1	40	15	20
X_2	10	20	30

23.

	Y_1	Y_2
X_1	0	3
X_2	-4	0
X_3	-2	5

24.

	Y_1	Y_2	Y_3
X_1	0	6	2
X_2	3	-1	5

INSTRUCTIONS FOR PROBLEMS 25–28

Give a graphical representation of each of the following games. Graphically determine the value of the game and the optimal mixed strategy for the player who has only two alternatives.

25.

	Y_1	Y_2	Y_3
X_1	-4	8	2
X_2	6	-2	0

26.

	Y_1	Y_2
X_1	-4	6
X_2	8	-6
X_3	5	0

27.

	Y_1	Y_2	Y_3
X_1	-2	2	5
X_2	10	-2	-5

28.

	Y_1	Y_2
X_1	-4	2
X_2	0	-4
X_3	2	-10

INSTRUCTIONS FOR PROBLEMS 29–32

Use the simplex method of linear programming to determine the value of the game and the optimal mixed strategy for player Y.

29.

	Y_1	Y_2
X_1	2	12
X_2	14	0
X_3	11	6

30.

	Y_1	Y_2	Y_3
X_1	-1	3	6
X_2	11	-1	-4

31.

	Y_1	Y_2	Y_3
X_1	0	1	-1
X_2	-1	0	1
X_3	1	-1	0

32.

	Y_1	Y_2	Y_3
X_1	0	4	2
X_2	2	1	4
X_3	3	3	1

INSTRUCTIONS FOR PROBLEMS 33–35

These problems are considered games against nature, and no probabilities can be associated with the various states of nature. What is the proper strategy under each of the four decision criteria — minimax, maximax, LaPlace, and minimax regret? Under what conditions might the decision maker use a particular one of these criteria?

33. The Martin Company is planning to choose one of three advertising strategies for a new product. It is expected that sales will depend not only on the strategy chosen, but also on economic conditions. No probabilities can be assigned to the three possible economic states. The payoff table is as follows:

	S_1	S_2	S_3
X_1	40	170	150
X_2	80	30	190
X_3	60	90	120

34. The local student club is planning to raise money next Saturday by offering

services to a nearby residential community. The club must decide on car washing, grass cutting, or window washing. The estimated return to the club depends on weather conditions. The probability of occurrence of each condition is unknown. The following table gives the estimated return for each alternative under each weather condition.

	Weather conditions		
	S_1	S_2	S_3
Car washing X_1	50	35	65
Grass cutting X_2	80	40	30
Window washing X_3	30	75	45

35. The Fisher Company has been asked to present a display at a local fair. The location of the display at the fair is unknown, so the company cannot predict whether the visitors to the display will be primarily children, teenagers, young adults, or retired people. The company has three displays to choose from. The consumer reaction to each display is expected to depend on the type of visitors. The expected consumer reaction for each display and each type of audience is given in the accompanying table. Discuss the relevance of each criterion in a situation such as this.

	Children S_1	Teenagers S_2	Young adults S_3	Retired people S_4
X_1	bad	average	good	excellent
X_2	average	good	average	average
X_3	bad	good	average	good

Supplementary readings

Agee, M. H., R. E. Taylor, and P. E. Torgenson. *Quantitative Analysis for Management Decisions*. Englewood Cliffs, N.J.: Prentice-Hall, 1976.

Braverman, J. D. *Probability, Logic, and Management Decisions*. New York: McGraw-Hill, 1975.

Lapin, L. L. *Quantitative Methods for Business Decisions*. New York: Harcourt Brace Jovanovich, 1976.

Levin, R. I., and R. B. Des Jardins. *Theory of Games and Strategies*. Scranton, Pa.: International Textbook, 1970.

Levin, R. I., and C. A. Kirkpatrick. *Quantitative Approaches to Management*, 3rd ed. New York: McGraw-Hill, 1975.

Luce, R. D., and H. Raiffa. *Games and Decisions*. New York: Harcourt Brace Jovanovich, 1973.

Owen, G. *Game Theory*. Philadelphia: Saunders, 1968.

Shubik, M. *The Uses and Methods of Game Theory*. New York: American Elsevier, 1975.

Turban, E., and J. R. Meredith. *Fundamentals of Management Science*. Dallas, Texas: Business Publications, 1977.

Williams, J. D. *The Complete Strategist*, rev. ed. New York: McGraw-Hill, 1966.

Chapter 14

Utilizing tables and statistical distributions

At various locations in this book, we have assumed that the reader was familiar with statistical distributions such as the normal, binomial, and Poisson distributions. We also assumed that the reader knew how to use the tables given in the Appendix. This chapter is provided for those who feel they need to know more about these topics.

The normal distribution

The best-known statistical distribution is the normal distribution, which is represented by the bell-shaped curve. The major reason for the widespread use of the normal curve is that it is very often a good approximation of reality. Many real distributions, both discrete and continuous, can be approximated by the normal distribution. Both the heights and the weights of individuals of the same age and sex tend to be normally distributed. Student grade-point averages, daily sales values, and golf scores in a professional tournament also tend to be normally distributed. Since the normal curve closely approximates many business phenomena, we can often use it in decision analysis.

Characteristics of the normal distribution

Each normal distribution is characterized by an arithmetic mean and a standard deviation. The *arithmetic mean* is a measure of central tendency; that is, it is the value around which the majority of measurements are clustered. The Greek letter μ (mu) is used to represent the arithmetic mean. Suppose we want to describe the daily demand for milkshakes at a local restaurant. Figure 14.1 shows pictorial representations of two different demand situations.

The curve on the left represents a situation wherein the daily demand measurements tend to cluster around a value of 20. On most days, the number of milkshakes demanded was "close" to 20. In the curve on the right, the arithmetic mean is 50, and most of the daily demand values cluster around this value. Thus, the arithmetic mean is a measure of the

Figure 14.1 *Representations of two normal distributions with different arithmetic means*

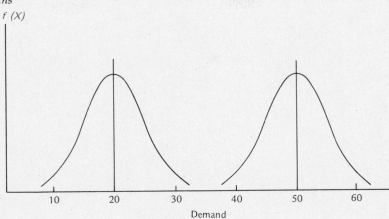

central tendency of a distribution, or the value around which the measurements tend to cluster.

Figure 14.2 shows pictorial representations of two demand situations that have the same arithmetic mean. The distribution shown on the left, however, is more widely dispersed than the distribution shown on the right. The *standard deviation* is a measure of the amount of dispersion about the mean. It is normally represented by the Greek letter σ (sigma). Since it is more widely dispersed, the distribution on the left in Figure 14.2 has a larger standard deviation than the distribution on the right.

Taken together, the mean and the standard deviation provide a method of determining what percent of measurements lie between any two values.[1] For example, if we start at the mean and travel 1 standard deviation unit in each direction, we will encompass approximately 68% of all daily demand values. Suppose past daily demand has averaged (arithmetic mean) 60 milkshakes a day with a standard deviation of 8 milkshakes. We know that approximately 68% of all daily demand values have been between 52 and 68, that is, (60 − 8) to (60 + 8).

---

[1]Although we will not use it in our discussion, you may be interested in the formula for the normal probability density function.

$$f(X) = \frac{e^{-(X-\mu)^2/2\sigma^2}}{\sigma\sqrt{2\pi}} \quad (-\infty < X < +\infty)$$

The symbols e and π represent irrational numbers the values of which are approximately 2.7183 and 3.1416 respectively. The symbols μ and σ are the mean and the standard deviation of the distribution. Statistical tables utilize the standardized normal distribution where $\mu = 0$ and $\sigma = 1$.

Figure 14.2 *Representations of two normal distributions with identical means and different standard deviations*

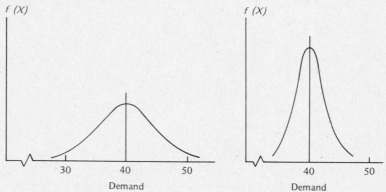

The mean plus or minus 2 standard deviation units encompasses approximately 95% of all daily demand values. Thus, approximately 95% of all daily demand values have been between 44 and 76. An important implication is that on any given day, the probability of demand being between 52 and 68 is approximately .68. Likewise, the probability of demand being between 44 and 76 on any given day is approximately .95.

Utilizing the normal distribution table

The 68% and 95% values we just discussed were approximations. We can obtain more specific values by using Table A in the Appendix. This table lists the areas between the mean μ and a specified number of standard deviation units to one side of the mean. This distance in standard deviation units is referred to as the *Z value* and can be computed as follows:

$$Z = \frac{X - \mu}{\sigma}$$

The probability distribution for Z is known as the *standardized normal distribution*. The arithmetic mean of the standardized normal distribution is 0, and the standard deviation is 1.

To illustrate the use of Table A, we will continue to examine the same demand distribution that we have been discussing. Past daily demand had a mean value of 60 units and a standard deviation of 8 units. Several examples will be given, and they are graphically displayed in Figure 14.3.

As our first example, let us use Table A in the Appendix to find *the percent of daily demand values that have been between 60 and 70*, as shown in Figure 14.3(a). With Table A, we always work from the mean to a specific value. Thus, the first task is to find the number of standard deviation units (distance) between the mean value of 60 and the demand value of 70. Since the standard deviation has a value of 8, this distance is easily obtained.

$$Z = \frac{X - \mu}{\sigma} = \frac{70 - 60}{8} = 1.25$$

From Table A in the Appendix, the area value corresponding to a Z value of 1.25 is .3943. This tells us that the area under the curve between the mean and 1.25 standard deviation units to the right (or left) of the mean contains 39.43% of the area under the curve. Thus, we know that 39.43% of the past daily demand values were between 60 and 70. This

Figure 14.3 *Determining probabilities by using the normal curve*

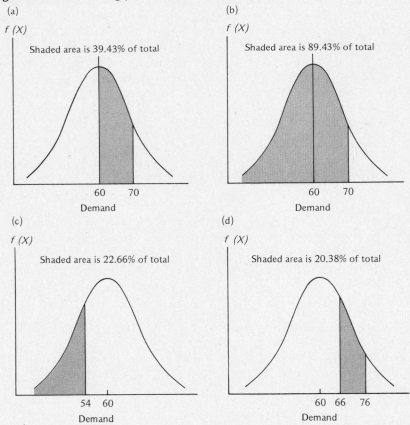

means that the probability of a particular demand value being between 60 and 70 is also .3943.

Since the mean represents the center of distribution, 50% of all measurements lie above (and below) the mean. If we wish to determine *what percent of the days demand has been 70 or less,* as shown in Figure 14.3(b), we simply add the percent of days the demand has been 60 or less (50%) to the percent of days the demand has been between 60 and 70 (39.43%). Demand has been for 70 or less on 89.43% of the days.

Figure 14.3(c) illustrates a situation wherein we are looking for the *percent of demand values that are 54 or less.* There are .75 standard deviation units between the mean (60) and 54; that is, $Z = (54 - 60)/8 = -.75$. Thus, 27.34% of all measurements are between 54 and 60. Since 50% of all measurements are less than the mean (60), the percent of measurements less than 54 is 22.66, that is $(50.00 - 27.34)$.

As a final example, suppose we need to know the *percent of days that demand was between 66 and 76.* First, we use Table A to find the percent of measurements between 60 and 76. $Z = (76 - 60)/8 = 2.0$. From Table A, .4772 is the area value corresponding to a Z value of 2.0. Thus, two standard deviation units from the mean include 47.72% of the measurements.

Second, the distance from the mean to 66 is .75 standard deviation units; that is, $(66 - 60)/8 = .75$. From Table A, this includes 27.34% of the measurements. We can obtain the percent of measurements between 66 and 76 by subtracting 27.34 from 47.72. Thus, the percent of measurements from 66 to 76 is 20.38.

Sample problem 14.1 WOLTER'S VARIETY STORE

Assume that past daily demand for an item at Wolter's Variety Store has been normally distributed with an arithmetic mean of 380 and a standard deviation of 60. Determine what percent of past daily demand values have been:

1. 400 or more
2. 420 or less
3. 290 or less
4. between 320 and 500

SOLUTION
1. $(400 - 380)/60 = .33$; Area 380–400 = .1293
   Area 400 or more = .5000 − .1293 = .3707
2. $(420 - 380)/60 = .67$; Area 380–420 = .2486
   Area 420 or less = .5000 + .2486 = .7486
3. $(290 - 380)/60 = -1.50$; Area 290–380 = .4332
   Area 290 or less = .5000 − .4332 = .0668
4. $(500 - 380)/60 = 2.00$; Area 380–500 = .4772
   $(320 - 380)/60 = -1.00$; Area 320–380 = .3413
   Area 320–500 = .4772 + .3413 = .8185

The binomial distribution

The binomial distribution is another well-known statistical distribution. Such events as coin flipping, basketball free-throw shooting, dichotomous consumer-preference analysis, and scores on true–false examinations can be adequately represented by the binomial distribution.

A process that gives rise to the binomial distribution is sometimes referred to as a Bernoulli process. It is characterized by repeated trials occurring under the following conditions:

1. Each trial has only two possible outcomes. We will refer to one outcome as a success and to the other as a failure.
2. The probability of a particular outcome remains fixed from trial to trial. We shall refer to the probability of a success on any one trial as p and the probability of failure as q, which is $(1 - p)$.
3. The trials are independent.

The binomial probability formula

The binomial distribution can be used to obtain the probability of achieving a specified number of successes in a given number of trials. The formula used to obtain these probabilities is as follows:

$$P(r) = \frac{n!}{r!(n - r)!} p^r q^{n-r}$$

where:

p = Probability of success on any trial

q = Probability of failure on any trial

n = Total number of trials

r = Number of successes in n trials.

As an example, assume that 6 fair coins are tossed and a head is considered a success. We will use the formula to determine the probability of obtaining exactly 2 heads. That is, the number of successes, r, is equal to 2. In this case, $p = 1/2$, $q = 1/2$, $r = 2$, and $n = 6$.

$$P(2) = \frac{6!}{2!(4)!} \cdot \left(\frac{1}{2}\right)^2 \left(\frac{1}{2}\right)^4$$

$$P(2) = \frac{720}{(2)(24)} \cdot \left(\frac{1}{4}\right) \left(\frac{1}{16}\right)$$

$$P(2) = 15(.015625) = .2344$$

By changing the value of r, we can use this formula to obtain the probabilities of achieving any number of successes between 0 and 6. The results appear in Table 14.1.

Table 14.1 *Binomial probabilities for n = 6,
p = .5*

Number of heads r	Probability P(r)
0	.0156
1	.0938
2	.2344
3	.3125
4	.2344
5	.0937
6	.0156
	1.0000

We can use this example to explain the structure of the binomial formula. The first term,

$$\frac{n!}{r!(n - r)!}$$

is the number of different ways in which r successes can be obtained in n trials. There are 15 different ways in which 2 heads can occur in 6 tosses of a coin. One sequence of outcomes is head, head, tail, tail, tail, and tail. Another sequence is head, tail, tail, tail, tail, and head. The second term in the formula, $p^r q^{n-r}$, is the probability of obtaining any one of the arrangements of r successes and $(n - r)$ failures. The probability of getting any particular arrangement of 2 heads and 4 tails is $(.5)^2(.5)^4$, or .015625.

As a second example, consider a production line that produces 70% acceptable parts and 30% defective parts. Five parts are sampled. What is the probability that the lot will contain exactly 3 acceptable parts? We will define "obtaining an acceptable part" as a success. Thus, $p = .7$, $q = .3$, $n = 5$, and $r = 3$.

$$P(3) = \frac{5!}{3!(2)!} (.7)^3 (.3)^2$$

$$P(3) = \frac{(120)(.343)(.09)}{(6)(2)} = .3087$$

We can obtain the probabilities of getting other numbers of successes by changing the value of r in the formula. The results appear in Table 14.2.

It should be evident that a binomial probability problem may be worked in either of two ways. For example, it is known that women

Table 14.2 *Binomial probabilities for the production line example,* $n = 5$, $p = .7$

Acceptable parts r	Defective parts $n - r$	Probability $P(r)$
0	5	.0024
1	4	.0284
2	3	.1323
3	2	.3087
4	1	.3601
5	0	.1681
		1.0000

purchase 60% of a particular food item in a restaurant and men purchase the other 40%. Each purchase is independent of other purchases. Suppose 4 units of this item are sold. What is the probability that exactly 3 units were purchased by women? We can define a success as "a purchase by a woman." Thus, $p = .6$, $q = .4$, $n = 4$, and $r = 3$.

$$P(r) = \frac{n!}{r!(n-r)!} p^r q^{n-r}$$

$$P(3) = \frac{4!}{(3!)(1!)} (.6)^3 (.4)^1$$

$$P(3) = \frac{24}{(6)(1)} (.216)(.4)$$

$$P(3) = .3456$$

In this example, we determined the probability that exactly 3 units were purchased by women. Obviously, the fourth unit must have been purchased by a man. We could have restated the same question as follows: "What is the probability that exactly 1 unit will be purchased by a man?" In this case, we can define a success as "a purchase by a man." Thus, $p = .4$, $q = .6$, $n = 4$, and $r = 1$. Since the two questions are exactly the same, we should obtain the same answer.

$$P(r) = \frac{n!}{r!(n-r)!} p^r q^{(n-r)}$$

$$P(1) = \frac{4!}{(1!)(3!)} (.4)^1 (.6)^3$$

$$P(1) = \frac{24}{(1)(6)} (.4)(.216)$$

$$P(1) = .3456$$

Characteristics of the binomial distribution

A histogram of our coin-tossing example appears in Figure 14.4. This is a graphical display of the probability of achieving any number of heads between 0 and 6. This distribution is symmetrical, but the binomial distribution will be symmetrical only in the special case where $p = q = .5$.

Figure 14.5 is a histogram of the production line example where p, the probability of an acceptable part, is equal to .7. In this example, p does not equal q and the distribution is not symmetrical.

Each binomial distribution is characterized by an arithmetic mean and a standard deviation. The mean number of successes in a binomial distribution is np, and the standard deviation is $\sqrt{npq}$. In the production line example, the expected value, or mean number of successes (acceptable parts), is determined as follows:

$$\mu = np = 5(.7) = 3.5$$

The standard deviation of the distribution is

$$\sigma = \sqrt{npq} = \sqrt{(5)(.7)(.3)} = \sqrt{1.05} = 1.02$$

Figure 14.4 *Histogram of binomial distribution for n = 6, p = .5*

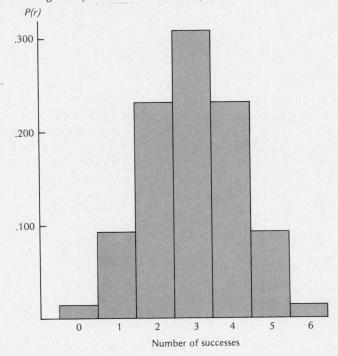

Figure 14.5 *Histogram for the production line example, n = 5, p = .7*

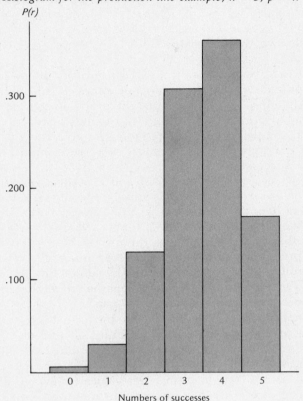

Using the cumulative binomial table

As the number of trials in the binomial experiment grows large, it becomes very burdensome to use the binomial formula to calculate probabilities. Tables for the binomial distribution have been generated and are available to help in these situations. Table B in the Appendix is a cumulative probability table for the binomial distribution. It gives the probabilities of r or more successes during n trials.

To illustrate the use of Table B, consider the following example. It is known that only 35% of the voters in a certain city favor candidate Smith. If 25 voters are selected at random, find the probability that:

1. Ten or more voters will favor candidate Smith
2. At least 5, but fewer than 10 voters will favor Smith
3. Exactly 8 voters will favor Smith

From Table B, we can determine the probability value for $n = 25$, $p = .35$, and $r \geq 10$. This value is .3697 and is the probability that 10 or more voters will favor candidate Smith.[2] This example illustrates the advantage of the cumulative tables. If we used a table of individual probabilities, we would have to add together all of the relevant probabilities. In this example, we would have to add the probabilities of exactly 10, exactly 11, . . . , all the way to 25.

Part 2 of this example illustrates the use of a cumulative table to obtain the probability that the number of successes will fall into a given range, that is, $p(j \leqslant r < k)$. Note that the probability is for j to be less than or equal to r ($j \leqslant r$ or $r \geqslant j$) but for r to be strictly less than k ($r < k$). Using a cumulative probability table, we obtain $p(j \leqslant r < k)$ by subtracting the probability of k or more successes from the probability of j or more successes.

In this example, p and n remain .35 and 25 respectively. If $r = 5$, the probability of 5 or more successes is found from Table B to be .9679. The probability of 10 or more successes is .3697. The probability of at least 5 but fewer than 10 successes is .5982, that is (.9679 − .3697).

Part 3 of this example illustrates the use of the cumulative table to obtain the probability of exactly r successes in n trials. We can obtain this probability from a cumulative table by subtracting the probability of obtaining ($r + 1$) or more successes from the probability of obtaining r or more successes. In this example, $r = 8$ and ($r + 1$) = 9. The value of n and p remain 25 and .35. From Table B, the probability of obtaining 8 or more successes is .6939. The probability of obtaining 9 or more successes is .5332. Thus, the probability of obtaining exactly 8 successes is .1607, that is (.6939 − .5332).

Table B does not contain probability values for events wherein the value of p is greater than .5. Thus, we must define a success to be the event that has a probability equal to or less than .5. As an example, consider a spinning game wheel that lands red 45% of the time and green 55% of the time. Since a payoff is made on green, we want to know the probability of:

1. Exactly 4 greens in 7 spins
2. Four or more greens in 7 spins

The red outcome is the only outcome with a probability of .5 or less. Thus, we must define a success as "obtain a red" and let $p = .45$. Part 1 asks for the probability of 4 greens in 7 spins. This is the same as 3 reds in 7 spins. Thus, $p = .45$, $n = 7$, and $r = 3$. The probability of 3 or more reds is .6836. The probability of 4 or more reds is .3917. The probability of exactly 3 reds (and consequently exactly 4 greens) is .2919, that is (.6836 − .3917).

[2]All values in Table B in the Appendix give the probability of r or more successes in n trials.

Part 2 asks for the probability of 4 or more greens, that is, 4, 5, 6, or 7 greens. This is the same as 3 or fewer reds: the number of reds will be 0 or greater, but less than 4. From Table B, the probability of 0 or more reds is 1.000, and the probability of 4 or more reds is .3917. Thus, the probability of 3 or fewer reds (and consequently 4 or more greens) is .6083, that is (1.000 − .3917).

Sample problem 14.2   BRODERICK'S MARKETING COMPANY

1. Mary Jones, a sales representative for Broderick's Marketing Company, is known to sell a product on 35% of her sales calls. She makes 15 calls a day. Find the probability that:
    a. She will make 5 or more sales
    b. She will make exactly 5 sales
    c. She will make more than 4 but fewer than 10 sales
2. Bill Jones is a door-to-door sales representative. In a given neighborhood, he finds someone at home on 90% of his sales calls. He makes 20 calls a day. Find the probability that:
    a. He will find someone at home on exactly 18 of his calls
    b. He will find someone at home on all of his calls
    c. He will find someone at home on 15 or fewer of his calls

SOLUTION
1. $p = .35$, $q = .65$, $n = 15$
    a. Probability of 5 or more = .6481
    b. Probability of 5 or more = .6481; Probability of 6 or more = .4357;
       Probability of exactly 5 = (.6481 − .4357) = .2124
    c. Probability of 5 or more = .6481; Probability of 10 or more = .0124;
       Probability of 5 to 9 = (.6481 − .0124) = .6357
2. A success is no one at home.
    $p = .10$, $n = 20$
    a. Probability of 2 or more = .6083; Probability of 3 or more = .3231
       Probability of exactly 2 = (.6083 − .3231) = .2852
    b. Probability of 0 or more = 1.0000; Probability of 1 or more = .8784
       Probability of exactly 0 = (1.0000 − .8784) = .1216
    c. Probability of 5 or more = .0432

Normal approximation to the binomial

In some cases, it may be convenient to approximate the binomial distribution with the normal distribution. Consider the example we used before about the number of voters favoring candidate Smith. It is known that 35% of the voters in a given city favor candidate Smith. If 25 voters are selected at random, what is the probability that 10 or more voters will favor candidate Smith?

First, we must know the mean and the standard deviation of the distribution being approximated. In this case,

$$\mu = np = (25)(.35) = 8.75$$

$$\sigma = \sqrt{npq} = \sqrt{(25)(.35)(.65)} = 2.38$$

The binomial distribution is discrete. If a histogram were drawn, the block representing exactly 10 voters would extend from 9.5 to 10.5 on the histogram. Thus, to determine the probability of exactly 10 voters favoring Smith, we would need the area under the curve from 9.5 to 10.5. To find the probability of 10 or more, we need all of the area to the right of 9.5. We can determine this by first finding the area under the curve between the mean (8.75) and 9.5.

$$Z = \frac{X - \mu}{\sigma} = \frac{9.5 - 8.75}{2.38} = .32$$

A Z value of .32 corresponds to an area of .1255. We subtract this value from .5000: .5000 − .1255 = .3745. The probability of 10 or more favoring Smith is .3745. This approximation is close to the .3697 value we had determined by using the binomial tables.

As a second example, we shall approximate the probability of at least 5 but fewer than 10 voters favoring Smith. To do this, we must find the area between 4.5 and 9.5. First, we find the area between the mean (8.75) and 4.5.

$$Z = \frac{X - \mu}{\sigma} = \frac{4.5 - 8.75}{2.38} = -1.79$$

The corresponding area is .4633.

The Z value for the area between 8.75 and 9.5 has been previously determined to be .32. The corresponding area is .1255. Thus, the probability that at least 5 but fewer than 10 voters will favor Smith is approximately .5888, that is (.4633 + .1255 = .5888). Compare this to the actual value of .5982 that we had obtained from Table B in the Appendix.

In this example, the normal distribution is a reasonable approximation to the binomial. This will not always be the case, particularly if n is small or if p is close to either 0 or 1. Generally, the approximation will improve as n grows larger and as p (or q) becomes closer to .5. A good rule of thumb is that the approximation should not be used unless the values ($\mu \pm 2\sigma$) lie between 0 and n. In our example,

$$\mu + 2\sigma = 8.75 + 2(2.38) = 13.51$$

$$\mu - 2\sigma = 8.75 - 2(2.38) = 3.99$$

Since 3.99 and 13.51 both lie between 0 and 25 (which is n), the approximation should be reasonably good.

The Poisson distribution

The Poisson distribution is another statistical distribution often used in managerial analysis. This distribution is best known for its use in queuing, or waiting-line, problems. It is used to estimate probabilities of arrivals of cars at tollbooths, customers at supermarket checkouts, and planes at airports. The use of the Poisson distribution is not limited to queuing theory. It has also been used to estimate demand for certain products, defects on a production line, and the number of accidents in a specific period of time. The Poisson distribution can also be used as an approximation to the binomial distribution.

The Poisson distribution is much like the binomial distribution, except that we think of n as very large and p as very small. For example, consider the production of cloth fabric. A given square yard may contain no blemishes, or it may contain 1, 2, or even more minor defects. Although we can count the defects, it is impossible to count the nonblemished spots. The best we can say is that there is a very large number of them. The probability of a blemish on any one spot is very small.

The Poisson distribution is discrete. From the probability function for the Poisson distribution, we can obtain the probability of a specified number of occurrences per unit of measurement. The probability function is

$$P(x) = \frac{e^{-\lambda}\lambda^x}{x!}$$

where:

x = Given number of occurrences during a specified time period

$P(x)$ = Probability of that given number of occurrences during a specified time period

λ = Average or mean number of occurrences during a specified time period (the Greek letter lambda)

e = 2.718 . . . , a mathematical constant, the base of the Napierian logarithm system

An illustration of the Poisson distribution

We will illustrate the Poisson distribution by considering the following example. Studies have revealed that the number of early morning calls to a particular switchboard is Poisson distributed with a mean of 1.5 calls per minute. Our task is to determine the probability that during any given minute the switchboard will receive no calls, 1 call, 2 calls, etc.

First, we will calculate the probability that 2 calls will come in during a particular minute; that is

$$P(2) = \frac{(1.5)^2 \; e^{-1.5}}{2!} = .2510$$

This calculation is difficult, because it involves raising a number to a fractional power. Nevertheless, it can be used to determine that the probability of 2 calls in a given minute is .2510. Poisson probability tables, such as Table C in the Appendix, have been generated so we do not have to make these calculations. Table C is the easiest to use of the tables in the Appendix. We can read the probability of 2 calls directly from the table by finding the column corresponding to the average or expected number of occurrences during the specified time period. In Table C, we locate the column with an expected value of 1.5 and read the probability of exactly 2 calls from the "$x = 2$" row. This value is .2510. Likewise, the probabilities of receiving no calls, 1 call, and 3 calls can also be read directly from the table as .2231, .3347, and .1255.

The Poisson probabilities for this example are given in Table 14.3, and the distribution is illustrated in Figure 14.6. The mean of the Poisson distribution is, of course, λ. It is curious to note that the standard deviation of this distribution is the square root of the mean. Thus,

$$\sigma = \sqrt{\lambda}$$

Table 14.3 *Probabilities of a given number of calls per minute; Poisson distribution with λ = 1.5*

Calls per minute	Probability
0	.2231
1	.3347
2	.2510
3	.1255
4	.0471
5	.0141
6	.0035
7	.0008
8 or more	.0002
	1.0000

Figure 14.6 *Histogram for the switchboard example, a Poisson distribution with* $\lambda = 1.5$

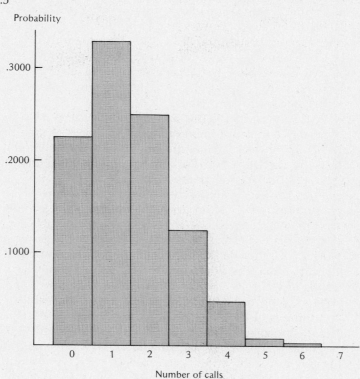

Sample problem 14.3   *KEISER'S FLOOR TILE*

A particular type of floor tile is decorated with gold dots randomly placed on the tile. The number of dots per square inch is Poisson distributed with an average value of 3 dots per square inch. Find the probability that a particular square inch will have:
1. Exactly 3 dots
2. Exactly 5 dots
3. 8 or more dots

SOLUTION
From Table C, the answers are:
1. .2240
2. .1008
3. .0081 + .0027 + .0008 + .0002 + .0001 = .0119

Binomial approximation to the Poisson

We can gain further appreciation of the Poisson process by comparing it with the Bernoulli process and the associated binomial distribution. In a Bernoulli process, a finite number of trials take place. Each trial has only two possible outcomes, and the probability of obtaining a success on a given trial is constant. In such cases, we can use the binomial formula to compute the probability of obtaining any number of successes in a specified number of trials.

In some instances, such as the arrival of customers at a service facility, it is possible to count the number of successes or arrivals, but not the number of times an arrival did not occur. The essential difference between the Bernoulli and Poisson processes is our inability to determine the number of trials in the latter case.

It is possible to use the binomial distribution as an approximation to the Poisson by viewing very short time periods, such as 1 minute, as a Bernoulli trial in which either no arrivals or 1 arrival can occur. For example, the second column of Table 14.4 shows the Poisson arrival probabilities for a 20-minute period when the mean arrival rate is 2. These probabilities may be approximated by subdividing the period into 20 intervals of 1 minute each and treating each minute as a trial in which there is a 0.1 probability of 1 arrival and a 0.9 probability of no arrivals. The number of trials, n, and the probability of a success, p, have been selected to ensure that the mean of the binomial distribution, $(n \times p)$, is equal to the mean arrival rate, λ. We can then use the binomial formula to compute the probability of obtaining any specific number of arrivals in 20 trials or minutes. These probabilities are shown in column 3 of Table 14.4.

Table 14.4 *Binomial approximation of Poisson arrival probabilities*

Number of arrivals in the period	Poisson probability $(\lambda = 2)$	Binomial probability $(n = 20, p = .1)$	Binomial probability $(n = 100, p = .02)$
0	.1353	.1216	.1326
1	.2707	.2701	.2707
2	.2707	.2852	.2734
3	.1804	.1901	.1823
4	.0902	.0898	.0902
5	.0361	.0319	.0353
6	.0120	.0089	.0114
7	.0034	.0020	.0032
8	.0009	.0003	.0007
9	.0002	.0001	.0002

The error source in this approximation results from the fact that it is possible to get more than 1 arrival in 1 minute of time. This error may be reduced by working with smaller time periods. If the 20-minute period is broken into 100 equal segments, and the probability of an arrival in a given period is adjusted to .02 so that $(n \times p)$ still equals 2, we can use the binomial formula to compute the probabilities in column 4. Comparison of columns 2 and 4 shows that this second approximation is quite close.

We can make further improvements in the approximation by further reducing the length of the divided segments. As the number of trials or segments, n, is allowed to grow without limit, and the probability of a success, p, is reduced to maintain a constant mean, $(n \times p)$, the binomial distribution approaches the Poisson distribution as its limiting form.

Problems and exercises

1. Explain the following terms:

   normal distribution   arithmetic mean
   bell-shaped curve   standard deviation
   standardized distribution   cumulative probabilities
   Z value   Bernoulli process
   binomial distribution   Poisson distribution

   INSTRUCTIONS FOR PROBLEMS 2–7
   Each question is concerned with the normal distribution. Use Table A in the Appendix.

2. The number of customers visiting a retail establishment on a given day is approximately normally distributed with a mean of 150 and a standard deviation of 20. Find the probability that during a given day:
   a. The number of customers is 150 or more
   b. The number of customers is between 155 and 180
   c. The number of customers is less than 142
   d. The number of customers is between 140 and 150

3. A football coach at a prep school is interested in the weights of the males enrolled. These weights are approximately normally distributed with a mean of 120 pounds and a standard deviation of 10 pounds. There are 1000 males enrolled. Estimate the number whose weights are:
   a. Less than 100 pounds   c. Between 128 and 138 pounds
   b. More than 115 pounds   d. Greater than 138 pounds

4. Scores on a particular test are approximately normally distributed with a mean of 500 and a standard deviation of 100. Estimate the percentage of scores that are:

   a. 750 or more   c. Between 325 and 425
   b. Between 425 and 575   d. 500 or greater

5. The useful lives of radio tubes of a particular type are approximately normally distributed with a mean of 400 hours. It is known that 28.81% of the tubes last between 400 and 440 hours. How many tubes last fewer than 300 hours?

6. Scores on a particular exam are approximately normally distributed with a mean of 200 and a standard deviation of 40. A particular student scored better than 89.43% of the students. What was the score of this student?

7. Daily demand for a product at a particular industry is normally distributed with a mean of 32. It is known that on 54.68% of the days, demand is between 26 and 38. What is the standard deviation of this demand?

INSTRUCTIONS FOR PROBLEMS 8–14
Each question is concerned with the binomial distribution. Use the appropriate tables in the Appendix.

8. A particular salesperson is successful on 25% of all calls. On a given day, 15 calls are made. Determine the probability that:
   a. 5 or more sales were made   c. No sales were made
   b. Exactly 4 sales were made

9. A production line is known to produce 85% good parts and 15% defective parts. Twelve parts are sampled. What is the probability of obtaining:
   a. 3 or fewer defective parts   c. Exactly 4 defective parts
   b. 10 or fewer good parts   d. Exactly 11 good parts

10. It is known that a particular basketball player can make free throws with 90% accuracy. If 20 free throws are shot, determine the probability that:
   a. All 20 shots will be made   c. 16 or fewer shots will be made
   b. Exactly 18 shots will be made

11. A biased coin lands heads on 20% of the tosses and tails on 80% of the tosses. The biased coin is flipped 4 times. What is the probability of obtaining exactly 1 head? Use Table B, and check your answer using the binomial probability formula.

12. A particular production line yields 90% good parts and 10% defective parts. Three parts are sampled. What is the probability that they will all be good parts? Use Table B, and check your answer using the binomial probability formula.

13. Refer to problem 10. Use the normal curve to answer parts (b) and (c). (*Hint:* Let $\mu = np$ and $\sigma = \sqrt{npq}$.) For part (b), find the area between 17.5 and 18.5. Suppose 100 free throws are attempted. What is the probability of making 85 or more?

14. Refer to problem 8. Use the normal curve to answer parts (a) and (b). (*Hint:* Let $\mu = np$ and $\sigma = \sqrt{npq}$.) For part (b), find the area between 3.5 and 4.5. Suppose 400 calls are made. What is the probability of making 120 or more sales?

INSTRUCTIONS FOR PROBLEMS 15–19

The following questions are concerned with the Poisson distribution. Use the appropriate tables in the Appendix.

15. Defects on a particular paper machine are measured in terms of number of defects per 100 linear feet. Defects are Poisson distributed with a mean of 3.0. What is the probability that on a particular 100 feet of paper the number of defects will be 0? 1? 2? 3? 4? 5? 6? 7? 8? 9? What is the probability that there will be 3 or fewer defects in a given segment?

16. Car arrivals at a parking lot are Poisson distributed with a mean of .5 arrivals per minute. For a given minute, determine the probabilities of 0, 1, 2, 3, 4, and 5 arrivals.

17. Telephone calls at a particular switchboard are Poisson distributed with a mean of 4 calls per minute. Give a probability distribution showing the probabilities of 0 through 10 arrivals in any given minute.

18. Arrivals at a tollbooth are Poisson distributed with a mean of 1 arrival per minute. Use Table C to determine the probability that the number of arrivals will be 1, or 2, or 3. Approximate these answers by using the binomial distribution. Divide the minute into 10 equal segments, and assume that the probability of 1 arrival during a 6-second segment is .10 and the probability of no arrival is .90. Use the binomial table for $n = 10$ and $p = .10$. Repeat the approximation with $n = 20$ and $p = .05$.

19. Consider problem 16. Use the binomial distribution to approximate the probability that the number of arrivals will be 2 or less. Use $n = 5$ and $p = .10$. Repeat with $n = 10$ and $p = .05$. Compare the results with your answers in problem 16.

Supplementary readings

Bell, C. E. *Quantitative Methods for Administration.* Homewood, Ill.: Irwin, 1977.

Cook, T. M., and R. A. Russell. *Introduction to Management Science.* Englewood Cliffs, N.J.: Prentice-Hall, 1977.

Hadley, G. *Introduction to Business Statistics.* San Francisco: Holden-Day, 1968.

Mendenhall, W., and J. E. Reinmuth. *Statistics for Management and Economics.* Belmont, Calif.: Wadsworth, 1971.

Schlaifer, R. *Introduction to Statistics for Business Decisions.* New York: McGraw-Hill, 1961.

Spurr, W. A., and C. P. Bonini. *Statistical Analysis for Business Decisions.* Homewood, Ill.: Irwin, 1973.

Chapter 15

Implementation and model selection

Chapters 1–14 of this book were concerned with management science models and their application to business, industry, government, and other organizations. They did not deal specifically with the problems of implementation and model selection. Implementing is using management science to get the job done, and it requires a great deal of managerial skill. It encompasses behavioral, organizational, and technical facets. Implementation is not the job of the management scientist alone. It is properly accomplished through the joint efforts of the management scientist, top management, and operating personnel.

Model selection is primarily the concern of management science personnel. It is often considered more of an art than a science. Skill in model selection increases with increasing knowledge of, and experience in, developing and implementing management science procedures. We hope that the following material will help the reader to better understand the difficulties, techniques, and rewards of proper implementation and model selection.

Implementation

Management science models are of little value unless they are used to assist in solving real problems. Thus, implementation may be the most important aspect of quantitative managerial analysis. Simply defined, *implementation* is putting a solution to work. Implementation should be the most rewarding aspect of a management science project. It can also be the most difficult.

Twenty-five years ago, successful implementation of operations research projects was much more difficult than it is today. In those days, top management was often skeptical of the practicability of efforts in quantitative managerial analysis. Many executives considered the work esoteric and not worthy of implementation. As a result, the successful practitioner had to be both a scientific expert and a successful salesman.

In the past few years, the situation has changed, largely due to a growing record of success for management science projects. Quantitative methods have been used in almost every function of business, such as production, personnel, and marketing. The list of successful projects comes from many types of industries, as well as from government and nonprofit organizations.

Despite the improvement, today's practitioners are still often faced with difficult situations when they try to implement the findings of an operations research study. Some of these problems result from vestiges of skepticism that still remain. More often, however, they are caused by conflicting organizational or behavioral demands on personnel. Consequently, effective implementation requires the application of behavioral, scientific, and organizational skills.

There is no golden rule of implementation. But experience indicates that certain conditions, such as those illustrated in Figure 15.1, foster a climate that facilitates implementation. A number of these are discussed in the following sections.

Figure 15.1 *Improving the implementation climate*

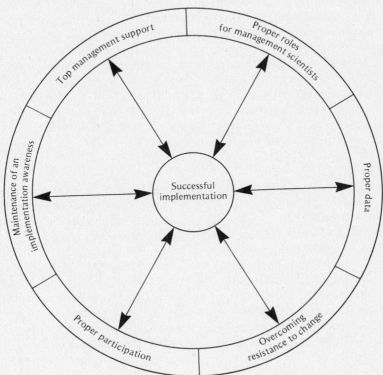

Support from top management

It is important that management science personnel and projects receive the support of management, particularly top management. Without this support, it is difficult to obtain cooperation from the people who are actually implementing the project. Operating personnel often gauge the effort they should devote to a project by the amount of interest that top management shows in the activity. Without this discernible interest, a project tends to lose its credibility and consequently the support of operating personnel.

Support from top management is demonstrated by the status given the project, willingness to implement the findings of the study, and the resources committed to the activity. Too often, however, verbal support is undercut by inadequate resources and reluctance to implement findings. Such actions usually result in a gradual deterioration of the management science function within the organization.

In addition to project support, it is important that management science personnel have a status similar to corresponding operating personnel. In many organizations, management scientists operate as a staff department. In such cases, it is important that this department receive proper recognition and support from top management.

A good relationship with top management is often demonstrated by the funding of the unit and the location of the unit in the organizational structure. Obviously, if this unit is headed by a vice president or someone reporting to a vice president it has more visible support than if it occupies a lower level in the organizational hierarchy. Support is also demonstrated by the use that top management makes of the management science team. An unused department appears to lack the faith of management. This is true for operations research groups as well as other departments within the organization.

Management scientists in the organization

There are two basic ways of structuring management science talent within an organization. As we have noted, these individuals may be placed in a single unit. Alternatively, they may be dispersed throughout the organization. In the early days of operations research, it was standard procedure to create a management science group that served as a staff unit. This procedure is still followed in many organizations today. In these organizations, there seems to be a correlation between the status of the group and the degree of successful implementation of management science projects. As the group goes up the organizational chart, the status of the team improves and so does the success ratio of projects that it undertakes. Many personnel perceive the location of the group in the organization as a measure of management support for management science.

Today, there is a trend toward the second approach, assignment of management science personnel throughout the organization. This gives management scientists operating experience and responsibility. It puts them on an operating team and tends to destroy the idea that members of management science groups have their heads in the clouds and cannot adapt to applied problems. There is also long-range value in this approach. It gives management science personnel the opportunity to move up the ladder in other areas of the organization. Ultimately, this will provide the organization with more managerial personnel who are familiar with the advantages and limitations of quantitative managerial analysis.

Regardless of the type of structure, implementation is aided by having the right type and the right amount of management scientists in the organization. Experience indicates that a good rule to follow at first is to have too few rather than too many management scientists. Acceptance is enhanced if there is a high demand on the technical expert's time. A bad climate develops when management science personnel appear to be combing the organization for problems to justify their existence.

Properly filling management science positions is a challenging and sometimes difficult task. A good rule is to try to obtain a team of individuals who will complement each other and the organization. This is true even if the individuals are dispersed throughout the organization. It may be wise not to bring in people who are technically oriented to the exclusion of all other skills. Management scientists must interact with all segments of the firm. They need to understand operating and behavioral problems. Many members of the organization's management science group should have the talent to eventually move into line positions or into other support groups.

It is also a good idea to have some management science personnel who have had previous experience in other areas of the firm. In fact, some people within the organization may have the skills to join the management science team. Little or no operating experience among operations research personnel gives the impression that this is merely a technical group convened to solve theoretical problems. Finally, management science people should be active and interested in making a major impact on problem solving within the organization. After all, their primary task, like that of everyone else, is to contribute to the performance of the organization.

Maintaining awareness of implementation

In Chapter 1, we defined the four stages of the management science process as problem analysis, model building, model solving, and model implementation. Although implementation is the final stage, it is important for the management science team to consider the task of implementation while they are performing the functions associated with the first three stages of the process.

In analyzing a problem, the management scientist must consider the desired objectives, the factors relevant to obtaining these desired objectives, and the ultimate cost of the solution. At this initial stage, implementation *must* be considered. It will do little good to spend time, money, and effort to analyze elements of a problem that are beyond the control of the decision maker. More fruitful results can be obtained by identifying and concentrating on factors that are under the control of those who actually implement the project.

The management scientist must also give careful thought to the expected cost of the problem-solving process. A potential project should not be undertaken unless the expected savings exceed the cost of obtaining these savings. In other words, project optimization needs to include the solution cost. The goal is to maximize the results obtained from implementing a solution less the costs incurred in developing that solution.

The next stages in the management science process are concerned with building and solving an appropriate model. Quite often, a particular problem may be amenable to analysis with the aid of several different types of management science models. Ease of implementation should be a major factor in choosing a particular type of model. If operating personnel are familiar with and have accepted a particular type of model, this factor should weigh heavily in model selection. In some cases, the model may have to be rerun (often under varying conditions) by individuals who are not management science personnel. The model should not be so complex that it exceeds the capabilities of existing operating personnel and operating equipment.

Implementation considerations are also important in designing the solution process and the format in which the solution is presented. For example, if implementation requires continual reruns of the model, then money and time must be spent to obtain an efficient solution process. If the solution procedure is a one-time effort, then less consideration need be given to the efficiency of the process. The results obtained must be presented in a format that can be used by operating personnel and operating equipment. Too often, a management science team reaches the implementation stage before realizing that the solution simply cannot be implemented in its present form. The necessary restructuring results in added costs, which no organization wants.

Data for management science projects

Management science techniques are often criticized because their implementation requires data that are inaccessible, unreliable, or too costly to obtain. Improvements in computers and the development of proper management information systems have gone far to reduce this deficiency. A computerized management information system is basically a set of computer hardware and software used to provide information for managerial decision making. Its purpose is to generate, process, store, and make available data that are useful to management. It should provide current as well as historical data.

It is very important that management scientists be able to use this data, so the system must be designed to satisfy the needs of management science personnel as well as other groups in the organization. Technical personnel must understand where the information comes from, how it is processed, its accuracy, and its timeliness. In many cases, the success of a project will depend on the quality of the data used. It is important that management science personnel understand these data and use them properly. Management scientists must contribute to as well as draw on the system. Projects should be designed to feed useful data back into the system. Given what it costs to acquire good information, it is best not to lose it.

Management information systems, coupled with time-sharing computer facilities, have greatly enhanced quantitative managerial analysis. It is now possible to monitor business transactions on a continuous basis. Accurate and timely information is almost immediately available. The proper use of management science models depends on this information. In the future, more and more managers will have access to management information systems and time-sharing terminals. This interface between people, machines, and information should improve decision making immensely.

The need for participation

Successful implementation requires the active participation of top management, operating management, and operating personnel. Top management must take the initiative in implementing management science projects. It is responsible for determining and satisfying overall organizational goals and objectives. It must ensure that projects are directed toward these organizational goals, rather than toward the interests of an individual manager or a segment of the organization. Top management usually selects the projects assigned to a management science group. It also may define what constitutes successful operation by this group.

Operating management must be directly involved in management science projects. These managers will eventually be responsible for operating the system after the management science specialist has left. Lasting success depends on the operating manager's knowledge and confidence in the system. Thus, these managers should be consulted and brought in on the formulation and evaluation stages of the project.

They should be clearly aware of the benefits to be gained from the project, as well as its weaknesses and the limitations and constraints it may place on the overall operation of the organization.

Finally, the project must be accepted by operating personnel. Ultimately, the operators implement the system. Their acceptance and knowledge of a system are vital to its success.

Resistance to change

Some people in organizations have a built-in resistance to change. It is often claimed that such resistance is natural, but this is not true. Left alone, people do change. They enjoy introducing variety into their work and personal lives. Resistance arises when change threatens an existing and relatively satisfying social system, as changes in status, employment conditions, or authority relationships may.

The introduction of a management science project into an organization is the type of change that is often resisted by management and operating personnel. Quite often, management science projects cause changes in technology, which means a change in social relationships. Furthermore, this change is perceived as imposed by narrow specialists who are insensitive to the needs of the people in the organization. This lack of confidence enforces and magnifies the individual's tendency to resist change.

In many cases, fear of change is not justified. Thus, it is the perceived threat rather than the actual threat that causes the problem. The best way of dealing with the situation is to eliminate the perceived threat by explaining the ramifications of the proposed project and the effect it is expected to have on operating personnel. In some cases, implementation will require changes in job functions. The negative aspects of these changes can often be overcome, or at least mitigated, by reassignment of duties, job rotation, or retraining of personnel. Planning for these personnel changes should be an integral part of planning the total management science project.

The best way to overcome fear of change is for top management and management scientists to show honesty, openness, and respect for all personnel. Once a mutual understanding is reached, it is much easier to cope with the realities of change.

Model selection

Each chapter of this book concentrates on a particular topic or set of related topics, and the problems and exercises at the end of each chapter correspond to the material within the chapter. For example, the topic of Chapter 5 is linear programming. We can be confident that the exercises for this chapter relate to linear programming. It is highly unlikely that these end-of-chapter exercises will be designed to test the reader's skill in simulation or queuing theory, so it requires little skill to select the proper model for these problems. Unfortunately, proper model selection is much more difficult in a real situation.

Quantitative managerial analysis is often referred to as management science. There is, however, a good deal of artistry in the successful application of management science. Much of this artistic skill is concerned with selecting the proper management science model. This skill improves with experience in using and implementing real management science projects. A prerequisite is an appreciation for, and an understanding of, the role that management science plays in managerial analysis. Such understanding requires knowledge of the basic elements of management problems that are suitable for quantitative managerial analysis. It also requires knowledge of the types of models available, their advantages and limitations, and their suitability for analyzing particular types of management problems.

It would be nice if we could add an additional chapter giving a simple explanation of how to select a proper model for a particular problem. Regrettably, it is impossible to develop a checklist to guide the reader infallibly toward selection of the proper model. In the remaining sections, however, we have tried to provide material that will be helpful in model selection.

First, we discuss the necessity of maintaining a problem orientation. Second, we review the models presented in this book, highlighting a few points the reader should have retained from each chapter. Third, we present eight groups or classes of management science problems that are often encountered in managerial analysis. We then show the relationships between problem type and model type. Finally, random problems appear at the end of this chapter to assist the reader in developing skill in model selection. In this chapter, unlike the others, the reader's knowledge of management science provides the only hints about what model or procedure to apply to a given problem.

Maintaining a problem orientation

The practicing management scientist should remember that his or her primary goal is to help the organization solve its problems as efficiently and effectively as possible. The technique is important only to the extent that it provides a good and useful solution at a reasonable cost.

There are several guidelines that are useful in developing and maintaining a problem orientation. The first is to resist the temptation to make the problem fit the model. Most of us have a preference for a certain type of technique, such as linear programming or simulation. We would like to use our favorite model on every problem. Even worse, we tend to seek out problems that fit the model, even if they do not exist! Of course, this should not be done. A problem should first be defined and analyzed and then an appropriate technique selected.

In model selection, it is important to appreciate the characteristics of the problem and the assumptions underlying the model. Errors can be made in either direction. Some analysts use their favorite model even though the assumptions underlying this model are so far from the characteristics of the problem that erroneous results are almost guaranteed. The opposite can also be true. We can get so involved in matching problem characteristics to model characteristics that we never get the job done. Always remember that the best model is a useful model.

There are many problems that can be analyzed by the use of several different management science techniques. In such cases, it is best to use the simpler and more economical of the models available. The reason for economy is apparent. Simplicity usually enhances the implementation process. It also provides other personnel with a better understanding of the interface between management science and operating problems.

Review of text material and models presented

Many mathematical models could have been included in a textbook of this type. We used the following criteria in selecting topics to cover. First, we presented those techniques that are most commonly used, such as linear programming, network analysis, and simulation. Second, we selected some models, such as decision theory and game theory, because of their contribution to the reader's general understanding of decision-making techniques. Finally, we chose not to include models that require knowledge of advanced mathematics. These criteria led to the selection of models that are in keeping with the objectives of the text. Many references are available for readers who wish to explore more complex models or a wider variety of quantitative procedures.

Chapters 2 and 3 are concerned with topics that are useful in understanding and making decisions when a condition of certainty does not exist. This section explores topics such as decision processes, decision trees, probability formulas, probability revision, and the value of information. These chapters make up a unit on a body of information that is often referred to as *decision theory*. Here, the reader should become familiar with the decision process, the uncertainties involved in this process, and the use of statistics and other techniques for improving one's skill in decision making.

Inventory models are the topic of Chapter 4. The section on simple inventory models is important for several reasons. First, similar but generally more complex models are widely used today. Second, the skills developed in building inventory models are useful in constructing other types of management models. Finally, inventory models illustrate the concept of balancing two contrasting types of costs in order to obtain the lowest total cost. This third concept appears in many types of decision situations.

The latter part of Chapter 4 is concerned with *inventory decisions made under uncertainty*. It should reinforce the concepts presented in Chapters 2 and 3. In this chapter, the reader should develop a better understanding of model formulation, a better appreciation for the use of probabilities in decision making, and a greater awareness of the application of management science models to actual problems.

Chapters 5, 6, and 7 constitute a unit on *linear programming models.* One reason why this section is important is that linear programming is perhaps the most widely used management science model. In its most general form, linear programming is a method of determining an optimal allocation of limited resources among competing demands. Many types of managerial problems fit this general format. They include production scheduling, blending, distribution, and dynamic or time-staged problems.

The linear programming section is important for other reasons. First, the reader should understand the relationship between economic reasoning and mathematical programming. The section on postoptimality analysis emphasizes that a great deal of valuable information besides the optimal solution can be obtained from mathematical programming. Second, this material should continue to reinforce the reader's knowledge of model building. Third, the reader should know the versatility, strengths, and limitations of mathematical models and the results obtained from them. Finally, the chapter on *transportation and assignment models* illustrates the advantages of using appropriate special-purpose algorithms.

It is true that Chapters 5, 6, and 7 are user-oriented in the sense that these models are quite commonly applied to real situations. This textbook would fall short of its mission if the reader only learned about the theory of linear programming. Understanding should run deeper, including knowledge of the applications of mathematical programming and how it is useful to the decision maker.

The material in Chapters 8 and 9 expands on the topics presented in the linear programming section. Chapter 8 introduces three types of mathematical programming procedures: *goal, integer,* and *dynamic programming.* These are well-known programming routines. Their introduction gives the reader a better understanding of the algorithms that are available for special types of problems. It should also point out the power and flexibility of mathematical programming.

Network models, including PERT and CPM, are covered in Chapter 9. These models are useful when we are managing a project that consists of a set of interrelated activities, such as a large construction project. A network model is often the first model that many individuals encounter in their vocational experience. It is important to understand the concepts and method of analysis utilized in this popular type of management science model.

Queuing theory, the study of waiting lines, is the subject of Chapter 10. Readers readily recognize the importance of this subject. People wait at banks, supermarkets, and tollbooths. The analysis used here is somewhat different from the procedures we discussed before in that it is descriptive rather than normative. Queuing models generate data that help describe a process, such as the average length of a line or the average wait per customer. Managers use these data in their decision making. Quite often, they are combined with economic data to suggest a quasioptimal solution. It is important to understand the factors that underlie the waiting process: the alternating busy and idle periods, the variations in service and arrival times, the configuration of the queue, and the variations in the service discipline.

Chapter 11 is concerned with *simulation.* It introduces a substantially different method of quantitative managerial analysis. The techniques previously discussed were analytical; they were models that could be solved. Many managerial problems are too complex for standard analytical methods, and a simulation model may be the only logical alternative available to the decision maker. It is important for the reader to understand the basic elements of the simulation process, the uncertainties involved in the results obtained, and the wide area of potential use.

Markov analysis and *game theory* are the last two management science concepts discussed in this book. They are covered in Chapters 12 and 13. They probably have fewer direct applications than any of the other techniques. Both, however, provide a convenient framework for the study and understanding of problems faced by management personnel. Markov analysis is used to describe and predict movements in a dynamic system. Such systems may include automobile locations, customer preferences, and bank accounts. Game theory is used to describe and study decision making in competitive situations. In both of these chapters, the knowledge of concepts involved is more important than their direct application to real problems. In short, these chapters should help the reader develop logical thinking patterns to use in dealing with competitive or dynamic situations.

Finally, we should again note that this book is only an introduction to quantitative managerial analysis. Many advanced textbooks are available. They discuss more complex models, such as calculus-based techniques, nonlinear programming, and advanced probabilistic models.

The models discussed in this textbook are the models you will use most often. They should provide a good basis for understanding management science.

Classification of problems

A common mistake is to identify or associate a problem with a particular type of model, such as a linear programming problem or a simulation problem. Problems are often amenable to analysis by more than one management science technique. Thus, a good classification of problems should be based on something other than the models typically used in analyzing them.

Several taxonomies of management science models have been developed. The general procedure is first to classify a model as stochastic or deterministic. If it is deterministic, it is classified as linear or nonlinear. This process can be continued through many subclasses of models. Figure 15.2 illustrates the procedure, using only the models discussed in this textbook. Unfortunately, this system is of little help in learning and explaining model selection. A better approach is to pinpoint certain

Figure 15.2 *A taxonomy of management science models (limited to models discussed in this text)*

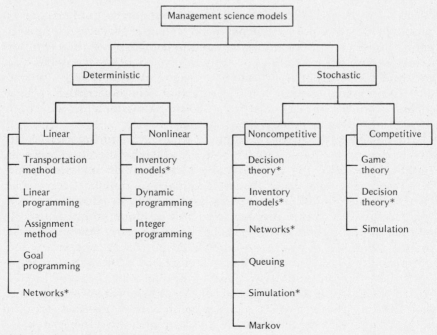

* Appears in two or more categories

Figure 15.3 *Classification of management science problems*

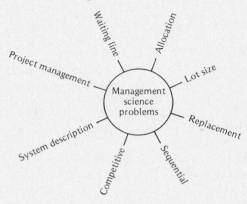

classes of problems that have been repeatedly encountered by management scientists (Figure 15.3). We can then identify models that have been successfully used in analyzing these situations. The problems discussed in the following sections are not mutually exclusive. Many real situations contain elements from several different classifications.

Allocation problems This is one of the most common types of managerial problems. In allocation problems, management is concerned with allocating limited resources among competing ends in a way that will best achieve some predetermined objective. A manager faces an allocation problem each time it is necessary to decide at what level to operate competing activities within an organization. These activities (departments, products, or machines) are often competing for a limited supply of such resources as money, labor, or time.

The Bell Metal Company example in Chapter 5 and the Rick Martin investment problem in Chapter 8 both illustrate the allocation problem. In the first example, the decision maker had to properly allocate production resources (brass, lamp shades, and machine time) to two production processes. Linear programming was used to assist in this allocation. In the Rick Martin problem, dynamic programming was used to allocate a scarce commodity ($60,000) among four competing investment alternatives. In both cases, the allocation was made in a way that optimized the decision maker's stated objective.

The distribution problem is a form of the allocation problem, but it is common enough to warrant special consideration. In distribution problems, the emphasis is on moving a commodity from its sources to several competing destinations. The allocation to these destinations is made in a way that will achieve some objective, such as minimizing cost. The Kappa Tile Company problem in Chapter 7 illustrates the movement of a commodity from manufacturing plants to distributors. The Hill Company problem in the same chapter is an example of allocating or assigning jobs to machines.

Many types of management situations fall into the general category of allocation problems. They include budgeting, portfolio selection, rationing of natural resources, media selection, and site selection. The common ingredient in all these problems is the need to allocate scarce resources to competing ends.

Lot-size problems Managers are often faced with determining how much of a commodity to manufacture, purchase, sell, or use. Lot-size analysis can be used in these and similar situations. The common characteristic of lot-size problems is the need to balance two or more contrasting types of cost in such a way that the sum of these costs is minimized.

The classic example of this situation is referred to as the "newsboy problem." It refers to the newsboy who makes a daily purchase of newspapers and then peddles them on the street corner. It is extremely important to purchase the right quantity of newspapers. If too many are purchased, an obsolescence cost is incurred because newspapers not sold on a given day must be discarded. Conversely, if too few are purchased, the newsboy has an opportunity cost, the lost profit that could have been made by buying and selling more newspapers. The right amount is the quantity that minimizes the sum of these costs.

John's Little Peach Market in Chapter 2 and the East Orange Nursery in Chapter 4 both have to solve lot-size problems. The first example is almost identical to the newsboy problem. The commodity is perishable peaches instead of newspapers. Otherwise, the analysis is the same.

The East Orange Nursery problem is an inventory problem. Two contrasting types of costs are involved. Ordering a large supply of inventory results in a large holding cost, or carrying cost. Decreasing the order quantity decreases this carrying cost but increases ordering cost, because the firm must place more orders per year. The manager must seek a policy that will minimize the sum of these two contrasting costs.

The lot-size problem is commonly associated with inventory analysis, but many other real situations fall in this category. The decision maker faces a problem with the same general characteristics when determining the number of clerks to use in a stockroom, the amount of cash to keep in a cash register, the number of seats on an airline route, or the size of a new manufacturing plant. In fact, some of the other classes of problems, such as the replacement problem, closely resemble the lot-size problem in that they tend to minimize the sum of related cost functions. They have other characteristics, however, that set them apart from the typical problem in this category.

Replacement problems Replacement problems deal with the proper time to take a particular action. They almost always contain probabilistic elements, and they usually deal with replacing items that fail or are used up over a period of time. In a sense, everything is perishable and all perishable items must be replaced. This is true of apples, light bulbs, heavy machinery, buildings, and even people. The development of proper replacement policies is an important aspect of the operation of any organization.

The Kent Company example in Chapter 3 is a typical replacement problem. This company uses a large number of sensitive industrial thermometers. These thermometers have useful lives that range from 0 to 6 months. The company can replace the thermometers as they burn out, or they can adopt a policy of periodic mass replacement at given time intervals. The task is to determine whether periodic mass replacement is the best policy and, if so, what is the proper replacement interval.

The example of Patterson Auto Supply in Chapter 4 is also a replacement problem. Here, the manager is facing an uncertain demand for a product. The objective is to find the proper time to begin the process of replenishing the supply of inventory.

Replacement problems are quite common in everyday life. We must decide when to eat, when to refuel our car, when to buy new clothes, and when to take out the garbage (which is a replacement problem in reverse). Industries must decide when to buy new equipment. Municipal governments must replace fire trucks and police cars.

Sequential decision problems In many managerial situations, a decision maker faces a series or sequence of interrelated decisions. Future decisions often depend on the decision made at an earlier stage in the sequence. The opposite is also true, so the impact of later decisions must be evaluated before the earlier decisions are made. The objective is to determine an overall policy or approach that will maximize the benefits resulting from the total set of decisions that must be made.

Janice Adams' problem in Chapter 8 is a typical example of a sequential problem. Senator Adams is attempting to cross the United States by making a series of short flights. Each flight moves her from one time zone to another (from Eastern Standard Time to Central Standard Time, for instance). At the end of each flight, a decision must be made about the destination of the next flight. Obviously, these decisions are related. The objective is to find the set of decisions that will minimize total flying time.

Dynamic programming was used to solve Janice Adams' problem. The nature of this technique makes it particularly suitable for analyzing situations involving a set of sequenced and interrelated decisions. In many situations, however, other management science procedures may be simpler or otherwise more appropriate. In Chapter 6 linear programming was used to obtain a production schedule for four successive periods for the Baur Company. Simulation was used in Chapter 11 to devise and formulate an inventory policy that encompassed a number of time periods. The McMillan Company problem in Chapter 2 illustrates the use of decision theory to analyze a management situation consisting of several sequential decisions.

It is easy to visualize other examples of industrial problems involving sequential decisions. The task of effectively scheduling several jobs through a number of different machines is a particularly difficult sequential problem. Other examples include investment decisions and product development decisions. An entering college student faces a sequential decision when determining what term to take a particular course. The replacement problem takes on the characteristics of a sequential problem when the manager must plan for a series of related replacements. For example, a ship steaming around the world may have to determine a master refueling plan before beginning the trip.

Competitive situations A manager faces a competitive situation whenever the outcome of the decision is affected not only by the manager's action but also by the action or decision of an outside party. The outside party is generally an opponent, as we find in baseball, or a competitor, as we find in business. In some cases, however, the outside party may be a nonhostile "competitor," such as inclement weather or equipment failures.

The Lauver's Garage example in Chapter 13 illustrates a simple competitive situation. In this example, each of two competitors is trying to better his market position by selecting the proper advertising strategy. A decision cannot be made in isolation, however, because the result is affected not only by the decision made by the individual, but also by the decision made by the competitor. The Fred's Green Frog Catering example in the same chapter is another illustration of a competitive situation. In this example, however, the opponent is nature. Competition against nature may pose special problems, because the opponent is unpredictable.

Competitive situations are common in everyday life. Football, advertising, pricing, and political campaigns all call for selection of the proper strategy. Other examples include the selection and programming of network television shows, military strategy, collective bargaining, and site selection by competitors such as banks and movie theatres.

System description problems Management is often more concerned with understanding and predicting the behavior of a system than with solving for an optimal solution. Ultimately, of course, the manager will use this knowledge of the system to approach a quasioptimal solution. Initially, however, the emphasis is on description rather than optimization.

The Bill's Car Wash example in Chapter 11 is a classic example of a system description model. Here, simulation is used to describe, under varying conditions, such operating characteristics as the percent of time the system was idle, the average time spent waiting by a customer, and the percent of customers lost due to a shortage of waiting facilities.

Although simulation is the management science technique most often associated with systems description, other types of analysis are often used. In the Browning Company problem in Chapter 10, queuing formulas were used to provide information similar to that obtained in the Bill's Car Wash example. In the Woody's Pest Control example in Chapter 12, Markov analysis was used to predict and describe market-share data for a series of successive time periods. Probability theory was used in Chapter 3 to describe the state of a machine calibration in the example of Wales Machine Parts, Inc.

System description models are quite common. They teach us to fly airplanes and to understand our economic system. They are used in the design of roadways, agricultural systems, and urban complexes. It is not unusual for an individual to want to learn more about a process or system. These models help by providing a description, often under varying conditions, of the system we are examining.

Project management problems Project management problems are distinguished from other types of management problems by their nonrepetitive nature. A project is usually a one-time effort. It consists of a set of interrelated activities that a decision maker must plan and control. Projects can be quite large and can involve significant amounts of money, people, time, and other resources. A scientific approach to project management has long been sought by managers. The first steps in this direction came with Gantt charts around the turn of the century. Significant further improvements, however, did not come until the 1950s, when management science entered its rapid growth stage.

The JASS Company problem in Chapter 9 is an example of a project management situation. Here, a decision maker is faced with expediting and controlling a market research study that consists of eight related activities. Janice Adams' problem in Chapter 8 can also be thought of as a project management problem. In this situation, the objective is to find an optimal itinerary for travel across the United States.

The application of quantitative managerial analysis to project management is well known. More people are probably familiar with this application of management science than with any other type of operations research activity. Government contractors are almost always required to use a scheduling technique such as CPM or PERT. Construction work is the most commonly discussed example of project management. The coordination required among plumbers, carpenters, and electricians is obvious. Other examples of project management include product development, organizational design, and planning for the introduction of a new computer to be used by the organization.

Waiting-line problems Waiting lines are often considered a special type of management science problem. Many situations fall into this category. People wait in line almost every day at banks, tollbooths, supermarkets, and so on. Machines also wait for service, airplanes wait for runways, and messages wait for an open circuit.

The English Chemical Company problem in Chapter 10 and the Hunt Company problem in Chapter 12 are both examples of waiting-line problems. In English Chemical, chemists wait in line to draw supplies from a chemical storeroom. Queuing formulas are used to develop a solution that will minimize total cost. At the Hunt Company, machines are waiting in line for service at a machine repair facility. Markov analysis is used to analyze this problem. The objective is similar to that found in the English Chemical Company problem: to design a service system that will minimize the sum of the cost of waiting and the cost of rendering service.

Many waiting-line problems resemble the lot-size problem in that the objective is often to balance two contrasting types of costs. It is expensive to wait in line. This cost can be reduced by speeding up the service system, but this modification usually increases service cost. Thus, the procedure is to find an appropriate facility that will minimize the sum of the two relevant costs.

This class of problem also resembles system description problems. Quite often, the manager is not looking for an optimal solution in the sense that we use the term in an allocation problem. Knowledge of operating characteristics (such as average length of the line or average waiting time) may be more important to the manager than obtaining a solution that is optimal in the tradition sense.

The relationship between model types and problem types

The foregoing discussion should have made it clear that there is not a one-to-one relationship between models and problem classifications. Some models, such as simulation, can be used to analyze problem situations from several of the categories we have just described. Likewise, all categories contain some situations amenable to analysis by several different management science models. There is, however, a relationship among categories and models. It would be unwise to try to specify the exact nature of this relationship, but Table 15.1 should help the reader better understand the process of model selection.

Summary

Today, an introductory course in quantitative methods is a required part of almost all university curricula in business and public administration. The reason for this academic interest in quantitative methods is their use and importance in business, government, and other organizations. Experience has shown that management science can assist in decision making in all types of organizations. It is important for graduates of programs in administration to have a working knowledge of management science, including the types of situations amenable to quantitative analysis, the management science techniques available, and the conditions that limit the effective use of these techniques. We hope that this book has contributed to this understanding.

Table 15.1 *Relationship between problem type and model type*

Chapter	Model type	Allocation	Lot size	Replacement	Sequential	Competitive	System description	Project management	Waiting line
2, 3	Decision theory			X	X	X			
4	Inventory		X	X					
5, 6, 7, 8	Linear programming	X			X	X		X	
8	Dynamic programming	X		X	X				
9	Networks					X		X	
10	Queues			X			X		X
11	Simulation	X	X	X	X	X	X	X	X
12	Markov				X	X	X		
13	Games					X			

Problems and exercises

1. Explain the following terms:

   implementation   allocation problems
   participation   distribution problems
   artistic ability   lot-size problems
   prototype problems   replacement problems
   competitive situations   description models

   INSTRUCTIONS FOR PROBLEMS 2–20
   Describe the procedure you would follow if faced with each of the following
   situations. In some cases, the solution procedure is quite simple. In other
   cases, the calculations are complex and tedious and should not be undertaken without computer assistance.

2. The Ahmad Company must plan its production schedule for the months of
   January, February, March, and April. The company works on a contract
   basis and has agreed to supply the following quantities on the last day of
   the month: January, 1000; February, 600; March, 1700; and April, 900. No
   additional sales are expected. The company will have no inventory of this
   item on January 1 and must also have none on May 1. Production capacity
   for this item is 800 units per month without overtime. If overtime is used,
   400 additional units can be manufactured monthly. Cost of production
   during January and February is $10 per unit on regular time and $14 per
   unit on overtime. It is anticipated that a new labor contract will increase
   each of these costs by $2 per unit in March and April. There is no setup cost
   involved in the production operation. Items produced in one month can be
   used to meet the sales quota at the end of that same month, or they can be
   held in inventory to meet demand in a later month. There is a $3 charge for
   holding a unit of inventory from one month to the next.

3. The Begley Company ships material from a central manufacturing location
   to four distributors, which are located on the north, east, south, and west
   sides of town. The company maintains a fleet of 26 trucks, which it uses to
   transport the material from plant to distributors. This fleet consists of 9
   large trucks with a capacity of 5 tons each, 12 medium-sized trucks with a
   capacity of 2 tons each, and 5 small trucks with a capacity of 1 ton each. On a
   particular day, the north, east, south, and west distributors require 15, 10,
   20, and 8 tons of material respectively. The costs of sending each type of
   truck to each distributor are as follows:

	North	East	South	West
Big	80	63	92	75
Medium	50	60	55	42
Small	20	15	38	22

4. The Henderson Company must decide how to allocate 4 available salespeople to the company's 4 sales territories. At the present time, there is no requirement that each territory have at least 1 salesperson. In fact, any number of the 4 available people may be assigned to any territory. The estimated sales results (in thousands of dollars per month) for various possible assignments are as follows:

Number of salespeople	Territory			
	A	B	C	D
0	5	4	8	3
1	10	12	12	9
2	13	18	15	14
3	15	19	17	17
4	16	20	18	20

5. The Smith Amusement Company has a game that is played as follows. Two dice are rolled and the sum of the spots is obtained (2, 3, . . . , 12). The player then rerolls the pair of dice. The sum of the spots on this roll is added to the sums of all previous rolls. For example, a 7 on the first roll plus an 11 on the second roll would total 18. The player may continue to roll or may stop at any time and let his or her final score be represented by the sum of dots on the final roll and all previous rolls. Points are awarded on the basis of the player's final score as follows:

Score	Points	Score	Points
More than 30	0	25	5
30	10	24	4
29	9	23	3
28	8	22	2
27	7	21	1
26	6	Less than 21	0

A player wishes to determine a decision rule that would indicate when to continue rolling and when to stop rolling. For example, a decision rule (but not necessarily the optimal one) would be to continue rolling if the score is 25 or less and to stop rolling if the score is 26 or more.

6. The Moore Company sells holiday gifts by mail. The company has a mailing list of 9000 potential customers. Each holiday season, the company solicits purchases by sending a catalog to all of these potential customers. It has found that if a customer orders from one catalog, there is a .60 probability that she or he will order from the next catalog. If a customer does not order from a catalog, there is a .20 probability that this customer will order from

the next catalog and a .80 probability that he or she will not. Typically, the average profit per customer order is $10. Three alternatives have been proposed to increase the firm's profitability. The first is to send new catalogs only to those customers who purchased from the previous catalog. The cost of preparing and mailing a catalog to a customer is $1. A second proposal is designed to encourage customers to purchase in consecutive periods. Any person who purchases from one catalog is given a $1 credit toward a purchase from the next catalog. This is expected to raise the probability of a customer purchasing from two consecutive catalogs from .6 to .7. It would not affect the probability to purchase of a person who did *not* purchase from the previous catalog. This would remain at .20. A third alternative is aimed at the nonpurchaser. Each person who does not purchase is sent a special advertisement that accompanies the next catalog. This adds $2 to the cost of solicitation for these people. It is expected to raise the purchase probability to .40. It would not affect the repurchase probability of those who bought from the previous catalog.

7. The Jacobs Company produces large industrial furnaces. Demand for the months of May, June, July, and August is expected to be for 4, 5, 3, and 2 units respectively. There is 1 unit in inventory on May 1. There is no requirement for any inventory to be held on the last day of August. The variable cost of producing a furnace is $2000. However, the firm incurs a setup cost of $10,000 each month in which 1 or more units are produced. The company estimates that it costs $2000 to hold a unit in inventory from one month to the next. Production capacity is limited to 5 units in any given month.

8. During the season, Mr. Well makes a daily purchase of fresh shrimp at an Eastern seaport. He transports the shrimp to an inland city and sells them to local fish markets. Mr. Well is promised a given percentage of a particular boat's daily catch. He must purchase his entire daily allotment of shrimp or give up his source of supply. Furthermore, he must buy at the going price and sell at the going rate. He has no control over purchasing price, selling price, or sales. It is also known that these three variables are independent, that is, their values are not related. Mr. Well has applied for an equipment loan at a new bank. Ms. Harmond, the loan officer, knows that daily operating expenses amount to $200. From past data, she has also determined the following probabilities for Mr. Well's daily purchase price, selling price, and sales volume.

Purchase price	Probability	Selling price	Probability	Sales volume	Probability
$1.00	.2	$1.00	.1	400 lbs.	.4
1.50	.6	2.00	.5	500	.3
2.00	.2	3.00	.4	600	.3

9. Consider problem 8. Ms. Harmond has acquired new data that improve and refine the probability estimates associated with Mr. Well's purchase price, selling price, and sales volume. These items are still considered independent.

Purchase price	Probability	Selling price	Probability	Sales volume	Probability
$1.20	.1	$ .80	.1	350	.1
1.30	.1	1.10	.1	400	.1
1.40	.1	1.40	.1	450	.2
1.50	.1	1.70	.2	500	.2
1.60	.1	2.00	.2	550	.2
1.70	.2	2.30	.1	600	.1
1.80	.1	2.60	.1	650	.1
1.90	.1	2.90	.1		
2.00	.1				

10. The Draper Company has $400,000 to invest. It is considering four investment alternatives, as follows:

Investment	Yield (%)	Risk factor (%)
Mortgages	9	4
Consumer loans	12	5
Type A bonds	8	3
Type B bonds	6	2

The combined risk factor of all loans cannot exceed 3.5%. The amount of money allocated to bonds must constitute at least 50% of total investment. Consumer loans and both types of bonds can be purchased in any quantity from $0 to $400,000. Mortgages, however, can only be purchased in lot sizes of $100,000.

11. The Thompson Company utilizes 72 units per year (6 per month) of a large electrical motor. It is considering purchasing these motors from an out-of-town dealer at a cost of $200 per unit. This dealer will supply the company the motors in any lot size from 1 to 480. The Thompson Company believes that holding cost is equal to 18% of average inventory value. It also believes that it costs $100 to place and receive an order from this out-of-town vendor. The Thompson Company is also considering an offer from a local supplier. The price per unit is higher at $250 per unit. When this local supplier receives an order, it fills the order at a rate of 10 motors per month.

The Thompson Company estimates that the ordering cost when buying from this local supplier is $50 per order.

12. The McDonald Company manufactures and sells desk pipe lighters. Variable costs of production and distribution amount to $2 per unit. The firm receives $7 per unit for each unit sold. The company has recently experienced a large number of consumer complaints that the striker mechanism failed to operate correctly. At such times, the company repairs the lighters free of charge. The company estimates the cost of repair to be $20, which includes the actual repair cost, a goodwill cost, and a $2.90 charge for a deluxe striker mechanism. There is almost no chance of this deluxe mechanism failing. Experience has indicated that approximately 10% of the regular mechanisms fail. The company assumes that all failures will be returned. The company is concerned about the high return rate and is considering two alternative proposals. The first is to substitute the deluxe mechanism for the regular mechanism in every lighter. This would add $2.50 to the cost of each lighter, because the regular mechanism costs $.40. The second proposal is to test the regular mechanisms before installing them. A testing company has agreed to test each mechanism for $.40 per item. They will classify each item as either grade A or grade B. The McDonald Company would use only grade A items. From experience, it is known that 80% of the items fall into the class A category. Furthermore, it is known that only 5% of those items classified as grade A will fail and result in the consumer returning the item.

13. The Alexander Company sells "pure branch water" to wholesale customers. These customers arrive in their own tank trucks. All customers use identical trucks. The Alexander Company has a pumping system able to fill 10 trucks per hour. At the present time, trucks arrive randomly at the rate of 8 per hour. In recent years, the popularity of branch water has increased dramatically, and planners anticipate that over the next several years, the arrival rate will increase to 10 trucks per hour. At the present time, operating costs are $40 per hour. The owner of the company hates to see trucks wait in line. A bid has been received on increasing the capacity of the pumping system to 12, 14, or 16 trucks per hour. The operating costs would increase to $50, $62, or $75, depending on the capacity chosen.

14. The Chastain Company has two manufacturing plants that both produce wrought iron chairs. It ships these items from its plants to 4 distributors located in the north, east, south, and west sections of the state. The costs of shipping a chair from each factory to each warehouse are as follows:

Factories	Warehouses			
	North	East	South	West
1	$6	$2	$5	$3
2	1	5	2	4

The cost of production at factory 1 is $10 per unit for the first 10,000 chairs and $14 per unit for the next 15,000 chairs. Plant capacity is 25,000 chairs. The cost of production at plant 2 is $8 per unit for the first 8000 chairs and $15 per unit for the next 12,000 chairs. Plant capacity is 20,000 units. Distributor requirements for the following year are 8000 chairs for the north and east distributors, 10,000 chairs for the south distributor, and 14,000 chairs for the west distributor. Any distributor may buy from an outside source at a price of $30 per chair. This includes transportation costs.

15. The Brinkworth Company operates a large retail merchandising establishment that is open 24 hours every day. The company has estimated the minimum number of clerks needed during each 4-hour period. These estimates are as follows:

Time period	Clerks needed
8 A.M. to noon	80
Noon to 4 P.M.	100
4 P.M. to 8 P.M.	40
8 P.M. to midnight	60
Midnight to 4 A.M.	20
4 A.M. to 8 A.M.	40

A clerk usually works one of the 8-hour shifts that begin at 8 A.M., noon, 4 P.M., 8 P.M., midnight, or 4 A.M. The clerks' standard rate of pay is $6 per hour. This rate is paid for all hours worked between 8 A.M. and 6 P.M. A premium of $1 per hour is paid for every hour worked between 6 P.M. and 10 P.M. A premium of $2 per hour is paid for every hour worked between 10 P.M. and 8 A.M. the next morning.

16. The Hodges Company produces and sells wheelbarrows. For the past several years, sales of wheelbarrows have averaged 4000 units per year. The company expects demand to increase slowly for the next several years. At the present time, the company purchases tires for these units from a nearby supplier at a cost of $6 per tire. The company is committed to buying at least 2000 tires per year. The Hodges Company is considering manufacturing its own tires. A careful analysis of cost data indicates that this would result in fixed cost of $10,000 per year and a variable cost of $4 per tire.

17. The Wing Company is trying to determine if it should set up a new production line to manufacture items for the bicentennial celebration of a particular state. Management feels that all profits from this operation must be made in a one-year period. The setup cost for the operation is $200,000. The company plans a profit contribution of $1 per unit on each unit produced and sold. It is anticipated that demand will be for either 100,000 units or 400,000 units and that these two possibilities are equally likely.

One alternative available to the company is to purchase a market research study before building the production line. At the moment, it is uncertain what this study would cost.

18. Consider the example in problem 17. Assume that the marketing research firm that wants to sell information to the Wing Company has a track record of being correct 80% of the time. In other words, if they say demand will be high, we can assume there is a probability of .80 that demand will be for 400,000 units and a probability of .20 that demand will be for 100,000 units. Likewise, if they say demand will be low, we can assign a probability of .80 to sales of 100,000 units and a probability of .20 to sales of 400,000 units.

19. The Fisher Company sells one-volume encyclopedias. The company purchases the books for $20 and sells them for $30. Carrying cost is assumed to be 15% of average inventory value. Annual demand is for 12,000 units. The company presently orders in lot sizes of 2000 units. The company is concerned about the large number of stockouts it has experienced in the past. It feels that the number of stockouts should be significantly reduced. Demand during past reorder periods has averaged 500 units. It is believed that this demand is normally distributed with a standard deviation of 70 units.

20. The McNair Company is a large manufacturer of paper used in cardboard boxes. The paper is produced in large rolls 11 feet wide. This large roll is then cut into smaller rolls, which have widths of either 5 feet, 4 feet, or 3 feet. For example, an 11-foot roll can be cut into 1 five-foot roll and 2 three-foot rolls, 1 five-foot roll and 1 four-foot roll, 3 three-foot rolls, etc. In the latter two examples, there would be a waste or "trim" roll 2 feet wide. This trim cannot be sold and must be recycled through the machine. The company makes up a daily production schedule. Today's orders are for 480 five-foot rolls, 390 four-foot rolls, and 600 three-foot rolls.

Supplementary readings

Bell, C. E. *Quantitative Methods for Administration.* Homewood, Ill.: Irwin, 1977.

Budnick, F. S., R. Mojena, and T. E. Vollman. *Principles of Operations Research for Management.* Homewood, Ill.: Irwin, 1977.

Cook, T. M., and R. A. Russell. *Introduction to Management Science.* Englewood Cliffs, N.J.: Prentice-Hall, 1977.

Grayson, C. J. "Management Science and Business Practice." *Harvard Business Review,* 51 (July–August 1973), 41–48.

Hammond, J. S. "The Roles of the Manager and Management Scientist in Successful Implementation." *Sloan Management Review,* 15 (Winter 1974), 1–24.

Harvey, A. "Factors Making for Implementation Success and Failure." *Management Science,* 11 (April 1965), B89–97.

Lapin, L. L. *Quantitative Methods for Business Decisions*. New York: Harcourt Brace Jovanovich, 1976.

Lee, S. M., and L. J. Moore. *Introduction to Decision Science*. New York: Petrocelli/Charter, 1975.

McCoubrey, C. A., and M. Sulg. "OR/MS Implementation at Converse Rubber." *Sloan Management Review*, 17 (Winter 1976), 63–76.

Radnor, M., A. H. Rubenstein, and D. A. Tansik. "Implementation in Operating Research and R & D in Government and Business Organizations." *Operations Research*, 18 (November–December 1970), 967–997.

Turban, E., and J. R. Meredith. *Fundamentals of Management Science*. Dallas, Texas: Business Publications, 1977.

Wagner, H. M. *Principles of Management Science*. Englewood Cliffs, N.J.: Prentice-Hall, 1975.

Wagner, H. M. "The ABC's of OR." *Operations Research*, 6 (October 1971), 1259–1281.

Appendix

Table A *Areas under the normal curve*

Z	.00	.01	.02	.03	.04	.05	.06	.07	.08	.09
0.0	0.0	0.0040	0.0080	0.0120	0.0160	0.0199	0.0239	0.0279	0.0319	0.0359
0.10	0.0398	0.0438	0.0478	0.0517	0.0557	0.0596	0.0636	0.0675	0.0714	0.0753
0.20	0.0793	0.0832	0.0871	0.0910	0.0948	0.0987	0.1026	0.1064	0.1103	0.1141
0.30	0.1179	0.1217	0.1255	0.1293	0.1331	0.1368	0.1406	0.1443	0.1480	0.1517
0.40	0.1554	0.1591	0.1628	0.1664	0.1700	0.1736	0.1772	0.1808	0.1844	0.1879
0.50	0.1915	0.1950	0.1985	0.2019	0.2054	0.2088	0.2123	0.2157	0.2190	0.2224
0.60	0.2257	0.2291	0.2324	0.2357	0.2389	0.2422	0.2454	0.2486	0.2517	0.2549
0.70	0.2580	0.2611	0.2642	0.2673	0.2703	0.2734	0.2764	0.2793	0.2823	0.2852
0.80	0.2881	0.2910	0.2939	0.2967	0.2995	0.3023	0.3051	0.3078	0.3106	0.3133
0.90	0.3159	0.3186	0.3212	0.3238	0.3264	0.3289	0.3315	0.3340	0.3365	0.3389
1.00	0.3413	0.3438	0.3461	0.3485	0.3508	0.3531	0.3554	0.3577	0.3599	0.3621
1.10	0.3643	0.3665	0.3686	0.3708	0.3729	0.3749	0.3770	0.3790	0.3810	0.3830
1.20	0.3849	0.3869	0.3888	0.3907	0.3925	0.3943	0.3962	0.3980	0.3997	0.4015
1.30	0.4032	0.4049	0.4066	0.4082	0.4099	0.4115	0.4131	0.4147	0.4162	0.4177
1.40	0.4192	0.4207	0.4222	0.4236	0.4251	0.4265	0.4279	0.4292	0.4306	0.4319
1.50	0.4332	0.4345	0.4357	0.4370	0.4382	0.4394	0.4406	0.4418	0.4429	0.4441
1.60	0.4452	0.4463	0.4474	0.4484	0.4495	0.4505	0.4515	0.4525	0.4535	0.4545
1.70	0.4554	0.4564	0.4573	0.4582	0.4591	0.4599	0.4608	0.4616	0.4625	0.4633
1.80	0.4641	0.4649	0.4656	0.4664	0.4671	0.4678	0.4686	0.4693	0.4699	0.4706
1.90	0.4713	0.4719	0.4726	0.4732	0.4738	0.4744	0.4750	0.4756	0.4761	0.4767
2.00	0.4772	0.4778	0.4783	0.4788	0.4793	0.4798	0.4803	0.4808	0.4812	0.4817
2.10	0.4821	0.4826	0.4830	0.4834	0.4838	0.4842	0.4846	0.4850	0.4854	0.4857
2.20	0.4861	0.4864	0.4868	0.4871	0.4875	0.4878	0.4881	0.4884	0.4887	0.4890
2.30	0.4893	0.4896	0.4898	0.4901	0.4904	0.4906	0.4909	0.4911	0.4913	0.4916
2.40	0.4918	0.4920	0.4922	0.4925	0.4927	0.4929	0.4931	0.4932	0.4934	0.4936
2.50	0.4938	0.4940	0.4941	0.4943	0.4945	0.4946	0.4948	0.4949	0.4951	0.4952
2.60	0.4953	0.4955	0.4956	0.4957	0.4959	0.4960	0.4961	0.4962	0.4963	0.4964
2.70	0.4965	0.4966	0.4967	0.4968	0.4969	0.4970	0.4971	0.4972	0.4973	0.4974
2.80	0.4974	0.4975	0.4976	0.4977	0.4977	0.4978	0.4979	0.4979	0.4980	0.4981
2.90	0.4981	0.4982	0.4982	0.4983	0.4984	0.4984	0.4985	0.4985	0.4986	0.4986
3.00	0.4986	0.4987	0.4987	0.4988	0.4988	0.4989	0.4989	0.4989	0.4990	0.4990
3.10	0.4990	0.4991	0.4991	0.4991	0.4992	0.4992	0.4992	0.4992	0.4993	0.4993
3.20	0.4993	0.4993	0.4994	0.4994	0.4994	0.4994	0.4994	0.4995	0.4995	0.4995
3.30	0.4995	0.4995	0.4995	0.4996	0.4996	0.4996	0.4996	0.4996	0.4996	0.4997
3.40	0.4997	0.4997	0.4997	0.4997	0.4997	0.4997	0.4997	0.4997	0.4997	0.4998
3.50	0.4998	0.4998	0.4998	0.4998	0.4998	0.4998	0.4998	0.4998	0.4998	0.4998

p

n	r	.05	.10	.15	.20	.25	.30	.35	.40	.45	.50
1	0	1.0000	1.0000	1.0000	1.0000	1.0000	1.0000	1.0000	1.0000	1.0000	1.0000
	1	0.0500	0.1000	0.1500	0.2000	0.2500	0.3000	0.3500	0.4000	0.4500	0.5000
2	0	1.0000	1.0000	1.0000	1.0000	1.0000	1.0000	1.0000	1.0000	1.0000	1.0000
	1	0.0975	0.1900	0.2775	0.3600	0.4375	0.5100	0.5775	0.6400	0.6975	0.7500
	2	0.0025	0.0100	0.0225	0.0400	0.0625	0.0900	0.1225	0.1600	0.2025	0.2500
3	0	1.0000	1.0000	1.0000	1.0000	1.0000	1.0000	1.0000	1.0000	1.0000	1.0000
	1	0.1426	0.2710	0.3859	0.4880	0.5781	0.6570	0.7254	0.7840	0.8336	0.8750
	2	0.0072	0.0280	0.0607	0.1040	0.1562	0.2160	0.2817	0.3520	0.4252	0.5000
	3	0.0001	0.0010	0.0034	0.0080	0.0156	0.0270	0.0429	0.0640	0.0911	0.1250
4	0	1.0000	1.0000	1.0000	1.0000	1.0000	1.0000	1.0000	1.0000	1.0000	1.0000
	1	0.1855	0.3439	0.4780	0.5904	0.6836	0.7599	0.8215	0.8704	0.9085	0.9375
	2	0.0140	0.0523	0.1095	0.1808	0.2617	0.3483	0.4370	0.5248	0.6090	0.6875
	3	0.0005	0.0037	0.0120	0.0272	0.0508	0.0837	0.1265	0.1792	0.2415	0.3125
	4	0.0000	0.0001	0.0005	0.0016	0.0039	0.0081	0.0150	0.0256	0.0410	0.0625
5	0	1.0000	1.0000	1.0000	1.0000	1.0000	1.0000	1.0000	1.0000	1.0000	1.0000
	1	0.2262	0.4095	0.5563	0.6723	0.7627	0.8319	0.8840	0.9222	0.9497	0.9687
	2	0.0226	0.0815	0.1648	0.2627	0.3672	0.4718	0.5716	0.6630	0.7438	0.8125
	3	0.0012	0.0086	0.0266	0.0579	0.1035	0.1631	0.2352	0.3174	0.4069	0.5000
	4	0.0000	0.0005	0.0022	0.0067	0.0156	0.0308	0.0540	0.0870	0.1312	0.1875
	5	0.0000	0.0000	0.0001	0.0003	0.0010	0.0024	0.0053	0.0102	0.0185	0.0312
6	0	1.0000	1.0000	1.0000	1.0000	1.0000	1.0000	1.0000	1.0000	1.0000	1.0000
	1	0.2649	0.4686	0.6229	0.7379	0.8220	0.8824	0.9246	0.9533	0.9723	0.9844
	2	0.0328	0.1143	0.2235	0.3446	0.4661	0.5798	0.6809	0.7667	0.8364	0.8906
	3	0.0022	0.0158	0.0473	0.0989	0.1694	0.2557	0.3529	0.4557	0.5585	0.6562
	4	0.0001	0.0013	0.0059	0.0170	0.0376	0.0705	0.1174	0.1792	0.2553	0.3437
	5	0.0000	0.0001	0.0004	0.0016	0.0046	0.0109	0.0223	0.0410	0.0692	0.1094
	6	0.0000	0.0000	0.0000	0.0001	0.0002	0.0007	0.0018	0.0041	0.0083	0.0156
7	0	1.0000	1.0000	1.0000	1.0000	1.0000	1.0000	1.0000	1.0000	1.0000	1.0000
	1	0.3017	0.5217	0.6794	0.7903	0.8665	0.9176	0.9510	0.9720	0.9848	0.9922
	2	0.0444	0.1497	0.2834	0.4233	0.5551	0.6706	0.7662	0.8414	0.8976	0.9375
	3	0.0038	0.0257	0.0738	0.1480	0.2436	0.3529	0.4677	0.5801	0.6836	0.7734
	4	0.0002	0.0027	0.0121	0.0333	0.0706	0.1260	0.1998	0.2898	0.3917	0.5000
	5	0.0000	0.0002	0.0012	0.0047	0.0129	0.0288	0.0556	0.0963	0.1529	0.2266
	6	0.0000	0.0000	0.0001	0.0004	0.0013	0.0038	0.0090	0.0188	0.0357	0.0625
	7	0.0000	0.0000	0.0000	0.0000	0.0001	0.0002	0.0006	0.0016	0.0037	0.0078
8	0	1.0000	1.0000	1.0000	1.0000	1.0000	1.0000	1.0000	1.0000	1.0000	1.0000
	1	0.3366	0.5695	0.7275	0.8322	0.8999	0.9424	0.9681	0.9832	0.9916	0.9961
	2	0.0572	0.1869	0.3428	0.4967	0.6329	0.7447	0.8309	0.8936	0.9368	0.964d
	3	0.0058	0.0381	0.1052	0.2031	0.3215	0.4482	0.5722	0.6846	0.7799	0.8555
	4	0.0004	0.0050	0.0214	0.0563	0.1138	0.1941	0.2936	0.4059	0.5230	0.6367
	5	0.0000	0.0004	0.0029	0.0104	0.0273	0.0580	0.1061	0.1737	0.2604	0.3633
	6	0.0000	0.0000	0.0002	0.0012	0.0042	0.0113	0.0253	0.0498	0.0885	0.1445
	7	0.0000	0.0000	0.0000	0.0001	0.0004	0.0013	0.0036	0.0085	0.0181	0.0352
	8	0.0000	0.0000	0.0000	0.0000	0.0000	0.0001	0.0002	0.0007	0.0017	0.0039
9	0	1.0000	1.0000	1.0000	1.0000	1.0000	1.0000	1.0000	1.0000	1.0000	1.0000
	1	0.3698	0.6126	0.7684	0.8658	0.9249	0.9596	0.9793	0.9899	0.9954	0.9980
	2	0.0712	0.2252	0.4005	0.5638	0.6997	0.8040	0.8789	0.9295	0.9615	0.9805
	3	0.0084	0.0530	0.1409	0.2618	0.3993	0.5372	0.6627	0.7682	0.8505	0.9102
	4	0.0006	0.0083	0.0339	0.0856	0.1657	0.2703	0.3911	0.5174	0.6386	0.7461

						p					
n	*r*	.05	.10	.15	.20	.25	.30	.35	.40	.45	.50
	5	0.0000	0.0009	0.0056	0.0196	0.0489	0.0988	0.1717	0.2666	0.3786	0.5000
	6	0.0000	0.0001	0.0006	0.0031	0.0100	0.0253	0.0536	0.0994	0.1658	0.2539
	7	0.0000	0.0000	0.0000	0.0003	0.0013	0.0043	0.0112	0.0250	0.0498	0.0898
	8	0.0000	0.0000	0.0000	0.0000	0.0001	0.0004	0.0014	0.0038	0.0091	0.0195
	9	0.0000	0.0000	0.0000	0.0000	0.0000	0.0000	0.0001	0.0003	0.0008	0.0020
10	0	1.0000	1.0000	1.0000	1.0000	1.0000	1.0000	1.0000	1.0000	1.0000	1.0000
	1	0.4013	0.6513	0.8031	0.8926	0.9437	0.9718	0.9865	0.9940	0.9975	0.9990
	2	0.0861	0.2639	0.4557	0.6242	0.7560	0.8507	0.9140	0.9536	0.9767	0.9893
	3	0.0115	0.0702	0.1798	0.3222	0.4744	0.6172	0.7384	0.8327	0.9004	0.9453
	4	0.0010	0.0128	0.0500	0.1209	0.2241	0.3504	0.4862	0.6177	0.7340	0.8281
	5	0.0001	0.0016	0.0099	0.0328	0.0781	0.1503	0.2485	0.3669	0.4956	0.6230
	6	0.0000	0.0001	0.0014	0.0064	0.0197	0.0473	0.0949	0.1662	0.2616	0.3770
	7	0.0000	0.0000	0.0001	0.0009	0.0035	0.0106	0.0260	0.0548	0.1020	0.1719
	8	0.0000	0.0000	0.0000	0.0001	0.0004	0.0016	0.0048	0.0123	0.0274	0.0547
	9	0.0000	0.0000	0.0000	0.0000	0.0000	0.0001	0.0005	0.0017	0.0045	0.0107
	10	0.0000	0.0000	0.0000	0.0000	0.0000	0.0000	0.0000	0.0001	0.0003	0.0010
11	0	1.0000	1.0000	1.0000	1.0000	1.0000	1.0000	1.0000	1.0000	1.0000	1.0000
	1	0.4312	0.6862	0.8327	0.9141	0.9578	0.9802	0.9912	0.9964	0.9986	0.9995
	2	0.1019	0.3026	0.5078	0.6779	0.8029	0.8870	0.9394	0.9698	0.9861	0.9941
	3	0.0152	0.0896	0.2212	0.3826	0.5448	0.6873	0.7999	0.8811	0.9348	0.9673
	4	0.0016	0.0185	0.0694	0.1611	0.2867	0.4304	0.5744	0.7037	0.8089	0.8867
	5	0.0001	0.0028	0.0159	0.0504	0.1146	0.2103	0.3317	0.4672	0.6029	0.7256
	6	0.0000	0.0003	0.0027	0.0117	0.0343	0.0782	0.1487	0.2465	0.3669	0.5000
	7	0.0000	0.0000	0.0003	0.0020	0.0076	0.0216	0.0501	0.0994	0.1738	0.2744
	8	0.0000	0.0000	0.0000	0.0002	0.0012	0.0043	0.0122	0.0293	0.0610	0.1133
	9	0.0000	0.0000	0.0000	0.0000	0.0001	0.0006	0.0020	0.0059	0.0148	0.0327
	10	0.0000	0.0000	0.0000	0.0000	0.0000	0.0000	0.0002	0.0007	0.0022	0.0059
	11	0.0000	0.0000	0.0000	0.0000	0.0000	0.0000	0.0000	0.0000	0.0002	0.0005
12	0	1.0000	1.0000	1.0000	1.0000	1.0000	1.0000	1.0000	1.0000	1.0000	1.0000
	1	0.4596	0.7176	0.8578	0.9313	0.9683	0.9862	0.9943	0.9978	0.9992	0.9998
	2	0.1184	0.3410	0.5565	0.7251	0.8416	0.9150	0.9576	0.9804	0.9917	0.9968
	3	0.0196	0.1109	0.2642	0.4417	0.6093	0.7472	0.8487	0.9166	0.9579	0.9807
	4	0.0022	0.0256	0.0922	0.2054	0.3512	0.5075	0.6533	0.7747	0.8655	0.9270
	5	0.0002	0.0043	0.0239	0.0726	0.1576	0.2763	0.4167	0.5618	0.6956	0.8062
	6	0.0000	0.0005	0.0046	0.0194	0.0544	0.1178	0.2127	0.3348	0.4731	0.6128
	7	0.0000	0.0001	0.0007	0.0039	0.0143	0.0386	0.0846	0.1582	0.2607	0.3872
	8	0.0000	0.0000	0.0001	0.0006	0.0028	0.0095	0.0255	0.0573	0.1117	0.1938
	9	0.0000	0.0000	0.0000	0.0001	0.0004	0.0017	0.0056	0.0153	0.0356	0.0730
	10	0.0000	0.0000	0.0000	0.0000	0.0000	0.0002	0.0008	0.0028	0.0079	0.0193
	11	0.0000	0.0000	0.0000	0.0000	0.0000	0.0000	0.0001	0.0003	0.0011	0.0032
	12	0.0000	0.0000	0.0000	0.0000	0.0000	0.0000	0.0000	0.0000	0.0001	0.0002
13	0	1.0000	1.0000	1.0000	1.0000	1.0000	1.0000	1.0000	1.0000	1.0000	1.0000
	1	0.4867	0.7458	0.8791	0.9450	0.9762	0.9903	0.9963	0.9987	0.9996	0.9999
	2	0.1354	0.3787	0.6017	0.7664	0.8733	0.9363	0.9704	0.9874	0.9951	0.9983
	3	0.0245	0.1339	0.3080	0.4983	0.6674	0.7975	0.8868	0.9421	0.9731	0.9888
	4	0.0031	0.0342	0.1180	0.2527	0.4157	0.5794	0.7217	0.8314	0.9071	0.9539
	5	0.0003	0.0065	0.0342	0.0991	0.2060	0.3457	0.4995	0.6470	0.7720	0.8666
	6	0.0000	0.0009	0.0075	0.0300	0.0802	0.1654	0.2841	0.4256	0.5732	0.7095
	7	0.0000	0.0001	0.0013	0.0070	0.0243	0.0624	0.1295	0.2288	0.3563	0.5000
	8	0.0000	0.0000	0.0002	0.0012	0.0056	0.0182	0.0462	0.0977	0.1788	0.2905
	9	0.0000	0.0000	0.0000	0.0002	0.0010	0.0040	0.0126	0.0321	0.0698	0.1334

p

n	r	.05	.10	.15	.20	.25	.30	.35	.40	.45	.50
	10	0.0000	0.0000	0.0000	0.0000	0.0001	0.0007	0.0025	0.0078	0.0203	0.0461
	11	0.0000	0.0000	0.0000	0.0000	0.0000	0.0001	0.0003	0.0013	0.0041	0.0112
	12	0.0000	0.0000	0.0000	0.0000	0.0000	0.0000	0.0000	0.0001	0.0005	0.0017
	13	0.0000	0.0000	0.0000	0.0000	0.0000	0.0000	0.0000	0.0000	0.0000	0.0001
14	0	1.0000	1.0000	1.0000	1.0000	1.0000	1.0000	1.0000	1.0000	1.0000	1.0000
	1	0.5123	0.7712	0.8972	0.9560	0.9822	0.9932	0.9976	0.9992	0.9998	0.9999
	2	0.1530	0.4154	0.6433	0.8021	0.8990	0.9525	0.9795	0.9919	0.9971	0.9991
	3	0.0301	0.1584	0.3521	0.5519	0.7189	0.8392	0.9161	0.9602	0.9830	0.9935
	4	0.0042	0.0441	0.1465	0.3018	0.4787	0.6448	0.7795	0.8757	0.9368	0.9713
	5	0.0004	0.0092	0.0467	0.1298	0.2585	0.4158	0.5773	0.7207	0.8328	0.9102
	6	0.0000	0.0015	0.0115	0.0439	0.1117	0.2195	0.3595	0.5141	0.6627	0.7880
	7	0.0000	0.0002	0.0022	0.0116	0.0383	0.0933	0.1836	0.3075	0.4539	0.6047
	8	0.0000	0.0000	0.0003	0.0024	0.0103	0.0315	0.0753	0.1501	0.2586	0.3953
	9	0.0000	0.0000	0.0000	0.0004	0.0022	0.0083	0.0243	0.0583	0.1189	0.2120
	10	0.0000	0.0000	0.0000	0.0000	0.0003	0.0017	0.0060	0.0175	0.0426	0.0898
	11	0.0000	0.0000	0.0000	0.0000	0.0000	0.0002	0.0011	0.0039	0.0114	0.0287
	12	0.0000	0.0000	0.0000	0.0000	0.0000	0.0000	0.0001	0.0006	0.0022	0.0065
	13	0.0000	0.0000	0.0000	0.0000	0.0000	0.0000	0.0000	0.0001	0.0003	0.0009
	14	0.0000	0.0000	0.0000	0.0000	0.0000	0.0000	0.0000	0.0000	0.0000	0.0001
15	0	1.0000	1.0000	1.0000	1.0000	1.0000	1.0000	1.0000	1.0000	1.0000	1.0000
	1	0.5367	0.7941	0.9126	0.9648	0.9866	0.9953	0.9984	0.9995	0.9999	1.0000
	2	0.1710	0.4510	0.6814	0.8329	0.9198	0.9647	0.9858	0.9948	0.9983	0.9995
	3	0.0362	0.1841	0.3958	0.6020	0.7639	0.8732	0.9383	0.9729	0.9893	0.9963
	4	0.0055	0.0556	0.1773	0.3518	0.5387	0.7031	0.8273	0.9095	0.9576	0.9824
	5	0.0006	0.0127	0.0617	0.1642	0.3135	0.4845	0.6481	0.7827	0.8796	0.9408
	6	0.0001	0.0022	0.0168	0.0611	0.1484	0.2784	0.4357	0.5968	0.7392	0.8491
	7	0.0000	0.0003	0.0036	0.0181	0.0566	0.1311	0.2452	0.3902	0.5478	0.6964
	8	0.0000	0.0000	0.0006	0.0042	0.0173	0.0500	0.1132	0.2131	0.3465	0.5000
	9	0.0000	0.0000	0.0001	0.0008	0.0042	0.0152	0.0422	0.0950	0.1818	0.3036
	10	0.0000	0.0000	0.0000	0.0001	0.0008	0.0037	0.0124	0.0338	0.0769	0.1509
	11	0.0000	0.0000	0.0000	0.0000	0.0001	0.0007	0.0028	0.0093	0.0255	0.0592
	12	0.0000	0.0000	0.0000	0.0000	0.0000	0.0001	0.0005	0.0019	0.0063	0.0176
	13	0.0000	0.0000	0.0000	0.0000	0.0000	0.0000	0.0001	0.0003	0.0011	0.0037
	14	0.0000	0.0000	0.0000	0.0000	0.0000	0.0000	0.0000	0.0000	0.0001	0.0005
	15	0.0000	0.0000	0.0000	0.0000	0.0000	0.0000	0.0000	0.0000	0.0000	0.0000
16	0	1.0000	1.0000	1.0000	1.0000	1.0000	1.0000	1.0000	1.0000	1.0000	1.0000
	1	0.5599	0.8147	0.9257	0.9719	0.9900	0.9967	0.9990	0.9997	0.9999	1.0000
	2	0.1892	0.4853	0.7161	0.8593	0.9365	0.9739	0.9902	0.9967	0.9990	0.9997
	3	0.0429	0.2108	0.4386	0.6482	0.8029	0.9006	0.9549	0.9817	0.9934	0.9979
	4	0.0070	0.0684	0.2101	0.4019	0.5950	0.7541	0.8661	0.9349	0.9719	0.9894
	5	0.0009	0.0170	0.0791	0.2018	0.3698	0.5501	0.7108	0.8334	0.9147	0.9616
	6	0.0001	0.0033	0.0235	0.0817	0.1897	0.3402	0.5100	0.6712	0.8024	0.8949
	7	0.0000	0.0005	0.0056	0.0267	0.0796	0.1753	0.3119	0.4728	0.6340	0.7727
	8	0.0000	0.0001	0.0011	0.0070	0.0271	0.0744	0.1594	0.2839	0.4371	0.5982
	9	0.0000	0.0000	0.0002	0.0015	0.0075	0.0257	0.0671	0.1423	0.2559	0.4018
	10	0.0000	0.0000	0.0000	0.0002	0.0016	0.0071	0.0229	0.0583	0.1241	0.2272
	11	0.0000	0.0000	0.0000	0.0000	0.0003	0.0016	0.0062	0.0191	0.0486	0.1051
	12	0.0000	0.0000	0.0000	0.0000	0.0000	0.0003	0.0013	0.0049	0.0149	0.0384
	13	0.0000	0.0000	0.0000	0.0000	0.0000	0.0000	0.0002	0.0009	0.0035	0.0106
	14	0.0000	0.0000	0.0000	0.0000	0.0000	0.0000	0.0000	0.0001	0.0006	0.0021
	15	0.0000	0.0000	0.0000	0.0000	0.0000	0.0000	0.0000	0.0000	0.0001	0.0003
	16	0.0000	0.0000	0.0000	0.0000	0.0000	0.0000	0.0000	0.0000	0.0000	0.0000

p

n	r	.05	.10	.15	.20	.25	.30	.35	.40	.45	.50
20	0	1.0000	1.0000	1.0000	1.0000	1.0000	1.0000	1.0000	1.0000	1.0000	1.0000
	1	0.6415	0.8784	0.9612	0.9885	0.9968	0.9992	0.9998	1.0000	1.0000	1.0000
	2	0.2642	0.6083	0.8244	0.9308	0.9757	0.9924	0.9979	0.9995	0.9999	1.0000
	3	0.0755	0.3231	0.5951	0.7939	0.9087	0.9645	0.9879	0.9964	0.9991	0.9998
	4	0.0159	0.1330	0.3523	0.5885	0.7748	0.8929	0.9556	0.9840	0.9951	0.9987
	5	0.0026	0.0432	0.1702	0.3704	0.5852	0.7625	0.8818	0.9490	0.9811	0.9941
	6	0.0003	0.0113	0.0673	0.1958	0.3828	0.5836	0.7546	0.8744	0.9447	0.9793
	7	0.0000	0.0024	0.0219	0.0867	0.2142	0.3920	0.5834	0.7500	0.8701	0.9423
	8	0.0000	0.0004	0.0059	0.0321	0.1018	0.2277	0.3990	0.5841	0.7480	0.8684
	9	0.0000	0.0001	0.0013	0.0100	0.0409	0.1133	0.2376	0.4044	0.5857	0.7483
	10	0.0000	0.0000	0.0002	0.0026	0.0139	0.0480	0.1218	0.2447	0.4086	0.5881
	11	0.0000	0.0000	0.0000	0.0006	0.0039	0.0171	0.0532	0.1275	0.2493	0.4119
	12	0.0000	0.0000	0.0000	0.0001	0.0009	0.0051	0.0196	0.0565	0.1308	0.2517
	13	0.0000	0.0000	0.0000	0.0000	0.0002	0.0013	0.0060	0.0210	0.0580	0.1316
	14	0.0000	0.0000	0.0000	0.0000	0.0000	0.0003	0.0015	0.0065	0.0214	0.0577
	15	0.0000	0.0000	0.0000	0.0000	0.0000	0.0000	0.0003	0.0016	0.0064	0.0207
	16	0.0000	0.0000	0.0000	0.0000	0.0000	0.0000	0.0000	0.0003	0.0015	0.0059
	17	0.0000	0.0000	0.0000	0.0000	0.0000	0.0000	0.0000	0.0000	0.0003	0.0013
	18	0.0000	0.0000	0.0000	0.0000	0.0000	0.0000	0.0000	0.0000	0.0000	0.0002
	19	0.0000	0.0000	0.0000	0.0000	0.0000	0.0000	0.0000	0.0000	0.0000	0.0000
	20	0.0000	0.0000	0.0000	0.0000	0.0000	0.0000	0.0000	0.0000	0.0000	0.0000
21	0	1.0000	1.0000	1.0000	1.0000	1.0000	1.0000	1.0000	1.0000	1.0000	1.0000
	1	0.6594	0.8906	0.9671	0.9908	0.9976	0.9994	0.9999	1.0000	1.0000	1.0000
	2	0.2830	0.6353	0.8450	0.9424	0.9810	0.9944	0.9985	0.9997	0.9999	1.0000
	3	0.0849	0.3516	0.6295	0.8213	0.9255	0.9729	0.9914	0.9976	0.9994	0.9999
	4	0.0189	0.1520	0.3887	0.6296	0.8083	0.9144	0.9669	0.9890	0.9969	0.9993
	5	0.0032	0.0522	0.1975	0.4140	0.6326	0.8016	0.9076	0.9630	0.9874	0.9964
	6	0.0004	0.0144	0.0827	0.2307	0.4334	0.6373	0.7991	0.9043	0.9611	0.9867
	7	0.0000	0.0033	0.0287	0.1085	0.2564	0.4495	0.6433	0.7998	0.9036	0.9608
	8	0.0000	0.0006	0.0083	0.0431	0.1299	0.2770	0.4635	0.6505	0.8029	0.9054
	9	0.0000	0.0001	0.0020	0.0144	0.0561	0.1476	0.2941	0.4763	0.6587	0.8083
	10	0.0000	0.0000	0.0004	0.0041	0.0206	0.0676	0.1623	0.3086	0.4883	0.6682
	11	0.0000	0.0000	0.0001	0.0010	0.0064	0.0264	0.0772	0.1744	0.3210	0.5000
	12	0.0000	0.0000	0.0000	0.0002	0.0017	0.0087	0.0313	0.0849	0.1841	0.3318
	13	0.0000	0.0000	0.0000	0.0000	0.0004	0.0024	0.0108	0.0352	0.0908	0.1917
	14	0.0000	0.0000	0.0000	0.0000	0.0001	0.0006	0.0031	0.0123	0.0379	0.0946
	15	0.0000	0.0000	0.0000	0.0000	0.0000	0.0001	0.0007	0.0036	0.0132	0.0392
	16	0.0000	0.0000	0.0000	0.0000	0.0000	0.0000	0.0001	0.0008	0.0037	0.0133
	17	0.0000	0.0000	0.0000	0.0000	0.0000	0.0000	0.0000	0.0002	0.0008	0.0036
	18	0.0000	0.0000	0.0000	0.0000	0.0000	0.0000	0.0000	0.0000	0.0001	0.0007
	19	0.0000	0.0000	0.0000	0.0000	0.0000	0.0000	0.0000	0.0000	0.0000	0.0001
	20	0.0000	0.0000	0.0000	0.0000	0.0000	0.0000	0.0000	0.0000	0.0000	0.0000
	21	0.0000	0.0000	0.0000	0.0000	0.0000	0.0000	0.0000	0.0000	0.0000	0.0000
22	0	1.0000	1.0000	1.0000	1.0000	1.0000	1.0000	1.0000	1.0000	1.0000	1.0000
	1	0.6765	0.9015	0.9720	0.9926	0.9982	0.9996	0.9999	1.0000	1.0000	1.0000
	2	0.3018	0.6608	0.8633	0.9520	0.9851	0.9959	0.9990	0.9998	1.0000	1.0000
	3	0.0948	0.3800	0.6618	0.8455	0.9393	0.9793	0.9939	0.9984	0.9997	0.9999
	4	0.0222	0.1719	0.4248	0.6680	0.8376	0.9319	0.9755	0.9924	0.9980	0.9996
	5	0.0040	0.0621	0.2262	0.4571	0.6765	0.8354	0.9284	0.9734	0.9917	0.9978
	6	0.0006	0.0182	0.0999	0.2674	0.4832	0.6866	0.8371	0.9278	0.9729	0.9915
	7	0.0001	0.0044	0.0368	0.1330	0.3006	0.5058	0.6978	0.8416	0.9295	0.9738
	8	0.0000	0.0009	0.0114	0.0561	0.1615	0.3287	0.5264	0.7102	0.8482	0.9331
	9	0.0000	0.0001	0.0030	0.0201	0.0746	0.1865	0.3534	0.5460	0.7236	0.8569

p

n	r	.05	.10	.15	.20	.25	.30	.35	.40	.45	.50
25	0	1.0000	1.0000	1.0000	1.0000	1.0000	1.0000	1.0000	1.0000	1.0000	1.0000
	1	0.7226	0.9282	0.9828	0.9962	0.9992	0.9999	1.0000	1.0000	1.0000	1.0000
	2	0.3576	0.7288	0.9069	0.9726	0.9930	0.9984	0.9997	0.9999	1.0000	1.0000
	3	0.1271	0.4629	0.7463	0.9018	0.9679	0.9910	0.9979	0.9996	0.9999	1.0000
	4	0.0341	0.2364	0.5289	0.7660	0.9038	0.9668	0.9903	0.9976	0.9995	0.9999
	5	0.0072	0.0980	0.3179	0.5793	0.7863	0.9095	0.9679	0.9905	0.9977	0.9995
	6	0.0012	0.0334	0.1615	0.3833	0.6217	0.8065	0.9174	0.9706	0.9914	0.9980
	7	0.0002	0.0095	0.0695	0.2200	0.4389	0.6593	0.8266	0.9264	0.9742	0.9927
	8	0.0000	0.0023	0.0255	0.1091	0.2735	0.4881	0.6939	0.8464	0.9361	0.9784
	9	0.0000	0.0005	0.0080	0.0468	0.1494	0.3231	0.5332	0.7265	0.8660	0.9461
	10	0.0000	0.0001	0.0021	0.0173	0.0713	0.1894	0.3697	0.5754	0.7576	0.8852
	11	0.0000	0.0000	0.0005	0.0056	0.0297	0.0978	0.2288	0.4142	0.6157	0.7878
	12	0.0000	0.0000	0.0001	0.0015	0.0107	0.0442	0.1254	0.2677	0.4574	0.6550
	13	0.0000	0.0000	0.0000	0.0004	0.0034	0.0175	0.0604	0.1538	0.3063	0.5000
	14	0.0000	0.0000	0.0000	0.0001	0.0009	0.0060	0.0255	0.0778	0.1827	0.3450
	15	0.0000	0.0000	0.0000	0.0000	0.0002	0.0018	0.0093	0.0344	0.0960	0.2122
	16	0.0000	0.0000	0.0000	0.0000	0.0000	0.0005	0.0029	0.0132	0.0440	0.1148
	17	0.0000	0.0000	0.0000	0.0000	0.0000	0.0001	0.0008	0.0043	0.0174	0.0539
	18	0.0000	0.0000	0.0000	0.0000	0.0000	0.0000	0.0002	0.0012	0.0058	0.0216
	19	0.0000	0.0000	0.0000	0.0000	0.0000	0.0000	0.0000	0.0003	0.0016	0.0073
	20	0.0000	0.0000	0.0000	0.0000	0.0000	0.0000	0.0000	0.0001	0.0004	0.0020
	21	0.0000	0.0000	0.0000	0.0000	0.0000	0.0000	0.0000	0.0000	0.0001	0.0005
	22	0.0000	0.0000	0.0000	0.0000	0.0000	0.0000	0.0000	0.0000	0.0000	0.0001
	23	0.0000	0.0000	0.0000	0.0000	0.0000	0.0000	0.0000	0.0000	0.0000	0.0000
	24	0.0000	0.0000	0.0000	0.0000	0.0000	0.0000	0.0000	0.0000	0.0000	0.0000
	25	0.0000	0.0000	0.0000	0.0000	0.0000	0.0000	0.0000	0.0000	0.0000	0.0000

Table C *Poisson probabilities—noncumulative*

λ

X	.001	.002	.003	.004	.005	.006	.007	.008	.009	.010	.011	.012	.013	.014	.015	.016	.017	.018	.019
0	.9990	.9980	.9970	.9960	.9950	.9940	.9930	.9920	.9910	.9901	.9891	.9881	.9871	.9861	.9851	.9841	.9831	.9822	.9812
1	.0010	.0020	.0030	.0040	.0050	.0060	.0070	.0079	.0089	.0099	.0109	.0119	.0128	.0138	.0148	.0157	.0167	.0177	.0186
2	.0000	.0000	.0000	.0000	.0000	.0000	.0000	.0000	.0000	.0000	.0001	.0001	.0001	.0001	.0001	.0001	.0001	.0002	.0002

X	.020	.030	.040	.050	.060	.070	.080	.090	.100	.110	.120	.130	.140	.150	.160	.170	.180	.190	.200
0	.9802	.9704	.9608	.9512	.9418	.9324	.9231	.9139	.9048	.8958	.8869	.8781	.8694	.8607	.8521	.8437	.8353	.8270	.8187
1	.0196	.0291	.0384	.0476	.0565	.0653	.0738	.0823	.0905	.0985	.1064	.1142	.1217	.1291	.1363	.1434	.1503	.1571	.1637
2	.0002	.0004	.0008	.0012	.0017	.0023	.0030	.0037	.0045	.0054	.0064	.0074	.0085	.0097	.0109	.0122	.0135	.0149	.0164
3	.0000	.0000	.0000	.0000	.0000	.0001	.0001	.0001	.0002	.0002	.0003	.0003	.0004	.0005	.0006	.0007	.0008	.0009	.0011
4	.0000	.0000	.0000	.0000	.0000	.0000	.0000	.0000	.0000	.0000	.0000	.0000	.0000	.0000	.0000	.0000	.0000	.0000	.0001

X	.210	.220	.230	.240	.250	.260	.270	.280	.290	.300	.310	.320	.330	.340	.350	.360	.370	.380	.390
0	.8106	.8025	.7945	.7866	.7788	.7711	.7634	.7558	.7483	.7408	.7334	.7261	.7189	.7118	.7047	.6977	.6907	.6839	.6771
1	.1702	.1766	.1827	.1888	.1947	.2005	.2061	.2116	.2170	.2222	.2274	.2324	.2372	.2420	.2466	.2512	.2556	.2599	.2641
2	.0179	.0194	.0210	.0227	.0243	.0261	.0278	.0296	.0315	.0333	.0352	.0372	.0391	.0411	.0432	.0452	.0473	.0494	.0515
3	.0013	.0014	.0016	.0018	.0020	.0023	.0025	.0028	.0030	.0033	.0036	.0040	.0043	.0047	.0050	.0054	.0058	.0063	.0067
4	.0001	.0001	.0001	.0001	.0001	.0001	.0002	.0002	.0002	.0003	.0003	.0003	.0004	.0004	.0004	.0005	.0005	.0006	.0007
5	.0000	.0000	.0000	.0000	.0000	.0000	.0000	.0000	.0000	.0000	.0000	.0000	.0000	.0000	.0000	.0000	.0000	.0000	.0001

X	0.40	0.45	0.50	0.55	0.60	0.65	0.70	0.75	0.80	0.85	0.90	0.95	1.00	1.05	1.10	1.15	1.20	1.25	1.30
0	.6703	.6376	.6065	.5769	.5488	.5220	.4966	.4724	.4493	.4274	.4066	.3867	.3679	.3499	.3329	.3166	.3012	.2865	.2725
1	.2681	.2869	.3033	.3173	.3293	.3393	.3476	.3543	.3595	.3633	.3659	.3674	.3679	.3674	.3662	.3641	.3614	.3581	.3543
2	.0536	.0646	.0758	.0873	.0988	.1103	.1217	.1329	.1438	.1544	.1647	.1745	.1839	.1929	.2014	.2094	.2169	.2238	.2303
3	.0072	.0097	.0126	.0160	.0198	.0239	.0284	.0332	.0383	.0437	.0494	.0553	.0613	.0675	.0738	.0803	.0867	.0933	.0998
4	.0007	.0011	.0016	.0022	.0030	.0039	.0050	.0062	.0077	.0093	.0111	.0131	.0153	.0177	.0203	.0231	.0260	.0291	.0324
5	.0001	.0001	.0002	.0002	.0004	.0005	.0007	.0009	.0012	.0016	.0020	.0025	.0031	.0037	.0045	.0053	.0062	.0073	.0084
6	.0000	.0000	.0000	.0000	.0000	.0001	.0001	.0001	.0002	.0002	.0003	.0004	.0005	.0007	.0008	.0010	.0012	.0015	.0018
7	.0000	.0000	.0000	.0000	.0000	.0000	.0000	.0000	.0000	.0000	.0000	.0001	.0001	.0001	.0001	.0002	.0002	.0003	.0003
8	.0000	.0000	.0000	.0000	.0000	.0000	.0000	.0000	.0000	.0000	.0000	.0000	.0000	.0000	.0000	.0000	.0000	.0000	.0001

λ

X	1.4	1.5	1.6	1.7	1.8	1.9	2.0	2.1	2.2	2.3	2.4	2.5	2.6	2.7	2.8	2.9	3.0	3.1	3.2
0	.2466	.2231	.2019	.1827	.1653	.1496	.1353	.1225	.1108	.1003	.0907	.0821	.0743	.0672	.0608	.0550	.0498	.0450	.0408
1	.3452	.3347	.3230	.3106	.2975	.2842	.2707	.2572	.2438	.2306	.2177	.2052	.1931	.1815	.1703	.1596	.1494	.1397	.1304
2	.2417	.2510	.2584	.2640	.2678	.2700	.2707	.2700	.2681	.2652	.2613	.2565	.2510	.2450	.2384	.2314	.2240	.2165	.2087
3	.1128	.1255	.1378	.1496	.1607	.1710	.1804	.1890	.1966	.2033	.2090	.2138	.2176	.2205	.2225	.2237	.2240	.2237	.2226
4	.0395	.0471	.0551	.0636	.0723	.0812	.0902	.0992	.1082	.1169	.1254	.1336	.1414	.1488	.1557	.1622	.1680	.1733	.1781
5	.0111	.0141	.0176	.0216	.0260	.0309	.0361	.0417	.0476	.0538	.0602	.0668	.0735	.0804	.0872	.0940	.1008	.1075	.1140
6	.0026	.0035	.0047	.0061	.0078	.0098	.0120	.0146	.0174	.0206	.0241	.0278	.0319	.0362	.0407	.0455	.0504	.0555	.0608
7	.0005	.0008	.0011	.0015	.0020	.0027	.0034	.0044	.0055	.0068	.0083	.0099	.0118	.0139	.0163	.0188	.0216	.0246	.0278
8	.0001	.0001	.0002	.0003	.0005	.0006	.0009	.0011	.0015	.0019	.0025	.0031	.0038	.0047	.0057	.0068	.0081	.0095	.0111
9	.0000	.0000	.0000	.0001	.0001	.0001	.0002	.0003	.0004	.0005	.0007	.0009	.0011	.0014	.0018	.0022	.0027	.0033	.0040
10	.0000	.0000	.0000	.0000	.0000	.0000	.0000	.0001	.0001	.0001	.0002	.0002	.0003	.0004	.0005	.0006	.0008	.0010	.0013
11	.0000	.0000	.0000	.0000	.0000	.0000	.0000	.0000	.0000	.0000	.0000	.0000	.0001	.0001	.0001	.0002	.0002	.0003	.0004
12	.0000	.0000	.0000	.0000	.0000	.0000	.0000	.0000	.0000	.0000	.0000	.0000	.0000	.0000	.0000	.0000	.0001	.0001	.0001

X	3.3	3.4	3.5	3.6	3.7	3.8	3.9	4.0	4.1	4.2	4.3	4.4	4.5	4.6	4.7	4.8	4.9	5.0	5.1
0	.0369	.0334	.0302	.0273	.0247	.0224	.0202	.0183	.0166	.0150	.0136	.0123	.0111	.0101	.0091	.0082	.0074	.0067	.0061
1	.1217	.1135	.1057	.0984	.0915	.0850	.0789	.0733	.0679	.0630	.0583	.0540	.0500	.0462	.0427	.0395	.0365	.0337	.0311
2	.2008	.1929	.1850	.1771	.1692	.1615	.1539	.1465	.1393	.1323	.1254	.1188	.1125	.1063	.1005	.0948	.0894	.0842	.0793
3	.2209	.2186	.2158	.2125	.2087	.2046	.2001	.1954	.1904	.1852	.1798	.1743	.1687	.1631	.1574	.1517	.1460	.1404	.1348
4	.1823	.1858	.1888	.1912	.1931	.1944	.1951	.1954	.1951	.1944	.1933	.1917	.1898	.1875	.1849	.1820	.1789	.1755	.1719
5	.1203	.1264	.1322	.1377	.1429	.1477	.1522	.1563	.1600	.1633	.1662	.1687	.1708	.1725	.1738	.1747	.1753	.1755	.1753
6	.0662	.0716	.0771	.0826	.0881	.0936	.0989	.1042	.1093	.1143	.1191	.1237	.1281	.1323	.1362	.1398	.1432	.1462	.1490
7	.0312	.0348	.0385	.0425	.0466	.0508	.0551	.0595	.0640	.0686	.0732	.0778	.0824	.0869	.0914	.0959	.1002	.1044	.1086
8	.0129	.0148	.0169	.0191	.0215	.0241	.0269	.0298	.0328	.0360	.0393	.0428	.0463	.0500	.0537	.0575	.0614	.0653	.0692
9	.0047	.0056	.0066	.0076	.0089	.0102	.0116	.0132	.0150	.0168	.0188	.0209	.0232	.0255	.0280	.0307	.0334	.0363	.0392
10	.0016	.0019	.0023	.0028	.0033	.0039	.0045	.0053	.0061	.0071	.0081	.0092	.0104	.0118	.0132	.0147	.0164	.0181	.0200
11	.0005	.0006	.0007	.0009	.0011	.0013	.0016	.0019	.0023	.0027	.0032	.0037	.0043	.0049	.0056	.0064	.0073	.0082	.0093
12	.0001	.0002	.0002	.0003	.0003	.0004	.0005	.0006	.0008	.0009	.0011	.0013	.0016	.0019	.0022	.0026	.0030	.0034	.0039
13	.0000	.0000	.0001	.0001	.0001	.0001	.0002	.0002	.0002	.0003	.0004	.0005	.0006	.0007	.0008	.0009	.0011	.0013	.0015
14	.0000	.0000	.0000	.0000	.0000	.0000	.0000	.0001	.0001	.0001	.0001	.0001	.0002	.0002	.0003	.0003	.0004	.0005	.0006
15	.0000	.0000	.0000	.0000	.0000	.0000	.0000	.0000	.0000	.0000	.0000	.0000	.0001	.0001	.0001	.0001	.0001	.0002	.0002
16	.0000	.0000	.0000	.0000	.0000	.0000	.0000	.0000	.0000	.0000	.0000	.0000	.0000	.0000	.0000	.0000	.0000	.0001	.0001

λ

X	5.2	5.3	5.4	5.5	5.6	5.7	5.8	5.9	6.0	6.1	6.2	6.3	6.4	6.5	6.6	6.7	6.8	6.9	7.0
0	.0055	.0050	.0045	.0041	.0037	.0033	.0030	.0027	.0025	.0022	.0020	.0018	.0017	.0015	.0014	.0012	.0011	.0010	.0009
1	.0287	.0265	.0244	.0225	.0207	.0191	.0176	.0162	.0149	.0137	.0126	.0116	.0106	.0098	.0090	.0082	.0076	.0070	.0064
2	.0746	.0701	.0659	.0618	.0580	.0544	.0509	.0477	.0446	.0417	.0390	.0364	.0340	.0318	.0296	.0276	.0258	.0240	.0223
3	.1293	.1239	.1185	.1133	.1082	.1033	.0985	.0938	.0892	.0848	.0806	.0765	.0726	.0688	.0652	.0617	.0584	.0552	.0521
4	.1681	.1641	.1600	.1558	.1515	.1472	.1428	.1383	.1339	.1294	.1249	.1205	.1162	.1118	.1076	.1034	.0992	.0952	.0912
5	.1748	.1740	.1728	.1714	.1697	.1678	.1656	.1632	.1606	.1579	.1549	.1519	.1487	.1454	.1420	.1385	.1349	.1314	.1277
6	.1515	.1537	.1555	.1571	.1584	.1594	.1601	.1605	.1606	.1605	.1601	.1595	.1586	.1575	.1562	.1546	.1529	.1511	.1490
7	.1125	.1163	.1200	.1234	.1267	.1298	.1326	.1353	.1377	.1399	.1418	.1435	.1450	.1462	.1472	.1480	.1486	.1489	.1490
8	.0731	.0771	.0810	.0849	.0887	.0925	.0962	.0998	.1033	.1066	.1099	.1130	.1160	.1188	.1215	.1240	.1263	.1284	.1304
9	.0423	.0454	.0486	.0519	.0552	.0586	.0620	.0654	.0688	.0723	.0757	.0791	.0825	.0858	.0891	.0923	.0954	.0985	.1014
10	.0220	.0241	.0262	.0285	.0309	.0334	.0359	.0386	.0413	.0441	.0469	.0498	.0528	.0558	.0588	.0618	.0649	.0679	.0710
11	.0104	.0116	.0129	.0143	.0157	.0173	.0190	.0207	.0225	.0244	.0265	.0285	.0307	.0330	.0353	.0377	.0401	.0426	.0452
12	.0045	.0051	.0058	.0065	.0073	.0082	.0092	.0102	.0113	.0124	.0137	.0150	.0164	.0179	.0194	.0210	.0227	.0245	.0263
13	.0018	.0021	.0024	.0028	.0032	.0036	.0041	.0046	.0052	.0058	.0065	.0073	.0081	.0089	.0099	.0108	.0119	.0130	.0142
14	.0007	.0008	.0009	.0011	.0013	.0015	.0017	.0019	.0022	.0025	.0029	.0033	.0037	.0041	.0046	.0052	.0058	.0064	.0071
15	.0002	.0003	.0003	.0004	.0005	.0006	.0007	.0008	.0009	.0010	.0012	.0014	.0016	.0018	.0020	.0023	.0026	.0029	.0033
16	.0001	.0001	.0001	.0001	.0002	.0002	.0002	.0003	.0003	.0004	.0005	.0005	.0006	.0007	.0008	.0010	.0011	.0013	.0014
17	.0000	.0000	.0000	.0001	.0001	.0001	.0001	.0001	.0001	.0001	.0002	.0002	.0002	.0003	.0003	.0004	.0004	.0005	.0006
18	.0000	.0000	.0000	.0000	.0000	.0000	.0000	.0000	.0000	.0000	.0001	.0001	.0001	.0001	.0001	.0001	.0002	.0002	.0002
19	.0000	.0000	.0000	.0000	.0000	.0000	.0000	.0000	.0000	.0000	.0000	.0000	.0000	.0000	.0000	.0001	.0001	.0001	.0001

X	7.5	8.0	8.5	9.0	9.5	10.0	10.5	11.0	11.5	12.0	12.5	13.0	13.5	14.0	14.5	15.0	20.0	25.0	30.0
0	.0006	.0003	.0002	.0001	.0001	.0000	.0000	.0000	.0000	.0000	.0000	.0000	.0000	.0000	.0000	.0000	.0000	.0000	.0000
1	.0041	.0027	.0017	.0011	.0007	.0005	.0003	.0002	.0001	.0001	.0000	.0000	.0000	.0000	.0000	.0000	.0000	.0000	.0000
2	.0156	.0107	.0074	.0050	.0034	.0023	.0015	.0010	.0007	.0004	.0003	.0002	.0001	.0001	.0001	.0001	.0000	.0000	.0000
3	.0389	.0286	.0208	.0150	.0107	.0076	.0053	.0037	.0026	.0018	.0012	.0008	.0006	.0004	.0003	.0002	.0000	.0000	.0000
4	.0729	.0573	.0443	.0337	.0254	.0189	.0139	.0102	.0074	.0053	.0038	.0027	.0019	.0013	.0009	.0006	.0000	.0000	.0000
5	.1094	.0916	.0752	.0607	.0483	.0378	.0293	.0224	.0170	.0127	.0095	.0070	.0051	.0037	.0027	.0019	.0001	.0000	.0000
6	.1367	.1221	.1066	.0911	.0764	.0631	.0513	.0411	.0325	.0255	.0197	.0152	.0115	.0087	.0065	.0048	.0002	.0000	.0000
7	.1465	.1396	.1294	.1171	.1037	.0901	.0769	.0646	.0535	.0437	.0353	.0281	.0222	.0174	.0135	.0104	.0005	.0000	.0000
8	.1373	.1396	.1375	.1318	.1232	.1126	.1009	.0888	.0769	.0655	.0553	.0457	.0375	.0304	.0244	.0194	.0013	.0001	.0000
9	.1144	.1241	.1299	.1318	.1300	.1251	.1177	.1085	.0982	.0874	.0765	.0661	.0563	.0473	.0394	.0324	.0029	.0001	.0000
10	.0858	.0993	.1104	.1186	.1235	.1251	.1236	.1194	.1129	.1048	.0956	.0859	.0760	.0663	.0571	.0486	.0058	.0004	.0000
11	.0585	.0722	.0853	.0970	.1067	.1137	.1180	.1194	.1181	.1144	.1087	.1015	.0932	.0844	.0753	.0663	.0106	.0008	.0000
12	.0366	.0481	.0604	.0728	.0844	.0948	.1032	.1094	.1131	.1144	.1132	.1099	.1049	.0984	.0910	.0829	.0176	.0017	.0001
13	.0211	.0296	.0395	.0504	.0617	.0729	.0834	.0926	.1001	.1056	.1089	.1099	.1089	.1060	.1014	.0956	.0271	.0033	.0002
14	.0113	.0169	.0240	.0324	.0419	.0521	.0625	.0728	.0822	.0905	.0972	.1021	.1050	.1060	.1051	.1024	.0387	.0059	.0005

λ

	7.5	8.0	8.5	9.0	9.5	10.0	10.5	11.0	11.5	12.0	12.5	13.0	13.5	14.0	14.5	15.0	20.0	25.0	30.0
15	.0057	.0090	.0136	.0194	.0265	.0347	.0438	.0534	.0630	.0724	.0810	.0885	.0945	.0989	.1016	.1024	.0516	.0099	.0010
16	.0026	.0045	.0072	.0109	.0157	.0217	.0287	.0367	.0453	.0543	.0633	.0719	.0798	.0866	.0920	.0960	.0646	.0155	.0019
17	.0012	.0021	.0036	.0058	.0088	.0128	.0177	.0237	.0306	.0383	.0465	.0550	.0633	.0713	.0785	.0847	.0760	.0227	.0034
18	.0005	.0009	.0017	.0029	.0046	.0071	.0104	.0145	.0196	.0255	.0323	.0397	.0475	.0554	.0632	.0706	.0844	.0316	.0057
19	.0002	.0004	.0008	.0014	.0023	.0037	.0057	.0084	.0119	.0161	.0213	.0272	.0337	.0409	.0483	.0557	.0888	.0415	.0089
20	.0001	.0002	.0003	.0006	.0011	.0019	.0030	.0046	.0068	.0097	.0133	.0177	.0228	.0286	.0350	.0418	.0888	.0519	.0134
21	.0000	.0001	.0001	.0003	.0005	.0009	.0015	.0024	.0037	.0055	.0079	.0109	.0146	.0191	.0242	.0299	.0846	.0618	.0192
22	.0000	.0000	.0001	.0001	.0002	.0004	.0007	.0012	.0020	.0030	.0045	.0065	.0090	.0121	.0159	.0204	.0769	.0702	.0261
23	.0000	.0000	.0000	.0000	.0001	.0002	.0003	.0006	.0010	.0016	.0024	.0037	.0053	.0074	.0100	.0133	.0669	.0763	.0341
24	.0000	.0000	.0000	.0000	.0000	.0001	.0001	.0003	.0005	.0008	.0013	.0020	.0030	.0043	.0061	.0083	.0557	.0795	.0426
25	.0000	.0000	.0000	.0000	.0000	.0000	.0001	.0001	.0002	.0004	.0006	.0010	.0016	.0024	.0035	.0050	.0446	.0795	.0511
26	.0000	.0000	.0000	.0000	.0000	.0000	.0000	.0000	.0001	.0002	.0003	.0005	.0008	.0013	.0020	.0029	.0343	.0765	.0590
27	.0000	.0000	.0000	.0000	.0000	.0000	.0000	.0000	.0000	.0001	.0001	.0002	.0004	.0007	.0011	.0016	.0254	.0708	.0655
28	.0000	.0000	.0000	.0000	.0000	.0000	.0000	.0000	.0000	.0000	.0000	.0001	.0002	.0003	.0005	.0009	.0181	.0632	.0702
29	.0000	.0000	.0000	.0000	.0000	.0000	.0000	.0000	.0000	.0000	.0000	.0001	.0001	.0002	.0003	.0004	.0125	.0545	.0726
30	.0000	.0000	.0000	.0000	.0000	.0000	.0000	.0000	.0000	.0000	.0000	.0000	.0000	.0001	.0001	.0002	.0083	.0454	.0726
31	.0000	.0000	.0000	.0000	.0000	.0000	.0000	.0000	.0000	.0000	.0000	.0000	.0000	.0000	.0001	.0001	.0054	.0366	.0703
32	.0000	.0000	.0000	.0000	.0000	.0000	.0000	.0000	.0000	.0000	.0000	.0000	.0000	.0000	.0000	.0001	.0034	.0286	.0659
33	.0000	.0000	.0000	.0000	.0000	.0000	.0000	.0000	.0000	.0000	.0000	.0000	.0000	.0000	.0000	.0000	.0020	.0217	.0599
34	.0000	.0000	.0000	.0000	.0000	.0000	.0000	.0000	.0000	.0000	.0000	.0000	.0000	.0000	.0000	.0000	.0012	.0159	.0529
35	.0000	.0000	.0000	.0000	.0000	.0000	.0000	.0000	.0000	.0000	.0000	.0000	.0000	.0000	.0000	.0000	.0007	.0114	.0453
36	.0000	.0000	.0000	.0000	.0000	.0000	.0000	.0000	.0000	.0000	.0000	.0000	.0000	.0000	.0000	.0000	.0004	.0079	.0378
37	.0000	.0000	.0000	.0000	.0000	.0000	.0000	.0000	.0000	.0000	.0000	.0000	.0000	.0000	.0000	.0000	.0002	.0053	.0306
38	.0000	.0000	.0000	.0000	.0000	.0000	.0000	.0000	.0000	.0000	.0000	.0000	.0000	.0000	.0000	.0000	.0001	.0035	.0242
39	.0000	.0000	.0000	.0000	.0000	.0000	.0000	.0000	.0000	.0000	.0000	.0000	.0000	.0000	.0000	.0000	.0001	.0023	.0186
40	.0000	.0000	.0000	.0000	.0000	.0000	.0000	.0000	.0000	.0000	.0000	.0000	.0000	.0000	.0000	.0000	.0000	.0014	.0139
41	.0000	.0000	.0000	.0000	.0000	.0000	.0000	.0000	.0000	.0000	.0000	.0000	.0000	.0000	.0000	.0000	.0000	.0009	.0102
42	.0000	.0000	.0000	.0000	.0000	.0000	.0000	.0000	.0000	.0000	.0000	.0000	.0000	.0000	.0000	.0000	.0000	.0005	.0073
43	.0000	.0000	.0000	.0000	.0000	.0000	.0000	.0000	.0000	.0000	.0000	.0000	.0000	.0000	.0000	.0000	.0000	.0003	.0051
44	.0000	.0000	.0000	.0000	.0000	.0000	.0000	.0000	.0000	.0000	.0000	.0000	.0000	.0000	.0000	.0000	.0000	.0002	.0035
45	.0000	.0000	.0000	.0000	.0000	.0000	.0000	.0000	.0000	.0000	.0000	.0000	.0000	.0000	.0000	.0000	.0000	.0001	.0023
46	.0000	.0000	.0000	.0000	.0000	.0000	.0000	.0000	.0000	.0000	.0000	.0000	.0000	.0000	.0000	.0000	.0000	.0001	.0015
47	.0000	.0000	.0000	.0000	.0000	.0000	.0000	.0000	.0000	.0000	.0000	.0000	.0000	.0000	.0000	.0000	.0000	.0000	.0010
48	.0000	.0000	.0000	.0000	.0000	.0000	.0000	.0000	.0000	.0000	.0000	.0000	.0000	.0000	.0000	.0000	.0000	.0000	.0006
49	.0000	.0000	.0000	.0000	.0000	.0000	.0000	.0000	.0000	.0000	.0000	.0000	.0000	.0000	.0000	.0000	.0000	.0000	.0004
50	.0000	.0000	.0000	.0000	.0000	.0000	.0000	.0000	.0000	.0000	.0000	.0000	.0000	.0000	.0000	.0000	.0000	.0000	.0002
51	.0000	.0000	.0000	.0000	.0000	.0000	.0000	.0000	.0000	.0000	.0000	.0000	.0000	.0000	.0000	.0000	.0000	.0000	.0001
52	.0000	.0000	.0000	.0000	.0000	.0000	.0000	.0000	.0000	.0000	.0000	.0000	.0000	.0000	.0000	.0000	.0000	.0000	.0001